SMITH WIGGLESWORTH

SMITH WIGGLESWORTH

The Complete Collection of His Life Teachings

compiled by Roberts Liardon

Albury Publishing
Tulsa, Oklahoma

Unless otherwise indicated, all Scripture quotations are taken from the *King James Version* of the Bible.

Smith Wigglesworth: The Complete Collection of His Life Teachings
ISBN 1-57778-024-8
Copyright © 1996 by
Roberts Liardon
P.O. Box 30710
Laguna Hills, California 92654

6th Printing
Published by ALBURY PUBLISHING
P.O. Box 470406
Tulsa, Oklahoma 74147-0406

CONTENTS

FOREWORD

I am privileged to be the granddaughter of the "apostle of faith," my grandfather, the late Smith Wigglesworth. I remember him as a stately old gentleman immaculately dressed. His shoes were specially made — size six — and were always highly polished.

In the home, Grandfather was gentle and would weep as the younger grandchildren came in to greet him after one of his preaching tours in Britain or abroad. He would sit in his easy chair with a rug over his knees and the New Testament in his hand. He brought each of us a *Newbury Bible* and wrote on the front page: "Trusting that this will be the choicest of all books to you."

On Wednesday evenings my father, who was Grandfather's eldest son, and Father's two younger brothers, Ernest and Harold, would meet to sit and listen to Grandfather expound the Scriptures. He would recount some of his experiences concerning his healing ministry abroad. I was privileged to be present at some of these sittings. The presence of the Lord was so intense that I would prefer to leave the house quietly and walk through the Park, taking the quiet road home, in order not to meet people and by conversation break the holy presence of God.

At the age of seventeen Grandfather asked me to stand by his chair and said, "If you surrender your life to God, He will send you all over the world." I am surprised in looking back over my life now to find how many countries I have actually visited — including New Zealand. In that beautiful country I realized my grandfather's greatness in God, through the testimonies being given. Many healings had taken place, and after forty years the privileged people were still well. A number of people wanted to give me a hug because they were so thrilled to meet the off-spring of Smith Wigglesworth — the man of God.

Grandfather died as he lived, without complaint, leaving us all a legacy of tried faith. It is my heart's desire that all who read this excellent book will be inspired to have the same fervent faith in God.

Alice Berry

Neé Wigglesworth

Granddaughter of Smith Wigglesworth

INTRODUCTION

Dr. Lester Sumrall once told me a personal story about Smith Wigglesworth that illustrates his bold and unashamed personality. He told me how Wigglesworth would frequently travel with his daughter Alice. She had a hearing problem and would often sit and listen to her father's sermons with a "hearing horn." Once, a man yelled from the audience: "Wigglesworth! If you are such a healer in the power of God, then why does your daughter need a hearing horn?" Unshaken by the question, Wigglesworth looked to the man and said, "When you can tell me why Elijah was bald, I'll tell you why Alice needs a hearing horn."

Smith Wigglesworth never minced his words, and he was never shaken by religious persecution. I admire that quality in Smith Wigglesworth. In fact, I've always loved his ministry. I am continually blessed by the mixture of his boldness, his faith, and his compassion. As I've traveled throughout the world, I've found that others have never grown tired of his ministry. Smith Wigglesworth had a true Pentecostal ministry with no man-made strings attached. Walking in an astounding measure of anointing, Wigglesworth never waited for special camp meetings to show the power of God. Instead, he daily demonstrated the book of Acts, producing countless salvations and miracles in his ministry.

While on earth, we will never have the opportunity to sit in a Wigglesworth meeting. That's one reason I am publishing this book. I want you to experience how it would have been to be a part of the congregation and receive the Word and the Spirit from Wigglesworth. I have purposely left these manuscripts in their original form. Wigglesworth's ministry shook nations and became world-renowned for the incredible strength, anointing, and insight he carried.

Many of these sermons from my private collection were recorded in shorthand by Wigglesworth's stenographers, and we've translated them into this form for publication. This book is comprised of messages that were preached in many countries around the world, including the United States, Europe, South Africa, and Australia.

In this book you will experience Smith Wigglesworth's actual ministry. You will notice that many times throughout his sermons he would inspirationally sing out melodies that came from the strength of his spirit.

Other times, he would begin to speak in tongues and then interpret what the Spirit of God spoke through him. He had a wonderful habit of submitting to the Holy Spirit and yielding to the gifts of the Spirit. Though manifestations such as these are repeatedly illustrated in the New Testament, they are specifically mentioned in 1 Corinthians 12.

In my book, *God's Generals: Why They Succeeded and Why Some Failed*, I tell Wigglesworth's story in a condensed, yet very dramatic manner. In that book, his particular chapter thoroughly explains his character make-up and the challenges he faced in that generation.

Not long ago, I was in South Africa where I met with Wigglesworth's granddaughter and great-granddaughter. They are both in the ministry with their husbands, and I ministered at their church. I told them about the unpublished manuscripts I had in my possession and offered his family my complete collection for their own rights and publication usage. Recognizing my genuine love for their grandfather, and seeing the anointing God had given me to minister about these Generals, they told me to publish the sermons myself.

With their blessing and support, I dedicate these sermons, which have never been published in one book volume, to the Wigglesworth family — and to future generations of bold, aggressive reformers whose true citizenship is in heaven. May you turn the world upside down with the Kingdom of God.

Roberts Liardon

"Only melted gold is minted."

THE CONFIDENCE THAT WE HAVE IN HIM

August 1914

I n 1 John 5:14,15, I read a very wonderful word:

And this is the confidence that we have in him, that, if we ask any thing according to his will, he heareth us: and if we know that he hear us, whatsoever we ask, we know that we have the petitions that we desired of him.

It is necessary that we find our bearings in this Word. There is nothing that will bring to you such confidence as a life that is well-pleasing to Him. When Daniel's life pleased God he could ask to be kept in the lions' den. But you cannot ask with confidence until there is a perfect union between you and God, as there was always perfect union between God and Jesus. The foundation is confidence in and fidelity to God. Some people think that Jesus wept because of the love that He had for Lazarus, but that could not be. Jesus knew that these people who were around the grave, and even Martha, had not come to the realization that whatever He would ask of the Father He would give Him. Their unbelief brought brokenness and sadness to the heart of Jesus; and He wept because of this. The moment you pray you find that the heavens are opened. If you have to wait for the heavens to be opened something is wrong.

I tell you what makes us lose the confidence is disobedience to God and His laws. Jesus said it was because of them who stood around that He prayed; but He knew that He heard Him always. And because He knew that His Father heard Him always, He knew that the dead could come forth. There are times when there seems to be a stone wall in front of us, as black as midnight, and there is nothing left but confidence in God. There is no feeling. What you must do is to have a fidelity and confidence to believe that He will not fail, and cannot fail. We shall never get anywhere if we depend upon our feelings. There is something a thousand times better than feelings, and it is the naked Word of God.

There is a divine revelation within you, that came in when you were born from above, and this is a real faith. To be born into the new kingdom is to be born into a new faith. Paul speaks of two classes of brethren, one of whom are obedient, and the other disobedient. The obedient always obey God when He first speaks. It is the people of God that He will use to make the world know that there is a God. The just shall live by faith. You cannot talk about things which you have never experienced. It seems to me that God has a process of training us. You cannot take people into the depths of God unless you have been broken yourself. I have been broken and broken and broken. Praise God that He is near to them that are of a broken heart. You must have a brokenness to get into the depths of God.

There is a rest of faith, there is a faith that rests in confidence on God. God's promises never fail. "...faith cometh by hearing, and hearing by the word of God" (Romans 10:17). The Word of God can create a resistless faith, a faith that is never daunted, a faith that never gives up, and never fails.

We fail to realize the largeness of our Father's measure, and we forget that He has a measure which cannot be exhausted. It pleases Him when we ask for most. "How much more." It is the much more that God shows me. I see that God has a plan of healing. It is on the line of perfect confidence in Him. The confidence comes not from our much speaking, but it comes because of our fellowship with Him. There is a wonderful fellowship with Jesus. The chief thing is to be sure that we take time for communion with Him. There is a communion with Jesus that is life, and that is better than preaching. If God tells you definitely to do anything, do it, but be sure it is God that tells you.

I used to work with a man, who had been a Baptist minister for twenty years. He was one of the sweetest souls I ever met. He was getting to be an old man, and I used to walk by his side, and listen to his instruction. God made the Word in his hand as a two-edged sword to me, and I used to say, "Yes, Lord." If the sword ever comes to you, never straighten yourselves up against it, but let it pierce you. You must be yielded to the Word of God. The Word will work out love in our hearts, and when practical love is in our hearts there is no room to vaunt ourselves. We see ourselves as nothing when we get lost in this divine love. This man of God used to prune and prune me with the sword of God, and it is just as sweet to me today as it was then. I praise God for the sword that cuts us, and for a tender conscience. Oh, for that sweetness of fellowship with Jesus that when you hurt a brother by word or act you could never let it rest until you make it right. First, we need to be converted and to become as little children, and to have the hard heart taken away; to have a heart that is broken and melted with the love of God.

The man of whom I have been speaking came to me and said, "The doctor says that this is the last day that my wife has to live." I said, "Oh, Mr. C., why don't you believe God?" He replied, "I have looked at you when you talked, and have wept, and said, 'Father, if You could give me this confidence, I would be so happy.'" I said, "Could you trust God?" I felt that the Lord would heal her. I sent to a man and asked if he would come with me to a dying woman, and I believed that if two of us would go and anoint her according to James 5:14,15 she would be raised up. This man said, "Oh, why do you come to me? I could not believe, although I believe the Lord would be sure to heal her if you would go." Then I sent to another man and asked him to go with me, and told him that whatever his impression was to be sure to go on and pray right through. We entered the house. I asked this man to pray first; he cried in his desperation, and prayed that this man might be comforted after he was left with these little motherless children, and that he might be strengthened to bear his sorrow! I could hardly wait until he had finished; my whole being was moved, I thought what an awful thing to bring this man all this way to pray that kind of a prayer. What was the matter with him? He was looking at the dying woman instead of looking at God. You can never pray "the prayer of faith" if you look at the person who is needing it; there is only one place to look and that is to Jesus.

The Lord wants to help us this afternoon to learn this truth and to keep our eyes on Him. When this man had finished, I said to Mr. C., "Now you pray." He took up the thread where the other man left off, and went on with the same kind of prayer; he got so down beneath the burden I thought he would never rise again, and I was glad when he got through. I could not have borne it much longer, it all seemed the most out of order of anything I ever heard; my soul was stirred. I was anxious for God to get a chance to do something and to have His way. I did not wait to pray but rushed up to the bed and tipped up the oil bottle, pouring nearly the whole contents on the woman, and I saw Jesus just above the bed with the sweetest smile on His face, and I said to her, "Woman,

Jesus Christ makes you whole." And she was not only healed, but was raised up in that very hour.

Oh, beloved, may God help us this afternoon to get our eyes off the conditions and symptoms, no matter how bad they may be, and get them fastened upon Him, and then we shall be able to pray the prayer of faith.

Published in *Triumphs of Faith*

urn with me to the fourth chapter of Luke, verse 18:

The Spirit of the Lord is upon me, because he hath anointed me to preach the gospel to the poor; he hath sent me to heal the brokenhearted, to preach deliverance to the captives, and recovering of sight to the blind, to set at liberty them that are bruised.

THE SPIRIT OF THE LORD IS UPON ME

September 1914

Jesus took up the book in the temple and read these words, and impressed the fact because of the manifestation of the work He was doing. I believe God is bringing us to a place where we know the Spirit of the Lord is upon us. If we have not got to that place, God wants to bring us to the fact of what Jesus said in John 14, "...I will pray the Father, and he shall give you another Comforter, that he may abide with you for ever" (v. 16). Because the Spirit of the Lord came upon Him who is our head, we must see to it that we receive the same anointing, and that the same Spirit is upon us. The devil will cause us to lose the victory if we allow ourselves to be defeated by him. But it is a fact that the Spirit of the Lord is upon us, and as for me I have no message apart from the message He will give, and I believe then the signs He speaks of will follow. I believe that Jesus was the "Sent forth" One from God, and the propitiation for the sins of the whole world, and we see the manifestation of the Spirit resting upon Him so that His ministry was with power. May God awaken us to the fact that this is the only place where there is any ministry of power.

In asking the Lord what to say to this people, it came to me to arouse them to the fact that the Comforter has come. He is come; and He has come to abide forever. Are you going to be defeated by the devil? No, for the Comforter has come that we may receive and give forth the signs which must follow, so that we may not by any means be deceived by the wiles of the devil. There is no limit as to what we may become if we dwell and live in the Spirit. In the Spirit of prayer we are taken from earth right away into heaven. In the Spirit the Word of God seems to unfold in a wonderful way, and it is only in the Spirit that the love of God is shed abroad in us. We feel as we speak in the Spirit that the fire which burned in the hearts of the two men on their way to Emmaus, when Jesus walked with them, is burning in our heart. It is sure to come to pass when we walk with Him, our hearts will burn; it is the same power of the Spirit. They could not understand it then, but a few hours later they saw Him break the bread, and their eyes were opened.

But, beloved, our hearts ought to always burn. There is a place where we can live in the unction and the clothing of the Spirit, where our words will be clothed with power. "...be not drunk with wine...but be filled with the Spirit" (Ephesians 5:18). It is a wonderful privilege; and I see that it was necessary for John to be in the Spirit on the Isle of Patmos for the revelation to be made clear to him.

What does it mean to this generation for us to be kept in the Spirit? All human reasoning and all human knowledge cannot be compared to the power of the life that is lived in the Spirit. We have power to loose, and power to bind in the Spirit. There is a place where the Holy Ghost can put us where we cannot be anywhere else but in the Spirit. But if we breathe His thoughts into our thoughts, and live in the unction of the Holy Spirit as He lived, then there will be evidences that we are in Him; and His works we will do. But it is only in the Spirit.

Now I read in Matthew's gospel of a power which we have not yet claimed, and we shall not be able to claim this manifestation of the Spirit unless we live in the Spirit. He says, "I will give you power to bind and I will give you power to loose." When are you able to bind and able to loose? It is only in the Spirit. You cannot bind things in the human or with the natural mind. This power was never off from Jesus. I feel as I preach to you tonight that there is a great lack of it in most of us. God help us! "The Spirit of the Lord is upon me." Beloved, there was a great purpose in this Spirit being on Him, and there is a special purpose in your being baptized in the Spirit. We must not forget that we are members of His body and by this wonderful baptismal power, we are partakers of His divine nature.

In the revelation it came this way, that I saw Adam and Eve driven out of the Garden and a flaming sword at every side to keep them from entering into the Garden. But I saw that all around me was a flaming sword keeping me from evil, and it seemed this would be true if I would claim it, and I said, "Lord, I will." The flaming sword was around about me delivering me from the power of hell. So we are preserved from evil. He is like a wall of fire around about us; then why should we fear? What a wonderful salvation! What a wonderful deliverer!

Notice Ezekiel chapter 37. The only need of Ezekiel was to be in the Spirit, and while he was in the Spirit it came to him to prophesy to the dry bones and say, "O ye dry bones, hear the word of the Lord" (Ezekiel 37:4). And as he prophesies according to the Lord's command he sees an "exceeding great army" rising up about him. The prophet obeyed God's command, and all we have to do is exactly this, obey God. What is impossible with man is possible with God.

I pray God that your spirit, soul and body may be preserved holy, and that you may be always on fire, and always ready with the unction on you. If this is not so we are out of divine order, and we ought to cry to Him until the glory comes back upon us.

"The Spirit of the Lord is upon me." There must have been a reason why it was upon Him. First of all, it says here, "...because he hath anointed me to preach the gospel to the poor; he hath sent me to heal the brokenhearted..." What a Gospel! "...to preach deliverance to the captives...." What a wonderful Spirit was upon Him! "...and recovering of sight to the blind, to set at liberty them that are bruised, to preach the acceptable year of the Lord" (Luke 4:18,19). You missionaries who are going to India and Africa and China and other places have a wonderful Gospel to take to these people who know nothing about God; a Gospel of salvation and healing and deliverance. If you want to know how it works, look at Paul among the Barbarians; when the viper came out of the fire and lit on Paul's hand, they watched to see him swell up and die, but when he neither swelled up nor died, they said, "These are gods." When you go forth to these dark lands where the Holy Ghost has sent you to preach the unsearchable riches of Christ, to loose the bands of Satan and set the captives free, be sure you can say, "The Spirit of the Lord is upon me," and remember that Christ is made unto us not only salvation but wisdom and redemption. "Filled with God, yes, filled with God, pardoned and cleansed and filled with God." Filled with God leaves no room for doubting or fearing. We have no idea of all that means, to be filled with God. It means emptied of self. Do you know what it means to be filled with God? It means you have no fear, for when you are filled with God you are filled with love, and perfect love casts out fear.

I want to know more about this manifestation of the power of the Holy Spirit. Let us follow Paul farther; here we find the chief of the island had the bloody flux, and when Paul ministered to him he was healed, and they laded Paul with everything to take away. When we think the church is so poor and needy, we forget that the spirit of intercession can unlock every safe in the world. What did God do for the children of Israel? He took them to vineyards and lands flowing with milk and honey, and all they did was to walk in and take possession. If we will only live in the Spirit and the unction of the Spirit, there will be no lack. There is only lack where faith is not substance, but the Word says faith is the substance, and whatsoever is not of faith is sin. Things will surely come to pass if you will believe this. You have not to try to bring Him down; He is down; you have not to try to bring Him here; He is here. If we will obey the Lord there is nothing He will not give us since He has given us Jesus. The Spirit will have to reveal to us that fact that, because He has given us Jesus, He has given us *all things*.

"The Spirit of the Lord is upon me." It is true, we must be filled with the Spirit. Father, teach us what that means! It was only because He had a knowledge of it that He could stand and say before those men, to the demon, "Come out of him." Who is the man that is willing to lay down all that he may have God's all? Begin to seek and don't stop seeking until you know the Spirit of the Lord is upon you. "I thank Thee, Father, Thou hast hid these things from the wise and prudent, and revealed them unto babes." If you are in the babe class tonight, the

Spirit must have revealed to you your lack. We need to seek with all our hearts. We need to be made flames of fire.

Published in *Triumphs of Faith*

WHAT WILT THOU HAVE ME TO DO?

October 1914

Read Acts 19. As soon as Paul saw the light from heaven above the brightness of the sun, he said, "Lord, what wilt thou have me to do?" (Acts 9:6). And as soon as he was willing to yield he was in a condition where God could meet his need; where God could display His power; where God could have the man. Oh, beloved, are you saying today, "What wilt thou have me to do?" The place of yieldedness is just where God wants us.

People are saying, "I want the baptism, I want healing, I would like to know of a certainly that I am a child of God," and I see nothing, absolutely nothing in the way except unyieldedness to the plan of God. The condition was met which Paul demanded, and instantly when he laid hands on them they were filled with the Spirit and spake in other tongues and prophesied (Acts 19:6). The only thing needed was just to be in the condition where God could come in. The main thing today that God wants is obedience. When you begin yielding and yielding to God He has a plan for your life, and you come in to that wonderful place where all you have to do is to eat the fruits of Canaan. I am convinced that Paul must have been in divine order as well as those men, and Paul had a mission right away to the whole of Asia.

Brothers and sisters, it is the call of God that counts. Paul was in the call of God. Oh, I believe God wants to stir somebody's heart today to obedience; it may be for China or India or Africa, but the thing God is looking for is obedience.

"What wilt thou have me to do?" (Acts 9:6).

...God wrought special miracles by the hands of Paul: so that from his body were brought unto the sick handkerchiefs or aprons, and the diseases departed from them, and the evil spirits went out of them.

Acts 19:11,12

If God can have His way today, the ministry of somebody will begin; it always begins as soon as you yield. Paul had been bringing many people to prison, but God brought Paul to such a place of yieldedness and brokenness that he cried out, "What wilt thou have me to do?" (Acts 9:6). Paul's choice was to be a bondservant for Jesus Christ. Beloved, are you willing that God shall have His way today? God said, "I will shew him how great things he must suffer for my name's sake" (Acts 9:16). But Paul saw that these things were working out a far more exceeding weight of glory. You people who have come for a touch from God, are you willing to follow Him; will you obey Him?

When the prodigal son had returned and the father had killed the fatted calf and made a feast for him, the elder brother was angry and said, "...thou never gavest me a kid, that I might make merry with my friends," (Luke 15:29) but the father said to him, "...all that I have is thine" (v. 31). He could kill a fatted calf at any time. Beloved, all in the Father's house is ours, but it will come only through obedience. And when He can trust us, we will not come behind in anything.

"...God wrought special miracles by the hands of Paul" (Acts 19:11). Let us notice the handkerchiefs that went from his body; it means to say that when he touched and sent them forth, God wrought special miracles through them, and diseases departed from the sick, and evil spirits went out of them. Is it not lovely? I believe after we lay hands on these handkerchiefs and pray over them, that they should be handled very sacredly, and even as the one carries them they will bring life, if they are carried in faith to the suffering one. The very effect of it, if you only believed, would change your own body as you carried it.

A woman came to me one day and said, "My husband is such a trial to me; the first salary he gets he spends it in drink, and then he cannot do his work and comes home; I love him very much, what can be done?" I said, "If I were you I would take a handkerchief and would place it under his head when he went to sleep at night, and say nothing to him, but have a living faith." We anointed a handkerchief in the name of Jesus, and she put it under his head. Oh, beloved, there is a way to reach these wayward ones. The next morning on his way to work he called for a glass of beer; he lifted it to his lips, but he thought there was something wrong with it, and he put it down and went out. He went to another saloon, and another, and did the same thing. He came home sober. His wife was gladly surprised and he told her the story; how it had affected him. That was the turning point in his life; it meant not only giving up drink, but it meant his salvation.

God wants to change our faith today. He wants us to see it is not obtained by struggling and working and pining. "...the Father himself loveth you..." (John 16:27). "...Himself took our infirmities, and bare our sicknesses" (Matthew 8:17). "Come unto me, all ye that labour and are heavy laden, and I will give you rest" (Matthew 11:28).

Who is the man that will take the place of Paul, and yield and yield and yield, until God so possesses him in such a way that from his body virtue shall flow to the sick and suffering? It will have to be the virtue of Christ that flows. Don't think there is some magic virtue in the handkerchief or you will miss the virtue; it is the living faith in the man who lays the handkerchief on his body, and the power of God through that faith. Praise God, we may lay hold of this living faith today. "The blood has never lost its power." As we get in touch with Jesus, wonderful things will take place; and what else? We shall get nearer and nearer to Him.

There is another side to it. "...exorcists, took upon them to call over them which had evil spirits the name of the Lord Jesus, saying, We adjure you by Jesus whom Paul preacheth...and the evil spirit answered and said, Jesus I know, and Paul I know; but who are ye?" (Acts 19:13,15). I beseech you in the name of Jesus, especially those of you who are baptized, to awaken up to the fact that you have power if God is with you; but there must be a resemblance between you and Jesus. The evil spirit said, "...Jesus I know, and Paul I know; but who are ye?" (Acts 19:15). Paul had the resemblance.

You are not going to get it without having His presence; His presence changes you. You are not going to be able to get the results without the marks of the Lord Jesus. The man must have the divine power within himself; devils will take no notice of any power if they do not see the

Christ. "Jesus I know, and Paul I know; but who are ye?" The difference between these men was they had not the marks of Christ, so the manifestation of the power of Christ was not seen.

You want power: don't take the wrong way. Don't take it as power because you speak in tongues, and if God has given you revelations along certain lines don't take that for the power; or if you have even laid hands on the sick and they have been healed, don't take that for the power. "The Spirit of the Lord is upon me..." (Luke 4:18); that alone is the power. Don't be deceived; there is a place to get where you know the Spirit is upon you, so you will be able to do the works which are wrought by this blessed Spirit of God in you, and the manifestation of His power shall be seen, and people will believe in the Lord.

What will make men believe the divine promises of God? Beloved, let me say to you today, God wants you to be ministering spirits, and it means to be clothed with another power. And this divine power, you know when it is there, and you know when it goes forth. The baptism of Jesus must bring us to have a single eye to the glory of God; everything else is wasted time and wasted energy. Beloved, we can reach it; it is a high mark but we can get to it. You ask how? "What wilt thou have me to do?" That is the plan. It means a perfect surrender to the call of God, and perfect obedience.

A dear young Russian came to England. He did not know the language, but learned it quickly and was very much used and blessed of God; and as the wonderful manifestations of the power of God were seen, they pressed upon him to know the secret of his power, but he felt it was so sacred between him and God he should not tell it, but they pressed him so much he finally said to them: "First God called me, and His presence was so precious, that I said to God at every call I would obey Him, and I yielded, and yielded, and yielded, until I realized that I was simply clothed with another power altogether, and I realized that God took me, tongue, thoughts and everything, and I was not myself but it was Christ working through me." How many of you today have known that God has called you over and over, and has put His hand upon you, but you have not yielded? How many of you have had the breathing of His power within you, calling you to prayer, and you have to confess you have failed?

I went to a house one afternoon where I had been called, and met a man at the door. He said, "My wife has not been out of bed for eight months; she is paralyzed. She has been looking so much for you to come, she is hoping God will raise her up." I went in and rebuked the devil's power. She said, "I know I am healed; if you go out I will get up." I left the house, and went away not hearing anything more about her. I went to a meeting that night, and a man jumped up and said he had something he wanted to say; he had to go to catch a train but wanted to talk first. He said, "I come to this city once a week, and I visit the sick all over the city. There is a woman I have been visiting and I was very much distressed about her; she was paralyzed and has lain on that bed many months, and when I went there today she was up doing her work." I tell this story because I want you to see Jesus.

We had a letter which came to our house to say that a young man was very ill. He had been to our Mission a few years before with a very bad foot; he had no shoe on, but a piece of leather fastened on the foot. God healed him that day. Three years after, something else came upon him. What it was I don't know, but his heart failed, and he was helpless; he could not rise or dress or do anything for himself, and in that condition he called his sister and told her to write and see if I would pray. My wife said to go, and she believed God would give me that life. I went, and when I got to this place I found the whole country was expecting me; they had said that when I came this man would be healed. I said to the woman when I arrived, "I have come." "Yes," she said, "but it is too late." "Is he alive?" I asked, "Yes, just alive," she said. I went in and put my hands upon him, and said, "Martin." He just breathed slightly, and whispered, "The doctor said if I move from this position I will never move again." I said, "Do you know the Scripture says, 'God is the strength of my heart, and my portion for ever'?" (Psalm 73:26). He said, "Shall I get up?" I said, "No."

That day was spent in prayer and ministering the Word. I found a great state of unbelief in that house, but I saw Martin had faith to be healed. His sister was home from the asylum. God held me there to pray for that place. I said to the family, "Get Martin's clothes ready; I believe he is to be raised up." I felt the unbelief. I went to the chapel and had prayer with a number of people around there, and before noon they too believed Martin would be healed. When I returned I said, "Are his clothes ready?" They said, "No." I said, "Oh, will you hinder God's work in this house?" I went in to Martin's room all alone. I said, "I believe God will do a new thing today. I believe when I lay hands on you the glory of heaven will fill the place." I laid my hands on him in the name of the Father, Son, and Holy Ghost, and immediately the glory of the Lord filled the room, and I went headlong to the floor. I did not see what took place on the bed, or in the room, but this young man began to shout out, "Glory, glory!" and I heard him say, "for Thy glory, Lord," and that man stood before me perfectly healed. He went to the door and opened it and his father stood there. He said, "Father, the Lord has raised me up," and the father fell to the floor and cried for salvation. The young woman brought out of the asylum was perfectly healed at that moment by the power of God in that house.

God wants us to see that the power of God coming upon people has something more in it than we have yet known. The power to heal and to baptize is in this place, but you must say, "Lord, what wilt thou have me to do?" You say it is four months before the harvest. If you had the eyes of Jesus you would see that the harvest is already here. The devil will say you can't have faith; you tell him he is a liar. The Holy Ghost wants you for the purpose of manifesting Jesus through you. Oh, may you never be the same again! The Holy Spirit moving upon us will make us to be like Him, and we will truly say, "Lord, what wilt thou have me to do?"

Published in *Triumphs of Faith*

SPIRITUAL GIFTS
November 1914

See the twelfth chapter of First Corinthians. "Now concerning spiritual gifts, brethren, I would not have you ignorant" (v. 1). Now when the Holy Ghost says that, He expects us to understand what the gifts are, and He wants us to understand that the church may be able to profit thereby.

"...no man can say Jesus is the Lord, but by the Holy Ghost" (1 Corinthians 12:3). Whenever I have come in touch with people who have acknowledged the Lord Jesus, I have known whether they knew anything about the Spirit of God, for every spirit which is of God testifies of Jesus, and you will always be able to tell by that their spiritual condition. If they do not confess that Jesus was manifested in the flesh, you may know that they have not the Spirit of God. Beloved, on the contrary, we find out that every spirit that confesses that Jesus is the Lord, is by the Holy Ghost.

> *...there are diversities of operations, but it is the same God which worketh all in all. But the manifestation of the Spirit is given to every man to profit withal.*
>
> *1 Corinthians 12:6,7*

Everyone who has received the Holy Ghost has within him great possibilities and unlimited power; also great possessions, not only of things which are present, but also of things which are to come. The Holy Ghost has power to equip you for every emergency. The reason people are not thus equipped is that they do not receive Him and do not yield to Him; they are timid and doubt, and in the measure that they doubt, they go down. But if you yield to His leadings and do not doubt, it will lead you to success and victory; you will grow in grace and will have not only a controlling power, but you will have a revealing power of the mind and purposes which God has for you. I see where all things are in the power of the Holy Ghost, and I must not fail to give you the same truth.

We must remember that we have entered into the manifestation of the glory of God, and in that is great power and strength. Many might be far ahead of where they are this morning but they have doubted. If by any means the enemy can come in and make you believe a lie, he will do so. We have had to struggle to maintain our standing in our salvation, for the enemy would beat us out of that if possible. It is in the closeness of the association and oneness with Christ where there is no fear, but perfect confidence all the time. The child of God need not go back a day for his experience, for the presence of the Lord is with him and the Holy Ghost is in him and in mighty power, if he will believe; and I see that we should stir one another up and provoke one another to good works.

The Pentecostal people have a "know" in their experience. We know that we have the Spirit abiding within and if we are not moved upon by the Spirit, we move the Spirit; that is what we mean by stirring up the

Spirit. And yet it is not we, but the living faith within us, it is the Spirit who stirs Himself up. Where are we living? I do not mean in the natural order. We are a spiritual people, a royal priesthood, a holy people.

If we find that there is unbelief in us we must search our hearts to see why it is there. Where there is a living faith, there is no unbelief, and we go on from faith to faith until it becomes as natural to live there as can be. But if you try to live faith before you are just, you will fail, for "the just shall live by faith," (Romans 1:17) and when you are just, it is a natural consequence for you to live by faith. It is easy; it is joyful; it is more than that, it is our life, and spiritual inheritance.

> *For to one is given by the Spirit the word of wisdom; to another the word of knowledge by the same Spirit.*
>
> *1 Corinthians 12:8*

If the Spirit can stir you up this morning, you will come short in no gift. God wants you to see that we need not come behind in any gift, and wants to bring us to a place where we will be on fire because of what He has called us to. We ought always to move the tent every night; we cannot stay in one place; the land is before us; there are wonderful possessions. He says, "They are yours; go in and claim them."

Paul prayed that we might be "able to comprehend with all saints," (Ephesians 3:18) and I see that place where Paul was in the Holy Ghost and I believe that God is calling us today to comprehend as much as Paul comprehended. It is in the perfect will of God that we should possess the needed gifts, but there must be unity between God and you. When the gifts are in evidence, the whole church is built up, Christ being the head. Jesus said, "I come to do Thy will, O my God!" and as we surrender in that way God will be delighted to hand to us the gift which is necessary. The more we realize that God has furnished us with a gift, the more completely we will be united with Jesus, so that people will be conscious of Him rather than of His gift.

Oh, beloved, if it is not all of the Holy Ghost and if we are not so lost and controlled in the ministry of the gift, that it is only to be Jesus, it will all be a failure and come to naught. There was none so self-conscious as they who said, "In Thy name we have cast out devils." They were so controlled by the natural and the thought that they had done it all, that God was not in it. But when He comes forth and does it, it is all right.

There is a place in the Holy Ghost where we will not allow unbelief to affect us, for God has all power in heaven and earth. And now that I am in the secret knowledge of this power I stand in a place where my faith is not to be limited, because I have the knowledge that He is in me and I in Him. Some of you come from your homes with broken hearts, you have a longing for something to strengthen you in conditions which exist there, and a power to make these conditions different. You say you are unequally yoked together. You have a mighty power that is greater than all natural power. You can take victory over your homes, and your husbands, and children and you must do it in the Lord's way. Suppose you do see many things that ought to be different; if it is your cross you must take it and win the victory for God; it can be done, for greater is He that is in you than all the power of hell. I reckon that any man filled with the Holy Ghost is equal to a legion of devils any day.

A man in Glasgow got up and said, "I have power to cast out devils." A man full of devils got up and came to him, and this man did everything he could, but could not cast out the devils. Do you want to cast out devils? You be sure it is the Holy Ghost that does it. You know that spirit of divination followed Paul three days. The Holy Ghost has His dwelling place within me and is stirring up my heart and life to adore Jesus. Other things must be left behind; I must adore Him.

God says, "Every one that asketh receiveth." What do you ask for? What is the motive? In the fourth chapter of James we read that they asked amiss, that they might consume it on their own lusts. There is a need for the gifts, and God will reveal to you what you ought to have, and you ought never to be satisfied until you receive it. It is important that we know we can do nothing of ourselves; but we may know that we are clothed with the power of God so we are not in the natural man in a sense, but as we go forth in this power things will take place as they took place in the days of the disciples. When I received the new birth at eight years of age it was so precious and lovely; I have never lost the knowledge of my acceptance with God since that time. Brothers and sisters, there was a work that God wrought in me when I tarried for the baptism, which has been wonderful. I was in a strange position; I had testified to having received the baptism of the Holy Spirit for sixteen years and had the anointing of the Spirit; I could not speak without it. My wife would come to me and say, "They are waiting for you to come out and speak to the people." I would say, "I cannot and will not come without the anointing of the Spirit." I can see now I was calling the anointing the baptism; but when the Holy Spirit came into my body until I could not give satisfaction to the glory that was in me, God took this tongue, and I spoke as the Spirit gave utterance which brought perfect satisfaction to me. When He comes in He abides. I then began to reach out as the Holy Ghost showed me.

In the call of Elisha God saw the young man's willingness to obey. The twelve yoke of oxen, the plow and all soon came to naught and all bridges had to be burned behind him. Brother, the Lord has called you. Are you separated from the old things? You cannot go without. As Elisha went on with Elijah, he heard the wonderful things of his ministry, and he was longing for the time when he would take his master's place. The time was coming. His master said to him, "I am going to Gilgal today, I want you to remain here." "Master," he said, "I must go with you." I find that other people knew something about it for they said to him, "Do you know the Master is going to be taken away from you today?" He said, "Hold your peace, I know it." Later on the master said, "I want to go on to Bethel; you stay here." But Elisha says, "No, I will not leave thee" (see 2 Kings 2). Something had been revealed to Elisha. Perhaps God is drawing you to do something; you feel it. Then Elijah said, "The Lord hath sent me to Jordan; you stay here." It was the spirit of the old man that was stirring up the young man. If you see zeal in somebody else, get on a stretch for it; it is for you. I am recognizing that God is wanting all the members of His body joined together; and He makes us feel in these days when a person is failing to go on with God, we must have that member.

When they came to the Jordan Elijah switched his mantle over it, and they passed over, and no doubt Elisha said, "I must follow his steps." And when they had gone over, the old man said, "You have done well, you would not stay back; what is the real desire of your heart? I feel I am going to leave you; ask what you like now before I leave you." "Master," he says, "I have seen all that you have done; Master, I want twice as much as you have." I believe it is the fainthearted that do not get much. As they went on up the hill down comes the chariot of fire, nearer and nearer, and when it lights, the old man jumps in, and the young man says, "Father, Father, Father," and down comes the mantle. What have you asked for? Are you satisfied to go on in the old way now when the Holy Spirit has come to give you an unlimited supply of power, and He says, "What will you have?"

We see Peter so filled with the Holy Ghost that his shadow falling on sick people heals them (Acts 5:15). What do you want? He asked and he got it. Elisha comes down and he says, "I don't feel any different," but he had the knowledge that feelings are not to be counted for anything; some of you people are looking at your feelings all the time. He came to the waters as an ordinary man, then in the knowledge that he possessed the mantle (not in any feelings about it) he said, "Where is the God of Elijah?" and he put his feet down. When you put your feet down and say you are going to have a double portion, you will get it. After he had crossed, there were the young men again (they always come where there is power) and they said, "The spirit of Elijah doth rest upon Elisha."

You are to have the gifts, and claim them, and the Lord will certainly change your life and you will be new men and women. Are you asking for a double portion this morning? I trust that no one shall come behind in any gift. You say, "I have asked; do you think God will be pleased to have me ask again?" Yes, do before Him; ask again, and we may this morning go forth in the Spirit of the mantle, and it shall be no longer I, but the Holy Ghost, and we shall see and know His power because we believe.

Published in *Triumphs of Faith*

THOU ART THE CHRIST

November 1914

I need not say how pleased I am to be among you again. We are coming in contact this afternoon with a living Christ. It is upon this Rock God is building His Church, and the gates of hell shall not prevail against it

f wonderful possibilities because of this Rock. Take a stand
is afternoon that this Rock cannot be overthrown.

ne to a meeting where I was, who was paralyzed and was
years old. But the power of God came into her, and she
thened and blessed after prayer she rushed up and down in
vay. Brothers and sisters, what I see in this woman's heal-
tration of what God will do. I am trusting that we shall all
hened today in the power of God that we shall not allow
fear to come into our hearts; but you will know that you
new by a living faith, and there is in that faith within you
omplish wonderful things for God. I want to say that the
ful and marvelous faith is the simple faith of a little child.
aith that dares. There is a boldness that comes and we say,
healed."

ht his son to my meeting, and he was all drawn to one side
its for years. The father said, "Can you do anything for my
aid, "In the name of Jesus, yes, he can be healed"; and I
ecause of the Rock it could be done. There is a Spirit that
us, and this is nothing less than the life of Him who gave
s, for He is the Rock-life in us. I wonder if you wait until
power sweeps over you before you have power to bind;
power. The Rock is within you, you have power to bind
loose because you consist of that Rock. What you have to
on that fact and use the power. Will you do it?

r, in the name of Jesus, I bind the evil spirit in this young
at name of Jesus! We make too little use of that name.
dren cried "Hosanna." If we would let ourselves go, and
ise and *praise* Him, God would give us the shout of vic-
t meeting the father brought the young man again, and
eed to ask if he was delivered; the brightness of his face,
g of the father's face told the story. I said, "Is it all right
said, "Yes." Oh, I see it is needed so much, this power to
r to loose. Brothers and sisters, wherever you are you can
e. God wants to change your name this afternoon from
mas to prevailing Israel.

(Matthew 16:18). We are more confident today than we were yesterday. God is building us up in this faith, so that we are living in great expectation. He is bringing us into a place with Himself where we can say, "I have seen God." I have been asking God to send us His Word that is on fire; something that will live in our hearts, that will abide with us forever. It is important that every day we should lay some new foundation that can never be uprooted. Oh, for a living touch from God, and a new inspiration of power, and a deeper sense of His love! I have been thinking about the sixteenth chapter of Matthew, and Peter's answer to Jesus when He asked His disciples the question, "Whom say ye that I am?" (Matthew 16:15); and Peter answered saying, "Thou art the Christ, the Son of the living God" (v. 16).

Beloved friends, do you know Him this afternoon? Has this revelation come to your heart? Do you call Him Lord? Do you find comfort in the fact that He is yours? "Whom say ye that I am?" The Master knew what was in their thoughts before He asked them. This fact makes me long more and more to be really true; God is seeing right into my heart and reads my thoughts. There is something in what Jesus said to Peter that is applicable to us this afternoon:

> *Blessed art thou, Simon Barjona: for flesh and blood hath not revealed it unto thee, but my Father which is in heaven.*
> *Matthew 16:17*

If you can call Jesus Lord this afternoon, it is by the Holy Ghost. And so there ought to be within us this afternoon a deep response that says, "Thou art the Christ." When we can say this from our hearts it makes us know that we are not born of flesh and blood, but of the Spirit of the living God. If you will go back to the time when you first had the knowledge that you were born of God, you will see that there was within you a deep cry for your Father; you found you had a heavenly Father. If you want to know the real success of any life it will be because of this knowledge, "Thou art the Christ." This knowledge is the rock foundation, "and the gates of hell shall not prevail against it. And I will give unto thee the keys of the kingdom of heaven" (Matthew 16:18,19).

It is about this rock, this blessed foundation-truth, that I want to speak this afternoon; this knowledge of our personal acceptance with God;

this life of faith that we have come into. It is because of this rock foundation that we have this living faith, and that foundation cannot be overthrown. He has given us power to bind and loose. Everyone that has come down to this rock foundation ought to be in this position. I want you to go away from this meeting knowing that you are on this rock foundation and able to bind and able to loose; and to have that living faith that you can pray and *know* you have the answer because of God's promises, and the fact that Jesus said, "If ye believe." It is on this rock that our faith must be based, and this will never fail; God has established it forever.

From that time forth began Jesus to show unto his disciples, how that he must go unto Jerusalem, and suffer many things...and be killed, and be raised again the third day. Then Peter took him, and began to rebuke him, saying, Be it far from thee, Lord: this shall not be unto thee. But he turned, and said unto Peter, Get thee behind me, Satan...Then said Jesus unto his disciples, If any man will come after me, let him deny himself, and take up his cross, and follow me.

Matthew 16:21-24

We find the fundamental truths of all the ages were planted right in the life of Peter. We see evidences of the spiritual power to which he had attained, and we also see the natural power working. Jesus saw that He must suffer if He would reach that spiritual life which God intended Him to reach. So Jesus said, "I must go forward; your words, Peter, are an offense to Me." So if you seek to save yourself it is an offense to God. God has been impressing it upon me more and more that if I seek at any time favor of men, or earthly power, I shall lose favor with God, and I cannot have faith. Jesus said, "How can ye believe if ye seek honor one of another?" God is speaking to us, every one, and trying to get us to cut the shore lines. There is only one place where we can get the mind and will of God; it is alone with God; if you look to anybody else you cannot get it. If we seek to save ourselves we shall never reach the place where we will be able to bind and loose. There is a close companionship between you and Jesus that nobody knows about, where every day you have to choose or refuse. It is in the narrow way that you get the power to bind and the power to loose. I know that He was separated from His own kith and kin,

A young woman was brought to me who had a cancer; she had gotten very low. People need cheering up. This young woman was cast down. I said to her, "Cheer up"; but I could not get her to cheer up, so in the name of Jesus I bound this evil power, and then laid hands on her and said, "Sister, you are free." Then she arose and asked if she might say something, and she rubbed the place where the cancer had been and said, "It is all gone."

Oh, brothers and sisters, I want you to see that power is yours. God is delighted when we use the power He has given us. I believe every child of God has a measure of this power, but there is a fuller manifestation of the power when they get so filled that they speak in tongues. I want you to press on till you get the fulness. We must send these people home, Mrs. Montgomery, with a loaf of bread and a flagon of wine, as David did those people (2 Samuel 6:19).

When shall we see all the people filled with the Holy Ghost, and the things done as they were in the Acts of the apostles? It will be when all the people shall say, "Lord, thou art God." I want you to come into a place of such relationship with God that you will know your prayers are answered, because He has promised.

I dropped into a cobbler's shop one morning, and there was a man who had his eyes covered with a green shade, and they were so inflamed he was suffering terribly. He said, "I cannot rest anywhere." I did not ask him what he believed, but laid down my Bible, and put my hands on those poor suffering eyes in the name of Jesus. He said, "This is strange; I have no pain; I am free." Do you think the human mind can do that? I say, "No." We do these things with a consciousness that God will answer, and He is pleased with that kind of service.

A boy came into the meeting on crutches; he had a broken ankle; several of us joined in prayer, and with joy I saw that boy so healed that he put his crutches under his arm and walked away.

Beloved, Jesus is coming soon; there are so many things that seem to say, "He is at the door." Will you use the power of the Rock within you, for His glory?

Address given in Oakland, California

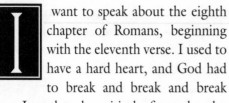

SONS AND JOINT-HEIRS

February 1915

I want to speak about the eighth chapter of Romans, beginning with the eleventh verse. I used to have a hard heart, and God had to break and break and break me. I used to be critical of people who preached divine healing, and did certain things which I thought they should not do. Then God began to put me through a testing and to break me; I went down before God, and then the hardness was taken away and all bitterness. I believe God wants to get all the grit and hardness out of us.

> *...if the Spirit of him that raised up Jesus from the dead dwell in you, he that raised up Christ from the dead shall also quicken your mortal bodies by his Spirit that dwelleth in you.*
>
> Romans 8:11

The power of God here is dealing with our "mortal bodies," but I see the power of the Spirit today wants to quicken us both in spirit and body.

> *...If ye live after the flesh, ye shall die: but if ye THROUGH THE SPIRIT do mortify the deeds of the body, ye shall live. For as many as are led by the Spirit of God, they are the sons of God. For ye have not received the spirit of bondage again to fear; but ye have received the spirit of adoption, whereby we cry, Abba, Father...And if children, then heirs; heirs of God, and joint-heirs with Christ....*
>
> Romans 8:13-15,17

The thought that specially comes to me today is that of sonship. The Spirit brings us to a place where we see that we are sons of God. And because of this glorious position we are not only sons but heirs, and not only heirs, but joint-heirs. And because of that, I want you to see that *all* the promises of God are yea and amen to you through Jesus in the Holy Ghost. If the Spirit of God that raised Jesus from the dead is in you, that power of the Spirit is going to quicken your mortal body. And it brings me into a living place to believe that as an adopted child I may lay hold of the promises. I see two wonderful things: I see deliverance for the body, and I see also the power of the Spirit in sonship is raising me up, and pressing me onward to translation through faith in the Lord Jesus Christ.

I want to read two verses in the seventeenth chapter of John:

> *These words spake Jesus, and lifted up his eyes to heaven, and said, Father, the hour is come; glorify thy Son, that thy Son also may glorify thee: As thou hast given him power over all flesh, that he should give eternal life to as many as thou hast given him. And this is life eternal, that they might know thee the only true God, and Jesus Christ, whom thou hast sent.*
>
> *Verses 1-3*

It is no small thing to be brought into fellowship with the Father through Jesus Christ. The Spirit that is in you not only puts to death all other power, but He is showing us our privilege and bringing us into a faith that we can claim all we need. The moment a man comes into the knowledge of Christ he is made an heir of heaven. By the Spirit he is being changed into the image of the Son of God, and it is in that image that we can definitely look into the face of the Father and see that the things we ask for are done.

> *...if children, then heirs; heirs of God, and joint-heirs with Christ; if so be that we suffer with him, that we may be also glorified together. For I reckon that the sufferings of this present time are not worthy to be compared with the glory that shall be revealed in us.*
>
> *Romans 8:17,18*

And the glory is not only going to be revealed, but it is already revealed in us. We are being changed from glory to glory. I want you to go away from this camp meeting in the knowledge of your sonship. I want you to go away knowing that the Spirit which raised up Jesus from the dead is dwelling in your mortal body, and making you a son. "...we shall be like him; for we shall see him as he is" (1 John 3:2). It does not mean that we shall have faces like Jesus, but have the same Spirit. When they look at us and see the glory, they will say, "Yes, it is the same Spirit," for they will see the lustre of the glory of Jesus Christ. Beloved, we are being changed.

> *For the earnest expectation of the creature waiteth for the man-ifestation of the sons of God.*
>
> Romans 8:19

Every one of us who is born of God, and has the power of the Holy Spirit in him, is longing for the manifestation of the sonship. You say, when shall these things come forth? So Paul gets into the expectation of it and says:

> *...the whole creation groaneth and travaileth in pain together until now...even we ourselves groan...waiting for the adoption, to wit, the redemption of our body.*
>
> Romans 8:22,23

Brothers and sisters, within me this afternoon, there is a cry and a long-ing for deliverance. Praise God, it is coming! There is a true sense even now in which you may live in the resurrection power. The Holy Spirit is working in us and bringing us to a condition where we know He is doing a work in us. I never felt so near heaven as last night when the house was shaking with an earthquake, and I thought my Lord might come. More than crossing the sea and seeing my children, I would rather see Jesus. "For the creature was made subject to vanity..." (Romans 8:20). Praise God, we are delivered by the power of the Spirit.

> *Because the creature itself also shall be delivered from the bondage of corruption into the glorious liberty of the children of God.*
>
> Romans 8:21

Do not say, how can this be and that be? The sovereign grace and power of God are equal to all these things. I changed by the power of the Holy Spirit, that I know there is a bigger man in me than the natural man.

> *And not only they, but ourselves also, which have the firstfruits of the Spirit, even we ourselves groan within ourselves, waiting for the adoption....*
>
> Romans 8:23

Brothers and sisters, are you really waiting? The baptism of the Holy Spirit links heaven to earth, and God wants us to be so filled with the Spirit, and walk in the Spirit, that while we live here on earth our heads will be right up in heaven. Brothers and sisters, the Spirit can give you patience to wait. The baptism in the Holy Ghost is the essential power in the body which will bring rest from all your weariness, and give you a hopeful expectation that each day may be the day we go up with Him. We must not be foolish people folding our hands and giving up everything. I find there is no time like the present to be up and active. "...the Spirit also helpeth our infirmities..." (Romans 8:26). We have need for our infirmities to be helped by the Spirit, in order that the body should not be taxed out of measure. The Holy Spirit Himself will pray through you and bring to your remembrance the things you ought to pray for, according to the mind of the Spirit. Is there a person in this place who says I have no need of the Holy Ghost?

A young man came into the meeting last night and I asked him where he stood. He said, "I am satisfied." I said, "You are in a sad condition; there is nothing anywhere for a man who is satisfied. It is only the hungry and thirsty that God says shall receive and shall be filled." "Blessed are they which do hunger and thirst after righteousness: for they shall be filled" (Matthew 5:6).

The highest purpose God has for us is that we shall be transformed into the image of His Son. We have seen in a measure God's purpose in filling us with the Spirit, that He might bring about in us the image of His Son.

> *For whom he did foreknow, he also did predestinate to be conformed to the image of his Son, that he might be the firstborn among many brethren. Moreover whom he did predestinate, them he also called: and whom he called, them he also justified; and whom he justified, them he also glorified.*
>
> *Romans 8:29,30*

Where are you this afternoon; are you standing on that? I believe there are two classes of people, the whosever will and the whosever won't. I want you to examine yourselves this afternoon and see where you stand, and if you stand on these truths which God has given, you will be amazed to see how God will make everything move so that you may be conformed to the image of His Son.

> *But when it pleased God, who separated me from my mother's womb, and called me by his grace, to reveal his Son in me, that I might preach him among the heathen....*
>
> *Galatians 1:15,16*

It is a sad thing today to see how people are astonished at the workings of God. Millions of years ago He purposed in His heart to do this mighty thing in us. Are you going to refuse it, or are you going to yield? I thank God He predestinated me to be saved, and it is a case of whosever will, and whosoever will not believe. You see it is a mystery, but God purposed it before the foundation of the world. And if you yield, He will put in you a living faith, and you cannot get away from the power of it. Oh, brothers and sisters, let us come a little nearer. How amazing it is that we can be so transformed that the thoughts of Christ will be first in our minds. How blessed that when everybody around you is interested in everything else, you are thinking about Jesus Christ. Brothers and sisters, let us get a little nearer still.

I want to say this afternoon it is the purpose of God that you should rise into the place of sonship. Don't miss the purpose God has in His heart for you. If you could only realize that God wants to make of you the firstfruits, and separate you unto Himself. God has lifted some of you up over and over again. It is amazing how God in His mercy has restored and restored, "...and whom he called, them he also justified: and whom he justified, them he also glorified" (Romans 8:30). The glorification is still going on, and is going to exceed what it is now.

Within your heart this afternoon there surely must be a response to this call. "What shall we then say to these things? If God be for us, who can be against us?" (Romans 8:31). It does not matter who is against us. If there are millions against you, God has purposed it and will bring you right through to glory. "What shall we say then to these things?" (v. 31). Human wisdom has to stand still. It is with the heart that man believeth unto righteousness.

> *He that spared not his own Son, but delivered him up for us all,*
> *how shall he not with him also freely give us all things?*
> *Romans 8:32*

Brothers and sisters, what do you want? That is the question. What have you come here for? We have seen God work in horribly diseased bodies. Our God is able to heal and to "...freely give us *all things*" (v. 32).

"Who shall lay any thing to the charge of God's elect?" (Romans 8:33). I tell you, it is a bad business for the man who puts his hand upon God's anointed. "Who is he that condemneth?" (v. 34). How much of that there is today; brother condemning brother, everybody condemning one another. You also go about condemning yourself. The devil is the accuser of the brethren. But there is power in the blood to free us and keep us and to bring us healing. Do not let the enemy cripple you and bind you. Why don't you believe God's Word? There is a blessed place for you in the Holy Ghost. Instead of condemning you, Christ is interceding for you.

> *For I am persuaded, that neither death, nor life, nor angels, nor*
> *principalities, nor powers, nor things present, nor things to come,*
> *nor height, nor depth, nor any other creature, shall be able to sep-*
> *arate us from the love of God, which is in Christ Jesus our Lord.*
> *Romans 8:38,39*

Beloved, you are in a wonderful place. I want you to take home this afternoon the knowledge that because God has called you and chosen you, He wants you to know today that you have power with Him, and because you are sons, and joint-heirs, you have a right to healing for your bodies, and to be delivered from all the power of the enemy.

Published in *Triumphs of Faith*

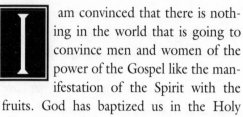

THE POWER OF THE GOSPEL

July 1915

I am convinced that there is nothing in the world that is going to convince men and women of the power of the Gospel like the manifestation of the Spirit with the fruits. God has baptized us in the Holy Ghost for a purpose, that He may show His mighty power in human flesh, as He did in Jesus, and He is bringing us to a place where He may manifest these gifts.

> *...no man speaking by the Spirit of God calleth Jesus accursed: and no man can say that Jesus is the Lord, but by the Holy Ghost.*
> *1 Corinthians 12:3*

Every man who does not speak the truth concerning this Word, which is Jesus, makes Him the accursed; so all we have to do is to have the revelation of the Word in our hearts and there will be no fear of our being led astray, because this Word is nothing else but Jesus. In the gospel of St. John you read that the Word was God, and He became flesh and dwelt amongst us and we beheld His glory, the glory of the only begotten Son of the Father. So it is revealed that He is the Son of God — the Word of God. This Word (pointing to the Bible) is nothing else than the Word of God, and everything that confesses it not you can put down straight away, without getting mixed up at all, that it is not of the Holy Ghost and consequently you can wipe out all such things. There is no difficulty about saving yourselves, because the Word of God will always save.

> *Now there are diversities of gifts, but the same Spirit. And there are diversities of administrations, but the same Lord. And there are diversities of operations, but it is the same God which worketh all in all. But the manifestation of the Spirit is given to every man to profit withal.*
> *1 Corinthians 12:4-7*

My heart is in this business. I am brought face to face with the fact that now the Holy Ghost is dwelling within me, that He is dwelling in my body, and as John says in his epistle, the unction of the Holy One is within. The unction of the Holy One is the Holy Spirit manifested in us. So we see that straight away within us there is the power to make manifest and bring forth those gifts which He has promised, and these gifts will be manifested in proportion as we live in the unction of the Spirit of God. Thus we shall find out that those gifts must be manifested.

My brother here (Mr. Moser) was suffering from want of sleep. He had had no full night of sleep for a long time. I said last night, "I command thee in the name of Jesus to sleep." When he came this morning he was well, he had had a good night's sleep. A man came to me in Toronto and said he had not had a night's rest for three years and that he had lost the power to sleep. He also said he had lost his business; what could we do for him? I said, "I command you in the name of the Lord Jesus to go home and sleep." Without questioning me further he went home, and at eight o'clock the next morning he rung me up and said, "Can I see you? I want to see you soon. I have been sleeping at night." So he came, and then said, "Can you give me power to get my business back?" I said, "Come to the meeting tonight." He said, "I will." He came, and the power of the Lord filled the place. Conviction settled upon that man. A call was made to the altar. He came, but fell on the way. God saved him, and that was the turning point in his life and for his business. Beloved, the power of the Holy Ghost is within us to profit withal. He says,

> *To one is given by the Spirit the word of wisdom; to another the word of knowledge by the same Spirit; to another faith by the same Spirit; to another the gifts of healing by the same Spirit; to another the working of miracles; to another prophecy; to another discerning of spirits; to another divers kinds of tongues; to another the interpretation of tongues: But all these worketh that one and the selfsame Spirit, dividing to every man severally as he will.*
>
> *1 Corinthians 12:8-11*

Paul distinctly says that it is possible for any one man not to come behind in any gift according to the measure of faith as he receives of the Lord Jesus. No doubt some of you present have sometimes thought what a blessed thing it would be if you had been the Virgin Mary. Listen, "Blessed is the womb that bare thee, and the paps which thou hast sucked. But he said, Yea rather, blessed are they that hear the word of God, and keep it" (Luke 11:27,28). You see a higher position than Mary's is attained through simple faith in what the Scriptures say.

If we receive the Word of God as it is given to us, there will be power in our bodies to claim the gifts of God, and it will amaze the world when they see the power of God manifested through these gifts. I believe we are coming to a time when these gifts will be more distinctly manifested. What can be more convincing? Aye, He is a lovely Jesus. He went forth from place to place, rebuking demons, healing the sick, and doing other wonderful things. What was the reason? God was with Him.

Wherever there is a child of God who dare receive the Word of God and cherish it, there is God made manifest in the flesh, for the Word of God is life and spirit and brings us into a place where we know that we have power with God and with men, in proportion to our loyalty of faith in the Word of God.

Now, beloved, I feel somehow that we have missed the greatest principle which underlies the baptism of the Holy Spirit. The greatest principle is that God the Holy Ghost came into my body to make manifest the mighty works of God and that I may profit withal. Not one gift alone, but as God the Holy Ghost abides in my body I find He fills it, and then one can truly say it is the unction of the Holy One. It so fills us that we feel we can command demons to come out of persons possessed; and when I lay hands on the sick in the name of the Lord Jesus I realize that this body is the outer coil merely and that within is the Son of God. For I receive the Word of Christ and Christ is in me, the power of God is in me, and the Holy Ghost is making that Word a living Word, and the Holy Ghost makes me say, "Come out!" It is not Wigglesworth. It is the power of the Holy Ghost that makes manifest the glorious presence of Christ.

Published in *Flames of Fire*

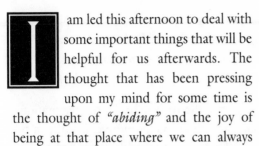

THE PLACE OF VICTORY

January 1916

I am led this afternoon to deal with some important things that will be helpful for us afterwards. The thought that has been pressing upon my mind for some time is the thought of *"abiding"* and the joy of being at that place where we can always count upon being in the *presence of power*, where we know God's presence is with us, leading to the place where *victory is assured*. That is the important truth I have been led to think of, and we are here to get hold of the thought that if we keep in the right place with God, God can do anything with us.

I am going to turn to two or three passages of Scripture. The first is Luke 4, first verse:

> *And Jesus being full of the Holy Ghost returned from Jordan, and was led by the Spirit into the wilderness.*

Mark speaks about being driven by the Spirit. Whatever either Mark or Luke means, there is one thing certain, and that is this, there is a power, a majesty, falling on Jesus, and He is no longer the same man — He has now *received this mighty anointing power of God* and in this place He realizes that the only thing for Him to do is to *submit*, and as He submits He is more and more *covered with the power*, and led by the Spirit. The Holy Spirit takes Him away into the wilderness, with its darkness and great privations. For forty days He was without food, but because of the presence and the power within and on Him, He is certain of victory. With this power He faces the wild beasts of the wilderness and the privations as to every human sustenance, and then at the end of forty days, in that holy attainment, He is brought into a state of persecution and trial such as probably has never attacked a man before. And in that place where He is, God sustains Him mightily. With what? With this holy — and I want you to think about it — this holy, *blessed unction* which is upon Jesus, and which so brings prophecy to bear upon Satan that Jesus is like the pen of a ready writer, and slays Satan every time with prophecy.

> *...Jesus returned in the power of the Spirit into Galilee: and there went out a fame of him through all the region round about. And he taught in their synagogues, being glorified of all.*
>
> *Luke 4:14,15*

I want you to understand that after the trials, after all the temptations, and everything, He came out more full of God, more clothed with the Spirit, more ready for the fight. The enduement with power had such an effect upon Him that other people saw it and flocked to hear Him, and great blessings came to the land. He is among His kinsfolk and relations, and in the spirit of this kind of holy attainment He goes into the synagogue. There was delivered to Him a roll of the book, and He read:

> *The Spirit of the Lord is upon me, for he hath anointed me to preach the gospel to the poor....*
>
> *Luke 4:18*

I want you to keep before you where the anointing came from. How was He anointed? How did it come to Him? You know how that was. And in just the same manner I see that the Holy Ghost also *fell upon the disciples at Pentecost.* I see that they were anointed with the same power, and I see that they went forth and success attended their ministry until the *power of God swept through the whole earth.* I want you to see that it was because of this unction, this power, that when Peter and John spoke to the lame man at the gate of the temple, he was able to rise and leap for joy. The Holy Ghost, coming upon an individual, is capable of changing him, and fertilizing his spiritual life, and filling him with such power, and grace, that he may not be able to say what could not happen. What can happen, what is possible, if we reach this place and keep in it — abide in it?

Some people have an idea that they have to be doing something. I beseech you, by the power of the Holy Ghost today, that you see that there is one thing only that is going to accomplish the purposes of God, and that is *being in the Spirit.* I don't care how dry the land is; I don't care how thirsty the land is, or how many vessels or how few, that are round about, I beseech you in the name of Jesus, that you keep in the Spirit. That's the secret.

"Son of man, can these bones live? And I answered, O Lord God, Thou knowest" (Ezekiel 37:3). When you are in the Spirit and the dry bones are round about you, and barren conditions all about you, and you think everything is exactly opposite to your desires, and you can see no deliverance by human power, then, knowing your condition is known to God and that God wants men and women who are willing to submit and submit, and yield and yield to the Holy Spirit until their bodies are saturated and soaked with God, you realize that God your Father has you in such a condition that at any moment He can reveal His will to you.

Now I want you to understand that there is something more in it. I want you to see that God is everything to us, and I believe that we have come to a place where we have to submit ourselves to the mighty unctionizing power of God and where we shall see we are in the will of God. And I pray God the Holy Ghost that if He does one thing among us this afternoon, it will be to show us our leanness, our farness from this place. Not that we are not in the running for it, but what we want is a great *hunger and thirst for God*. He said, "O ye dry bones, hear the word of the Lord" (Ezekiel 37:4). I would like you to understand that God speaks first, and He speaks so loud and clear and so distinct that this man who was filled with the Spirit hears every word. I want you to understand that there is not a move in the valley; until the word of the Lord is uttered, the bones are as dry as at the beginning. But what is the matter? God has spoken and the message has gone forth. What is it? Ah! it is only that the Word of God has gone forth *through His servant the prophet*. The world has to be brought to a knowledge of the truth, but that will only be brought about *through human instrumentality*, and that will be when the human instrument is at a place where he will say all that the Holy Spirit directs him to say.

The man rose up, and clothed with divine power, he began to speak, he began to prophesy; then there was a rattling among the bones; bone to bone at the voice of the man filled with the Spirit of the living God. God had given him the victory. God in like manner wants to give us the victory. What does the Word say? "Be still, and know that I am God," (Psalm 46:10) the place of tranquility, where we know that He is controlling and moving us by the mighty power of His Spirit.

Beloved, that is the place which we reach. This prophecy is for us. Truly God wants to begin this in us. There are many dry places, what is that to do with you? The Lord's hand is not shortened that it cannot save. It is man's extremity that God finds to be His opportunity, and it is for His Word to awaken. "...all things are possible to him that believeth" (Mark 9:23). But if we are to do the will of God at the right time and place, we must get into the Spirit and so give God a fair chance.

"So I prophesied as I was commanded..." (Ezekiel 37:7). He just did what he was told to do. It takes more to live in that place than any other I know of — to live in that place where you hear God's voice. It is only by the power of the Holy Spirit that you can do as you are told quickly. "...and as I prophesied, there was a noise, and behold a shaking, and the bones came together, bone to his bone" (Ezekiel 37:7).

There is something worth your notice in this. It is only the Spirit that can make the crooked straight. Only yield so that He may have full control of all you are. We must get to that place where we shall see God and know His voice when He sends us with a message that brings life, power, and victory. "...and [they] stood up upon their feet, an exceeding great army" (Ezekiel 37:10).

Published in *Flames of Fire*

THE MIGHT OF THE SPIRIT

September 1916

Shall we turn to the first chapter of the Acts of the apostles?

The former treatise have I made, O Theophilus, of all that Jesus began both to do and teach, until the day in which he was taken up, after that he through the Holy Ghost had given commandments unto the apostles whom he had chosen: To whom also he shewed himself alive after his passion by many infallible proofs...And, being assembled together with them, commanded them that they should not depart from Jerusalem, but wait for the promise of the Father, which, saith he, ye have heard of me.

> *For John truly baptized with water; but ye shall be baptized with the Holy Ghost not many days hence. When they therefore were come together, they asked of him, saying, Lord, wilt thou at this time restore again the kingdom to Israel? And he said unto them, It is not for you to know the times or the seasons, which the Father hath put in his own power. But ye shall receive power, after that the Holy Ghost is come upon you: and ye shall be witnesses unto me both in Jerusalem, and in all Judaea, and in Samaria, and unto the uttermost part of the earth.*
>
> *Acts 1:1-8*

This morning I understand that our subject is *Power for Service*, and *Power in Service*. It is a very wonderful subject, and possibly we shall not be able today to define all its lines. But there is so much in it that we are comprehending now what was once blank; there is much now that we know about, that we are not feeling after, not thinking about, not speaking so much about as something not yet quite clear; but we are speaking the things we do know, and testifying to the things which we have seen. Now we are on the Rock. We are understanding now what Peter received on that memorable day when our Lord said to him, "...thou art Peter, and upon this rock I will build my church; and the gates of hell shall not prevail against it" (Matthew 16:18).

We are standing now on the foundation, the Rock, Christ, the Word, the living Word. The power is contained in substance there. Christ is the substance of our faith. He is the hope of our inheritance, He is the substance and sum of our whole convention, and outside that we are altogether outside the plan of the great ideal of this convention. *Christ the centre.* "...ye shall receive power, after that the Holy Ghost is come upon you..." (Acts 1:8). Jesus was living in the knowledge of the power. The Spirit of the Lord was upon Him.

These are some of the important lines that I want, God breathing through me, to deal with today — the fact of power being there, the fact of a knowledge of the power, the fact of the substance being there, the fact of that which is being created, or breathed in, or formed by God Himself in the individual. We have come into a new order, we are dwelling in a place where Christ is the whole substance, where man is but the carcass or the clay, and the Word of God the temple. Within the

temple there is a living principle laid down of rock, the Word of the living God, formed in us, and a thousand times more mighty than "me," in thought, in language, in activity, in movement; there is an unction, a force, a power mightier than dynamite, more strong than the mightiest gun that has ever been made, and able to resist the greatest pressure that the devil can bring against it. Mighty power has no might against this almighty power. When we speak about evil power, we speak about mighty power; when we speak about almighty power, we speak about a substance of rock dynamite diffusing through the human, displaying its might and bringing everything into insignificance.

I want you to think well out what I am saying. I want us this morning to be able to lay everything down on the Word. They that "...know their God shall be strong, and do exploits" (Daniel 11:32). The Holy Ghost has come with one definite purpose, to reveal unto us the Father and the Son in all Their different branches of helpfulness to humanity, displaying almighty power that the weak may be made strong; bringing sickness into such a display of the revelation of the blood of Christ, of the atonement on Calvary, that the evil power of disease is conquered and cleared out.

There is in this baptism of the Holy Ghost a holy boldness; not superstition, but a boldness which stands unflinchingly and really on what the Word of God says. To have holy boldness is to live in the Holy Ghost, to get to know the principles that are worked out by Him. It says that "Jesus began to teach." He did not have to begin to teach in order that they might understand His plan, but He began to teach. Then I must understand that as He lived in this blessed, sweet fellowship with His Father, and worked and operated because His Father worked, therefore I must learn that the blessed principles of divine order are in me, and that I am existing only for Him, so long as I am not. He is, and ought to be always in pre-eminence. Then there is no fear. Perfect love, perfect knowledge of God, of Jesus, brings me to the state where there is no fear. Now there is another order which is Christ working in me and bringing every thought into subjection, every desire into a divine plan of desire, and now I am working on a new plan — Christ performing, and "me" ceasing, and the work accomplished.

You say "How?" I am going to mention a few things for the helpfulness of our morning. You cannot have holy boldness without you know God; and do not attempt to exercise it without you know Him. Daniel would never have entered into the lions' den if he had not known God. What did the king say? The king said this: "Daniel...is thy God, whom thou servest continually, able to deliver thee?" (Daniel 6:20). "O king, live for ever. My God hath sent his angel, and hath shut the lions' mouths, that they have not hurt me..." (Daniel 6:21,22). The mouths of the lions were not shut in the den; and yet they were. The lions' mouths were shut when the decree was signed. You will always find that victory is at the moment when you open the door of your heart to believing.

I landed one day in a place where there was a great deal of strife and friction. I had a letter of introduction to a stranger, and did not know a single person in the place. I brought a letter to this man and he read it, and he said, "This letter is from [a brother in the Lord] of Cleveland. I know him. The letter mentions much about you. There will be an open door for you here. Instantly after that he said, "Go out and visit these different people" — he gave me their names — "and then come back to dinner."

As soon as I got back a little bit late, he said, "I am sorry you are late for dinner, we have had dinner, and for this reason: A young man has been here heartbroken. He was going to marry a beautiful young woman. She is dying, and the doctor is by her side and cannot help her. That young man has promised to be here and will be here in a minute. You better get ready." "I am ready now." Just as I commenced my dinner, in came this man brokenhearted. I did not question him. I went with him, and we got to the house. The mother met me at the door brokenhearted. I said to her, "Cheer up. Shew me the girl, take me to her; it will be all right in a minute or two. I was taken right into the house upstairs, and there in bed the young woman lay. She was just a travailing, poor soul. I said to her, "It will be all right in a minute or two." Then I said, "Come out!" And instantly she was healed. Holy boldness!

What do you mean by holy boldness? We may say that there is a divine position where the human may dwell, and where he has such a knowledge of God that he knows God will not fail him. It is not a miracle, though it seems sometimes almost as if it has a measure of it. It does not act sometimes exactly as the human mind would have it to act. God does not act that way. It is very often in quite an opposite line altogether. What I want you to know is this — God has a plan for His child. What came out of that case that I have just mentioned? There is the secret.

The doctor came a short time after that girl had been healed, and could not understand it. He saw this young woman, and she was dressed and downstairs in ten minutes after having been made well. While she was dressing, other four people were definitely healed. What was God's purpose? That young doctor had been investigating this power of healing, and he could not find a single person who was able to heal thus. He said to the young woman, "Are you down?" "Yes." "Come here. A young man" — she called me a young man — "from England has been brought, and I was instantly healed." "Come here," and then he took her and pressed his long finger into the soft of that tumor. It would have made her scream had she still had appendicitis. But he could not feel any symptom, and he said, "This is God, this is God."

Anything else? Yes. They had built a new place there, and they had not it full. But the leader said, "I am going to prophesy that our place won't hold the people." Neither would it. Anything else? Yes, God healed over two hundred people in that place. Brothers and sisters, it is not we. I am as conscious as anything that it is just as Jesus said in the fourteenth chapter of John's gospel:

> *...the words that I speak unto you I speak not of myself: but the Father that dwelleth in me, he doeth the works.*
>
> *John 14:10*

Is not that beautiful? Just think of it, some of you people who have been so busy in arranging plans for preaching. Think how wonderful it is when the Holy Ghost comes and takes possession, and just utters through you such things as are needed.

Some people say, "Do these things last?" Praise God, His truth never fails to last; it goes on lasting. I had a letter the other day from Albany, about seventy miles from Oregon. This person had never written to me since I was there. The letter ran like this: "You remember my taking you to my wife's brother who had lost all power of reason and everything." Drink and the power of the devil had laid hold on him. "My brother has been perfectly whole ever since, and has never tasted alcohol." "Ye shall have power." Glory to God! I realize this: that if I will be still, God can work; if I will be sure that I pay the price, and not come out of the divine order, God will surely work.

Let me say a word to your hearts. Most of us here this morning are diligently seeking God's best. We feel that we would pay any price for His best. God knows my heart. I have not an atom of desire outside the perfect will of God, and God knows that. But Wigglesworth, like everybody else, occasionally has to come to this: "What is up with me? I do not feel the unction;" and if there is anything to repent of, I get right down before God and get it out. You cannot cover sins over, or cover faults over; they must be gotten to the bottom of. You cannot have the unction, and the Holy Ghost power, and the life of Christ, and the manifest glory — it cannot come excepting through self-abasement, complete renunciation of self, with God only enthroned, and Wigglesworth dead. It must be of God, and if he will only examine the conditions and act upon them, I tell you things would come off wonderfully.

TONGUES AND INTERPRETATION: "The deliverances of the Lord are as high as the righteousness of heaven; the purity of His saints as white as the linen; and the divine principles of His gracious will can only flow out when He is enthroned within. Christ first, last, always Christ. Through Christ and by the name of Jesus, whatever you shall ask in My name I will do."

I repeat, people sometimes say, "Do these things last, is this thing permanent?" The baptism of the Holy Ghost in my life is as a river flowing on. Eight years ago, and the tide rises higher and higher. Holiness, purity of heart, divine thoughts and revelations of God, are far in advance of what they were even a short time ago. We are living in a divine place where the Lord is blessedly having His way. I want you to hear what I have got to say about one or two things. Some people can have things rubbed out, but I want God Almighty to do something now that cannot be rubbed out. We are definitely told in the Word of God that if we ask of the Holy Spirit, He will give. We hear people give that out quite easily, but I find that many people who dwell upon that do not get it. I know when a man is baptized of the Holy Ghost. There is a kindred spirit with a person who is baptized of the Holy Ghost that there is not in any other person. The Holy Ghost is given to those who obey.

That obey what? What Jesus said. What did Jesus say? "Tarry, till ye receive." Is not that clear? That is Scripture. You need not have anything more scriptural than that.

Now the reason why God the Holy Ghost brings me into this place this morning is because I love the church of God; and when I hear men and women who are saved as much as I am — when I hear them on a line that I know is not according to the Spirit of God, I know exactly what spirit they are of. God save us from building up on our own imagination. Let us build up on what the Word of God says. We shall never be strong except as we believe what God says. If God tells me that Paul was the chiefest of sinners, I say I will believe it, I will believe it forever. Whatever the Holy Ghost says through His Word, I believe it, and keep to it, and I will not move from it. And the Holy Ghost says I will have power after He comes upon me through Jesus.

TONGUES AND INTERPRETATION: "They that fear the Lord and they that keep His commandments shall have the goodness of the land; and they that will do His will shall know the doctrine, and God will declare unto their hearts the perfectness of His way. For there is a way that seemeth right unto a man, but the way of that is death; but the way of righteousness bringeth to pass that God's Word is true."

I am so pleased because there is a thought coming into my heart that you ought all to know. I believe there is a great need today of finding our place in the Holy Ghost. It would save us from such a lot of burdens and many things. I am going to give you a little illustration. There is a dear woman at our house who looks after my affairs. Everlastingly she becomes a real slave servant. I often think she does so much that is not needed. She is a slave servant; that is her disposition. There are many of them. We have a lot in our place that God has been blessing, and who have come out to speak for Him in different places. She thought she ought to do the same. There were many invitations, and she took one of these invitations on. She looked timid and said she had to take this service. I got up with the needed boldness and set to work to strip away that which was causing this timidity. With her heart full, she went out and got someone else, and instantly she found relief. She came back with her face beaming. "What's up?" I asked. She said, "I've got relieved." The burden was gone.

Some people, just because they have been baptized with the Holy Ghost and with fire, think they have to go and be preachers. It is a thousand pities that it is so. It is good that that desire is in your heart, but it may not be God's purpose for you. If you would get to know your place in the Holy Ghost, it would save you from struggles and burdens, and relieve the whole situation. Get to know your place in the Holy Ghost and God will bless you.

There are hearts here crushed because they are not able to sing like our Welsh brother. But it would not do for us all to be like him. We should be breaking all the pots in the house if we were all like him. We have all to get to know our position in the Holy Ghost. God can work it so beautifully, and harmonize it so that there will not be a thing out of order. God will put you in the place you are to occupy, if you will ask and trust Him for it; and you will live in the Holy Ghost so that His glory shall be always upon you. If you miss it, say, like David, "Lord, restore unto me the joy of thy salvation" (Psalm 51:12). If you feel out of touch with God, get back to Calvary, keep near the cross; let the God of glory glorify Himself in you.

It is marvelous how all the gifts of the Spirit may be manifested in some people. Everybody acquainted with me knows that I was short of speech and slow at everything, and all out of order. My wife used to preach, and I carried the babies and the boots and everything. Then there came a time when my wife could not be there and I was forced to roll in some-how, and I rolled in, and was very glad to roll out many a time. But it is marvelous now. As a vocation God has allowed every one of the nine gifts to be ministered through me. There is not a single gift but what has been ministered through me. What I mean is this. You won't hear me say that I have got these gifts, but living in the Holy Ghost, you are in a place in which God can manifest anything at any needed moment. You may live in that glorious attitude, and then it is heaven to live, it is heaven to eat, it is heaven to sleep, it is heaven all the time; and when heaven comes it will never be a breaking of the casket, but only more fulness, for already the kingdom of heaven is within.

My speech is a heart speech this morning. It is no good my speaking without I speak from the heart. I have put my hands to this work, and I feel that God the Holy Ghost has done something, and I want just to speak about it in closing. I know you will believe it, I know it is true. God has helped me to go into different places and bring about revivals. Over and over again, revivals begin with people who are baptized, and God does great things. Last night there was in one of these rooms a preacher. There he was. He knelt down. He was a stiff as a board. You want to have discernment to see whether there is reality. He was frightened to let go. I said, "Come, brother, receive the Holy Ghost." "I cannot." "You are not in earnest, you are not real; there is no business about you, you must begin to move. Receive the Holy Ghost." Then with a knowledge that he was being really stirred up, according to God's divine order, I put my hands on him and said, "Receive the Holy Ghost," and God the Holy Ghost shook him from top to bottom, inside out, and what a wonderful baptism he had!

Brothers and sisters, do you want the Holy Ghost? Some hymns are sung about the breath of the Holy Ghost. We read that "Jesus breathed upon them," and they received the unction in the breathing. As people breathe in the Holy Ghost they become so possessed with the power of God that they have no possessions in themselves; they simply fall into God, and God takes possession of everything — hands and feet and body and tongue for the glory of God. My heart yearns for you to be so filled with the divine power of the Holy Ghost that you will go back from these meetings into your own meetings and assemblies in the order of God — not taking notice of your fulness, but having the fact remaining in you that you have power, and letting the Word of God so act upon the power that God will let it flow through you to others. By what? His way. You cannot baptize people, but His way can do it. How? Receive ye the Holy Ghost; let Him have His way.

Published in *Flames of Fire*

THE WAY TO OVERCOME... BELIEVE!

1917

irst John 5. The greatest weakness in the world is unbelief. The greatest power is the faith that worketh by love. Love, mercy, and grace bind faith. There is no fear in love and no question as to being caught up when Jesus comes. The world is filled with fear, torment, remorse, and brokenness, but faith and love are sure to overcome. "Who is he that overcometh the world, but he that believeth that Jesus is the Son of God?" (1 John 5:5). God hath established the earth and humanity on the lines of faith. As you come into line, fear is cast out, the Word of God comes into operation and you find bedrock. The way to overcome is to believe Jesus is the Son of God. The commandments are wrapped up in it.

When there is a fidelity between you and God and the love of God is so real that you feel you could do anything for Jesus, all the promises are yea and amen to those who believe. Your life is centered there. Always overcoming what is in the world.

Who keepeth the commandments? The born of God. "Ye are of God, little children, and have overcome them: because greater is he that is in you, than he that is in the world" (1 John 4:4). They that believe, love. When did He love us? When we were in the mire. What did He say? Thy sins are forgiven thee. Why did He say it? Because He loved us. What for? That He might bring many sons into glory. His object? That we might be with Him forever. All the pathway is an education for this high vocation and calling. This hidden mystery of love to us, the undeserving! For our sins the double blessing. "...whatsoever is born of God overcometh the world: and this is the victory...even our faith" (1 John 5:4). He who believeth — to believe is to overcome. On the way to Emmaus Jesus, beginning from Moses and all the prophets, interpreted to them in all the Scriptures the things concerning Himself (Luke 24:27). He is the root! In Him is life. When we receive Christ, we receive God and the promises (Galatians 3:29), that we might receive the promise of the Spirit through faith. I am heir to all the promises because I believe. A great heirship! I overcome because I believe the truth. The truth makes me free.

TONGUES AND INTERPRETATION: "It is God who exalteth, God who maketh rich. The Lord in His mighty arms bears thee up — it is the Lord that encompasseth round about thee. When I am weak, then I am strong."

No wavering! This is the principle. He who believes is definite, and because Jesus is in it, it will come to pass. He is the same yesterday, today, and forever (Hebrews 13:8). They that are poor in spirit are heirs to all. There is no limit to the power, for God is rich to all who call upon Him. Not the will of the flesh, but of God (John 1:13). Put in your claim for your children, your families, your co-workers, that many sons may be brought to glory (Hebrews 2:10), for it is all on the principle of faith. There is nothing in my life or ambition equal to my salvation, a spiritual revelation from heaven according to the power of God, and it does not matter how many flashlights Satan sends through the human mind; roll all on the blood. Who overcomes? He who believes Jesus is the Son (1 John 5:5). God calls in the person with no credentials, it's the order of faith, He who believeth overcometh — will be caught up. The Holy Ghost gives revelation all along the line. He that is not against us is for us, and some of the most godly have not touched Pentecost yet. We must have a good heart especially to the household of faith. "...If any man love the world, the love of the Father is not in him" (1 John 2:15). The root principle of all truth in the human heart is Christ, and when grafted deeply there are a thousand lives you may win. Jesus is the way, the truth, and the life (John 14:6), the secret to every hard problem in the world.

You can't do it! Joseph could not! Everything depends on the principles in your heart. If God dwells in us the principle is light, it comprehends darkness. If thine eye be single, thy whole body shall be full of light, breaking through the hardest thing. "Herein is our love made perfect, that we may have boldness in the day of judgment: because as he is, so are we in this world (1 John 4:17) — for faith has full capacity. When man is pure and it is easy to detect darkness, he that hath this hope purifieth himself (1 John 3:3).

TONGUES AND INTERPRETATION: "God confirms in us faith that we may be refined in the world, having neither spot nor blemish nor any such thing. It is all on the line of faith, he that hath faith overcomes — it is the Lord Who purifieth and bringeth where the fire burns up all the dross, and anoints with fresh oil; see to it that ye keep pure. God is separating us for Himself.

"...I will give you a mouth and wisdom, which all your adversaries will not be able to gainsay nor resist" (Luke 21:15). The Holy Spirit will tell you in the moment what you shall say. The world will not understand you, and you will find as you go on with God that you do not understand fully. We cannot comprehend what we are saved to, or from. None can express the joy of God's indwelling. The Holy Spirit can say through you the need of the moment. The world knoweth us not because it knew Him not.

"Who is he that overcometh the world, but he that believeth Jesus is the Son of God?" (1 John 5:5). A place of confidence in God, a place of prayer, a place of knowledge, that we have what we ask, because we keep His commandments and do the things that are pleasing in His sight. Enoch before his translation had the testimony, he had been well-pleasing unto God. We overcome by believing.

Published in *Flames of Fire*

FAITH IS THE SUBSTANCE!

February 4, 1917

Hebrews 11. Faith is the evidence, the assurance that the word that God hath said is true. It is the gift of God. Unclouded faith has entered in to prove all things and believe all things. "...all men have not faith" (2 Thessalonians 3:2). Those of faith in God are determined that no man shall take their crown. They see the promise. See the thing there and claim it from God. It is always more than one can carry! It not only helps you, but all who believe the report. A living Word, quickened by a living faith, brings forth the evidence, which though not seen is there. Men of grace have found glory begun below.

God rocked in a man makes a man rocked in God and so submitted to God that there is no carefulness. Moses with his face-to-face communion could say, "If these men die the common death of all men...then the

Lord hath not sent me" (Numbers 16:29) — justice against all mourners, grumblers and unbelievers. God can so fill a man with His Spirit that he can laugh and believe in the face of a thousand difficulties. Joshua dealt with the wedge of gold and the Babylonish garment, but sin had to be removed and the saints must ever say Amen! to the judgments of God which work out His purpose. He spake and it was done, for faith is a sub-stitutionary work of grace and an imputed righteousness. "They that trust in the Lord shall be as mount Zion, which cannot be removed, but abideth for ever" (Psalm 125:1), because they have kept His Word. Keep His Word at all costs. Faith! The substance of faith wrought out by the will of God within you, a living faith given by God. We are so saved that all things are possible. Nothing of this world existed, it was brought forth by the Word of God. Faith is creative. The walls of Jericho will fall, Abel offered his offering on the lines that God approved. If we have any faith it is through the blood of Jesus. God has respect to the blood. Will not God avenge His own elect (Luke 18:7)? Yea, I tell you, He will avenge them speedily (v. 8). Who are they? Blood-bought ones — greater than John — by faith Enoch pleased God — Peter on the mount said, "...let us make three tabernacles...there was a cloud that overshadowed them...they saw no man any more, save Jesus only..." (Mark 9:5,7,8).

Jesus is all we need. Faith is loyalty to Jesus, belief on the basis of the blood. Because of this testimony of faith God moved with Jesus.

Noah was a preacher of righteousness 120 years; he never wavered or lost the reality of God. There was no sea near, but God had said He would send a flood, it was sufficient. The fear of God has a principle in it which brings peace. Real faith has perfect peace and joy and a shout at any time. It always sees the victory. Real faith built the ark, but real faith did not shut the door. God did that. He does what you cannot do. When they were all in, God shut the door. When God shuts no man can open. When you are all shut in, it is sure to come to pass. As the large ship on the ocean rocks in the storm, the natural man says fearfully, "Do you think we shall ever land?" but to the man of God — peace. He holdeth the sea in the hollow of His hand.

Peace, perfect peace, in this dark world of sin, in the world tribulation, but in Me, peace. The men of grace have found glory begun below. Through all the unrest of the times? Yes! "Thou wilt keep him in perfect peace, whose mind is stayed on thee..." (Isaiah 26:3). "...perfect love casteth out fear... (1 John 4:18). Perfect love, perfect peace.

God said to Abraham: "Go" and he went. He was a stranger in the land, but God brought him into possession because he believed. All this is for us, for them it was natural lives, for us spiritual progress, and we are both to be perfected together. The Word of the Lord endureth forever. Did they get in? Yes! Have you? When they believed God worked out a plan. But now they desire a better country, wherefore God is not ashamed to be called their God, He hath prepared for them a city. A baptism of the Holy Ghost according to the Word.

The just shall hold constant communion with God and be so wrought upon by the Spirit; and by the Spirit shall works of righteousness be manifested from strength to strength, judging all things and holding fast that which is good. "...Eye hath not seen, nor ear heard, neither have entered into the heart of man, the things which God hath prepared for them that love him. But God hath revealed them unto us by his Spirit: for the Spirit searcheth all things, yea, the deep things of God" (1 Corinthians 2:9,10). A substance of faith beyond all that has gone before — they desire a better country — that is, a heavenly. They saw — were persuaded — embraced — confessed, i.e., they lived in the power of them. Truly, beloved, God hath prepared for us wonderful things.

Address given at Rowland Street Mission

NOT DRUNK BUT FILLED
April 1917

phesians 5:18-20. I must see to it that I am filled with the Holy Spirit's power and be careful not to rest in any gift. We have here the contrary spectacle in a man drunk with wine. What are the special characteristics of a man so possessed? He is not careful, he is under the control of another spirit managing him and believes. We must be careful not to choose but to let God's Holy Spirit manage our lives, not to smooth down and explain away, but to stir up the gift and allow God's Spirit to disturb us and disturb us and disturb us until we yield and yield and yield and the possibility in God's

mind for us becomes an established fact in our lives, with the rivers in evidence meeting the need of a dying world. The drunken man is not careful what people think or who sees him or what language he utters — he is under the control of another. So let us be careful not to take control. God's Spirit which is upon me, filling me, is better than my best, and will press me on to a zeal for God as was manifested in my Lord. His disciples remembered it was written "...the zeal of thine house hath eaten me up..." (Psalm 69:9).

Oh! to be pressed on thus. Unreserved for God, to use my mouth, my brain, my all! To be filled with the Holy Ghost. Is it for me? Oh, yes! "...the promise is unto you, and to your children, and to all that are afar off, even as many as the Lord our God shall call" (Acts 2:39). One passion must possess me—to be filled with the Holy Spirit. Are we so thoughtful! thoughtless! for God to have us all to Himself. "Speaking to yourselves in psalms and hymns and spiritual songs, singing and making melody in your heart to the Lord" (Ephesians 5:19). A drunken man has his thoughts, his mouth, his body, under the control of another. So my thoughts, my mouth, my body, must be under the control of God's Holy Spirit. Is it not lovely? Spiritual songs — the tongue of the learned; we cannot rest until we are quite full.

What has the Holy Ghost come to do? To reprove the world of sin. "...when he is come, he will reprove the world of sin..." (John 16:8). Now! Through His indwelling pressure in the hearts of His children. "...know ye not that your body is the temple of the Holy Ghost...therefore glorify God in your body..." (1 Corinthians 6:19,20). We cannot reprove the world of sin unless we keep in the place where He can rest in His love and joy over us with singing. "He brought me to the banqueting house, and his banner over me was love" (Song of Solomon 2:4). "Giving thanks always for all things unto God and the Father in the name of the Lord Jesus Christ" (Ephesians 5:20). If we are filled with the Spirit, in the hard place where the test comes like the three Hebrew children — our testimony is, "...we are not careful to answer thee in this matter...our God whom we serve is able to deliver us from the burning fiery furnace, and he will deliver us..." (Daniel 3:16,17). You cannot give thanks under such circumstances unless you are filled with the Spirit. Ye are not your own.

Mother! Mother! Mother! My brother has broken the basin upstairs — all the house in a tumult! You can quieten them in the Spirit and still give thanks. Paul said, "I know both how to be abased, and I know how to abound..." (Philippians 4:12), "...as having nothing, and yet possessing all things" (2 Corinthians 6:10). He had no need to draw on the bank when he had something, but to have nothing is a rich place, it is a wonderful process! — it only comes to drunken people. Here is a drunken man singing, muttering, talking, what is it? It is another spirit. So the spiritual man can rest in the Holy Ghost and give thanks.

Oh! beloved, to have nothing and yet to possess all things. Poor, yet when I feel so, it turns me on to the resources of God — to make many rich! What a condition to be in, to grow in. You know a man at first takes one glass, then twenty glasses, but when seasoned with the grace of God, taking in, taking in, until we can rejoice in the hard corner, grace increasing in us from the boundless, endless source, it's wonderful! Only those can give thanks whom God has in control. He abideth a quickening spirit, an increasing power when once the Lord has laid hold of us, bringing us to a place of rest in Him. Let us rejoice, giving thanks all the time — this is the will of God.

What is God's will towards me: when He gave me Jesus He gave me all. Lay me down a law where it will always work! Continue to believe Jesus is the Son of God. Can you make yourself drunk? We can believe! Simplicity will do it — yieldedness will do it — faith will assist it. The man drunk with wine says everybody is drunk but him. May God the Holy Ghost make me so unconscious of my condition in the Spirit, so hungry, so thirsty, that I see everyone has more than me. God can do it, it means much. Jesus says — "I give you My life, it is to become in you a production of what I am." "...be not drunk with wine...but be filled with the Spirit" (Ephesians 5:18).

Published in *Flames of Fire*

ccording to his abundant mercy hath begotten us again unto a lively hope by the resurrection of Jesus Christ from the dead.

1 Peter 1:3

OUR LIVING HOPE

May-June 1917

In 1 Corinthians 15 we read of the glorious fact of Christ the firstfruits. A farmer goes over his land eagerly scanning the first ears of corn that show themselves above the soil because he knows, as the first beginnings, so may the harvest be. And just in the measure as Jesus Christ is risen from the dead, so are we. "...as he is, so are we in this world" (1 John 4:17). Christ is now getting the church ready for translation. Here we read in Peter, we are "...begotten...again unto a lively hope by the resurrection of Jesus Christ from the dead." Oh, to be changed — a living fact in the body. Just as in the flesh Jesus triumphed by the Spirit. Oh, to be like Him! What a living hope it is!

Paul and Peter were very little together, but both were inspired to bring before the vision of the church this wonderful truth of the living being changed. If Christ rose not, our faith is vain, we are yet in our sins, it has no foundation. But Christ has risen and become the firstfruits, and we have now the glorious hope that we shall be so changed. We who were not a people are now the people of God. Born out of due time, out of the mire, to be among princes. Beloved, God wants us to see the preciousness of it. It will drive away the dullness of life; it is here set above all other things. Jesus gave all for this treasure. He purchased the field because of the pearl, the pearl of great price — the substratum of humanity. Jesus purchased it, and we are the pearl of great price for all time. Our inheritance is in heaven, and in 1 Thessalonians 4:18 we are told to comfort one another with these words.

What can you have better in the world than the hope that in a little while the change will come. It seems such a short time since I was a boy; in a little while I shall be changed by His grace and be more than a conqueror in an inheritance incorruptible, undefiled, that fadeth not away (1 Peter 1:4). The inheritance is in you, something that is done for you, accomplished by God for you; a work of God wrought out for us by Himself, an inheritance incorruptible. When my daughter was in Africa she often wrote of things "corroding." We have a corruptible nature, but, as the natural decays, the spiritual man is at work. As the corruptible is doing its work, we are changing.

When will it be seen? When Jesus comes. Most beautiful of all, we shall be like Him. What is the process? Grace! What can work it out? Love! Love! Love! It cannot be rendered in human phrases. God so loved that He gave Jesus.

There is something very wonderful about being undefiled, there in the presence of my King to be undefiled, never to change, only to be more beautiful. Unless we know something about grace and the omnipotence of His love, we should never be able to grasp it. Love, fathomless as the sea. Grace flowing for you and for me.

He has prepared a place for us, a place which will fit in beautifully, with no fear of anyone else taking it; reserved. When I went to certain meeting I had a seat reserved and numbered. I could walk in any time. What is there in the reserving? Having a place where we can see Him; the very seat we would have chosen. He knows just what we want! There will be no brokenness or jar or wish to have come sooner. He has made us for the place. The beginning of all joys. He loved me so; no jar throughout all eternity. Will you be there? Is it possible for us to miss it? We are kept by the power of God, through faith, unto a salvation ready to be revealed in the last time (1 Peter 1:5).

What is there peculiar about it? The fulness of perfection, the ideal of love — the beatitudes worked in. The poor in spirit, the mourners, the meek, the hungry and thirsty, the merciful, the pure — all ready to be revealed at the appearing of Jesus Christ (1 Peter 1:6,7). You could not remain there but for the purifying, the perfecting, the establishing; working out His perfect will when ready! Refined enough, you will go. But there is something to be done yet to establish you, to make you purer. A great price has been paid. The trial of your faith is more precious than gold that perisheth. (Men are losing their heads for gold.) And we must give all, yield all, as our Great Refiner puts us again and again in the melting pot; what for? To lose the chaff, that the pure gold of His presence is so clearly seen and His glorious image reflected. From glory to glory even by the Spirit of the Lord. We must be steadfast, immovable, until all His purposes are wrought out.

Praising God on this line in a meeting is a different thing to the time when you are faced with a hard career; there must be no perishing though we are tried by fire. What is going to appear at the appearing of Jesus? Faith! Faith! The establishing of your heart by the grace of the Spirit, not to crush, but to refine; not to destroy, but to enlarge you. Oh, beloved, to make you know the enemy as a defeated foe, and Jesus not only conquering but displaying the spoils of conquest. The pure in heart shall see God. If thine eye be single, thy whole body shall be full of light. What is it? Loyalty to the Word by the power of the blood. You know your inheritance within you is more powerful than all that is without. How many have gone to the stake and through fiery persecution? Did they desire it? Faith tried by fire had power to stand all ridicule, all slander. The faith of the Son of God who, for the joy that was set before Him, endured the cross. Oh, the joy of pleasing Him. No trial, no darkness; nothing too hard for me. If only I may see the image of my Lord in it again and again. He removes the skimmings until in the melting pot His face is seen. When it reflects Him, it is pure. Who is looking into our hearts? Who is the refiner? My Lord. He will only remove that which will hinder. Oh, I know the love of God is working out in my heart a great purpose of reality.

I remember going to the Crystal Palace when General Booth had a review of representatives of the Salvation Army from all nations. It was a grand sight as company after company with all their peculiar characteristics passed a certain place where he could view them. It was a wonderful scene. We are going to be presented to Him. The trials are getting us ready for the procession and the presentation. We are to be a joy to look at, to be to His praise and glory. No one will be there but the tried by fire. Is it worth it? Yes, a thousand times. Oh, the ecstasy of exalted pleasure. God thus reveals Himself to our hearts.

Verse 22 [of 1 Peter 1] speaks of unfeigned faith and unfeigned love. What it means to have unfeigned faith! When ill-used, put to shame, or whatever the process, it never alters, only to be more refined, more like unto Him. Unfeigned love full of appreciation for those who do not see eye to eye with you. "Father, forgive them." Remember Stephen: "...lay not this sin to their charge..." (Acts 7:60). Unfeigned love is the greatest thing God can bestow on my heart.

Verse 23 [1 Peter 1] shows we are saved by a power incorruptible — a process always refining, a grace always enlarging, a glory always increasing, thus we are made neither barren nor unfruitful, in the knowledge of our Lord Jesus Christ. The spirits of just men made perfect are garnered in the treasury of the Most High. Purified as sons. To go out no more. To be as He is — holy, blameless. Through all eternity to gaze upon Him with pure, unfeigned love. God glorified in the midst as the whole company of heaven cries out: "...Holy, holy, holy, Lord God Almighty..." (Revelation 4:8). "...And this is the word which by the gospel is preached unto you" (1 Peter 1:25).

How can we be sad, or hang our heads, or be distressed? Oh, if we only knew how rich we are! Blessed be the name of the Lord.

Address given at Bowland Street Mission, March 1917
Published in *Confidence*

OUR GREAT NEED
Paul's Vision and the Baptism in the Holy Ghost
November-December 1917

I want to speak this afternoon of Pentecost and the fulness of the Spirit, and of what God is able to do with any man who is yielded to Him. We are here today for one purpose, and that is to kindle one another with a holier zeal than ever has possessed us before. I believe there is a greater need for us today in the world than ever. There is a more broken spirit abroad in our land than for a long time past, and no one can meet the need today but the man filled with God. God has promised to fill us. You may be filled with the mighty power of God, and yet in a way not realize it, and yet know that you are being used by a power apart from yourself, a power that keeps you from self-exhibition. Just as the sun by its mighty power brings certain resources to nature, so I believe the power of God in the human soul, the power filling it with Himself, is capable, by living faith, of bringing about what otherwise could never be accomplished. May God by His Spirit this afternoon prepare us for what He has to say.

PART I

I want to draw your attention to Acts 26:12-19, where we are told of the light from heaven and the voice which arrested Paul on his way to Damascus, and of his conversion, and of the commission given to him to go unto the Gentiles to turn them from darkness to light, and from the power of Satan unto God, and of the fact that he was not disobedient unto the heavenly vision. You remember how it is stated in Acts 9, that for three days after this vision Paul was blind; he was in a state in which he could not see, in a state of brokenheartedness, I suppose. And then God had him.

It is a wonderful thing when God gets you. You are not much good for anything until God gets you. When God gets you, you are loose and you are bound; you are free, but you can act only as He wills for you to act; and when you act only for Him, there is in the process that which brings out something mighty for all time.

Well, Paul had first to come to this time of crying, weeping, contrition, heartmeltedness, yieldedness. He had done all he could in the natural, but the natural had only brought him to a broken place, to blindness, to helplessness, and this must come out of Paul's life before he could have the life of God. When we have altogether parted with our own, as it were, then there is a possibility of God's likeness being made manifest in us, of the water of life filling us, and not only fertilizing our own life, but

FLOWING FROM US AS A RIVER

that will touch others; and no one can tell what a river can do when it is set aflow by God, because when God is in the plan, everything works mightily and harmoniously. I pray God the Holy Ghost that at all times I should cease from anything except that thing which God wants to bring out, and not I.

There are so many wonderful things about a life filled with the Holy Ghost that one feels almost as if one were a machine and could never stop speaking of them. There are so many opportunities and such greater forces that can never come along any other line. When Jesus has come to a place where He will not make bread for Himself, I find that

He reaches a place where He can make bread for thousands. And when I come to a place where I will not do anything for myself, then God will do something for me and

I WILL GLADLY DO ANYTHING FOR HIM

that He may desire me to do. That is in the order of the baptism. It is when we cease to clothe ourselves that God clothes us, and it is the clothing wherewith He clothes us that covers all our nakedness.

In his helplessness and brokenness Paul cries: "Lord, what wilt Thou have me to do?" That cry reached to heaven, and as a result there came a holy man, touched with the same fire and zeal that filled his Master, and he laid his hands upon Paul and said, "Receive thy sight, and be filled with the Holy Ghost."

TONGUES AND INTERPRETATION: "The living touch of the river of the life of God is that which makes all things akin, and brings a celestial glory into the human heart, and phrases that meet the kindled desire therein."

When God moves a man, his body becomes akin with celestial glory all the time, and the man says things as he is led by the Holy Ghost who fills him. When we are filled with the Holy Ghost we go forth to see things accomplished that we could never see otherwise. First of all, Paul has a vision. There is always a vision in the baptism of the Spirit. But visions are no good to me except I make them real, except I claim them as they come, except I make them my own; and if your whole desire is to carry out what the Spirit has revealed to you by vision, it will surely come to pass. Lots of people lack the power because they do not keep the vision, because they do not allow the fire which has come to infuse into them and continue to burn. There must be

A CONTINUOUS BURNING ON THE ALTAR

Holy Ghost power in a man is meant to be an increasing force, an enlargement. God has never anything of a diminishing type. He is always going on. And I am going on. Are you going on? It is necessary, I tell you, to go on. You must not stop in the plains; there are far greater things for you on the hilltops than in the plains.

Jesus took particular care of Paul; He did not rush him through the business. Some people think that everything ought to be done

IN A TREMENDOUS HURRY.

With God it is not so. God takes plenty of time, and He has a wonderful way of developing things as He goes along. Nothing that you undertake will fail, if only you do not forget what He has told you, and if you act upon it. You really cannot forget that which the Holy Ghost brings right into your heart as His purpose for you. A man baptized by the Holy Ghost is no longer a natural man; he is forced by the Spirit, he is turned into another man. Joshua and Caleb could not say anything less than that "God, who has taken us and let us see the land, He will surely give us the land."

Where are you fixed? Is God the Holy Ghost arranging things for you, or are you arranging things according to your own plan? A man filled with the Holy Ghost has ceased to be, in a sense; he has come to a rest, he has come to where God is working, to a place where He can "stand still and see the salvation of the Lord." What do I mean? I mean that such a man has ceased from his own works and abilities and associations. He will not trust his own heart; he relies only on the omnipotent power of the Most High, he is girded with Another. The man baptized with the Holy Ghost will always

KEEP IN TOUCH WITH THE MASTER

in the passing crowd, or wherever he may be. He has no room for anything that steps lower than the unction that was on his Master, or for anything that hinders him from being about his Master's business. If you are baptized by the Holy Ghost, you have no spiritual food apart from the Word of God, you have no resources but those that are heavenly; you have been "planted" with Christ, and have "risen with Him," and you are "seated with Him in heavenly places; your language is a heavenly language, your source of inspiration is a heavenly touch; God is enthroned in your whole life, and you see things "from above," and not from below.

A man who is baptized with the Holy Ghost has a Jesus mission. He knows his vocation, the plan of his life. God speaks to him so definitely and really that there is no mistaking about it. Thank God for the knowledge which fixes me so solidly upon God's Word that I cannot be moved from it by any storm that may rage. The revelation of Jesus to my soul by the Holy Ghost brings me to a place where I am willing, if need be,

To Die on What the Word Says.

The three Hebrew children said "...we are not careful to answer thee in this matter" (Daniel 3:16); and when a man of God by the Spirit is quickened he never moves toward, or depends upon, natural resources. The furnace "one seven times more" heated is of no consequence to the men who have heard the voice of God; the lions' den has no fearfulness for the man who opens his windows and talks to his Father. The people who live in the unction of the Spirit are taken out of the world in the sense that they are kept in the world without being defiled by the evil of the world.

PART II

But let us come back to this wonderful vision that Paul had. I want you to see how carefully the Lord deals with him. "But rise, and stand upon thy feet: for I have appeared unto thee for this purpose, to make thee a minister and a witness both of these things which thou hast seen, and of those things in the which I will appear unto thee" (Acts 26:16). Do not you see how carefully the Lord works? He shows Paul the vision as far as Paul can take it in, and then He says: "There are other things in the day which I will again appear unto thee." Did He ever appear unto Paul after that? Certainly He did. But Paul never lost this vision; he kept it up, so to speak. What was there in the vision that held him in such close association with Jesus Christ that he was ready for every activity to which he was led by the Holy Ghost? There were certain things he had to do. Look, for instance, at Galatians 1:15,16. There you will find a very wonderful word — a word that has had a great impression upon me in relation to the subject of

The Continuation of the Baptism.

"...when it pleased God, who separated me from my mother's womb, and called me by his grace, to reveal his Son in me, that I might preach him among the heathen; immediately I conferred not with flesh and blood." Now read together the words: "Therefore I was not disobedient to the heavenly vision," and "I conferred not with flesh and blood."

There is no man here this afternoon who can be clothed in the Spirit, and catch the fire and zeal of the Master every day and many times in the day, without he ceases in every way to be connected with the "arm of flesh" which would draw him aside from the power of God. Many men have lost the glory because they have been taken up with the natural. If we are going to accomplish in the Spirit the thing God has purposed for us, we can never turn again to the flesh. If we are Spirit-filled, God has cut us short and brought us into relationship with Himself, joined us to Another, and now He is all in all to us. You may have

A VISION OF THE LORD

all the time you are in a railway train, or in a tramcar, or walking down a street. It is possible to be lonely in the world and to be a Christian, without what? Without you cease to be a natural man. I mean that the Christian ought to have such an unction as to realize at any moment, whether in the presence of others or alone, that he is with God. He can have a vision in the tramcar, or in the railway train, even if he has to stand with others in front or behind him; or he can have a vision if he is there alone.

Nehemiah stood before the king because of trouble in Jerusalem which had nigh broken his heart. He was sorrowful, and it affected his countenance; but he was so near to God that he could say: "I have communed with the God of heaven." And if we believers are to go forth and fulfill God's purpose with us, the Holy Spirit must be constantly filling us and moving upon us until our whole being is on fire with the presence and power of God. That is the order of the baptism of the Holy Ghost. The man is then ready for every emergency.

Now it is a most blessed thought — it struck me as I was reading at our assembly on Sunday morning — that in the holy, radiant glory of the vision that was filling Paul's soul (Acts 20) the people became so hungry after it that until midnight they drank in at the fountain of his life, and as he was pouring forth a young man fell down from the third loft, and Paul, in the same glorious fashion, as always, went down and embraced him and pressed the very life from himself into the young man, and brought him back to life. Always equipment for emergency, a blessed, holy equipment by God! Someone calls at your door and wants to see you particularly; but you

CANNOT BE SEEN TILL YOU ARE THROUGH WITH GOD.

Living in the Holy Ghost, walking in the divine likeness, having no confidence in the flesh, but growing in the grace and knowledge of God, and going on from one state of glorious perfection unto another state of perfection — that is it. You cannot compare the Holy Ghost to anything less, but something more, than ever you thought about with all your thoughts. That is the reason why the Holy Ghost has to come into us to give us divine revelations for the moment. The man that is a "partaker of the divine nature" has come into a relationship where God imparts His divine mind for the comprehension of His love and of the fellowship of His Son. We are only powerful as we know that source, we are only strong as we behold the beatitudes and all the wonderful things and graces of the Spirit.

PART III

It was a necessity that Jesus should live with His disciples for three years, and walk in and out amongst them and manifest His glory, and show it forth day by day. I will show you why it was a necessity. Those men believed in God. But this Messiah had continually, day by day, to bring Himself into their vision, into their mind, into their very nature. He had

TO PRESS HIMSELF

right into their life to make them a success after He had ascended to heaven. He had to show them how wonderfully and gracefully and peacefully He could move the crowds. You remember that the house to which they brought the sick of the palsy, and in which He was speaking to the people, was so crowded that they could not come nigh unto Him except by uncovering the roof and dropping the man through. The way to the cities was so pressed with the people who were following Jesus and His disciples, that He and they could hardly get along, but He always had time to stop and perform some good deed on the journey thither. What He had to bring home to the minds and hearts of the disciples was that He was truly the Son of God. They never could accomplish what they had to accomplish until He had proved that to them, and until He had soared to the glory. They could only manifest Him to others when He had imparted His life into

The very Core of Their Nature

and make others confess that they were astonished, and that "we never saw things like this." It was the Son of God travelling in the greatness of His strength to manifest before those disciples the keynote of truth that no one could gainsay. They had been with Him and seen His desire, His craving, His lust to serve God. Yes, He lusted to be like God in the world, manifesting Him so that they might see what Philip had missed when Jesus said to him, "Hast thou not seen the Father?" He wanted them to be clothed with the Spirit, baptized by the Spirit.

Some people get a wrong notion of the baptism. The baptism is nothing less than the third person of the blessed Trinity coming down from the glory, the executive Spirit of the triune God indwelling your body, revealing the truth to you, and causing you sometimes to say "Ah!" till your bowels yearn with compassion, as Jesus yearned, to travail as He travailed, to mourn as He mourned, to groan as He groaned. It cannot be otherwise with you. You cannot get this thing along a merely passive line. It does not come that way. But, glory be to God, it does come. O that God might bring from our hearts the cry for such

A Deluge of the Spirit

that we could not get away till we were ready for Him to fulfill His purpose in us and for us.

I had a wonderful revelation of the power of God this last week. If there is anything I know about this baptism it is this: that it is such a force of conviction in my life that I am carried, as it were, through the very depths of it. Sometimes we have to think; at other times we have not time to think, and it is when we are at our wits' end that God comes and brings deliverance. When you are at your wits' end, and you throw yourself on the omnipotent power of God, what a wonderful transformation there is in a moment.

An Incident

I went to a house where they were very much distressed. It is a peculiar thing, but it is true, that the Spirit of the Lord upon one either binds people together or makes them tremendously fidgety or restless, that they have to come to some place of decision. I know nothing like the mighty power of the Spirit; it works so harmoniously with the will of

God. I was talking to the people in that house, and a young woman was there, and she said, "Oh, father, I ought to have relief today. I am sitting here and I do know what to say, but somehow I feel that this whole trouble ought to go today." "What trouble?" I said. "For six years I have not been able to drink. I cannot drink. I go to the tea-table and cannot drink. My body has gone down." I knew what it was. It was

A DEVIL IN THE THROAT

You say, "You must be very careful." Well, I don't care whom I affront by saying that; I believe the devil is the root of all evil, and it is a serious thing for a beautiful young woman who had perfect health, otherwise to be, as a result of that one thing, so disorganized in her mind and body. I knew it was the power of Satan. How did I know? Because it attacked her at a vital point, and it got her mind on that point, and when it got her mind on that point she went downhill, and she said, "I dare not drink; if I do I shall choke."

I asked the father and mother to go out, and then I said to the young woman, "You will be free and you will drink as much as you want as soon as I have done with you, if you will believe. As sure as you are there you will drink as much as you want." Our brethren are going out into the streets tonight, and I may be amongst them, and they will be preaching, and they will say definitely, "Everyone that believeth can be saved." They will mean, everyone that believeth can be healed. The same truth. They will emphasize it over and over again. They have no more right to emphasize that than I have a right to say, "He was wounded for my transgressions, He was bruised." So I said to her, "Now, dare you believe?" "Yes, I believe that in the name of Jesus you can cast the evil power out." I then laid my hands upon her, and I said:

"IT'S DONE; YOU DRINK."

She went laughingly, "Praise God," and drew the first glass of water and drank. "Mother! father! brother!" she said, "I've drunk one glass!" There was joy in the house. What did it? It was the living faith of the Son of God. Oh, if we only know how rich we are, and how near we are at the fountain of life! "...all things are possible to him that believeth" (Mark 9:23).

When Eneas, who had kept his bed eight years, was told by Peter to "Arise and make thy bed," and he arose immediately, what did it? A life clothed with the Spirit.

TONGUES AND INTERPRETATION: "The living water is falling and making manifest the Christ mission to those who will enter in by a living faith. Nothing can hinder the life-flow to those who believe, for all things are possible to them that believe."

I wonder how many people there are here this afternoon who have missed the point. If I talked to you for a short time you would probably say to me, "I had a wonderful vision when I was baptized." I want you to notice that this vision that Jesus gave to Paul was right on the threshold of his baptism. An inspired life is always on the very open door of the quickenings of that life by the Spirit. I want you to notice also that when a man is born of God, or when, as it were, God is born into the man, and he becomes a quickened soul to carry out the convictions of the life of the Spirit of God in him — when he is born of God, instantly on the threshold of this new birth there comes a vision of what his life is to be. The question is whether you dare go through with it, whether you are going to hold on to the very thing the Holy Ghost brought to you, and never lose sight of it, but press on in a life of devotion to God and of fellowship and unity with Him.

A WARNING

That is what Paul did, that is what Jesus did, and that is what we all have to do. In this connection I want to say advisedly that when we are baptized with the gift of tongues, we must not allow tongues to entertain us, nor be entertained with speaking in tongues. When you have accomplished one thing in the purpose of God for you, He means you to go forward and accomplish another. As soon as you accomplish one thing, it is, so to speak, no more to you, and God will enlarge you and fit you for the next thing He wants you to do.

WHEN I WAS BAPTIZED IN THE HOLY GHOST

there was the unfolding of a new era of my life, and I passed into that and rejoiced in the fact of it, and others with me. But the moment I reached that, God had been ready with another ministry for me. If you are careful to watch for God, God is always caring for you. Jesus said,

"If you honor Me here, I will honor you yonder." Whatever it may be that you are working out for God here, He is working out a far greater, a divine, glory for you. You have no need to be constantly talking of what you are going to appear like in the glory. The chief thing you are to watch is that you realize within yourself a deeper manifestation of the power of God today than yesterday, that you have something more clear today of the mind of the Spirit than you had the day before, that nothing comes between you and God to cloud your mind. You are to see a

VISION OF THE GLORY OF GOD

more today than yesterday, and to be living in such a state of bliss that it is heavenly to live. Paul lived in that ecstasy because he got into a place where the Holy Ghost could enlarge him more and more. I find that, if I continually keep my mind upon God, He unfolds things to me, and if I obediently walk before God and keep my heart pure and clean and holy and right, He will always be lifting me higher than I have ever expected to be.

PART IV

How does it come? On this line. In Romans 12:1, Paul speaks about a certain place being reached — he speaks about an altar on which he had laid himself. When he had experienced the mercies of the Lord, he could do no other than make a presentation of his body on the altar, and it was always to be on the altar and never to be taken off. As soon as he got there he was at the place where the Holy Ghost could bring out of him "things new and old," and, as we read in his epistles, "things" which Peter said were "hard to be understood." How was that? Because he so lived in the Spirit that God brought His mind into Paul's mind, so that the apostle could write and speak, as an oracle of the Holy Ghost, things which had never been in print before, things portraying the mind of God; and we read them today and drink them in as a river, and we come out of the epistles, as it were, clothed with mighty power, the power of God Himself. How does it come? It comes when we are in

A PLACE LOW ENOUGH,

and where God can pour in, pour in, pour in. Paul could say that not one thing that God had spoken of him had failed. In Acts 26, and Romans 15, you will find that he accomplished the whole of what Jesus said he would accomplish, when he was reorganized, or filled, or infilled by the mighty power of God. God wants to do the same for you and for me, according to the gifts He has bestowed upon us. Shall we stop short of what He says we ought to be — shall we cease to come into line with the Mind which is always thinking for our best — shall we cease to humble ourselves before Him who took the way of the cross for us — shall we cease to withhold ourselves from Him who could weep over the doomed city, from the Lord Jesus Christ who "trod the winepress alone." Shall we cease to give Him our all? To what profit will it be if we hold back anything from Him who gives us a thousand times more than ever He asks from us? In Hebrews 2 He says He is going to bring many sons to glory. It means that He is going to clothe them with His glory. Let that be your vision. If you have lost the vision, He is tender to those who cry to Him; from the broken heart

HE NEVER TURNS AWAY,

and they that seek Him with a whole heart will find Him.

As I speak to you this afternoon I feel somehow that my heart is very much enlarged, that my compassion for my Lord is intensified, that nothing is too hard. The people in the days of the apostles took joyfully the spoiling of their goods, and I feel there is a measure of grace given to the man who says, "I will go all the way with Jesus." What is that measure of grace? It is a girding with hopefulness in pressing forward to the goal that God would have us reach. But it is important that we forget not Paul's words, "...that no man take thy crown" (Revelation 3:11). He saw there was a possibility lest any man who had been the means of sowing the good seed of the Gospel should lose that for which God had apprehended him.

In closing, let me remind you that the Holy Ghost has brought us here. For what purpose has He brought us? Can anyone have come here, either seeker or speaker, without a cry to God to make some men today, as it were, flames of fire? My passion is that God shall endue this convention with such an unction and cry that you won't be satisfied until you feel the very members of your body all on fire with a Spirit-kindled unity. It is not too late to don the girdle today, it is not too late to put on the armour of God, to put on the shield, to

PUT ON THE SANDALS

better than ever before. This afternoon God wants me to know, and you to know, that experimentally we have only touched the very frill, the very edge, of this outpouring of the Spirit. If we do not allow God to fill us with Himself He will choose somebody else. If we do not fall into line with the will of God, there will be somebody else who will. God is able to raise up men to carry out His behests. The children were crying out one day, and the disciples rebuked them. "No," He said, "if these were to hold their peace, the very stones," of which He could make bread — He could make them cry out.

I HAVE A JESUS LIKE THAT,

who can speak the word, and the thing is done; I have a Jesus indwelling me and vitalizing me with a faith that believes it is true; I have a Jesus within me who has never let me get faint-hearted or weary. Let us press on in faith along the line of God's will, and the outpouring which we have longed to see will come. Cheer up, hold on, never let go the vision; be sure it is for you just as much as for anybody else, and God will surely make it come to pass. Never look down, because then you will only see the ground and miss the vision. All blessings come from above; therefore keep your eye on Jesus. Never weary. If you do not fall out by the way, He will be with you to strengthen you in the way. Hallelujah!

Address given in Kingsway Hall, London, May 28, 1917
Published in *Confidence*

EXCEEDINGLY ABOVE ALL YOU CAN ASK OR THINK

January-March 1918

Read Ephesians 3 carefully. This is a lovely chapter on Paul's mission to the Gentiles. God has grafted us (Gentiles) in. In other ages (vv. 5,6) it was not made known that the Gentiles should be fellow heirs, whereof he was made a minister by the effectual working of His power (v. 7). This power in Paul wrought a very effectual work, it worked in him to such effect that he was the least of all saints; that to him was given this grace of mystery and revelation. It came forth as a living reality of a living substance indwelling him.

> *To the intent that now unto the principalities and powers in heavenly places might be known by the church the manifold wisdom of God.*
>
> *Ephesians 3:10*

WISDOM

This wisdom of God is only revealed in the depths of humiliation where the Holy Ghost has full charge. There alone it is that the vision comes to all His saints. We are now in the process of revelation. You must let the Holy Ghost have His perfect office. A new order of breathing. First a calculation of the mind — I can go no further, I give myself to a new order, the manifold wisdom of God "in whom we have boldness and access with confidence by the faith of him" (Ephesians 3:12). Boldness brings us into a place of access, confidence, laying hold, taking all off the table and making it ours. The Holy Ghost in the human body unfolding the mystery that we might know and have the revelation according to the will of God. The flesh brought to a place of nonexistence, that in the life of this man should come out the mighty power of God to usward. Paul can get no further. He says — "...I bow my knees unto the Father..." (Ephesians 3:14).

PRAYER

Jude also speaks of praying in the Holy Ghost. There is no natural line of thought here, not one point in particular upon which the mind can rest, but that which is predicted from the throne of glory, then the tongue, then all the divine attributes are displayed above all, exceedingly above all, that the glory of God may be revealed in the face of Jesus. Ye are His workmanship, created for His glory. God cannot display the greater glory except through those co-equal in the glory. The Holy Ghost is the ideal and brings out the very essence of heaven through the human soul. Oh, the need of the baptism of the Holy Ghost (Paul was held in the Spirit: may it be so in our case) — there is no difference; he was willing for all things, bound in the spirit — here we have the greatest liberty that can come to humanity, all the liberty of heaven open, the family in heaven and earth (Ephesians 3:15). I love that thought that the veil is so thin that the tie is closer than ever, Christ with them, they with us. One is on earth; what a loftiness, a reverence, a holiness! A wonderful thing is this wedlock and fellowship in the Spirit — now an infinite mind of fulfillment and glory. "Are they not all ministering spirits?" (Hebrews 1:14). Who can help us as those tried with us? As the body is so fitly framed together by the effectual working of His power, we are all one, nothing separates us, but we *look for the appearing of Jesus*. He is there in the glory, they are with Him. "For the Lord himself shall descend from heaven with a shout...and the dead in Christ shall rise first: then we which are alive and remain shall be caught up together with them in the clouds, to meet the Lord in the air: and so shall we ever be with the Lord" (1 Thessalonians 4:16,17).

We can only pray as the Holy Ghost gives utterance. Here the Holy Ghost gives the highest principles through this prayer that the purposes of salvation are a continuous working and an increasing power all the time. The day that is coming will declare all things. Strengthened by the Spirit according to the riches of His glory.

GLORY

What is the glory? All the glory that ever comes is from Him. You have the glory in the measure that you have the Son of glory in you. If you are filled with Jesus, you are filled with the glory. When we have the spirit of wisdom and revelation in the knowledge of Him, there is nothing to hinder the Holy Ghost having the control of the whole being. "That Christ may dwell in your hearts by faith..." (Ephesians 3:17). Faith is the production of all things. The Holy Ghost indwelling and enlarging until the whole body is filled with Christ, and we are coming there in a very remarkable way. Did the Holy Ghost ever utter a prayer that no power could answer? In John 17:21 Jesus says, "That they all may be one; as thou, Father, art in me, and I in thee, that they also may be one in us...." What works in us through being one with Him, rooted and grounded? Perfect love, and perfect love has justice wrapped up in it, and the day is coming when

The Saints Will Say "Amen"

to the judgments of God. Justice will do it. All the wood, hay, and stubble must be destroyed, but, rooted and grounded in the Word, I am a production of what God is forming and I can stay the gates of hell and laugh in the face of calamity and say, "…all things work together for good to them that love God…" (Romans 8:28); rooted and grounded in love. So-and-so may leave me, but if I am grounded, it is for my good and nothing can be against me but myself. We live for the glory of God. The Lord, it is He that establisheth, strengtheneth and upholdeth, making strong that which is weak and enabling them to stand in the difficulty, and in the day of battle. God is with thee to do far exceeding above all you can ask or think.

Faith

Are we children of circumstances, or children of faith? If we are on natural lines, we are troubled at the wind blowing, as it blows it whispers fearfulness; but if you are rooted and grounded you can stand the tests, and it is only then that you prove what is the breadth and length and depth and height, and know the love of Christ (Ephesians 3:18,19). It is an addition sum to meet every missionary's needs, to display God's power, enlarging that which needs to be quickened. Breadth: the whole man seeing God is sufficient in every state. The length of things: God is in everything. Oh, the depths! But God is in the depths! The heights! God is always lifting you, and the revelation of the mind in that verse is enough for any in any circumstances to triumph, able to do exceedingly abundantly above all that you can ask or think (v. 20), not according to the mind of Paul but according to the revelation of the Spirit (v. 19). Filled unto all the fulness of God. The natural capacity when filled with simplicity has within it an enlargement of itself, but this fulness is an ideal power of God in the human soul; every part of you is enlarged by the Spirit. God is there instead of you to make you full, and you are full as your faith reaches out to the measure. "Filled unto all the fulness of God."

The power of the Lord was present to heal, fulness of power pressed out of them unto others. In Acts 1 we see a power of the Holy Ghost filling Jesus. He became lighter and lighter until

HE WAS LIFTED BACK

to where He was before, in the presence of God. Jesus Christ manifest in the flesh, the power of God in human form. The fulness of the God-head bodily manifested in Jesus. John says He was the light of life, increasing in fulness until wafted away entirely, in substance the fulness of God. Exceedingly abundantly above all we can ask or think (v. 20). How can it be fulfilled in me, you say? It is filled there in the glory! But it's a tremendous thing! God will have to do something! Beloved, it is not according to your mind at all, but according to the mind of God, according to the revelation of the Spirit. Above all you could ask or think! The blood has been poured out.

THE HOLY GHOST HAS BEEN SENT DOWN

Verily, we are not worthy, but He is worthy! It's above all you can ask! How can it be possible? God puts it in your heart! He can do it.

We have been hearing much about war loan and interest, but if you will follow on, God will add and enlarge and enlarge and lift you all the time, adding compound interest. Five percent! No! A thousand percent, a million percent! If thou wilt, if holiness is the purpose of your heart, it shall be, for God *is* in His place. Will you be in the plan according to the power that worketh, working in you? (v. 20). Whatever you are at any time, it will be by His effectual power, lifting, controlling, carrying you in constant rest and peace; it is according to the power that wor-keth in you. "Unto him be glory in the church by Christ Jesus through-out all ages, world without end. Amen" (v. 21).

Published in *Confidence*

I n days gone by God's people have been persecuted, hunted. In Hebrews 11:38 we read of those of whom the world was not worthy, they wandered in deserts and mountains and wilderness and caves of the earth. We live in golden days in comparison. Days of sunshine, prosperity, and hopefulness.

ACTS 20

February 4, 1918

A NEW PLANE

Those who have passed on before wore such beautiful crowns in such times of strain and stress. Tidal waves of blessing come as the Holy Ghost has His way in these human bodies and produces in us an eternal working. The baptism of the Holy Ghost is a new plane, a covering with the divine presence, a power burning in our very bones. It is very wonderful to be in the place where the truths of the Holy Ghost are so advanced. The day will soon dawn and the Daystar appear, and our one regret will be our lost opportunity of witnessing for God. May God make us a worthy people embracing every opportunity. For Paul had determined to sail by Ephesus, because he would not spend the time in Asia, for he hasted if it were possible for him to be at Jerusalem the day of Pentecost. He remembered the days of Acts 9 verse 3 when as he journeyed — suddenly there shined round about him a light from heaven and the Lord saying unto Ananias, "Arise, and go into the street which is called Straight, and enquire in the house of Judas for one called Saul, of Tarsus: for, behold, he prayeth" (v. 11). "And Ananias went his way, and entered into the house; and putting his hands on him said, Brother Saul, the Lord, even Jesus, that appeared unto thee in the way as thou camest, hath sent me, that thou mightest receive thy sight, and be filled with the Holy Ghost. And immediately there fell from his eyes as it had been scales: and he received sight forthwith, and arose, and was baptized" (vv. 17,18).

Paul was stirred as he remembered this mighty baptism in the Spirit, the victory that it had brought him into, the power to preach the Gospel unlimited, unhindered, effectually working in us. The mighty unction of the Holy Spirit abode upon him. So at Troas,

> *...Paul preached unto [the church], ready to depart on the morrow; and continued his speech until midnight. And there were many lights in the upper chamber, where they were gathered together. And there sat in a window a certain young man named Eutychus, being fallen into a deep sleep: and as Paul was long preaching, he sunk down with sleep, and fell down from the third loft, and was taken up dead. And Paul went down, and fell on him, and embracing him said, Trouble not yourselves; for his life is in him. When he therefore was come up again, and had broken bread, and eaten, and talked a long*

while, even till break of day, so he departed. And they brought the young man alive, and were not a little comforted.

Acts 20:7-12

Thus Paul with the unction of the Spirit upon him went down and fell on the young man, embracing him in the power of the Spirit, *he returns and finishes his address.*

The day of Pentecost. The day of Pentecost, near at hand. Oh, what memories it had for Paul! We are all looking forward to Easter to when the Holy Ghost fell as at the beginning, where the cross of Calvary made an open door for all hearts to be saved, a few days afterward the resurrection of our Lord, then the wonderful descent of the Holy Ghost, to enlarge the hearts of all the people to live so in the Spirit, that there should be new vision, new revelation, new equipment, new men. The baptism of the Holy Ghost means a new creation after the order of the Spirit.

TONGUES AND INTERPRETATION: "For the Lord descended Himself by the power of the Spirit. He shall not speak of Himself, and He will show you things to come. The baptism of the Holy Ghost is to fulfill in these bodies a new order — to everyone by a new power, to change from one state of grace to another — even by the Spirit of the Lord. So Paul "...hasted, if it were possible for him, to be at Jerusalem the day of Pentecost" (v. 16).

HIS PROMISE TO FILL THE HUNGRY

Remember, beloved, many of the people living remembered the falling of the power in Acts 2. There is a wonderful unctionizing force when all the people of God baptized with the Holy Ghost come together. What are conventions for? They are for the meeting of the need of the hungry and the thirsty after God. Oh, this longing cry in the hearts of the people that cannot be satisfied but with more of God. On that memorable journey from Jerusalem to Damascus, Paul had seen the risen Christ, and *by the anointing* of the Spirit became the greatest missionary enterpriser the world has ever seen.

Oh yes! There is something in unity, there is something in fellowship, there is something in being of one accord! Is the church today at such a place to receive? No! But God is in such a place to give. Who to? Only to thirsty souls, the hungry. He has promised to fill the hungry with good things. Then it will be always. Convention, what is it! A condition of not falling asleep, a condition of continual longing after God for a real outpouring of His Spirit. So Paul hastened if it were possible for him, to be at Jerusalem the day of Pentecost (v. 16). They expected wonderful things when they were once more in the upper room. Paul had seen Jesus by revelation on the road to Damascus by he wanted to meet with those who had seen Him as He walked the streets, as He healed the sick and raised the dead. Would you not like to talk with anyone that had seen Him? What was His face like? What was His manner? How did He speak? "...Never man spake like this man" (John 7:46). Lots of people had seen Him around the table and in the roadways and could testify to His wonderful works. No wonder. Paul hastened if it were possible for him to be at Jerusalem the day of Pentecost.

What was the plan as the disciples gathered together? Preaching and telling the marvelous things that had happened. "...Eye hath not seen, nor ear heard, neither have entered into the heart of man, the things which God hath prepared for them that love him. But God hath revealed them unto us by his Spirit..." (1 Corinthians 2:9,10). The Holy Ghost revealing. The Holy Ghost strengthening all the time. Back to Pentecost all the time.

An old man once stood up in a meeting and was referring to one and another who had passed on. He said, "All the good people are gone now." Another brother standing up exclaimed — "Thank God that's a lie." Oh yes! There are lots of people on the earth today, and in our meeting tonight that have seen Jesus. And if we wait until Easter we shall see many more who will have seen Jesus. Jesus by the power of the Holy Ghost is making me understand we are only in the beginnings of Pentecost yet. Get back to Pentecost. Keep in the unction. Paul hasted, if it were possible for him, to be at Jerusalem the day of Pentecost. Pentecost, the place where God can bestow such a measure of His love, without limit, He giveth not the Spirit by measure (John 3:34).

SEPARATING FORCE

And now, behold, I go bound in the spirit unto Jerusalem, not knowing the things that shall befall me there: save that the Holy Ghost witnesseth in every city, saying that bonds and afflictions abide me. But none of these things move me, neither count I my life dear unto myself, so that I might finish my course with joy, and the ministry, which I have received of the Lord Jesus, to testify the gospel of the grace of God.

Acts 20:22-24

The baptism of the Holy Ghost is not only the great essential power for victorious life and service, it is a separating force. Jesus said a man's foes should be oftentimes those of his own household (Matthew 10:36). It means separation as sure as you live, if you follow the narrow way that leadeth unto life. It means persecution, but if you follow holy, you will have no room for any but Jesus — bound in the Spirit — on, on, on. Another side: the world narrows up to you. There are thousands of believers which mean well, do not see the need of the baptism of the Holy Ghost. So in the first place the old company has no room for you, but in the second place the Holy Ghost binds you. You have no room, only to go the way of the Spirit, in conformity to the will of God, you are bound to go the narrow way. I have never seen the Holy Ghost change His position. Simplicity in living, nonconformity to the world. You will not find God begin in the Spirit and leading back to the flesh. You have no liberty to go back? If you want to turn back, ask yourself where you are going to. What does Paul say? I go bound in the Spirit unto Jerusalem's bonds, afflictions — none of these things move me, neither count I my life dear unto myself. That I might finish my course with joy and the ministry which I have received of the Lord Jesus to testify the Gospel of the grace of God. The way, the way of the cross — separation from the flesh, nonconformity to the world — but with an ever deepening and enlarging in that abounding fulness of life that flows from the throne of God.

You must be in the order of seeing Him who is invisible (Hebrews 11:27), your mind operated by the Spirit, your desires under the control of the Spirit, your plans narrowed down by the Spirit (Daniel 10) Comeliness turned into corruption. Then it is a wonderfully broad way, very broad, a perfection of order. An entrenchment in the living God, bound in the Spirit! Can we take it in? There are depths we could fathom, I know it means bonds and afflictions (Acts 20:23). Shall I draw back? I cannot. Do you not see in Paul's willingness Jesus in a new form? Jesus again on the earth? This is the way we are bound to go. Paul calls himself the bondslave of Jesus Christ. But we are not obeyed! We could throw all over! Could I? Yes, I could! But I cannot! Separated bondslave, you cannot go back. It costs much to come, but it costs a thousand times more to retreat.

Oh, it's a costly thing to follow Jesus. Once having tasted the hidden manna, once having seen His face. It cost you your life to go out. "...to whom shall we go? thou hast the words of eternal life" (John 6:68).

The Lord is that Spirit, which has not only come in, but has embraced you and called you truly in the Spirit, that you might be a choice virgin betrothed to another, even Christ.

DEVOTED HEARTS

Shall we come out? No! Do you want to be unclothed? What a dreadful thing if nakedness is seen. What is it to be naked? To have a name! To be! And not to be! Lord, save us. Oh, for hearts that throb after the divine call. I love my Master. I will not go out free.

This is no mean meeting; the Holy Ghost gently falls upon us. The Spirit of the Living God yearns over us with tender compassion. God the Holy Ghost overshadows us. Some may say, "I want to get so near! I'll pay any price to come in to this holy place!" Dear ones, you cannot take off your filthy garments. Christ unclothes! He clothes upon! Oh, breathe every breath in the Holy Ghost. The old taken away — the bringing in of another — to never lose the fragrance of the divine presence, to fan and fan and fan until the Holy Ghost makes us living flames of fire carrying salvation everywhere, healing everywhere, the baptism of the Holy Ghost everywhere. On fire, bound forever, God thrilling the life.

TONGUES AND INTERPRETATION: "It is the Lord Himself which has the choice of my heart, pruning to bring forth to His glory an eternal harvest gathered in forever."

There is something beautiful in the gift of tongues with interpretation — joyfulness experience — sweet harmony – establishing, joy – lifting and making our hearts strong in Himself. The day is not far distant when we may have to stand very firm to what God is taking us on to. War, pestilence, famine; the order has not been altered since the world began.

These are trying times for the believer, the world wants less of God. There is a great deal of trial of faith. Are we going to be found faithful? Two lines will help you. Faith! Baptism of the Holy Ghost! An establishment against shot or shell or evil wind from any source.

So established that we are ready and willing to be tried when the day comes, whichever side the Spirit presses. There is always the thought,

Jesus may come before that day so that one is likely as the other. God will strengthen thy heart in the trial, in the evil day. He will never leave His own. Every man burned at the stake for the faith has been a seed, a light, a torch, bringing in a new order. Let us keep the vision clear — pure in heart, upward, onward, heavenward, until the day break and the shadows flee way (Song of Solomon 2:17).

Jesus is the loveliest on earth. The Holy Ghost clothes Him. He met the need of all. You belong to the church of the firstborn, the establishment of that wonderful place in the glory. Will you promise God nothing shall come between you and the throne — the heart of God and the mind of the Spirit. God has a choice for everyone who swears to his own hurt and changes not. A pressing right in.

Is not Jesus beautiful? Could anything cloud that brow? He has the joy of heaven for us. From victory unto victory. Your faces are a picture of what they will be in the glory — let us be jealous. Setting to our seals that God is true, until that day when we shall abide with Him forever. Set thine house in order, thou must go your way; follow Him. The building is going up. The top stone must be put on. Grace, grace unto it.

Address given at Bowland Street Mission

NEW WINE
April-June 1918

It is a settled thing in the glory that in the fulness of time the latter rain has to be greater than the former. Some of our hearts have been greatly moved by the former rain, but it is the latter rain we are crying out for. What will it be when the fulness comes and the heart of God is satisfied?

> *...and [they] began to speak with other tongues, as the Spirit gave them utterance.*
>
> Acts 2:4

What a lovely thought that the Holy Ghost had such partiality that the Word was all His! We are having to learn, whether we like it or not, that our end is God's beginning. Then it is all God, and the Lord Jesus stands forth in the midst with such divine glory and men are impelled, filled, led so perfectly. Nothing else will meet the need of the world.

There is something beautiful about Peter and John when we read that people took knowledge of them, that they had been with Jesus. There was something so real, so after the order of the Master.

> *Now when they saw the boldness of Peter and John, and perceived that they were unlearned and ignorant men, they marvelled; and they took knowledge of them, that they had been with Jesus.*
>
> *Acts 4:13*

May all in the temple glorify Jesus; it can be so.

The one thing marked more than anything else in the life of Jesus was the fact that the people glorified God in Him, and when God is glorified and gets the right of way and thoughts of His people, everyone is as He is, filled with God. Whatever it costs it must be. Let it be so. Filled with God! The only thing to help people is to tell out the latest thing God has given us from the glory. There is nothing outside salvation. We are filled, immersed, clothed upon; there must be nothing felt, seen, spoken about, but the mighty power of the Holy Ghost. We are new creatures in Christ Jesus, baptized into a new nature.

> *He that believeth on me...out of his belly shall flow rivers of living water.*
>
> *John 7:38*

The very life of the risen Christ in everything, moving us to do His will.

There is something not touched yet, but praise God for the thirst to be in this meeting! Praise God, the thirst is of God, the desire is of God, the plan is of God, the purpose is of God. God's plan, God's thought, God's vessel, and God's servant. In the world to meet the need; but not of the world or of its spirit.

God incarnate in humanity. Partakers of the divine nature to manifest the life of Jesus to the world.

> *Others mocking said, These men are full of new wine.*
>
> *Acts 2:13*

That is what we want, you say? "...Never man spake like this man" (John 7:46). "New wine": a new order, new inspiration, new manifestation. New, new, new, new wine. A power all new of itself, as if you were born, as you are, into a new day, a new creation.

It has a freshness about it! It has a beauty about it! It has a quality about it! To create in others the desire for the same taste. Some saw! But three thousand felt, tasted, and enjoyed. Some looked on! Others drinking with a new faith never before seen — a new manifestation, a new realization all divine, a new thing straight from heaven, from the throne of the glorified Lord. It is God's mind to fill us with that wine, to make us ready to burst forth with new rivers, fresh energy, no tired feeling.

God manifest in the flesh — that is what we want, and it is what God wants, and it satisfies everybody. All the people said, "We have never seen anything like it." The disciples rejoiced in it being new; others were brokenhearted, crying out, "...said unto Peter and to the rest of the apostles, Men and brethren, what shall we do?" (Acts 2:37).

> *Then Peter said unto them, Repent, and be baptized every one of you in the name of Jesus Christ for the remission of sins, and ye shall receive the gift of the Holy Ghost. For the promise is unto you, and to your children, and to all that are afar off, even as many as the Lord our God shall call. And with many other words did he testify and exhort, saying, Save yourselves from this untoward generation.*
>
> *Acts 2:38-40*

What shall we do? Men and brethren, what shall we do? Believe! Stretch out! Press on! Let there be a new entering in, a new passion to have it. We must be beside ourselves; we must drink deeply of the new wine, that multitudes may be satisfied and find satisfaction too.

The new wine is to have a new bottle* — the necessity of a new vessel. If anything of the old is left, not put to death, destroyed, there will be a rending and a breaking. The new wine and the old bottle will not work in harmony. It must be new wine and a new wineskin, then there will be nothing to drop off when Jesus comes.

> *For the Lord himself shall descend from heaven with a shout,*
> *with the voice of the archangel, and with the trump of God: and*
> *the dead in Christ shall rise first: then we which are alive and*
> *remain shall be caught up together with them in the clouds, to*
> *meet the Lord in the air: and so shall we ever be with the Lord.*
>
> *1 Thessalonians 4:16,17*

The body being so operated by the Spirit in the process of changing until we are like unto Him.

> *Who shall change our vile body, that it may be fashioned like*
> *unto his glorious body, according to the working whereby he is*
> *able even to subdue all things unto himself.*
>
> *Philippians 3:21*

I desire you to be all so filled with the Spirit at this Convention; so hungry, so thirsty, that nothing will satisfy us but seeing Jesus. Getting more thirsty every day, more dry every day, until the floods come, and the Master passes by, ministering unto us and through us, and through us the same life, the same inspiration, that as He is, so are we in this world.

He was straitened, but it was accomplished. It meant strong crying and tears — the cross manward, but the glory heavenward. Glory descending on a cross! Verily, great is the mystery of godliness. He cried, "It is finished." Let the cry never be stopped until the heart of Jesus is satisfied, until His plan for humanity is reached in the sons of God being manifested and the earth filled with the knowledge of the glory of the Lord as the waters cover the sea. Amen. Amen. Amen.

*The wine in Palestine was kept in wineskins, which in time lost their elasticity, and so would split when the new wine fermented. New wine must be in new wineskins.

Published in *Confidence*

From April 18th (Good Friday) for *ten days* is to be held (D.V.) the Bradford Easter Devotional Convention. Brother Smith Wigglesworth is, of course, to be the Convener. Meetings: 10:30, 3:00, and 7:00.

THE BRADFORD CONVENTION
Bowland Street Mission, Manningham Lane
April-June 1919

SPEAKERS:

Mr. Thomas Myerscough (Preston)

Mr. Boulton (Hull)

Pastor Jeays (Cheltenham)

Miss Morrell

Mrs. Crisp (London)

Mr. and Mrs. Walshaw (Halifax)

Rev. W. Reed (Glasgow)

Brother Reef Griffiths (Wales)

Brother James Tetchner (Horden)

Probably there will also be present other brethren and missionaries. Brother Wigglesworth writes: "There are many enquiries for rooms, and there is great interest in many quarters, and all seem full of expectation. We are bidding well for a £500 offering, and there seems every evidence that by faith we shall reach this amount. I am being much used, and God is helping me to rebuke the 'flu' demons. Many are healed who apparently were dying."

Address: Bro. Smith Wigglesworth, 70 Victor Road, Manningham, Bradford.

Announcement published in *Confidence*

nd Jacob was left alone; and there wrestled a man with him until the breaking of the day.

Genesis 32:24

A Straightened Place Which Revealeth the Face of God

April-June 1919

As we look back over our spiritual career we shall always see there has been a good deal of our own day, and that the end of our day was the beginning of God's day. "Can two walk together, except they be agreed?" (Amos 3:3). "...flesh and blood cannot inherit the kingdom of God; neither doth corruption inherit incorruption (1 Corinthians 15:50), and we cannot enter into the deep things of God until we are free from our own ideas and ways.

Jacob! The name means supplanter, and when Jacob came to the end of his way God had a way. How slow we are to see that there is a better day. Beloved, the glory is never so wonderful as when God has His plan and we are helpless and throw down our sword and give up our authority to another. Jacob was a great worker, and he would go through any hardship if he could have his way. In many ways he had his way, and in ignorance how gloriously God preserved him from calamity. There is a good and there is a better, but God has a best, a higher standard for us than we have yet attained. It is a better thing if it is God's plan and not ours.

Jacob and his mother had a plan to secure the birthright and the blessing, and his father agreed to his going to Padan-aram, but God planned the ladder and the angels. "...the land whereon thou liest, to thee will I give it...I am with thee, and will keep thee in all places whither thou goest, and will bring thee again into this land; for I will not leave thee, until I have done that which I have spoken to thee of" (Genesis 28:13,15). What a good thing for the lad, in the midst of the changes, God obtained the right place. The planning for the birthright had not been a nice thing, but here at Bethel he found God was with him.

Many things may happen in our lives, but when the veil is lifted and we see the glory of God, His tender compassion over us all the time, to be where God is, how wonderful it is. Bethel was the place where the ladder was set up twenty-one years before. Twenty-one years of wandering and fighting and struggling. Listen to his conversation with his wives. "…your father hath deceived me, and changed my wages ten times; but God suffered him not to hurt me" (Genesis 31:7). To his father-in-law: "Except the God of my father…had been with me, surely thou hadst sent me away now empty. God hath seen mine affliction and the labour of my hands…" (Genesis 31:42). Jacob had been out in the bitter frost at night watching the flocks. He was a thrifty man, a worker, a planner, a supplanter. We see the whole thing around us in the world today — supplanters. There may be a measure of blessing, but God is not first in their lives. We are not judging them, but there is a better way, better than our best — God's way. God first!

> *There is a way that seemeth right unto a man, but the end thereof are the ways of death.*
>
> Proverbs 16:25

But there is a way that God establisheth, and I want us to keep that way before us this morning — the way that God establisheth. In our own natural planning and way we may have much blessing, of a kind; but oh, beloved, the trials, the hardships, the barrenness, the things missed which God could not give us! I realize this morning by the Holy Ghost, I realize by the anointing of the Spirit that there is a freshness, a glow, a planning in God where you can know that God is with you all the time. Can we know that God is with us all the time? Yes! Yes! Yes! I tell you there is a place to reach where all that God has for us can flow through us to a needy world all the time.

> *For as the heavens are higher than the earth, so are my ways higher than your ways, and my thoughts than your thoughts.*
>
> Isaiah 55:9

"And Jacob was left alone; and there wrestled a man with him until the breaking of the day" (Genesis 32:24). Oh, to be left alone! Alone with God! In the context we read that several things had gone on. His wives had gone on, his children had gone on, all had gone on. His sheep and oxen had gone on, his camels and asses had gone on, all had gone on. He was alone. You will often find you are alone. Whether you like it or not, your wives will go on, your children will go on, your cattle will go on. Jacob was left alone. His wife could not make atonement for him, his children could not make atonement for him, his money was useless to help him.

"And Jacob was left alone; and there wrestled a man with him until the breaking of the day" (Genesis 32:24). What made Jacob come to that place of loneliness, weakness, and knowledge of himself? The memory of the grace with which God had met him twenty-one years before, when he saw the ladder and the angels and heard the voice of God: "And, behold, I am with thee, and will keep thee in all places whither thou goest, and will bring thee again into this land; for I will not leave thee, until I have done that which I have spoken to thee of" (Genesis 28:15). He remembered God's mercy and grace.

Here he was returning to meet Esau. His brother had become very rich, he was a chief, he had been blessed abundantly in the things of this world, he had authority and power to bind all Jacob had and to take vengeance upon him. Jacob knew this. He knew also that there was only one way of deliverance. What was it? The mind of God. "No one can deliver me but God." God had met him twenty-one years before, when he went out empty. He had come back with wives and children and goods, but he was lean in soul and impoverished in spirit. Jacob said to himself, "If I do not get a blessing from God I can never meet Esau," and he made up his mind he would not go on until he knew that he had favor with God. Jacob was left alone, and unless we get alone with God, we shall surely perish. God interposes where strife is at an end; the way of revelation is plain, and the Holy Ghost's plan is so clear, that we have to say it was God after all.

Jacob was left alone. He knelt alone. The picture is so real to me. Alone! Alone! Alone! He began to think. He thought about the ladder and the angels. I think as he began to pray, his tongue would cleave to the roof of his mouth. Jacob had to get rid of a lot of things. It had all been Jacob! Jacob! Jacob! He got alone with God and he knew it. If you get alone with God, what a place of revelation! Alone with God! Jacob was left alone, alone with God. We stay too long with our relations, our camels, and our sheep. Jacob was left alone. It would be afternoon. Hour after hour passed. He began to feel the presence of God. But God was getting disappointed with Jacob.

If ever God is disappointed with you when you tarry in His presence, it will be because you are not white-hot. If you do not get hotter, and hotter, and hotter, you disappoint God. If God is with you and you know it, be in earnest. Pray! Pray! Pray! Lay hold! "...hold fast the confidence and the rejoicing of the hope firm unto the end" (Hebrews 3:6). If you do not, you disappoint God.

Jacob was that way. God said, "You are not real enough; you are not hot enough; you are too ordinary; you are no good to Me unless you are filled with zeal — white hot!" He said, "Let me go, for the day breaketh." Jacob knew if God went without blessing him, Esau could not be met. If you are left alone — alone with God — and you cannot get to a place of victory, it is a terrible time. You must never let go, whatever you are seeking — fresh revelation, light on the path, some particular need — never let go. Victory is ours if we are in earnest enough. All must pass on, nothing less will please God. "Let me go, the day breaketh!" He was wrestling with equal strength. Nothing is obtained that way.

You must always master that which you are wrestling with. If darkness covers you, if it is fresh revelation you need, or your mind to be relieved, always get the victory. God says you are not in earnest enough. "Oh," you say, "the Word does not say that." But it was God's mind. In wrestling the strength is in the neck, chest, and thigh; the thigh is the strength of all. So God touched his thigh. That strength gone, defeat is sure. What did Jacob do? He hung on. God means to have a people severed by the power of His power, so hold fast; He will never leave go. And if we do leave go, we shall fall short.

Jacob said, "...I will not let thee go, except thou bless me" (Genesis 32:26). And God blessed him. "...Thy name shall be called no more Jacob, but Israel..." (Genesis 32:28). Now a new order is beginning, sons of God. How wonderful the change of Jacob to Israel! Israel! Victory all the time; God building all the time; God enough all the time. Power over Esau, power over the world, power over the cattle. The cattle are nothing to him now. All is in subjection as he comes out of the great night of trial. The sun rises upon him. Oh, that God may take us on, the sun rising, God supplanting all!

What after that? Read how God blessed and honored him. Esau meets him. No fighting now — what a blessed state of grace! They kissed each other. "When a man's ways please the Lord, he maketh even his enemies to be at peace with him" (Proverbs 16:7). "What about all these cattle, Jacob?" "Oh, it's a present."

"Oh, I have plenty; I don't want your cattle. What a joy it is to see your face again! What a wonderful change! Who wrought it?" "God."

"...when he saw that he prevailed not against him..." (Genesis 32:25). Could he hold God? Can you hold God? — it is irreverent to say so — oh, yes, you can. Sincerity can hold Him, dependence can hold Him, weakness can hold Him. When you are weak, then are you strong (2 Corinthians 12:10). I'll tell you what cannot hold Him. Self-righteousness cannot hold Him, pride cannot hold Him, assumption cannot hold Him, high-mindedness cannot hold Him — thinking you are something when you are nothing, puffed up in your imagination. Nothing but sincerity! You can hold Him in the closet, in the prayer meeting, everywhere. "...if any man hear my voice, and open the door, I will come in to him, and will sup with him, and he with me" (Revelation 3:20).

Can you hold Him? There may be a thought, sometimes, that He has left you. Oh, no! He does not leave Jacob, Israel. What changed his name? The wrestling? What changed his name? The holding on, the clinging, the brokenness of spirit? If you do not help me, I am no good, no good for the world's need. I am no longer salt. Jacob obtained the blessing on two lines: the favor of God, and a yieldedness of will. God's Spirit was working in him to bring him to a place of helplessness — God co-working to bring him to Bethel, the place of victory. Jacob remembered Bethel, and through all the mischievous conditions he had kept his vow.

When we make vows and keep them, how God helps us. We must call upon God and give Him account of the promise. "And Jacob called the name of the place Peniel: for I have seen God face to face, and my life is preserved" (Genesis 32:30). How did he know? Do you know when God blesseth you, when you have victory? But twenty years afterwards the vision of the ladder and the angels! How did he know?

We must have a perfect knowledge of what God has for us. He knew that he had the favor of God, and that no man could hurt him. Let us in all our seeking see we have the favor of God, walking day by day beneath an open heaven. Keeping His commandments, walking in the Spirit, tender in our hearts, lovable, appreciated by God; if so, we shall be appreciated by others and our ministry will be a blessing to those who hear. God bless you. God bless — for Jesus' sake.

Published in *Confidence*

 hen said they unto him, What shall we do, that we might work the works of God? Jesus answered and said unto them, This is the work of God, that ye believe on him whom he hath sent.

John 6:28,29

FAITH BASED UPON KNOWLEDGE

October-December 1919

"This is the work of God, that ye believe."
Nothing in the world glorifies God so much as simple rest of faith in what God's Word says. Jesus said, "...My Father worketh hitherto, and I work" (John 5:17). He saw the way the Father did the works; it was on the ground- work of knowledge, faith based upon knowledge. When I know Him, there are any amount of promises I can lay hold of, then there is no struggle, "For [he] that asketh receiveth; and he that seeketh findeth; and to him that knocketh it shall be opened" (Matthew 7:8).

Jesus lived to manifest God's glory in the earth, to show forth what God was like, that many sons might be brought to glory (Hebrews 2:10).

John the Baptist came as a forerunner, testifying beforehand to the coming revelation of the Son. The Son came, and in the power of the Holy Ghost revealed faith. The Living God has chosen us in the midst of His people. The power is not of us, but of God. Yes, beloved, it is the power of another within us (Hebrews 10:13).

JESUS THE SON OF GOD

Just in the measure we are clothed and covered and hidden in Him, is His inner working manifested. Jesus said, "...My Father worketh hitherto, and I work" (John 5:17). Oh, the joy of the knowledge of it! To know Him. We know if we look back how God has taken us on. We love to shout "Hallelujah," pressed out beyond measure by the Spirit, as He brings us face to face with reality, His blessed Holy Spirit dwelling in us and manifesting the works. I must know the sovereignty of His grace and the manifestation of His power. Where am I? I am in Him; He is in God. The Holy Ghost, the great Revealer of the Son. Three persons dwelling in man. The Holy Spirit is in us for revelation to manifest the Christ of God. Therefore be it known unto you, He that dwelleth in God doeth the works (John 14:10). The law of the Spirit of life having made us free from the law of sin and death (Romans 8:2).

The Spirit working in righteousness, bringing us to the place where

ALL UNBELIEF IS DETHRONED,

and Christ is made the head of the Corner. "...this is the Lord's doing, and it is marvellous in our eyes" (Matthew 21:42). It is a glorious fact, we are in God's presence, possessed by Him; we are not our own, we are clothed with Another. What for? For the deliverance of the people. Many can testify to the day and hour when they were delivered from sickness by a supernatural power. Some would have passed away with influenza if God had not intervened, but God stepped in with a new revelation, showing us we are born from above, born by a new power, God dwelling in us superseding the old. "If ye shall ask any thing in my name, I *will do it*" (John 14:14). Ask and receive, and your joy shall be full, if ye dare to believe (John 16:24). "...What shall we do, that we might work the works of God? This is the work of God, that ye believe on him whom he hath sent" (John 6:28,29). God is more anxious to answer than we are to ask. I am speaking of faith based upon knowledge.

A TESTIMONY

I was healed of appendicitis, and that because of the knowledge of it; faith based upon the knowledge of the experience of it. Where I have ministered to others, God has met and answered according to His will. It is in our trust and our knowledge of the power of God — the knowledge that

God will not fail us if we will only believe. "...speak the word only, and my servant shall be healed" (Matthew 8:8). Jesus said unto the centurion, "Go thy way; as thou hast believed, so be it done unto thee. And his servant was healed in the selfsame hour" (Matthew 8:13).

An Instance

In one place where I was staying a young man came in telling us his sweetheart was dying; there was no hope. I said, "Only believe." What was it? Faith based upon knowledge. I knew that what God had done for me He could do for her. We went to the house. Her sufferings were terrible to witness. I said, "In the name of Jesus come out of her." She cried, "Mother, Mother, I am well." Then I said that the only way to make us believe it was to get up and dress. Presently she came down dressed. The doctor came in and examined her carefully. He said, "This is of God; this is the finger of God." It was faith based upon knowledge.

If I received a check for £1000, and knew only imperfectly the character of the man that sent it, I should be careful of the man that sent it, I should be careful not to reckon on it until it was honored. Jesus did great works because of His knowledge of His Father. Faith begets knowledge, fellowship, communion. If you see imperfect faith, full of doubt, a wavering condition, it always comes of

Imperfect Knowledge.

Jesus said,

> *Father...I knew that thou hearest me always: but because of the people which stand by I said it, that they may believe that thou hast sent me...he cried with a loud voice, Lazarus, come forth.*
> *John 11:41-43*

> *And God wrought special miracles by the hands of Paul: so that from his body were brought unto the sick handkerchiefs or aprons, and the diseases departed from them, and the evil spirits went out of them.*
> *Acts 19:11,12*

For our conversation is in heaven from whence also we look for the Savior.

Who shall fashion anew the body of our humiliation that it may be conformed to the body of His glory, according to the working whereby He is able to subdue all things unto Himself? How God has cared for me these twelve years, and blessed me, giving me such a sense of His presence! When we depend upon God how bountiful He is, giving us enough and to spare for others. Lately God has enabled me to take victory on new lines, a living-in-Holy Ghost attitude in a new way. As we meet, immediately the glory falls. The Holy Ghost has the latest news from the Godhead, and has designed for us the right place at the right time. Events happen in a remarkable way. You drop in where the need is.

There have been several mental cases lately. How difficult they are naturally, but how easy for God to deal with. One lady came, saying, "Just over the way there is a young man terribly afflicted,

DEMENTED,

with no rest day or night." I went with a very imperfect knowledge as to what I had to do, but in the weak places God helps our infirmities. I rebuked the demon in the name of Jesus, then I said, "I'll come again tomorrow." Next day when I went he was with his father in the field and quite well.

Another case. Fifty miles away there was a fine young man, twenty-five years of age. He had lost his reason, could have no communication with his mother, and he was always wandering up and down. I knew God was waiting to bless. I cast out the demon-power, and heard long after he had become quite well. Thus the blessed Holy Spirit takes us on from one place to another. So many things happen, I live in heaven on earth. Just the other day, at Coventry, God relieved the people. Thus He takes us on and on and on.

Do not wait for inspiration if you are in need; the Holy Ghost is here, and you can have perfect deliverance as you sit in your seats.

I was taken to three persons, one in care of an attendant. As I entered the room there was a terrible din, quarreling, such a noise it seemed as if all the powers of hell were stirred. I had to wait God's time. The Holy Ghost rose in me at the right time, and the three were delivered, and at night were singing praises to God. There had to be activity and testimony. Let it be known unto you this Man Christ is the same today. Which man? God's Man Who has to have the glory, power, and dominion. "For he must reign, till he hath put all enemies under his feet" (1 Corinthians 15:25). When He reigns in you, you know how to obey, how to work in conjunction with His will, His power, His light, His life, having faith based upon knowledge, we know He has come. "...ye shall receive power, after that the Holy Ghost is come upon you..." (Acts 1:8). We are in the experience of it.

Sometimes a live word comes unto me, in the presence of a need, a revelation of the Spirit to my mind, "Thou shalt be loosed." Loosed now? It looks like presumption, but God is with the man who dares to stand upon His Word. I remember, for instance, a person who had not been able to smell anything for four years. I said, "You will smell now if you believe." This stirred another who had not smelled for twenty years. I said, "You will smell tonight." She went about smelling everything, and was quite excited. Next day she gave her testimony. Another came and asked, "Was it possible for God to heal her ears?" The drums were removed. I said, "Only believe." She went down into the audience in great distress; others were healed, but she could not hear. The next night she came again. She said, "I am going to believe tonight." The glory fell. The first time she came feeling; the second time she came believing.

At one place there was a man anointed for [a] rupture. He came the next night, rose in the meeting saying, "This man is an impostor; he is deceiving the people. He told me last night I was healed; I am worse than ever today." I spoke to the evil power that held the man and rebuked it, telling the man he was indeed healed. He was a mason. Next day he testified to lifting heavy weights, and that God had met him. "...with his stripes we are healed" (Isaiah 53:5). He hath made to light on Him the iniquity of us all. It was the Word of God, not me he was against.

"...What shall we do, that we might work the works of God? Jesus answered and said unto them, This is the work of God, that ye believe on him whom he hath sent" (John 6:28,29). Anything else? Yes. He took our infirmities and healed all our diseases. I myself am a marvel of healing. If I fail to glorify God, the stones would cry out.

> Salvation is for all,
>
> Healing is for all.
>
> Baptism of the Holy Ghost is for all.

Reckon yourselves dead indeed unto sin, but alive unto God.

"The world has to be brought to a knowledge of the truth, but that will only be brought about *through human instrumentality.*"

By His grace get the victory every time. It is possible to live holy.

> He breaks the power of canceled sin,
> He sets the prisoner free;
> His blood can make the foulest clean,
> His blood avails for me.

...What shall we do, that we might work the works of God? Jesus answered and said unto them, This is the work of God, that ye believe on him whom he hath sent.

John 6:28,29.

Published in *Confidence*

e are glad of cathedrals and churches, but God does not dwell in temples made by hands but in the fleshly tables of the heart.

Now! Now! Now!

1921

WHERE CHRIST REIGNS!

Here is true worship. God is a Spirit: and they that worship him must worship him in spirit and in truth — the Father seeketh such to worship Him (John 4:23,24). The church is the body of Christ; its worship is a heart worship, a longing to come into the presence of God. God sees our hearts and will open our understanding. The Lord delighteth in His people. He wants us to come to a place of undisturbed rest and peace — an undisturbed position — it is only in God! Only simplicity will bring us there. Jesus said when He uplifted the baby, "Except ye be converted, and become as little children, ye shall not enter into the kingdom of heaven" (Matthew 18:3). It is not to have the child's mind, but the child's spirit: meekness, gentleness. It is the only place to meet God. He will give us that place of worship.

How my heart cries out for a living faith with a deep vision of God. The world cannot produce it. A place where we see the Lord — that when we pray we know God hears. Asking God and believing for the answer, having no fear but a living faith to come into the presence of God. In His presence is fulness of joy and at His right hand are pleasures forevermore (Psalm 16:11).

God is looking for a people He can reveal Himself in. It is wonderful for me to be here. I used to have a tremendous temper, going white with passion. My whole nature was outside God that way. God knew His child could never be of service to the world unless he was wholly sanctified. I was difficult to please at the table. My wife was a good cook, but there was always something wrong; but after God sanctified me I heard her testify in a meeting; from that time I was pleased with everything.

I had men working for me (I wanted to be a good testimony to them), and one day they waited after work was over and said, "we would like that spirit you have." It is our human spirit that has to be controlled by the Holy Spirit. There is a place of death and life where Christ reigns in the body. Then all is well. This Word is full of stimulation. It is by faith, into a place of grace, that all may see us new. Behold! Behold! Behold! What is it? The Holy Ghost arousing our attention. He has something special to say. Behold, if you will believe you can be sons of God in likeness — character, spirit, longings, acts until all know you are a son of God.

Now the Spirit of God can change our nature. God is Creator. His Word is creative, and if you believe today — a creative power changing the whole nature. Sons of God. You cannot reach this altitude only by faith. No man can keep himself. The God of almightiness spreads His covering over you, saying, "I am able to do all things, and all things are possible to him that believeth." The old nature is so difficult to manage. You have been ashamed of it many a time, but the Lord Himself will come. He says, "Come unto me, and I will give the rest, peace, strength. I will change you. I will operate upon you by My power, making you a new creation if you will believe." Leave it there, leave it there. Take your burden to the Lord and leave it there. Learn of Me, for I am meek and lowly in heart, and ye shall find rest unto your souls. The world has no rest, it is full of troubles; but in Me a peace which passeth understanding with an inward flow of divine power changing your nature until you can live, move and act in the power of God. Therefore the world knoweth you not because it knew Him not.

What does it mean? I have lived in one house fifty years. I have preached from my own doorstep — all around know me. They know me when they need someone to pray, when there is trouble, when they need a word of wisdom. But at Christmas time when they call their friends, would they call me? No! Why? They would say, "He is sure to want a prayer meeting, but we what to finish up with a dance."

Wherever Jesus came, sin was revealed and men don't like sin revealed. Sin separates from God forever. You are in a good place when you weep before God, repenting over the least thing. If you have spoken unkindly, you realized it was not like the Lord. Your keen conscience has taken you to prayer. It is a wonderful thing to have a keen conscience. When everything is wrong, you cry unto the Lord! It is when we are close to God that our hearts are revealed. God intends us to live in purity, seeing Him all the time. How can we?

> *Beloved, now are we the sons of God, and it doth not yet appear what we shall be: but we know that, when he shall appear, we shall be like him; for we shall see him as he is. And every man that hath this hope in him purifieth himself, even as he is pure.*

> *1 John 3:2,3*

WHAT AN OFFERING!

It is the hope of the church, as the Bridegroom to the bride, our Lord Who has died for us, the Lamb of God, Who became poor for us that we might be made rich. What an offering! He has suffered for us, been buried for us, risen for us, jealous for us. How we love Him. He is coming again. I am praying God will create sons in this meeting. "To as many as believe on Him, to them gave He power to become sons of God." When we believe, we receive Him. When you receive Him anything may take place. "All things are possible to him that believeth." Paul says of some that they came behind in no gift, comprehending with all saints over sin, clean and pure, having a boldness in humility, a place in God in sobriety.

When I am leaving anywhere by train or ship, people come to see [me] off; I preach to them. It is God's plan to me; it is an order. The captain hears; the stewards hear. "Oh!" they say. "Another on board." The world thinks there is something wrong with you if you are full of zeal for God.

A young man came and asked me to take part in a sweep. I said, "I am preaching on Sunday. Would you come if I did?" He said, "No." Later, there was an entertainment. I said I would take part. It was the strangest thing for me. I said I would sing. I saw men dressed as clergy entertaining the people with foolishness. I was troubled; I cried to God. Then came my turn just before the dance. A young woman came to take my book; she was half dressed. She said, "I cannot play that." I said, "Never worry." I said, "Oh! If I could only tell you how I love Him! I am sure that you would make Him yours today." There was no dance. They began weeping, and six young men gave their hearts to God in my cabin.

The world does not know us, but we are sons of God with power. Jesus is the chance, and as we look for Him our life is changed. He is God's Son. What is the object of my ministry? No man that sins has power. Sin makes a man weak — takes away his dignity and power. With joy in the Holy Ghost — filled with joy. It is God's plan. Heaven open. No condemnation. If you pray, you know He hears. If you read the Word of God, it is all alive. Remember this: sin dethrones, but purity strengthens. Temptation is not sin, but the devil is a liar and tries to take away peace. You must live in the Word of God. There is now no condemnation. Who is he that can condemn you, Christ that died!!!

He won't condemn you. He died to love you. Don't condemn yourself. If there is anything wrong, come to the blood.

> *...if we walk in the light, as he is in the light, we have fellowship one with another, and the blood of Jesus Christ his Son cleanseth us from all sin.*
>
> *1 John 1:7*

Jesus was manifested to destroy the works of the devil. You can come this morning into a new experience of God. All fear God, and God creates in our hearts such a love for Jesus that we are living in a new realm — sons of God with power, filled with all the fulness of God. If our hearts condemn us not, we have confidence towards God, and whatsoever we ask we receive of Him, because He keeps His commandments and does those things that are pleasing in His sight. Hereby we know that He abideth in us by the Spirit which He has given us.

Paul went to impart some spiritual gifts. Did Paul give gifts? No! The Holy Ghost gives gifts, and Jesus gives gifts. No man can give a gift.

I am here ministering faith on the line of an act. Before leaving home I received a wire, would I go to Liverpool. There was a woman with cancer and gallstones down with much discouragement. If I know God is sending me, my faith rises. The woman said, "I have no hope." "Well," I said, "I have not come from Bradford to go home with a bad report." God said to me, "Establish her in the fact of the new birth." When she had the assurance that her sin was gone and she was born again, she said, "That is everything to me. Cancer is nothing now. I have got Jesus. The battle was won. God delivered her, and she was free and up and dressed and happy in Jesus.

When God speaks, it is as a nail in a sure place. Will you believe that God makes you His sons? Life and immortality are ours in the Gospel. This is our inheritance through the blood of Jesus — life forevermore. Believe, and the Lord will transmit life right through you, that you may be waiting for His coming witnessing unto Him.

Address given in Colombier, Switzerland

IMMERSED IN THE HOLY GHOST
May 1921

The baptism of the Holy Ghost is a great beginning. I think the best word we can say is, "Lord, what wilt Thou have me to do?" The greatest difficulty today with us is to be held in the place where it shall be God only. It is so easy to get our own mind to work. The working of the Holy Ghost is so different. I believe there is a mind of Christ, and we may be so immersed in the Spirit that we are all the day asking, "What wilt Thou have me to do?"

This has been a day in the Holy Ghost. The last three months have been the greatest days of my life. I used to think if I could see such and such things worked I should be satisfied; but I have seen greater things than I ever expected to see, and I am more hungry to see greater things yet. The great thing at conventions is to get us so immersed in God that we may see signs and wonders in the name of the Lord Jesus; a place where death has taken place and we are not, for God has taken us. If God has taken hold of us we will be changed by His power and might. You can depend on it, the Ethiopian will be changed. I find God has a plan to turn the world upside down, where we are not.

When I have been at my wit's end, and have seen God open the door, I have felt I should never doubt God again. I have been taken to another place that was worse still. There is no place for us, and yet a place where God is, where the Holy Ghost is just showing forth and displaying His graces; a place where we will never come out, where we are always immersed in the Spirit, the glory of God being seen upon us. It is wonderful! There is a power behind the scenes that moves things. God can work in such a marvelous way....

I believe we have yet to learn what it would be with a Pentecostal Church in England that understood truly the work of intercession. I believe God the Holy Ghost wants to teach us that it is not only the people on the platform who can move things by prayer. You people, the Lord can move things through you. We have to learn the power of the breath of the Holy Ghost. If I am filled with the Holy Ghost, He will formulate the word that will come into my heart. The sound of my voice is only by the breath that goes through it. When I was in a little room at Bern waiting for my passport, I found a lot of people, but I couldn't speak to them. So I got hold of three men and pulled them unto me. They stared, but I got them on their knees. Then we prayed, and the revival began. I couldn't talk to them, but I could show them the way to talk to Someone else.

God will move upon the people to make them see the glory of God just as it was when Jesus walked in this world, and I believe the Holy Ghost will do special wonders and miracles in these last days. I was taken to see a young woman who was very ill. The young man who showed me the way said, "I am afraid we shall not be able to do much here, because of her mother, and the doctors are coming." I said, "This is what God has brought me here for," and when I prayed the young woman was instantly healed by the power of God. God the Holy Ghost says in our hearts today that it is only He who can do it. After that we got crowds, and I ministered to the sick among them for two hours.

The secret for the future is living and moving in the power of the Holy Ghost. One thing I rejoice in is that there need not be an hour or a moment when I do not know the Holy Ghost is upon me. Oh, this glorious life in God is beyond expression; it is God manifest in the flesh. Oh, this glorious unction of the Holy Ghost — that we move by the Spirit. He should be our continual life. The Holy Ghost has the last thoughts of anything that God wants to give. Glory to God for the Holy Ghost! We must see that we live in the place where we say, "What wilt Thou have me to do?" and are in the place where He can work in us to will and to do of His good pleasure.

Published in *Triumphs of Faith*

 he Lord give us patience to take in this Word. It is a very marvelous Word, and God wants us to fully comprehend the fulness of what it means to us all. The great plan of God's salvation is redemption in its fulness.

FAITH
Romans 4
1922

There are things in this chapter that will bring a revelation of what God means for the man who believes. While I know prayer is wonderful, and not only changes things but changes *you*, while I know the man of prayer can go right in and take the blessing from God, yet I tell you that if we grasp this truth that we have before us, we shall find that faith is the greatest inheritance of all.

May God give us faith that will bring this glorious inheritance into our hearts; for, beloved, it is true that the just shall live by faith; and do not forget that it takes a just man to live by faith, and may the Lord reveal to us the fulness of this truth that God gave to Abraham.

THAT BLESSED PLACE

Twenty-five years Abraham had the promise that God would give him a son. Twenty-five years he stood face to face with God on the promise, expecting every year to have a son. There was Sarah becoming weaker, his own stamina and body becoming more frail, and natural conditions so changing both Sarah and him that, so far as they could see, there was no such thing as seeing their bodies bring forth fruit. And, if they had looked at their bodies as some people do theirs, they would probably have remained like they were forever. But Abraham dared not look either at Sarah or himself in that respect. He had to look at God. You cannot find anywhere that God ever failed. And He wants to bring us into that blessed place of faith, changing us into a real substance of faith, till we are so like-minded that whatever we ask we believe we receive, and our joy becomes full because we believe. I want you to see how God covered Abraham because he believed.

Hear what God said to Abraham, and then see how Abraham acts. He was amongst his own people and his own kindred, and God said to him, "Come out, Abraham, come out!" And Abraham obeyed, and came out, not knowing whither he was going. You say, "He was the biggest ass that ever God had under His hands." You will never go through with God on any lines except by believing Him. It is, "Thus saith the Lord" every time; and you will see the plan of God come right through when you dare believe. He came right out of his own country, and God was with him. Because he believed God, God overshadowed him. I am as confident as possible that if we could get to the place of believing God, we need not have a dog in the yard or a lock on the door. All this is unbelief. God is able to manage the whole business. It doesn't matter how many thieves are about; they cannot break through nor steal where God is.

I want, by the help of God, to lead you into the truth, for there is nothing but the truth can set you free, but truth can always do it. It is impossible, if God covers you with His righteousness, for anything to happen to you, contrary to the mind of God.

When God sets His seal upon you, the devil dare not break it. He dare not break in where you are. You know what a "seal" is, don't you? Now, then, when God puts His seal upon you, the devil has no power there. He dare not break that seal and go through; and God puts His seal upon the man that believes Him. There are two kinds of righteousness. There is a righteousness which is according to the law, the keeping of the law; but there is a better righteousness than that. You ask, "What could be better than keeping the law"? The righteousness that sees God and obeys Him in everything! The righteousness that believes that every prayer uttered is going to bring the answer from God. There is a righteousness which is made known only to the heart that knows God. There is a side to the inner man that God can reveal only to the man that believes Him.

We have any amount of scriptural illustrations to show us how God worked with those people who believed Him. I have any amount of definite instances in my life where God came, where God was, where God worked, where God planned. And here is one of the greatest plans of all, where God works in this man (Abraham) exactly opposite to human nature. There were many good points about Sarah, but she had not reached the place. She laughed, and then denied having done so, and when they waited a time and she saw that their bodies were growing frailer, she said: "Now it will be just as good for you to take Hagar for a wife and bring forth a son through her." But that was not the seed of Abraham that God spoke about, and that caused a great deal of trouble in the house of Abraham; and there are times when you dare not take your wife's advice. The man who walks with God can only afford to take God's leadings, and when He leads you it is direct and clear, and the evidence is so real that every day you know that God is with you unfolding His plan to you. It is lovely to be in the will of God.

TONGUES AND INTERPRETATION: "Glory to God! He is the Lord of Hosts Who cometh forth into the heart of the human life of man, and speaks according to His divine plan, and as you live in the Spirit, you live in the process of God's mind, and act according to His divine will."

A HIGHER ORDER

And so there is a higher order than the natural man, and God wants to bring us into this higher order, where we will believe Him. In the first place, God promised Abraham a son. Could a child be born into the world, except on the line of the natural law? It was when all natural law was finished, and when there was no substance in these two persons, that the law of the Spirit brought forth a son. It was the law of faith in God Who had promised.

And then we are brought to the time when our blessed Lord was conceived. I hear Mary saying to the angel, "Lord, be it unto me according to thy word" (Luke 1:38), so that the man Christ Jesus was brought forth on the same lines. Tonight I see before me faces I know, and I can see that these men are born, not of blood, neither by the will of the flesh, but of God. We have the same law in our midst tonight. Born of God! And sometimes I see that this power within us is greater when we are weak than when we are strong; and this power was greater in Abraham day by day than when he was strong.

Looking at him, Sarah would shake her head and say: "I never saw anybody so thin and weak and helpless in my life. No, Abraham, I have been looking at you, and you seem to be going right down." But Abraham refused to look at his own body or that of Sarah; he believed the promise that it should be. Some of you people have come for healing. You know as well as possible that, according to the natural life, there is no virtue in your body to give you that health. You know also that the ailment from which you suffer has so drained your life and energy that there is no help at all in you; but God says that you shall be healed if you *believe*. It makes no difference how your body is. It was exactly the helplessness of Sarah and Abraham that brought the glorious fact that a son was born, and I want you to see what sort of a son he was.

He was the son of Abraham. The seed of the whole, believing church — his seed as innumerable as the sands upon the seashore. God wants you to know tonight that there is no limitation with Him, and to bring us to a place where there will be no limitation in us. This state would be brought about by the working of the Omnipotent in the human body; working in us continually — greater than any science or any power in the world — and bringing us into the place to comprehend God and man.

I want you to see tonight that Romans 4:16 has a great touch for us all. You look at it: "Therefore it is of faith, that it might be by grace; to the end the promise might be sure to all the seed; not to that only which is of the law, but to that also which is of the faith of Abraham; who is the father of us all." Think about those words, "Therefore it is of faith, that it might be by grace." Some of you would like a touch in your bodies; some would like a touch in your spirit; some would like to be baptized in the Holy Ghost; some want to be filled with all God's power. There it is for you.

> *That the blessing of Abraham might come on the Gentiles through Jesus Christ; that we might receive the promise of the Spirit through faith.*
>
> *Galatians 3:14*

Now come on the lines of faith again. I want you to see tonight that you can be healed if you will hear the Word. Now there are some people here for healing; maybe some want salvation, maybe others want sanctification and the baptism of the Spirit. This Word says it is by faith, that it might be by grace. Grace is omnipotence; it is activity, benevolence, mercy. It is truth, perfection, and God's inheritance in the soul that can believe. God gives us a negative side. What is it? It is by faith. Grace is God. You open the door by faith, and God comes in with all you want, and it cannot be otherwise, for it is "of faith, that it might be by grace." It cannot be by grace unless you say it shall be so.

This is believing, and most people want healing by feeling. It cannot be. Some even want salvation on the same lines, and they say, "Oh, if I could feel I was saved, brother!" It will never come that way. There are three things that work together. The first is faith. Faith can always bring a fact, and a fact can always bring joy, and so God brings you into this meeting to hear the Scriptures, which can make you wise unto salvation, which can open your understanding and make you so that if you will hear the truth, you will go out with what you want. So that you have power to shut the door, and power to open the door. Let us now take another verse more mighty still, step by step, and you will find it is very wonderful.

GOD IS

Here is Sarah — her body is dead — and Abraham — his body is dead. "As it is written, I have made thee a father of many nations... (Romans 4:17). "Now," says Abraham, "God has made me a father of many nations, and there is no hope of a son according to the natural law — no hope whatever." But here God says, "I have made thee a father of many nations," and yet he has no son, and during the past twenty years of waiting, conditions have grown more and more hopeless, and yet the promise was made. Now how long have you been with your rheumatism and believing? How long have you been waiting for the promise and it has not come? Had you need to wait? Look here! I want to tell you that all the people who are saved are blessed with faithful Abraham. Abraham is the great substance of the whole keynote of Scripture — a man that dared for twenty-five years [to] believe God when everything went worse every day. Oh, it is lovely. It is perfect. I do not know anything in the Scriptures so marvelous, so far-reaching, and so full of the substance of living reality, to change us if we will believe God. He will make us so different. This blessed incarnation of living faith which changes us and makes us know that God *is*, and that He is a rewarder of them that diligently seek Him. God is a reality. God is true, and in Him there is no lie, neither shadow of turning. Oh, it is good! I do love to think about such truths as this.

Oh, beloved, there is not a subject in the whole Bible that makes my body aflame with passion after God and His righteousness as this. I see He never fails. He wants the man to believe, and then the man shall never fail. Oh, the loveliness of the character of God!

"The father of many nations!" You talk about your infirmities...look at this! I have never felt I have had an infirmity since I understood this chapter. Oh God, help me. I feel more like weeping than talking tonight. My cup runneth over as I see the magnitude of this living God. "(As it is written, I have made thee a father of many nations,) before him whom he believed, even God, who quickeneth the dead, and calleth those things which be not as though they were." "I won't look at my body. I won't look at my infirmities. I believe God will make the whole thing right. What matter if I have not heard for over twenty years? I believe my ears will be perfect." God is reality, and wants us to know that if we will believe it shall be perfect. "Who quickeneth that which is dead, and calleth those things which be not as though they were." No limitation of possibility. Then God tested them still further than that. Oh, it is blessed to know you are tested. It is the greatest thing in the world to be tested. You never know what you are made of till you are tested. Some people say, "Oh, I don't know why my lot is such a heavy one," and God puts them into the fire again. He knows how to do it. I can tell you, He is a blessed God. There is not such a thing as a groan when God gets hold of you. There is no such thing as want to them who trust the Lord. When we really get in the will of God, He can make our enemies to be at peace with us. It is wonderful.

Brothers, I wonder if you really believe that God can quicken that which is dead? I have seen it any amount of times. The more there was no hope, Abraham believed in hope. Sometimes Satan will blear your minds and interfere with your perception that would bring right in between you and God the obscure condition; but God is able to change the whole position if you will let Him have a chance. Turn your back on every sense of unbelief, and believe God. There are some who would like to feel the presence of the touch of God; God will bring it to you. Now, I wish people could come to this place. Oh, Abraham had a good time; the more he was squeezed, the more he rejoiced; and being not weak in faith, he considered not his own body, which was now dead, when he was about 100 years old, neither yet the deadness of Sarah's womb. He staggered not through unbelief, but was strong in faith, giving God the glory (Romans 4:19,20). God knows. He has a plan. He has a way. Dare you trust Him? He knows.

I am here — saved by the power of God because of the promise that God made to Abraham; as the countless sands upon the seashore and as the stars in multitude and glory, the seed of thy son shall be! It is for us tonight, beloved. The Scripture says to us that the delaying of the promise and the testing of Abraham was the seed of all the world to be who believed in God. And, being fully persuaded that that which He had promised He was able to perform. Therefore, it was imputed unto him for righteousness, and not to him only, but to all the people who will believe God (Romans 4:21-24).

THE SEED OF THE PROMISE
AND THE SEED OF THE FLESH

We have another place in the Scriptures, and I want to touch this now. Isaac was born. And you find that, right in that house where Isaac was and where Ishmael was, there was the seed of promise and the seed of flesh; and you find there is strife and trouble right there, for Ishmael was teasing Isaac. And you will find, my dear friends, as sure as anything, there is nothing that is going to hold you except the Isaac life — the seed of Abraham. You will find that the flesh-life will always have to be cast out. "And Sarah said, Cast out Hagar and her son." It was very hard to do, but it had to be done. You say, "How hard!" Yes, but how long had it to be? Till submission came! There will always be jealousy and strife in your hearts and lives till flesh is destroyed — till Isaac controls and rules in authority over the whole body; and when Isaac–power reigns over you, you will find that the whole of your life is full of peace and joy. And then comes the time when this son grew up a fine young man, perhaps twenty years of age — we are not told — but then came another test.

God says to Abraham, "Take thy son Isaac, and offer him to Me upon the mount that I will shew thee." Do you think that Abraham told anybody of that? No, I am sure he didn't. He was near to his heart, and God said he had to offer him on the altar, and there he was — Isaac, the heart of his heart — and God said he was to be the seed of all living. What had he to do but to believe that, just as miraculously as Isaac came into the world, God could even raise him though he were slain. Did he tell Sarah about the thing? No, I am certain he did not, or else he would not have got away with that boy. There would have been such a trial in the home. I believe he kept it to himself. When God tells you a secret don't tell anyone else. God will, perchance, tell you to go and lay hands on some sick one. Go, do it, and don't tell anyone.

One thing I know is that Satan does not know my thoughts; he only knows what I let out of my mouth. Sometimes he suggests thoughts in order to get to know, but I can see that God can captivate my thoughts in such a way that they may be entirely for Him. When God gets upon your hearts you will see that every thought is captive, that everything is brought into obedience, and is brought into a place where you are in dominion because Christ is enthroned in your life (2 Corinthians 10:4,5). Some people God reveals deep and special things to. Keep your counsel before God.

Now, beloved, I see this: Abraham could offer Isaac. Now tell me how. I believe in this meeting that God wants me to tell you how, in order that you may know something about your trials. Some think they are tried more than other people. If you knew the value of it, you would praise God for trial more than for anything. It is the trial that is used to purify you; it is in the fiery furnace of affliction that God gets you in the place where He can use you. The person that has no trials and no difficulties is the person whom God dare not allow Satan to touch, because he could not stand temptation; but Jesus will not allow any man to be tempted more than he is able to bear. The Scriptures are the strongest evidence of anything you can have. Before Abraham offered Isaac he was tried, and God knew he could do it. And before God puts you through the furnace of afflictions, He knows you will go through. Not one single temptation cometh to any man more than he is able to bear; and with the temptation God is always there to help you through. Don't you see that was exactly the position in the case of Abraham?

If you know you need the baptism of the Holy Spirit, and you know it is in the Scriptures, never rest till God gives it [to] you. If you know it is scriptural for you to be healed of every weakness, never rest until God makes it yours. If you know that the Scriptures teach holiness, purity, and divine likeness — overcoming under all conditions — never rest till you are an overcomer. If you know that men have gone in and have seen the face of God, who have had the vision revealed, have had the whole of the Scriptures made life in their lives, never rest till you come to it. You say, "Have you a Scripture to prove it?" Yes, the Scripture says, "That ye may apprehend with all saints what is the depth, length, breadth and height of the love of God."

TONGUES AND INTERPRETATION: "Oh, hallelujah! This blessed inheritance of the Spirit is come to profit withal; teaching you all things, and making you understand the will of God cometh not by observation; but holy men of old spoke and wrote as the Spirit gave them power and utterance, and so today the Holy Ghost must fill us with this same initiative of God."

We must live in the fire; we must hate sin; we must love righteousness; we must live with God, for He says we have to be blameless and harmless amidst the crooked positions of the world. Beloved, I look at you tonight, and I say God is able to confirm all I have been speaking about trials and testings, which are the greatest blessings you can have. God wants to make sons everywhere like unto Jesus. Jesus was a type of the sonship that we have to attain unto. I don't know how I feel when I am speaking about the loftiness of the character of Jesus, Who was a first-fruit to make us pure and holy. And I see Jesus going about clothed with power. I see likewise, every child of God in this place clothed with power, and I see every detail. Jesus was just the firstfruit — and I know that is the pattern of God.

God has not given us a pattern which it would be impossible to copy. Beloved, He hated sin — which is the greatest luxury we can have in our lives. If I have a hatred for sin, I have something which is worth millions of pounds. Oh, the blood of Jesus Christ, God's Son, cleanseth us from *all* sin. Beloved, I feel somehow that that is the hope of the church for the future — being purified, made like unto Jesus, pure in heart, pure in thought. Then when you lay your hands upon the sick, *Satan has no power.* When you command him to leave, *he has to go.* What a redemption! What a baptism! *What an unction!* It is ecstasies of delight beyond all expression for the soul to live and move in Him Who is our being.

Address given at Good News Hall
Melbourne, Australia

R omans 8. For a short time I want specially to speak to the people in this meeting who are saved. God wants us to be holy. He wants us to be filled with a power that keeps us holy. He wants us to have a revelation of what sin and death are, and what the Spirit and the life of the Spirit are.

FILLED WITH GOD
Romans 8
1922

NO CONDEMNATION

Look at the first two verses. They are full of matter — sufficient to keep us for two hours tonight, but we must move on in order to help everybody. But look at these verses for a moment:

> *There is therefore now no condemnation to them which are in Christ Jesus, who walk not after the flesh, but after the Spirit. For the law of the Spirit of life in Christ Jesus hath made me free from the law of sin and death.*
>
> Romans 8:1,2

"No condemnation." This is the primary word for me tonight because it means so much — it has everything within it. If you are without condemnation you are in a place where you can pray through — where you have a revelation of Christ. For Him to be in you brings you to a place where you cannot but follow the divine leadings of the Spirit of Christ, and where you have no fellowship with the world. And I want you to see that the Spirit of the Lord would reveal unto us this fact, that if you love the world you cannot love God, and the love of God cannot be in you. So God wants a straight cut tonight. Why does God want a straight cut? Because if you are "in Christ" you are a "new creation." You are in Him, you belong to a new creation in the Spirit. Therefore you walk in the Spirit and are free from condemnation.

So the Spirit of the Lord tonight wants you without condemnation, and desires to bring you into revelation. Now what will it mean? Much every way, because God wants all His people to be targets, to be lights, to be like cities set on a hill which cannot be hid; to be so "in God" for the world's redemption that the world may know that ye belong to God. That is the law of the Spirit. What will it do? The law of the Spirit of life in Christ Jesus will make you free from the law of sin and death. Sin will have no dominion over you. You will have no desire to sin, and it will be as true in your case as it was in Jesus' when He said: "Satan cometh, but findeth nothing in Me." He cannot condemn; he has no power. His power is destroyed in the tenth verse. What does it say? "...the body is dead because of sin; but the Spirit is life because of righteousness." To be "filled with God" means that you are free — full of joy, peace, blessing, enduement, strength of character, moulded afresh in God and trans-formed by His mighty power till you *live*. Yet not you, but "Another lives in you," manifesting His power through you as sons of God.

Notice these two laws: the law of the Spirit of life in Christ Jesus making you free from the law of sin and death. The same law is in you as was in you before, but it is dead. You are just the same man, only quickened — the same flesh, but it is dead. You are a new creation — a new creature. Created in God afresh after the image of Christ. Now, beloved, some people come into line with this but do not understand their inheritance and go down; but instead of you being weak and going down, you have got to rise triumphantly over it. You say, "Show us the law." I will, God helping me. It is found in the seventh chapter of Romans, the last verse:

> *I thank God through Jesus Christ our Lord. So then with the mind*
> *I myself serve the law of God; but with the flesh the law of sin.*

Is it a sin to work? No, it is not a sin to work. Work is ordained by God. It is an honor to work. I find that there are two ways to work. One way is working in the flesh, but the child of God should never allow himself to come into the flesh when God has taken him in the Spirit. God wants to show you that there is a place where you can live in the Spirit and not be subject to the flesh. Live in the Spirit till sin has no dominion. Sin reigneth unto death; but Christ reigns, and so we reign in Christ, over sin and death (Romans 5:20,21). Reigning in life.

BLESSED REDEMPTION

There is not a person here who, if he is sick, is reigning in life. There is satanic power reigning there, but God wants you to know that you have to reign. God made you like Himself, and Jesus bought back for us in the Garden of Gethsemane everything that was lost in the Garden of Eden, and restored it to us in His agony. He bought that blessed redemption. When I think of "redemption," I wonder if there is anything greater than the Garden of Eden, when Adam and Eve had fellowship with God, and He came down and walked with them in the cool of the evening. Is there anything greater?

Yes, redemption is greater. How? Anything that is local is never so great. When God was in the Garden, Adam was local; but the moment a man is born again he is free, and lives in heavenly places. He has no destination except the glory. Redemption is greater than the Garden, and God wants you to know that He wants you to come into this glorious redemption, not only for the salvation of your soul, but also your body — to know that it is redeemed from the curse of the law, to know that you have been made free, to know that God's Son has set you free. Hallelujah! Free from the law of sin and death! How is it accomplished? The third and fourth verses tell us. Let us look at them. These are master verses:

> *For what the law could not do, in that it was weak through the flesh, God sending his own Son in the likeness of sinful flesh, and for sin, condemned sin in the flesh: that the righteousness of the law might be fulfilled in us, who walk not after the flesh, but after the Spirit.*

Righteousness fulfilled in us! Brother! Sister! I tell you there is a redemption. There is an atonement in Christ — a personality of Christ to dwell in you. There is a God-likeness for you to attain to — a blessed resemblance of Christ in you, if you will believe the Word of God. The Word is sufficient for you. Eat it; devour it. It is the living Word of God.

Jesus was manifested to destroy the works of the devil. God so manifested His fulness in Jesus that He walked this earth glorified and filled with God. In the first place, He was with God and was called "the Word." In the second place, He and God became so "One" in their operation that they said it was "God." Then the cooperation of oneness was so manifest that there was nothing done without the other. They cooperated in the working of power. Then you must see that before the foundation of the world this plan of redemption was all completed, and set in order before the fall. Notice that this redemption had to be so mighty, and to redeem us all so perfectly, that there should be no lack in the whole redemption. Let us see how it comes about. First, He became flesh; then He was filled with the Holy Ghost; then He became the voice and the operation of the Word by the power of God through the Holy Ghost. He became "the Authority."

Let me go further. You are born of an incorruptible power — the power of God's Word — by His personality and His nature. Ye are begotten of God and are not your own. You are now incarnated; and you can believe that you have passed from death unto life and become an heir of God, a joint-heir with Christ, in the measure that you believe His Word. The natural flesh has been changed for a new order; the first order was the natural Adamic order, the last order is Christ — the heavenly order. And now you become changed by a heavenly power existing in an earthly body; a power that can never die; it can never see corruption, and it cannot be lost. If you are born of God, you are born of the power of the Word and not of man. I want you to see that you are born of a power which exists in you, a power of which God took and made the world that you are in. It is the law of the Spirit of life in Christ Jesus that makes us free from the law of sin and death. Did you accept it?

I want you all to see that what I have been preaching for two weeks in this place is all biblical. Divine life, divine healing, satanic powers. If you will only believe it you are secure, for there is a greater power in you than in all the world. Power over sin; power over death.

There are two laws. Let us look at the law without the Spirit — the law of sin. Here is a man tonight who has never known regeneration, he is led captive by the devil at his will. There is no power that can convert men except the power of the blood of Jesus. Men try without it; science tries without it; all have tried without it; but all are left shaking on the brink of hell — without it. Nothing can deliver you but the blood of the

Lamb. "Free from the law of sin and death by the Spirit of life in Christ Jesus." Clean hearts, pure lives.

Brothers, the carnal life is not subject to the will of God, neither indeed can be. Carnality is selfishness — uncleanness. It cannot be subject to God; it will not believe; it interferes with you; it binds and keeps you in bondage. But, beloved, God destroys carnality. He destroys the work of the flesh. How? By a new life which is so much better, by a peace which passes all understanding, by a joy which is unspeakable and full of glory. It cannot be told. Everything that God does is too big to tell. His grace is too big. His love is too big. Why, it takes all heaven. His salvation is too big to be told. One cannot understand. It is so vast, mighty, and wonderful — so "in God." God gives us the power to understand it. Yes, of course, He does. Do you not know that ours is an abundant God? His love is far exceeding and abundant above all that we could ask or think (Ephesians 3:20). Hear! After ye were illuminated — Glory to God — ye were quickened by the Spirit, looking forward to a day of rapture, when you will be caught up and lifted into the presence of God. You cannot think of God on any small line. God's lines are magnitude — wonderful, glorious. God can manifest them in our hearts with a greater fulness than we are able to express. Let me touch an important point; Christ Jesus has borne the cross for us — there is no need for us to bear it. He has borne the curse, for "cursed is every one that hangeth on a tree" (Galatians 3:13). The curse covered everything. When Christ was in the grave, the Word says that He was raised from the grave by the operation of God through the Spirit. He was quickened by the Spirit in the grave, and so the same Spirit dwelling in you shall quicken your mortal bodies. Jesus rose by the quickening power of the Holy Ghost, "But if the Spirit of him that raised up Jesus from the dead dwell in you, he that raised up Christ from the dead shall also quicken your mortal bodies...(Romans 8:11)." What does it mean? Now, it is not an immortal body you have got. Immortality can only be obtained in resurrection order. He will quicken your mortal body.

If you will allow Jesus to have control of your bodies, you will find that His Spirit will quicken you, will loose you; He will show you that it is the mortal body that has to be quickened. Talk about divine healing! You can't get it out of the Scriptures for they are full of it. I see this. Everyone who is healed by the power of God — especially believers —

will find their healing an incentive to make them purer and holier. If divine healing was only to make you whole, it would be worth nothing. Divine healing is a divine act of the providence of God coming into your mortal bodies and touching them with almightiness. Could you remain the same? No. Like me, you will go out to worship and serve God. That is why I am here in Australia — because of the healing of God in this mortal body. I am not here to build new orders of things. I see the fact that God would have me preach so that everyone who hears me should go back to his own home with energy and power of God and the revelation of Christ. It is fact that the more you are held in bondage, the more you shut your eyes to the truth, the Bible becomes a blank instead of life and joy. The moment you yield yourself, the Bible becomes a new Book; it becomes revelation, so that we have the fulness of redemption going right through our bodies in every way. Filled with all the fulness of the Godhead bodily.

> Filled with God! Yes, filled with God,
> Pardoned and cleansed and filled with God.
> Filled with God! Yes, filled with God,
> Emptied of self and filled with God!

DEAD TO SELF

A young monk came one day to his father superior and asked: "Father, what is it to be dead to self?" The father replied: "I cannot explain it now; but I have a duty for you to perform. Brother Martin died last week and is buried in the churchyard of our order. Go to his grave, standing close beside it, repeat in a loud voice all the good things you ever heard of him. After this, say all the flattering things you can invent; and attribute to him every saintly grace and virtue, without regard to truth; and report the result to me."

The young monk went to do his bidding, wondering what all this could mean. Soon he returned and the father asked him what had transpired. "Why, nothing," replied the young man. "I did as you told me and that was all." Did Brother Martin make no replay?" asked the superior. "Of course he did not, for he was dead," said the monk. The elder shook his head thoughtfully, saying: "That is very strange. Go again tomorrow at the same hour, and repeat at the graveside all the evil you ever heard concerning Brother Martin. Add to that the worst slander and calumny your mind can imagine, and report the result to me."

Again the young man obeyed, and brought back the same report. He had heaped unlimited abuse on the head of Brother Martin and yet had received no reply. "From Brother Martin you may learn," said the father, "what it is to be dead to self. Neither flattery nor abuse has moved him, for he is dead. So the disciple who is dead to self will be insensible to these things, hearing neither voice of praise nor retaliation but all personal feeling will be lost in the service of Christ."

Address given in Melbourne, Australia
Published in *Pentecostal Testimony*

LOVE
1922

I want to turn this morning to the last verse of the thirteenth chapter of First Corinthians, and the first three verses of the fourteenth chapter. I want you to see that the primary thought in this passage is that when love is in perfect progress, other things will work in harmony, for prophetic utterances are of no value unless perfectly covered by divine love.

Jesus was so full of love to His Father and love to us that that love never failed to accomplish its purpose. It works in us and through us by the power of the Father's love in Him. This is what must come into our lives. Christ is to be the all-in-all of all things. All our doings, sayings, workings must be in Him and unto Him. Then our prophetic utterances will be well-pleasing to God. Pentecostal people sometimes make prophetic utterance a side issue. They think they are obliged to rise up and speak because the Spirit is upon them. That is not true — and again it is true. If they are in the right place — hidden away in Christ, saturated with His love — they will have such unction as to be balanced and always have spiritual utterance that pleases Him. It will all be to edification.

"Follow after charity [love], and desire spiritual gifts, but rather that ye may prophesy" (1 Corinthians 14:1). Moses said, I would "...that all the Lord's people were prophets, and that the Lord would put his spirit upon them!" (Numbers 11:29). And this is to me a revelation that God would have us in such a spiritual, holy place that He can take our words and so fill them with divine power that we speak in the Spirit right along in prophetic utterance. Beloved, there is human language on the human plane, and there is a divine incoming into the same language so that it is changed by spiritual power and made to live to those who hear. That divine touch of prophetic utterance will never come on any line except being filled with the Spirit. If you wish to be anything for God, do not miss the plan. You cannot afford to be on ordinary lines. You must realize that within you there is a power of the Spirit that is forming everything you require.

Perhaps you have not heard what our experience was in the early days of the Christian Mission in England which turned out to be the Salvation Army. I have never seen anything like it in my life. The power of God rested upon the worst characters and they were saved. It reached every class. Drunkards were saved right and left and the next day when they were put up for testimony their testimony thrilled the place so that the power of God fell upon others who in turn became witnesses to the salvation of Christ. There was no such thing as a building large enough to hold the work. The meetings were in open marketplaces, and they put big wagons there for platforms. The people who were saved the night before would speak and the power of God would fall.

I maintain that we are in a different order and a higher, yet we lack. We have too much preaching and too little testifying. You can never get a live Pentecostal church with a preacher every night preaching, preaching, preaching. The people become weary of preaching. But they never tire of the whole place being on fire. Therefore I can understand the exhortation "that ye may prophesy." You must awake out of your lethargy. There is no room for a man in the Pentecostal Movement who has settled on his lees. If you come to a Pentecostal meeting and sit through it unmoved, you are not in the Spirit, and dearth will fall on the church.

When the Holy Ghost comes in His fulness He comes into a man to move him so that he knows he has to speak now in a different way. "...when he, the Spirit of truth, is come, he will guide you into all truth..." (John 16:13). The Holy Ghost is inspiration, revelation, manifestation, operation. When a man comes into the fulness of the Holy Ghost he is in perfect order, built on a scriptural foundation. I have failed to find any man who understood the 12th, 13th and 14th chapters of First Corinthians unless he had been baptized in the Holy Ghost. When a man gets baptized with the Holy Ghost, he speaks from a deep inward conviction, by the power of the Spirit, a revelation of that Scripture.

God wants to make us on fire in the Spirit, speaking burning words. He wants to make all that a man has so prophetic in all its bearings that he will always speak as an oracle of God. There ought to be something within him that shines through him with a vital power that makes men know he has seen God, and they feel God has come into their midst.

One day in a railroad carriage I was drawing near to Cardiff and washed my hands and face because I knew the moment I jumped off the train I should have to rush to get to the meeting. I had just a little season of prayer while washing. Meanwhile the carriage had filled up with people who got on at Newport. When I returned there were two ministerial gentlemen with the accustomed white collars. These two parsons cried out under conviction of sin, and in ten minutes' time the whole place was bathed in prayer and conviction.

We should be filled with the Holy Ghost to such an extent it would always be so. To be filled with the Holy Ghost and fire is a higher order different from anything else. I often kneel before God thinking, "Now what is the burden of my heart?" The Lord knows more than I do about the burden, and the moment I kneel down I lose all my English. I am in the presence of God and He takes me right on to victory. Talk about this praying in the Holy Ghost, there is nothing like it! There is a secret about it. It is a secret between you and God. It is purely a Holy Ghost utterance. Let me tell you an incident of what it does. It does such marvelous things.

Brother Burton, who is associated with my son-in-law in Africa, has a wonderful work going on in the Congo. When they were going there to break up the new ground they lost one man on the way, and then Burton was laid low. He seemed dead, and they started on broken-heartedly. But looking around they saw him coming on just as lively as though he had never had a touch of fever. "What has happened?" they shouted. "Tell us!" He said, "From my head right down there came a warmth of life through my body, and here I am perfectly well."

Afterwards Burton visited England and when he was at a meeting a woman said to him, "Do you keep a diary?" "Yes," he answered. "I wish you would look at your diary," she continued, "and tell me what happened on a certain day," (giving the date). While he was looking it up she went on, "I saw you lying as one dead, and I was broken down before God in your behalf and was praying for you when the Spirit filled me and there I was speaking in an unknown tongue, and when I got through I saw you looking perfectly well." Burton found in his diary that it was the very hour of his recovery. What we need is more of the Holy Ghost. Oh, let it be no longer we but the Spirit who prays!

Two African boys were brought to us from the Congo, and my daughter said to me, "Father, will you take the boys around?" Well, it was a job because they could not speak a word of English. When I was walking with these boys I kept saying, "Praise the Lord, Amen." After a while they caught on to it. So when I said, "Praise the Lord," they would say, "Amen." We boarded a car which was full of people and the boys were at one end and I at the other. They would shout, "Praise the Lord!" and I would respond, "Amen," and we kept it up through the town. The boys were having a great time. When they sought the baptism of the Holy Ghost we had a glorious time. By the way, these "boys" were thirty years old. The Holy Ghost fell on them and gave them a new language, so different from their own. It was wonderful. They were full of the Spirit and joyful beyond words. They said, "When we were saved it was good, very good; but now it is more good, more so!" O beloved! I know God wants us all to have this "more so" salvation. It is not a measure but a pressed down measure; and not only a pressed down measure but a measure shaken together and running over. The baptism of the Spirit is an overflowing cup. Praise the Lord!

People who are baptized in the Holy Ghost can have a wonderful time in song. I have seen it, especially in England. If we only understood it better we should have greater chorals than ever were sung, far better than man ever made. I have heard singing in the Spirit with such rarity of music as I have never heard elsewhere, music from the deepest bass to octaves higher than you ever hear in the natural. All is in perfect harmony and it makes you think of a big organ, only more massive, more beautiful. Everyone gets to weeping and rejoicing and is solemnized by the presence of God, so that there is nothing in the flesh. The people are melted down at such times. I pray God we may all come to understand this in its fulness.

Message given at Glad Tidings Tabernacle and Bible Training School
San Francisco, California

ORDINATION
1922

Ye have not chosen me, but I have chosen you, and ordained you, that ye should go and bring forth fruit, and that your fruit should remain: that whatsoever ye shall ask the Father in my name, he may give it you.
John 15:16

YOUR POSITION

God wants, by the power of the Spirit, to reveal unto us our position in Christ. We see Jesus foreshadowing blessings that were to come. Most of His ministry was a type of what the believer was to enter into. Let us see what God had in His mind to do through His Son for us. Oh, to realize the fact of "ordination"! What will bring it; shall we stand before God? He wants us to be right up to date in everything, and the Spirit of the Lord shall be able to bring before our minds, this morning, what is the mind of the Spirit concerning us, so that we may step into all the privileges. God wants a strong people. Remember the charge God gave Joshua. He said: "Be full of courage; be neither dismayed nor discouraged" — and then He gave him the charge. If God forecasts anything for you, He will give the power to carry it through. So, after He had given Joshua the word, He said: "Now it will depend upon your living, day and night meditating upon the Word of God." As you come into this blessed state of holy reverence for the Word of God, it will build you up also, and make you strong.

"Then thou shalt have good success." And He told Joshua that, in this state of grace, whenever he put his foot down, not to let it slide back but to put the other foot ready for going forward. The devil brings back to people's minds those things which they did so long ago, and there they are, thinking about them day and night! There are two things certain, and a third thing which is more valuable than either of the two. One is that you never forget them; and the third is that God *has forgotten them*. The question is whether we are going to believe God, or the devil, or ourselves. God says they are passed, cleansed, *gone*! You cannot go on with God till you stand on His Word as "cleansed," with the heart made pure. Standing on this blessed Rock, you can step forward and make inroads into the devil's camp, and overthrow all his tactics, and bring desolation to his power as you realize that *your sin is done and finished with*.

God has ordained us. Then people allow Satan to say to them: "Yes, that was the disciples' order." I tell you, this morning, beloved, that God's order is for the church. What He said to the disciples, He says to us. If you can believe, God has ordained by the Holy Ghost to fill us and clothe us till we know we are the chosen of God, precious in His sight to bear the vessels of the Lord, to be, not only co-workers with Him, but to stand in our lot in the way, dividing the powers of Satan. This salvation is too big and great for any mind to take in. It is only the flash of eternity, the divine light of heaven, the Spirit of the living God with that infinite mind, that can flash into the caverns of the human soul, till we see the whole heaven, and are changed by His power till there is not a weak point, not an unbelieving attitude; because the Word has so changed us that we are a perfect pattern of the new covenant of Christ.

The ordination was finished, but there was a lack of power. The credentials were all right, but the power was not there. **"I have ordained you; I have chosen you that you should go and bring forth fruit, and that your fruit should remain, that whatsoever ye shall ask the Father in My name, He may give it you."** I believe God wants us to know that our fruit has to remain. Beloved, we should recognize that our prayers are in vain unless we really expect what we ask to be granted to us.

"The Word profited nothing, not being mixed with faith in them that heard it"; but, tonight, may God give us the word of faith, and you shall know for a fact that there is a great change in you. Even the preacher himself will be changed as he reads and preaches the Word. The Word quickens the preacher, the hearer, and everybody. The Word giveth life, and God wants it to be so live in you that you will be moved as it is preached. Oh, it is lovely to think that God can change in a moment, and can heal in a moment. When God begins, who can hinder? Sometimes a thing comes before me, and I realize that nothing but the Word of God can do it. I meet all classes of people — people who have no faith — and I find the Word of God quickens them, even those who have no knowledge of salvation. You often notice hoardings with advertisements which would make it appear as if the thing advertised would cure everything. Oh, the Gospel of the Lord Jesus Christ does cure everything. One day in Toronto, at the close of the service, I saw one of the leaders rush out as though something had happened, and when I got home, I found he had brought a man to me who was in a very strange way. He was a man of fine physique, and looked quite all right. But his nerves were shattered throughout, and he asked me if I could do anything for a man who had not slept properly for three years. He said: "I have a business, a beautiful ranch and home — it is all going. My whole nervous system is just in an awful state, and without something happening, I shall lose everything." He stood in front of me, and asked for help. I said: "Go home and sleep." He remonstrated, but I insisted that, without further remonstration, he must obey my command and *go*. He went home, got into bed, fell asleep, and slept all night. In fact, he told me afterwards that his wife had to wake him.

He came along to see me again, and said: "I have slept all night; I am a new man. The whole situation is changed now. I want to ask you another question. Can you get my money back? My business back? Can you get my house put in order again?" I said, "Yes — everything. You shan't lose a thing. You be at the meeting tonight." I knew this man was a perfect stranger to salvation and knew nothing about it. He was in the audience and I preached — not to him, for God has a better plan than for me to preach to any one person in a meeting. If God speaks, the whole thing will be done. He finishes the work, and I have come here tonight only to speak for God. I am not seeking what to say to you, am not trying to think of stories to tell you. God is the operator of my mind, and I am telling you all that He tells me to tell you. I am chargeable to Him for you and must be faithful to you.

I preached the Gospel, which is the power of God unto salvation and as I preached, this man became very uneasy and as I preached on, he became more and more restless; seemed as though he could not bear to sit in his seat, and as I gave the altar call, he came rushing forward for salvation and for healing, and as he started to come he fell in the way, the shot had gone so deeply into him that he could not get away.

Oh, it is lovely. "Men and brethren," they said, "What shall we do?" It must be something more mighty than moving your brain. Except it moves your hearts it is no good. He must bring into your hearts a real longing for Himself, you cannot be saved by feelings, or on the lines of excitement. You can only be saved by the Word of the Lord. And this man fell there by the way, and I said: "Nobody touch him! No one speak to him. Keep your hands off the man. God has him in hand." Oh, God made a fine job of him, and if you go to Toronto today, you will find that man worshipping the Lord, and a wonderful citizen, out of the clutches of Satan, everything squared up. Oh, when God begins to move, everything is soon in order.

SEEK AND FIND

But seek ye first the kingdom of God, and his righteousness; and all these things shall be added unto you.

Matthew 6:33

"And, behold, there came a man named Jairus..." (Luke 8:41). I would like you to notice this man and his wife tonight. They have a daughter whose needs nothing can meet. They have heard quite a lot about Jesus, and I fancy I hear the woman say to her husband: "There's only one thing left; if you could see Jesus, our daughter would live." My brother, my sister, tonight I tell you: "If you see Jesus, you will live. You will; and you can see Him here tonight. God can so reveal Him to your hearts that while you are in this place you will be able to see Jesus. He is in the midst; the power of God is over us. No man can say after this meeting, 'No man shewed me the way.' The Holy Ghost will shew you the way of salvation, and oh, it is a wonderful way."

Think about Him. Did you ever think about Him? Talk about love! There is no love like His! His love has never changed. He loved us while we were yet sinners, and then He died for us. Nobody is saved when they are good, they are always saved when they are bad. God has a way of revealing our hearts to us, and when we see ourselves as sinners He applies the balm. Is it possible for anybody to seek Jesus and not find Him? Is it? Jairus went to seek Jesus. It is not possible for you to seek Jesus in this meeting without finding Him. They that seek Him find Him just the same as this man did. Glory to God! There is nothing in the world so lovely as the knowledge that God reaches out, and those who seek Him find Him and He finds them. Remember there are always two seekers. The moment you begin, you will find God begins. When the prodigal began to turn home, the Father turned towards him. Praise the Lord!

And he found Him in the way, and he said unto Him: "...My little daughter lieth at the point of death...come and lay thy hands on her...and she shall live" (Mark 5:23), and Jesus said: "I will come."

Oh, I do wish I was like Jesus. When I think that we left behind us at Melbourne over 100 who were invalid and helpless and could not come to the meetings, and we had no time to go to them. Oh, how my heart aches for those circumstanced like them! Jesus said, "I will come." Eh, it is lovely! Brother, you never need be afraid that He will not find you if you seek Him. I tell you, my dear ones, it is impossible for God to fail you. If you hear the Word of God tonight, it will so stimulate you that you will know as sure as you live tonight that God will bring you out of this condition. It is impossible to know the Word of God without knowing that He will meet you.

And just as they were travelling along the road toward the house of Jairus, and there was a great pack of people all around Jesus, then we read about this woman (Luke 8:43). Hers is rather an interesting case. There is a little bit of arithmetic here I would like you to notice. The woman had an issue of blood for twelve years, and when she began to be sick she had money. The physicians took all her money, and left her worse than they found her! Now, I believe that doctors ought to be paid when they cure their patients — and not before. You may all go on the same game and finish up just where this woman did, and so there ought to be a fresh arrangement. I am not against the doctors. They have a work that no one else in the world has to do. Apart from salvation they have a great suffering world of trials and sickness and sorrow to help. The world is full of trouble, and they are in the midst of it, for "In the world is tribulation;" but Jesus says: "In Me there shall be peace," and there is no peace where there is disease, so if you get His peace, you will be free from disease! "In the world — tribulation; but in *Me*, peace!"

I can just imagine some of those people had been saying to this woman: "Oh, if you had only been with us today! We have seen such wonderful things; we are sure you would have been healed. I thought about you." And as they told this woman all about what Jesus had done that day, she said: "Oh, if I was only able to touch His garment, I believe I should be whole also." Is it possible? This woman was worse than she had been twelve years before. Beloved, I tell you it is impossible for a single soul in this meeting to have an inward desire of seeing and meeting with Jesus, but what they will both see and feel and *know* Him.

God's Word is true. "They that seek Me shall find Me." And this woman was so moved upon by these stories, that day by day she longed to see Jesus, and glory to God, the day came. There was a great cry: all the people were thronging and surrounding Him on all sides and rushing out of the houses and saying, "Oh, there He is!" She pushed her way in and *touched Him*, and the touch did it. God wants reality in your hearts tonight, bringing you into the same determination to touch *Jesus!*

Jesus knew that if He left the congregation in that position and ascended on high, no one in Adelaide would have been satisfied that they could be healed unless they could "touch Him," so He changed the order of it, and turned round and said: "Who touched Me?" And Peter said: "That's a nice thing to say, why, all the people are leaning upon you; everybody's leaning on you." "Yes," he says, "But somebody touched Me."

Oh, there's a difference! You may lean about all your lives; but one atom of faith will do it. Come out of yourselves tonight. No longer have an imaginary faith — get a reality, *believe*, and God will do it! So Peter said: "What do You mean, Lord?" And He says, "Someone has touched Me!" And then the woman turned round and said: "Yes, it was I; but I am so different now, the moment I touched You, I was made whole!!" Ah! He answered her, "Go in peace, thy faith hath made thee whole." Notice, not "thy touch," "thy faith," and brother, tonight it is faith.

DIVINE POSSIBILITY

Oh, blessed be God, "a living faith." You say, "Oh, tell me how to get it." Brother, you can have it for 6d. What? "The Bible; the *Word of God*."

It is faith. It is the living principle of faith. His Word was the authority of faith. "If thou canst believe." Believe what? Believe what the Word says. They came and asked Him, saying: "Tell us how we may work the works of God." He said: "This is the work of God, that ye *believe* Him whom God hath sent." This is the work of God. Oh, beloved, I should be a poor man without the Word of God; but I am rich:

> "My heavenly Bank, my Heavenly Bank,
> The House of God's treasure and store;
> I have plenty up there — I'm a real millionaire,
> And I will go poor no more."

Oh, the Word of God — the living Word — the precious, precious, Word of God. Jesus said, "Search the scriptures, for in them ye think ye have eternal life: and they are they which testify of me" (John 5:39). Hallelujah! And just when everyone was getting to see that Jesus was everything, into the midst of the throng the devil came. Yes, he always comes at a busy time. Four or five people rushed from the house of Jairus right into the presence of Jesus, and took hold of Jairus and said, "Look here! Don't trouble Jesus anymore; your daughter is dead. He can do nothing for a dead daughter," but Jesus said, "Only believe!" And God, help us tonight to believe. Only to believe! Oh, what blessing it is if we believe. Allow God to divest you of everything tonight, beloved. Allow the Word to sink into your heart. Allow it to drive away everything else. There is eternal life here tonight for you who will believe.

Your faces are an inspiration, as I look at you and see your eternal destiny and I see that God, the Holy Ghost, can make every person in the meeting without exception "heirs and joint-heirs" with Him tonight. You can be saved by the power of the faith that I am speaking to you about. Only believe. You cannot save yourself. The more you try in your own strength, the more you get fixed up; but oh, if you will believe God will save you, He will do it. You shall know tonight that God saves. Oh, bless the Lord, oh, my soul, and all that is within me bless His holy name!

Sometimes we are tested on the lines of faith. For twenty-five years Abraham believed God. He said to him, "Thy wife shall have a son." Every year his wife grew weaker. He saw the wrinkles and her puny weak condition. Did he look at it? No — he looked at the promise. For twenty-five years God tested him; but he gave glory to God, and considered neither Sarah's body nor his own and as he did so, God said: "Yes, Abraham." Hearken what the Word says: "Now it was not written for his sake alone...but for us also...[who] believe on him that raised up Jesus our Lord from the dead; who was delivered for our offences, and was raised again for our justification" (Romans 4:23-25).

All who believe are blessed with faithful Abraham and God wants to show us tonight that nothing is impossible to those who believe. I would like God to reveal Himself to us tonight. People say to me, "How long will it be before I am healed?" And I ask: "How long will it be before you believe God?" I would like you to see those ten lepers. Look at them for a moment. You never saw such a regiment in your life. Some were blind; some lame and maimed; and there they were, all wanting to get to Jesus! They saw Him and shouted at Him, for they were not allowed to go near, and they shouted and said, "Jesus, Thou Son of David, have mercy upon us." And He shouted and answered them thus: "Go, shew thyself to the priest." Was it an impossibility? Yes, humanly speaking; but the lame were helped by those who were not lame, and the blind by those who could see, and the whole regiment went their way, and *as they went* they were healed. As they believed, they were healed. Hallelujah! And one said: "I'm not going any farther; I'm not going to see the priest; I'm going back to see the man who did it," and he turned back, and said: "I'm one of the ten." "Well," said Jesus, "Where are the other nine? Are you the only one coming to give God glory?" That is the way with people today. They get saved and healed and they don't tell it out for the glory of God. How is it that people don't tell what God has done for them?

> The Lord told His disciples to proclaim everywhere,
> The Gospel of redemption to hearts o'erwhelmed with care.
> "But tarry at Jerusalem till pow'r from heaven descend,
> And lo, will I be with you, even till the world doth end.

These signs shall follow them that believe upon My name — Go, preach ye the Gospel, then will I confirm the same.

Address given in Adelaide

THE BIBLE EVIDENCE OF THE BAPTISM OF THE SPIRIT

May 27, 1922

There is much controversy today as regards the genuineness of this Pentecostal work, but there is nothing so convincing as the fact that over fifteen years ago a revival on Holy Ghost lines began and has never ceased. You will find that in every clime throughout the world God has poured out His Spirit in a remarkable way in a line parallel with the glorious revival that inaugurated the church of the first century. People, who could not understand what God was doing when He kept them concentrated in prayer, wondered as these days were being brought about by the Holy Ghost, and found themselves in exactly the same place and entering into an identical experience as the apostles on the day of Pentecost.

Our Lord Jesus said to His disciples,

> *...behold, I send the promise of my Father upon you: but tarry ye in the city of Jerusalem, until ye be endued with power from on high.*
> *Luke 24:49*

God promised through the prophet Joel, "...I will pour out my spirit upon all flesh...upon the servants and upon the handmaids in those days will I pour out my spirit" (Joel 2:28,29). As there is a widespread misconception concerning this receiving of the Holy Spirit, I believe the Lord would have us examine the scriptures on this subject.

You know, beloved, it had to be something on the line of solid facts to move me. I was as certain as possible that I had received the Holy Ghost, and was absolutely rigid in this conviction. When this Pentecostal outpouring began in England I went to Sunderland and met with the people who had assembled for the purpose of receiving the Holy Ghost. I was continuously in those meetings causing disturbances until the people wished I had never come. They said that I was disturbing the whole conditions. But I was hungry and thirsty for God, and had gone to Sunderland because I heard that God was pouring out His Spirit in a new way. I heard that God had now visited His people, had manifested His power and that people were speaking in tongues as on the day of Pentecost.

When I got to this place I said, "I cannot understand this meeting. I have left a meeting in Bradford all on fire for God. The fire fell last night and we were all laid out under the power of God. I have come here for tongues, and I don't hear them — I don't hear anything."

"Oh!" they said, "when you get baptized with the Holy Ghost you will speak in tongues." "Oh, is that it?" said I, "When the presence of God came upon me, my tongue was loosened, and really I felt as I went in the open air to preach that I had a new tongue." "Ah no," they said, "that is not it." "What is it, then?" I asked. They said, "When you get baptized in the Holy Ghost — ." "I am baptized," I interjected, "and there is no one here who can persuade me that I am not baptized." So I was up against them and they were up against me.

I remember a man getting up and saying, "You know, brothers and sisters, I was here three weeks and then the Lord baptized me with the Holy Ghost and I began to speak with other tongues." I said, "Let us hear it. That's what I'm here for." But he would not talk in tongues. I was doing what others are doing today, confusing the twelfth chapter of 1 Corinthians with the second chapter of Acts. These two chapters deal with different things: one with the gifts of the Spirit, and the other with the baptism of the Spirit with the accompanying sign. I did not understand this and so I said to the man, "Let's hear you speak in tongues." But he could not. He had not received the "gift" of tongues, but the baptism.

As the days passed I became more and more hungry. I had opposed the meetings so much, but the Lord was gracious, and I shall ever remember that last day — the day I was to leave. God was with me so much that last night. They were to have a meeting and I went, but I could not rest. I went to the Vicarage, and there in the library I said to Mrs. Boddy, "I cannot rest any longer, I must have these tongues." She replied, "Brother Wigglesworth, it is not the tongues you need but the baptism. If you will allow God to baptize you, the other will be all right." "My dear sister, I know I am baptized," I said. "You know that I have to leave here at 4 o'clock, please lay hands on me that I may receive the tongues."

She rose up and laid her hands on me and the fire fell. I said, "The fire's falling." Then came a persistent knock at the door, and she had to go out. That was the best thing that could have happened, for I was *alone with God*. Then He gave me a revelation. Oh, it was wonderful! He showed me an empty cross and Jesus glorified. I do thank God that the cross is empty, that Christ is no more on the cross. It was there that He bore the curse, for it is written, "...Cursed is every one that hangeth on a tree" (Galatians 3:13). He became sin for us that we might be made the righteousness of God in Him, and now, there He is in the glory. Then I saw that God had purified me. It seemed that God gave me a new vision, and I saw a perfect being within me with mouth open saying, "Clean, Clean! Clean!" When I began to repeat it I found myself speaking in other tongues. The joy was so great that when I came to utter it, my tongue failed, and I began to worship God in other tongues as the Spirit gave me utterance.

It was all as beautiful and peaceful as when Jesus said, "Peace, be still!" and the tranquility of that moment and the joy surpassed anything I had ever known up to that moment. But, Hallelujah! These days have grown with greater, mightier, more wonderful divine manifestations and power. That was but the beginning. There is no end to this kind of beginning. You will never get an end to the Holy Ghost till you are landed in the glory — till you are right in the presence of God for ever. And even then we shall ever be conscious of His presence.

What had I received? I had received the Bible evidence. This Bible evidence is wonderful to me. I knew I had received the very evidence of the Spirit's incoming that the apostles received on the day of Pentecost. I knew that everything I had had up to that time was in the nature of an anointing bringing me in line with God in preparation, but now I knew I had the Biblical baptism in the Spirit. It had the backing of the Scriptures. You are always right if you have the backing of the Scriptures, and you are never right if you have not a foundation for your testimony in the Word of God.

For many years I have thrown out a challenge to any person who can prove to me that he has the baptism without speaking in tongues as the Spirit gives utterance — to prove it by the Word that he has been baptized in the Holy Ghost without the Bible evidence, but so far no one has accepted the challenge. I only say this because so many were like I was, they have a rigid idea that they have received the baptism without the Bible evidence. The Lord Jesus wants those who preach the Word to have the Word in evidence. Don't be misled by anything else. Have a Bible proof for all you have, and then you will be in a place where no man can move you.

I was so full of joy that I wired home to say that I had received the Holy Ghost. As soon as I got home, my boy came running up to me and said, "Father, have you received the Holy Ghost?" I said, "Yes, my boy." He said, "Let's hear you speak in tongues." But I could not. Why? I had received the baptism in the Spirit with the speaking in tongues as the Bible evidence according to Acts 2:4, and had not received the gift of tongues according to 1 Corinthians 12. I had received the Giver of all gifts. At some time later when I was helping some souls to seek and receive the baptism of the Spirit, God gave me the gift of tongues so that I could speak at any time. I could speak, but will not — no never! I must allow the Holy Ghost to use the gift. It should be so, so that we shall only have divine utterances by the Spirit. I would be very sorry to use a gift, but the Giver has all power to use the whole nine gifts.

I want to take you to the Scriptures to prove my position. There are businessmen here, and they know that in cases of law, where there are two clear witnesses they could win a case before any judge in Australia. On the clear evidence of two witnesses any judge will give a verdict. What has God given us? Three clear witnesses on the baptism in the Holy Spirit — more than are necessary in law courts.

The first is in Acts 2:4,

> *...they were all filled with the Holy Ghost, and began to speak with other tongues, as the Spirit gave them utterance.*

Here we have the original pattern. And God gave to Peter an eternal word that couples this experience with the promise that went before. "This is that." And God wants you to have that — nothing less than that. He wants you to receive the baptism in the Holy Spirit according to this original Pentecostal pattern.

In Acts 10 we have another witness. Peter is in the house of Cornelius. Cornelius had had a vision of an holy angel and had sent for Peter. A person said to me one day, "You don't admit that I am filled and baptized with the Holy Ghost. Why, I was ten days and ten nights on my back before the Lord and He was flooding my soul with joy." I said, "Praise the Lord, sister, that was only the beginning. The disciples were tarrying that time, and they were still, and the mighty power of God fell upon them then and the Bible tells what happened when the power fell." And that is just what happened in the house of Cornelius. The Holy Ghost fell on all them which heard the Word. "And they of the circumcision which believed were astonished, as many as came with Peter, because that on the Gentiles also was poured out the gift of the Holy Ghost" (Acts 10:45). What convinced these prejudiced Jews that the Holy Ghost had come? "For they heard them speak with tongues, and magnify God..." (Acts 10:46). There was no other way for them to know. This evidence could not be contradicted. It is the Bible evidence.

If some people in this district had an angel come and talk to them as Cornelius had, they would say that they knew they were baptized. Do not be fooled by anything. Be sure that what you receive is according to the Word of God.

We have heard two witnesses, and that is sufficient to satisfy the world. But God goes one better. Let us look at Acts 19:6,

> *And when Paul had laid his hands upon them, the Holy Ghost came on them; and they spake with tongues, and prophesied.*

These Ephesians received the identical Bible evidence as the apostles at the beginning and they prophesied in addition. Three times the Scriptures show us this evidence of the baptism in the Spirit. I do not magnify tongues. No, by God's grace, I magnify the Giver of tongues. And I magnify above all Him whom the Holy Ghost has come to reveal to us, the Lord Jesus Christ. He it is who sends the Holy Spirit, and I magnify Him because He makes no difference between us and those at the beginning.

But what are the tongues for? Look at the second verse of 1 Corinthians 14 and you will see a very blessed truth. Oh, Hallelujah! Have you been there, beloved? I tell you, God wants to take you there. "...he that speaketh in an unknown tongue speaketh not unto men, but unto God: for no man understandeth him; howbeit in the spirit he speaketh mysteries." It goes on to say, "He that speaketh in an unknown tongue edifieth himself..." (v. 4).

Enter into the promises of God. It is your inheritance. You will do more in one year if you are really filled with the Holy Ghost than you could do in fifty years apart from him. I pray that you may be so filled with Him that it will not be possible for you to move without a revival of some kind resulting.

Published in *The Pentecostal Evangel*

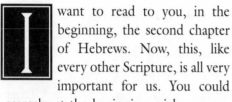

FILLED WITH GOD
Hebrews 2
August 1922

I want to read to you, in the beginning, the second chapter of Hebrews. Now, this, like every other Scripture, is all very important for us. You could scarcely, at the beginning, pick any special Scripture out of this we have read, it is all so full of truth, it means so much to us, and we must understand that God, in these times, wants to bring us into perfect life, that we need never, under any circumstances, go outside of His Word for anything.

Some people only come with a very small thought concerning God's fulness, and a lot of people are satisfied with a thimbleful, and you can just imagine God saying, "Oh, if they only knew how much they could take away!" Other people come with a larger vessel, and they go away satisfied, but you can feel how much God is longing for us to have such a desire for more, such a longing as only God Himself can satisfy. I suppose you women would have a good idea of what I mean from the illustration of a screaming child being taken about from one to another, but never satisfied till it gets to the bosom of its mother. You will find that there is no peace, no help, no source of strength, no power, no life, nothing can satisfy the cry of the child of God but the Word of God. God has a special way of satisfying the cry of His children. He is waiting to open to us the windows of heaven until He has so moved in the depths of our hearts that everything unlike Himself has been destroyed. There need no one in this place go away dry, dry. God wants you to be filled. My brother, my sister, God wants you today to be like a watered garden, filled with the fragrance of His own heavenly joy, till you know at last you have touched immensity. The Son of God came for no other purpose than to lift and lift, and mold and fashion and remold, until we are just after His mind.

I know that the dry ground can have floods, and may God save me from ever wanting anything less than a flood. I will not stoop for small things when I have such a big God. Through the blood of Christ's atonement we may have riches and riches. We need the warming atmosphere of the Spirit's power to bring us closer and closer until nothing but God can satisfy, and then we may have some idea of what God has left after we have taken all that we can. It is only like a sparrow taking a drink of the ocean and then looking around and saying, "What a vast ocean! What a lot more I could have taken if I had only had room."

You may have sometimes things you can use, and not know it. Don't you know that you could be dying of thirst right in a river of plenty? There was once a vessel in the mouth of the Amazon River. They thought they were still in the ocean, and they were dying of thirst, some of them nearly mad. They saw a ship and asked if they would give them some water, for some of them were dying of thirst, and they replied, "Dip your bucket right over; you are in the mouth of the river." There are any amount of people today in the midst of a great river of life, but they are dying of thirst, because they do not dip down and take it. Dear brother, you may have the Word, but you need an awakened spirit. The Word is not alive until it is moved upon by the Spirit of God, and in the right sense it becomes Spirit and life when it is touched by His hand alone.

Oh, beloved, there is a stream that maketh glad the city of God. There is a stream of life that makes everything move. There is a touch of divine life and likeness through the Word of God that comes nowhere else. There is a death which has no life in it; and there is a death-likeness with Christ which is full of life.

Oh, beloved, there is no such thing as an end to God's beginnings. But we must be in it; we must know it. It is not a touch; it is not a breath; it is the Almighty God; it is a Person; it is the Holy One dwelling in the temple not made with hands. Oh, beloved, He touches and it is done. He is the same God over all, rich unto all who call upon Him. Pentecost is the last thing that God has to touch the earth with. The baptism is the last thing; if you do not get this you are living in a weak and impoverished condition which is no good to yourself or anybody else. May God move us on to a place where there is no measure to this fulness that He wants to give us. God exalted Jesus and gave Him a name above every name. You notice that everything has been put under Him.

It is about eight years since I was in Oakland and in that time I have seen thousands and thousands healed by the power of God. Last year in Sweden, the last five months of the year, we had over 7,000 people saved by the power of God. The tide is rolling in; let us see to it today that we get right out into the tide, for it will bear you. The bosom of God's love is the center of all things. Get your eyes off yourself; lift them up high and see the Lord, for in the Lord there is everlasting strength.

If you went to see a doctor, the more you told him the more he would know, but when you come to Doctor Jesus, He knows all from the beginning, and He never gives you the wrong medicine. I went to see one today, and someone said, "Here is a person who has been poisoned through and through by a doctor giving him the wrong medicine." Jesus sends His healing power and brings His restoring grace, and so there is nothing to fear. The only thing that is wrong is your wrong conception of the mightiness of His redemption.

He was wounded that He might be touched with a feeling of your infirmities. He took your flesh and laid it upon the cross that He might destroy "...him that had the power of death, that is, the devil; And deliver them who through fear of death were all their lifetime subject to bondage" (Hebrews 2:14,15). You will find that almost all the ailments that you are heir to come on satanic lines, and they must be dealt with as satanic; they must be cast out. Do not listen to what Satan says to you, for the devil is a liar from the beginning. If people would only listen to the truth of God they would find out they were over the devil, over all satanic forces; they would realize that every evil spirit was subject to them; they would find out that they were always in the place of triumph, and they would "reign in life" by King Jesus.

Never live in a less place than where God has called you to, and He has called you up on high to live with Him. God has designed that everything shall be subject to man. Through Christ He has given you power over all the power of the enemy. He has wrought out your eternal redemption.

I was finishing a meeting one day in Switzerland. And when we had finished the meeting and had ministered to all the sick, we went out to see some people. Two boys came to us and said that there was a blind man present at the meeting this afternoon, who had heard all the words of the preacher, and said he was surprised that he had not been prayed for. They went on to say this blind man had heard so much that he would not leave that place until he could see. I said, "This is positively unique. God will do something today for that man."

We got to the place. This blind man said he never had seen; he was born blind, but because of the Word preached in the afternoon he was not going home until he could see. If ever I have joy it is when I have a lot of people who will not be satisfied until they get all they have come for. With great joy I anointed him that day and laid hands on his eyes, and then immediately God opened his eyes. It was very strange how he acted. There were some electric lights. First he counted them; then he counted us. Oh, the ecstatic pleasure that every moment was created in that man because of his sight! It made us all feel like weeping and dancing and shouting. Then he pulled out his watch, and said that for years he had been feeling the watch for the time, by the raised figures, but now he could look at it and tell us the time. Then, looking as if he was awakened from some deep sleep, or some long, strange dream, he awakened to the fact that he had never seen the face of his father and mother, and he went to the door and rushed out. At night he was the first in the meeting. All the people knew him as the blind man, and I had to give him a long time to talk about his new sight.

Beloved, I wonder how much you want to take away today. You could not carry it if it was substance, but there is something about the grace and the power and the blessings of God that can be carried, no matter how big they are. Oh, what a Savior; what a place we are in, by grace, that He may come in to commune with us. He is willing to say to every heart, "Peace, be still," and to every weak body, "Be strong."

Are you going halfway; or are you going right to the end? Be not today deceived by Satan, but believe God.

Published in *Triumphs of Faith*

HE IS RISEN

August 1922

cripture Reading: Acts 4:1-32. Brothers and sisters, God anointed Jesus, who went about doing good, for God was with Him; and today we know for a fact He is the risen Christ. There is something about this risen, royal, glorified Christ that God means to confirm in our hearts today. The power of the risen Christ makes our hearts move and burn, and we know that there is within us that eternal working by the power of the Spirit. Oh, beloved, it is eternal life to know Jesus! Surely the kingdom of darkness is shaken when we come into touch with that loftiness, that holiness, that divine integrity of our Master who was so filled with power, and the grace of God was upon Him. This blessed divine inheritance is for us. Surely God wants every one of us to catch fire. We must grasp new realities, we must cease from our murmurings; we must get into the place of triumph and exaltation.

We have before us this Scripture, "And when they had prayed, the place was shaken where they were assembled together..." (Acts 4:31). You talk about a church that cannot shout — it will never be shaken. You can write over it, "Ichabod, the glory has departed." It is only when men have learned the secret of the power of praying, and of magnifying God that God comes forth. I have heard people say, "Oh, I praise the Lord inwardly," and nothing comes forth outwardly.

There was a man who had a large business in London. He was a great churchgoer. The church was wonderfully decorated and cushioned and everything was comfortable enough to make him sleep. His business increased and he was full of prosperity, but seemed always in a nightmare, and could not tell what was after him. One day he left his office to walk round the building. When he got to the door, he saw the boy who minded the door jumping and whistling. "I wish I felt like that," he said to himself. He returned to his business, but his head was in a whirl. "Oh," he said, "I will go and look at the boy again." Again he went and looked at the boy who was whistling and jumping. "I want to see you in the office," he said to the boy.

"How is it," he asked the boy, when he got into the office, "that you can always whistle and be happy?" "I cannot help it, master," replied the boy. "Where did you get it?" "I got it at the Pentecostal Mission." "Where is it?" And the boy told him about it. This man came to the Pentecostal church and heard about the power of God. He was broken up and God did a wonderful thing for that man, changing him altogether, and one day he was in his office in the midst of his business and he found himself whistling and jumping. He had changed his position.

Beloved, it cannot come out unless it is within. It is God who transforms the heart and life, and there must be an inward working of the power of God, or it cannot come forth outwardly. We must understand this that the power of Pentecost, as it came in the first order, was to loose men. People are tired of smoke and deadness, tired of imitations. We want realities, men who have God within them, men who are always filled with God. This is a more needy day than any, and men should be filled with the Holy Ghost.

We must be like our Master. We must have definiteness about all we say. We must have an inward confidence and knowledge that we are God's property, bought and paid for by the precious blood of Jesus, and now the inheritance is in us. People may know that Jesus died and that He rose again, and yet they may not have salvation. Beloved, you must have the witness. You may know today that you are born again for he that believeth hath the witness of the Spirit in him. It is true today that Jesus was raised up by the power of the Holy Ghost. It is true today that we in this place are risen by the power of the Spirit. It is true that we are preaching to you divine power that can raise you up, and God can set you free from all your weakness. God wants you to know how to take the victory and shout in the face of the devil and say, "Lord, it is done." I will read Acts 4:24,31.

> *And when they heard that, they lifted up their voice to God with one accord, and said, Lord, thou art God...And when they had prayed, the place was shaken where they were assembled together; and they were all filled with the Holy Ghost, and they spake the word of God with boldness.*

That is a wonderful time. That is a real revival. A proper convention. God means for us to have life. The people perceived something remarkable in the power of God changing these fishermen on the day of Pentecost.

Brothers and sisters, it is the Holy Ghost. We must not say this is an influence; He is the Personality and power, and presence of the third Person of the Trinity. Many of us have been longing for years for God to come forth and now He is coming forth. The tide is rising everywhere. God is pouring out His Spirit in the hearts of all flesh and they are crying before God. The day is at hand. God is fulfilling His promises.

Oh, it is lovely, the incarnation of a regeneration, a state of changing from nature to grace, from the power of Satan to God. Ye which are natural, made supernatural by the divine touch of Him who came to raise you from the dead. The Holy Spirit comes to abide. He comes to reveal the fulness of God. Verily, the Holy Ghost is shedding abroad in our hearts the love of God, and He takes of the things of Jesus and shows them unto us.

I know this great salvation that God has given us today is so large that one feels his whole body is enraptured. Dare you leap into the power of faith this afternoon? Dare you take your inheritance in God? Dare you believe God? Dare you stand upon the record of His Word? If thou wilt believe thou shalt see the glory of God. "...all things are possible to him that believeth" (Mark 9:23). Dare you come near today and say that God will sanctify your body and make it holy? He wants you to have a pure body, a holy body, a separated body, a body presented on the altar of God that you may be no longer conformed to this world, but transformed and renewed after His image.

I believe there are people here who will be put in the place where they will have to stand upon God's Word. You will be sifted as wheat. You will be tried as though some strange thing happened unto you. You will be put in most difficult places where all hell seems round about you, but God will sustain and empower you, and bring you into an unlimited place of faith. God will not allow you to be "...tempted above that ye are able; but will with the temptation also make a way to escape, that ye may be able to bear it" (1 Corinthians 10:13). God will surely tell you when you have been tried sufficiently to bring you out as pure gold. Every trial is to prepare you for a greater position for God. Your tried faith will make you know that you will have the faith of God to go through the next trial. Who is going to live dormant, weak, trifling, slow, indolent, prayerless, Bible-less lives when you know you must go through these things? And if you are to be made perfect in weakness, you must be tried as by fire in order to know that no man is able to win a victory, only by the power of God in him. The Holy Spirit will lead us day by day. You will know that these light afflictions, which are but for a moment, are working out for us an eternal weight of glory.

Oh, beloved, what are we going to do with this day? We must have a high tide this afternoon. We must have people receive the Holy Ghost, we must have people healed in their seats, we must see God come forth. Some of you have been longing for the Holy Ghost. God can baptize you just where you are. There may be some here who have not yet tasted of the grace of God. Close beside thee is the water of life. Have a drink, brother, sister, for God says, "...And let him that is athirst come. And whosoever will, let him take the water of life freely" (Revelation 22:17).

"If we love one another, God dwelleth in us, and his love is perfected in us" (1 John 4:12).

Sermon preached at Glad Tidings Tabernacle and Bible Training School
San Francisco, California

LIKE PRECIOUS FAITH

August 1, 1922

God will do great things for us if we are prepared to receive them from Him. We are dull of comprehension because we let the cares of this world blind our eyes, but if we keep open to God, He has a greater plan for us in the future than we have seen or ever have dreamed about in the past. It is God's delight to fulfil to us impossibilities because of His omnipotence, and when we reach the place where He alone has the right of way in all things, then all mists and misunderstandings will clear away.

I have been asking the Lord for His message for you this morning, and I believe He would have me turn to the second epistle of Peter, first chapter, beginning with the first verse:

> *Simon Peter, a servant and an apostle of Jesus Christ, to them that have obtained like precious faith with us through the righteousness of God and our Saviour Jesus Christ: Grace and peace be multiplied unto you through the knowledge of God, and of Jesus our Lord, According as his divine power hath given unto us all things that pertain unto life and godliness, through the knowledge of him that hath called us to glory and virtue: Whereby are given unto us exceeding great and precious promises: that by these ye might be partakers of the divine nature, having escaped the corruption that is in the world through lust. And beside this, giving all diligence, add to your faith virtue; and to virtue knowledge; and to knowledge temperance; and to temperance patience; and to patience godliness; And to godliness brotherly kindness; and to brotherly kindness charity. For if these things be in you, and abound, they make you that ye shall neither be barren nor unfruitful in the knowledge of our Lord Jesus Christ.*
>
> *Verses 1-8*

Probably there is not a greater word that anyone could bring to an audience than this word, "*like precious faith.*" "Like Precious Faith" means that God, who is from everlasting to everlasting, has always had people that He could trust; that He could illuminate, that He could enlarge until there was nothing within them that would hinder the power of God. Now this "Like Precious Faith" is the gift that God is willing to impart to all of us. He wants us to have this faith in order that we may "subdue kingdoms," "work righteousness," and, if it should be necessary, "stop the mouths of lions" (Hebrews 11:33).

We should be able under all circumstances to triumph. Not that we have any help in ourselves, but our help comes only from God, and if our help is only in God then we are always strong and never weak. It is always those people who are full of faith who have a "good report," who never murmur, who are in the place of victory, who are not in the place of human order, but of divine order in God. He is the Author of our faith, and our faith is always based on "thus saith the Lord."

This "Like Precious Faith" is for all. There is a word in the third chapter of Ephesians which is very good for us to consider: that you "may be able to comprehend with all saints..." (Ephesians 3:18). What does this "Like Precious Faith" mean to you this morning? Every one here is receiving a blessing because of the faith of Abraham. But remember this, this "Like Precious Faith" is the same that Abraham had. This "Like Precious Faith" is the substance of the power of eternal life which is given to us through the Word. You may not be able to use this faith because of some hindrance in your life. I have had a thousand road engines come over my life to break me up and bring me to the place where this faith could operate within me. There is no way into the deep things of God, only through a broken spirit. When we are thus broken, we cease forever from our own works for Another, even Christ, has taken the reign. Faith in God, and power with God, come to us through the knowledge of the Word of God. Whatever we may think about it, it is true that we are no better than our faith. Whatever your estimation is of your own ability, of your own righteousness, or of your work in any way, you are no better than your faith.

How wonderful is this faith that overcomes the world! "He that believeth that Jesus is the Son of God overcomes the world!" But how does he overcome the world? If you believe in Him you are purified as He is pure. You are strengthened because He is strong. You are made whole because He is whole. All of His fulness may come into you because of the revelation of Himself. Faith is the living principle of the Word of God. If we yield ourselves up to be led by the Holy Spirit we shall be divinely led into the deep things of God, and the truths and revelations and all His mind will be made so clear unto us that we shall live by faith in Christ.

God has no thought of anything on a small scale. In the passage which we have read this morning are these words, "Grace and peace be '*multiplied*' unto you through the knowledge of God, and of Jesus our Lord" (2 Peter 1:2). God's Word is always on the line of multiplication, and so I believe the Lord wants us on that line this morning. We see "Like Precious Faith" is to be obtained "through the righteousness of God and our Savior Jesus Christ." God's Word is without change. We are to be filled with the righteousness of God on the authority of the

Word. His righteousness is from everlasting to everlasting, the same, yesterday and today and forever.

If I limit the Lord, He cannot work within me, but if I open myself to God then He will surely fill me and flow through me.

We must have this "Like Precious Faith" in order to have our prayers answered. If we ask anything according to God's will, we are told that He hears us, and if we know that He hears us, then we know we have the petitions that we desire. Oh, brothers, sisters, we must go into the presence of God and get from Him the answer to our prayers. Hear what Mark 11:24 says,

> *...What things soever ye desire, when ye pray, believe that ye receive them, and ye shall have them.*

In the twenty-third verse we see mountains removed, difficulties all cleared away. When? When the man believes in his heart and refuses to doubt. We must have the reality, we must know God, we must be able to go into His presence and converse with God.

This "Like Precious Faith" goes on multiplying in grace and in peace through the knowledge of God. It places our feet on the Rock, and brings us to an unlimited place in our faith. This faith makes you dare to do anything with and for God. Remember that you can only be built up on the Word of God. If you build yourself on imagination or your own thoughts you will go wrong.

The Bible is the Word of God: supernatural in origin, eternal in duration, inexpressible in valor, infinite in scope, regenerative in power, infallible in authority, universal in interest, personal in application, inspired in totality. Read it through, write it down, pray it in, work it out, and then pass it on. Truly it is the Word of God. It brings into man the personality of God; it changes the man until he becomes the epistle of God. It transforms his mind, changes his character, takes him on from grace to grace, and gives him an inheritance in the Spirit. God comes in, dwells in, walks in, talks through, and sups with him.

Your peace be multiplied! You are to rejoice greatly. Oh! the bride ought to rejoice to hear the Bridegroom's voice. How we love our Bridegroom and how He loves us! How adorable He is and how sweet is His countenance. At the presence of Jesus, all else goes.

Oh, my brother, my sister, we have the greatest tide of all our life. There is no tide like the power of the "latter rain." We must not fail to see what remarkable things God has for every one of us.

Beloved, I would like to press into your heart this morning the truth that God has no room for an ordinary man. God wants to take the ordinary man and put him through the sieve and bring him out into a place of extraordinary faith. The cry of our souls can be satisfied only with God. The great plan of God is to satisfy you, and then give you the vision of something higher.

If ever you stop at any point, pick up at the place where you failed, and begin again under the refining light, and power and zeal of heaven and all things will be brought to you, for He will condescend to meet you.

Remember, beloved, it is not what you are but what God wants you to be. What shall we do? Shall we not dedicate ourselves afresh to God? Every new revelation brings a new dedication.

Let us seek *Him*.

Sermon preached at Glad Tidings Tabernacle and Bible Training School
San Francisco, California

 ONGUES AND INTERPRETATION: "Fear not, neither be thou dismayed, for the God who has led, shall descend upon thee, shall surely carry thee where thou wouldst not. But to this end He has

FAITH
Part 1
August 2, 1922

called thee out to take thee on, to move upon thee with divine unction of the Spirit that thou shouldst not be entertained by nature, but caught up with Him to hear His words, to speak His truth, to have His mind, to know His will, to commune and be still, to see Him who is invisible, to be able to pour out to others the great stream of life, to quicken everything wherever it moves. For the Spirit is not given by measure but He is given to us by faith, the measureless measure that we may know Him, and the power of His resurrection in the coming day. And now is the day set for us which is the opening for the coming day."

I believe the Lord would have me speak to you this morning the lines of faith, so I shall read a few verses to you from Hebrews 11:

> *Now faith is the substance of things hoped for, the evidence of things not seen. For by it the elders obtained a good report. Through faith we understand that the worlds were framed by the word of God, so that things which are seen were not made of things which do appear. By faith Abel offered unto God a more excellent sacrifice than Cain, by which he obtained witness that he was righteous, God testifying of his gifts: and by it he being dead yet speaketh. By faith Enoch was translated that he should not see death; and was not found, because God had translated him: for before his translation he had this testimony, that he pleased God. But without faith it is impossible to please him: for he that cometh to God must believe that he is, and that he is a rewarder of them that diligently seek him.*
>
> *Hebrews 11:1-6*

I think that is as far as we will be able to get this morning. I have been much complexed whether I should continue the yesterday morning subject, but the Lord seems to turn that into this channel this morning. So may the Lord open unto us today His good treasures.

You know, beloved, that there are many wonderful treasures in the storehouse of God that we have not yet gotten. But praise God, we have the promise in Corinthians,

> *...Eye hath not seen, nor ear heard, neither have entered into the heart of man, the things which God hath prepared for them that love him.*
>
> *1 Corinthians 2:9*

I pray God, this morning, that there may be within us a deep hunger and thirst with the penetration which is centered entirely upon the axle of Him, for surely He is all and in all. I pray God that we may be able to understand the opening of this chapter.

Now faith is the substance of things hoped for, the evidence of things not seen. For by it the elders obtained a good report. Through faith we understand that the worlds were framed by the word of God, so that things which are seen were not made of things which do appear.

Hebrews 11:1-3

Now beloved, you will clearly see this morning, that God wants to bring us to a foundation. If we are ever going to make any progress in divine life we shall have to have a real foundation. And there is no foundation, only the foundation of faith for us.

All our movements, and all that ever will come to us, which is of any importance, will be because we have a *Rock*. And if you are on the Rock, no powers can move you. And the need of today is the Rock to have our faith firm upon.

On any line of principle of your faith you must have something established in you to bring that forth. And there is no establishment outside God's Word for you. Everything else is sand. Everything else shall sunder.

If you build upon anything else but the Word of God, on imaginations, sentimentality, or any feelings, or any special joy, it will mean nothing without you have a foundation, and the foundation will have to be in the Word of God.

I was once going on a tram to Blackpool. It is one of our fashionable resorts, and many people go there because of the high tides, and the wonderful sights they get as the ocean throws up its large, massive mountain of sea.

When we were going on the tram, I looked over and said to a builder, "The men are building those houses upon the sands." "Oh," he said, "you don't know. You are not a builder. Don't you know that we can pound that sand till it becomes like rock?" I said, "Nonsense!"

I saw the argument was not going to profit, so I dropped it. By and by we reached Blackpool where the mountainous waves come over. I was looking and taking notice of so many things. I saw a row of houses that had fallen flat, and drawing the attention of this man I said, "Oh, look at those houses. See how flat they are." He forgot our previous conversation, saying, "You know here we have very large tides, and these houses being on the sands, when the floods came, they fell."

Beloved, it won't do. We must have something better than sand, and everything is sand except the Word. There isn't anything that will remain — we are told the heaven and earth will be melted up as a scroll as fervent heat. But we are told the Word of God shall be forever, and not one jot or tittle of the Word of God shall fail. And if there is anything that is satisfying me today more than another, it is, "...thy word is settled in heaven" (Psalm 119:89).

And another Word in the 138th Psalm says, "...thou hast magnified thy word above all thy name" (v. 2). The very establishment for me is the Word of God. It is not on any other line.

Let us come to the principle of it. If you turn to John's gospel you will find a wonderful word there. It is worth our notice and great consideration this morning.

I would like to see more Bibles than I see. It is important. If I left my house without my purse, I should naturally return for it because it might be of importance. My brothers, your Bible is worth ten million purses and their contents, and you had better turn back for your Testament or Bible, rather than for your purse. It is more important that you have the Word of life.

Some people say, "I have it inside." People are not satisfied sometimes, you must give them chapter and verse, and ask them to read it for themselves. It is important that the people should know and we ought to be able to give a good account always of the hope that is within us.

Now beloved, I would turn to this first chapter of John this morning for a moment, for our edification, because it will help us so much. I want to make a real basis this morning for you to build upon, that when we leave this meeting you will know exactly where you are.

In the beginning was the Word, and the Word was with God,
and the Word was God. The same was in the beginning with

God. All things were made by him; and without him was not any thing made that was made.

John 1:1-3

There we have the foundation of all things, which is the Word. It is a substance. It is a power. It is more than relationship. It is personality. It is a divine injunction to every soul that enters into this privilege to be born of this Word, to be created by this Word, to have a knowledge of this Word. What it means to us will be very important for us.

For remember, it is a substance, it is an evidence of things not seen. It bringeth about that which you cannot see. It brings forth that which is not there, and takes away that that is there, and substitutes it.

God took the Word and made the world of the things which did not appear. And we live in the world which was made by the Word of God, and it is inhabited by millions of people. And you say it is a substance. Jesus, the Word of God, made it of the things which did not appear.

And there is not anything made that is made that has not been made by that Word. And when we come to the truth of what that Word means, we shall be able not only to build but to know, not only to know, but to have. For if there is anything helping me today more than another, it is the fact I am living in facts, I am moving in facts, I am in the knowledge of the principles of the Most High.

God is making manifest His power. God is a reality and proving His mightiness in the midst of us. And as we open ourselves to divine revelation, and get rid of all things which are not of the Spirit, then we shall understand how mightily God can take us on in the Spirit, and move the things which are, and bring the things which are not, into prominence.

Oh, the riches, the depths of the wisdom of the Most High God! May this morning enlarge us. Jabus knew that there were divine principles that we need to know, and he says, "Enlarge me."

David knew that there was mightiness beyond and within, and he says, "Thou hast dealt bountifully with me," knowing that all the springs came from God that were in Him, which made His face to shine.

And God is an inward witness of a power, of a truth, of a revelation, of an inward presence, of a divine knowledge. He is! He is!

Then I must understand. I must clearly understand. I must have a basis of knowledge for everything that I say. We must, as preachers, never preach what we think. We must say what we know. Any man can think. You must be beyond the thinking. You must be in the teaching. You must have the knowledge.

And God wants to make us so in fidelity with Him that He unvails Himself. He rolls the clouds away, the mists disappear at His presence. He is almighty in His movements.

God has nothing small. He is all large, immensity of wisdom, unfolding the mysteries and the grandeur of His design of plan for humanity, that humanity may sink into insignificance, and the mightiness of the mighty power of God may move upon us till we are the sons of God with power, in revelation, and might, and strength in the knowledge of God.

Oh, this wonderful salvation! Now let us think about it, it is so beautiful. Seeing then that God took the Word — what was the Word? The Word was Jesus. The Word became flesh and dwelt among us. And we beheld and saw the glory of God.

I think John has a wonderful word on this which is to edification at this moment. Very powerful in its revelation to me so often as I gaze into the perfect law of liberty. Let me read you one verse, or perhaps more than one from the first epistle of John:

> *That which was from the beginning, which we have heard, which we have seen with our eyes, which we have looked upon, and our hands have handled, of the Word of life; (For the life was manifested, and we have seen it, and bear witness, and shew unto you that eternal life, which was with the Father, and was manifested unto us;) That which we have seen and heard declare we unto you, that ye also may have fellowship with us: and truly our fellowship is with the Father, and with His Son Jesus Christ.*
>
> *1 John 1:1-3*

Oh, beloved, He is the Word! He is the principle of God. He is the revelation sent forth from God. All fulness dwelt in Him. This is a grand word, of His fulness we have all received, and grace for grace.

In weakness, strength. In poverty, wealth. Oh, brother, this Word! It is a flame of fire. It may burn in your bones. It may move in every tissue of your life. It may bring out of you so forcibly the plan and purpose and life of God, till you cease to be, for God has taken you.

It is a fact we may be taken, hallelujah! into all the knowledge of the wisdom of God. Then I want to build, if I am created anew, for it is a great creation. It took nine months to bring us forth into the world after we were conceived, but it only takes one moment to beget us as sons. The first formation was a long period of nine months. The second formation is a moment, is an act, is a faith, for "He that believeth hath." And as you receive Him, you are begotten, not made.

Oh, the fact that I am begotten again, wonderful! Begotten of the same seed that begot Him. Remember, as He was conceived in the womb by the Holy Ghost, so we were conceived the moment we believed, and became in a principle of the like-mindedness of an open door to become sons of God with promise.

And oh! how the whole creation groaneth for sonship! There is a word in Romans, I think it would help us this morning to read it. Some knowledge of sonship, it is a beautiful word. I have so often looked at it with pleasure, for it is such a pleasure to me to read the Word of God. Oh, the hidden treasures there are! What a feast to have the Word of God! "Man shall not live by bread alone, but by every Word of God."

How we need the Word! The Word is life. Now, think about this first word here. The 4th verse is very beautiful. I will read the 3rd and 4th:

> *Concerning his Son Jesus Christ our Lord, which was made of the seed of David according to the flesh; And declared to be the Son of God with power, according to the spirit of holiness, by the resurrection from the dead.*

> *Romans 1:3,4*

Oh, what a climax of beatitudes there is here! How beautiful! God, breathe upon us this morning this holy, inward way after His passion. Hear it. "Declared to be the Son of God with power."

Sons must have power. We must have power with God, power with man. We must be above all the world. We must have power over Satan, power over the evils. I want you just this moment to think with me because it will help you with this thought.

You can never make evil pure. Anything which is evil never becomes pure in that sense. There is no such a thing as ever creating impurity into purity. The carnal mind is never subject to the will of God, and cannot be. There is only one thing, it must be destroyed.

But I want you to go with me to when God cast out that which was not pure. I want you to think about Satan in the glory with all the chances, and nothing spoiled him but his pride. And pride is an awful thing. Pride in the heart, thinking we are something when we are nothing. Building up a human constitution out of our own.

Oh, yes, it is true the devil is ever trying to make you think what you are. You never find God doing it. It is always Satan who comes on and says, "What a wonderful address you gave! How wonderful he did that, and how wonderful he prayed, and sung that song." It is all of the devil. There is not an atom of God in it, not from beginning to end.

And if we only knew how much we could preach better, if we only would not miss the revelation. And Paul, in order that he might never miss the revelation, said, "Therefore I have never ceased, I have kept that."

Oh, the vision is so needy today, more needy than anything that man should have the visions of God. The people have always perished when there has been no vision. God wants us to have visions, and revelations, and manifestations.

You cannot have the Holy Ghost without having manifestations. You cannot have the Holy Ghost without having revelations. You cannot have the Holy Ghost without being turned into another nature. It was the only credential that Joshua and Caleb could enter the land because they were of another spirit.

And we must live in an unction, in a power, in a transformation, and a divine attainment where we cease to be, where God becomes enthroned so richly.

TONGUES AND INTERPRETATION: "It is He! He came forth, emptied Himself of all, but love brought to us the grace, and then offered by Himself to purge us that we might be entire and free from all things. That we should see Him who was invisible, and changed by the power which is divine, and be lost to everything but the immensity of the mightiness of a God-likeness, for we must be in the world sons of God with promise."

We must be, we must be! We must not say it is not for me. Oh no, we must say it is for us.

And God cast Satan out. Oh, I do thank God for that. Yes, beloved, but God could not have cast him out if he had even been equal of power. I tell you, beloved, we can never bind the strong man till we are in the place of binding.

Thank God, Satan had to come out. Yes, and how did he come out? By the Word of His power. And beloved, if we get to know, and understand the principles of our inheritance by faith, we shall find out Satan will always be cast out by the same power that cast him out in the beginning. He will be cast out to the end because Satan has not become more holy but more vile.

If you think about the last day upon the earth, you will find out that the greatest war — not Armageddon, the war beyond that — will be betwixt the hosts of Satan and the hosts of God. And how will it take place? With swords, dynamite, or any other human power? No, by the brightness of His presence, the holiness of His holiness, the purity of His purity, where darkness cannot remain, where sin cannot stand, where only holiness, purity will remain. All else will flee from the presence of God into the abyss forever.

And God has saved us with this Word of power over the powers of sin. I know there is a teaching and a need of teaching of the personality of the presence of the fidelity of the Word of God with power. And we need to eat and drink of this Word. We need to feed upon it in our hearts. We need that holy revelation that ought always to take away the mists from our eyes and reveal Him.

Remember beloved, don't forget that every day must be a day of advancement. If you have not made any advancement since yesterday, in a measure you are a backslider. There is only one way for you between Calvary and the glory, and it is forward. It is every day forward. It is no day back. It is advancement with God. It is cooperation with Him in the Spirit.

Beloved, we must see these things, because if we live on the same plane, day after day, the vision is stale, the principles lose their earnestness. But we must be like those who are catching the vision of the Master day by day. And we must make inroads into every passion that would interfere, and bring everything to the slaughter that is not holy. For God would have us in these days to know that He wishes to seat us on High. Don't forget it.

The principles remain with us if we will only obey, to seat us on High, hallelujah! And let us still go on building because we must build this morning. We must know our foundation. We must be able to take the Word of God, and so make it clear to people because we shall be confronted with evil powers.

I am continually confronted with things which God must clear away. Every day something comes before me that has to be dealt with on these lines. For instance, when I was at Cazadero seven or eight years ago, amongst the first people who came to me in those meetings, was a man who was stone deaf. And every time we had the meeting — suppose I was rising up to say a few words, this man would take his chair from off the ordinary row and place it right in front of me. And the devil used to say, "Now, you are done." I said, "No, I am not done. It is finished."

The man was as deaf as possible for three weeks. And then in the meeting, as we were singing about three weeks afterwards, this man became tremendously disturbed as though in a storm. He looked in every direction, and then he became as one who had almost lost his mind.

And then he took a leap. He started on the run and went out amongst the people, and right up one of the hills. When he got about 60 yards away he heard singing. And the Lord said, "Thy ears are open."

And he came back, and we were still singing. That stopped our singing. And then he told us that when his ears were opened, he could not understand what it was. There was such a tremendous noise he could not understand it whatever. He thought something had happened to the world, and so he ran out of the whole thing. Then when he got away he heard singing.

Oh, the devil said for three weeks, "You cannot do it." I said, "It is done!" As though God would ever forget! As though God could forget! As if it were possible for God to ever ignore our prayers!

The most trying time is the most helpful time. Most preachers say something about Daniel, and about the Hebrew children, and especially about Moses when he was in a tried corner. Beloved, if you read the

Scriptures you will never find anything about the easy time. All the glories come out of hard times.

And if you are really reconstructed it will be in a hard time, it won't be in a singing meeting, but at a time when you think all things are dried up, when you think there is no hope for you, and you have passed everything, then that is the time that God makes the man, when tried by fire, that God purges you, takes the dross away, and brings forth the pure gold. *Only melted gold is minted.* Only moistened clay receives the mold. Only softened wax receives the seal. Only broken, contrite hearts receive the mark as the potter turns us on his wheel, shaped and burnt to take and keep the heavenly mold, the stamp of God's pure gold.

We must have the stamp of our blessed Lord who was marred more than any man. And when He touched human weakness it was reconstructed. He spoke out of the depths of trial and mockery, and became the initiative of a world's redemption. Never man spake like He spake! He was full of order and made all things move till they said, "We never saw it on this like."

He was truly the Son of God with power, with blessing, with life, with maturity, that He could take the weakest and make them into strong and strength.

God is here this morning in power, in blessing, in might, and saying to thee, my brother, and to you, my sister, "What is it? What is thy request?"

Oh, He is so precious! He never fails! He is so wonderful! He always touched the needy place. He is so gentle. He never breaks the bruised reed. He is so rich in His mighty benevolence that He makes the smoking flax to flame.

May God move us this morning to see that He must have out of us choice. Oh, how precious He is! There is no word so precious to me as when He said, "I have desired to eat this with you before I suffer."

Oh, that lovely, benevolent, wonderful Jesus! Oh, before the garden experience, with the knowledge of it before the cross, and Gethsemane, there that love of Jesus, that holy Jesus, could say, With desire! It was the joy that was set before Him. Shall it be missed? Is it possible for it to be missed? That joy that was set before Him of making us fully matured saints of God, with power over the powers of the enemy, filled with the might of His Spirit.

Surely this is our God, for there is no God answers like this. Beloved, let me entreat you this morning to pay any price. Never mind what it costs, it is worth it all, to have His smile, to have His presence. Nay verily, more than that, to have the same desire that He had to win others for Him.

When I see His great desire to win me, I say, "Lord, remold me like that. Make me have the desire of salvation for others at any cost." Thank God He went through. He did not look back. He went right on.

Oh, you never need to be afraid of joining yourself to this Nazarene, for He is always a King. When He was dying He was a King. Yes, if ever any man spoke in tongues, Jesus spoke in tongues, for there was no interpretation. And if any man ever spoke truth He spoke the truth when He said, "It is finished."

Thank God it is finished. And I know, because it is finished, everything is mine. Thank God, everything is mine, things in heaven, things in earth, things under the earth. He is all power over all. He is in all. He is through all. Thank God He is for all.

And I say to you without contradiction, that Jesus has so much more for you than you have any conception. Just as the two sons of Zebedee, did they know what they asked? Certainly, they had no conception of their asking.

Jesus said, "Are ye able to drink of the cup that I shall drink of and to be baptized with the baptism that I am baptized with? They say unto Him, We are able." Were they able? No, but it was their heart. Have a big heart! Have a big yes! Have a big "I will!" Have a great desire though you are blind to what is to follow.

And they wondered what He had. I believe that all believers want the same. Did they drink? Yes, He said they would. Did they see His baptism? Yes, He said they would. But they had no idea what it meant, what the cup was.

But the cup was drunk to the dregs. Yes, His cup was different. But because of His cup, our cup runneth over. Oh, surely goodness and mercy shall follow thee. Thy cup shall run over.

There may be many cups before the cup is full. But oh, hallelujah, any way, only let it be His will and His way, not my way. Oh, for His way only, and His plan, His will only.

I feel we have gotten very little out of the subject, but oh, what shall we say? What are we going to do? Brothers, let the mantle fall from Him on you today. "If thou see me when I go, it shall be." And Elisha kept his eye on Elijah. The mantle is to fall, my brother; the mantle of power, the mantle of blessing.

And I ask you today, seeing that you have this spiritual revelation in the body, in the earthly tabernacle, what are you going to do? If the body is yielded sufficiently till it becomes perfectly the temple of the Spirit, then the fulness will flow, and the life shall be yielded to you, given to you as you need.

May God mold us all to believe it is possible this morning not only for the rivers but the mightiness of the expanselessness of that mighty ocean of His to flow through us.

You do as you are led to do. The altar rail is before you. No pressure ought to be needed for you as you see your need before God, and know He is here to supply your need. Wherefore, why should we have to be entreated to seek the best of all when God is waiting to give without measure to each and all.

Do as the Lord leads you, and we will be still before Him to let Him direct you in whatever way.

Glad Tidings Tabernacle and Bible Training School
San Francisco, California

 I believe the Lord would be magnified and be pleased if we are to continue our subject we had yesterday morning from the eleventh chapter of Hebrews. I will read from the first verse:

FAITH
Part 2
August 3, 1922

Now faith is the substance of things hoped for, the
evidence of things not seen. For by it the elders obtained a good

report. Through faith we understand that the worlds were framed by the word of God, so that things which are seen were not made of things which do appear. By faith Abel offered unto God a more excellent sacrifice than Cain, by which he obtained witness that he was righteous, God testifying of his gifts: and by it he being dead yet speaketh. By faith Enoch was translated that he should not see death; and was not found, because God had translated him: for before his translation he had this testimony, that he pleased God. But without faith it is impossible to please him: for he that cometh to God must believe that he is, and that he is a rewarder of them that diligently seek him. By faith Noah, being warned of God of things not seen as yet, moved with fear, prepared an ark to the saving of his house; by the which he condemned the world, and became heir of the righteousness which is by faith. By faith Abraham, when he was called to go out into a place which he should after receive for an inheritance, obeyed; and he went out, not knowing whither he went. By faith he sojourned in the land of promise, as in a strange country, dwelling in tabernacles with Isaac and Jacob, the heirs with him of the same promise: For he looked for a city which hath foundations, whose builder and maker is God.

Hebrews 11:1-10

I believe that there is only one way to all the treasures of God, and it is the way of faith. There is only one principle underlying all the attributes and all the beatitudes of the mighty ascension into the glories of Christ, and it is by faith. All the promises are Yea and Amen to them that believe.

And God wants this morning, by His own way — for He has a way and it never comes human, it always comes on divine principles, you cannot know God by nature. You get to know God by an open door of grace.

He has made a way. It is a beautiful way, that all His saints can enter in by that way and find rest. The way is the way of faith, there isn't any other way. If you climb up any other way, you cannot work it out.

There [are] several things that are coming before me from time to time, and I find that it is all a failure without its base is right on the rock Christ Jesus. He is the only way, the truth, and the life. But praise God, He is the truth, He is the life, and His Word is Spirit and life-giving. And when we understand it in its true order to us we find that it is not only the Word of life but it quickeneth, it openeth, it filleth, it moveth, it changeth, and it brings us into a place where we dare to say, Amen!

You know, beloved, there is a lot in an Amen. You know you never get but still you have an Amen inside. There was such a difference between Zacharias and Mary. I find you can have zeal without faith. And I find you can have any amount of things without faith.

As I looked into the twelfth chapter of the Acts of the apostles, I find that the people that were waiting all night praying for Peter to come out of prison had zeal but they had not faith. They were so zealous that they even gave themselves only to eat the unleavened bread, and went to prayer. And it seemed all the time that there was much that could be commended to us all this morning, but there was one thing missing. It was faith. You will find that Rhoda had more faith than all the rest of them. When the knock came at the door, she ran to it and the moment she heard Peter's voice she ran back again with joy, saying, "Peter stood before the gate."

And all the people said, "You are mad. It isn't so." And she made mention of what she saw. There was no faith at all. But they said, "Well, God has perhaps sent an angel." But Rhoda said, "It is Peter." And Peter continued knocking. And they went and found it was so. They had zeal but no faith. And I believe there is quite a difference.

God wants to bring us into an activity where we shall in a living way take hold of God on the lines of solidity, that which rests and sees the plan of God always.

Zacharias and Elizabeth surely wanted a son, but even when the angel came and told Zacharias he was full of unbelief. And the angel said, "Because thou hast not believed, thou shalt be dumb."

But look at Mary. When the angel came to Mary, Mary said, "...be it unto me according to thy word." And it was the beginning of the Amen, and the presentation of the Amen was when she nursed Jesus.

Believe that there can be a real Amen in your life that can bring to pass. And God wants us with the Amen that never knows anything else than Amen, an inward Amen, a mighty moving Amen, a God-likeness Amen. That which says, "It is," because God has spoken. It cannot be otherwise. It is impossible to be otherwise.

Beloved, I see all the plan of life where God comes in and vindicates His power, makes His presence felt. It is not by crying, nor groaning. It is because we believe. And yet, I have nothing to say about it. Sometimes it takes God a long time to bring us through the groaning, crying, before we can believe.

I know this as clearly as anything, that no man in this place can change God. You cannot change Him. There is a word in Finney's lectures which is very good, and it says, "Can a man who is full of sin and all kinds of ruin in his life, change God when he comes out to pray?" No, it is impossible. But as this man labors in prayer, and groans, and travails, because his tremendous sin is weighing him down, he becomes broken in the presence of God, and when properly melted in the perfect harmony with the divine plan of God, then God can work in that clay. He could not before.

Prayer changes hearts but it never changes God. God is the same today and forever, full of love, full of entreaty, full of helpfulness. Always in the presence of God as you come you have what you come for. You take it away. You can use it at your disposal.

And there is nothing you can find in the Scriptures where God ever charges you for what you have done with what He has given you. God upbraids no man, but you can come and come again, and God is willing to give if you believe.

TONGUES AND INTERPRETATION: "It is the living God. It is the God of power who changes things, changes us. It is He Who has formed us, not we ourselves, and transformed us because it is He Who comes in and makes the vessel ready for the immensity of its power working through us, transforming us into His will, His plan, for He delighteth in us."

God delighteth in us. When a man's ways please the Lord, then He makes all things to move accordingly.

Now we come to the Word, this blessed Word, this holy Word. I want to go to the 5th verse of the 11th [chapter] of Hebrews. We were dealing with the two first verses yesterday.

> *By faith Enoch was translated that he should not see death; and was not found, because God had translated him: for before his translation he had this testimony, that he pleased God.*

When I was in Sweden, the Lord worked mightily there in a very blessed way — after one or two addresses the leaders called me and they said, "We have heard very strange things about you, and we would like to know whether they are true because we can see the doors are opening to you. We can see that God is with you, and God is moving, and we know that it will be a great blessing to Sweden."

"Well," I said, "what is it?"

"Well," they said, "we have heard from good authority that you preach that you have the resurrection body." When I was in France I had an interpreter that believed this thing, and I found out after I had preached once or twice through the interpreter that she gave her own expressions. And of course I did not know but I said, "Nevertheless, I will tell you what I really believe. If I had the testimony of Enoch I should be off. I would like it and I would like to go. Evidently there is no one in Sweden has it or they would be off, because the moment Enoch had the testimony to please God, off he went."

I pray that God will so quicken our faith for we have a far way to go maybe before we are ready. It was in the mind of God, translation. But remember translation comes on the lines of holy obedience and walk with pleasure with a perfectness of God. Walking together with God in the Spirit. Some others have had touches of it. It is lovely, it is delightful to think about those moments as we have walked with God and had communion with Him, when our words were lifted, and we were not made to make them, but God made them.

Oh, that smile of divine communication which is truly of God, where we speak to Him in the Spirit, and where the Spirit lifts and lifts and lifts, and takes us in. Oh, beloved, there is a place of God where God can bring us in, and I pray that God by His Spirit, may move us so we will strive to be where Enoch was as he walked with God.

As Paul divinely puts it by the Spirit, I don't believe that any person in this place hasn't an open door into everything that is in the Scriptures. I believe the Scriptures are for us. And in order that we may apply our hearts to understand the truth I say, Oh, for an inroad of the mighty revolution of the human heart to break it so that God can plan afresh and make all within us say, Amen! What a blessed experience it is truly.

There are two kinds of faith, God wants to let us see. I am not speaking about natural things this morning but divine things. There is a natural faith and there is a saving faith. The saving faith is the gift of God. All people are born with the natural faith. But this supernatural faith is the gift of God.

And yet there are limitations in this faith. But faith which has no limitation in God, bring it to us this morning in the 26th chapter of the Acts of the apostles. This is a very wonderful chapter. I want to define, or express, or bring into prominence this morning the difference between the natural faith and this faith that I am going to read about, beginning at the 16th verse:

> *But rise, and stand upon thy feet: for I have appeared unto thee for this purpose, to make thee a minister and a witness both of these things which thou hast seen, and of those things in the which I will appear unto thee; Delivering thee from the people, and from the Gentiles, unto whom now I send thee, To open their eyes, and to turn them from darkness to light, and from the power of Satan unto God, that they may receive forgiveness of sins, and inheritance among them which are sanctified by faith that is in me.*
>
> *Acts 26:16-18*

Is that the faith of Paul? No, it is the faith which the Holy Ghost is giving. We may have very much of revelation of a divine plan of God through the gifts in the Lord's order, when He speaks to me I will open out on the gifts.

But beloved, I see here just a touch of the line of the gifts, where Paul, through the revelation, and through the open door that was given to him on the way to Damascus, saw he had the faith of salvation. Then I notice as Ananias laid his hands upon him, there came a power, the promise of the Holy Ghost and filled this body.

And then I notice in that order of the Spirit, he walked in the comfort of the Holy Ghost, which is a wonderful comfort. Oh, tell me if you can, is there anything to compare to that which Jesus said, When He comes "...he shall teach you all things, and bring all things to your remembrance..." (John 14:26). Surely this is a Comforter. Surely He is the Comforter who can bring to our memory, to our mind, all the things that He said.

And all the way He worked is the divine plan of the Spirit to reveal unto us till every one of us, without exception, tastes of this angelic mighty touch of the heavenly as He moves upon us.

Oh, beloved, the baptism of the Holy Ghost is the essential mighty touch of revelation of the wonders, for God the Holy Ghost has no limitations on these lines. But when the soul is ready to enter into His life, there is a breaking up of fallow ground and a moving of the mists away, bringing us into the perfect day of the light of God.

And I say that Paul was moved upon by this power, and yet Jesus said unto him, "As you go you will be changed, and in the changing I will take you from revelation to revelation, open door to open door and the accomplishment will be as My faith is committed unto thee."

Oh, hallelujah, there is saving faith. There is the gift of faith. It is the faith of Jesus which brings to us as we press in and on with God, a place where we can always know it is God.

I want just to put before you this difference between our faith and the faith of Jesus. Our faith comes to an end. Most people in this place have come to a place where they have said, "Lord, I can go no further. I have gone so far, now I can go no further. I have used all the faith I have, and I have just to stop now and wait."

Well, brother, thank God that we have this faith. But there is another faith. I remember one day being in Lan——shire, and going around to see some sick people. I was taken into a house where there was a young woman lying on her bed, a very helpless case. It was a case where the reason had gone, and many things were manifested there which were satanic, and I knew it.

She was only a young woman, a beautiful child. Then the husband quite a young man, came in with a baby and he leaned over to kiss the wife. The moment he did she threw herself over on the other side of the bed, just as a lunatic would do, with no consciousness of the presence of the husband.

That was very heart-breaking. And then he took the baby and pressed the baby's lips to the mother. Again another wild kind of thing happened. So he said to a sister who was attending her, "Have you anybody to help?" "Oh," they said, "we have had everything."

But I said, "Have you no spiritual help?" And her husband stormed out and said, "Help? You think that we believe in God after we have had seven weeks of no sleep, of maniac conditions? You think that we believe God? You are mistaken. You have come to the wrong house."

And then a young woman about eighteen or so just grinned at me and passed out of the door, and that finished the whole business. That brought me to a place of compassion for this woman that something had to be done, did not matter what it was.

And then with my faith — oh, thank God for the faith. I began to penetrate the heavens, and I was soon out of that house I will tell you, for I never saw a man get anything from God who prayed on the earth. If you get anything from God you will have to pray into heaven for it is all there. If you are living on the earth and expect things from heaven it will never come. If you want to touch the ideal you must live in ideal principles.

And as I saw in the presence of God the limitations of my faith, there came another faith, a faith that could not be denied, a faith that took the promise, a faith that believed God's Word. And I came from that presence back again to earth, but not the same man, under the same condition confronting me but in the name of Jesus, with a faith that could shake hell and move anything else.

I said, "Come out of her in the name of Jesus!" And she rolled over and fell asleep and wakened in fourteen hours, perfectly sane and perfectly whole. Oh, there is faith. The faith that is in me. And Jesus wants to bring us all this morning into a place in line with God where we cease to be, for God must have the right of way, of thought, of purpose. God must have the way.

Beloved, I say there is a process on this line. Enoch walked with God. That must have been all these hundreds of years as he was penetrating, and going through, and laying hold, and believing, and seeing that he had gotten to such cooperation and touch with God that things moved on earth, and was moving towards heaven. And surely God came for the last time.

It was not possible for him to stop any longer. Oh, hallelujah! And I believe that God this morning wants to so bring all of us into line with His will that we may see signs, and wonders, and divers miracles and gifts of the Holy Ghost. For this is a wonderful day, the day of the Holy Ghost. It is a blessed day. If you would ask me any time, "When would you have liked to come to earth?" Just now! Oh, yes, it suits me beautifully to know that the Holy Ghost can fill the body. Just to be a temple of the Spirit! Just to manifest the glory of God! Brother, it is truly an ideal summit, and everyone can reach out their hand and God will take and lift us on.

For the heart that is longing this morning, God makes the longing cry. Sometimes we have an idea that there is some specialty in us that does it. No, beloved. If you have anything at all worth having it is because God has love to give you.

According to the fifteenth chapter of First Corinthians everybody who dies — I see there is a place where they have fallen short somehow to me. It can never appear as the right thing, as it is sown in dishonor. Seems to be truly that God will raise it in power, the same power God would raise it in is the power that God wants to keep us in, so as we should not be sown in dishonor.

I truly say that there is a plan of God for this purpose, of this life. Enoch walked with God. God wants to raise the conditions of saints to walk with Him, and talk with Him. I don't want to build anything about myself, but it is truly true if you found me outside of conversation with man, I am in conversation with God.

One thing God has given to me from my youth up, and I am so thankful, God has never given me a taste or a relish for any book but the Bible. And I can say before God, I have never read a book but the Bible, so I know nothing about books. As I have peeped into books I have seen in them just one thing that good people said, "Well, that is a good book." Oh, but how much better to get the Book of books which contains nothing but

God. If a book is commended because it has something about God in it, how much more shall the Word of God be the food of the soul, the strengthening of the believer, and the building up of the human order of character with God, so that all the time he is being changed by the Spirit of the Lord from one state of glory into another.

This is the ideal principle of God. I have a word to say about those who have gone, because Paul says, "It is better to go than to stop." But oh, I am looking forward, and hasting unto, and believing the fact that He is coming again.

And this hope in me brings me to the same place as the man of faith who looked for a city which human hands had not made. There is a city which human hands have not made, and by faith we have a right to claim our position right along as we go, and to these glorious positions.

I will turn now from this fifth verse to the sixth, also a beautiful verse of Hebrews 11:

> *But without faith it is impossible to please him: for he that cometh to God must believe that he is, and that he is a rewarder of them that diligently seek him.*
>
> *Hebrews 11:6*

I often think that we make great failures on this line because of an imperfect understanding of His Word. I can see it is impossible to please God on any lines but faith, for everything which is not of faith is sin.

So God wants us all to see this morning the plan of faith is the ideal and principle of God. And when I remember and keep in my thoughts these beautiful words in the twelfth chapter of this same epistle, it is wonderful as I read this second verse:

> *Looking unto Jesus the author and finisher of our faith....*

He is the author of faith. Jesus became the author of faith. God worked the plan through Him by forming the worlds, making everything that there was by the Word of His power. Jesus was the Word, Christ. God so manifested this power in the world, forming the worlds by the word of Jesus.

I see that on this divine line of principle of God, God hath chosen Him and ordained Him, and clothed Him, and made Him greater than all because of one principle, and on this principle only. Because of the joy, it was the love of God that gave. It was the joy of the Lord to save.

And because of this exceeding, abundant joy of saving the whole world, He became the author of a living faith. And everyone in this place is changed by this faith from grace to grace. We become divine inheritances of the promises, and we become the substance. We can become all and in all.

One ideal only, God is working in this, this holy principle of faith. It is divine.

TONGUES AND INTERPRETATION: "It is God installated through the flesh, quickened by His Spirit, molded by His will, till it is so in order, till God's Son could not come without we went for His life is in us."

Thank God for that interpretation. God's Son, this life, this faith, could not move from the glory without I move from the earth. And right in the heaven we should meet.

This faith, this principle, this life, this inheritance, this truth, this eternal power working in us mightily by His Spirit! Oh, thank God for His Word! Live it, moved by His Word.

We shall become flat, and anemic, and helpless without this Word, dormant and so helpless to take hold. You are not any good for anything apart from the Word. The Word is everything. The Word has to become everything. When the heavens and the earth are melted away then we shall be as bright, and brighter than the day, and going on to be consistent because of the Word of God.

Oh, when we know it is quick, and powerful, and sharper than any two-edged sword, dividing asunder soul and spirit, joints and marrow, and thoughts of the heart! God's Word is like a sword piercing through. Who could have a stiff knee if they believed in that Word?

The Word is so divinely appointed for us. Think about it. How it severs the soul and the spirit! Take it in. Think it out. Work it out. It is divine. See it, truth.

The soul which has all the animal, all the carnal, all the selfishness, all the evil things, thank God for the truth to the Word, that the soul will never inherit that place. The soul must go from whence it came. It is earthly, sensual. But the two-edged sword divides it so it shall have no power. And over it, ruling it, controlling it, bringing it always to death, is the Spirit of the life of Jesus.

Jesus poured out His soul unto death. Flesh and blood shall not inherit the kingdom of heaven. So I see it is necessary for us to have the Word of God piercing even to dividing asunder soul and spirit.

Then I notice the joints and marrow must have the Word of God to quicken the very marrow. Oh, how many people in Australia came to me with double-curvature of the spine, and instantly they were healed, and made straight as I put hands upon them. But no man is able, but the divine Son of God and His power moved upon these curvatures of the spine, and straightened them. Oh, the mighty power of the Word of God!

God must have us in these days so separated on every line as we proceed on the lines of God, and see that the Word of God must bring forth. As it destroys it brings forth. You can never live if you have never been dead. You must die if you want to live. It was the very death of Jesus that raised Him to the highest height of glory.

Every death-likeness is a likeness to the Son of God. And all the time the Word of God must quicken, flow through, and move upon us till these ideals are in us, till we move in them, live in them.

TONGUES AND INTERPRETATION: "The living God is lifting thee out of thyself into Himself."

We must be taken out of the ordinary. We must be brought into the extraordinary. We must live in a glorious position, over the flesh and the devil, and everything of the world. God has ordained us, clothed us within, and manifested upon us His glory that we may be the sons with promise, of Son-likeness to Him.

Oh, what an ideal! What a Savior! What an ideal Savior! And to be like Him! Oh, yes, we can be like Him. This is the ideal principle, God to make us like Him!

Then I see another truth. He that cometh to God — How do you come to God? Where is God? Is He in the ceiling? In the elements? Is He in the air? In the wind? Where is God? He that cometh to God — Where is He? *God is in you.* Oh, hallelujah! And you will find the Spirit of the living God in you, which is the prayer circle, which is the lifting power, which is the revelation element, which is the divine power which lifts you.

He that cometh to God is. He is already in the place where the Holy Ghost takes the prayers and swings them out according to the mind of the Spirit. For who hath known the mind of Christ, or who is able to make intercession but the mind of the Spirit of the living God. He maketh intercession. Where is He? He is in us.

Oh, this baptism of the Holy Ghost is an inward presence of the personality of God, which lifts, prays, takes hold, lives in, with a tranquility of peace and power that rests and says, "It is all right."

God answers prayer because the Holy Ghost prays and your advocate is Jesus, and the Father the Judge of all. There He is. Is it possible for any prayer to be missed on those lines? Let us be sure that we are in this place this morning.

"He that cometh to God must believe that He is, and that He is a rewarder of them that diligently seek Him." Must believe that God is. You cannot help it. You must believe He is already in the temple.

But some people have not yet entered into the experience because they have never come out. But God said to Abraham, "Come out, Come out." And if you have never known the voice of God to come out, you may be a long time in the wilderness before you come in.

Now look at the ridiculousness of Abraham, that is the human side. Look at it in verse 8: "By faith Abraham, when he was called to go out into a place which he should after receive for an inheritance, obeyed; and he went out..." (Hebrews 11:8). What a silly man he was!

"...not knowing whither he went." Why, that was the very secret of power. Everything was there. If there is anything that I know which is worth knowing, it is that which I don't know about God which He is always making me to know.

There is something about being after God's mind till we will be all the time what He wants us to be. God has ordered it so. God has planned it so. God wills it. So God has no other method or plan of saving ruined man except by man.

And when man remains in the place which God has called him out, so that he can be a perfect man, substitute of God's plan for the man, then the man will surely reach the attitude where God has said, "Come out, for I have a place for thee and thou canst never reach the place without Me. But I am willing that thou shouldst be for Me that I may be for thee."

Oh, this God of grace! Oh, this willingness for God to let us see His face! Oh, this longing of my soul which cannot be satisfied without more of God! Oh, it is this, more of God I want! I feel that I am the youngest man in the world.

Without God does something I should be an awful failure. But surely He will do it. He has brought us in that He might take us out. And God will never leave us in an unfinished plane.

It is all divine order. As surely as Jesus came, it is divine order that I should come at this time to San Francisco. There is nothing wrong in the plan of God. It is all in perfect order. To think that God can make a mistake is the biggest blunder that a man makes in his life. God makes no mistakes. But when we are in the will of God the plan works out admirably because it is divine, thought out by the almightiness of God.

Oh, beloved, have you come out yet? You say, "Out of what?" Out of that you know you didn't want to be in. Why should I answer your questions when you can answer them yourselves. It would be a waste of time. No need of going on that line.

But God knows where you are and where you ought to be. Many of you heard the voice of God long ago, but still you have not obeyed. Will you come out? God says, "Come out!" But you say, "Where shall I go to? Where shall I come out?" Come out into God! Unto God! Oh, hallelujah!

I would like to say so many more things to you this morning, but I think it is just about time to come out. It is such a mistake to hold on, hearing His voice and not obeying. But oh, when we obey, it is so sweet when we obey! So I will cease at this time because God has something better probably teaching you in the Spirit as you obey His call, obey His "Come out."

God has something better for you than I can tell you. Oh, I say to you, Come out, and I will leave you to either sit still or come out. Amen!

Message given at Glad Tidings Tabernacle and Bible Training School
San Francisco, California

I believe the Lord would be very pleased in His leadings, this morning, to take us to first chapter of Second Peter again, that we may see what the mind of the Lord is concerning us in that chapter. I will read from the first verse:

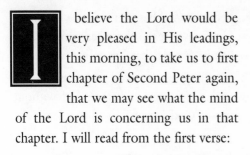

OUR INHERITANCE

August 4, 1922

> *Simon Peter, a servant and an apostle of Jesus Christ, to them that have obtained like precious faith with us through the righteousness of God and our Savior Jesus Christ: Grace and peace be multiplied unto you through the knowledge of God, and of Jesus our Lord, According as his divine power hath given unto us all things that pertain unto life and godliness, through the knowledge of him that hath called us to glory and virtue: Whereby are given unto us exceeding great and precious promises; that by these ye might be partakers of the divine nature, having escaped the corruption that is in the world through lust. And beside this, giving all diligence, add to your faith virtue; and to virtue knowledge; And to knowledge temperance; and to temperance patience; and to patience godliness; And to godliness brotherly kindness; and to brotherly kindness charity. For if these things be in you, and abound, they make you that ye shall neither be barren nor unfruitful in the knowledge of our Lord Jesus Christ.*
>
> 2 Peter 1:1-8

I believe the Lord wants us to know our inheritance this morning. You know there is such a thing as having something left to you. For instance, many people make wills, and they leave testators to carry out their wills. When the person is dead, very often those people who have had the property left to them, never get it, because of unfaithful stewards, who have been left in charge.

But there is one will that has been left, and He who made the whole will is our Lord Jesus Christ. After He was dead He rose to carry out His own will. And now we may have all that has been left to us by Him, all the inheritances, all the blessings, all the power, all the life, and all the victory. All the promises are ours because He is risen.

Because He is risen as a faithful High Priest, He is here to help us this morning to understand what it means by these divine principles that we have been reading. I pray God that we may have a clear knowledge today of what God means for us in these days, for He has called us to great banquets, and we must always have a good appetite at the Lord's banquets.

It is a serious thing to come to a banquet of the Lord, and have an anemic stomach, something that cannot take anything. We must have great appetites. We must have longing desires. We must have very thirsty conditions, and hungry souls when we come to the Lord's table. And then we can have what is laid up for us. We can be strengthened by the might of the power of God in the inner man. May the Lord take us into His treasures now. Suppose we turn to the third verse:

> *According as his divine power hath given unto us all things*
> *that pertain unto life and godliness, through the knowledge of*
> *him that hath called us to glory and virtue.*
>
> *2 Peter 1:3*

We will find out that the main staff of this portion of truth as it comes before us this morning, will always be in the unfolding of the Christ. All the fulness is in Him. All the glories surround Him. All the divine virtue flows from Him.

And we must understand that God is bringing us into the place that we may understand what He means by "pertaining unto life and godliness, through the knowledge of Him."

Now, this morning, God has brought us from one step to another. I see the first days He gave us a glimpse of faith which was given to us. Then I noticed the next days He gave us assurance of the faith on the principles of the groundwork of Christ being the foundation of all things. And now the Lord wants to show us how this virtue can remain in us. We must reach, we must attain to this virtue.

What is virtue? Oh, brother, sister, if I have to take you this morning into the virtue, I must let you know that Paul touched these divine powers, because he speaks to us in the third chapter of Ephesians of that power. He calls it the effectual working of the powers of God, which is the Holy Ghost, which is the divine infilling, which has to fill the whole body till the body is filled with life, and virtue, and grace, and power, and faith.

There are no limitations. He is the executive of the kingdom of heaven. He has power in our body as we open ourselves to Him. He has all fulness to display because He displays it on the fulness. He has the measureless measure, as He reveals Him to us as the measure.

So beloved, God wants us to see this day that we must understand, whatever it costs, whatever it means, we must have a personal incoming of this life of God, this Holy Ghost, this divine person.

And I want you to think what it really means to receive the Holy Ghost. We are born again of the incorruptible Word, which is Christ. It is an incorruptible Word. It liveth and abideth forever. And we are born again of that incorruptible power. It is God's plan for us. It is a further divine power than the human mind has ever been able to receive. We must have a divine mind to take in divine things. We must be made divine in order to understand all things which are divine.

We must understand that this matter must return into grace. We must understand this body must be changed into a body as a temple of the Spirit. And we must understand that even the mind must be the mind of Christ. And we must understand that the very inner moving and crying must be of the divine plan, for God has come to change us into the same image, into the same process of power.

Just as He was in this world, so are we to be. John clearly saw it. And if we could only take another step, and this step is an important step for us this morning. As He is so are we. There is a step further. I find that God has always, in order to encourage His people, been speaking to them of the future tense.

You remember that Jesus lived in the present tense, but always spoke in a future tense. And beloved, there is a future tense. But I believe we must come now to the place of present tense. Whatever God has designed for man we must claim it as now, and we shall always have greater manifestations of power if we are living now instead of living future. Living in a now power, a now blessing, a now God, a now heaven, a now glory, a now virtue.

TONGUES AND INTERPRETATION: "It is the Spirit that worketh in us all these divine plans, that He may build us on the foundations of the living Word which liveth, which always quickeneth, and moveth. Builds high, higher, higher, into and with love. It is always in a higher sense because God has no lower means."

He wants us to go higher and higher. Oh, for a heavenly sight this morning, a divine touch of God, of Jesus. It is the divine touch! One touch of deity, one flash of light, one moment in the presence of Him, one touch of infinite, and united, it makes us mighty in a moment to see all things as He sees them.

TONGUES AND INTERPRETATION: "Oh, it is that which God hath for me, that I must never cease till I reach that which He has for me, for I must be for others as He wants me to be."

Oh, this divine, this virtue! It is eminently real, and we have no sense of its presence, and that is what I believe we ought to be in. There are so many things in the Scriptures that bring to my mind these things. You take, for instance, the sixth chapter of the Acts of the apostles, and you see Stephen, "A man full of faith and of the Holy Ghost."

And you take Barnabas and read of him. Barnabas was a good man filled with the Holy Ghost and faith. It seems to me that God has a plan through holiness that you cannot get into, that plan only by holiness. It seems there is a pure place, a pure heart where it sees God. There is a divine place of purity, where the unclean never put their feet.

But God has a way, it is called the way of holiness, and He can bring us into that place. He has a divine longing to bring us into that place where we hear the voice of God, we see the form of God, we understand the way of God, and we walk in communion with God. These are the places where divine virtue flows.

Once at a very late open air meeting, I was being pressed beyond measure, as it were. God was saving the people and I returned home. Oh, the joy of pointing people to Jesus! Oh, the joy of living in this life. There is a life which seems right to men, but oh, it isn't that life. There is a life which is only taken in and lived out, moved in by God alone.

When I went home, they said to me, "Aunt Mary is going home, and Uncle Sam would like you to see her before she bids farewell." I went down there, and not knowing anything, only as it were, "Goodbye." Only I was impressed as I neared the bed to stretch out my hand. Oh, that hand! What there is in a hand. What there is in a person by the power of God no one can tell. We must live in this, that God can see it through.

As my hand touched her hand, the divine virtue of heaven flowed through the death form conditions, and brought her into perfect life, perfect as ever she was, instantaneously brought back from death into life, and joy, and peace. Oh brothers, there is a virtue, there is a truth, God must manifest His power till everything we touch moves at the powers of God. Paul knew it, the apostles had a clear conception of it, Jesus spoke about it. The woman felt it as she touched Him in the skirts of His garment. The virtue went through.

Oh, if there is anything in the Scriptures that is moving me to understand, it is that there is a transmitting condition, there is a power that goes through the human body to another body. I see that it is in perfect conjunction with the Scriptures that we lay hands on the sick, and they shall recover.

There is a truth in John's gospel — oh, sometimes I think we have never understood it, but maybe God has revealed it to some of us, and I would like to give it to you this morning. John's gospel has many wonderful things to say to us. I will just turn to the third chapter of John and I will read from the eleventh verse:

> *Verily, verily, I say unto thee, We speak that we do know, and testify that we have seen; and ye receive not our witness. If I have told you earthly things, and ye believe not, how shall ye believe, if I tell you of heavenly things? And no man hath ascended up to heaven, but he that came down from heaven, even the Son of man which is in heaven.*
>
> *John 3:11-13*

Do you see there are three things there that we must clearly understand this morning. It is a privilege to everyone, a great truth. If I told you earthly things, and you cannot understand them, supposing I tell you heavenly things? He goes on, on this line of thought. Supposing you see the Son of man return unto the place from whence He came.

But here in this divine order, I wish you to see a great principle. He says, "If I have told you earthly things, and you cannot understand them, how will you understand if I tell you heavenly things?" He says, "The Son of man cometh down, the Son of man is down, the Son of man is up."

Now, you see that electric light there is only showing forth the brilliancy because of the dynamo. It has a receiver and transmitter. There you have the naked wires, but the power of the dynamo is sending forth through those naked wires brilliancy.

I want you to notice that in the glory there are all the powers of God. Every man who is born of God is receiving life from God. Inside the vessel is the bare wire with revelation, and all illumination, and in order to keep it perfect it is always returning from whence it came. It cometh down, it is down, and it is always the same. And so is everyone who is born of God. He is kept alive by a power which he cannot see but feel, which power is generated in the glory, and comes down into earthen vessels, and is received back to the throne of God.

And oh, all the time we are receiving and transmitting — just as we stop for a moment to place our hands upon a needy case, the supernatural goes through the case, and brings forth life. So God would have us know that there is a divine glory, a divine virtue, a perfect knowledge, an inward conception of an ideal which has always been made in the glory.

The Holy Ghost is the great incentive to us all. He receives all/He disburses all, and reechoes back the wonderful manifestations, after He has had the call. So we must have life in this glorious order of the Spirit, united, illuminated, transformed all the time by this glorious regenerating power of the Spirit of life of God.

May God open the door for us this morning to see that it is for us all, such a manifestation of the life and of the power of God, to be given us till there shall be neither barrenness nor unfruitfulness, but rather an unbending unto all His will. Oh, hallelujah!

TONGUES AND INTERPRETATION: "It is that which God has designed from the beginning. It is no new thing. It is as old as God. It lasts as long as eternity. We are, we shall be, forever with Him. He has created us for this purpose that we should be the sons of God with power, with promise, with life, for all the world."

Thank God for that interpretation.

Oh brothers, oh sisters, don't tell me that we have got the fulness. Oh, the fulness of the Spirit, an immeasurable measure! Oh, don't tell me there are any limitations of it. It comes in floods we cannot contain. I drink and drink and drink again, and still we yet are dry.

Oh saints of God, the more of this joy they get, the more they require, the more they desire. It is God in you that longs for all the fulness of God to come into you, praise His name. But we must be partakers of it.

I want you to see this morning that there are two words here that are closely connected together. Beautiful words, and they are full of need for this moment for us. Let me read them: "Through the knowledge of Him that hath called us to glory and virtue."

A lot of people have a great misunderstanding about glory. Glory is always an expression. Therefore there are of necessity three things that ought to take place in the baptism. In the baptism it was a necessity that the moving by the mighty rushing wind should be made manifest in the upper room. And then it was also of importance that they should be clothed with tongues as of fire. Then it should also be of importance that the body should receive not only the fire but also the rushing wind, the personality of the Spirit in the wind. The divine order is in the wind, and all the manifestation of the glory is in the wind.

Now let me express it. You see there is always this, the inward man receives the Holy Ghost with great joy and blessedness, instantly. He cannot express it. It is beyond His expression. Then the power of the Spirit, which is the Word — when you speak about words you say you heard so many words. I want you to notice when the Holy Ghost is in the body this divine power, this personality, this breath of God, takes of the things of Jesus, and utters them by this expressive wind and sends forth as a river the utterances of the Spirit.

Then again, when the body is filled with joy, sometimes it is so inexpressible, being thrown on the canvas of the mind, the canvas of the mind has great power to move the operation of the tongue to bring out the very depths of the inward hearts, power, love, joy, to us. By the same process the Spirit over all, which is the breath of God, brings forth the manifestation of the glory.

Sometimes when God speaks there is always a glory, it always comes. Peter speaks here about being in the Holy Mount, in Second Peter 1:16,17:

> *For we have not followed cunningly devised fables, when we made known unto you the power and coming of our Lord Jesus Christ, but were eyewitnesses of his majesty. For he received from God the Father honour and glory, when there came such a voice to him from the excellent glory....*

Sometimes people wonder how it is and why it is that the Holy Ghost is always expressing Himself in words. It cannot be otherwise. You couldn't understand it otherwise. You cannot understand God by shakings, and yet shakings may be in perfect order sometimes. There isn't any manifestation of the body — your shakings, your rollings, your jumpings, and all kinds of things which are allowed, are no manifestation of God. Only the utterances are manifestations of God. The others may be so mixed with the flesh and the Spirit, it would take a great deal of divine intuition and divine revelation to discriminate between the Spirit and flesh in those things.

But you can always tell when the Spirit moves, and brings forth the utterances. They are always the utterances that shall magnify God, and not waving of hands, not shakings of body. But the Holy Ghost has a perfect plan. He comes right through every man who is so filled, and brings divine utterances that we may understand what the mind of the Lord is.

Perhaps I might take you to three expressions in the Bible on this line. First of all I would take you to the ninth verse of the sixteenth Psalm. You notice all my addresses I give unto you are on inspiration. There is no preconception of things in my mind worked out for a meeting. I dare not do it. If I did it I would get out of the plan of God. I have to come to you with the bare Word of God, and expect the Holy Ghost to lighten it up.

I must read into my heart the perfect law of liberty, but if I came to you with a fixed arrangement of an address, the whole thing would be as natural as me. But I cannot afford to be natural. I can only afford to be supernatural now. I cannot afford to be anything less than being in the Holy Ghost order.

If I turn to any other plan then I am losing the unction, the power, the revelation, of what God has. When I come into the presence of God, He does take the things of the Spirit and reveals them to me. Our hearts are comforted and built up. And there is no way to warm a heart more than by the heart that first touched the flame. There must be the heavenly fire burnings, inward movings.

We are born of the Spirit, and nothing but the Spirit of God can feed that spiritual life. We must live in it, feed in it, walk in it, talk in it, sleep in it, hallelujah! We must always be in the Holy Ghost. "When I am awake, I am with thee. When I am asleep, my heart talketh."

There is a place in the Holy Ghost for man where God has him up in His place, and he is lost to every man, but he is never lost to God. God can find him any time He wants him. Oh, hallelujah!

I want you to turn to three Scriptures. I am now upon the glory I want to manifest today so that we may not be deceived about the glory.

"Therefore my heart is glad, and my glory rejoiceth..." (Psalm 16:9).

Now there is something that has made the rejoicing bring forth the glory. It was because his heart was glad. We will further turn to the 108th Psalm, and that will bring another side of it, first verse: "O God, my heart is fixed; I will sing and give praise, even with my glory."

So you see, glory is a manifestation of language. It is when the body is filled with the powers of God, then the only thing that can express the glory is the tongue. And God has given us the tongue that we can express the glory, the glory of God.

Glory is not halo. It is presence, and the presence always comes by the tongue which brings forth the revelations of God. You find in Acts also another side to this. We read in Acts 2:25,26:

> *For David speaketh concerning him, I foresaw the Lord always before my face, for he is on my right hand, that I should not be moved: Therefore did my heart rejoice, and my tongue was glad....*

You will always find that God works on these lines. God first brings into us His power, then He gives us verbal expressions by the same Spirit of the moving within us to bring the manifestation out of us just as it is within us. Therefore, "...out of the abundance of the heart the mouth speaketh" (Matthew 12:34).

What is all this about this morning? I want you to notice this, that virtue and glory will be inexpressible conditions sometimes. You will find out that virtue has to be transmitted, and you will find out that glory has to be expressed. And so God, by filling us with the Holy Ghost, has brought into us this which He has in the glory, that out of us may come forth that which He has in the glory. And everything He has in the glory the Holy Ghost — the Holy Ghost understands the latest things, and brings through the heart of a man that is filled with God the latest thought.

The world's needs, our manifestations, revivals, all conditions, are first settled in heaven, then worked out on the earth. So we must be in touch with God Almighty to bring out on the face of the earth all the things that God has in the heavens. This is an ideal for us, and God help us not to forsake the sense of holy communion, entering into the closet in privacy, that publicly He may manifest His glory.

We must see the face of the Lord. We must understand the workings of the Lord. There are things that God says to me that I know must take place. It doesn't matter what people say. I have been face to face with some of the most trying moments of men's lives when it meant so much to me if I kept the vision, and if I held fast to that which God had said.

A man must be in an immovable condition. The voice of God must mean to him more than what he sees, feels, or what people say. He must have an originality born in heaven, transmitted by tongues, or expressed in some way. We must bring heaven to earth. God has us for that purpose. Turn again to 2 Peter 1:4:

> "Whereby are given unto us exceeding great and precious promises: that by these ye might be partakers of the divine nature, having escaped the corruption that is in the world through lust."

We must enter into this because we have to be partakers of His divine nature. Turn to the eighth of Romans for one verse. There is a law there that God wants us to understand, it is a law of the Spirit of life. You see, there are two laws, but the law of the Spirit of life in Christ Jesus is different from the law of sin and death. One is that which looks on the divine principles which makes me know that I am free.

Now let me turn to that law of life of the Spirit, unto this Word for a moment. This same life which is the law of the Spirit of life, must bring us into the same attitude of being partakers of His divine nature. You see, it is a divine life. I have two lives. I have a spiritual life and I have a natural life.

And I hope no one will ever be so foolish in this meeting as to believe the natural life is done away with. You will always have it as long as you are here. It may be there for great advantages. For instance, I thank God for my natural life this morning which has moved me and helped me to dress myself. I thank God for the natural life which has brought us here. It is the natural body that brought your spiritual perception into a holy meeting, and your natural body is necessary to bring you to a place where you can feed your spiritual desires.

But we must understand the natural matter has only to play out a certain plan, and it is always to be for the advancement of the Spirit of the living God to have control of our bodies. The spiritual life is so mighty in all its branches to bring to death the natural man till the man when it is brought to a place of real death, the righteousness of the Spirit of the life of God can so permeate the whole body till the virtues of Christ are as much in His fingers as in His hand. It is the divine life, the divine virtue of our Lord Jesus Christ.

And then while we walk about it is truly true that we have no desire for the world, because our desires are greater than the world. You cannot fascinate a man of God with gold, or houses, or lands. We seek a country, a city which hands have not made, eternal in the heavens. And if this mortal body shall be put off, the heavenly body shall be put on. And we are waiting and longing with an expression, with an inward joy, with a great leap of life, waiting to jump into that.

TONGUES AND INTERPRETATION: "He has designed the plan. He has the unfolding of the purpose. He is the grandeur of the principles. He lays the foundation of the spiritual life, quickened always by His own life, for He is our life, and when He shall appear we shall be like Him. He shall appear!"

Beloved, there is a longing in the soul, there is a travail in the spirit, there is a yielding of the will, there is the blending of the life which only gives utterances as He wishes. And this morning, I believe God the Holy Ghost is bringing us to a longing for these utterances in the Spirit.

Oh, this is a lovely verse. See, there is so much depth in it for us. Oh, but it is all real from heaven. It is as divinely appointed for this meeting as when the Holy Ghost was upon Peter, and He brings it out for us. I will read it again for it is to me life, marrow. To me it is like the breath. It moves me. I must live in this grace.

"According as his divine power," there it is again, "hath given unto us all things that pertain unto life and godliness." Oh, what wonderful things He has given us, "through the knowledge of him that hath called us to glory and virtue."

You cannot get away from Him. He is the center of all things. He moves the earth, transforms beings, can live in every mind, plan every thought. Oh, He is there all the time.

"Through the knowledge of him that hath called us to glory and virtue: Whereby are given unto us exceeding great and precious promises...."

The Holy Ghost has only language — there is no language on the earth, no man can form language, it takes the Holy Ghost to form language. You will find if you go to the epistle, when Paul has finished, he is full of the might of the Spirit, the Spirit breathing through him. And yet he comes to a place where he feels he must stop. For there are greater things than he can even utter only by the oratory coming forth on the line of prayer. Prayer, the breath of the Almighty breathing through the human soul. There He breathes through Paul.

You find in the last of Ephesians 3, three words which no human man could ever think, no human man could ever plan with pen and ink, so mighty, so of God when it speaks about being able to do all things, greater things, more than you can ask, abundantly more, "exceeding abundantly above all that we ask or think."

The mighty God of revelation through a man! There the Holy Ghost gave these words of grandeur to stir our hearts, to move our affections to transform us altogether. This is ideal! This is God. Shall we teach them? Shall we have them? Oh, they are ours. Will they remain ours? Oh, brother, God has never put anything over on a pole you could not reach. God has brought His plan down to man, and if we are prepared this morning, oh, what there is!

I feel sometimes we have just as much as we can digest, yet there are such divine nuggets of precious truth held before our hearts, so full that it makes you understand that there are yet heights, and depths, and lengths, and breadths of the knowledge of God that God hath laid up for us. Oh brother, we might truly say,

> "My heavenly bank, my heavenly bank,
> The house of God's treasure and store.
> I have plenty in here, I'm a real millionaire."

Glory, it is all in here. Never to be poverty struck anymore. An inward knowledge of an unfolding of a greater bank than ever the Rothchild's or any other child ever knew about. There it is stored up, nugget upon nugget, weights of glory, expression of the countenance of the invisible Christ to be seen.

God is shaking the earth, and the foundations of all nationalities and making us all the time to understand that there is a principle in the Scriptures that may bring to man that which frees him from the natural order of every institution, and brings him unto a place of holiness, righteousness, and peace of God which passeth all human understanding. We must touch it. We must reach it. Praise God!

One thing is certain. God has brought us in on purpose to take us on. God has brought us here this morning, and you say, "How shall I be able to get all these things that are laid up for me?" Brother, sister, I know no other way. A broken and a contrite heart God will not despise.

A man said to me last night, "Don't you think I am baptized with the Holy Ghost?" I said, "I don't know anything about you." "I am willing," he said, "for anything." Then I knew he was not baptized. I never saw a man willing for everything and anything that got anything. The man that gets anything is the man who goes after one thing. "One thing have I desired of the Lord, that will I seek after...." (Psalm 27:4). Whatever you want, make it one thing and get it.

What do you want this morning? Make it one thing. You know better than I what you want, and God knows what you want, and that one thing you require is for you this morning. May God help you to move from your seats where you are and get that one thing. Set it in your mind you will know this morning the powers of the world to come, and you will see, for truly when Daniel set his mind to get all the things which were provided, God gave an abundance of other things which have not yet been fulfilled.

So I ask you this morning one thing, "Ask, and it shall be given you; seek, and ye shall find; knock, and it shall be opened unto you: For every one that asketh receiveth; and he that seeketh findeth; and to him that knocketh it shall be opened" (Matthew 7:7,8).

May God help you to take your own course, to do as the Spirit leads you, and we will leave the meeting in the hands of God.

Message given at Glad Tidings Tabernacle and Bible Training School
San Francisco, California

 want to speak to you this morning from the fourth chapter of
Ephesians. We will begin reading from the first verse:

OUR CALLING
Part 1
August 18, 1922

*I therefore, the prisoner of the Lord,
beseech you that ye walk worthy of the
vocation wherewith ye are called, With all lowliness and meekness, with longsuffering, forbearing one another in love; Endeavoring to keep the unity of the Spirit in the bond of peace. There is
one body, and one Spirit, even as ye are called in one hope of your
calling; One Lord, one faith, one baptism, One God and Father*

of all, who is above all, and through all, and in you all. But unto every one of us is given grace according to the measure of the gift of Christ. Wherefore he saith, When he ascended up on high, he led captivity captive, and gave gifts unto men. (Now that he ascended, what is it but that he also descended first into the lower parts of the earth? He that descended is the same also that ascended up far above all heavens, that he might fill all things.) And he gave some, apostles; and some, prophets; and some, evangelists; and some, pastors and teachers; For the perfecting of the saints, for the work of the ministry, for the edifying of the body of Christ: Till we all come in the unity of the faith, and of the knowledge of the Son of God, unto a perfect man, unto the measure of the stature of the fulness of Christ.

Ephesians 4:1-13

Beloved, we have for several mornings been speaking concerning the gifts. And I believe that the Lord would have us this morning further consider another side of the gifts. I shall be more or less speaking to preachers, and to those who desire to be preachers. I would like to utter those same words Paul utters in 1 Corinthians 14:5:

I would that ye all spake with tongues, but rather that ye prophesied....

I believe there is no way to make proclamation but by the Spirit. And I believe that they that are sent are called and chosen of God to be sent. And so as we go forth into this chapter, I trust that everyone will understand what his vocation is in the Spirit, and what the Lord demands of us as preachers.

We should be able in the face of God and the presence of His people to behave ourselves so comely and pleasing to the Lord that we always leave behind us a life of blessing and power without gendering strife.

It is a great choice to become a preacher of the Gospel, to handle the Word of life. We that handle the Word of life ought to be well built on the lines of common sense, judgment, and not given to anything which is contrary to the Word of God. There should be in us all the time such deep reverence towards God and His Word that under all circumstances we would not forfeit our principles on the lines of faith that God had revealed unto us by the truth.

Today I believe God will show us how wonderful we may be in the order of the Spirit for God wants us to be always in the Spirit so rightly dividing the Word of truth that all who hear it shall be like strength to weakness. It shall bring oil to the troubled heart. It shall bring rest. The Word of God shall make us know that having done all we may stand in the trial.

God would have us to know that there is strength by the power of the Spirit, of an equipment of character to bring us into like-mindedness with the Lord. We must know to be baptized in the Holy Ghost is to leave your own life, as it were, out of all questioning; leave yourself out of all pleasing, and in the name of Jesus come into like-mindedness.

How He pleased God! How He brought heaven to earth, and all earth moved at the mightiness of the presence of heaven in the midst. We must see our vocation in the Spirit, for God hath chosen us. We must remember that it is a great choice. Turning to the tenth chapter of Romans, we read:

> *And how shall they preach, except they be sent? ...How beautiful are the feet of them that preach the gospel of peace, and bring glad tidings of good things!*
>
> *Romans 10:15*

We want to be sent. It is a great thing to be called of God to preach the unsearchable riches of Christ. You have in this land, and we have in our land, men of note and of authority, who are looked to on the lines of socialistic problems. I often think that Lloyd George has a wonderful time but not a time like a preacher. He only preaches of natural sources but the man who handles the Word of God preaches life immortality that swallows up life. When we come into this blessed life we know we are teaching principles and ideals which are for life eternal.

God has given to us in the Spirit, and behold, we are spiritual children today, and we must know that we have to be spiritual all the time. God forbid that we should ever be like the Galatian church, after we have been in the Spirit, we could come in the flesh. You are allowed to go into the Spirit but you are never allowed to come in the flesh after you have been in the Spirit.

And so God gives such an idea of this high order in the Spirit that we may be moved by its power to see how we may change strength and come into all the line of faith in God. Let me turn to the first verse of this wonderful fourth chapter of Ephesians:

> *I therefore, the prisoner of the Lord, beseech you that ye walk worthy of the vocation wherewith ye are called.*

Here is Paul in prison. If I can take a word from anybody, I can take it from anyone who is in prison. I have never read a book but the Bible, but there are some things I have read out of *Pilgrims Progress* which have helped me very much. It was when he was in prison that God wakened him on so many wonderful lines of thought. How Paul must have read the Word right in the hearts of those who came and went when he was bound with chains for two full years. He could speak about a fulness, freedom, power, and joy although he was bound with chains.

My brothers, there is something in the Gospel different from anything else. And if these men could go through such hardships — read the first epistle of Peter and you will see how they were scattered. God says that the world wasn't worthy of such material as God was filling with His power that were in dens and caves of the earth.

Oh, brother and sister, there have been some wonderful gems passed through the world touched by the Master's hand. There have been some wonderful men in the world who have caught the glory as the rays have shone from His lips by the power of His expression. As they beheld Him they have been fascinated with Him. And I can fairly see as Peter drew near the time of his departure, as Jesus said:

> *...When thou wast young, thou girdedst thyself, and walkedst whither thou wouldest: but when thou shalt be old, thou shalt stretch forth thy hands, and another shall gird thee, and carry thee whither thou wouldest not.*
>
> *John 21:18*

And as Peter drew near to the portals of glory, he wished to die with his head downwards. My word! What grace incarnated in a human casket that it should have such ideals of worship.

Oh, beloved, God is a real essence of joy to us in a time when it seems barrenness, when it seems nothing can help us but the light from heaven far above the brightness of the sun. Then that touches you, then that changes you, and you realize nothing is worthwhile but that.

How he speaks to us when he is in prison, about "the vocation wherewith ye are called, with all lowliness and meekness" (Ephesians 4:1,2). He speaks unto the preacher. Let no person in this place think that he cannot become a preacher. Let none think he cannot reach this ideal of lowliness and meekness. God can bring us there.

Some preachers get an idea that nobody ought to say a word till they are established. I like to hear the bleating of the lambs. I like to hear the life of the young believer. I like to hear something coming right from heaven into the soul as they rise the first time with tears coming down their eyes, telling of the love of Jesus.

The Holy Ghost fell upon a young man outside a church. He went into the church where they were all so sedate. If anything had to move in that church out of the ordinary, my word! It would be extraordinary. And this young man with his fulness of life and zeal for the Master got into ejaculating and praising the Lord, and making manifest the joy of the Lord, and he disturbed the old saints.

An old man one day was reading the Psalms quietly. It touched a young man sitting behind him who was filled with the Holy Ghost. And the young man shouted, "Glory!" Said the old man, "Do you call that religion?"

The father of the young man to whom we referred was one of the deacons of the church. The other deacons got round him and said, "You must talk to your boy, and give him to understand that he has to wait till he is established before he manifests those things."

So his father had a long talk with the boy, and told him what the deacons said. "You know," he said, "I must respect the deacons, and they have told me they won't hate this thing. You have to wait till you are established."

As they neared their home their horse made a full stop. He tried to make it go forward and back but the horse would not move for anything.

"What is up with the horse?" asked the father of the son. "Father," replied the boy, "this horse has got established."

I pray God the Holy Ghost that we will not get established in that way. God, loose us up from these old, critical, long-faced, poisoned kind of countenances, which haven't seen daylight for many days. They come into the sanctuary and are in a terrible way. May the Lord save Pentecost from going to dry rot. Yea, deliver us from any line of sentimentality, anything which is not reality. For remember, we must have reality of supernatural quickening till we are sane and active, and not in any way dormant, but filled with life, God working in us mightily by His Spirit.

We must always be on the transforming position, not on the conforming condition, always renewing the mind, always renovated by the mighty thoughts of God, always being brought into line with that which God has said to us by the Spirit, "This is the way, walk ye in it." "Walk in the Spirit, and ye shall not fulfill the lusts of the flesh."

Lord, how shall we do it? Can a man be meek and lowly, and filled with joy? Do they work together? "Out of the abundance of the heart the mouth speaketh." The depths of God come in, in lowliness and meekness and make the heart love. There is no heart can love like the heart that God has touched.

Oh, that love that is made to love the sinner! There is no love like it. I always feel I can spend any time with the sinner. Oh, brother, there is a love which is God's love! There is a love which only comes by the principles of the Word of God. "He loved us and gave Himself for us."

When that meekness and lowliness of mind take hold, the preacher is moved by His Creator to speak from heart to heart and move the people. For without we are moved by an inward power and ideal of principles, we are never worth. We must have ideals which come from the throne of God. We must live in the throne, live on the throne, and let Him be enthroned, and then He will lift us to the throne.

TONGUES AND INTERPRETATION: "Out of the depths He has called us, into the heights He has brought us, unto the uttermost He has saved us to make us kings and priests unto God. For we are His property, His own, His loved ones. Therefore He wants to clothe us upon, with the gifts of the Spirit, and make us worthy for His ministry."

Glory to God! Thank the Lord!

"With all lowliness and meekness, with longsuffering, forbearing one another in love" (Ephesians 4:2).

Oh, how it is needed, "forbearing one another in love." Oh, how this is contrary to hardness of heart; how this is contrary to the evil powers; how this is contrary to the natural mind. It is a divine revelation, and you cannot forbear till you know how He has been with you in the same thing. It is God's love toward you that makes tender, compassionate love one toward another.

It is only the broken, contrite heart which has received the mark of God. It is only those in that secluded place where He speaks to thee alone, and encourages thee when thou art down and out, and when no hand is stretched out to thee, He stretches out His hand with mercy and brings thee into a place of compassion. And now, you cannot think evil; now you cannot in any way act hard. God has brought you into long-suffering, with tenderness, with love.

Oh, this love, brother! Many a time my two brothers have been under conviction and have wept under conviction as I have tried to bring them into the light. But up till now neither of them is in the light. I believe God will bring them.

In the church of God, where a soul is on fire, kindled with the love of God, there is a deeper love between me and that brother than there is between me and my earthly brother. Oh, this love that I am speaking about is divine love, it is not human love. It is higher than human love, it is more devoted to God. It will not betray. It is true in everything. You can depend upon it. It won't change its character. It will be exactly as He would act for you will act with the same spirit, for as He is so are ye in this world.

As you rise into association with Him in the Spirit, as you walk with Him in the light as He is in the Light, then the fellowship becomes unique in all its plan. I pray God that He will help us to understand it that we shall be able to put off and put on. We shall be able to be clothed upon as we have never been, with another majestic touch, with another ideal of heaven.

No one can love like God. And when He takes us into this divine love we shall exactly understand this Word, this verse, for it is full of entreaty, it is full of passion and compassion, it has every touch of Jesus right in it. It is so lovely:

"With all lowliness and meekness, with longsuffering, forbearing one another in love."

Isn't it glorious? You cannot find it anywhere else. You cannot get these pictures in any place you go to. I challenge you to go into any library in the world and find words coined or brought forth like these words, without they are copied from this Word. It isn't in nature's garden, it is in God's. It is the Spirit explaining, for He alone can explain this ideal of beatitudes. They are marvelous, they are beautiful, they are full of grandeur, they are God's. Hallelujah!

I hope you are having a good time, for it is just filling me with new wine this morning. Oh, it is lovely!

"Endeavouring to keep the unity of the Spirit in the bond of peace" (Ephesians 4:3).

This is one of the main principles of this chapter. Beloved, let us keep in mind this very thought today. I am speaking this morning, by the grace of God, to the preacher. It should never be known that any preacher caused any distraction, or detraction, or any split, or disunion in a meeting. The preacher has lost his unction and his glory if he ever stoops to anything that would weaken the assembly in any way.

The greatest weakness of any preacher is to draw men to himself. It is a fascinating point, but you must be away from fascination. If you don't crucify your "old man" on every line, you are not going into divine lines with God. When they wanted to make Jesus king, He withdrew Himself to pray. Why? It was a human desire of the people. What did He want? His Kingdom was a spiritual Kingdom. He was to reign over demon powers. He was to have power over the passions of human life. He was to reign so supremely over everything which is earthly, that all the people might know He was divine.

He is our pattern, beloved. When they want to make anything of us, He will give you grace to refuse it. The way to get out is to find there is

"Be not afraid to ask, because God is on the throne
waiting to answer your request."

nothing in the earth which is worthy of Him; that there is no one in the world who is able to understand but He; that everything will crumble to the dust and become worthless. Only that which is divine will last.

Every time you draw anyone to yourself it has a touch of earth. It does not speak of the highest realm of thought of God. There is something about it which cannot bear the light of the Word of God. Keep men's eyes off you, but get their eyes on the Lord. Live in the world without a touch or taint of any natural thing moving you. Live high in the order and authority of God, and see that everything is bearing you on to greater heights and depths and greater knowledge of the love of God.

You will help any assembly you go to, and everybody will get a blessing and will see how much richer they are because you brought them Jesus. Only Jesus! And He is too big for any assembly, and He is little enough to fill every heart. We will always go on to learn of Him. Whatever we know, the knowledge is so small to what He has to give us. And so God's plan for us in giving us Jesus, is all things, for all things consist in Him.

"All things were made by him; and without him was not any thing made that was made" (John 1:3).

"...in him we live, and move, and have our being..." (Acts 17:28).

And when it is a spiritual being and an activity of holiness, see how wonderfully we grow in the Lord. Oh, it is just lovely!

TONGUES AND INTERPRETATION: "Yea, it is the Lord Himself. He comes forth clothed upon to clothe thee in thy weakness, to strengthen thee in thy helplessness, to uphold thee in the limitation of thy knowledge, to unfold the mysteries of the Kingdom in the dire straits where two ways meet, and you know not where to go. He says, 'This is the way.' When thou art in such a straitened place that no hand but God is able to lead thee out, then He comes to thee and says, 'Be strong and fear not, for I am with thee.'"

Hallelujah! Praise the Lord of glory! He is the everlasting King, and will reign forever and ever and ever. Glory! Glory! Amen!

TONGUES AND INTERPRETATION: "God has spoken and He will make it clear, for He is in the midst of thee to open out thy mind and reveal unto thee all the mysteries of the Kingdom, for the God of grace is with thee. For God is greater than all unto thee. He is making thy way straight before thee, for the Lord is He that comforteth thee as He comforted Israel, and will lead thee into His power, for His right hand is with thee to keep thee in all thy ways lest thou shouldst dash thy foot against a stone, for the Lord will uphold thee."

How beautiful is the Scripture coming to us this morning! How lively it appears to us! And now we can understand something about the fourteenth chapter of First Corinthians:

> *...I will pray with the spirit, and I will pray with the understanding also: I will sing with the spirit, and I will sing with the understanding also.*
>
> *Verse 15*

So God is bringing us right into the fulness of the Pentecostal power as given in the first days. God wants us to know that after we have been brought into this divine life with Christ, we are able to speak in the Spirit, and we are able to sing in the Spirit; we are able to speak with the understanding, and sing with the understanding also. Ah, hallelujah this good day!

I think I ought to say a few more words concerning: "Endeavouring to keep the unity of the Spirit in the bond of peace" (Ephesians 4:3).

Beloved, I want you, above all things, to remember that the church is one body. She has many members, and we are all members of that one body. At any cost we must not break up the body but rather keep the body in perfect unity. Never try to get the applause of the people by any natural thing. Yours is a spiritual work. Yours has to be a spiritual breath. Your word has to be the Word of God. Your counsel to the church has to be so that it cannot be gainsaid. You have to have such solid, holy reverence on every line so that every time you handle anybody you handle them for God, and you handle the church as the church of God. By that means you keep the church bound together.

As the church is bound together in one Spirit, they grow into that temple in the Lord, and they all have one voice, one desire, and one plan. And when they want souls saved, they are all of one mind. I am speaking now about spiritual power. You get them into the mind of the Spirit with Christ, and all their desires will be the same desires of Christ the Head. And so nothing can break the church on those lines.

As preachers you must never try to save yourself on any line. You must always be above mentioning a financial matter on your side. Always before God in the secret place mention your need, but never bring it to an assembly; if you do, you drop in the estimation of the assembly. You are allowed to tell any need belonging to the assembly or the church management, but on a personal line never refer to yourself on the platform.

If you preach faith you must live it, and a man is not supposed to preach without he preach a living faith. And he must so impress it upon the people that they will always know God has taken us on for a special plan, and that we are not ordinary men. After we are called of God and chosen for Him, we are not again to have ordinary men's plans. We ought to have ideals of God only.

Another thing which I think is perhaps more essential to you than anything else: you preachers, never drop into an assembly and say the Lord sent you, because sometimes the assembly has as much on as she can manage. But it is right for you to get your orders from heaven, and for God to switch the same order somewhere else that will make the first call and you will be dropping into the call. Never make a call without you are really sent. Be sure you are sent of God.

Brothers, can you be out of God's will when you hear His voice? "My sheep hear My voice, and they follow Me." Oh, that God today shall help us by the mind of the Spirit to understand. I believe God has a message on fire. He has men clothed by God. He has men sent by God. Will you be the men? Will you be the women?

You ask, "Can I be the man? Can I be the woman?" Yes, God says, "Many are called, but few are chosen." Are you the chosen ones? Those who desire to be chosen, will you allow God to choose you? Then He will put His hand upon you. And in the choice He will give you wisdom, He will lead you forth, He will stand by you in the straitened corner, He will lead you every step of the way, for the Lord's anointed shall go forth and bring forth fruit, and their fruit shall remain.

TONGUES AND INTERPRETATION: "Behold, now is the day of decision. Yield now while the moment of pressure by the presence of God comes. Yield now and make your consecration to God."

The altar is ready now for all who will obey.

Message given at Glad Tidings Tabernacle and Bible Training School
San Francisco, California

TONGUES AND INTERPRETATION: "The Lord is that Spirit that moves in the regenerated, and brings us to the place where fire can begin and burn, and separate, and transform, and make you all know that God has made an inroad into every order. Because we have to be divine, spiritual, changed, and on fire to catch all the rays of His life, first, burning out; second, transforming; and third, making you fit to live or die."

OUR CALLING
Part 2
August 22, 1922

Oh, thank God for that interpretation.

I want to turn your attention again to the fourth chapter of Ephesians, to continue our subject of last week. I will read from the first verse:

> *I therefore, the prisoner of the Lord, beseech you that ye walk worthy of the vocation wherewith ye are called, With all lowliness and meekness, with longsuffering, forbearing one another in love; Endeavoring to keep the unity of the Spirit in the bond of peace. There is one body, and one Spirit, even as ye are called in one hope of your calling; One Lord, one faith, one baptism. One God and Father of all, who is above all, and through all, and in you all. But unto every one of us is given grace according to the measure of the gift of Christ. Wherefore he saith, When he ascended up on high, he led captivity captive, and gave gifts unto men. (Now that he ascended, what is it but that he also descended first into the lower parts of the earth? He that descended is the same also*

that ascended up far above all heavens, that he might fill all things.) And he gave some, apostles; and some, prophets; and some, evangelists; and some, pastors and teachers; For the perfecting of the saints, for the work of the ministry, for the edifying of the body of Christ: Till we all come in the unity of the faith, and of the knowledge of the Son of God, unto a perfect man, unto the measure of the stature of the fulness of Christ.

Ephesians 4:1-13

I believe the Lord, this morning as on the last morning, especially wants me to emphasize facts which will be a blessing and a strengthening to the preachers. If there is anything of importance it is to the preachers because God must have us in the place of building and edifying the Church. And we must be in that order of the Spirit that God can work through us for the needs of the Church.

As it was only out of the brokenness of Paul's life that blessing came forth, so it is out of the emptiness, and brokenness, and yieldedness of our lives that God can bring forth all His glories through us to others. And as our brother said this morning on the platform, except we pass on what we receive we shall lose it. If we didn't lose it, it would become stagnant.

Virtue is always manifested through blessing which you have passed on. Nothing will be of any importance to you except that which you pass on to others. So God wants us to be so in the order of the Spirit that when He breaks upon us the alabaster box of ointments of His precious anointing which He has for every child of His, He wants us to be filled with perfumes of holy incense that we may be poured out for others and that others may receive the graces of the Spirit, and all the church may be edified. And there shall never be known in Glad Tidings Tabernacle one dry day, but there shall always be freshness and life which makes all hearts burn together as you know the Lord has talked with you once more.

We must have this inward burning desire for more of God. We must not be at any stationary point. We must always have the highest power telescopes looking and hasting unto that which God has called us to that He may perfect that forever.

Oh, what a blessed inheritance of the Spirit God has for us in these days, that we should be no longer barren, nor unfruitful, but rather filled with all fulness, unlimited, increasing with all increasings, with a measureless measure of the might of the Spirit in the inner man, so that we are always like a great river pressing on and healing everything that it touches. Oh, let it be so today!

TONGUES AND INTERPRETATION: "The Lord has awakened in us the divine touches of His spiritual favor to make us know He is here with all you require if you are ready to take it."

But are we ready to take it? If we are, then God can give us wonderful things. We must be always in that hunger ready for every touch of God. Last week you remember we were dwelling on verse three: "Endeavouring to keep the unity of the Spirit in the bond of peace."

It was a very precious word to us because it meant that under any circumstances we would not have our way but God's way. We have it for the person and for the Church.

Whatever God means us to be, He means us to be peacemakers. Yes, love without alloy; that which, always at its own expense, goes to help another and pays the price for it. I shall not find a Scripture which will help me so much on this line as Matthew 5:23,24:

> *Therefore if thou bring thy gift to the altar, and there rememberest that thy brother hath aught against thee;*
>
> *Leave there thy gift before the altar, and go thy way; first be reconciled to thy brother, and then come and offer thy gift.*

Most Christians are satisfied with the first line of it, but the second line is deeper. Most people believe it is perfectly right if you have offended another, to go to that one and say, "Please forgive me," and you gain your brother when you take that part. But this is a deeper sense: "If thou...rememberest that thy brother hath ought against thee," go forgive him his transgressions. It is so much deeper than getting your own side right, to go and get their side right by forgiving them all they have done.

That will be a stepping stone to very rich grace on the line of "keeping the unity of the Spirit in the bond of peace." Someone says, "I cannot forgive her because she did that, and the brother said that. You know the brother didn't recognize me at all. And he has never smiled at me for at least six months." Poor thing! God help you through evil report and good report. God can take us right through if we get to the right side of grace.

My brother, when you get to the place of forgiving your brother who hath ought against you, you will find that is the greatest ideal of going on to perfection, and the Lord will help us "to keep the unity of the Spirit in the bond of peace."

I like that "bond of peace." It is an inward bond between you and the child of God. "Bond of peace." Hallelujah! Oh, glory to God!

> *There is one body, and one Spirit, even as ye are called in one hope of your calling.*
>
> Ephesians 4:4

We must recognize there is only one body. It seems to me that God would at one time have made such an inroad into all nations on the lines of the truth through the Plymouth brethren, if they had only recognized that there was more in the body than just the Plymouth brethren. You will never gain interest without you see that in every church there will be a nucleus which has as real a God as you have.

It is only on these lines I believe that the longsuffering of God waiteth for the precious fruit. And the longsuffering of God is with the believers who have an idea that only those in Glad Tidings Hall are right, or those in Oakland, or those in England. It is all foolishness.

Fancy people sitting round the table and reckoning that that table is the only table. What about hundreds of people I know who are sitting round the table every day and taking the bread and the wine? Brother, the body of Christ consists of all who are in Christ.

While we know the Holy Ghost is the only power that can take the Church up, we know the Holy Ghost will go with the Church. The Scriptures are very definite in saying that all that are Christ's at His coming will be changed. It doesn't seem to be that we can be all Christ's without something is done, and God will sweep away so many things which are spoiling things. We must get to perfect love, and we will see that God can make even those in Caesar's household our souls, glory to God!

TONGUES AND INTERPRETATION: "It is the Spirit that joins us and makes us one. It is the health of the Spirit that goes through the body that quickens the body and makes it appear as one."

Oh, the body appearing as one body! The same joy, the same peace, the same hope! No division, all one in Christ! What a body! Who can make a body like that? Seems to me that this body is made deep in the cross. Hundreds of people are carrying a cross on watch guard, or around their necks. I could never carry a cross, He has carried the cross, He has borne the shame. I find right there in that atoning blood there is cleansing and purifying, and taking away every dross, and everything that will mar the vessel, and He is making a vessel unto honor fit for the Master's use, joined up in that body, one body.

Let us be careful that we do not in any way defile the body because God is chastening the body and fitly framing it and bringing it together. The body of Christ will rise. You ask, "How will it rise?" It will rise in millions, and billions, and trillions, more than any man can number. It will be a perfect body.

Oh, there is one body! Ah, it is a lovely body. I look at you, I see you. I look in your faces and I know there is a closer association than one can tell or speak about. Oh, brother, there is something deeper down in the spirit of the regenerated person when the dross of life and the flesh falls off.

Oh, there will be a similitude, a likeness, a perfection of holiness, of love! Oh God, take away the rudiments, the weaknesses, all the depravities.

"Now ye are the body of Christ, and members in particular" (1 Corinthians 12:27).

I like the word, particular, meaning to say there is just the right place for us. God sees us in that place. He is making us fit in that place so that for all time we shall have a wonderful place in that body. Ah, it is so lovely!

Oh, these exhaustless things! Brothers, sisters, it isn't the message, it is the heart. It isn't the heart, it is the Christ. It isn't the Christ, it is the

God. It isn't the God, it is the whole Body. Deeper and more precious than we have any conception of!

> *There is one body, and one Spirit, even as ye are called in one hope of your calling.*
>
> *Ephesians 4:4*

I feel that God would have me say a word about the calling. Many people get called and they have missed because they are dull of hearing. There is something in the call, beloved. "Many are called, but few are chosen." I want a big heart this morning to believe that all shall be chosen. You ask, "Can it be so?" Yes, beloved, it can, not few chosen, but many chosen.

And how shall the choice be? The choice is always your choice first. You will find that gifts are your choice first. You will find that salvation is your choice. God has made it all but you have to choose. And so God wants you especially this morning to make an inward call, to have a great intercessory condition of beseeching the Holy One to prepare you for that wonderful mystical Body.

Called! Beloved, I know some people have an idea (and it is a great mistake), because they are not successful in everything they touch, because they have failed in so many things they have been desirous to go forward in, because they don't seem to aspire in prayer as some, and perhaps don't enter into the fulness of tongues, that there is no hope for them in this calling.

Satan comes and says, "Look at that black catalogue of helpless infirmities! You never expect to be in that calling!" Yes, you can, brother! God has it in the Scriptures. Oh, my brother, it is the weakness made strong! It is the last that can be made first. What will make the whole different? When we confess our helplessness. He says He feeds the hungry with good things, but the satisfied He sends away empty.

If you want to grow in grace and in the knowledge of the grace of God, get hungry enough to be fed, be thirsty enough to cry, be broken enough you cannot have anything in the world without He comes Himself. I was reading last night in my Bible, it was so lovely, "And God shall wipe away all tears from their eyes..." (Revelation 21:4).

Ah, you say, that will be there. Thank God there are two "theres." Hallelujah! Let God do it this morning. Let Him wipe away all tears. Let Him comfort thy heart. Let Him strengthen thy weakness. Let Him cause thee to come into the place of profit. Let Him help thee into the place God has chosen for thee, for "many are called, but few are chosen." But God has a big choice.

He is a big Jesus! If I could measure Him I would be very small. But I cannot measure Him, and I know He is very large. I am glad I cannot measure Jesus but I am glad I can touch Him all the same. The fifth verse:

> *One Lord, one faith, one baptism.*
>
> *Ephesians 4:5*

I must touch the thought of baptism this morning. We must get away from the thought of water baptism when we are in the epistles. If water baptism is at all mentioned in any way, it is always mentioned as a past tense. We must always remember this, beloved, that while water baptism, in my opinion, is essential, "He that believeth, and is baptized, shall be saved." I wouldn't say for a moment a man could not be saved without he was baptized in water, because it would be contrary to Scripture. Yet I see there is a blending. If we turn to the third chapter of John's gospel we find:

> *...Except a man be born of water and of the Spirit, he cannot enter into the kingdom of God.*
>
> *John 3:5b*

I believe God would have us to know that we never ought to put aside water baptism, but believe it is in perfect conjunction and in operation with the working of the Spirit that we may be buried with Him.

But oh, the baptism in the Holy Ghost! The baptism of fire! The baptism of power! The baptism of oneness! The baptism of association! The baptism of communion! The baptism of the Spirit of life which takes the man, shakes him through, builds him up, and makes him know he is a new creature in the Spirit, worshipping God in the Spirit.

If my preaching and the preaching of those who come on this platform emphasizes the facts of being baptized with the Holy Ghost, and you only have touches of it, if you stop at that, you will be almost as though you were missing the calling. John said by the Spirit:

...He that cometh after me is preferred before me....

John 1:15

I indeed baptize you with water unto repentance: but he that cometh after me is mightier than I...he shall baptize you with the Holy Ghost, and with fire.

Matthew 3:11

By all means if you can tarry, you ought to tarry. If you have the Spirit's power upon you, go into that room or somewhere else and never cease till God finishes the work. Outside the Pentecostal church where there isn't a revival spirit, and where people are not born again, you will find the church becomes dead, dry, and barren, and helpless. They enter into entertainments and all kinds of teas. They live on a natural association and lose their grand, glorious hope.

I come to the Pentecostal church. Without the Pentecostal church is having an increase on the lines of salvation, without it is having continuous baptisms in the Holy Ghost, and a continuous pressure into the Kingdom, that church will become dry, lukewarm, helpless, and you will wonder what church it is.

But every night if somebody rises up in testimony saying they received the Holy Ghost, and others say, "Oh, last night I was saved," that church is ripening. She will not flounder. She is ripening for greater things, for God will take that church.

Beloved, you are responsible for this, the platform is not responsible. The whole Church is responsible to keep this place on fire. If you have come into this meeting, if you are baptized with the Holy Ghost, without an unction upon you and ready so that you feel like bursting into tongues, or having a psalm, hymn, or some spiritual song, without you have a tongue or interpretation, without something is taking place on these lines you have fallen from the grace of the Pentecostal position.

You talk about a message. God has given us a message this morning if you dare hear it. We dare say in the open air and everywhere that we are Pentecostal. If we are Pentecostal we shall be Biblical Pentecostal. What is Biblical Pentecost? It is found in the fourteenth chapter of First Corinthians, 26th verse:

> *How is it then, brethren? when ye come together, every one of you hath a psalm, hath a doctrine, hath a tongue, hath a revelation, hath an interpretation. Let all things be done unto edifying.*

It is an injunction for a Pentecostal continuance in the Corinthian church. Supposing that was the case of this Pentecostal church, it would not be possible for sinners to come in without being saved, or for people coming in not having the baptism without having a hunger and thirst to come into that fulness. It must be so. God must bring us to a place where we have not a name, but have the position that brings the name.

How many of you felt speaking in tongues as you came into the room this morning? Praise God, there are some. How many of you have a psalm burning through you and feel like rehearsing it in the streets? Praise God, that is very well. How many of you sung a hymn as you came along? Praise the Lord, glory to God! You are going on very well. But don't you see this is what we have to continue. There has to be a continuance of such things.

TONGUES AND INTERPRETATION: "The hope of the Church is springing up of the Spirit through the Word. Therefore, as many of you as are living in the Spirit are putting to death the flesh. You are quickened by the Spirit and live in the realms of His grace."

Praise the Lord, it is the grace of our Lord Jesus. Hallelujah! We can sing, "I will never be cross anymore." Beloved, it is the most wonderful thing on earth when God touches you with this new life in the Spirit. Oh, then whether you are on the streets, or roadways, or trains, it doesn't matter where, you are in the Spirit, you are ready to be caught up.

Oh, beloved, here we are this morning, "one body," praise the Lord! One spirit, one baptism. I am crying to God for these meetings because I believe God can do a great thing in a moment when we are all brought into line of the Spirit. It wouldn't surprise me whatever happened.

I have been in meetings for ten days when the attention has been on the gifts, and the people have gotten so worked up, as it were, in the Spirit that they felt something had to happen on a new line else they couldn't live. And it has happened. I believe these and other meetings are bringing us to a place of great expectancy.

"One Lord, one faith, one baptism" (Ephesians 4:5).

Just in the proportion that you have the Spirit unfolding to you, "One Lord, one faith, one baptism," you have the Holy Ghost so incarnated in you bringing into you a revelation of the Word. Nothing else can do it, for the Spirit gave the Word through Jesus. Jesus spoke by the Spirit that was in Him, He being the Word. The Spirit brought out all the Word of this life. Then we must have the Spirit.

If you take up John's gospel you will find that when He came it wasn't to speak about Himself but to bring forth all He said. Just as we have the measure of the Spirit, there will be no measure of unbelief. We shall have faith. The Church will rise to the highest position when there is no schism in the Body of the lines of unbelief. When we all, with one heart, and one faith, believe the Word as it is spoken, then signs, and wonders, and divers miracles will be manifested everywhere. One accord: "One Lord, one faith, one baptism." Hallelujah!

The next verse I think probably is one of the primary verses of all:

> *One God and Father of all, who is above all, and through all, and in you all.*
>
> *Ephesians 4:6*

If this spiritual life be in us, we will find we have no fear. We would have no nervous debility, it would vanish. Every time you have fear, it is imperfect love. Every time you have nervous weaknesses, you will find it is a departing from an inner circle of true faith in God. We read in 1 John 4:18:

> *There is no fear in love; but perfect love casteth out fear: because fear hath torment. He that feareth is not made perfect in love.*

Then you can get a very good word in the sixteenth verse of the same chapter:

> *...God is love; and he that dwelleth in love dwelleth in God, and God in him.*

Where is the man? He is swallowed up in God. And when God takes hold of us on these lines it is remarkable to see we are encircled and overshadowed by Him.

TONGUES AND INTERPRETATION: "I feel we must magnify the Lord in the Spirit."

When the believer sees that God is over all, take a real glance at that. Think about God being through all. See if any satanic powers can work against you. But just think about another step; He is in you all. How can the devil have a chance with the body when God is "in you all"? Hallelujah! Glory!

Don't you see the groundwork, the great base, the rock of the principles of these Scriptures, how they make us know that we are not barren, we cannot be unfruitful, but we must always be abounding and in the joy of the Lord. We lack because we are short of truth.

When this truth of God lays hold the man, he is no longer a man. What is he? He is a divine construction. He has a new perception of the ideals of God. He has a new measurement. Now he sees God is over all things. Now he sees that God is through all things. The whole world can join in a league of nations, they can do as they like, but the Word of God abideth forever.

"In you all." Think of that, God is in you all. Who is God? Who is the Holy Spirit? Who is Jesus? Is it possible to have any conception of the mightiness of the power of God? And yet you take the thoughts of Jesus and see that all the embodiment of the fulness was right in Him. And I have Him. I have the Holy Ghost also which is as great in equality for those three are one, and joined equally in power. They never twaddle on their conditions but are perfectly one.

When the Spirit comes in the body, how many are there in the body? You have Jesus already. When you are baptized you have the Holy Ghost. And now God is in you all. Hallelujah! Talk about Samson carrying the gates, if you know your position you will take both the city and the gates. Go in and possess every part of the land, for surely there is a land of gladness, a land of pleasure, a land of peace.

And remember, brothers; when the Holy Ghost gets an end of us, and we just utter the Spirit's power and the Spirit's words, we find out it is always more and more and more. Oh, yes, we will magnify the Lord on all these lines. If we don't the stones will begin to cry out against us.

> *But unto every one of us is given grace according to the measure of the gift of Christ.*
>
> Ephesians 4:7

This is a great summing up. Oh, brother, I wish you to see Jesus this morning because if we don't see Him we miss a great deal. Grace and gifts are equally abounding there. It is as you set your strength on Jesus, it is as you allow the Holy Ghost to penetrate every thought bringing always on the canvas of the mind a perfect picture of holiness, purity, righteousness, that you enter into Him and become entitled to all the riches of God.

How do you measure up this morning? God gives a measure. Oh, this is a lovely word:

> *But unto every one of us is given grace according to the measure of the gift of Christ.*
>
> Ephesians 4:7

I know that salvation, while it is a perfect work, is an insulation which may have any amount of volts behind it. In the time when they laid bare wires, when they were getting electric power from Niagara, they tell me there was a city whose lights suddenly went out. Following the wires they came to a place where a cat had gotten on the wires, and the lights were stopped. I find that the dynamo of heaven can be stopped with a less thing than a cat. An impure thought across the mind stops the circulation. An act stops the growth of the believer. I like Hebrews 4:12:

> *For the word of God is quick, and powerful, and sharper than any twoedged sword, piercing even to the dividing asunder of soul and spirit, and of the joints and marrow, and is a discerner of the thoughts and intents of the heart.*

Then I find in 2 Corinthians 10:5 these words:

Casting down imaginations, and every high thing that exalteth itself against the knowledge of God, and bringing into captivity every thought to the obedience of Christ.

So I find if I am going to have all the revelations of Jesus brought to me, I am going to attain to all that God has for me through a pure heart, a clean heart, right thoughts, and an inward affection towards Him. Then heaven bursts through my human frame, and all the rays of heaven flow through my body. Hallelujah! My word, it is lovely!

The measure of the gift of Christ remains with you. I cannot go on with inspiration without I am going on with God in perfection. I cannot know the mind of the natural and the mysteries of the hidden things with God without I have power to penetrate everything between me and heaven. And there is nothing goes through but a pure heart, for the pure in heart shall see God.

Oh, it is lovely! And I see that the pure heart can come into such closeness with God that the graces are so enriched, and the measure of Christ becomes so increased that you know you are going on to possess all things.

Nothing comes up in my mind so beautiful as a soul just developing in their first love to want to preach to all people. In Revelation, one church is reproved for having lost its first love. And I believe that God would have us to know that this first love, the great love which Jesus gives us with which to love others, is the primary stepping stone to all these things that we had this morning. I don't know whether there is such a one here who has never lost that first love.

The preacher, I love him. The young man I love. Oh, how I love the youth who is developing in his character and longing to become a preacher. If you ask me if I have a choice in my whole life, I say, yes, I have a choice for a young preacher. I love them. God has perfect positions of development for the preacher.

The young preacher may have greater inward longings to get people saved than he has power over his depravities. And they are hindered in their pursuit into this grandeur of God. I want to take you to a place where there is wonderful safety and security.

God will take into captivity him who is captive to weaknesses, and to failures, and to the power of Satan which has interfered with the young or old life that is longing to preach the glories of Christ. God will take him into captivity if he will let Him for God has gifts for him. He takes the captive into captivity and surrounds him, keeps him, chastens him, purifies him, cleanses him, washes him. And He is making prophets of such, and apostles of such, and evangelists of such.

God has never been able to make goodness only out of helplessness lest we should glorify through the flesh. God destroys every line of flesh that no flesh can glory in His sight. If we have any glory, we will glory in the Lord.

Do you want to be preachers? Nay, verily, I know you do. There isn't a child in this place who does not want to bear the glad tidings.

> *...How beautiful are the feet of them that preach the gospel of peace, and bring glad tidings of good things!*
>
> Romans 10:15

Oh, glad tidings! What does it mean? Eternal salvation. You talk about gold mines, and diamonds, and precious stones! Oh, my brother, to save one soul from death! Oh, to be the means of saving many! God has for us a richer treasure than we have any idea of. Don't say you cannot reach it, brother, sister. Never look at yourself, get a great vision of the Master. Let His love so penetrate you that you will absolutely make everything death but Him. And as you see Him in His glory, you will see how God can take you.

I believe that there are many in this place that God is taking hold of this morning. My brother, don't fail God, but by the measure of faith in Christ let your hand be outstretched, let your eye be fixed with an eternal fixedness, let an inward passion grip you with the same zeal that took the Lord. And let your mind forget all the past, come into like-mindedness with Jesus and let Him clothe you.

> *Wherefore he saith, When he ascended up on high, he led captivity captive, and gave gifts unto men.*
>
> Ephesians 4:8

He has gifts for men. You ask, what kind of men? Rebels also. Did they desire to be rebels? No. Sometimes there are transgressions who break our hearts and make us groan and travail. Was it our desire? No. God looks right through the very canvas of your whole life history, and He has set His mind upon you. I would like you preachers to know:

> *...Eye hath not seen, nor ear heard, neither have entered into the heart of man, the things which God hath prepared for them that love him.*
>
> *1 Corinthians 2:9*

Your weakness has to be riddled through like the chaff before the wind, and every corn shall bring forth pure grain after God's mind. So the fire will burn as an oven, and burn up the stubble, but the wheat shall be gathered into the garner, the treasury of the most High God, and He Himself shall lay hold of us.

What is it for? The perfecting of the saints. Oh, to think that that brokenness of thine is to be so made like Him, that weakness of thine to be made so strong like Him! Thou hast to bear the image of the Lord in every iota. We have to have the mind of Christ in perfection, in beauty.

Beloved, don't fail and shrivel because of the hand of God upon thee, but think that God must purify thee for the perfecting of the saints. Oh, Jesus will help us this morning. Oh, beloved, what are you going to do with this golden opportunity, with this inward pressure of a cry of God in thy soul? Are you going to let others be crowned, and you lose the crown? Are you willing to be brought into captivity today for God?

Verily, this morning must decide some things. If you are not baptized you must seek the baptism of the Spirit of God. And if there is anything which has marred the fruit, or interfered with all His plan, I beseech you this morning to let the blood so cover, let the anointing of Christ so come, let the vision of Christ so be seen that you will have a measure that shall take all that God has for you.

Message given at Glad Tidings Tabernacle and Bible Training School
San Francisco, California

YE ARE OUR EPISTLE

August 23, 1922

I want to read to you this morning the third chapter of Second Corinthians:

Do we begin again to commend ourselves? or need we, as some others, epistles of commendation to you, or letters of commendation from you? Ye are our epistle written in our hearts, known and read of all men: Forasmuch as ye are manifestly declared to be the epistle of Christ ministered by us, written not with ink, but with the Spirit of the living God; not in tables of stone, but in fleshy tables of the heart. And such trust have we through Christ to God-ward: Not that we are sufficient of ourselves to think any thing as of ourselves; but our sufficiency is of God; Who also hath made us able ministers of the new testament; not of the letter, but of the spirit: for the letter killeth, but the spirit giveth life. But if the ministration of death, written and engraven in stones, was glorious, so that the children of Israel could not stedfastly behold the face of Moses for the glory of his countenance; which glory was to be done away: How shall not the ministration of the spirit be rather glorious? For if the ministration of condemnation be glory, much more doth the ministration of righteousness exceed in glory. For even that which was made glorious had no glory in this respect, by reason of the glory that excelleth. For if that which is done away was glorious, much more that which remaineth is glorious. Seeing then that we have such hope, we use great plainness of speech: And not as Moses, which put a vail over his face, that the children of Israel could not stedfastly look to the end of that which is abolished: But their minds were blinded: for until this day remaineth the same vail untaken away in the reading of the old testament; which vail is done away in Christ. But even unto this day, when Moses is read, the vail is upon their heart. Nevertheless when it shall turn to the Lord, the vail shall be taken away. Now the Lord is that Spirit: and where the Spirit of the Lord is, there is liberty. But we all, with open face beholding as in a glass the glory of the Lord, are

> *changed into the same image from glory to glory, even as by the*
> *Spirit of the Lord.*
>
> *2 Corinthians 3:1-18*

We have this morning one of those high water marks of very deep things of God in the Spirit. I believe the Lord will reveal to us these truths as our hearts are open and responsive to the Spirit's leadings.

But let not any man think he shall receive anything of the Lord only on the lines of a spiritual revelation, for there is nothing that will profit you, or bring you to a place of blessing except that which denounces or brings to death the natural order that the supernatural plan of God may be in perfect order in you.

The Lord of hosts camps round about us this morning, with songs of deliverance that we may see face to face the glories of His grace in a new way, for God hath not brought us into cunningly devised fables but in these days He is rolling away the mists and clouds, and every difficulty that we may understand the mind and will of God.

If we are going to catch the best of God, there must be in this meeting a spiritual desire, the open ear, the understanding heart. The vail must be lifted. We must see the Lord in that perfectness of being glorified in the midst of us. As we enter into these things of the Spirit we must clearly see that we are not going to be able to understand these mysteries that God is unfolding to us, only on the lines of being filled with the Spirit.

Even when these special meetings close, the pastor and everybody else will find that we must all the time grow in grace. We must see that God has nothing for us on the old lines. The new plan, the new revelation, the new victories are before us. The ground must be gained, supernatural things must be attained. All carnal things, and evil powers, and spiritual wickedness in high places must be dethroned. We must come into the line of the Spirit by the will of God in these days.

Let us just turn to the Word which is so beautiful and so expressive in so many ways.

> *Do we begin again to commend ourselves? or need we, as some*
> *others, epistles of commendation to you, or letters of commenda-*

tion from you? Ye are our epistle written in our hearts, known and read of all men: Forasmuch as ye are manifestly declared to be the epistle of Christ ministered by us, written not with ink, but with the Spirit of the living God; not in tables of stone, but in fleshy tables of the heart. And such trust have we through Christ to God-ward.

2 Corinthians 3:1-4

I want this morning to dwell upon these words for a short time: "Forasmuch as ye are manifestly declared to be the epistle of Christ."

What an ideal position that now the sons of God are being manifested; now the glory is being seen; now the Word of God is becoming an expressed purpose in life till the life has ceased and the Word has begun to live in them.

How truly this position was in the life of Paul when he came to a climax when he said: "I am crucified with Christ: nevertheless I live; yet not I, but Christ liveth in me: and the life which I now live in the flesh I live by the faith of the Son of God, who loved me, and gave himself for me" (Galatians 2:20).

How can Christ live in you? There is no way for Christ to live in you only by the manifested Word in you, through you, manifestly declaring every day that you are a living epistle of the Word of God. Beloved, God would have us to see that no man is perfected or equipped on any lines only as the living Word abides in Him.

It is the living Christ, it is the divine likeness to God, it is the express image of Him, and the Word is the only factor that works out in you and brings forth these glories of identification between you and Christ. It is the Word dwelling in your hearts, richly by faith.

We may begin at Genesis, go right through the Pentateuch, and the other Scriptures, and be able to rehearse them, but without they are a living factor within us, they will be a dead letter. Everything that comes to us must be quickened by the Spirit. "The letter killeth, but the Spirit giveth life."

We must have life in everything. Who knows how to pray but as the Spirit prayeth? What kind of prayer does the Spirit pray? The Spirit always brings to your remembrance the mind of the Scriptures, and brings forth all your cry and your need better than your words. The Spirit always takes the Word of God and brings your heart, and mind, and soul, and cry, and need into the presence of God.

So we are not able to pray only as the Spirit prays, and the Spirit only prays according to the will of God, and the will of God is all in the Word of God. No man is able to speak according to the mind of God and bring forth the deep things of God out of his own mind. The following Scripture rightly divides the Word of truth:

> *Forasmuch as ye are manifestly declared to be the epistle of Christ ministered by us, written not with ink, but with the Spirit of the living God; not in tables of stone, but in fleshly tables of the heart.*
>
> *2 Corinthians 3:3*

God help us to understand this, for it is out of the heart that all things proceed. When we have entered in with God into the mind of the Spirit, we will find God ravishes our hearts.

> *Do ye think that the scripture saith in vain, The spirit that dwelleth in us lusteth to envy?*
>
> *James 4:5*

I have been pondering over that for years, but now I can see that the Holy Ghost so graciously, so extravagantly, puts everything to one side that He may ravish our hearts with a great inward cry after Jesus. The Holy Spirit "lusteth to envy" for you to have all the divine will of God in Christ Jesus right in your hearts.

When I speak about the "fleshly tables of the heart," I mean the inward love. Nothing is so sweet to me as to know that the heart yearns with compassion. Eyes may see, ears may hear, but you may be immovable on those two lines without you have an inward cry where "deep calleth unto deep."

When God gets into the depths of our hearts, He purifies every intention of the thoughts and the joys. We are told in the Word it is joy unspeakable and full of glory.

Beloved, it is truth that the commandments were written on tables of stone. Moses, like a great big, loving father over Israel, had a heart full of joy because God had showed him a plan where Israel could be made to partake of great things through these commandments. But God says, "Not in tables of stone," which made the face of Moses to shine with great joy. Deeper than that, more wonderful than that: the commandments in our hearts; the deep love of God in our hearts, the deep movings of eternity rolling in and bringing God in. Hallelujah!

Oh, beloved, let God the Holy Ghost have His way today in so unfolding to us all the grandeurs of His glory.

TONGUES AND INTERPRETATION: "The Spirit, He Himself, it is He, that waketh thee morning by morning and unfolds unto thee in thy heart, tenderness, compassion and love towards thy Maker till thou dost weep before Him and say to Him, in the spirit, 'Thou art mine! Thou art mine!'"

Yes, He is mine! Beloved, He is mine!

"And such trust have we through Christ to God-ward:

"Not that we are sufficient of ourselves to think any thing as of ourselves; but our sufficiency is of God." (vv. 4,5).

Ah, it is lovely! Those verses are to keep to pass over. Beloved, that is a climax of divine exaltation that is so much different from human exaltation.

> The end is not yet, praise the Lord!
> The end is not yet, praise the Lord!
> Your blessings He is bestowing,
> And my cup is overflowing,
> And the end is not yet, praise the Lord!

We want to get to a place where we are beyond trusting in ourselves. Beloved, there is so much failure in self-assurances. It is not bad to have good things on the lines of satisfaction, but we must never have anything on the human that we rest upon. There is only one sure place to rest upon, and our trust is in God.

In Thy name we go. In Thee we trust. And God brings us off in victory. When we have no confidence in ourselves to trust in ourselves but when our whole trust rests upon the authority of the mighty God, He has promised to be with us at all times, and to make the path straight, and to make all the mountains a way. Then we understand how it is that David could say, "Thy gentleness hath made me great."

Ah, thou lover of souls! We have no confidence in the flesh. Our confidence can only be stayed and relied in the One who never fails, in the One who knows the end from the beginning, in the One who is able to come in at the midnight hour as easy as in the noonday, and make the night and the day alike to the man who rests completely in the will of God, knowing that "all things work together for good to them that love Him," and trust in Him. And such trust have we in Him.

This is the worthy position where God would have all souls to be. We should find that we would not run His errands and make mistakes; we would not be dropping down in the wrong place. We would find our life was as surely in the canon of thought with God as the leading of the children of Israel through the wilderness. And we should be able to say, Not one good thing hath the Lord withheld from me (Psalm 84:11), and "...all the promises of God in him are yea, and in him Amen, unto the glory of God by us" (2 Corinthians 1:20).

The Lord has helped me to have no confidence in myself, but to wholly trust in Him, bless His name!

> *Who also hath made us able ministers of the new testament; not of the letter, but of the spirit: for the letter killeth, but the spirit giveth life. But if the ministration of death, written and engraven in stones, was glorious, so that the children of Israel could not stedfastly behold the face of Moses for the glory of his countenance; which glory was to be done away: How shall not the ministration of the spirit be rather glorious? For if the ministration of condemnation be glory, much more doth the ministration of righteousness exceed in glory.*
>
> *2 Corinthians 3:6-9*

Let us enter into these great words on the line of holy thoughtfulness. If I go on with God He wants me to understand all His deep things. He doesn't want anybody in the Pentecostal church to be novices, or to deal with the Word of God on natural grounds. We can understand the Word of God only by the Spirit of God.

We cannot define, or separate, or deeply investigate and unfold this holy plan of God without we have the life of God, the thought of God, the Spirit of God, and the revelation of God. The Word of Truth is pure, spiritual, and divine. If you try to divide it on natural grounds you will only finish up on natural lines for natural man, but you will never satisfy a Pentecostal Assembly.

The people who are spiritual can only be fed on spiritual material. So if you are expecting your messages to catch fire you will have to have them on fire. You won't have to light the message up in the meeting. You will have to bring the message red-hot, burning, living. The message must be direct from heaven. It must be as truly, "Thus saith the Lord," as the Scriptures which are, "Thus saith the Lord," because you will only speak as the Spirit gives utterance, and you will always be giving fresh revelation. You will never be stale on any line, whatever you say will be fruitful, elevating the mind, lifting the people, and all the people will want more.

To come into this we must see that we not only need the baptism of the Spirit but we need to come to a place where there is only the baptism of the Spirit left. Look at the first verse of the fourth chapter of Luke and you will catch this beautiful truth:

> *And Jesus being full of the Holy Ghost returned from Jordan,*
> *and was led by the Spirit into the wilderness.*

But look at Mark 1:12 and you will find He was driven of the Spirit into the wilderness:

> *And immediately the Spirit driveth him into the wilderness.*

In John's gospel Jesus says He does not speak or act of Himself:

...the words that I speak unto you I speak not of myself: but the Father that dwelleth in me, he doeth the works.

John 14:10

We must know that the baptism of the Spirit immerses us into an intensity of zeal, into a likeness to Jesus, to make us into pure, running metal so hot for God that it travels like oil from vessel to vessel. This divine line of the Spirit will let us see that we have ceased and we have begun. We are at the end for a beginning. We are down and out, and God is in and out.

There isn't a thing in the world can help us in this meeting. There isn't a natural thought that can be of any use here. There isn't a thing that is carnal, earthly, natural, that can ever live in these meetings. It must only have one pronouncement, it has to die eternally because there is no other plan for a baptized soul, only dead indeed.

God, help us to see then that we may be filled with the letter without being filled with the Spirit. We may be filled with knowledge without having divine knowledge. And we may be filled with wonderful things on natural lines and still remain a natural man. But you cannot do it in this truth that I am dealing with this morning. No man is able to walk this way without He is in the Spirit. He must live in the Spirit and he must realize all the time that he is growing in that same ideal of his Master, in season and out of season, always beholding the face of the Master, Jesus.

David says, "I foresaw the Lord for He was on my right hand that I should not be moved. Then my tongue was glad." Praise the Lord!

For even that which was made glorious had no glory in this respect, by reason of the glory that excelleth. For if that which is done away was glorious, much more that which remaineth is glorious.

2 Corinthians 3:10,11

I notice here that the one has to be done away, and the other has to increase. One day I was having a good time on this chapter. I had a lot of people before me who were living on the 39 Articles and Infant Baptism, and all kinds of things. The Lord showed me that all these things had to be done away. I find there is no place into all the further plan with God without you absolutely putting them to one side. "Done away."

Is it possible to do away with the commandments? Yes and no. If they are not so done away with you that you have no consciousness of keeping commandments, then they are not done away. If you know you are living holy, you don't know what holiness is. If you know you are keeping commandments, you don't know what keeping commandments is.

These things are done away. God has brought us in to be holy without knowing it, and keeping the whole truth without knowing it, living in it, moving in it, acting in it, a new creation in the Spirit. The old things are done away. If there is any trouble in you at all, it shows you have not come to the place where you are at rest.

"Done away." God, help us to see it. If the teaching is a bit too high for you, ask the Lord to open your eyes to come into it. For there is no man here has power in prayer, or has power in life with God if he is trying to keep the commandments. They are done away, brother. And thank God, the very doing away with them is fixing them deeper in our hearts than ever before. For out of the depths we cry unto God, and in the depths has He turned righteousness in, and uncleanness out. It is unto the depths we cry unto God in these things. May God lead us all every step of the way in His divine leading.

PART TWO

I am going to commence with the sixth verse of the third chapter of Second Corinthians, lest you stop in "the letter."

> *Who also hath made us able ministers of the new testament; not of the letter, but of the spirit: for the letter killeth, but the spirit giveth life. But if the ministration of death, written and engraven in stones, was glorious, so that the children of Israel could not stedfastly behold the face of Moses for the glory of his countenance; which glory was to be done away: How shall not the ministration of the spirit be rather glorious? For if the ministration of condemnation be glory, much more doth the ministration of righteousness exceed in glory. For even that which was made glorious had no glory in this respect, by reason of the glory that excelleth. For if that which is done away was glorious, much more that which remaineth is glorious. Seeing then that*

we have such hope, we use great plainness of speech: And not as Moses, which put a vail over his face, that the children of Israel could not stedfastly look to the end of that which is abolished: But their minds were blinded: for until this day remaineth the same vail untaken away in the reading of the old testament; which vail is done away in Christ. But even unto this day, when Moses is read, the vail is upon their heart. Nevertheless when it shall turn to the Lord, the vail shall be taken away. Now the Lord is that Spirit: and where the Spirit of the Lord is, there is liberty. But we all, with open face beholding as in a glass the glory of the Lord, are changed into the same image from glory to glory, even as by the Spirit of the Lord.

2 Corinthians 3:6-18

Think about that: even the glory that was on the face of Moses had to be done away for what reason? For something that had exceeding glory. I am positive we have no conception of the depths and heights of the liberties and blessings and incarnations of the Spirit. We must attain to these positions of godliness and we must be partakers of His divine nature. Praise the Lord!

How shall not the ministration of the spirit be rather glorious? For if the ministration of condemnation be glory, much more doth the ministration of righteousness exceed in glory.

2 Corinthians 3:8,9

The Lord help us now on this. I see the truth as it was brought to them in the law as we read last Sunday morning. Paul had something to glory in when he kept the law, and was blameless, but he said he threw that to one side to win Him which is greater even than that.

Now we come to the truth of this: what is there in the law that isn't glorious? Nothing. It was so glorious that Moses was filled with joy in the expectation of what it was. But what is ours in the excellence of glory? It is this, that we live, we move, we reign over all things and it isn't "Do, do, do." It is a "Will, will, will." And I rejoice to do. It is no more, "Thou shalt not." It is a will. "I delight to do Thy will, O God!" So it is far exceeding in glory. And beloved, in our hearts there is exceeding glory. Oh, the joy of this celestial touch this morning!

TONGUES AND INTERPRETATION: "The living God who is chastening us after this manner, is always building us after His manner that there may be no spot in us. For the Lord Himself has designed the plan, and is working out in us His divine mind, and is taking the man and transforming him in this plan till he loses his identity in the mighty God of possibilities."

Hallelujah! We praise Thee, O God. And we will praise Him forever.

> Far above all,
> Far above all,
> God hath exalted Him,
> Far above all.

Amen! Glory to God! Thank God for that interpretation. I shall be glad to read that, I don't know what I said, only I know the joy of it.

Oh, yes, it exceeds in glory. It is an excellent glory. When Peter is rehearsing that wonderful day in the mount, he says, "There came such a voice to Him from the excellent glory." And so we are hearing this morning from the excellent glory. It is so lovely.

If I come along to you this morning and say, "Whatever you do, you must try to be holy," I should miss it. I should be altogether outside of this plan. But I take the words of the epistle this morning by the Holy Ghost that says, "Be ye holy."

It is as easy as possible to be holy, but you can never be holy by trying to be. But when you lose your heart and another takes your heart, and you lose your desires and He takes the desires, then you live in that sunshine of bliss which no mortal can ever touch.

Divine immortality swallows up all natural mortality. And God wants us to see that we have to be entirely eaten up by this holy zeal of God so that every day we walk in the Spirit. It is lovely to walk in the Spirit, then ye shall not fulfill any part of the law but the Spirit will cause you to dwell in safety and rejoice inwardly, and praise God reverently, and make you know that you are an increasing force of immortality swallowing up life. Hallelujah!

Ah, it is lovely! I will never be cross anymore.

Beloved, it is impossible to go on with God and have the old life jumping up. Glory to God!

> *For if the ministration of condemnation be glory, much more*
> *doth the ministration of righteousness exceed in glory.*
> *2 Corinthians 3:9*

This is a beautiful word. I want to speak about "righteousness" now. There is nothing so beautiful as righteousness. You cannot touch these beatitudes we are dwelling on this morning without seeing the excellent glory exists right in the Christ. All the excellent glory is in Him. All righteousness is in Him.

Everything that pertains to holiness, and godliness, everything that denounces and brings to death the natural, everything that makes you know you have ceased to be forever, is always in the knowledge of an endless power of a risen Christ.

I want you to notice there is an excellent glory about it. Whenever you look at Jesus you can look at so many different facts of His life. I see Him in those forty days, with wonderful truth, infallible proof of His ministry. What was the ministry of Christ? When you come to the very essence of His ministry it was the righteousness of His purpose. The excellence of His ministry was the glory that covered Him. His Word was convincing, inflexible, divine with a personality of an eternal endurance. It never failed.

The righteousness of God. If He said it, it was there. He said it and it stood fast. It was an immutable condition with Him. When God spake it was done. And His righteousness abideth. God must have us there. We must be people of our word. People ought to be able to depend upon our word.

If there were only five saved in a meeting we should never say there were six. If there were five baptized we should never say there were seven. If the building would hold 500 people we should never say it was packed and had a thousand in it. He is establishing righteousness in our hearts that we shall not exaggerate on any line.

Jesus was true inwardly and outwardly. He is the way, the truth and the life, and on these things we can build; on these things we can pray; on these things we can live. When we know that our own heart condemneth us not, we can say to the mountain, "Be removed." But when our own hearts condemn us, there is no power in prayer, no power in preaching, or in anything. We are just sounding brass and tinkling cymbals.

May God the Holy Ghost show us there must be a ministry of righteousness. We ought to stand by our signature, and abide by it. And if we were cut through they would find pure gold right through us. That is what I call righteousness. He was righteousness through and through. He is lovely! Oh, truly, He is beautiful!

One thing God wants to fix in our hearts is to be like Him. Be like Him in character. Don't be troubled so much about your faces but be more concerned about your hearts. All the powder won't change the heart. All the adorning of silks and satins won't make purity. Beloved, if I was going down a road and I saw a fox tail sticking out of a hole I shouldn't ask anybody what there was inside. And if there is anything hanging outside, you know what there is inside. Righteousness in the inward parts. Pure through and through.

Hearken! There is an excellent glory attached to it. We read:

> *For if the ministration of condemnation be glory, much more doth the ministration of righteousness exceed in glory.*
>
> *2 Corinthians 3:9*

The Bible is the plumbline of everything. And without we are plumbed right up with the Word of God, we will fail in the measure in which we are not righteous. And so may God the Holy Ghost bring us, this morning, into that blessed ministry of righteousness. Amen! Glory to God!

> *For even that which was made glorious had no glory in this respect, by reason of the glory that excelleth.*
>
> *2 Corinthians 3:10*

Come again right to the law. I see that it was truly a schoolmaster that brought us to Christ. I like the thought of it, that law is beautiful, law is established in the earth. As far as possible in every country and town, you will find the law has something to do with keeping things straight. And in a measure the city has some kind of sobriety because of the law.

But beloved, we are belonging to a higher, to a nobler citizenship, and it isn't an earthly citizenship, for our citizenship is in heaven. So we must see thee is an excellent glory about this position we are holding this morning. For if the natural law will keep an earthly city in somewhat moderate conditions, what will the excellent glory be in the divine relationship of the citizenship to which we belong?

What I mean by excellent glory, it outshines. It makes all the people feel a longing to go. What there is about the excellent glory is this: the earth is filled with broken hearts, but the excellent glory is filled with redeemed men and women, filled with the excellency of the graces of the glory of God. Oh, glorious is the excellent glory! Ah, praise the Lord, oh my soul! Hallelujah!

> *For if that which is done away was glorious, much more that which remaineth is glorious. Seeing then that we have such hope, we use great plainness of speech: And not as Moses, which put a vail over his face, that the children of Israel could not stedfastly look to the end of that which is abolished.*
>
> *2 Corinthians 3:11-13*

Yesterday morning I was preaching to preachers, but we can see that this message is for the perfecting of preachers. The man who is going on with God will have no mix-up in his oratory. He will be so plain and precise, and divine in his leadings, that everything will have a lift towards the glory. And you will always realize he will not play about to satisfy human curiosity. He must have his mind upon higher things altogether, and he must see God would not have him loiter about. He must "use great plainness of speech." He must be a man who knows his message. He must know what God has in His mind in the Spirit, not in the letter, because no man that is going to speak by the Spirit of God knows what God is going to say in the meeting.

He is there a vessel for honor, His mouthpiece, and all contained there is of God. And therefore, he stands in the presence of God, and God speaks and uses him. But hearken! God is a Spirit working within the human life with thought, with might, with truth and life, and brings out of the great treasury of His mightiness into the human life, into the heart, and sends it right through onto the canvas of the mind, and the language comes out according to the operation of the Spirit of God.

Beloved, shall we any more try any lines but the divine? Every man is not just in the same order, but I could say to the man with faith that there is a touch of faith for that man to come into as a spiritual orator. He has to forget all he has put on his notes because of a higher order of notes.

I always say you cannot sing victory on a minor key. And you never can have a spiritual horizon on a low note. If your life isn't constant pitch, you will never ring the bells of heaven. You must always be in tune with God, and then the music will come out as sweet as possible.

Let us get away from going into libraries and filling our minds with human theology. Not that I want to discourage anybody, but it would pay the best man here, I don't care who he is, to go home and set fire to his library. You say that is a silly thing? I would not have said it if I had not the best thing to put into it after it is burned down. I don't say, Go home and do it straightway. Think over it first. The more you think over it the more you will want to burn it.

I am not here for any other purpose than for the glory of God. God forbid! I have known so many people who have been barren and helpless, and they have used other people's material on the platform. If you ever turn to another man's material you have dropped from the higher sense of an orator from heaven.

We must now be the mouthpiece of God, not by letter but by the Spirit. And we must be so in the will of God that God rejoices over us with singing. Isn't it lovely? We are going forward a little. Let us turn now to the thirteenth and fourteenth verses:

And not as Moses, which put a vail over his face, that the children of Israel could not stedfastly look to the end of that which is abolished:

But their minds were blinded: for until this day remaineth the same vail untaken away in the reading of the old testament; which vail is done away in Christ.

2 Corinthians 3:13,14

I have nothing to say about the Jew except this: that I know I am saved by the blood of a Jew. I owe my Bible to the Jews, for the Jews have kept it for us. We have a Savior who was a Jew. The first proclamation of the Gospel was of the Jews. I know that I owe everything to the Jew today, but I see that the Jew will never have the key to unlock the Scriptures till he sees Jesus. The moment he does he will see this truth that Jesus gave to Peter:

And I say also unto thee, That thou art Peter, and upon this rock I will build my church...And I will give unto thee the keys of the kingdom of heaven....

Matthew 16:18,19

And I will give thee the key of truth, the key to unvail. The key was brought in the moment Peter saw the Lord. The moment they see Christ, the whole of the Scriptures is opened out to the Jew. That will be a great day when the Jews see the Lord. They will see Him!

But their minds were blinded: for until this day remaineth the same vail untaken away in the reading of the old testament; which vail is done away in Christ.

But even unto this day, when Moses is read, the vail is upon their heart.

2 Corinthians 3:14,15

God doesn't say the vail is upon their mind, but upon their heart. And beloved, God can never save a man through his mind. He saves him through his heart. He can never bring all the glories into a man's life by his mind. He must touch the deep things of his heart.

> *Nevertheless when it shall turn to the Lord, the vail shall be taken away. Now the Lord is that Spirit: and where the Spirit of the Lord is, there is liberty. But we all, with open face beholding as in a glass the glory of the Lord, are changed into the same image from glory to glory, even as by the Spirit of the Lord.*
>
> *2 Corinthians 3:16-18*

I must speak about liberty first. There are two kinds of liberty, two kinds of grace. We must never use liberty but we must be in the place where liberty can use us. If we use liberty we shall be as dead as possible, and it will all end up in a fizzle.

But if we are in the Spirit, the Lord of life is the same Spirit. I believe it is right to jump for joy but don't jump till the joy makes you jump because if you do you will jump flat. If you jump as the joy makes you jump you will bounce up again.

In the Spirit I know there is any amount of divine plan. If the Pentecostal people had only come into it in meekness and in the true knowledge of God, it would all be so manifest that every heart in the meeting would be moved by that Spirit.

> *Now the Lord is that Spirit: and where the Spirit of the Lord is, there is liberty.*
>
> *2 Corinthians 3:17*

Liberty has a thousand sides to it, but there is no liberty which is going to help the people so much as testimony. I find people who don't know how to testify right. We must testify only as the Spirit gives utterance. We find in Revelation that the testimony of Jesus is the spirit of prophecy.

When your flesh is keeping you down, but your heart is so full it is lifting you up — have you ever been like that? The flesh has been fastening you to the seat but your heart has been bubbling over. At last the heart has had more power and you have risen up.

And then in that heart affection for Jesus in the Spirit of love and in the knowledge of truth, you begin to testify, and when you have done you sit down. Liberty used wrongly goes on when you finished and spoils the meeting. You are not to use your liberty except for the glory of God.

So many churches are spoiled by long prayers, and long testimonies. The speaker can tell, if he keeps in the Spirit, when he should sit down. When you begin to rehearse yourself, the people get wearied and tired and they wish you would sit down. The unction ceases, they sit down worse than when they rose up.

It is nice for a man to begin cold, and warm up as he goes on. When he catches fire and sits down in the midst of it he will keep the fire afterwards. Look! It is lovely to pray, and it is a joy to hear you pray, but when you go on after you are done, all the people are tired of it.

So God wants us to know that we are not to use liberty because we have it to use, but we are to let the liberty use us, and we should know when to end.

This excellent glory should go on to a liberality to everybody, and this would prove that all the Church is in liberty. The Church ought to be free so that the people always go away feeling, "Oh, I wish the meeting had gone on for another hour." Or, "What a glorious time we had at that prayer meeting!" Or, "Wasn't that testimony meeting a revelation!" That is the way to finish up. Never finish up with something too long, finish up with something too short. Then everybody comes again to piece up where they left off.

The last verse is the most glorious of all for us:

> *But we all, with open face beholding as in a glass the glory of the Lord, are changed into the same image from glory to glory, even as by the Spirit of the Lord.*
>
> *2 Corinthians 3:18*

So there are glories upon glories, and joys upon joys, exceeding joyous and abundance of joys, and a measureless measure of all the lot. Beloved, we get the word so wonderfully in our hearts that it absolutely changes us in everything. And we so feast on the Word of the Lord, so eat and digest the truth, so inwardly eat of Him, till we are absolutely changed every day from one state to another.

As we look into the perfect mirror of the face of the Lord we are changed from one state of grace to another, from glory to glory. You will never find anything else but the Word of God that takes you there. So you cannot afford to put aside that Word.

I beseech you, beloved, that you come short of none of these beatitudes we have been speaking of, in your life. These grand truths of the Word of God must be your testimony, must be your life, your pattern. You must be in it, in fact you are of it. "Ye are...the epistle of Christ," God says to you by the Spirit. Then let us see that we put off everything that by the grace of God we may put on everything.

Where there is a standard which hasn't been reached in your life, God in His grace, by His mercy and your yieldedness, can fit you for that place that you can never be prepared for only by a broken heart and a contrite spirit, yielding to the will of God. If you will come with a whole heart to the throne of grace, God will meet you and build you on His spiritual plane. Amen. Praise the Lord!

Message given at Glad Tidings Tabernacle and Bible Training School
San Francisco, California

I believe the Lord would be pleased for us to turn to the fourth chapter of Second Corinthians this morning and read from the sixteenth verse, concluding with the seventh verse of the fifth chapter:

CLOTHED UPON

September 15, 1922

For which cause we faint not; but though our outward man perish, yet the inward man is renewed day by day. For our light affliction, which is but for a moment, worketh for us a far more exceeding and eternal weight of glory; While we look not at the things which are seen, but at the things which are not seen: for the things which are seen are temporal; but the things which are not seen are eternal. For we know that if our earthly house of this tabernacle were dissolved, we have a building of God, an house not made with hands, eternal in the heavens. For in this we groan, earnestly desiring to be clothed upon with our house which is from heaven: If so be that being clothed we shall not be found naked. For we that are in this tabernacle do groan, being burdened: not for that we would be unclothed, but clothed upon, that mortality might be swallowed up of life. Now he that hath wrought us for the selfsame thing is God, who also hath given unto us the earnest of the Spirit. Therefore we are always confident, knowing that, whilst we are at home in the body, we are absent from the Lord: (For we walk by faith, not by sight.)

I believe the Lord has in His mind this morning the further freedom of life. There will nothing please the Lord so much as for us to come into our fulness of redemption, because I believe, "...the Lord is that Spirit: and where the Spirit of the Lord is, there is liberty" (2 Corinthians 3:17).

Liberty is beautiful when we never use it to satisfy ourselves but use liberty in the Lord. We must never transgress because of liberty. What I mean is this: to take opportunities because the Spirit of the Lord is upon me, it would be wrong. But it would be perfectly justifiable if I clearly allow the Spirit of the Lord to have His liberty with me, but not be unseemingly in liberty because the flesh has a more extravagant position than the Spirit has.

The Spirit's extravagant positions are always to edification, and strenthening of the character, and bringing us all more into conformity with the life of Christ. But the flesh conditions of extravagances always mar and bring the position of the saints into a place of trial for a moment. But as the Spirit of the Lord takes further hold of the person we may get liberty in it, but we are tried in the manifestations of it.

I believe we have come to such liberty of the Spirit that it shall be so pure it shall never bring a frown of distraction over another person's mind. I have seen so many people in the power of the Spirit, and yet with such a manifestation which was not elementary nor even helpful. I have seen people under the mighty power of the Holy Ghost who have waved their hands terrifically, and moved on the floor, and gone on in such a state that no one could say the body was not under the power.

There was more natural power than spiritual power, and the natural condition of the person, along with the spiritual condition, made a manifestation. Though we know the Spirit of the Lord was there, it was not that which would elevate, or please, or grant to the people a desire for more of that. It wasn't an edification of the Spirit.

If there are any here who have those manifestations, I want to help you. I don't want to hurt you. It is good that you should have the Spirit upon you. People need to be filled with the Spirit, but you have never a right to say you were obliged to do this or that or the other.

When people come up to me and say, "Oh, I was obliged to do that," I always know it was right and wrong. In the mind it was wrong to do it. If you were forced to do it, it was a good position but it was not right to do it if it was not bringing glory to God.

There isn't manifestation in the body that ever glorifies the Lord but the tongue. If you will seek to be free in the operation of the Spirit through the mouth, the tongue, which may be under subconscious conditions, brings out the glory of the Lord, and that will always be to edification, and consolation, and comfort.

But no other manifestation, and yet I believe that it is necessary to have all this at the beginning. It seems to be almost necessary for some people to have a kick. I have seen some people kick up with both heels, and made it so you could hardly see across the room.

When the Spirit is there the flesh must get out some way, and so we allow, because of experience, all these things at the beginning. But we believe the Holy Ghost brings a sound condition of mind, and the first thing must pass away in order that the divine position may remain.

And so there is kicking and waving, and all these things which take place at the incoming of the Holy Ghost, when the flesh and the Spirit are so in a position of controversy. One must decrease, and die, and the other must increase and multiply.

And consequently when you come into that attitude you are in a sound place of judgment and understand that now the Holy Ghost has come to take you on with God. Suppose I read this:

> *While we look not at the things which are seen, but at the things which are not seen: for the things which are seen are temporal; but the things which are not seen are eternal.*
>
> *2 Corinthians 4:18*

What would you think if at this place I have to stop because of a great kicking sensation, and I have to lie down on the floor for three hours before I can go on with the other position of the Spirit of the Lord because of my body and spirit disagreeing?

Suppose I had to read that in it. It is a proper translation on some lines. The glory of the Lord is upon me, and the Lord is speaking through me, but now I must stop to have a half hour of kicking. And all the people in the audience are waiting to see Wigglesworth kick through a half hour before he goes on. And I wonder if you would think that was in the will of God?

I don't believe the other is then, and I never believe you have a license to do it. I never believe that God would baptize you with the Holy Ghost and then make you to be a machine so you couldn't stop at any time, and begin at any time.

All these things which I am speaking about are necessary for you for further advancement in the Spirit. To me it is a very marvelous thing that the Spirit can have such mightiness over a body to kick out the flesh.

I have known some people when they have gone through that, God has begun with a new line. When the Lord baptized me with the Holy Ghost, at first there was so much flesh that needed to be done away, I went all around the dining room on my knees, clapping my hands, got through, and at the end of it was tongues. Then I stopped it because there was no more kick left. It couldn't go out through the feet and out through the mouth.

When the Holy Ghost gets full concentration of the operation of the human life He always works out divine wisdom. And when He gets perfect control of the life there flows through that divine source so that all the people may receive edification in the Spirit. If you act foolishly after you have had wisdom taught you nobody will give you much room.

"We then that are strong ought to bear the infirmities of the weak..." (Romans 15:1).

Some who come to these meetings have known nothing about the power of the Holy Ghost. They get saved, and are quickened, so after the Spirit comes upon them you will see all these things. And in love and grace you bear with them as newborn babes in the order of the Spirit, and rejoice with them in all that condition, because that is only a beginning to an end, because the Lord wouldn't have us to be anything but strong in the Lord, and in the power of His might, to help everyone in the midst of us.

I want to keep the four verses primary in your mind as I speak to you on the next verses:

> *For we know that if our earthly house of this tabernacle were dissolved, we have a building of God, an house not made with hands, eternal in the heavens. For in this we groan, earnestly desiring to be clothed upon with our house which is from heaven: If so be that being clothed we shall not be found naked. For we that are in this tabernacle do groan, being burdened: not for that we would be unclothed, but clothed upon, that mortality might be swallowed up of life.*
>
> *2 Corinthians 5:1-4*

This morning I feel I may speak to you with perfect freedom because I believe the Lord is helping us to catch a very deep spiritual condition.

I believe that we will all catch the truth that we are not our own, in the first place. In the second place we are belonging to a spiritual order, and that we don't belong to the earth.

And not only that, but our mind, our body, our whole position through the eternal Spirit, has to always be on the ascending position. To descend is to be conformed. To ascend is to be transformed.

And on this transforming condition, we may, by the power of the Spirit, as God shall give us revelation, be lifted up into a very blessed state of fellowship with God, of power with God. And in that place of power with God we shall have power with everything else, for all the power of the earth is first having power with God.

While we know we are heavenly citizens, while we know we have to have an exit, and have been preparing for an exit, yet in this position we must live in the place where we groan over everything that binds us from that loosing.

What will hold me? Association will hold me in this present world. I must have no earthly association. And you know it is as natural to have an earthly association as it is to live. Hold every earthly association at a distance. It must never tie me or bind me. It must never have any persuasion on me. Hear what the Scripture says: "...being made conformable unto his death" (Philippians 3:10).

What is the conforming unto the death of Jesus? It leads me to that death of separation, of yieldedness, of exchange where God takes me on and leaves the natural there. "While we look not at the things which are seen, but at the things which are not seen...."

Then I may grasp some idea of what it will mean if I am lost. I want, by the grace of God, to let us see that the dissolving is a great thought. There is a position here that we must clearly understand: "...not for that we would be unclothed, but clothed upon, that mortality might be swallowed up of life" (2 Corinthians 5:4).

That is a great word, mortality. While it is necessary, it is a hindrance. While mortality has done a great deal to produce everything we see, it is a hindrance if we live in it. It is a helpful position if we live over it.

Then I must understand how it can be swallowed up. I must know how that the old body, the old tendencies to natural order may be swallowed up. There is a verse here we must come to. It would serve us now:

> *Always bearing about in the body the dying of the Lord Jesus,*
> *that the life also of Jesus might be made manifest in our body.*
>
> *2 Corinthians 4:10*

What is that "dying of the Lord"? It is dying to desire. In the measure that we honor one another we lose faith in God. If you rely upon any man or woman or upon any human assistance to help you, you fall out of the greater purpose God has for you.

You must learn that no earthly source can ever assist you into this. You are going to this realm of life only by mortality being swallowed up of life, and the life that I live is lived by faith in the Son of God. Dying, living.

God will help us this morning. I know He will. I believe that the Lord will not let the preacher be anything more anymore. All these messages that God is giving me show me I am down and out. But thank God I am in and out. Truly so.

I dare not give way to my own self because I should only make a fool to appearances. But I tell you this life I am speaking about absolutely ravishes you. It absolutely severs you from earthly connections. It absolutely disjoins you from every helpfulness. And I can see now more than ever, this word:

"Ye have not yet resisted unto blood, striving against sin" (Hebrews 12:4).

The great striving of the blood, the very essence of the life, the Scripture says we have not, but I know it meant that we had not come there. But thank God we are in it in a measure.

Paul could see that if he had any communion with flesh and blood he couldn't go forward. It was of a necessity that the blood and the life of Mary, the mother of Jesus, of the Son of God, to come into this position:

> *...Who is my mother? and who are my brethren? And he stretched forth his hand toward his disciples, and said, Behold my mother and my brethren! For whosoever shall do the will of My Father which is in heaven, the same is my brother, and sister, and mother.*
>
> *Matthew 12:48-50*

Flesh and blood were nothing to Jesus. The body that brought Him forth was nothing to Him. God brought Him into the world as a seed of life. To Him that was His mother, that was His brother, that was His sister. But that is a higher ideal, that is a spiritual knowledge.

Take another touch of it. Here we find Jesus in the Garden of Gethsemane under two aspects. In a natural aspect He is instantly crying out, "If it be possible." The next moment in the divine aspect, "But for this cause came I unto this hour." And the other aspect had no more choice. He was off.

And when God the Holy Ghost brings us to see these truths we shall deny ourselves for the sake of the cross. We will deny ourselves of anything where our brother would stumble. We would annihilate ourselves on all lines of fleshly indulgences lest we should miss the great swallowing up of life. We would not even mention, or ever give sense to, anything on a natural order.

If God shall have choice with us this morning He shall lift us up into a higher state of grace than ever we have been. If a sister or a brother could catch this spiritual power this morning they could stand anything on the lines of ridicule by husband, and ridicule by wife.

When are we drawn aside and disturbed? When we don't reach the ideals in the Spirit. When we reach the ideals in the Spirit what does it matter? I find that the power of God sanctifies husband and wife.

One half of the trouble in the assemblies is the murmuring over the conditions they are in. There isn't a murmur in that Bible. If you reach that standard you will never murmur anymore. You will be above murmuring. You will be in the place where God is absolutely the exchanger of thought, and the exchanger of act, and the exchanger of your inward purity. He will be purifying you all the time, and lifting you higher, and you will know you are not of this world.

You are not of this world. If you want to stop in the world, you cannot go on with this. Your position in the world in your banking affairs, and everything else would have the least effect on you. Yet you would know everything would work for good if you climb the ladder of faith with God. God will keep the world in perfect order and make it out for you.

God cannot work for you, you are so mixed in the world He cannot get your eye. How can a man or woman get into these divine orders when he is troubled between the two things: he cannot let himself go and let God take him.

Let us read again from the seventeenth verse:

> *For our light affliction, which is but for a moment, worketh for us a far more exceeding and eternal weight of glory; While we*

look not at the things which are seen, but at the things which are not seen: for the things which are seen are temporal; but the things which are not seen are eternal. For we know that, if our earthly house of this tabernacle were dissolved, we have a building of God, an house not made with hands, eternal in the heavens.

I maintain that, by the grace of God, we are so rich, we are so abounding, we have such a treasure house, we have such a storehouse of God, we have such an unlimited faith to go in for all God has for it is ours. We are the choice of the earth, we are the precious fruit of the earth.

God has told us that all things shall work together for good to us. God has said that we should be the children of the Highest, and that we should be the meat of the earth. God has declared all that in His Word, and you will never reach those beatitudes if you lay hold of the bulrush, it will keep you down.

How am I to have all the treasures of heaven, and all the treasures of God? It is not to get my eyes on the things which are seen for they will fade away. I must get my eyes upon the things which are not seen for they will remain as long as God reigns.

Where are we? Are our eyes on the earth? You once had your eyes on the earth. All your members were in the earth working out the plan of the earth. But now there is a change taking place. I read in the Scriptures.

...that ye should be married to another, even to him who is raised from the dead, that we should bring forth fruit unto God.

Romans 7:4

You are joined unto another, you belong to another, you have a new life, you have a new place. God has changed you. Is it a living fact? If it is only a word it will finish up there, but if it is a spiritual fact, and you reign in it, you will go away from this meeting and say, "Thank God, I never knew I was so rich!" How to loose, how to bind in the Spirit! Great ideals.

I want you to see there are two planes in this: there is a swallowing up and a dissolving. I like the thought of dissolving. Will that dissolving take place while I live? Ye shall want to be no other way. When will the clothing take place that I may not be naked? It will take place while you live.

People take these conditions as not attainable while you live. All these are spiritual blessings attainable while you live. These beatitudes along with the fifth chapter of Matthew's gospel, dovetail so perfectly. And yet there are so many things in that fifth chapter of Matthew's gospel that we will have to wake up to see they are as practical as possible, and God will be able to trust us on these lines with them.

I want us to catch the idea of dissolving:

> *For we know that if our earthly house of this tabernacle were dissolved, we have a building of God, an house not made with hands, eternal in the heavens.*
>
> *2 Corinthians 5:1*

That is a perfect condition of a heavenly atmosphere and dwelling place. Let me take you there this morning. If I live on the earth I fail everything. If I continue on the earth, everything I do will be mortal and die. If I live in the heavenly things, in the heavenly place, everything I touch will become spiritual, vital, purified, and eternal.

I must see this morning by the faith of God how everything can be dissolved. I will take it first in its heavenly bearings because you will understand it better that way. I will take you on to the rapture, that is what all people get their minds on in this chapter. They say, "Some day we shall leave the earth, and everything will be dissolved, and we will be clothed upon with new bodies for heavenly conditions."

But let me come now to a new plane of it. What is the good of a white raiment to cover your nakedness that it may not be seen in heaven? You know very well that isn't a heavenly position. There will be no flesh in heaven. No nakedness will be seen in heaven. Then what does it really mean? That the power of God can so dwell in us that it can burn up everything which is not spiritual, and dissolve it to such a perfection of beauty and holiness as Jesus was. He walked up and down, and when Satan came he could find nothing in Him. He was perfectly dissolved on every natural line, and He lived in the Spirit over everything else. And as He is, so have we to be.

We shouldn't be troubled in the flesh. Was Jesus troubled in the flesh? Did He go forth with perfect victory? It is impossible for any avenue of flesh, or anything that you touch in your natural body to be helpful. Even your eyes have to be sanctified by the power of God that they strike fire every time you look at a sinner, and the sinner shall be changed.

We shall be clothed upon with a robe of righteousness in God that wherever we walk there will be a whiteness of effectiveness that shall bring people to a place of conviction of sin. You say, "There are so many things in my house that would have to be thrown out the window if Jesus came to my home." Would to God we could understand it for He is in the house all the time. All the things ought to go out the window that couldn't stand His eyes on them. Every impression of our hearts that brought trouble when He looked at us ought to go forever.

You ask, "What is it?" It is in the message I am preaching, it is in being "swallowed up of life." The great I *Am* in perfect holiness, is He an example only? By the grace of God He isn't only the example but He is the personality of a personator.

It is impossible for us to subdue kingdoms, it is impossible for the greater works to be accomplished, impossible for the Son of God to be making sons on earth only as we stand exactly in His place. It is lovely...and I must win Him. There isn't a place in Scripture that God spoke about that He hasn't for us to take us into, beloved.

TONGUES AND INTERPRETATION: "It is a whole burnt offering. It is a perfect sacrifice. It is a place where we are perfectly justified, where we have been partakers of His divine nature, and become personated with His holiness, where we still are there, and He is still in the place of working out His great purpose in us which is the work of God. For it is God who worketh in you to will and to do these things when we are still, and dissolved, and put to death, where only the life of Christ is being manifested."

And that is the interpretation of the Spirit. It is a lofty look, a lowly place.

See what it means, a whole burnt offering, a place of ashes, a place of helplessness, a place of wholehearted surrender where you refer not to yourself. You have no justification on any line. You are prepared to be slandered, to be set at naught by everybody. You are of no importance to anybody but to God. But because of His personality in you, He reserves you for Himself because you are godly, and He sets you on high because you have known His name. And He causes you to be the fruit out of His loins to bring forth His glory that you should not in any way rest in yourself, or have any confidence in yourself, but your confidence shall be in God. Ah, it is lovely.

> *...the Lord is that Spirit: and where the Spirit of the Lord is, there is liberty.*
>
> *2 Corinthians 3:17*

TONGUES AND INTERPRETATION: "And in the depths of the heart there comes forth to us this morning this truth: set thy house in order. See to it that thou dost not allow anything that could be there that He could see that He could be displeased with. Thy house is thy body, thy body is the temple of the Spirit."

See to it that you obey that message.

I wonder how much we know about groaning to be delivered? I think I could get a display of it this morning if I turn to Nehemiah. Jerusalem to the Jews was everything. Jerusalem to the Jews is a great deal now, but it is nothing to us any more than any city. Why? Theirs is an earthly type but ours is a heavenly. Our Jerusalem is the glory.

One day Nehemiah says that a report was brought to him:

> *That Hanani, one of my brethren, came, he and certain men of Judah; and I asked them concerning the Jews that had escaped, which were left of the captivity, and concerning Jerusalem. And they said unto me, The remnant that are left of the captivity there in the province are in great affliction and reproach: the wall of Jerusalem also is broken down, and the gates thereof are burned with fire. And it came to pass, when I heard these words, that I sat down and wept, and mourned certain days, and fasted, and prayed before the God of heaven.*
>
> *Nehemiah 1:2-4*

He did it till it brought the same thing that God's Word brings to us, it dissolved him. It brought everything of his old nature into a dissolved place where he went right through into the presence of God.

The moment the king saw it he asked, "What is up with thee, Nehemiah? I have never seen thy countenance changed like this." And Nehemiah was so near almightiness before the king, he could pray and move the heavens, and move the king, and move the world, till Jerusalem was restored.

He mourned. When we reach a place where the Spirit takes us to see our weakness, our depravity, our failings; when we mourn before God we shall be dissolved, and in the dissolving we shall be clothed upon with our house from heaven. And we shall walk in white, we shall be robed with a new robe, and this mortality will be swallowed up of life.

Beloved, Christ can bring every one of us, if we will, into an activity of a wholehearted dependency where God will never fail us but we shall reign in life, we shall travail and bring forth fruit. For Zion, when she travails, shall make the house of hell shake.

Shall we reach it? Our blessed Lord reached it. Every night He went alone and reached ideals and walked the world in white. He was clothed with the Holy Spirit from heaven. His comeliness was always being eaten up.

Daniel entered into the same negotiations with heaven by the same position of an inward aspiring, with a groaning, travailing position, till for three weeks he shook the heavens and moved Gabriel to come. He passed through all the regions of the damned to bring the message to him.

There was something so beautiful about the whole thing that even Daniel in his most holy, beautiful state, in the presence of Gabriel, became as corruption before him. And he strengthened him by his right hand, and lifted him up, and gave him the visions of the world's history which are to be fulfilled.

TONGUES AND INTERPRETATION: "The lamentable condition where God travails through the soul, touches by the Almighty the man of God like Gabriel, touches the human flesh, and changes it, and makes it bring forth and blossom even like the rose, out of death into life, the powers of God shall be."

You cannot get into life but out of death, and you cannot get into death but by life. The only way to go into fulness with God is for the life to swallow up the life. For the life to be swallowed up there must come nothing there but helplessness till the life strengthens the life. Instead of the natural life being strengthened the supernatural life comes forth with abounding conditions.

There has been much given this morning in the Spirit that has never been given before by me, and I know that God has brought that message through a travail, and it has come this morning for us. It will mean a lot more to us if we don't let these things slip.

Let us catch something from the sixteenth verse:

> *Wherefore henceforth know we no man after the flesh: yea, though we have known Christ after the flesh, yet now henceforth know we him no more.*
>
> *2 Corinthians 5:16*

To know no man any more after the flesh is a great thing. Beloved, we shall know no man any more on a natural line. Everything from this moment we will only know on the line of a spiritual basis. Conversation must be spiritual. The thing that distracts you is after you have had a real good feast, you go out and instead of knowing no man any more after the flesh so that everything is in spiritual fellowship and union, you lower the standard by talking about natural things.

If you ride with me in a railroad carriage you will have to pray or testify. If you don't you will hear a whole lot of talk that will lower the unction, and bring you into a kind of bondage, and make you feel you wish you were out of the carriage. Break in and have a prayer meeting and you turn the whole thing. Go in and pray till you know everybody is feeling the touch of it.

If you go out to dinner with anybody today, don't get sidetracked by having a long story of their ranches. You must only know one Man now, and that is Christ, and He hasn't any ranches, and He belongs to all the ranches. Live in the Spirit and all things will work together for good to you. If you live in the heavenly places and you will cause your ranches and all things to come out of difficulties, for God will fight for you.

"Know we no man after the flesh." I won't enter into anything that is lower than spiritual fidelity. When I am preaching spiritual unctionizing thoughts, I must see I lift my people into a place where I know the Spirit is leading me to know Jesus.

Supposing you know Jesus. What do you say? He lost out? No, He didn't. But there was a great deal put upon Him by the people who said:

> *Is not this the carpenter's son? is not his mother called Mary?*
> *and his brethren, James, and Joses, and Simon, and Judas?*
> *And his sisters, are they not all with us? Whence then hath this*
> *man all these things?*
>
> *Matthew 13:55,56*

They said, "He is only an ordinary man. He is born the same way. You see Him, there, what is He?"

You will never get anything that way. He wasn't an ordinary man if He was born out of the same loins. There were two sons born, and one was of promise, the other wasn't. But the son of promise got the blessings. You can never enter into God's conditions on any lines, only the spiritual.

For a time there was a cloud overshadowed Jesus because of His ancestry. With the Jews it overshadows Him today because the vail is over their eyes, but the vail will be lifted. With the Gentiles the vail is already lifted.

We see Him as the incarnation, as the Holy One of God, as the Son of God, as the only Begotten of the Father full of grace and truth. We see Him as the burden bearer, as our sanctifier, as our cleanser, as our baptizer. Know no man after the flesh but see Him! And as we behold Him in all His glory we shall rise, we cannot help but rise in the power of God.

Know no man after the flesh. You will draw people if you refuse to be contaminated. People want holiness. People want righteousness. People want purity. People have an inward longing to be clothed upon.

May the Lord lead you this morning to the supply of every need far more than you can ask or think. The Lord bless you as you are led to dedicate yourself afresh to God this very day. Amen.

Message given at Glad Tidings Tabernacle and Bible Training School
San Francisco, California

ow beloved, I believe the Lord wants me to read you a few verses from St. Mark's gospel. Turn to the second chapter, (here following the reading of the healing of the palsied man, borne of four and let down through the housetop at Jesus' feet).

PRESSING THROUGH

September 1922

> *And immediately he arose, took up the bed, and went forth before them all; insomuch that they were all amazed, and glorified God, saying, We never saw it on this fashion.*
>
> *Mark 2:12*

If anything stirs me in my life it is such words as these, "We never saw it on this fashion." Something ought to happen all the time so that people will say, "We never saw it like that." If there is anything that God is dissatisfied with, it is stationary conditions. So many people stop on the threshold, when God, in His great plan, is inviting them into His treasury. Oh, this treasury of the Most High, the unsearchable riches of Christ, this divine position which God wants to move us into so that we are altogether a new creation. You know that the flesh profiteth nothing. "...the carnal mind is enmity against God: for it is not subject to the law of God, neither indeed can be" (Romans 8:7). As we cease to live in the old life, and know the resurrection power of the Lord, we come into a place of rest, of faith, and joy and peace and blessing and life everlasting. Glory to God!

May the Lord give us a new vision of Himself, fresh touches of divine life and His presence that will shake off all that remains of the old life and bring us fully into His newness of life. May He reveal to us the greatness of His will concerning us, for there is no one who loves us like Him. Yes, beloved, there is no love like His, no compassion like His. He is filled with compassion, and never fails to take those who will fully obey Him into the promised land.

You know, beloved, in God's Word there is always more to follow, always more than we know, and oh, if we could only be babies this afternoon, with a childlike mind to take in all the mind of God, what wonderful things would happen. I wonder if you take the Bible just for yourself. It is grand. Never mind who takes only a part — you take it all. When we get such a thirst upon us that nothing can satisfy us but God, we shall have a royal time.

The child of God must have reality all the time. After the child of God comes into the sweetness of the perfume of the presence of God, he will have the hidden treasures of God and will always be feeding on that blessed unction of truth that will make life full of glory. Are you dry? There is no dry place in God, but all the good things come out of hard times. The harder the place you are in, the more blessedness can come out of it as we yield to His plan. Oh, if I had only known God's plan in its fulness I might never have had a tear in my life. God is so abundant, so full of love and mercy; there is no lack to them that trust in Him. As I bring you these words this afternoon on the lines of faith, I pray that God may give us some touch of reality, so that we may be able to trust Him all the way.

It is an ideal thing to get people to believe, when they ask, that they shall receive; but how could it be otherwise? It must be so when God says it. Now we have a beautiful word brought before us this afternoon in the case of this man with the palsy, a helpless man, and so infirm that he could not help himself to get to the place where Jesus was. Four men, whose hearts were full of compassion, carried the man to the house, but the house was full. Oh, I can see that house today as it was filled, jammed and crammed just as it was in Mexico (we had a wonderful time in Mexico, hadn't we, Brother Montgomery?), just as it was in Switzerland and in Sweden, in Norway and in Denmark. The places have been packed to hear the words of our Savior. There was no room, even by the door. It was crowded inside and crowded outside.

The men who were carrying the palsied man said, "What shall we do?" But there is always a way. I have never found faith to fail, never once. May God the Holy Ghost, this afternoon, give us a new touch of faith in God's unlimited power. May we have a living faith that will dare to trust Him and say, "Lord, I do believe."

There was no room, "not so much as about the door," (Mark 2:2) but these men said, "Let's go up on the housetop." Unbelieving people would say, "Oh, that is silly, ridiculous, foolish!" But the men of faith say, "We must have him in at all costs. It is nothing to move the roof.

Let's go up and go through." Lord, take us today, and let us go through; let us drop right into the arms of Jesus. It is a lovely place to drop into, out of your self-righteousness, out of your self-consciousness, out of your unbelief. Some people have been in a strange place of deadness for years, but God can shake them out of it. Thank God some of the molds have been broken. It is a blessed thing when the old mold gets broken, for God has a new mold, and how He can make perfect out of the imperfect by His own loving touch.

I tell you, my sister, my brother, that since the day that Christ's blood was shed; since the day of His atonement, He has paid the price to meet all the world's need and its cry of sorrow. Truly Jesus has met the need of the broken hearts and the sorrowful spirits, and also of the withered limbs and the broken bodies. God's dear Son paid the debt for all, for He took our infirmities and bare our sicknesses. In all points He was tempted like as we are, in order that He might be able to succor them that are tempted. I rejoice to bring Him to you today, in a new way it may be on some lines, even though it be in my crooked Yorkshire speech, and say to you that He is the only Jesus; He is the only plan; He is the only life; He is the only help; but thank God He has triumphed to the uttermost. He came to seek and to save that which was lost, and He heals all who come to Him.

As the palsied man is let down through the roof, there is a great commotion, and all the people are gazing up at this strange sight. We read, "When Jesus saw their faith, he said unto the sick of the palsy, Son, thy sins be forgiven thee" (Mark 2:5). What had the forgiveness of sins to do with the healing of this man? It had everything to do with it. Sin is at the root of disease. May the Lord cleanse us this afternoon from outward sin and from inbred sin, and take away from us all that hinders the power of God to work through us.

The scribes reasoned in their hearts thus, "...who can forgive sins but God only?" (v. 7). But the Lord answered the thoughts of their hearts by saying, "Whether is it easier to say to the sick of the palsy, Thy sins be forgiven thee; or to say, Arise, and take up thy bed, and walk? But that ye may know that the Son of man hath power on earth to forgive sins, (he saith to the sick of the palsy,) I say unto thee, Arise, and take up thy bed, and go thy way into thine house" (vv. 9-11).

Jesus had seen the weakness of that man, and his helplessness. He saw also the faith of these four men. There is something in this for us today. Many people will not be saved unless some of you are used to stir them up. Remember that you are your brother's keeper. We must take our brother to Jesus. When these men carried the palsied man, they pressed through until he could hear the voice of the Son of God, and liberty came to the captive. The man became strong by the power of God, arose, took up his bed, and went forth before them all.

Oh, beloved, I have seen wonderful things like this wrought by the power of God. We must never think about our God on small lines. He spoke the word one day and made the world of things which did not appear. That is the kind of a God we have, and He is just the same today. There is no change in Him. Oh, He is lovely and precious above all thought and comparison. There is none like Him.

I am certain today that nothing will profit you but that which you take by faith. God wants you to come into a close place with God where you will believe and claim the promises, for they are Yea and Amen to all that believe. Let us thank God for this full Gospel which is not hidden under a bushel today. Let us thank Him that He is bringing out the Gospel as in the days of His flesh. God is all the time working right in the very midst of us, but I want to know, what are you going to do with the Gospel today? There is greater blessing for you than you have ever received in your life. Do you believe it and will you receive it?

Published in *Triumphs of Faith*

THE FAITH THAT COMES FROM GOD

September 16, 1922

Read Hebrews 11:1-11. I believe that there is only one way to all the treasures of God, and that is the way of faith. By faith and faith alone do we enter into a knowledge of the attributes, become partakers of the beatitudes, and participate in the glories of our ascended Lord. All His promises are Yea and Amen to them who believe.

God would have us come to Him by His own way. That is through the open door of grace. A way has been made. It is a beautiful way, and all His saints can enter in by this way and find rest. God has prescribed that the just shall live by faith. I find that all is a failure that has not its base on the rock Christ Jesus. He is the only way, the truth, and the life. The way of faith is the Christ way, receiving Him in His fulness and walking in Him; receiving His quickening life that filleth, moveth, and changeth us, bringing us to a place where there is always an Amen in our hearts to all the will of God.

As I look into the twelfth chapter of Acts, I find that the people were praying all night for Peter to come out of prison. They had a zeal but no faith. They were to be commended for their zeal in spending their time in prayer without ceasing, but there was one thing missing. It was faith. Rhoda had more faith than the rest of them. When the knock came to the door, she ran to it, and the moment she heard Peter's voice, she ran back again with joy saying that Peter stood before the gate. And all the people said, "You are mad. It isn't so." But she constantly affirmed that it was even so. But they had not faith, and conjectured, "Well, God has sent His angel." But Peter continued knocking. They had zeal but no faith. And I believe there is quite a difference.

Zacharias and Elisabeth surely wanted a son, but even when the angel came and told Zacharias he was full of unbelief. And the angel said, "...thou shalt be dumb...because thou believest not my words..." (Luke 1:20).

But look at Mary. When the angel came to her, Mary said, "...be it unto me according to thy word..." (Luke 1:38). It was her Amen to the will of God. And God wants us with an Amen in our lives, an inward Amen, a mighty moving Amen, a God-inspired Amen, that which says, "It is, because God has spoken. It cannot be otherwise. It is impossible to be otherwise."

Let us examine this fifth verse of Hebrews 11: "By faith Enoch was translated that he should not see death; and was not found, because God had translated him: for before his translation he had this testimony, that he pleased God."

When I was in Sweden, the Lord worked mightily. After one or two addresses the leaders called me and said, "We have heard very strange things about you, and we would like to know if they are true. We can see that God is with you, and that God is moving, and we know that it will be a great blessing to Sweden."

"Well," I said, "what is it?"

"Well," they said, "we have heard from good authority that you preach that you have the resurrection body." When I was in France I had an interpreter that believed this thing, and I found out after I had preached once or twice through the interpreter that she gave her own expressions. And of course I did not know. I said to these brethren, "I tell you what my personal convictions are. I believe that if I had the testimony of Enoch I should be off. I believe that the moment Enoch had the testimony that he pleased God, off he went."

I pray that God will so quicken our faith, for translation is in the mind of God; but remember that translation comes on the line of holy obedience and a walk that is pleasing to God. This was true of Enoch. And I believe that we must have a like walk with God in the Spirit, having communion with Him, living under His divine smile, and I pray that God by His Spirit may so move us that we will be where Enoch was when he walked with God.

There are two kinds of faith. There is the natural faith. But the supernatural faith is the gift of God. In Acts 26:18, Paul is telling Agrippa of what the Lord said to him in commissioning him,

> *To open their eyes, and to turn them from darkness to light, and from the power of Satan unto God, that they may receive forgiveness of sins, and inheritance among them which are sanctified by faith that is in me.*

Is that the faith of Paul? No, it is the faith that the Holy Ghost is giving. It is the faith that He brings to us as we press in and on with God. I want to put before you this difference between our faith and the faith of Jesus. Our faith comes to an end. Most people in this place have come to where they have said, "Lord, I can go no further. I have gone so far and I can go no further. I have used all the faith I have, and I have just to stop now and wait."

I remember one day being in Lancashire, and going round to see some sick people. I was taken into a house where there was a young woman lying on a bed, a very helpless case. The reason had gone, and many things were manifested there which were satanic and I knew it. She was only a young woman, a beautiful child. The husband, quite a young man, came in with the baby, and he leaned over to kiss the wife. The moment he did, she threw herself over on the other side, just as a lunatic would do. That was very heartbreaking. Then he took the baby and pressed the baby's lips to the mother. Again another wild kind of thing happened. I asked one who was attending her, "Have you anybody to help?" "Oh," they said, "We have had everything." "But," I said, "have you no spiritual help?" Her husband stormed out and said, "Help? You think that we believe in God after we have had seven weeks of no sleep and maniac conditions. You think that we believe God. You are mistaken. You have come to the wrong house."

Then a young woman of about eighteen or so just grinned at me and passed out of the door, and that finished the whole business. That brought me to a place of compassion for the woman that something had to be done, no matter what it was. Then with my faith I began to penetrate the heavens, and I was soon out of that house I will tell you, for I never saw a man get anything from God who prayed on the earth. If you get anything from God you will have to pray into heaven for it is all there. If you are living in the earth realm and expect things from heaven, they will never come. And as I saw in the presence of God the limitations of my faith, there came another faith, a faith that could not be denied, a faith that took the promise, a faith that believed God's Word. And I came from that presence back again to earth, but not the same man under the conditions confronting me. God gave a faith that could shake hell and anything else.

I said, "Come out of her in the name of Jesus!" And she rolled over and fell asleep and wakened in fourteen hours perfectly sane and perfectly whole.

There is a process on this line. Enoch walked with God. That must have been all those years as he was penetrating, and going through, and laying hold, and believing and seeing and getting into such close cooperation and touch with God that things moved on earth and he began to move toward heaven. At last it was not possible for him to stop any longer. Oh, hallelujah!

In the fifteenth chapter of First Corinthians we read of the body being "sown with dishonor," to be raised in power. It seems to me that as we are looking for translation that the Lord would have us know something of that power now, and would have us kept in that power, so that we should not be sown in dishonor.

Enoch walked with God. God wants to raise the condition of saints so that they walk with Him and talk with Him. I don't want to build anything round myself, but it is true that if you find me outside of conversation with man, you will find me in conversation with God.

There in one thing that God has given me from my youth up, a taste and relish for my Bible. I can say before God, I have never read a book but my Bible, so I know nothing about books. It seems better to me to get the Book of books for food for your soul, for the strengthening of your faith and the building up of your character in God, so that all the time you are being changed and made meet to walk with God.

> *...without faith it is impossible to please him: for he that cometh to God must believe that he is, and that he is a rewarder of them that diligently seek him.*
>
> Hebrews 11:6

I can see that it is impossible to please Him on any lines but faith, for everything that is not of faith is sin. God wants us to see that the plan of faith is the ideal and principle of God. In this connection I love to keep in my thoughts the beautiful words in the second verse of the twelfth chapter of Hebrews: "Looking unto Jesus the author and finisher of our faith...." He is the author of faith. God worked through Him for the forming of the worlds. All things were made by Him, and without Him was not anything made that was made. And because of the exceeding abundant joy of providing for us so great salvation, He became the author of a living faith. And through this principle of living faith, looking unto Him who is the author and finisher of our faith, we are changed into the same image from glory to glory, even by the Spirit of the Lord.

God has something better for you than you have ever had in the past. Come out into all the fulness of faith and power and life and victory that He is willing to provide, as you forget the things of the past, and press right on for the prize of His calling in Christ Jesus.

Published in *The Pentecostal Evangel*

THE APPLAUSE OF THE WORLD VS. THE APPROVAL OF GOD

THE APPOINTED "HOUR"
Life Out of Death
November 5, 1922

This is a very blessed time for us to gather together in remembrance of the Lord. I want to remind you of this fact, that this is the only service we render to the Lord. All other services we attend are for us to get blessing from the Lord, but Jesus said, "This do in remembrance of Me." We have gathered together to commemorate that wonderful death, victory, and triumph, and the looking forward to the "glorious hope," and I want you, if it is possible at all, to get rid of your religion. It has been "religion" at all times that has slain and destroyed that which was good. When Satan entered into Judas, the only people who the devil could speak to through Judas were the priests, sad as it is to say it. They conspired to get him to betray Jesus, and the devil took money from these priests to put Jesus to death. Now it is a very serious thing, for we must clearly understand whether we are of the right spirit or not, for no man can be of the Spirit of Christ and persecute another; no man can have the true Spirit of Jesus and slay his brother, and no man can follow the Lord Jesus and have enmity in his heart. You cannot have Jesus and have bitterness and hatred, and persecute the believer.

It is possible for us, if we are not careful, to have within us an evil spirit of unbelief, and even in our best state it is possible for us to have enmity unless we are perfectly dead and let the life of the Lord lead us. You remember Jesus wanted to pass through a certain place as He was going to Jerusalem. Because He would not stop and preach to them concerning the Kingdom, they refused to allow Him to go through their section of the country. And the disciples which were with Jesus said to Him, "Shall we call down fire from heaven upon them as Elijah did?" (Luke 9:54). But Jesus turned and said, "Ye know not what manner of spirit ye are of" (v. 55). There they were, following Jesus and with Him all the time, but Jesus rebuked that spirit. I pray God that we may get this out of this service, that our knowledge of Jesus is pure love, and pure love to Jesus is death to self on all lines, body, soul and spirit. I believe if we are in the will of God, we will be perfectly directed at all times, and if we would know anything about the mighty works of Christ, we shall have to follow what Jesus said. Whatever He said came to pass.

Many things happened in the lives of the apostles to show His power over all flesh. In regard to paying tribute, Jesus said to Peter, "We are free, we can enter into the city without paying tribute; nevertheless, we will pay." I like that thought, that Jesus was so righteous on all lines. It helps me a great deal. Then Jesus told Peter to do a very hard thing. He said, "Take that hook and cast it into the sea. Draw out a fish and take from its gills a piece of silver for thee and Me." This was one of the hardest things Peter had to do. He had been fishing all his life, but never had he taken silver out of a fish's mouth. There were thousands and millions of fish in the sea, but one fish had to have a piece of silver in it. He went down to the sea as any natural man would, speculating and thinking, "How can it be?" But how could it not be, if Jesus said it would be? Then the perplexity would arise, "But how many fish there are, and which fish has the money?" Brother, if God speaks, it will be as He says.

What you need is to know the mind of God and the Word of God, and you will be so free you will never find a frown on your face, nor a tear in your eye. The more you know of the mightiness of revelation, the more does everything in the way of fearfulness pass away. To know God is to be in the place of triumph. To know God is to be in the place of rest. To know God is to be in the place of victory. No doubt many things were in Peter's mind that day, but thank God there was one fish, and he obeyed. Sometimes to obey in blindness brings the victory. Sometimes when perplexities arise in your mind, obedience means God working out the problem. Peter cast the hook into the sea, and it would have been amazing if you could have seen the disturbance the other fish made to move out of the way, all excepting the right one. Just one among the millions of fish God wanted. God may put His hand upon you in the midst of millions of people, but if He speaks to you, that thing that He says will be appointed.

On this occasion, Jesus said to Peter and the rest, that when they went out into the city they would see a man bearing a pitcher of water, and they should follow him. It was not customary in the East for men to carry anything on their heads. The women always did the carrying, but this had to be a man, and he had to have a pitcher. One day there was a man preaching and he said it was quite all right for Jesus to go and arrange for a colt to be tied there, and another preacher said it was quite easy to feed all those thousands of people, because the loaves in those days were so tremendously big, but he didn't tell them it was a little boy who had the five loaves. Unbelief can be very blind, but faith can see through a stone wall. Faith when it is moved by the power of God can laugh when trouble is on.

They said to the man with the pitcher, "Where is the guest chamber?" "How strange it is that you should ask," he replied. "I have been preparing that, wondering who wanted it." It is marvelous when God is leading how perfectly everything works into the plan. He was arranging everything. You think He cannot do that today for you? People who have been in perplexities for days and days, He knows how to deliver out of trouble; He knows how to be with you in the dark hour. He can make all things work together for good to them that love God. He has a way of arranging His plan, and when God comes in, you always know it was a day you lived in God. Oh, to live in God! There is a vast difference between living in God and living in speculation and hope. There is something better than hope; something better than speculation. "They that know their God shall be strong and do exploits," and God would have us to know Him.

"And when the hour was come, He sat down and the twelve apostles with Him." "When the hour was come" — that was the most wonderful hour. There never was an hour, never will be an hour like that hour. What hour was it? It was an hour of the passing of creation under the blood. It was an hour of destruction of demon power. It was an hour appointed of life coming out of death. It was an hour when all that ever lived came under a glorious covering of the blood. It was an hour when all the world was coming into emancipation by the blood. It was an hour in the world's history when it emerged from dark chaos, a wonderful hour! Praise God for that hour! Was it a dark hour? It was a dark hour for Him, but a wonderful light dawned for us. It was tremendously dark for the Son of Man, but praise God He came through it.

There are some things in the Scriptures which move me greatly. I am glad that Paul was a man. I am glad that Jesus was a Man. I am glad that Daniel was a man, and I am also glad that John was a man. You ask, "Why?" Because I see that whatever God has done for other men, He can do for me. And I find God has done such wonderful things for other men that I am always on the expectation that these things are possible for me. Think about this. It is a wonderful thought to me. Jesus said in that trying hour — hear it for a moment: "I have a desire to eat this Passover with you before I suffer." Desire? What could be His desire? His desire because of the salvation of the world. His desire because of dethronement of the powers of Satan. His desire because He knew He was going to conquer everything and make every man free who ever lived. It was a great desire, but what lay between it? Just between that and the cross lay Gethsemane! Some people say that Jesus died on the cross. It is perfectly true, but is that the only place? Jesus died in Gethsemane. That was the tragic moment! That was the place where He paid the debt. It was in Gethsemane, and Gethsemane was between Him and the cross. He had a desire to eat this Passover and knew Gethsemane was between Him and the cross.

I want you to think about Gethsemane. There alone, and with the tremendous weight, the awful effect of all sin and disease upon that body, He cries out, "If it be possible, let it pass." Oh, could it be! He could only save when He was man, but here, like a giant refreshed and coming out of a great chaos of darkness, He comes forth: "To this end I came." It was His purpose to die for the world. Oh, brother, will it ever be said to pass through your lips or your mind for a moment that you will not have a desire to serve Christ like that? Can you deign, under any circumstances to take your cross fully, to be in the place of any ridicule, any surrender, anything for the Man who said He desired to eat the Passover with His disciples, knowing what it meant? It can only come out of the depths of love we have for Him that we can say this morning, "Lord Jesus, I will follow." Oh, brother, there is something very wonderful in the decision in your heart! God knows the heart. You do not always have to be on the housetop to shout to indicate the condition of your heart. He knows your inward heart. You say, "I would be ashamed not to be willing to suffer for a Man who desired to suffer to save me." *"With desire,"* He says.

I know what it is to have the kingdom of heaven within you. He said that even the least in the kingdom of heaven is greater than John the Baptist, meaning those who are under the blood, those who have seen the Lord by faith, those who know by redemption they are made sons of God. I say to you, He will never taste again until we are there with Him. The Kingdom will never be complete — it could not be — until we are all there at that great Supper of the Lamb where there will be millions and trillions of redeemed, which no man can number. We shall be there when that Supper is taking place. I like to think of that.

I hope you will take one step into definite lines with God and believe it. It is an act of faith God wants to bring you into; a perfecting of that love that cannot fail to avail. It is a fact that He has opened the kingdom of heaven to all believers, and that He gives eternal life to them who believe. The Lord, the Omnipotent God, it is He that knoweth the end from the beginning, and has arranged by the blood of the Lamb to cover the guilty and make intercession for all believers. Oh, it is a wonderful inheritance of faith to find shelter under the blood of Jesus!

I want you to see that He says, "Do this in remembrance of Me." He took the cup. He took the bread, and He gave thanks. The very attitude of giving thanks for His shed blood, giving thanks for His broken body, overwhelms the heart. To think that my Lord could give thanks for His shed blood! To think that my Lord could give thanks for His broken body! Only divinity can reveal this sublime act unto the heart! The natural man cannot receive it, but the spiritual man, the man who has been created anew by faith in Christ, he is open to it. The man who believes God comes in is inborn with the eternal seed of truth and righteousness and faith, and from the moment he sees the truth on the lines of faith he is made a new creation. The flesh ceases, the spiritual man begins. One passes off, the other passes on, until a man is in the existence of God. I say the Lord brings a child of faith into a place of rest, causes him to sit with Him in heavenly places, gives him a language in the Spirit and makes him know he belongs no longer to the law of creation.

You see this bread which represents His broken body? The Lord knew He could not bring us any nearer to His broken body. Our bodies are made of bread. The body of Jesus was made of that bread, and He knew He could bring us no nearer. He took the natural elements and said,

"This bread represents my broken body." Now will it ever become that body of Christ? No, never. You cannot make it so. It is foolishness to believe it, but I take it as an emblem and when I eat it, the natural leads me into the supernatural, and instantly I begin to feed on the supernatural by faith. One leads me into the other.

Jesus said, "Take, eat, this is my body." I have a real knowledge of Christ through this emblem. May we take from the table of the riches of His promises. The riches of heaven are before us. Fear not, only believe, for God has opened the treasures of His holy Word.

(COMMUNION SERVICE)

As they were all gathered together, He looked on them and said right into their ears, "There is one of you which will betray Me." Jesus knew who would betray Him. He had known it for many, many months. They whispered to one another, "Who is it?" None of them had real confidence that it would not be he. That is the serious part about it; they had so little confidence in their ability to face the opposition that was before them, and they had no confidence it would not be one of them. Jesus knew. He had been talking to Judas many times, rebuking him, and telling him that his course would surely bring him to a bad end. He never had told any of His disciples, not even John who leaned on His breast. Now if that same spirit was in any church, it would purify the church. But I fear sometimes Satan gets the advantage and things are told before they are true. I believe God wants to so sanctify us, so separate us, that we will have that perfection of love that will not speak ill of a brother, that will not slander a brother whether it is true or not.

There was strife among them who should be the greatest, but He said, "He that is chief let him be as he that doth serve," and then He, the Master said, "I am among you as one that serveth." He, the noblest, the purest, He was the servant of all! Exercising lordship over another is not of God. We must learn in our hearts that fellowship, true righteousness loving one another and preferring one another must come into the church. Pentecost must outreach everything that ever has been, and we know it will if we are willing. But it cannot be if we will not. We can never be filled with the Holy Ghost so long as there is any human, craving desire for our own will. Selfishness must be destroyed. Jesus was perfect, the end of everything, and God will bring us all there. It is *giving* that pays; it is *helping* that pays; it is *loving* that pays; it is *putting your-self out of the way for another* that pays. "I am among you as one that serveth. Ye are they which have continued with Me in My temptations. And I appoint unto you a kingdom, as my Father hath appointed unto Me." I believe there is a day coming greater than anything any of us have any conception of. This is the testing road. This is the place where your whole body has to be covered with the wings of God that your nakedness shall not be seen. This is the thing that God is getting you ready for, the most wonderful thing your heart can conceive. How can you get into it? First of all, "Ye have continued with Me in My tempta-tions." He had been in trials, He had been in temptation. There is not one of us who is tempted beyond what He was. If a young man can be so pure that he cannot be tempted, he will never be fit to be made a judge, but God intends us to be so purified during these evil days that He can make us judges in the world to come. If we can be tried, if we can be tempted on any line, Jesus said, "Ye are they which have contin-ued with Me in My temptation." Have faith and God will keep you pure in the temptation. How shall we reach it? In Matthew 19:28, Jesus said,

> *...ye which have followed me, in the regeneration when the Son of man shall sit in the throne of his glory, ye also shall sit upon twelve thrones, judging the twelve tribes of Israel.*

"Follow in regeneration" — every day is a regeneration; every day is a day of advancement; every day is a place of choice. Every day you find yourself in need of fresh consecration. If you are in a place to yield, God moves you in the place of regeneration.

For years and years God has been making me appear to hundreds and thousands of people as a fool. I remember the day when He saved me and when He called me out. If there is a thing God wants to do today, He wants to be as real to you and me as He was to Abraham. After I was saved I joined myself up to a very lively lot of people who were full of a revival spirit, and it was marvelous how God blest. And then there came a lukewarmness and indifference, and God said to me as clearly as anything, "Come out." I obeyed and came out. The people said, "We cannot understand you. We need you now and you are leaving us." The Plymouth brethren at that time were in a Conference. The Word of God was with them in power, the love of God was with them unveiled. Baptism by immersion was revealed to me, and when my friends saw me go into the water they said I was altogether wrong. But God had called me and I obeyed. The day came when I saw that the brethren had dropped down to the letter, all letter, dry and barren.

At that time the Salvation Army was filled with love, filled with power, filled with zeal; every place a revival, and I joined up with them. For about six years the glory of God was there, and then the Lord said again, "Come out," and I was glad I came. It dropped right into a social movement and God has no place for a social movement. We are saved by regeneration and the man who is going on with God has no time for social reforms.

God moved on, and at that time there were many people who were receiving the baptism of the Holy Ghost without signs. Those days were "days of heaven on earth." God unfolded the truth, showed the way of sanctification by the power of the blood of Christ, and I saw in that the great inflow of the life of God. I thank God for that, but God came along again and said, "Come out." I obeyed God and went with what they called the "tongues" folks; they got the credit for having further light. I saw God advancing every movement I made, and I can see even in this Pentecostal work, except we see there is a real death, God will say to us, "Come out." Unless Pentecost wakes up to shake herself free from all worldly things and comes into a place of the divine-likeness with God, we will hear the voice of God, "Come out" and He will have something far better than this. I ask every one of you, will you hear the voice of God and come out? You ask, "What do you mean?" Everyone of you knows without exception, there is no word for Pentecost, only being on fire. If you are not on fire, you are not in the place of regeneration. It is only the fire of God that burns up the entanglements of the world.

When we came into this new work God spoke to us by the Spirit and we knew we had to reach the place of absolute yieldedness and cleansing, so that there would be nothing left. We were swept and garnished. Brother, that was only the beginning, and if you have not made tremendous progress in that holy zeal and power and compassion of God, we can truly say you have backslidden in heart. The backslider in heart is dead. He is not having the open vision. The backslider in heart is not seeing the Word of God more fresh every day. You can put it down that a man is a backslider in heart if he is not hated by the world. *If you have the applause of the world you are not having the approval of God.* I do not know whether you will receive it or not but my heart burns with this message, "changing in the regeneration" for in this changing you will get a place in the Kingdom to come where you shall be in authority; that place which God has prepared for us, that place which is beyond all human conception. We can catch a glimpse of that glory when we see how John worshipped the angel, and the angel said to him, "See thou do it not, for I am thy fellow-servant, of thy brethren the prophets." This angel is showing John the wonders of the glorious Kingdom and in his glorified state, John thought he was the Lord. I wonder if we dare believe for it.

Let me close with these words: as sure as we have borne the image of the earthly, we shall have the image of the heavenly. It means to us that everything of an earthly type has to cease, for the heavenly type is so wonderful in all its purity. God, full of love, full of purity, full of power! No power only on the lines of purity! No open door into heaven only on the lines of the conscience void of sin between man and God, the heavens open only where the Spirit of the Lord is so leading, so that flesh has no power, but we will live in the Spirit. God bless you and prepare you for greater days.

Communion Service
Stone Church

I s any sick among you? let him call for the elders of the church; and let them pray over him, anointing him with oil in the name of the Lord: And the prayer of faith shall save the sick, and the Lord shall raise him up; and if he hath committed sins, they shall be forgiven him.

James 5:14,15

I AM THE LORD THAT HEALETH THEE

November 11, 1922

We have in this precious Word a real basis for the truth of healing. In this scripture God gives very definite instructions to the sick. If you are sick, your part is to call for the elders of the church; it is their part to anoint and pray for you in faith, and then the whole situation rests with the Lord. When you have been anointed and prayed for, you can rest assured that the Lord will raise you up. It is the Word of God.

I believe that we all can see that the church cannot play with this business. If any turn away from these clear instructions they are in a place of tremendous danger. Those who refuse to obey do so to their unspeakable loss.

James tells us in connection with this, "...if any of you do err from the truth, and one convert him; let him know, that he which converteth the sinner from the error of his way shall save a soul from death..." (James 5:19,20). Many turn away from the Lord like King Asa, who sought the physicians in his sickness and consequently died, and I take it that this passage means that if one induces another to turn back to the Lord, he will save such from death and God will forgive a multitude of sins that they have committed. This scripture can also have a large application on the line of salvation. If you turn away from any part of God's truth, the enemy will certainly get an advantage over you.

Does the Lord meet those who look to Him for healing and obey the instructions set forth in James? Most assuredly. Let me tell you a story to show how He will undertake for the most extreme case.

One day I had been visiting the sick, and was with a friend of mine, an architect, when I saw a young man from his office coming down the road in a car holding in his hand a telegram. It contained a very urgent request that we go immediately and pray for a man who was dying. We went off in an auto as fast as possible and in about an hour and a half reached a large house in the country where the man who was dying resided. There were two staircases in that house, and it was extremely convenient, for the doctors could go up and down one, and my friend and I could go up and down the other, and so we had no occasion to meet one another.

I found on arrival that it was a case of this sort. The man's body had been broken, he was ruptured, and his bowels had been punctured in two places. The discharge from the bowels had formed abscesses and blood poisoning had set in. The man's face had turned green. Two doctors were in attendance, but they saw that the case was beyond their power. They had telegraphed to London for a great specialist, and, when we arrived, they were at the railway station awaiting his arrival.

The man was very near death and could not speak. I said to his wife, "If you desire, we will anoint and pray for him." She said, "That is why I sent for you." I anointed him in the name of the Lord and asked the Lord to raise him up. Apparently there was no change. God often hides what He does. From day to day we find that God is doing wonderful things, and we receive reports of healings that have taken place that we heard nothing about at the time of our meetings. Only last night a woman came into the meeting suffering terribly. Her whole arm was filled with poison, and her blood was so poisoned that it was certain to bring her to her death. We rebuked the thing, and she was here this morning and told us that she was without pain and had slept all night, a thing she had not done for two months. To God be all the praise. You will find He will do this kind of thing all along.

As soon as we anointed and prayed for this brother we went down the back staircase and the three doctors came up the front staircase. As we arrived downstairs, I said to my friend who had come with me, "Friend, let me have hold of your hands." We held each other's hands, and I said to him, "Look into my face and let us agree together according to Matthew 18:19 that this man should be brought out of this death." We laid the whole matter before God, and said, "Father, we believe."

Then the conflict began. The wife came down to us and said, "The doctors have got all their instruments out and they are about to operate." I cried, "What? Look here, he's your husband, and I tell you this, if those men operate on him, he will die. Go back and tell them you cannot allow it." She went back to the doctors and said, "Give me ten minutes." They said, "We can't afford to, the man is dying and it is your husband's only chance." She said, "I want ten minutes, and you don't touch his body until I have had them."

They went downstairs by one staircase and we went up by the other. I said to the woman, "This man is your husband, and he cannot speak for himself. It is now the time for you to put your whole trust in God and prove Him wholly true. You can save him from a thousand doctors. You must stand with God and for God in this critical hour." After that, we came down and the doctors went up. The wife faced those three doctors and said, "You shan't touch this man's body. He is my husband. I am sure that if you operate on him he will die, but he will live if you don't touch him."

Suddenly the man in the bed spoke. "God has done it," he said. They rolled back the bed clothes and the doctors examined him, and the abscesses were cut clear away. The nurse cleaned the place where they had been. The doctors could see the bowels still open and they said to the wife, "We know that you have great faith, and we can see that a miracle has taken place. But you must let us unite these broken parts and put in silver tubes, and we know that your husband will be all right after that, and it need not interfere with your faith at all." She said to them, "God has done the first thing and He can do the rest. No man shall touch him now." And God healed the whole thing. And that man is well and strong today. I can give his name and address to any who want it.

Do you ask by what power this was done? I would answer in the words of Peter, "...his name through faith in his name hath made this man strong..." (Acts 3:16). The anointing was done in the name of the Lord. And it is written, "The *Lord* shall raise him up." And He provides the double cure; even if sin has been the cause of the sickness, His Word declares, "If he have committed sins, they shall be forgiven."

You ask, "What is faith?" Faith is the principle of the Word of God. The Holy Spirit, who inspired the Word, is called the Spirit of Truth, and, as we receive with meekness the engrafted Word, faith springs up in our heart — faith in the sacrifice of Calvary; faith in the shed blood of Jesus; faith in the fact that He took our weakness upon Himself, has borne our sicknesses and carried our pains, and that He is our life today.

God has chosen us to help one another. We dare not be independent. He brings us to a place where we submit ourselves to one another. If we refuse to do this, we get away from the Word of God and out of the place of faith. I have been in this place once and I trust I shall never be there again. I went one time to a meeting. I was very, very sick, and I got worse and worse. I knew the perfect will of God was for me to humble myself and ask the elders to pray for me. I put it off and the meeting finished. I went home without being anointed and prayed with, and everyone in the house caught the thing I was suffering with.

My boys did not know anything else but to trust the Lord as the family Physician, and my youngest boy, George, cried out from the attic, "Dadda, come." I cried, "I cannot come. The whole thing is from me. I shall have to repent and ask the Lord to forgive me." I made up my mind to humble myself before the whole church. Then I rushed to the attic and laid my hands on my boy in the name of Jesus. I placed my hands on his head and the pain left and went lower down; he cried again, "Put your hands still lower." At last the pain went right down to the feet and as I placed my hand on the feet he was completely delivered. Some evil power had evidently gotten hold and as I laid my hands on the different parts of the body it left. (We have to see the difference between anointing the sick and casting out demons.) God will always be gracious when we humble ourselves before Him and come to a place of brokenness of spirit.

I was at a place one time ministering to a sick woman, and she said, "I'm very sick. I become all right for an hour, and then I have another attack." I saw that it was an evil power that was attacking her, and I learned something in that hour that I had never learned before. As I moved my hand down her body in the name of the Lord that evil power seemed to move just ahead of my hands and as I moved them down further and further the evil power went right out of her body and never returned.

I was in Havre in France and the power of God was being mightily manifested. A Greek named Felix attended the meeting and become very zealous for God. He was very anxious to get all the Catholics he could to the meeting in order that they should see that God was graciously visiting France. He found a certain bedridden woman who was fixed in a certain position and could not move, and he told her about the Lord healing at the meetings and that he would get me to come if she wished. She said, "My husband is a Catholic and he would never allow anyone who was not a Catholic to see me."

She asked her husband to allow me to come and told him what Felix had told her about the power of God working in our midst. He said, "I will have no Protestant enter my house." She said, "You know that the doctors cannot help me, and the priests cannot help, won't you let this man of God pray for me?" He finally consented and I went to the house. The simplicity of this woman and her childlike faith was beautiful to see.

I showed her my oil bottle and said to her, "Here is oil. It is a symbol of the Holy Ghost. When that comes upon you, the Holy Ghost will begin to work, and the Lord will raise you up." And God did something the moment the oil fell upon her. I looked toward the window and I saw Jesus. (I have seen Him often. There is no painting that is a bit like Him; no artist can ever depict the beauty of my lovely Lord.) The woman felt the power of God in her body and cried, "I'm free, my hands are free, my shoulders are free, and oh, I see Jesus! I'm free! I'm free!"

The vision vanished and the woman sat up in bed. Her legs were still bound, and I said to her, "I'll put my hands over your legs and you will be free entirely." And as I put my hands on those legs covered with bed clothes, I looked and saw the Lord again. She saw Him too and cried, "He's there again. I'm free! I'm free!" She rose from her bed and walked round the room praising God, and we were all in tears as we saw His wonderful works. The Lord shall raise them up when conditions are met.

When I was a young man I always loved the fellowship of old men, and was always careful to hear what they had to say. I had a friend, an old Baptist minister who was a wonderful preacher. I spent much of my time with him. One day he came to me and said, "My wife is dying." I said, "Brother Clark, why don't you believe God? God can raise her up if you will only believe Him." He asked me to come to his house, and I looked for someone to go with me.

I went to a certain rich man who was very zealous for God, and spent much money in opening up rescue missions, and I asked him to go with me. He said, "Never you mind me. You go yourself, but I don't take to this kind of business." Then I thought of a man who could pray by the hour. When he was on his knees he could go round the world three times and come out at the same place. I asked him to go with me and said to him, "You'll have a real chance this time. Keep at it, and quit when you're through." (Some go on longer after they are through.)

Brother Nichols, for that was his name, went with me and started praying. He asked the Lord to comfort the husband in his great bereavement and prayed for the orphans and a lot more on this line. I cried, "Oh, my God, stop this man." But there was no stopping him and he went on praying and there was not a particle of faith in anything he uttered. He did stop at last, and I said, "Brother Clark, it's now your turn to pray." He started, "Lord, answer the prayer of my brother and comfort me in this great bereavement and sorrow. Prepare me to face this great trial." I cried out, "My God, stop this man." The whole atmosphere was being charged with unbelief.

I had a glass bottle full of oil and I went up to the woman and poured the whole lot on her in the name of Jesus. Suddenly Jesus appeared, standing at the foot of the bed. He smiled and vanished. The woman stood up, perfectly healed, and she is a strong woman today.

We have a big God. We have a wonderful Jesus. We have a glorious Comforter. God's canopy is over you and will cover you at all times, preserving you from evil. Under His wings shalt thou trust. The Word of God is living and powerful and in its treasures you will find eternal life. If you dare trust this wonderful Lord, the Lord of life, you will find in Him everything you need.

So many are tampering with drugs, quacks, pills and plasters. Clear them all out and believe God. It is sufficient to believe God. You will find that if you dare trust Him, He will never fail. "The prayer of faith shall save the sick, and the *Lord* shall raise him up." Do you trust Him? He is worthy to be trusted.

I was one time asked to go to Weston-super-mare, a seaside resort in the West of England. I learned from a telegram that a man had lost his reason and had become a raving maniac, and they wanted me to go to pray for him. I arrived at the place, and the wife said to me, "Will you sleep with my husband?" I agreed, and in the middle of the night an evil power laid hold of him. It was awful. I put my hand on his head and his hair was like a lot of sticks. God gave deliverance — a temporary deliverance. At 6 o'clock the next morning, I felt that it was necessary that I should get out of that house for a short time.

The man saw me going and cried out, "If you leave me, there is no hope." But I felt that I had to go. As I went out I saw a woman with a Salvation Army bonnet on and I knew that she was going to their seven o'clock prayer meeting. I said to the Captain who was in charge of the meeting, when I saw he was about to give out a hymn, "Captain, don't sing. Let's get to prayer." He agreed, and I prayed my heart out, and then I grabbed my hat and rushed out of the hall. They all thought they had a madman in their prayer meeting that morning.

I went down to the end of the parade, and there was the man I had spent the night with, rushing down toward the sea, without a particle of clothing on, about to drown himself. I cried, "In the name of Jesus, come out of him." The man fell full length on the ground and that evil power went out of him never to return. His wife came rushing after him, and the husband was restored to her in a perfect mental condition.

There are evil powers, but Jesus is greater than all evil powers. There are tremendous diseases, but Jesus is healer. There is no case too hard for Him. The Lion of Judah shall break every chain. He came to relieve the oppressed and to set the captive free. He came to bring redemption, to make us as perfect as man was before the fall.

People want to know how to be kept by the power of God. Every position of grace into which you are led — forgiveness, healing, deliverance of any kind — will be contested by Satan. He will contend for your body. When you are saved, Satan will come round and say, "See, you are not saved." The devil is a liar. If he says you are not saved, it is a sure sign that you are.

You will remember the story of the man who was swept and garnished. The evil power had been swept out of him. But the man remained in a stationary position. If the Lord heals you, you dare not remain in a stationary position. The evil spirit came back to that man and found the house swept, and took seven others worse than himself, and the last stage of that man was worse than the first. Be sure and get filled with God. Get an Occupier. Be filled with the Spirit.

God has a million ways of undertaking for those who go to Him for help. He has deliverance for every captive. He loves you so much that He even says, "Before they call, I will answer." Don't turn Him away.

Published in *The Pentecostal Evangel*

ible reading, 2 Corinthians 3.

LIFE IN THE SPIRIT

November 25, 1922

We are told that we are to leave the first principles of the doctrine of Christ and go on to perfection, not laying again the foundation of repentance from dead works and the doctrine of baptisms and the other first principles (Hebrews 6:1,2). What would you think of a builder who was everlastingly pulling down his house and putting in fresh foundations? Never look back if you want the power of God in your life. You will find out that in the measure you have allowed yourself to look back you have missed that which God had for you.

The Holy Ghost shows us that we must never look back to the law of sin and death from which we have been delivered. God has brought us into a new order of things, a life of love and liberty in Christ Jesus that is beyond all human comprehension. Many are brought into this new life through the power of the Spirit of God, and then, like the Galatians, who ran well at the beginning, they try to perfect themselves on the lines of legalism. They go back from the life in the Spirit to a life on natural lines. God is not pleased with this, for He has no place for the man who has lost the vision. The only thing to do is to repent. Don't try to cover up anything. If you have been tripped up on any line, confess it out, and then look to God to bring you to a place of stability of faith where your whole walk will be in the Spirit.

We all ought to have a clear conviction that salvation is of the Lord. It is more than a human order of things. If the enemy can move you from a place of faith, he can get you outside the plan of God. The moment a man falls into sin, divine life ceases to flow, and his life becomes one of helplessness. But this is not God's thought for any of His children. Read the third chapter of John's first epistle and take your place as a son of God. Take the place of knowing that you are a son of God, and remember that, as your hope is set in Christ it should have a purifying effect on your life. The Holy Spirit says, "Whosoever is born of God doth not commit sin; for His seed remaineth in him: and he cannot sin, because he is born of God" (1 John 3:9). There is life and power in the seed of the Word that is implanted within. God is in that "cannot," and there is more power in that Word of His than in any human objections. God's thought for every one of us is that we shall reign in life by Jesus Christ. You must come to see how wonderful you are in God and how helpless you are in yourself.

God declared Himself more mighty than every opposing power when He cast out the powers of darkness from heaven. I want you to know that the same power that cast Satan out of heaven dwells in every man who is born of God. If you would but realize this, you would reign in life. When you see people laid out under an evil power, when you see the powers of evil manifesting themselves, always put the question, "Did Jesus come in the flesh?" I have never seen an evil power answer in the affirmative. When you know you have an evil spirit to deal with, you have power to cast it out. Believe it and act on it, for "...greater is he that is in you, than he that is in the world" (1 John 4:4). God means you to be in a place of overcoming, and has put a force within you whereby you may defeat the devil.

Temptations will come to all. If you are not worth tempting you are not worth powder and shot. Job said, "...when he hath tried me, I shall come forth as gold" (Job 23:10). In every temptation that comes, the Lord lets you be tempted up to the very hilt, but will never allow you to be defeated if you walk in obedience; for right in the midst of the temptation He will always "make a way to escape" (1 Corinthians 10:13).

TONGUES AND INTERPRETATION: "God comes forth and with His power sweeps away the refuge of lies and all the powers of darkness, and causes you always to triumph in Christ Jesus. The Lord loveth His saints and covers them with His almighty wings."

May God help us to see it. We cannot be to the praise of His glory until we are ready for trials, and are able to triumph in them. We cannot get away from the fact that sin came in by nature, but God comes into our nature and puts it into the place of death, that the Spirit of God may come into the temple in all His power and liberty, that right here in this present evil world Satan may be dethroned by the believer.

Satan is always endeavoring to bring the saints of God into disrepute, bringing against them railing accusations, but the Holy Ghost never comes with condemnation. He always reveals the blood of Christ. He always brings us help. The Lord Jesus referred to Him as the Comforter who would come. He is always on hand to help in the seasons of trial and test. The Holy Ghost is the lifting power of the church of Christ. And Paul tells us that we "...are manifestly declared to be the epistle of Christ...written not with ink, but with the Spirit of the living God; not in tables of stone, but in fleshy tables of the heart" (2 Corinthians 3:3). The Holy Ghost begins in the heart, right in the depths of human affections. He brings into the heart the riches of the revelation of Christ, implanting a purity and holiness there, so that out of its depths, praises well up continually.

The Holy Ghost will make us epistles of Christ, ever telling out that Jesus our Lord is our Redeemer and that He is ever before God as a newly slain Lamb. God has never put away that revelation. And because of the perfect atonement of that slain Lamb, there is salvation, healing and deliverance for all. Some people think that they have only to be cleansed once, but as we walk in the light, the blood of Jesus Christ is ever cleansing.

The very life of Christ has been put within us, and is moving within us — a perfect life. May the Lord help us to see the power of this life. The years of a man's life are threescore years and ten, and so in the natural order of things, my life will be finished in seven years, but I have begun a new life that will never end. "From everlasting to everlasting Thou art God." This is the life I have come into, and there is no end to this life. In me is working a power that is stronger than every power; Christ, the power of God, formed within me. I can see why we need to be clothed upon from above, for the life within me is a thousand times bigger than I am outside. There must be a tremendous expansion. I see, and cannot help seeing, that this thing cannot be understood on natural lines; no natural reason can comprehend the divine plan.

We are not sufficient to think anything as of ourselves, but our sufficiency is of God (2 Corinthians 3:5). If you go back, you miss the plan. We leave the old order of things. We can never have confidence in the flesh, we cannot touch that. We are in a new order, a spiritual order. It is a new life of absolute faith in the sufficiency of our God in everything that pertains to our salvation.

You could never come into this place and be a Seventh-day Adventist. The law has no place in you. You are set free from everything. At the same time, like Paul, you are "bound in the Spirit" so that you would not do anything to grieve the Lord.

Paul further tells us that He has made us "...able ministers of the new testament; not of the letter, but of the spirit: for the letter killeth, but the spirit giveth life" (2 Corinthians 3:6). It is one thing to read this, and another to have the revelation of it and to see the spiritual force of it. Any man can live in the letter and become dry and wordy, limited in knowledge of spiritual verities, and spend his time everlastingly in splitting hairs; but as soon as he touches the realm of the Spirit, all the dryness goes, all the spirit of criticism leaves. There can be no divisions in a life in the Spirit. The Spirit of God brings such pliability and such love! There is no love like the love in the Spirit. It is a pure, a holy, a divine love that is shed in our hearts by the Spirit. It loves to serve and to honor the Lord.

I can never estimate what the baptism of the Holy Ghost has been to me these past fifteen years. It seems that every year has had three years packed into it, so that I have had forty-five years of happy service since 1907. And it is getting better all the time. It is a luxury to be filled with the Spirit, and at the same time it is a divine command for us, not to be filled with wine wherein is excess, but to be filled with the Spirit. No Pentecostal person ought to get out of bed without being lost in the Spirit and speaking in tongues as the Spirit gives utterance. No one should come into the door of an assembly without speaking in tongues or having a psalm, or a note of praise. We emphasize that in the incoming of the Spirit He should so fill us that the last member in the body should be yielded to Him, and that no one is baptized in the Spirit without speaking in tongues as the Spirit gives utterance; and I maintain that with a constant filling, you will speak in tongues morning, noon and night. As you live in the Spirit when you walk down the steps of the house where you live, the devil will have to go before you. You will be more than a conqueror over the devil.

I see everything a failure except that which is done in the Spirit. But as you live in the Spirit, you move, act, eat, drink, and do everything to the glory of God. Our message is always this, "Be filled with the Spirit." This is God's place for you, and it is as far above the natural life as the heavens are above the earth. Yield yourselves for God to fill.

Moses had a tremendous trial with the people. They were always in trouble. But as he went up into the mount, and God unfolded to him the ten commandments, the glory fell. He rejoiced to bring those two tables of stone down from the mount, and his very countenance shone with the glory. He was bringing to Israel that which, if obeyed, would bring life.

I think of my Lord coming from heaven. I think all heaven was moved by the sight. The law of the letter was brought by Moses and it was made glorious, but all its glory was dimmed before the excelling glory which Jesus brought to us in the Spirit of life. The glory of Sinai paled before the glory of Pentecost. Those tables of stone with their, "Thou shalt not, thou shalt not," are done away; for they never brought life to anyone, and the Lord has brought in a new covenant, putting His law in our minds and writing it in our hearts, this new law of the Spirit of life. As the Holy Ghost comes in, He fills us with such love and liberty, and we shout for joy these words of this eleventh verse, "Done away! Done away!" Henceforth there is a new cry in our hearts, "I delight to do Thy will, O God." He taketh away the first, the ministration of death, written and engraven in stones, that He might establish the second, this ministration of righteousness, this life in the Spirit.

You ask, "Does a man who is filled with the Spirit cease to keep the commandments?" I simply repeat what the Spirit of God has told us here, that this ministration of death, written and engraven in stones (and you know that the ten commandments were written on stones), is *"done away."* The man who becomes a living epistle of Christ, written with the Spirit of the Living God, has ceased to be an adulterer, or a murderer or a covetous man; the will of God is his delight. I love to do the will of God, there is no irksomeness to it, it is no trial to pray, no trouble to read the Word of God, it is not a hard thing to go to the place of worship. With the psalmist you say, "I was glad when they said unto me, Let us go into the house of the Lord" (Psalm 122:1).

How does this new life work out? The thing works out because God works in you to will and to do of His own good pleasure (Philippians 2:13). There is a great difference between a pump and a spring. The law is a pump, the baptism is a spring. The old pump gets out of order, the parts perish, and the well runs dry. The letter killeth. But the spring is ever bubbling up and there is a ceaseless flow direct from the Throne of God. There is life.

It is written of Christ, "Thou lovest righteousness, and hatest wickedness." And in this new life in the Spirit, in this new covenant life, you love the things that are right and pure and holy, and shudder at all things that are wrong. Jesus was able to say, "...the prince of this world cometh, and hath nothing in me" (John 14:30). And the moment we are filled with the Spirit of God we are brought into like wonderful condition, and as we continue to be filled with the Spirit, the enemy cannot have an inch of territory in us.

Do you not believe that you can be so filled with the Spirit that a man who is not living right can be judged and convicted by your presence? As we go on in the life of the Spirit, it will be said of us, "In whose eyes a vile person is contemned..." (Psalm 15:4). Jesus lived there and moved in this realm, and His life was a constant reproof to the wickedness around. "But He was the Son of God," you say. God, through Him, has brought us into the place of sonship, and I believe that if He has a chance with the material, the Holy Ghost can make something of us, and bring us to the same place.

I don't want to boast. If I glory in anything it is only in the Lord who has been so gracious to me. But I remember one time stepping out of a railroad carriage to wash my hands. I had a season of prayer, and the Lord just filled me to overflowing with His love. I was going to a Convention in Ireland, and I could not get there fast enough. As I returned, I believe that the Spirit of the Lord was so heavily upon me that my face must have shone. (No man can tell himself when the Spirit transforms his very countenance.) There were two clerical men sitting together, and as I got into the carriage again, one of them cried out, "You convict me of sin." Within three minutes everyone in the carriage was crying to God for salvation. This thing has happened many times in my life. It is this ministration of the Spirit that Paul speaks of, this filling of the Spirit, that will make your life effective, so that even the people in the stores where you trade will want to leave your presence because they are brought under conviction.

We must move from everything of the letter. All that we do must be done under the anointing of the Spirit. The trouble has been that we as

Pentecostal people have been living in the letter. Believe what the Holy Spirit says through Paul — that all this ministration of condemnation that has hindered your liberty in Christ is done away. The law is *done away*! As far as you are concerned, all that old order of things is forever done away, and the Spirit of God has brought in a new life of purity and love. The Holy Ghost takes it for granted that you are finished with all the things of the old life when you become a new creation in Christ. In the life in the Spirit, the old allurements have lost their power. The devil will meet you at every turn, but the Spirit of God will always lift up a standard against him.

Oh, if God had His way, we would be like torches, purifying the very atmosphere wherever we go, moving back the forces of wickedness.

TONGUES AND INTERPRETATION: "The Lord is that Spirit. He moves in your heart. He shows you that the power within you is mightier than all the powers of darkness."

Done away! What do I mean? Will you be disloyal? You will be more than loyal. Will you grumble when you are treated badly? No, you will turn the other cheek. This is what you will always do when God lives in you. Leave yourselves in God's hands. Enter into yourselves in God's hands. Enter into rest.

> *For he that is entered into his rest, he also hath ceased from his own works, as God did from his.*
>
> *Hebrews 4:10*

Oh, this is a lovely rest! The whole life is a Sabbath. This is the only life that can glorify God. It is a life of joy, and every day is a day of heaven on earth.

There is a continued transformation in this life. Beholding the Lord and His glory, we are changed into the same image from glory to glory, even by the Spirit of the Lord. There is a continued unveiling, a constant revelation, a repeated clothing upon from above. I want you to promise God never to look back, never to go back to that which the Spirit has said is "done away." I made this promise to the Lord that I would never allow myself to doubt His Word.

There is one thing about a baby, it takes all that comes to it. A prudent man lets his reason cheat him out of God's best. But a baby takes all that its mother brings, and tries to swallow the bottle and all. The baby can't walk, but the mother carries it; the baby cannot dress itself, but the mother dresses it. The baby can't even talk. So in the life of the Spirit, God undertakes to do what we cannot do. We are carried along by Him, He clothes us, and He gives us utterance. Would that we all had the simplicity of the babes.

Published in *The Pentecostal Evangel*

ONLY BELIEVE
December 2, 1922

hen one dares to trust God on His bare Word, then peace flows freely, wavering is passed, there is nothing to be done, all is finished and you enter into possessions that cannot come in any other way. So keep the test before you and be still and see the salvation of God. Nothing but love counts, so be full of this all-prevailing charity that knows not fear and is blind to everything but the object of its perfect *choice*. Christ and Him alone.

Letter, Christmas 1922

HAVE FAITH IN GOD
December 9, 1922

or verily I say unto you, That whosoever shall say unto this mountain, Be thou removed, and be thou cast into the sea; and shall not doubt in his heart, but shall believe that those things which he saith shall come to pass; he shall have whatsoever he saith. Therefore I say unto you, What things soever ye desire, when ye pray, believe that ye receive them, and ye shall have them.

Mark 11:23,24

These are days when we need to have our faith strengthened, when we need to know God. God has designed that the just shall live by faith, no matter how he may be fettered. I know that God's Word is sufficient. One word from Him can change a nation. His Word is from everlasting to everlasting. It is through the entrance of this everlasting Word, this incorruptible seed, that we are born again, and come into this wonderful salvation. Man cannot live by bread alone, but must live by every word that proceedeth out of the mouth of God (Matthew 4:4). This is the food of faith. "...faith cometh by hearing, and hearing by the word of God" (Romans 10:17).

Everywhere men are trying to discredit the Bible and take from it all the miraculous. One preacher says, "Well, you know, Jesus arranged beforehand to have that colt tied where it was, and for the men to say just what they did." I tell you, God can arrange everything without going near. He can plan for you, and when He plans for you, all is peace. All things are possible if you will believe.

Another preacher said, "It was an easy thing for Jesus to feed the people with five loaves. The loaves were so big in those days that it was a simple matter to cut them into a thousand pieces each." But He forgot that one little boy brought those five loaves all the way in his lunch basket. There is nothing impossible with God. All the impossibility is with us when we measure God by the limitations of our unbelief.

We have a wonderful God, a God whose ways are past finding out, and whose grace and power are limitless. I was in Belfast one day and saw one of the brethren of the assembly. He said to me, "Wigglesworth, I am troubled. I have had a good deal of sorrow during the past five months. I had a woman in my assembly who could always pray the blessing of heaven down on our meetings. She is an old woman, but her presence is always an inspiration. But five months ago she fell and broke her thigh. The doctors put her into a plaster cast, and after five months they broke the cast. But the bones were not properly set and so she fell and broke the thigh again."

He took me to her house, and there was a woman lying in a bed on the right hand side of the room. I said to her, "Well, what about it now?" She said, "They have sent me home incurable. The doctors say that I am so old that my bones won't knit. There is no nutriment in my bones and they could never do anything for me, and they say I shall have to lie in bed for the rest of my life." I said to her, "Can you believe God?" She replied, "Yes, ever since I heard that you had come to Belfast my faith has been quickened. If you will pray, I will believe. I know there is no power on earth that can make the bones of my thigh knit, but I know there is nothing impossible with God." I said, "Do you believe He will meet you now?" She answered, "I do."

It is grand to see people believe God. God knew all about this leg and that it was broken in two places. I said to the woman, "When I pray, something will happen." Her husband was sitting there; he had been in his chair for four years and could not walk a step. He called out, "I don't believe. I won't believe. You will never get me to believe." I said, "All right," and laid my hands on his wife in the name of the Lord Jesus. The moment hands were laid upon her and she cried out, "I'm healed." I said, "I'm not going to assist you to rise. God will do it all." She arose and walked up and down the room, praising God.

The old man was amazed at what had happened to his wife, and he cried out, "Make me walk, make me walk." I said to him, "You old sinner, repent." He cried out, "Lord, You know I believe." I don't think he meant what he said; anyhow the Lord was full of compassion. If He marked our sins, where would any of us be? If we will meet the conditions, God will always meet us, if we believe all things are possible. I laid my hands on him and the power went right through the old man's body, and those legs, for the first time for four years received power to carry his body, and he walked up and down and in and out. He said, "Oh, what great things God has done for us tonight!"

"...What things soever ye desire, when ye pray, believe that ye receive them, and ye shall have them" (Mark 11:24). Desire toward God and you will have desires from God, and He will meet you on the line of those desires when you reach out in simple faith.

A man came to me in one of my meetings who had seen other people healed and wanted to be healed, too. He explained that his arm had been fixed in a certain position for many years and he could not move it. "Got any faith?" I asked. He said that he had a lot of faith. After prayer he was able to swing his arm round and round. But he was not satisfied and complained, "I feel a little bit of trouble just there," pointing to a certain place. I said, "Do you know what is the trouble with you?" He answered,

"No," I said, "Imperfect faith." "...What things soever ye desire, when ye pray, believe that ye receive them, and ye shall have them."

Did you believe before you were saved? So many people would be saved, but they want to feel saved first. There was never a man who felt saved before he believed. God's plan is always this, if you will believe, you shall see the glory of God. I believe God wants to bring us all to a definite place of unswerving faith and confidence in Himself.

Jesus here uses the figure of a mountain. Why does He say a mountain? If faith can remove a mountain, it can remove anything. The plan of God is so marvelous, that if you will only believe, all things are possible.

There is one special phrase to which I want to call your attention, "And shall not doubt in his heart." The heart is the mainspring. See that young man and that young woman. They have fallen in love at first sight. In a short while there is a deep affection, and a strong heart love, the one toward the other. What is a heart of love? A heart of faith. Faith and love are kin. In the measure that that young man and that young woman love one another they are true. One may go to the North and the other to the South, but because of their love they will be true to one another.

It is the same when there is a deep love in the heart toward the Lord Jesus Christ. In this new life into which God has brought us, Paul tells us that we have become dead to the law by the body of Christ, that we should be married to another, even to Him who is raised from the dead. God brings us into a place of perfect love and perfect faith. A man who is born of God is brought into an inward affection, a loyalty to the Lord Jesus that shrinks from anything impure. You see the purity of a man and woman when there is a deep natural affection between them; they disdain the very thought of either of them being untrue. I say that in the measure that a man has faith in Jesus he is pure. He that believeth that Jesus is the Christ overcometh the world. It is a faith that worketh by love.

Just as we have heart fellowship with our Lord, our faith cannot be daunted. We cannot doubt in our hearts. There comes, as we go on with God, a wonderful association, an impartation of His very life and nature within. As we read His Word and believe the promises that He has so graciously given to us, we are made partakers of His very essence and life. The Lord is made to us a Bridegroom, and we are His bride. His words to us are spirit and life, transforming us and changing us, expelling that which is natural and bringing in that which is divine.

It is impossible to comprehend the love of God as we think on natural lines. We must have the revelation from the Spirit of God. God giveth liberally. He that asketh, receiveth. God is willing to bestow on us all things that pertain to life and godliness. Oh, it was the love of God that brought Jesus. And it is this same love that helps you and me to believe. In every weakness God will be your strength. You who need His touch, remember that He loves you. Look, wretched, helpless, sick one, away to the God of all grace, whose very essence is love, who delights to give liberally all the inheritance of life and strength and power that you are in need of.

When I was in Switzerland the Lord was graciously working and healing many of the people. I was staying with Brother Reuss of Goldiwil and two policemen were sent to arrest me. The charge was that I was healing the people without a license. Mr. Reuss said to them, "I am sorry that he is not here just now, he is holding a meeting about two miles away, but before you arrest him I would like to show you something."

Brother Reuss took these two policemen down to one of the lower parts of that district, to a house with which they were familiar, for they had often gone to that place to arrest a certain woman who was constantly an inmate of the prison because of continually being engaged in drunken brawls. He took them to this woman and said to them, "This is one of the many cases of blessing that have come through the ministry of the man you have come to arrest. This woman came to our meeting in a drunken condition. Her body was broken, for she was ruptured in two places. While she was drunk, the evangelist laid his hands on her and asked God to heal her and deliver her." The woman joined in, "Yes, and God saved me, and I have not tasted a drop of liquor since." The policemen had a warrant for my arrest, but they said with disgust, "Let the doctors do this kind of thing." They turned and went away and that was the last we heard of them.

We have a Jesus who heals the brokenhearted, who lets the captives go free, who saves the very worst. Dare you, dare you, spurn this glorious Gospel of God for spirit, soul and body? Dare you spurn this grace? I realize that this full Gospel has in great measure been hid, this Gospel that brings liberty, this Gospel that brings souls out of bondage, this Gospel that brings perfect health to the body, this Gospel of entire salvation. Listen again to this word of Him who left the glory to bring us this great salvation, "...verily I say unto you, That whosoever shall say unto this mountain, Be thou removed...he shall have whatsoever he saith." Whatsoever!

I realize that God can never bless us on the lines of being hard-hearted, critical, or unforgiving. This will hinder faith quicker than anything. I remember being at a meeting where there were some people tarrying for the baptism — seeking for cleansing, for the moment a person is cleansed the Spirit will fall. There was one man with eyes red who was weeping bitterly. He said to me, "I shall have to leave. It is no good my staying without I change things. I have written a letter to my brother-in-law, and filled it with hard words, and this thing must first be straightened out." He went home and told his wife, "I'm going to write a letter to your brother and ask him to forgive me for writing to him the way I did." "You fool!" she said. "Never mind," he replied, "this thing is between God and me, and it has got to be cleared away." He wrote the letter and came again, and straightway God filled him with the Spirit.

I believe there are a great many people who would be healed, but they are harboring things in their hearts that are as a blight. Let these things go. Forgive, and the Lord will forgive you. There are many good people, people who mean well, but they have no power to do anything for God. There is just some little thing that came in their hearts years ago, and their faith has been paralyzed ever since. Bring everything to the light. God will sweep it all away if you will let Him. Let the precious blood of Christ cleanse from all sin. If you will but believe, God will meet you and bring into your lives the sunshine of His love.

Published in *The Pentecostal Evangel*

ible reading — Acts 5:1-20. Notice this expression that the Lord gives of the Gospel message — "the words of this life." It is the most wonderful life possible — the life of faith in the Son of God. This is the life where God is all

THE WORDS OF THIS LIFE

December 23, 1922

the time. He is round about and He is within. It is the life of many revelations and of many manifestations of God's Holy Spirit, a life in which the Lord is continually seen, known, felt and heard. It is a life without death, for "we have passed from death unto life." The very life of God has come within us. Where that life is within in its fulness, disease cannot exist. It would take me a month to tell out what there is in this wonderful life. Everyone can go in and possess and be possessed by this life.

It is possible for you to be within the vicinity of this life and yet miss it. It is possible for you to be in a place where God is pouring out His Spirit and yet miss the blessing that God is so willing to bestow. It all comes through shortness of revelation and through a misunderstanding of the infinite grace of God, and of the "God of all grace," who is willing to give to all who will reach out the hand of faith. This life that He freely bestows is a gift. Some think they have to earn it and they miss the whole thing. Oh, for a simple faith to receive all that God so lavishly offers. You can never be ordinary from the day you receive this life from above. You become extraordinary, filled with the extraordinary power of our extraordinary God.

Ananias and Sapphira were in this thing and yet they missed it. They thought that possibly the thing might fail. So they wanted to have a reserve for themselves in case it did turn out to be a failure. They were in the wonderful revival that God gave to the early church and yet they missed it. There are many people like them today who make vows to God in times of a great crisis in their lives. But they fail to keep their vows and in the end they become spiritually bankrupt. Blessed is the man who will swear to his own hurt and change not; who keeps the vow he has made to God; who is willing to lay his all at God's feet. The man who does this never becomes a lean soul. God has promised to "make fat his bones." There is no dry place for such a man; he is always fat and flourishing, and he becomes stronger and stronger. It pays to trust God with all and to make no reservation.

I wish I could make you see how great a God we have. Ananias and Sapphira were really doubting God and were questioning whether this work that He had begun would go through. They wanted to get some glory for selling their property, but because of their lack of faith they kept back part of the price in reserve in case the work of God should fail.

Many are doubting whether this Pentecostal revival will go through. Do you think this Pentecostal work will stop? Never. For fifteen years I have been in constant revival and I am sure that it will never stop. When John Stephenson made his first engine he took his sister Mary to see it. She looked at it and said to her brother, "John, it'll never go." He said to her, "Get in, Mary." She said again, "It'll never go." He said to her, "We'll see, you get in." Mary at last got in — the whistle blew, there was a puff and a rattle, and the engine started off. Then Mary cried out, "John, it'll never stop! It'll never stop!!"

People are looking on at this Pentecostal revival and they are very critical and they are saying, "It'll never go"; but when they are induced to come into the work, they one and all say, "It'll never stop." This revival of God is sweeping on and on and there is no stopping the current of life, of love, of inspiration, and of power.

TONGUES AND INTERPRETATION: "It is the living Word who has brought this. It is the Lamb in the midst, the same yesterday, today, and forever."

God has brought unlimited resources for everyone. Do not doubt. Hear with the ear of faith. God is in the midst. See that it is God who hath set forth that which you see and hear today.

I want you to see that in the early church, controlled by the power of the Holy Ghost, it was not possible for a lie to exist. The moment it came into the church, there was instant death. And as the power of the Holy Ghost increases in these days of the Latter Rain, it will be impossible for any man to remain in our midst with a lying spirit. God will purify the church; the Word of God will be in such power in healing and other spiritual manifestations, that great fear will be upon all those who see the same.

It seems to the natural mind a small thing for Ananias and Sapphira to want to have a little to fall back on; but I want to tell you that you can please God, and you can get things from God only on the line of a living faith. God never fails. God never can fail.

When I was in Bergen, Norway, there came to the meeting a young woman who was employed at the hospital as a nurse. A big cancer had developed on her nose, and the nose was enlarged and had become black and greatly inflamed. She came out for prayer and I said to her, "What is your condition?" She said, "I dare not touch my nose, it gives me so much pain." I said to all the people, "I want you to look at this nurse and notice her terrible condition. I believe that our God is merciful and that He is faithful, and that He will bring to naught this condition that the devil has brought about. I am going to curse this disease in the all-powerful name of Jesus. The pain will go. I believe God will give us an exhibition of His grace and I will ask this young woman to come to the meeting tomorrow night and declare what God has done for her."

Oh, the awfulness of sin! Oh, the awfulness of the power of sin! Oh, the awfulness of the consequences of the fall! When I see a cancer I always know it is an evil spirit. I can never believe it is otherwise. The same with tumors. Can this be the work of God? God help me to show you that this is the work of the devil, and to show you the way out.

I do not condemn people who sin. I don't scold people. I know what is back of the sin. I know that Satan is always going about as a roaring lion, seeking whom he may devour. I always remember the patience and love of the Lord Jesus Christ. When they brought to Him a woman that they had taken in adultery, telling Him that they had caught her in the very act, He simply stooped down and wrote on the ground. Then He quietly said, "He that is without sin among you, let him first cast a stone at her" (John 8:7). I have never seen a man without sin. "...all have sinned, and come short of the glory of God" (Romans 3:23). But I read in this blessed Gospel message that God hath laid upon Jesus the iniquity of us all, and when I see an evil condition I feel that I must stand in my office and rebuke the condition.

I laid my hands on the nose of that suffering nurse and cursed the evil power that was causing her so much distress. The next night the place was packed and the people were jammed together so that it seemed that there was not room for one more to come into that house. How God's rain fell upon us. How good God is, so full of grace and so full of love.

I saw the nurse in the audience and cried out, "Here's the woman with the nose." I asked her to come forward and she came and showed everyone what God had done. He had perfectly healed her. Oh, I tell you He is just the same Jesus. He is just the same today. All things are possible if you dare to trust God.

When the power of God came so mightily upon the early church, even in the death of Ananias and Sapphira, great fear came upon all the people. And when we are in the presence of God, when God is working mightily in our midst, there comes a great fear, a reverence, a holiness of life, a purity that fears to displease God. We read that no man durst join them, but God added to the church such as should be saved. I would rather have God add to our Pentecostal church than have all the town join it. God added daily to His own church.

The next thing that happened was that people became so assured that God was working that they knew that anything would be possible, and they brought their sick into the streets and laid them on beds and couches that at least the shadow of Peter passing by might overshadow them. Multitudes of sick people and those oppressed with evil spirits were brought to the apostles and God healed them every one. I do not believe that it was the shadow of Peter that healed, but the power of God was mightily present and the faith of the people was so aroused that they joined with one heart to believe God. God will always meet people on the line of faith.

God's tide is rising all over the earth. I had been preaching at Stavanger in Norway and was very tired and wanted a few hours' rest. I went to my next appointment, arriving at about 9:30 in the morning. My first meeting was to be at night. I said to my interpreter, "After we have had something to eat, let us go down to the fjords." We spent three or four hours down by the sea and at about 4:30 returned. We found the end of the street, which had a narrow entrance, just filled with autos, wagons, etc., containing invalids and sick people of every kind. I went up to the house and was told that the house was full of sick people. It reminded me of the scene that we read of in the fifth chapter of Acts. I began praying for the people in the street and God began to heal the people. How wonderfully He healed those people who were in the house. We sat down for a lunch and the telephone bell rang and someone at the other end was saying, "What shall we do? The town hall is already full, the police cannot control things." Beloved, the tide is rising, the fields are white unto harvest. God gave us a wonderful revival. I want to be in a mighty revival. I was in one mighty revival in Wales, and I long to be in a great revival that will eclipse anything we have ever thought of. I have faith to believe it is coming.

In that little Norwegian town the people were jammed together, and oh, how the power of God fell upon us. A cry went up from everyone, "Isn't this the revival?" Revival is coming. The breath of the Almighty is coming. The breath of God shows up every defect, and as it comes flowing in like a river everybody will need a fresh anointing, a fresh cleansing of the blood. You can depend upon it that that breath is upon us.

At one time I was at a meeting in Ireland. There were many sick carried to that meeting and helpless ones were helped there. There were many people in that place who were seeking for the baptism of the Holy Ghost. Some of them had been seeking for years. There were sinners there who were under mighty conviction. There came a moment when the breath of God swept through the meeting. In about ten minutes every sinner in the place was saved. Everyone who had been seeking the Holy Spirit was baptized, and every sick one was healed. God is a reality and His power can never fail. As our faith reaches out, God will meet us and the same rain will fall. It is the same blood that cleanseth, the same power, the same Holy Ghost, and the same Jesus made real through the power of the Holy Ghost! What would happen if we would believe God?

Right now the precious blood of the Lord Jesus Christ is efficacious to cleanse your heart and bring this life, this wonderful life of God, within you. The blood will make you every whit whole if you dare believe. The healing virtue of the blessed Son of God is right here for you, but so few will touch Him. The Bible is so full of entreaty for you to come and partake and receive the grace, the power, the strength, the righteousness, and the full redemption of Jesus Christ. He never fails to hear when we believe. This same Jesus is in our midst to touch and to loose thee.

At one place where I was, a lame man was brought to me who had been in bed for two years, with no hope of recovery. He was brought thirty miles to the meeting and he came up on crutches to be prayed for. His boy was also afflicted in the knees and they had four crutches between the two of them. The man's face was filled with torture. There is healing virtue in the Lord and He never fails to heal when we believe. In the name of Jesus — that name so full of virtue — I put my hand down on that leg that was so diseased. The man threw down his crutches and all were astonished as they saw him walking up and down without aid. The little boy called out to his father, "Papa, me; papa, me, me, me!" The little boy who was withered in both knees wanted a like touch. And the same Jesus was there to bring a real deliverance for the little captive. He was completely healed.

These were legs that were touched. If God will stretch out His mighty power to loose afflicted legs, what mercy will He extend to that soul of yours that must exist forever? Hear the Lord say,

> *The Spirit of the Lord is upon me, because he hath anointed me to preach the gospel to the poor; he hath sent me to heal the brokenhearted, to preach deliverance to the captives, and recovering of sight to the blind, to set at liberty them that are bruised.*
>
> *Luke 4:18*

He invites you, "Come unto me, all ye that labour and are heavy laden, and I will give you rest" (Matthew 11:28). God is willing in His great mercy to touch thy limbs with His mighty vital power, and if He is willing to do this, how much more anxious is He to deliver thee from the power of Satan and to make thee a child of the King. How much more necessary it is for you to be healed of your soul sickness than of your bodily ailments. And God is willing to give the double cure.

I was passing through the city of London one time, and Mr. Mundell, the secretary of the Pentecostal Missionary Union, got to know that I was there. He arranged for me to meet him at a certain place at 3:30 p.m. I was to meet a certain boy whose father and mother lived in the city of Salisbury. They had sent this young man to London to take care of their business. He had been a leader in Sunday school work but he had been betrayed and had fallen. Sin is awful and the wages of sin is death. But there is another side — the gift of God is eternal life.

This young man was in great distress; he had contracted a horrible disease and feared to tell anyone. There was nothing but death ahead for him. When the father and mother got to know of his condition they suffered inexpressible grief.

When we got to the house, Brother Mundell suggested that we get down to prayer. I said, "God does not say so, we are not going to pray yet. I want to quote a scripture, 'Fools, because of their transgression, and because of their iniquities, are afflicted. Their soul abhorreth all manner of meat; and they draw near unto the gates of death'" (Psalm 107:17,18). The young man cried out, "I am that fool." He broke down and told us the story of his fall. Oh, if men would only repent, and confess their sins, how God would stretch out His hand to heal and to save. The moment that young man repented, a great abscess burst, and God sent virtue into that young man's life, giving him a mighty deliverance.

God is gracious and not willing that any should perish. How many are willing to make a clean breast of their sins. I tell you that the moment you do this, God will open heaven. It is an easy thing for Him to save your soul and heal your disease if you will but come and shelter today in the secret place of the Most High. He will satisfy you with long life and show you His salvation. In His presence is fulness of joy, at His right hand there are pleasures forevermore. There is full redemption for all through the precious blood of the Son of God.

Published in *The Pentecostal Evangel*

WHAT IT MEANS TO BE FULL OF THE HOLY GHOST

January 6, 1923

Bible Reading — Acts 6.

In the days when the number of disciples began to be multiplied there arose a situation where the twelve had to make a definite decision not to occupy themselves with serving tables, but to give themselves continually to prayer and to the ministry of the Word. How important it is for all God's ministers to be continually in prayer, and constantly feeding on the Scriptures of truth. I often offer a reward to anyone who can catch me anywhere without my Bible or my Testament.

None of you can be strong in God unless you are diligently and constantly hearkening to what God has to say to you through His Word. You cannot know the power and the nature of God unless you partake of His inbreathed Word. Read it at morn and at night, and at every opportunity you get. After every meal, instead of indulging in unprofitable conversation round the table, read a chapter from the Word and then have a season of prayer. I endeavor to make a point of doing this no matter where or with whom I am staying.

The Psalmist said that he had hid God's Word in his heart, that he might not sin against Him; and you will find that the more of God's Word you hide in your heart, the easier it is to live a holy life. He also testified that God's Word had quickened him; and, as you receive God's Word into your being, your whole physical being will be quickened and you will be made strong. As you receive with meekness the Word, you will find faith upspringing within. And you will have life through the Word.

The twelve told the rest to look out seven men to look after the business end of things. They were to be men of honest report and filled with the Holy Ghost. These were just ordinary men who were chosen, but they were filled with the Holy Spirit, and this infilling always lifts a man to a plane above the ordinary. It does not take a cultured or a learned man to fill a position in God's church; what God requires is a yielded, consecrated, holy life, and He can make of such a flame of fire. Baptized with the Holy Ghost and fire!

The multitude chose out seven men to serve tables. They were doubtless faithful in their appointed tasks, but we see that God soon had a better choice for two of them. Philip was so full of the Holy Ghost that he could have a revival wherever God put him down. Man chose him to serve tables, but God chose him to win souls. Oh, if I could only stir you up to see that, as you are faithful in performing the humblest office, God can fill you with His Spirit and make you a chosen vessel for Himself, and promote you to a place of mighty ministry in the salvation of souls and in the healing of the sick. There is nothing impossible to a man filled with the Holy Ghost. It is beyond all human comprehension.

When you are filled with the power of the Holy Ghost, God will wonderfully work wherever you go.

When you are filled with the Spirit you will know the voice of God. I want to give you one illustration of this. When I was going out to Australia recently, our boat stopped at Aden and Bombay. In the first place the people came round the ship selling their wares, beautiful carpets and all sorts of oriental things. There was one man selling some ostrich feathers. As I was looking over the side of the ship watching the trading, a gentleman said to me, "Would you go shares with me in buying that bunch of feathers?" What did I want with feathers? I had no use for such things and no room for them either. But the gentleman put the question to me again, "Will you go shares with me in buying that bunch?" The Spirit of God said to me, "Do it."

The feathers were sold to us for three pounds, and the gentleman said, "I have no money on me, but if you will pay the man for them, I will send the cash down to you by the purser." I paid for the feathers and gave the gentleman his share. He was traveling first, and I was traveling second class. I said to him, "No, please don't give that money to the purser, I want you to bring it to me personally to my cabin." I said to the Lord, "What about these feathers?" He showed me that He had a purpose in my purchasing them.

At about 10 o'clock the gentleman came to my cabin and said, "I've brought the money." I said to him, "It is not your money that I want, it is your soul that I am seeking for God." Right there he opened up the whole plan of his life and began to seek God, and that morning he wept his way through to God's salvation.

You have no conception what God can do through you when you are filled with His Spirit. Every day and every hour you can have the divine leading of God. To be filled with the Holy Ghost means much in every way. I have seen some who have been suffering for years, and when they have been filled with the Holy Ghost everything of their sickness has passed away. The Spirit of God has made real to them the life of Jesus and they have been completely liberated of every sickness and infirmity.

Look at Stephen. He was just an ordinary man chosen to serve tables. But the Holy Ghost was in him and he was full of faith and power, and did great wonders and miracles among the people. There was no resisting the wisdom and the spirit by which he spake. How important it is that every man shall be filled with the Holy spirit.

TONGUES AND INTERPRETATION: "The divine will is that you shall be filled with God; for the power of the Spirit to fill you with the mightiness of God. There is nothing God will withhold to a man filled with the Holy Ghost."

I want to impress the importance of this upon you. It is not healing that I am presenting to you in these meetings — it is the living Christ. It is a glorious fact that the Son of God came down to bring liberty to the captives. And He it is who baptizes with the Holy Ghost and fire, who is shedding forth this which we are now seeing and hearing.

How is it that the moment you are filled with the Holy Ghost that persecution starts? It was so with the Lord Jesus Himself. We do not read of any persecutions before the Holy Spirit came down like a dove upon Him. Shortly after this we find that after preaching in His hometown they wanted to throw Him over the brow of a hill. It was the same with the twelve disciples. They had no persecution before the day of Pentecost, but after they were filled with the Spirit they were soon in prison. The devil and the priests of religion will always get stirred when a man is filled with the Spirit and does things in the power of the Spirit. And persecution is the greatest blessing to a church. When we have persecution we will have purity. If you desire to be filled with the Spirit you can count on one thing, and that is persecution. The Lord came to bring division, and even in your own household you may find three against two.

The Lord Jesus came to bring peace, and soon after you get peace within you get persecution without. If you remain stationary, the devil and his agents will not disturb you much. But when you press on and go the whole length with God, the enemy has you as a target. But God will vindicate you in the midst of the whole thing.

At a meeting I was holding, the Lord was working and many were being healed. A man saw what was taking place and remarked, "I'd like to try this thing." He came up for prayer and told me that his body was broken in two places. I laid my hands on him in the name of the Lord, and said to him, "Now, you believe God." The next night he was at the meeting and got up like a lion. He said, "I want to tell you people that this man here is deceiving you. He laid his hands on me last night for rupture in two places, but I'm not a bit better." I stopped him and said, "You are healed, your trouble is that you won't believe it."

He was at the meeting the next night and when there was opportunity for testimony this man arose. He said, "I'm a mason by trade. Today I was working with a laborer and he had to put a big stone in place. I helped him and did not feel any pain. I said to myself, 'How have I done it?' I went away to a place where I could strip, and I found that I was healed." I told the people, "Last night this man was against the Word of God, but now he believes it. It is true that these signs will follow them that believe, they shall lay hands on the sick and they shall recover. And all through the power that is in the name of Christ." It is the Spirit who has come to reveal the Word of God, and to make it spirit and life to us.

You people who are seeking the baptism are entering a place where you will have persecution. Your best friends will leave you — or those you may esteem your best friends. No good friend will ever leave you. But it is worthwhile. You enter into a realm of illumination, of revelation by the power of the Holy Ghost. He reveals the preciousness and the power of the blood of Christ. I find by the revelation of the Spirit that there is not one thing in me that the blood does not cleanse. I find that God sanctifies me by the blood and reveals the efficacy of the work by the Spirit.

Stephen was just an ordinary man clothed with the divine. He was full of faith and power, and great wonders and miracles were wrought by him. Oh, this life in the Holy Ghost! This life of deep, inward revelation, of transformation from one state to another, of growing in grace and in all knowledge and in the power of the Spirit, the life and the mind of Christ being renewed in you, and of constant revelations of the might of His power. It is only this kind of thing that will enable us to stand.

In this life, the Lord puts you in all sorts of places, and then reveals His power. I had been preaching in New York, and sailed one day for England on the Lusitania. As soon as I got on board I went down to my cabin. Two men were there, and one of them said, "Well, will I do for company?" He took out a bottle and poured out a glass of whiskey and drank it, and then he filled it up for me. "I never touch that stuff," I said. "How can you live without it?" he asked. "How could I live with it?" I asked. He admitted, "I have been under the influence of this stuff for months, and they say my 'inside is all shrivelled up,' and I know that

"Our purpose is to let the Holy Ghost glorify God
through us."

I am dying. I wish I could be delivered, but I just have to keep on drinking. Oh, if I could only be delivered! My father died in England and has given me his fortune, but what will the good of it be to me except to hasten me to my grave."

I said to this man, "Say the word, and you will be delivered." He inquired, "What do you mean?" I said, "Say the word, show that you are willing to be delivered and God will deliver you." But it was just as if I was talking to this platform for all the comprehension he showed. I said to him, "Stand still," and I laid my hands on his head in the name of Jesus and cursed that drink demon that was taking his life. He cried out, "I'm free! I'm free! I know I'm free!" He took two bottles of whiskey and threw them overboard, and God saved, sobered, and healed him. I was preaching all the way across. He sat beside me at the table. Previous to this he had not been able to eat, but every meal he went right through the menu. You only have to have a touch from Jesus to have a good time. The power of God is just the same today. To me, He's lovely. To me, He's saving health. To me, He's the lily of the valley. Oh, this blessed Nazarene, this King of kings! Hallelujah! Will you let Him have your will, will you let Him have you? If you will, all His power is at your disposal.

They were not able to resist the wisdom and spirit by which Stephen spake, and so, full of rage, they brought him to the council. And God filled his face with a ray of heaven's light. It is worth being filled with the Spirit, no matter what it costs. Read the seventh chapter, the mighty prophetic utterance by this holy man. Without fear he tells them, "Ye stiffnecked and uncircumcised in heart and ears, ye do always resist the Holy Ghost..." (Acts 7:51). And when they heard these things they were cut to the heart. There are two ways of being cut to the heart. Here they gnashed their teeth and cast him out of the city and stoned him. On the day of Pentecost, when they were cut or pricked at the heart they cried out, "What shall we do?" They took the opposite way. The devil, if he can have his way, will cause you to commit murder. If Jesus has His way, you will repent.

And Stephen, "...full of the Holy Ghost, looked up stedfastly into heaven, and saw the glory of God, and Jesus standing on the right hand of God" (Acts 7:55). Oh, this being full of the Holy Ghost! How much it means. I was riding for sixty miles one summer day and as I looked up in the heavens I had an open vision of Jesus all the way. It takes the Holy Ghost to give this.

Stephen cried out, "Lord, lay not this sin to their charge" (Acts 7:60). As he was full of the Spirit, he was full of love, and he manifested the very same compassion for his enemies that Jesus did at Calvary. This being filled with the Holy Ghost means much in every way. It means constant filling, quickening, and a new life continually. Oh, it's lovely! We have a wonderful Gospel and a great Savior! If you will be filled with the Holy Ghost, you will have a constant spring within, yea, as your faith centers in the Lord Jesus, from within you shall flow rivers of living water.

Published in *The Pentecostal Evangel*

THE POWER OF THE NAME

January 20, 1923

cripture reading: Acts 3:1-16. All things are possible through the name of Jesus. "...God also hath highly exalted him, and given him a name which is above every name: that at the name of Jesus every knee should bow..." (Philippians 2:9,10). There is power to overcome everything in the world through the name of Jesus. I am looking forward to a wonderful union through the name of Jesus. There is none other name under heaven given among men whereby we must be saved.

I want to instill into you the power, the virtue, and the glory of that name. Six people went into the house of a sick man to pray for him. He was an Episcopalian vicar, and lay in his bed utterly helpless, without even strength to help himself. He had read a little tract about healing and had heard about people praying for the sick and sent for these friends, who, he thought, could pray the prayer of faith. He was anointed according to James 5:14, but, because he had no immediate manifestation of healing, he wept bitterly. The six people walked out of the room, somewhat crestfallen to see the man lying there in an unchanged condition.

When they were outside, one of the six said, "There is one thing we might have done. I wish you would all go back with me and try it." They went back and all got together in a group. This brother said, "Let us whisper the name of Jesus." At first when they whispered this worthy name, nothing seemed to happen. But as they continued to whisper, "Jesus! Jesus! Jesus!" the power began to fall. As they saw that God was beginning to work, their faith and joy increased and they whispered the name louder and louder. As they did so the man arose from his bed and dressed himself. The secret was just this, those six people had gotten their eyes off the sick man, and they were just taken up with the Lord Jesus Himself, and their faith grasped the power that there is in His name. Oh, if people would only appreciate the power that there is in this name, there is no telling what would happen.

I know that through His name and through the power of His name we have access to God. The very face of Jesus fills the whole place with glory. All over the world there are people magnifying that name, and oh, what a joy it is for me to utter it.

One day I went up into a mountain to pray. I had a wonderful day. It was one of the high mountains of Wales. I heard of one man going up this mountain to pray, and the Spirit of the Lord met him so wonderfully that his face shone like that of an angel when he returned. Everyone in the village was talking about it. As I went up to this mountain and spent the day in the presence of the Lord, His wonderful power seemed to envelope and saturate and fill me.

Two years before this time there had come to our house two lads from Wales. They were just ordinary lads but they became very zealous for God. They came to our mission and saw some of the works of God. They said to me, "We would not be surprised if the Lord brings you down to Wales to raise our Lazarus." They explained that the leader of their assembly was a man who had spent his days working in a tin mine and his nights preaching, and the result was that he collapsed, went into consumption, and for four years he had been a helpless invalid, having to be fed with a spoon.

When I was up on that mountaintop I was reminded of the transfiguration scene, and I felt that the Lord's only purpose in taking us into the glory was to fit us for greater usefulness in the valley.

TONGUES AND INTERPRETATION: "The living God has chosen us for His divine inheritance, and He it is who is preparing us for our ministry, that it may be of God and not of man."

As I was on the mountaintop that day, the Lord said to me, "I want you to go and raise Lazarus." I told the brother who accompanied me of this, and when we got down to the valley, I wrote a postcard: "When I was up on the mountain praying today, God told me that I was to go and raise Lazarus." I addressed the postcard to the man in the place whose name had been given to me by the two lads. When we arrived at the place we went to the man to whom I had addressed the card. He looked at me and said, "Did you send this?" I said, "Yes." He said, "Do you think we believe in this? Here, take it." And he threw it at me.

The man called a servant and said, "Take this man and show him Lazarus." Then he said to me, "The moment you see him you will be ready to go home. Nothing will hold you." Everything he said was true from the natural viewpoint. The man was helpless. He was nothing but a mass of bones with skin stretched over them. There was no life to be seen. Everything in him spoke of decay.

I said to him, "Will you shout? You remember that at Jericho the people shouted while the walls were still up. God has like victory for you if you will only believe." But I could not get him to believe. There was not an atom of faith there. He had made up his mind not to have anything.

It is a blessed thing to learn that God's Word can never fail. Never hearken to human plans. God can work mightily when you persist in believing Him in spite of discouragements from the human standpoint. When I got back to the man whom I had sent the postcard, he asked, "Are you ready to go now?" "I am not moved by what I see. I am moved only by what I believe. I know this. No man looks if he believes. No man feels if he believes. The man who believes God has it. Every man who comes into the Pentecostal condition can laugh at all things and believe God."

There is something in the Pentecostal work that is different from anything else in the world. Somehow in Pentecost you know that God is a reality. Wherever the Holy Ghost has right of way, the gifts of the Spirit will be in manifestation; and where these gifts are never in manifestation, I question whether He is present. Pentecostal people are spoiled for anything else than Pentecostal meetings. We want none of the entertainments that the churches are offering. When God comes in He entertains us Himself. Entertained by the King of kings and Lord of lords!! Oh, it is wonderful.

There were difficult conditions in that Welsh village, and it seemed impossible to get the people to believe. "Ready to go home?" I was asked. But a man and a woman there asked us to come and stay with them. I said, "I want to know how many of you people can pray." No one wanted to pray. I asked if I could get seven people to pray with me for the poor man's deliverance. I said to the two people who were going to entertain us, "I will count on you two, and there is my friend and myself, and we need three others." I told the people that I trusted that some of them would awaken to their privilege and come in the morning and join us in prayer for the raising of Lazarus. It will never do to give way to human opinions. If God says a thing, you have to believe it.

I told the people that I would not eat anything that night. When I got to bed it seemed as if the devil tried to place on me everything that he had placed on that poor man in the bed. When I awoke I had a cough and all the weakness of a tubercular subject. I rolled out of bed on to the floor and cried out to God to deliver me from the power of the devil. I shouted loud enough to wake everybody in the house, but nobody was disturbed. God gave victory and I got back into bed again as free as ever I was in my life. At 5 o'clock the Lord awakened me and said to me, "Don't break bread until you break it round My table." At 6 o'clock He gave me these words, "And I will raise him up." I put my elbow into the fellow who was sleeping with me. He said "Ugh!" I put my elbow into him again and said, "Do you hear? The Lord says that He will raise him up."

At 8 o'clock they said to me, "Have a little refreshment." But I have found prayer and fasting the greatest joy, and you will always find it so when you are led by God. When we went to the house where Lazarus lived there were eight of us altogether. No one can prove to me that God does not always answer prayer. He always gives the exceeding abundant above all we ask or think.

I shall never forget how the power of God fell on us as we went into that sick man's room. Oh, it was lovely! As we circled round the bed I got one brother to hold the sick man's hand on one side and I held the other, and we each held the hand of the other next to us. I said, "We are not going to pray, we are just going to use the name of Jesus." We all knelt down and whispered that one word, "Jesus! Jesus! Jesus!" The power of God fell and then it lifted. Five times the power of God fell and then it remained. But the person who was in the bed was unmoved. Two years previous someone had come along and had tried to raise him up, and the devil had used his lack of success as a means of discouraging Lazarus. I said, "I don't care what the devil says; if God says he will raise you up it must be so. Forget everything else except what God says about Jesus."

The sixth time the power fell and the sick man's lips began moving and the tears began to fall. I said to him, "The power of God is here, it is yours to accept it." He said, "I have been bitter in my heart, and I know I have grieved the Spirit of God. Here I am helpless. I cannot lift my hands, nor even lift a spoon to my mouth." I said, "Repent, and God will hear you." He repented and cried out, "Oh God, let this be to Thy glory." As he said this the virtue of the Lord went right through him.

I have asked the Lord to never let me tell this story except as it was, for I realize that God can never bless exaggerations. As we again said, "Jesus! Jesus! Jesus!" the bed shook, and the man shook. I said to the people who were with me, "You can all go downstairs right away. This is all God. I'm not going to assist him." I sat and watched that man get up and dress himself. We sang the doxology as he walked down the steps. I said to him, "Now tell what has happened."

It was soon noised abroad that Lazarus had been raised up and the people came from Llanelli and all the district round to see him and hear his testimony. And God brought salvation to many. This man told right out in the open air what God had done, and as a result many were convicted and converted. All this came through the name of Jesus, through faith in His name, yea, the faith that is by Him gave this sick man perfect soundness in the presence of them all.

Peter and John were helpless, were illiterate, they had no college education. They had had some training with fish, and they had been with Jesus. To them had come a wonderful revelation of the power of the name of Jesus. They had handed out the bread and fish after Jesus had multiplied them. They had sat at the table with Him, and John had often gazed into His face. Peter had often to be rebuked, but Jesus manifested

His love to Peter through it all. Yea, He loved Peter, the wayward one. Oh, He's a wonderful lover! I have been wayward, I have been stubborn, I had an unmanageable temper at one time, but how patient He has been. I am here to tell you that there is power in Jesus and in His wondrous name to transform anyone, to heal anyone.

If only you will see Him as God's Lamb, as God's beloved Son who had laid upon Him the iniquity of us all, if only you will see that Jesus paid the whole price for our redemption that we might be free, you can enter into your purchased inheritance of salvation, of life, and of power.

Poor Peter, and poor John! They had no money! I don't think there is a person in this building as poor as Peter and John. But they had faith, they had the power of the Holy Ghost, they had God. You can have God even though you have nothing else. Even though you have lost your character you can have God. I have seen the worst men saved by the power of God.

I was one day preaching about the name of Jesus and there was a man leaning against a lamppost, listening. It took a lamppost to enable him to keep on his feet. We had finished our open air meeting, and the man was still leaning against the post. I asked him, "Are you sick?" He showed me his hand, and I saw that beneath his coat, he had a silver handled dagger. He told me that he was on his way to kill his unfaithful wife, but that he had heard me speaking about the power of the name of Jesus and could not get away. He said that he felt just helpless. I said, "Get you down." And there on the square, with people passing up and down, he got saved.

I took him to my home and put on him a new suit. I saw that there was something in that man that God could use. He said to me the next morning, "God has revealed Jesus to me; I see that all has been laid upon Jesus." I lent him some money, and he soon got together a wonderful little home. His faithless wife was living with another man, but he invited her back to the home that he had prepared for her. She came: and, where enmity and hatred had been before, the whole situation was transformed by love. God made that man a minister wherever he went. There is power in the name of Jesus everywhere. God can save to the uttermost.

There comes before me a meeting we had in Stockholm that I shall ever bear in my mind. There was a home for incurables there and one of the inmates was brought to the meeting. He had palsy and was shaking all over. He stood up before 3000 people and came to the platform, supported by two others. The power of God fell on him as I anointed him in the name of Jesus. The moment I touched him he dropped his crutch and began to walk in the name of Jesus. He walked down the steps and round that great building in view of all the people. There is nothing that our God cannot do. He will do everything if you will dare to believe.

Someone said to me, "Will you go to this Home for Incurables?" They took me there on my rest day. They brought out the sick people into a great corridor and in one hour the Lord set about twenty of them free.

The name of Jesus is so marvelous. Peter and John had no conception of all that was in that name; neither had the man, lame from his mother's womb who was laid daily at the gate; but they had faith to say, "In the name of Jesus Christ of Nazareth, rise up and walk." And as Peter took him by the right hand, and lifted him up, immediately his feet and ankle bones received strength, and he went into the temple with them, walking and leaping and praising God. God wants you to see more of this sort of thing done. How can it be done? Through His name, through faith in His name, through faith which is by Him.

Published in *The Pentecostal Evangel*

o speak all the words of this life. God has a plan for us in this life of the Spirit. This abundant life. Jesus came that we might have life. Satan comes to steal and kill and destroy, but God has for us abundance, full measure, pressed down, shaken together, overflowing, abundant measure, God filling us with His own personality — presence — making us salt and light and glory as revelation of Himself. God with us in all circumstances, afflictions, persecutions, in every trial girding us with truth. Christ the initiative, the Triune God, in control of our every thought, word, action, must be in line with Him with no weakness or failure. Our God — a God of might, light, revelation preparing us for heaven.

ACTS 5

February 23, 1923

For our life is hid with Christ in God, and when He who is our life shall be manifested, we also shall appear with Him in glory (Colossians 3:3,4).

> *For we know that if our earthly house of this tabernacle were dissolved, we have a building of God, an house not made with hands, eternal in the heavens. For in this we groan, earnestly desiring to be clothed upon with our house which is from heaven: If so be that being clothed we shall not be found naked. For we that are in this tabernacle do groan, being burdened: not for that we would be unclothed, but clothed upon, that mortality might be swallowed up of life. Now He that has wrought us for the selfsame thing is God, who also hath given unto us the earnest of the Spirit.*
>
> *2 Corinthians 5:1-5*

God's Word is a tremendous word, a productive word producing what it is. Power; producing God-likeness. We get to heaven through the Word of God, we have peace through the blood of His cross. Redemption is ours through the knowledge of the Word. I am saved because God's Word says so.

> *That if thou shalt confess with thy mouth the Lord Jesus, and shalt believe in thine heart that God hath raised him from the dead, thou shalt be saved.*
>
> *Romans 10:9*

If I am baptized with the Holy Spirit, it is because Jesus said, "...ye shall receive power, after that the Holy Ghost is come upon you..." (Acts 1:8). We must have one idea to be filled with the Holy Ghost, to be filled with God. God hath sent His Word to free us from the law of sin and death. Except we die we cannot live, except we cease to be, God cannot be.

A ROYAL PLAN

The Holy Ghost has a royal plan, a heavenly plan. He came to unveil the King to show the character of God, to unveil the precious blood. As I have the Holy Spirit within me, I see Jesus clothed for humanity. He was moved by the Spirit, led by the Spirit. We read of some who heard the

Word but were not profited, because faith was lacking in them. We must have a living faith in God's Word quickened by the Spirit. A man may be saved and still have a human spirit, with many who are spoken to about the baptism of the Holy Ghost, the human spirit at once arises against the Holy Ghost. The human spirit is not subject to the law of God, neither indeed can it be. The disciples at one time wanted to call down fire from heaven, Jesus said, "...Ye know not what manner of spirit ye are of" (Luke 9:55). The human spirit is not subject to the law of God.

The Holy Ghost came forth for one purpose to reveal unto us Jesus. He made Himself of no reputation, He was obedient unto death that God should forever have Him a token of submissive yieldedness, and God highly exalted Him and gave Him a name above every name. "Now he that hath wrought us for the selfsame thing is God, who also hath given us the earnest of the Spirit" (2 Corinthians 5:5). The clothing upon of the Spirit, human depravity covered, all contrary to the mind of God destroyed. God must have bodies for Himself, perfectly prepared by the Holy Ghost, for the day of the Lord. "For in this we groan, earnestly desiring to be clothed upon with our house which is from heaven" (2 Corinthians 5:2).

Is Paul speaking here of the coming of the Lord? No! Yet it is in conjunction, this condition of preparedness. The Holy Ghost is coming to take out a church and a perfect bride. The Holy Ghost must find in us perfect yieldedness with every human desire subjected to Him. No man can call Jesus Lord, but by the Holy Ghost. He has come to reveal Christ in us, that the glorious flow of the life of God may outflow rivers of living water to the thirsty land.

> *...if Christ be in you, the body is dead because of sin; but the Spirit is life because of righteousness.*
>
> *Romans 8:10*

This is that which God hath declared freedom from the law. If we love the world, the love of the Father is not in us.

> *For all that is in the world, the lust of the flesh, and the lust of the eyes, and the pride of life, is not of the Father, but is of the world.*
>
> *1 John 2:16*

NEW ORDER

The Spirit has to breathe in a new tenancy, a new order. The Holy Ghost came to give the vision of a life in which Jesus is perfected.

> *Who hath saved us, and called us with an holy calling, not according to our works, but according to his own purpose and grace, which was given us in Christ Jesus before the world began, But is now made manifest by the appearing of our Saviour Jesus Christ, who hath abolished death, and brought life...through the gospel.*
>
> *2 Timothy 1:9,10*

Saved, called to be saints, called with a holy calling, holy, pure, God-like — sons with power. It is a long time now since it was settled and death abolished, death has no more power — made known through the Gospel bringing in immortality. Mortality is a hindrance. Sin has no more domination over you. You reign in Christ, you appropriate His finished work. Don't groan and travail for a week. If you are in need "only believe." Don't fast to get some special thing, "only believe." It is according to your faith [that] God blesses you with faith. Have faith in God. If you are free in God, believe! Believe! And it shall be unto you even as you believe.

Awake thou that sleepest, put on light, open thine eyes. If ye then be risen with Christ, seek the things that are above where Christ is, seated at the right hand of God. Stir yourselves up, beloved! Where are you? I am risen with Christ, planted, it was a beautiful planting. Seated! God gives me the credit and I believe Him. Why should I doubt? Wherefore do you doubt, faith reigns. God makes it possible. How many receive the Holy Ghost and Satan gets a doubt in. Don't doubt, believe! There is power and strength in Him. Who dare believe God? Quit doubting street — live in faith, victory street. Jesus sent seventy away and they came back in victory. It takes God to make it real. Dare to believe until there is not a sick person, no sickness, everything withered and the life of Jesus implanted within. The righteous shall hold on his way. God has reserved him that is godly for Himself. Therefore lift up your heads — the devil makes you remember the day you failed, you would give the world to forget. God has forgotten. When He forgives, He forgets. *God wants to make us pillars, honourable, strong, holy.* God will take us on. I am enamoured with inspiration of the great fact of the possibility. God wants you to know that you are saved, cleansed, delivered, and marching to victory. Faith to believe! God has a plan! Set your affections on things above, get into the heavenly places with Christ.

> *...be not conformed to this world: but be ye transformed by the renewing of your mind....*
>
> Romans 12:2

You cannot repeat the name of Jesus too often, what a privilege to kneel and get right into heaven the moment we pray, where the glory descends and the fire burns and faith is active and the light dispels the darkness. What is darkness? What is mortality? Mortality hinders, but the life of Jesus eats up mortality. The Acts of the apostles deals with receiving the Holy Ghost and the epistles are written to believers baptised in the Holy Ghost.

When I was in New Zealand, some brethren came questioning about the baptism of the Holy Ghost. They quoted the epistles — but before we are in the experience of the epistles, we must go through the Acts. I asked them (1 Corinthians 14:2), when did you speak in mysteries? But they had not yet come into the baptism of the Holy Ghost.

Jesus was the light and the life of men, no man has this light and walketh in darkness. When Christ who is our life shall appear, we also shall appear with Him in glory. Where His life is, disease cannot remain. Is not He that indwells us greater than all? Is He greater? Yes, when He has full control. If one thing is permitted outside the will of God, it hinders in our standing against the powers of Satan. We must allow the Word of God to judge us, lest we stand condemned with the world. When He who is our life shall appear! Have I any life apart from Him? any joy — any fellowship apart from Him? Jesus said the prince of this world cometh and findeth nothing in Me. All that is contrary in [us] is withered by the indwelling life of the Son of God.

> *For we that are in this tabernacle do groan, being burdened: not for that we would be unclothed, but clothed upon, that mortality might be swallowed up of life.*
>
> 2 Corinthians 5:4

Are we ready, clothed upon, mortality swallowed up of life? If He came, who is our life, we should go. I know the Lord — I know the Lord laid His hand on me. He filled me with the Holy Ghost.

HEAVEN ON EARTH

I know the Lord laid His hand on me. It's heaven on earth. Heaven has begun with me. I am happy now — and free. Since the Comforter has come. The Comforter, the great revealer of the Kingdom. He came to give us the more abundant life. God has designed the plan, nothing really matters if the Lord loves us. God sets great store by us. The pure in heart see God. There are no stiff knees in the Spirit, or cough in the Holy Ghost — or pain. Nothing ails us if we are filled with the Spirit.

If the Spirit of Him that raised up Jesus from the dead dwells in you, He shall quicken your mortal bodies by His Spirit that dwelleth in you (Romans 8:11).

The way into the glory is through the flesh being rent, a separation unto God, freedom of spirit, rejoicing every day, free from the law of sin and death. The perfect law destroying the natural law. Spiritual activity taking in every passing ray, days of heaven upon earth, no sickness, not knowing we have a body, the life of God changing us, bringing us into the heavenly realm, where we reign over principalities and all evil, limitless, powerful, supernatural. If the natural body decays, the Spirit renews. Spiritual power increasing until with one mind and one heart, the glory is brought down over all the earth, right on into divine life, keeping the evidence. The whole life filled, this is Pentecost. The life of the Lord manifest wherever we are in bus or train, so filled with the life of Jesus unto perfection, rejoicing in hope of glory of God, always looking for translation. The life of the Lord in us as a magnet draws, His life eating up all else.

I must have the overflowing life in the Spirit, God is not pleased with less, it is a disgrace to be on an ordinary plan after we are filled with the Holy Ghost. We are to be salt in the earth, not lukewarm, hot which means seeing God, with eagerness, liberty, movement, and power. Believe! Believe! Amen.

Message preached in London, England

OUR RISEN CHRIST

March 31, 1923

Read the fourth chapter of Acts. Today we praise God for the fact that our glorious Jesus is the risen Christ. Those of us who have tasted the power of the indwelling Spirit know something of the manner in which the hearts those two disciples burned as they walked to Emmaus with their risen Lord as their companion.

Note the words of verse 31, "And when they had prayed, the place was shaken...." There are many churches where they never pray the kind of prayer that you read of here. A church that does not know how to pray and to shout will never be shaken. If you live in a place like that you may as well write "Ichabod — the glory of the Lord has departed" — over the threshold. It is only when men have learned the secret of prayer, of power, and of praise, that God comes forth. Some people say, "Well, I praise God inwardly," but if there is an abundance of praise in your heart, your mouth cannot help speaking it.

There was a man who had a large business in London who was a great churchgoer. The church he attended was beautifully decorated, and his pew was delightfully cushioned — just about enough to make it easy to sleep through the sermons. He was a prosperous man in business, but he had no peace in his heart. But there was a boy at his business who always looked happy. He was always jumping and whistling. One day he said to this boy, "I want to see you in my office." When the boy was in his office he asked him, "How is it that you can always whistle and be happy?" "I cannot help it," answered the boy. "Where did you get it?" asked the master. "I got it at the Pentecostal mission." "Where is that?" The boy told him, and the next thing was, that the man was attending. The Lord broke him up there, and in a short while he was entirely changed. One day, shortly after this, he found that, instead of being distracted by his business as he formerly had been, he was actually whistling and jumping. His whole position and his whole life had been changed.

The shout cannot come out unless it is in. There must first be the inner working of the power of God. It is He who changes the heart, and transforms the life, and before there is any real outward evidence there must be the inflow of divine life. Sometimes I say to people, "You weren't at meeting the other night." They reply, "Oh, yes, I was there in spirit." I say to them, "Well, come next time with your body also. We don't want a lot of spirits here and no bodies. We want you to come and get filled with God." When all the people will come and pray and praise as did these early disciples there will be something doing. People who come will catch fire and they will want to come again. But they will have no use for a place where everything has become formal, dry, and dead.

The power of Pentecost as it came at first came to loose men. God wants us free on every line. Men and women are tired of imitations; they want reality; they want to see people who have the living Christ within, and are filled with Holy Ghost power.

I received several letters and telegrams about a certain case, but when I arrived I was told I was too late. I said, "That cannot be. God has never sent me too late anywhere." God showed me when I went that something different would happen to anything I had seen previously. The people I went to were all strangers. I was introduced to a young man who lay helpless, and for whom there was no hope. The doctor had been to see him that morning and had declared that he would not live through the day. He lay with his face to the wall, and when I spoke to him he whispered, "I cannot turn over." His mother said that they had had to lift him out of bed on sheets for weeks, and that he was so weak and helpless that he had to stay in one position.

The young man said, "My heart is so weak." I assured him, "God is the strength of thy heart and thy portion forever. If you will believe God, it shall be so today."

Our Christ is risen. He is a living Christ who indwells us. We must not have this truth merely as a theory, Christ must be risen in us by the power of the Spirit. The power that raised Him from the dead must animate us, and as this glorious resurrection power surges through your being, you will be freed from all your weaknesses and you will become strong in the Lord and in the power of His might. There is a resurrection power that God wants you to have and to have today. Why not? Receive your portion here and now.

I said to these people, "I believe your son will rise today." They only laughed. People do not expect to see signs and wonders today as the disciples saw them of old. Has God changed? Or has our faith waned so that we are not expecting the greater works that Jesus promised? We must not harp on any minor key. Our message must rise to concert pitch, and there must be nothing left out of it that is in the Book.

It was winter time, and I said to the parents, "Will you get the boy's suit and bring it here?" They would not listen to the request, for they were expecting the boy to die. But I had gone to that place believing God. In Romans 4:17, we read of Abraham,

> ...(I have made thee a father of many nations,) before him whom he believed, even God, who quickeneth the dead, and calleth those things which be not as though they were.

God, help us to understand this. It is time people knew now to shout in faith as they contemplate the eternal power of our God to whom it is nothing to quicken and raise the dead. I come across some who would be giants in the power of God but they have no shout of faith. I find everywhere people who go down even when they are praying simply because they are just breathing sentences without uttering speech, and you cannot get victory that way. You must learn to take the victory and shout in the face of the devil, "It is done!" There is no man who can doubt if he learns to shout. When we know how to shout properly, things will be different, and tremendous things will happen. In Acts 4:24 we read, "...they lifted up their voice to God with one accord...." It surely must have been a loud prayer. We must know that God means us to have life. If there is anything in the world that has life in it, it is this Pentecostal revival we are in. I believe in the baptism of the Holy Ghost with the speaking in tongues, and I believe that every man who is baptized in the Holy Ghost will speak in other tongues as the Spirit gives him utterance. I believe in the Holy Ghost. And if you are filled with the Spirit, you will be superabounding in life — living waters will flow from you.

At last I persuaded the parents to bring the boy's clothes and lay them on the bed. From the natural viewpoint, the young man lay dying. I spoke to the afflicted one, "God has revealed to me that, as I lay my hands upon you, the place will be filled with the Holy Ghost, the bed will be shaken, you will be shaken and thrown out of bed by the power of the Holy Ghost, you will dress yourself and be strong." I said this to him in faith. I laid hands on him in the name of Jesus and instantly the power of God fell and filled the place. I felt helpless and fell flat on the floor. I knew nothing except that a short while after the place was shaken, I heard the young man walking over me and saying, "For Thy glory, Lord! For Thy glory, Lord!"

He dressed himself and cried, "God has healed me." The father fell, the mother fell, and another who was present fell also. God manifested His power that day in saving the whole household and healing the young man. It is the power of the risen Christ we need. That young man is today preaching the Gospel.

For years we have been longing for God to come forth, and, praise Him, He is coming forth. The tide is rising everywhere. I was in Switzerland not long ago, preaching in many places where the Pentecostal message had not been heard, and today there are nine new Pentecostal assemblies in different places going on blessedly for God. All over the world it is the same; this great Pentecostal work is in motion. You can hardly get to a place now where God is not pouring out His Spirit upon all flesh, and His promises never fail. Our Christ is risen. His salvation was not a thing done in a corner. Truly He was a man of glory who went to Calvary for us, in order that He might free us from all that would mar and hinder, that He might transform us by His grace, and bring us out from under the power of Satan into the glorious power of God. One touch of our risen Christ will raise the dead. Hallelujah!

Oh, this wonderful Jesus of ours! He comes and indwells us. He comes to abide. He it is who baptizes us with the Holy Ghost, and makes everything different. We are to be a kind of firstfruits unto God and are to be like Christ who is the firstfruit, walking in His footsteps, living in His power. What a salvation this is, having this risen Christ in us. I feel that everything else must go to nothingness, helplessness, and ruin. Even the best thought of holiness must be on the decrease in order that Christ may increase, and we live in another state, and all things are under the power of the Spirit.

Dare you take your inheritance from God? Dare you believe God? Dare you stand on the record of His Word? What is the record? If thou shalt believe, thou shalt see the glory of God. You will be sifted as wheat. You will be tried as though some strange thing tried you. You will be put in places where you will have to put your whole trust in God. There is no such thing as anyone being tried beyond what God will allow. There is no temptation that will come, but God will be with you right in the temptation to deliver you, and when you have been tried, He will bring you forth as gold. Every trial is to bring you to a greater position in God. The trial that tries your faith will take you on to the place where you will know that the faith of God will be forthcoming in the next test. No man is able to win any victory save through the power of the risen Christ within him. You will never be able to say, "I did this or that." You will desire to give God the glory for everything.

If you are sure of your ground, if you are counting on the presence of the living Christ within, you can laugh when you see things getting worse. God would have you settled and grounded in Christ, and you become steadfast and unmoveable in Him.

The Lord Jesus said, "...I have a baptism to be baptized with; and how am I straitened till it be accomplished!" (Luke 12:50). He assuredly straitened in the way, at Gethsemane, at the judgment hall, and, after that, at the cross, where He, through the eternal Spirit, offered Himself without spot to God. God will take us right on in like manner, and the Holy Spirit will lead every step of the way. God led Him right through to the empty tomb, to the ascension glory, to a place on the throne; and the Son of God will never be satisfied until He has us with Himself, sharing His glory and sharing His throne.

Published in *The Pentecostal Evangel*

THE GRACE OF LONGSUFFERING
Counterpart of "Gifts of Healing"
April 1923

This morning we will move on to the "gifts of healing." "To another faith by the same Spirit; to another the gifts of healing by the same Spirit" (1 Corinthians 12:9).

There is no use expecting to understand the gifts and to understand the epistles unless you have the Holy Ghost. All the epistles are written to a baptized people, and not to the unregenerated. They are written to those who have grown into a maturity as a manifestation of the Christ of God. Do not jump into the epistles before you have come in at the gate of the baptism of the Spirit. I believe that this teaching God is helping me to bring to you will move on you to become restless and discontented on every line till God has finished with you. If we want to know the mind of God through the epistles, there is nothing else to bring the truth but the revelation of the Spirit Himself. He gives the utterance; He opens the door. Don't live in a poverty state when we are all around, in and out, up and down, pressed out beyond measure with the rarest gems of the latest word from God. "Ask, and it shall be given you; seek, and ye shall find; knock, and it shall be opened unto you: For every one that asketh receiveth; and he that seeketh findeth; and to him that knocketh it shall be opened" (Matthew 7:7,8). There is the authority of God's Word. And remember, the authority of God's Word is Jesus. These are the utterances by the Spirit of Jesus to us this morning. I come to you with a great inward desire to wake you up to your great possibilities. Your responsibilities will be great, but not as great as your possibilities. You will always find that God is over-abundance on every line He touches for you, and He wants you to come into mind and thought with Him so that you are not straightened in yourselves. Be enlarged in God!

TONGUES AND INTERPRETATION: "It is that which God hath chosen for us, which is mightier than we. It is that which is bottomless, higher than the heights, more lovely than all beside. And God in a measure presses you out to believe all things that you may endure all things, and lay hold of eternal life through the power of the Spirit."

LONGSUFFERING AND AUTHORITY

The "gifts of healings" are wonderful gifts. There is a difference between having a gift of healing, and "gifts of healings." God wants us not to come behind in anything. I like this word, "gifts of healing." To have the accomplishment of these gifts I must bring myself to a conformity to the mind and will of God in purpose. It would be impossible to have "gifts of healing" unless you possessed that blessed fruit of "longsuffering." You will find these gifts run parallel with that which will bring them into operation without a leak.

But how will it be possible to minister the gifts of healing considering the peculiarities there are in the assemblies, and the many evil powers of Satan which confront us and possess bodies? The man who will go through with God and exercise the gifts of healing will have to be a man of longsuffering, always have a word of comfort. If the one who is in distress and helpless doesn't see eye to eye in everything, and doesn't get all he wants, longsuffering will bear and forbear. Longsuffering is a grace Jesus lived in and moved in. He was filled with compassion, and God will never be able to move us to the help of the needy one till we reach that place. Sometimes you might think by the way I went about praying for the sick that I was unloving and rough, but oh friends, you have no idea what I see behind the sickness and the afflicted. I am not dealing with the person, I am dealing with the satanic forces that are binding the afflicted. As far as the person goes, my heart is full of love and compassion for all, but I fail to see how you will ever reach a place where God will be able definitely to use you until you get angry at the devil.

One day a pet dog followed a lady out of her house and ran all around her feet. She said to the dog, "I cannot have you with me today." The dog wagged its tail and made a great fuss. "Go home, pet," she said, but it didn't go. At last she shouted roughly, "Go home!" and off it went. Some people play with the devil like that. "Poor thing!" The devil can stand all the comfort anybody in the world could give. Cast him out! You are not dealing with the person, you are dealing with the devil. If you say, with authority, "Come out, you demons, in the name of the

Lord!" they must come out. You will always be right when you dare to treat sickness as the devil's work and you will always be near the mark when you treat it as sin. Let Pentecostal people wake up to see that getting sick is caused by some misconduct; there is some neglect, something wrong somewhere, a weak place where Satan has had a chance to get in. And if we wake up to the real facts of it, we will be ashamed to say that we are sick because people will know we have been sinning.

FULNESS OF REDEMPTION

Gifts of healings are so varied in all lines you will find the gift of discernment often operated in connection therewith. And the manifestations of the Spirit are given to us that we may profit withal. You must never treat a cancer case as anything else than a living, evil spirit which is always destroying the body. It is one of the worst kinds I know. Not that the devil has anything good; every disease of the devil is bad, either to a greater or less degree, but this form of disease is one that you must cast out.

Among the first people I met in Victoria Hall was a woman who had a cancer in the breast. As soon as the cancer was cursed, it stopped bleeding because it was dead. The next thing that happened, the body cast it off, because the natural body has no room for dead matter. When it came out it was like a big ball with thousands of fibers. All these fibers had spread out into the flesh, but the moment the evil power was destroyed they had no power. Jesus gave us power to bind and power to loose; we must bind the evil powers and loose the afflicted and set them free. There are many cases where Satan has control of the mind, and those under satanic influence are not all in asylums.

I will tell you what freedom is: no person in this place who enjoys the fulness of the Spirit with a clear knowledge of redemption, should know that he has a body. You ought to be able to eat and sleep, digest your food, and not be conscious of your body; a living epistle of God's thought and mind, walking up and down the world without pain. That is redemption. To be fully in the will of God, the perfection of redemption, we should not have a pain of any kind.

I have had some experience along this line. When I was weak and helpless and friends were looking for me to die, it was in that straitened place that I saw the fulness of redemption. I read and re-read the ninety-first Psalm and claimed long life — "With long life will I satisfy him." What else? "And shew him my salvation." This is greater than long life. The salvation of God is deliverance from everything, and here I am. At twenty-five or thirty they were looking for me to die; now at sixty-three I feel young. So there is something more in this truth that I am preaching than mere words. God hath not designed us for anything else than to be firstfruits, sons of God with power over all the power of the enemy, living in the world but not of it.

BE SURE OF YOUR GROUND

We have to be careful in casting out demons, who shall give the command. Man may say, "Come out," but unless it is in the Spirit of God our words are vain. The devil always had a good time with me in the middle of the night, and tried to give me a bad time. I had a real conflict with evil powers, and the only deliverance I got was when I bound them in the name of the Lord.

I remember taking a man who was demon-possessed out for a walk one day. We were going through a thickly crowded place and this man became obstreperous. I squared him up and the devil came out of him, but I wasn't careful, and these demons fastened themselves on me right on the street there, so that I couldn't move. Sometimes when I am ministering on the platform and the powers of the devil attack me, the people think I am casting demons out of them, but I am casting them out of myself! The people couldn't understand when I cast that evil spirit out of that man on the street, but I understood. The man who had that difficulty is now preaching, and is one of the finest men we have. But it required someone to bind the strongman. You must be sure of your ground, and sure it is a mightier power than you that is destroying the devil. Take your position from the first epistle of John and say, "...greater is he that is in [me], than he that is in the world" (1 John 4:4). If you think it is you, you make a great mistake. It is your being filled with Him; He acting in the place of you; your thought, your mouth, your all becoming exercised by the Spirit of God.

At L. — in Norway we had a place seating 1,500 people. When we reached there it was packed and hundreds were unable to get in. The policemen were standing there, and I thought the first thing I would do would be to preach to the people outside and then go in. I addressed the policemen and said, "You see this condition. I have come with a message to help everybody, and it hurts me very much to find as many people outside as in; I want the promise of you police officials that you will give us the marketplace tomorrow. Will you do it?" They put up their hands that they would. It was a beautiful day in April, and there was a big stand in the woods about ten feet high in the great park, where thousands of people gathered. After the preaching we had some wonderful cases of healing. One man came one hundred miles, bringing his food with him. He hadn't passed anything through his stomach for over a month for there was a great cancer there. He was healed in the meeting and opening up his lunch began eating before all the people.

Then there was a young woman who came with a stiff hand. I cursed the spirit of infirmity and it was instantly cast out and the arm was free. She waved it over her head and said, "My father is the chief of police. I have been bound since I was a girl." At the close of the meeting Satan laid out two people with fits. That was my day! I jumped down to where they were and in the name of Jesus delivered them. People said, "Oh, isn't he rough," but when they saw those afflicted stand up and praise God, that was a time of rejoicing.

Oh, we must wake up, stretch ourselves out to believe God! Before God could bring me to this place He had to break me a thousand times. I have wept, I have groaned, I have travailed night after night till God broke me. Until God has mowed you down, you will never have this longsuffering for others.

When I was at Cardiff the Lord healed a woman right in the meeting. She was afflicted with ulceration, and while they were singing she fell full length and cried in such a way, I felt something must be done. I knelt down alongside of the woman, laid my hands on her body, and instantly the powers of the devil were destroyed and she was delivered from ulceration, rose up, and joined in the singing.

IN THE "GOING"

We have been seeing wonderful miracles in these last days, and they are only a little of what we are going to see. When I say "going to see" I do not want to throw something out ten years to come, nor even two years. I believe we are in the "going," right on the threshold of wonderful things.

You must not think that these gifts fall upon you like ripe cherries. You pay a price for everything you get from God. There is nothing worth having that you do not have to pay for, either temporally or spiritually. I remember when I was at Antwerp and Brussels. The power of God was very mighty upon me there. Coming through to London I called on some friends at [one place]. To show you the leading of the Lord, these friends said, "Oh, God sent you here. How much we need you!" They sent a wire to a place where there was a young man twenty-six years old, who had been in bed eighteen years. His body was so much bigger than an ordinary body, because of inactivity, and his legs were like a child's; instead of bone, there was gristle. He had never been able to dress himself. When they got the wire the father dressed him and he was sitting in a chair. I felt it was one of the opportunities of my life. I said to this young man, "What is the greatest desire of your heart?" "Oh," he said, "that I might be filled with the Holy Ghost!" I put my hands upon him and said, "Receive, receive ye the Holy Ghost." Instantly he became drunk with the Spirit, and fell off the chair like a big bag of potatoes. I saw what God could do with a helpless cripple. First, his head began shaking terrifically; then his back began moving very fast, and then his legs, just like being in a battery. Then he spoke clearly in tongues, and we wept and praised the Lord. His legs were still as they had been, by all appearances, and this is where I missed it. These "missings" sometimes are God's opportunities of teaching you important lessons. He will teach you through your weaknesses that which is not faith. It was not faith for me to look at that body, but human. The man who will work the works of God must never look at conditions, but at Jesus in whom everything is complete. I looked at the boy and there was absolutely no help. I turned to the Lord and said, "Lord, tell me what to do," and He did. He said, "Command him to walk in My name." This is where I missed it. I looked at his conditions and I got the father to help lift him up to see if his legs had strength. We did our best, but he and I together could not move him. Then the Lord showed me my mistake and I said, "God forgive." I got right down and repented, and said to the Lord, "Please tell me again." God is so good. He never leaves us to ourselves. Again He said to me, "Command him in My name to walk." So I shouted, "Arise and walk in the name of Jesus." Did he do it? No, I declare he never walked. He was lifted up by the power of God in a moment and he ran. The door was wide open; he ran out across the road into a field where he ran up and down and came back. Oh, it was a miracle!

There are miracles to be performed and these miracles will be accomplished by us when we understand the perfect plan of His spiritual graces which has come down to us. These things will come to us when we come to a place of brokenness, of surrender, of wholehearted yieldedness, where we decrease but where God has come to increase; and where we dwell and live in Him.

Will you allow Him to be the choice of your thoughts? Submit to Him, the God of all grace, that you may be well-furnished with faith for every good work, that the mind of the Lord may have free course in you, run and be glorified; that the heathen shall know, the uttermost parts of the earth shall be filled with the glory of the Lord as the waters cover the deep.

Published in *The Latter Rain Evangel*

PRESENT-TIME BLESSINGS FOR PRESENT-TIME SAINTS
April 14, 1923

Read with me the first twelve verses of Matthew 5, these verses that we generally call the "Beatitudes." Some tell us that Matthew 5 is a millennial chapter and that we cannot attain to these blessings at the present time. I believe that everyone who receives the baptism in the Spirit has a real foretaste and earnest of millennial blessing, but that here the Lord Jesus is setting forth present-day blessing that we can enjoy here and now.

It is a great joy for me to be speaking to baptized believers. We have not reached the height of God's mind, but my personal conviction is that we are nearer by far than we were fourteen years ago. If anyone had told me that I should be happier today than I was fourteen years ago when the Lord baptized me in the Spirit, I would not have believed him. But I see that God has more ahead for us, and that, so far, we have only touched the fringe of things. As we let the truth lay hold of us, we will press on for the mark ahead and enter more fully into our birthright — all that God says.

It seems to me that every time I open my Bible I get a new revelation of God's plan. God's Spirit takes man to a place of helplessness, and then reveals God as his all in all.

"Blessed are the poor in spirit: for theirs is the kingdom of heaven" (Matthew 5:3). This is one of the richest places into which Jesus brings us. The poor have a right to everything in heaven. "Theirs is." Dare you believe it? Yes, I dare. I believe, I know, that I was very poor. When God's Spirit comes in as the ruling, controlling power of the life, He gives us God's revelation of our inward poverty, and shows us that God has come with one purpose, to bring heaven's best to earth, and that with Jesus He will indeed "...freely give us all things" (Romans 8:32).

An old man and an old woman had lived together for seventy years. Someone said to them, "You must have seen many clouds during those days." They replied, "Where do the showers come from? You never get showers without clouds." It is only the Holy Ghost who can bring us to the place of realization of our poverty; but, every time He does it, He opens the windows of heaven and the showers of blessing fall.

But I must recognize the difference between my own spirit and the Holy Spirit. My own spirit can do certain things on natural lines, can even weep and pray and worship, but it is all on a human plane, and we must not depend on our own human thoughts and activities or on our own personality. If the baptism means anything to you, it should bring you to the death of the ordinary, where you are no longer putting faith in your own understanding; but, conscious of your own poverty, you are ever yielded to the Spirit. Then it is that your body becomes filled with heaven on earth.

"Blessed are they that mourn: for they shall be comforted" (Matthew 5:4). People get a wrong idea of mourning. Over in Switzerland they have a day set apart to take wreaths to graves. I laughed at the people's ignorance and said, "Why are you spending time around the graves? The people you love are not there. All that taking of flowers to the graves is not faith at all. Those who died in Christ are gone to be with Him, 'which,' Paul said, 'is far better.'"

My wife once said to me, "You watch me when I'm preaching. I get so near to heaven when I'm preaching that some day I'll be off." One night she was preaching and when she had finished, off she went. I was going to Glasgow and had said goodbye to her before she went to the meeting. As I was leaving the house, the doctor and policeman met me at the door and told me that she had fallen dead at the Mission door. I knew she had got what she wanted. I could not weep, but I was in tongues, praising the Lord. On natural lines she was everything to me; but I could not mourn on natural lines, but just laughed in the Spirit. The house was soon filled with people. The doctor said, "She is dead, and we can do no more for her." I went up to her lifeless corpse and commanded death to give her up, and she came back to me for a moment. Then God said to me, "She is Mine; her work is done." I knew what He meant.

They laid her in the coffin, and I brought my sons and my daughter into the room and said, "Is she there?" They said, "No, Father." I said, "We will cover her up." If you go mourning the loss of loved ones who have gone to be with Christ, I say it in love to you, you have never had the revelation of what Paul spoke of when he showed us that it is better to go than to stay. We read this in Scripture, but the trouble is that people will not believe it. When you believe God, you will say, "Whatever it is, it is all right. If Thou dost want to take the one I love, it is all right, Lord." Faith removes all tears of self-pity.

But there is a mourning in the Spirit. God will bring you to a place where things must be changed, and there is a mourning, an unutterable groaning until God comes. And the end of all real faith always is rejoicing. Jesus mourned over Jerusalem. He saw the conditions, He saw the unbelief, He saw the end of those who closed their ears to the Gospel. But God gave a promise that He should see the travail of His soul and be satisfied, and that He should see His seed. What happened on the day of Pentecost in Jerusalem was an earnest of what will be the results of His travail, to be multiplied a billionfold all down the ages in all the world. And as we enter in the Spirit into travail over conditions that are wrong, such mourning will ever bring results for God, and our joy will be complete in the satisfaction that is brought to Christ thereby.

"Blessed are the meek: for they shall inherit the earth" (Matthew 5:5). Moses was headstrong in his zeal for his own people, and it resulted in his killing a man. His heart was right in his desire to correct things, but he was working on natural lines, and when we work on natural lines we always fail. Moses had a mighty passion, and that is one of the best things in the world when God has control and it becomes a passion for souls to be born again; but apart from God it is one of the worst things. Paul had it to a tremendous extent, and, breathing out threatenings, he was hailing men and women to prison. But God changed it, and later we find him wishing himself accursed from Christ for the sake of his brethren, his kinsmen according to the flesh. God took the headstrong Moses and molded him into the meekest of men. He took the fiery Saul of Tarsus and made him the foremost exponent of grace. Oh, brothers, God can transform you in like manner, and plant in you a divine meekness and every other thing that you lack.

In our Sunday school we had a boy with red hair. His head was as red as fire and so was his temper. He was such a trial. He kicked his teachers and the superintendent. He was simply uncontrollable. The teachers had a meeting in which they discussed the matter of expelling him. They thought that God might undertake for that boy and so they decided to give him another chance. One day he had to be turned out, and he broke all the windows of the mission. He was worse outside than in. Sometime later we had a ten-day revival meeting. There was nothing much doing in that meeting and people thought it a waste of time, but there was one result — the red-headed lad got saved. After he was saved, the difficulty was to get rid of him at our house. He would be there until midnight crying to God to make him pliable and use him for His glory. God delivered the lad from his temper and made him one of the meekest, most beautiful boys you ever saw. For twenty years he has been a mighty missionary in China. God takes us just as we are and transforms us by His power.

I can remember the time when I used to go white with rage, and shake all over with temper. I could hardly hold myself together. I waited on God for ten days. In those ten days I was being emptied out and the life of the Lord Jesus was being wrought into me. My wife testified of the transformation that took place in my life, "I never saw such a change. I have never been able to cook anything since that time that has not pleased him. Nothing is too hot or too cold, everything is just right." God must come and reign supreme in your life. Will you let Him do it? He can do it, and He will if you will let Him. It is no use trying to tame the "old man." But

God can deal with him. The carnal mind will never be subjected to God, but God will bring it to the cross where it belongs, and will put in its place, the pure, the holy, the meek mind of the Master.

"Blessed are they which do hunger and thirst after righteousness: for they shall be filled" (Matthew 5:6). Note that word, "*shall* be filled." If you ever see a "shall" in the Bible, make it yours. Meet the conditions and God will fulfill His Word to you. The Spirit of God is crying, "Ho, every one that thirsteth, come ye to the waters, and he that hath no money; come ye, buy and eat; yea, come, buy wine and milk without money and without price" (Isaiah 55:1). The Spirit of God will take of the things of Christ and show them to you in order that you may have a longing for Christ in His fulness, and when there is that longing, God will not fail to fill you.

See that crowd of worshipers who have come up to the feast. They are going away utterly unsatisfied, but on the last day, the great day of the feast, Jesus stands up and cries, "If any man thirst, let him come unto me, and drink. He that believeth on me, as the scripture hath said, out of his belly shall flow rivers of living water" (John 7:37,38). Jesus knew that they were going away without the living water, and so He directs them to the true source of supply. Are you thirsty today? The living Christ still invites you to Himself, and I want to testify that He still satisfies the thirsty soul and still fills the hungry with good things.

In Switzerland, I learned of a man who met with the assembly of the Plymouth brethren. He attended their various meetings, and one morning, at their breaking of bread service, he arose and said, "Brethren, we have the Word, and I feel that we are living very much in the letter of it, but there is a hunger and thirst in my soul for something deeper, something more real than we have, and I cannot rest until I enter into it." The next Sunday this brother rose again and said, "We are all so poor here, there is no life in this assembly, and my heart is hungry for reality." He did this for several weeks until it got on the nerves of these people and they protested, "Sands, you are making us all miserable. You are spoiling our meetings, and there is only one thing for you to do, and that is to clear out."

That man went out of the meeting in a very sad condition. As he stood outside, one of his children asked him what was the matter, and he said, "To think that they should turn me out from their midst for being hungry and thirsty for more of God!" I did not know anything of this until afterward.

Some days later someone rushed up to Sands and said, "There is a man over here from England, and he is speaking about tongues and healing." Sands said, "I'll fix him. I'll go to the meeting and sit right up in the front and challenge him with the Scriptures. I'll dare him to preach these things in Switzerland. I'll publicly denounce him." So he came to the meetings. There he sat. He was so hungry and thirsty that he drank in every word that was said. His opposition soon petered out. The first morning he said to a friend, "This is what I want." He drank and drank of the Spirit. After three weeks he said, "God will have to do something new or I'll burst." He breathed in God and the Lord filled him to such an extent that he spoke in other tongues as the Spirit gave utterance. Sands is now preaching, and is in charge of a new Pentecostal assembly.

God is making people hungry and thirsty after His best. And everywhere He is filling the hungry and giving them that which the disciples received at the very beginning. Are you hungry? If you are, God promises that you shall be filled.

Published in *The Pentecostal Evangel*

I want you to see this morning two words that are closely connected; beautiful words and full of blessing this moment for us. Let me read them:

GLORY AND VIRTUE
May 1923

> "...*through the knowledge of him that hath called us to glory and virtue.*
> 2 Peter 1:3

People have a great misunderstanding about glory, though they often use the word. There are three things that ought to take place in the baptism. It was a necessity that the moving by the mighty rushing wind should be made manifest in the upper room; also that they should be clothed with tongues as of fire. Then that the body should receive, not only the fire, but also the rushing wind, the personality of the Spirit in the wind, and the manifestation of the glory is in the wind, or breath of God.

The inward man receives the Holy Ghost instantly with great joy and blessedness. He cannot express it. Then the power of the Spirit, this breath of God, takes of the things of Jesus and sends forth as a river the utterances of the Spirit. Again, when the body is filled with joy, sometimes so inexpressible, being thrown on the canvas of the mind, the canvas of the mind has great power to move the operation of the tongue to bring out the very depths of the inward heart's power, love, joy, to us. By the same process the Spirit, which is the breath of God, brings forth the manifestation of the glory.

Peter speaks in Second Peter 1:16,17:

> *For we have not followed cunningly devised fables, when we made known unto you the power and coming of our Lord Jesus Christ, but were eyewitnesses of his majesty. For he received from God the Father honour and glory, when there came such a voice to him from the excellent glory....*

Sometimes people wonder why it is that the Holy Ghost is always expressing Himself in words. It cannot be otherwise. You could not understand it otherwise. You cannot understand God by shakings, and yet shakings may be in perfect order sometimes. But you can always tell when the Spirit moves, and brings forth the utterances. They are always the utterances that shall magnify God. The Holy Ghost has a perfect plan. He comes right through every man who is so filled, and brings divine utterances that we may understand what the mind of the Lord is.

Perhaps I might take you to three expressions in the Bible upon the glory.

> *Therefore my heart is glad, and my glory rejoiceth....*
> Psalm 16:9

Something has made the rejoicing bring forth the glory. It was because his heart was glad. Turn to Psalm 108:1,

O God, my heart is fixed; I will sing and give praise, even with my glory.

You see, when the body is filled with the power of God, then the only thing that can express the glory is the tongue. Glory is presence, and the presence always comes by the tongue which brings forth the revelations of God.

You find in Acts 2:25,26 another side to this.

For David speaketh concerning him, I foresaw the Lord always before my face, for he is on my right hand, that I should not be moved: Therefore did my heart rejoice, and my tongue was glad....

God first brings into us His power, then He gives us verbal expressions by the same Spirit, the manifestation out of us just as it is within us. "...out of the abundance of the heart the mouth speaketh" (Matthew 12:34).

Virtue has to be transmitted, and glory has to expressed. So God, by filling us with the Holy Ghost, has brought into us this glory, that out of us may come forth the glory. The Holy Ghost understands everything Christ has in the glory and brings through the heart of man God's latest thought. The world's needs, our manifestations, revivals, all conditions, are first settled in heaven, then worked out on the earth. So we must be in touch with God Almighty to bring out on the face of the earth all the things that God has in the heavens. This is an ideal for us, and God help us not to forsake the sense of holy communion, entering into the closets in privacy, that publicly He may manifest His glory.

We must see the face of the Lord and understand His workings. There are things that God says to me that I know must take place. It does not matter what people say. I have been face to face with some of the most trying moments of men's lives, when it meant so much if I kept the vision, and held fast to what God had said. A man must be in an immoveable condition, and the voice of God must mean to him more than what he sees, feels, or what people say. He must have an originality born in heaven, transmitted or expressed in some way. We must bring heaven to earth.

Turn to 2 Peter 1:3:

According as his divine power hath given unto us all things
that pertain unto life and godliness, through the knowledge of
him that hath called us to glory and virtue.

Oh, this is a lovely verse. There is so much depth in it for us. It is all real from heaven. It is as divinely appointed for this meeting as when the Holy Ghost was upon Peter, and he brings it out for us. It is to me life; it is like the breath; it moves me. I must live in this grace. "According as his divine power," there it is again, "hath given unto us all things that pertain unto life and godliness." Oh, what wonderful things He has given us, "through the knowledge of him that hath called us to glory and virtue." You cannot get away from Him. He is the center of all things. He moves the earth, transforms beings, can live in every mind, plan every thought. Oh, He is there all the time.

You will find that Paul is full of the might of the Spirit breathing through him, and yet he comes to a place where he feels he must stop. For there are greater things than he can even utter only by prayer, the Almighty breathing through the human soul.

In the last of Ephesians 3 are these words which no human man could ever think or plan with pen and ink, so mighty, so of God when it speaks about His being able to do all things, "...exceeding abundantly above all that we ask or think..." (v. 20). The mighty God of revelation! The Holy Ghost gave these words of grandeur to stir our hearts, to move our affections, to transform us altogether. This is ideal! This is God. Shall we teach them? Shall we have them? Oh, they are ours. God has never put anything over on a pole where you could not reach it. He has brought His plan down to man, and if we are prepared this morning, oh, what there is for us! I feel sometimes we have just as much as we can digest, yet there are such divine nuggets of precious truth held before our hearts, it makes you understand that there are yet heights, and depths, and lengths, and breadths of the knowledge of God laid up for us. We might truly say,

> "My heavenly bank, my heavenly bank,
> The house of God's treasure and store.
> I have plenty in here; I'm a real millionaire."

Glory! Never to be poverty-struck anymore. An inward knowledge of a great bank than ever the Rothchilds, or any other, has known about. It is stored up, nugget upon nugget, weights of glory, expressions of the invisible Christ to be seen by men.

God is shaking the earth to its foundations, and making us to understand that there is a principle in the Scriptures that may bring to man freedom from the natural order, and bring him into a place of holiness, righteousness, and peace of God which passeth all human understanding. We must reach it. Praise God! God has brought us in on purpose to take us on. He has brought us here this morning, and you say, "How shall I be able to get all that is laid up for me?" Brother, sister, I know no other way — a broken and contrite heart He will not despise.

What do you want this morning? Be definite in your seeking. God knows what you need, and that one thing is for you this morning. Set it in your minds that you will know this morning the powers of the world to come.

> *Ask, and it shall be given you; seek, and ye shall find; knock, and it shall be opened unto you: for every one that asketh receiveth; and he that seeketh findeth; and to him that knocketh it shall be opened.*
>
> Matthew 7:7,8

Published in *Triumphs of Faith*

CONCERNING SPIRITUAL GIFTS

June 2, 1923

God wants us to enter into the rest of faith. He desires us to have all confidence in Himself. He purposes that His Word shall be established in our hearts; and, as we believe His Word, we will see that all things are possible.

In 1 Corinthians 12:1 we read,

> *Now concerning spiritual gifts, brethren, I would not have you ignorant.*

There is a great weakness in the church of Christ because of an awful ignorance concerning the Spirit of God and the gifts He has come to bring. God would have us powerful on all lines because of the revelation of the knowledge of His will concerning the power and manifestation of His Spirit. He would have us ever hungry to receive more and more of His Spirit. In times past I have arranged many conventions, and I have found that it is better to have a man on my platform who has not received the baptism but who is hungry for all that God has for him, than a man who has received the baptism and is satisfied and has settled down and become stationary and stagnant. But of course I would prefer a man who is baptized with the Holy Ghost and is still hungry for more of God. A man who is not hungry to receive more of God is out of order in any convention.

It is impossible to overestimate the importance of being filled with the Spirit. It is impossible for us to meet the conditions of the day, to walk in the light as He is in the light, to subdue kingdoms and work righteousness and bind the power of Satan unless we are filled with the Holy Ghost.

We read that in the early church "...they continued stedfastly in the apostles' doctrine and fellowship, and in breaking of bread, and in prayers" (Acts 2:42). It is important for us also to continue steadfastly in these same things. For some years I was associated with the Plymouth brethren. They are very strong on the Word, and are sound on water baptism, and they do not neglect the breaking of bread service, but have it every Lord's day morning as they had it in the early church. These people seem to have everything except the match. They have the wood, but they need the fire and they would be all ablaze. Because they lack the fire of the Holy Spirit, there is no life in their meetings. One young man who attended their meetings received the baptism with the speaking in other tongues as the Spirit gave utterance. The brethren were very upset about this and came to the father and said to him, "You must take your son aside and tell him to cease." They did not want any disturbance. The father told the son and said, "My boy, I have been attending this church for twenty years and have never seen anything of this kind. We are established in the truth and do not want anything new. We won't have it." The son replied, "If that is God's plan I will obey, but somehow or other I don't think it is." As they were going home the horse stood still; the wheels were in deep ruts. The father pulled at the reins but the horse did not move. He asked, "What do you think is up?" The son answered, "It has got established." God save us from becoming stationary.

God would have us to understand concerning spiritual gifts and to covet earnestly the best gifts, and also to enter into the more excellent way of the fruit of the Spirit. We must beseech God for these gifts. It is a serious thing to have the baptism and yet be stationary; to live two days in succession on the same spiritual plane is a tragedy. We must be willing to deny ourselves everything to receive the revelation of God's truth and to receive the fulness of the Spirit. Only that will satisfy God, and nothing less must satisfy us. A young Russian received the Holy Spirit and was mightily endued with power from on High. Some sisters were anxious to know the secret of his power. The secret of his power was continuous waiting upon God. As the Holy Ghost filled him, it seemed as though every breath became a prayer and so all his ministry was on an increasing line.

I knew a man who was full of the Holy Ghost and would only preach when he knew that he was mightily unctionized by the power of God. He was asked to preach at a Methodist church. He was staying at the minister's house and he said, "You go on to church and I will follow." The place was packed with people but this man did not turn up and the Methodist minister, becoming anxious, sent his little girl to inquire why he did not come. As she came to the bedroom door she heard him crying out three times, "I will not go." She went back and reported that she heard the man say three times that he would not go. The minister was troubled about it, but almost immediately after this the man came in, and, as he preached that night, the power of God was tremendously manifested. The preacher asked him, "Why did you tell my daughter that you were not coming?" He answered, "I know when I am filled. I am an ordinary man and I told the Lord that I dared not go and would not go until He gave me a fresh filling of the Spirit. The moment the glory filled me and overflowed I came to the meeting."

Yes, there is a power, a blessing, an assurance, a rest in the presence of the Holy Ghost. You can feel His presence and know that He is with you. You need not spend an hour without this inner knowledge of His holy presence. With His power upon you there can be no failure. You are above par all the time.

> *Ye know that ye were Gentiles, carried away unto these dumb idols, even as ye were led.*
>
> *1 Corinthians 12:2*

This is the Gentile day. When the Jews refused the blessings of God He scattered them, and He has grafted the Gentiles into the olive tree where the Jews were broken off. There never has been a time when God has been so favorable to a people who were not a people. He has brought in the Gentiles to carry out His purpose of preaching the Gospel to all nations and to receive the power of the Holy Ghost to accomplish this task. It is of the mercy of God that He has turned to the Gentiles and made us partakers of all the blessings that belong to the Jews; and here under this canopy of glory, because we believe, we get all the blessings of faithful Abraham.

> *Wherefore I give you to understand, that no man speaking by the Spirit of God calleth Jesus accursed: and that no man can say that Jesus is the Lord, but by the Holy Ghost.*
>
> *1 Corinthians 12:3*

There are many evil, deceiving spirits sent forth in these last days who endeavor to rob Jesus of His lordship and of His rightful place. Many are opening the doors to these latest devils, such as New Theology and New Thought and Christian Science. These evil cults deny the fundamental truths of God's Word. They all deny eternal punishment and all deny the deity of Jesus Christ. You will never see the baptism of the Holy Ghost come upon a man who accepts these errors. Neither will you see a Romanist receive. They put Mary in the place of the Holy Ghost. I would like you to produce a Romanist who knows that he is saved. No man can know he is saved by works. If you ever speak to a Romanist you will know that he is not definite on the line of the new birth. They cannot be. Another thing, you will never find a Russellite baptized in the Holy Ghost; nor a member of any other cult who does not put the Lord Jesus Christ pre-eminent above all.

The all important thing is to make Jesus Lord.* Men can grow lopsided by emphasizing the truth of divine healing. Man can get wrong by all the time preaching on water baptism. But we never go wrong in exalting the Lord Jesus Christ, giving Him the pre-eminent place and magnifying

Him as both Lord and Christ, yes, as very God of very God. As we are filled with the Holy Ghost our one desire is to magnify Him. We need to be filled with the Spirit to get the full revelation of the Lord Jesus Christ.

God's command is for us to be filled with the Spirit. We are no good if we only have a full cup. We need to have an overflowing cup all the time. It is a tragedy not to live in the fulness of overflowing. See that you never live below the overflowing tide.

"Now there are diversities of gifts, but the same Spirit" (1 Corinthians 12:4). Every manifestation of the Spirit is given that we might "profit withal." When the Holy Spirit is moving in an assembly and His gifts are in operation, everyone will receive profit. I have seen some who have been terribly switched. They believe in gifts, in prophecy, and they use these gifts apart from the power of the Holy Ghost. We must look to the Holy Spirit to show us the use of the gifts, what they are for, and when to use them, so that we may never use them without the power of the Holy Ghost. I do not know of anything which is so awful today as people using a gift without the power. Never do it. God save us from doing it.

A man who is filled with the Holy Ghost, while he may not be conscious of having any gift of the Spirit, can have the gifts made manifest through him. I have gone to many places to help and have found that under the unction of the Holy Spirit many wonderful things have happened in the midst when the glory of the Lord was upon the people. Any man who is filled with God and filled with His Spirit might at any moment have any of the nine gifts made manifest through him without knowing that he has a gift. Sometimes I have wondered whether it was better to be always full of the Holy Ghost and to see signs and wonders and miracles without any consciousness of possessing a gift, or whether it was better to know one has a gift. If you have received the gifts of the Spirit and they have been blessed, you should never under any circumstances use them without the power of God upon you pressing the gift through. Some have used the prophetic gift without the holy touch, and they have come into the realm of the natural, and it has brought ruin, caused dissatisfaction, broken hearts, upset assemblies. Do not seek the gifts unless you are purposed to abide in the Holy Spirit. They should be manifested only in the power of the Holy Spirit.

The Lord will allow you to be very drunk in His presence, but sober among people. I like to see people so filled with the Spirit that they are drunk like the 120 on the day of Pentecost, but I don't like to see people drunk in the wrong place. That is what troubles us, somebody being drunk in a place of worship where a lot of people come in that know nothing about the Word. If you allow yourself to be drunk there you send people away, they look at you instead of seeing God. They condemn the whole thing because you have not been sober at the right time. Paul writes, "For whether we be beside ourselves, it is to God: or whether we be sober, it is for your cause" (2 Corinthians 5:13). You can be beside yourself. You can go a bit further than being drunk. You can dance, if you will do it at the right time. So many things are commendable when all the people are in the Spirit. Many things are very foolish if the people round about you are not in the Spirit. We must be careful not to have a good time at the expense of somebody else. When you have a good time you must see that the spiritual conditions in the place lend themselves to help you and that the people are falling in line with you. Then you will find it always a blessing.

While it is right to covet earnestly the best gifts, you must recognize that the all important thing is to be filled with the power of the Holy Ghost Himself. You will never have trouble with people who are filled with the power of the Holy Ghost, but you will have a lot of trouble with people who have the gifts and have no power. The Lord wants us to come behind in no gift, but at the same time He wants us to be so filled with the Holy Ghost that it will be the Holy Spirit manifesting Himself through the gifts. Where the glory of God alone is desired, you can look for every needed gift to be made manifest. To glorify God is better than to idolize gifts. We prefer the Spirit of God to any gift; but we can look for the Trinity in manifestation, different gifts by the same Spirit, different administrations but the same Lord, diversities of operation but the same God working all in all. Can you conceive of what it will mean for our Triune God to be manifesting Himself in His fulness in our assemblies?

Watch that great locomotive boiler as it is filled with steam. You can see the engine letting off some of the steam as it remains stationary. It looks as though the whole thing might burst. You can see saints like that. They start to scream, but that is not to edification. But when the locomotive moves on, it serves the purpose for which it was built, and pulls along much traffic with it. It is wonderful to be filled with the power of the Holy Ghost, and for Him to serve His own purposes through us. Through our lips divine utterances flow, our hearts rejoice and our tongue is glad. It is an inward power within which is manifested in outward expression. Jesus Christ is glorified. As your faith in Him is quickened, from within you there will flow rivers of living water. The Holy Spirit will pour through you like a great river of life and thousands will be blessed because you are a yielded channel through whom the Spirit may flow.

> **...if thou shalt confess with thy mouth the Lord Jesus, and shalt believe in thine heart that God hath raised him from the dead, thou shalt be saved.*
>
> Romans 10:9

> *For TO THIS END Christ both died, and rose, and revived, THAT HE MIGHT BE LORD both of the dead and living.*
>
> Romans 14:9

> *[Christ Jesus]...humbled himself, and became obedient unto death, even the death of the cross. Wherefore God also hath highly exalted him, and given him a name which is above every name: That at the name of Jesus every knee should bow....And that every tongue should confess THAT JESUS CHRIST IS LORD, to the glory of God the Father.*
>
> Philippians 2:8-11

Published in *The Pentecostal Evangel*

od has given us much in these last days, and where much is given much will be required. The Lord has said to us,

THE GIFTS OF HEALING AND THE WORKING OF MIRACLES
August 4, 1923

Ye are the salt of the earth: but if the salt have lost his savour, wherewith shall it be salted? it is thenceforth good for nothing, but to be cast out, and to be trodden under foot of men.

Matthew 5:13

We see a thought on the same line when our Lord Jesus says,

If a man abide not in me, he is cast forth as a branch, and is withered; and men gather them, and cast them into the fire, and they are burned.

John 15:6

On the other hand He tells us,

If ye abide in me, and my words abide in you, ye shall ask what ye will, and it shall be done unto you.

John 15:7

If we do not move on with the Lord these days, and do not walk in the light of revealed truth, we shall become as the savorless salt, as a withered branch. This one thing we must do, forgetting those things that are behind, the past failures and the past blessings, we must reach forth for those things which are before, and press toward the mark for the prize of our high calling of God in Christ Jesus (Philippians 3:13,14).

For many years the Lord has been moving me on and keeping me from spiritual stagnation. When I was in the Wesleyan Methodist Church I was sure I was saved and was sure I was all right. The Lord said to me, "Come out," and I came out. When I was with the people known as the Brethren I was sure I was all right now. But the Lord said, "Come out." Then I went into the Salvation Army. At that time it was full of life and there were revivals everywhere. But the Salvation Army went into natural things and the great revivals that they had in those early days ceased. The Lord said to me, "Come out," and I came out. I have had to come out three times since. I believe that this Pentecostal revival that we are now in is the best thing that the Lord has on the earth today, and yet I believe that God has something out of this that is going to be still better. God has no use for any man who is not hungering and thirsting for yet more of Himself and His righteousness.

The Lord has told us to covet earnestly the best gifts, and we need to be covetous for those that will bring Him most glory. We need to see the gifts of healing and the working of miracles in operation today. Some say that it is necessary for us to have the gift of discernment in operation with the gifts of healing, but even apart from this gift I believe the Holy Ghost will have a divine revelation for us as we deal with the sick. Most people seem to have discernment, or think they have, and if they would turn it on themselves for twelve months they would never want to discern again. The gift of discernment is not criticism. I am satisfied that in Pentecostal circles today that our paramount need is more perfect love.

Perfect love will never want the preeminence in everything, it will never want to take the place of another, it will always be willing to take the back seat. If you go to a convention there is always someone who wants to give a message, who wants to be heard. If you have a desire to go to a convention you should have three things settled in your mind. Do I want to be heard? Do I want to be seen? Do I want anything on the line of finances? If I have these things in my heart, I have no right to be there. The one thing that must move us must be the constraining love of God to minister for Him. A preacher always loses out when he gets his mind on finances. It is well for Pentecostal preachers to avoid making much of finances except to stir up people to help our missionaries on financial lines. A preacher who gets big collections for the missionaries need never fear, the Lord will take care of his finances. A preacher should not land at a place and say that God had sent him. I am always fearful when I hear a man advertising this. If he is sent of God, the saints will know it. God has His plans for His servants and we must so live in His plans that He will place us where He wants us. If you seek nothing but the will of God, He will always put you in the right place at the right time. I want you to see that the gifts of healing and the working of miracles are part of the Spirit's plan and will come forth in operation as we are working along that plan. I must know the movement of the Spirit, and the voice of God. I must understand the will of God if I am to see the gifts of the Spirit in operation.

The gifts of healing are so varied. You may go and see ten people and every case is different. I am never happier in the Lord than when I am in a bedroom with a sick person. I have had more revelations of the Lord's presence when I have ministered to the sick at their bedsides than at any other time. It is as your heart goes out to the needy ones in deep compassion that the Lord manifests His presence. You are able to locate their position. It is then that you know that you must be filled with the Spirit to deal with the conditions before you.

Where people are in sickness you find frequently that they are dense about Scripture. They usually know three scriptures though. They know about Paul's thorn in the flesh, and that Paul told Timothy to take a little wine for his stomach's sake, and that Paul left someone sick somewhere; they forget his name, and don't remember the name of the place, and don't know where the chapter is. Most people think they have a thorn in the flesh. The chief thing in dealing with a person who is sick is to locate their exact position. As you are ministering under the Spirit's power, the Lord will let you see just that which will be the most helpful and the most faith-inspiring to them.

When I was in the plumbing business I enjoyed praying for the sick. Urgent calls would come and I would have no time to wash, and with my hands all black I would preach to these sick ones, my heart all aglow with love. Ah, you must have your heart in the thing when you pray for the sick. You have to get right to the bottom of the cancer with a divine compassion and then you will see the gifts of the Spirit in operation.

I was called at 10 o'clock one night to pray for a young person given up by the doctor who was dying of consumption. As I looked, I saw that unless God undertook it was impossible for her to live. I turned to the mother and said, "Well, Mother, you will have to go to bed." She said, "Oh, I have not had my clothes off for three weeks." I said to the daughters, "You will have to go to bed," but they did not want to go. It was the same with the son. I put on my overcoat and said, "Good-bye, I'm off." They said, "Oh, don't leave us." I said, "I can do nothing here." They said, "Oh, if you will stop, we will all go to bed." I knew that God would move nothing in an atmosphere of mere natural sympathy and unbelief.

They all went to bed and I stayed, and that was surely a time as I knelt by that bed face to face with death and with the devil. But God can change the hardest situation and make you know that He is almighty.

Then the fight came. It seemed as though the heavens were brass. I prayed from 11:00 P.M. to 3:30 in the morning. I saw the glimmering light on the face of the sufferer and saw her pass away. The devil said, "Now you are done for. You have come from Bradford and the girl has died on your hands." I said, "It can't be. God did not send me here for nothing. This is a time to change strength." I remembered that passage which said, "...men ought always to pray, and not to faint" (Luke 18:1). Death had taken place but I knew that my God was all powerful, and He that had split the Red Sea is just the same today. It was a time when I would not have "No," and God said "Yes." I looked at the window and at that moment the face of Jesus appeared. It seemed as though a million rays of light were coming from His face. As He looked at the one who had just passed away, the color came back to the face. She rolled over and fell asleep. Then I had a glorious time. In the morning she woke early, put on a dressing gown, and walked to the piano. She started to play and to sing a wonderful song. The mother and the sister and the brother had all come down to listen. The Lord had undertaken. A miracle had been wrought.

The Lord is calling us along this way. I am thanking God for difficult cases. The Lord has called us into heart union with Himself; He wants His bride to have one heart and one Spirit with Him and to do what He Himself loved to do. That case had to be a miracle. The lungs were gone, they were just in shreds, but the Lord restored lungs that were perfectly sound.

There is a fruit of the Spirit that must accompany the gift of healing and that is longsuffering. The man who is going through with God to be used in healing must be a man of longsuffering. He must be always ready with a word of comfort. If the sick one is in distress and helpless and does not see everything eye to eye with you, you must bear with them. Our Lord Jesus Christ was filled with compassion and lived and moved in a place of longsuffering, and we will have to get into this place if we are to help needy ones.

There are some times when you pray for the sick and you are apparently rough. But you are not dealing with a person, you are dealing with satanic forces that are binding the person. Your heart is full of love and compassion to all, but you are moved to a holy anger as you see the place the devil has taken in the body of the sick one, and you deal with his position with a real forcefulness. One day a pet dog followed a lady out of her house and ran all round her feet. She said to the dog, "My dear, I cannot have you with me today." The dog wagged its tail and made a big fuss. She said, "Go home, my dear." But the dog did not go. At last she shouted roughly, "Go home," and off it went. Some people deal with the devil like that. The devil can stand all the comfort you like to give him. Cast him out! You are dealing not with the person, you are dealing with the devil. Demon power must be dislodged in the name of the Lord. You are always right when you dare to deal with sickness as with the devil. Much sickness is caused by some misconduct, there is something wrong, there is some neglect somewhere, and Satan has had a chance to get in. It is necessary to repent and confess where you have given place to the devil, and then he can be dealt with.

When you deal with a cancer case, recognize that it is a living evil spirit that is destroying the body. I had to pray for a woman in Los Angeles one time who was suffering with cancer, and as soon as it was cursed it stopped bleeding. It was dead. The next thing that happened was that the natural body pressed it out, because the natural body had no room for dead matter. It came out like a great big ball with tens of thousands of fibers. All these fibers had been pressing into the flesh. These evil powers move to get further hold of the system, but the moment they are destroyed their hold is gone. Jesus said to His disciples that He gave them power to loose and power to bind. It is our privilege in the power of the Holy Ghost to loose the prisoners of Satan and to let the oppressed go free.

Take your position in the first epistle of John and declare, "...greater is he that is in [me], than he that is in the world" (1 John 4:4). Then recognize that it is not yourself that has to deal with the power of the devil, but the Greater One that is in you. Oh, what it means to be filled with Him. You can do nothing of yourself, but He that is in you will win the victory. Your being has become the temple of the Spirit. Your mouth, your mind, your whole being becomes exercised and worked upon by the Spirit of God.

I was called to a certain town in Norway. The hall seated about 1500 people. When I got to the place it was packed, and hundreds were trying to get in. There were some policemen there. The first thing I did was to preach to the people outside the building. Then I said to the policemen, "It hurts me very much that there are more people outside than inside and I feel I must preach to the people. I would like you to get me the marketplace to preach in." They secured for me a great park and a big stand was erected and I was able to preach to thousands. After the preaching, we had some wonderful cases of healing. One man came a hundred miles bringing his food with him. He had not been passing anything through his stomach for over a month as he had a great cancer on his stomach. He was healed at that meeting, and opening his parcel, he began eating before all the people. There was a young woman there with a stiff hand. Instead of the mother making the child use her arm, she had allowed the child to keep the arm dormant until it was stiff, and she had grown up to be a young woman and was like the woman that was bowed down with the spirit of infirmity. As she stood before me I cursed the spirit of infirmity in the name of Jesus. It was instantly cast out and the arm was free. Then she waved it all over. At the close of the meeting the devil laid out two people with fits. When the devil is manifesting himself, then is the time to deal with him. Both of these people were delivered, and when they stood up and thanked and praised the Lord, what a wonderful time we had.

We need to wake up and be on the stretch to believe God. Before God could bring me to this place, He has broken me a thousand times. I have wept, I have groaned. I have travailed many a night until God broke me. It seems to me that until God has moved you down you never can have this longsuffering for others. We can never have the gifts of healing and the working of miracles in operation only as we stand in the divine power that God gives us and we stand believing God, and having done all we still stand believing.

We have been seeing wonderful miracles these last days and they are only a little of what we are going to see. I believe that we are right on the threshold of wonderful things, but I want to emphasize that all these things will be through the power of the Holy Ghost. You must not think that these gifts will fall upon you like ripe cherries. There is a sense in which you have to pay the price for everything you get. We must be covetous for God's best gifts, and say Amen to any preparation the Lord takes us through, in order that we may be humble, useable vessels through whom He Himself can operate by means of the Spirit's power.

Published in *The Pentecostal Evangel*

DELIVERANCE TO THE CAPTIVES

October-December 1923

Our precious Lord Jesus has everything for everybody. Forgiveness from sin, healing of diseases and the fulness of the Spirit all come from one source — from the Lord Jesus Christ. Hear Him who is the same yesterday, today, and forever as He announces the purpose for which He came.

> *The Spirit of the Lord is upon me, because he hath anointed me to preach the gospel to the poor; he hath sent me to heal the brokenhearted, to preach deliverance to the captives, and recovering of sight to the blind, to set at liberty them that are bruised, To preach the acceptable year of the Lord.*
>
> *Luke 4:18,19*

Jesus had been baptized by John in Jordan, and the Holy Spirit had descended in a bodily shape like a dove upon Him. Being full of the Holy Ghost, He had been led by the Spirit into the wilderness, there to come off more than conqueror over the arch-enemy. Then He returned in the power of the Spirit to Galilee and preached in the synagogues, and at last He came to His old hometown, Nazareth, where He announced His mission in the words I have just quoted. For a brief while He ministered on the earth, and then gave His life a ransom for all. But God raised Him from the dead. And before He went to the glory, He told His disciples that they should receive the power of the

Holy Ghost upon them, too. Thus, through them, His gracious ministry would continue. This power of the Holy Ghost was not only for a few apostles, but even for them that are afar off, even as many as the Lord our God should call (Acts 2:39), even for us away down in this twentieth century. Some ask, "But was not this power just for the privileged few in the first century?" No. Read the Master's great commission as recorded by Mark, and you will see it is for them who believe.

After I had received the baptism of the Holy Ghost — and I know that I received, for the Lord gave me the Spirit in just the same way as He gave Him to the disciples at Jerusalem — I sought the mind of the Lord as to why I was baptized. One day I came home from work and went into the house and my wife asked me, "Which way did you come in?" I told her that I had come in at the back door. She said, "There is a woman upstairs and she has brought an old man of eighty to be prayed for. He is raving up there, and a great crowd is outside the front door, ringing the doorbell and wanting to know what is going on in the house." The Lord quietly whispered, "This is what I baptized you for."

I carefully opened the door of the room where the man was, desiring to be obedient to what my Lord would say to me. The man was crying and shouting in distress, "I am lost! I am lost! I have committed the unpardonable sin. I am lost! I am lost!" My wife said, "Dad, what shall we do?" The Spirit of the Lord moved me to cry out, "Come out, thou lying spirit." In a moment the evil spirit went, and the man was free. Deliverance to the captives! And the Lord said to me, "This is what I baptized you for."

There is a place where God, through the power of the Holy Ghost, reigns supreme in our lives. The Spirit reveals, unfolds, takes of the things of Christ and shows them to us, and prepares us to be more than a match for satanic forces.

When Nicodemus came to Jesus he said,

> *... we know that thou art a teacher come from God: for no man can do these miracles that thou doest, except God be with him. Jesus answered and said to him, Verily, verily, I say unto thee, Except a man be born again, he cannot see the kingdom of God.*

> *John 3:2,3*

Nicodemus was struck by the miracles wrought, and Jesus pointed out the necessity of a miracle being wrought with every man who would see the kingdom. When a man is born of God, is brought from darkness to light, a mighty miracle is wrought. Jesus saw every touch by God as a miracle, and so we may expect to see miracles wrought today. It is wonderful to have the Spirit of the Lord upon us. I would rather have the Spirit of God on me for five minutes than to receive a million dollars.

Do you see how Jesus mastered the devil in the wilderness? He knew He was the Son of God and Satan came along with an "if." How many times has Satan come along to you this way? He says, "After all, you may be deceived. You know you really are not a child of God." If the devil comes along and says that you are not saved, it is a pretty sure sign that you are. When he comes and tells you that you are not healed, it may be taken as good evidence that the Lord has sent His Word and healed you (Psalm 107:20). The devil knows that if he can capture your thought life, he has won a mighty victory over you. His great business is injecting thoughts, but if you are pure and holy you will instantly shrink from them. God wants us to let the mind that was in Christ Jesus, that pure, holy, humble mind of Christ, be in us.

I come across people everywhere I go who are held bound by deceptive conditions, and these conditions have come about simply because they have allowed the devil to make their minds the place of his stronghold. How are we to guard against this? The Lord has provided us with weapons that are mighty through God to the pulling down of these strongholds of the enemy, and by means of which every thought shall be brought into captivity to the obedience of Christ (2 Corinthians 10:4,5). The blood of Jesus Christ and His mighty name are an antidote to all the subtle seeds of unbelief that Satan would sow in your minds.

In the first chapter of Acts, we see that Jesus gave commandment to the disciples that they should wait for the promise of the Father, and He told them that not many days hence they would be baptized with the Holy Ghost. Luke tells us that he had written his former treatise concerning all that Jesus began both to do and teach. The ministry of Christ did not end at the cross, but the Acts and the epistles give us accounts of what He continued to do and teach through those whom He indwelt. And our blessed Lord Jesus is still alive, and continues His ministry through those who are filled with His Spirit. He is still healing the brokenhearted and delivering the captives through those on whom He places His Spirit.

I was traveling one day in a railway train in Sweden. At one station there boarded the train an old lady with her daughter. The old lady's expression was so troubled that I enquired what was the matter with her. I heard that she was going to the hospital to have her leg taken off. She began to weep as she told me that the doctors had said that there was no hope for her except through having her leg amputated. She was seventy years old. I said to my interpreter, "Tell her that Jesus can heal her." The instant this was said to her, it was as though a veil was taken off her face, it became so light.

We stopped at another station and the carriage filled up with people. There was a rush of men to board that train and the devil said, "You're done." But I knew I had the best proposition, for hard things are always opportunities to get to the Lord more glory when He manifests His power. Every trial is a blessing. There have been times when I have been pressed through circumstances and it seemed as if a dozen road engines were going over me, but I have found that the hardest things are just lifting places into the grace of God. We have such a lovely Jesus. He always proves Himself to be such a mighty Deliverer. He never fails to plan the best things for us.

The train began moving and I crouched down, and in the name of Jesus commanded the disease to leave. The old lady cried, "I'm healed; I know I'm healed." She stamped her leg and said, "I'm going to prove it." So when we stopped at another station she marched up and down, and shouted "I'm not going to the hospital." Once again our wonderful Jesus had proven Himself a Healer of the brokenhearted, a Deliverer of one that was bound.

At one time I was so bound that no human power could help me. My wife was looking for me to pass away. There was no help. At that time I had just had a faint glimpse of Jesus as the Healer. For six months I had been suffering from appendicitis, occasionally getting temporary relief. I went to the mission, of which I was pastor, but I was brought to the floor in awful agony, and they brought me home to my bed. All night I was praying, pleading for deliverance, but none came. My wife was sure it was my home call, and sent for a physician. He said that there was no possible chance for me — my body was too weak. Having had the appendicitis for six months, my whole system was drained, and, because of that, he thought that it was too late for an operation. He left my wife in a state of brokenheartedness.

After he left there came to our door a young man and an old lady. I knew that she was a woman of real prayer. They came upstairs to my room. This young man jumped on the bed and commanded the evil spirit to come out of me. He shouted, "Come out, you devil; I command you to come out in the name of Jesus!" There was no chance for an argument, or for me to tell him that I would never believe that there was a devil inside of me. The thing had to go in the name of Jesus, and it went, and I was instantly healed.

I arose and dressed and went downstairs. I was still in the plumbing business, and I asked my wife, "Is there any work in? I am all right now, and I am going to work." I found that there was a certain job to be done and I picked up my tools and went off to do it. Just after I left the doctor came in, put his plug hat down in the hall, and walked up to the bedroom. But the invalid was not there. "Where is Mr. Wigglesworth?" he asked. "Oh, doctor, he's gone out to work," said my wife. "You'll never see him alive again," said the doctor; "they'll bring him back a corpse."

Well, I'm the corpse.

Since that time the Lord has given me the privilege of praying for people with appendicitis in many parts of the world; and I have seen a great many people up and dressed within a quarter of an hour from the time I prayed for them. We have a living Christ who is willing to meet people on every line.

About eight years ago I met Brother Kerr, and he gave me a letter of introduction to a brother in Zion City named Cook. I took his letter to Brother Cook and he said, "God has sent you here." He gave me the addresses of six people and asked me to go and pray for them and meet him again at 12 o'clock. I got back at about 12:30, and he told me about a young man who was to be married the following Monday. His sweetheart was in Zion City dying of appendicitis. I went to the house and found that the physician had just been there and had pronounced that there was no hope. The mother was nearly distracted and was pulling her hair and saying, "Is there no deliverance?" I said to her, "Woman, believe God, and your daughter will be healed and be up and dressed in fifteen minutes." But the mother went on screaming.

They took me into the bedroom, and I prayed for the girl and commanded the evil spirit to depart in the name of Jesus. She cried, "I am healed." I said to her, "Do you want me to believe that you are healed? If you are healed, get up." She said, "You get out of the room, and I'll get up." In less than ten minutes the doctor came in. He wanted to know what had happened. She said, "A man came in and prayed for me, and I'm healed." The doctor pressed his finger right in the place that had been so sore, and the girl neither moaned nor cried. He said, "This is God." It made no difference whether he acknowledged it or not, I knew that God had worked. Our God is real in saving and healing power today. Our Jesus is just the same, yesterday, today, and forever (Hebrews 13:8). He saves and heals today just as of old, and He wants to be your Savior and your Healer.

Oh, if you would only believe God! What would happen? The greatest things. Some have never tasted the grace of God, have never had the peace of God. Unbelief robs them of these blessings. It is possible to hear and yet not conceive the truth. It is possible to read the Word and not share in the life it brings. It is necessary for us to have the Holy Ghost to unfold the Word and bring to us the life that is Christ. We can never fully understand the wonders of this redemption until we are full of the Holy Ghost.

I was once at an afternoon meeting. The Lord had been graciously with us and many had been healed by the power of God. Most of the people had gone home and I was left alone, when I saw a young man who evidently was hanging back to have a word. I asked, "What do you want?" He said, "I wonder if I could ask you to pray for me." I said, "What's the trouble?" He said, "Can't you smell?" The young fellow had gone into sin and was suffering the consequences. He said, "I have been turned out of two hospitals. I am broken out all over. I have abscesses all over me." And I could see that he had a bad breaking out at the nose. He said, "I heard you preach, and could not understand about this healing business, and was wondering if there was any hope for me."

I said to him, "Do you know Jesus?" He did not know the first thing about salvation, but I said to him, "Stand still." I placed my hands on his head and then on his loins and cursed that terrible disease in the name of Jesus. He cried out, "I know I'm healed. I can feel a warmth and a glow all over me." I said, "Who did it?" He said, "Your prayers." I said, "No, it was Jesus!" He said, "Was it He? Oh, Jesus! Jesus! Jesus save me." And that young man went away healed and saved. Oh, what a merciful God we have! What a wonderful Jesus is ours!

Are you oppressed? Cry out to God. It is always good for people to cry out. You may have to cry out. The Holy Ghost and the Word of God will bring to light every hidden, unclean thing that must be revealed. There is always a place of deliverance when you let God search out that which is spoiling and marring your life. That evil spirit that was in the man in the synagogues cried out, "Let us alone!" It was a singular thing that that evil spirit never cried out like that until Jesus rebuked the thing, saying, "Hold thy peace and come out of him"; and the man was delivered. He is just the same Jesus, exposing the powers of evil, delivering the captives and letting the oppressed go free, purifying them and cleansing their hearts. Those evil spirits that inhabited the man who had the legion did not want to be sent to the pit to be tormented before their time, and so they cried out to be sent into the swine. Hell is such an awful place that even the demons hate the thought of going there. How much more should men seek to be saved from the pit?

God is compassionate and says, "Seek ye the Lord while he may be found..." (Isaiah 55:6). And He has further stated, "For whosoever shall call upon the name of the Lord shall be saved" (Romans 10:13). Seek Him now, call on His name right now, and there is forgiveness, healing, redemption, deliverance, and everything you need for you right here and now, and that which will satisfy you throughout eternity.

Published in *Confidence*

or nothing really matters if the
Lord loves me;
And He does, He does.
For nothing really matters if the
Lord loves me;
And He does, He does.

KEEPING
THE VISION

December 6, 1923

Read the twentieth chapter of the Acts of the apostles, beginning at verse 7.

Encouragement? It is filled with encouragement. As I was saying to a few gathered together last night, this kind of blessed ministry with success, where God has put His hand upon us in such a way — I was describing to them, I met the same kind of thing in Switzerland where there were nine churches formed and another four being formed. I went back there and found all the people praising the Lord. Just as our brother tonight has asked these people to stand up who were healed through my ministry, they rose up. The same thing happened — just the same, the people are being healed during my absence. There is the sequel — there is the power manifested. I told you people when I was here before, if this work ceased you could count upon it that the mission had been Wigglesworth's; if it was of God it would not cease. Humanity is the failure everywhere, but when humanity is filled with God's divinity, there is no such thing as failure, and we know that the baptism of the Holy Ghost is not a failure. There are two sides to the baptism of the Holy Ghost. The first condition is that you possess the baptism, the second condition is that the baptism possesses you. This is my message tonight, being possessed by the Baptizer and not possessing the Baptizer. The first has to be before the second can be, and God can make the first to be tonight with these whom it has not been. God can so manifest His divine power in this meeting that every soul in this meeting can possess, if they are eligible, this blessed infilling of the baptism of the Holy Ghost. There is no limit to it, it has not to be measured, it is without measure, without limit, because it has God behind it, in the midst of it, and through it.

Taking the epistles and reading them through, I would say that God is through all in this work, God is under all in this work, and I believe that God is over all in this work, so I pray that the Holy Ghost tonight is in the first meeting that we are having before we meet for a convention, I trust at Christmas time.

I trust that this meeting shall be another witnessing, an inside witnessing of the Spirit's power, of the unction that is received, because every person in this place must see that they must be filled with the Holy Ghost. It is important; nay, it is more than important, you neglect it at your peril. I see people from time to time very slack, cold, and indifferent, and after they get filled with the Holy Ghost they become ablaze for God. I believe God wants the same proportion with every soul in this meeting, but greater than that, because we are in the Kingdom. John was not in the Kingdom and yet he was a bright and shining light, and when I read into this divine order of the Spirit, when I read into it, and what I feel that God would have me read into it, is that ministers of God are to be flames of fire, nothing less than flames, nothing less than holy, mighty instruments with burning messages, with a heart full of love, with a depth of consecration, where God has taken full charge of the body and it only exists that it may manifest the glory of God. Surely this is the ideal and purpose of this great plan of salvation for man, that we might be filled with all the fulness of God; ministers of life, standing in cooperation, God working mightily in us, proving and manifesting His grace, and the instrumentality of the saving power for humanity, for this glorious baptism is to be a witness of Jesus, and oh, beloved, beloved, we must reach the ideal identification with the Master. It is the same baptism, the same power, with the same revelation of the King of kings. God must fill us with this divine, glorious purpose for God, filled with God, manifest sons of God with power filling the earth.

TONGUES AND INTERPRETATION: "The Lord is the Life, the Truth, and the manifestation of bringing into life, and power of sonship, built upon the Rock, the Rock Christ Jesus, established with the truth of salvation, our heritage, for we have to go forth with ministry of life unto life, and death unto death, for the Holy Ghost is that ministry."

Beloved, I want us to turn to this wonderful Word of God tonight, I want you to see the equipment with power, I want you to keep your minds fixed upon this fact, it will help you, it will establish you. It will strengthen you if you carry into thought tonight, this Paul who was "born out of due time," this Paul who was plucked as a brand from the burning, this Paul whom God chose for an apostle to the Gentiles. I want you to see him, first as a persecutor, mad to destroy those people who were bringing glad tidings to the people. See how madly he rushed those people into the prisons, made them blaspheme that Holy name, then see this man changed by the power of the Christ and the Gospel of God. See him filled, impersonated, divinely built for God, filled with the Holy Ghost. You read the ninth chapter of Acts, you see how he was, as it were, called specially, but in order to come into line, to understand how he might be able to succor, to help the needy, God's Son said to Ananias, "For I will shew him how great things he must suffer for my name's sake" (Acts 9:16). Cooperated, or coupled up, joint union, you will find is the cup — two cups, the cup of suffering from heaven with a baptism of fire. Brother, I don't want you to think I mean suffering with diseases, I mean suffering in persecution, with slander, with strife, with bitterness, with revilings, and with many other evil ways of suffering, but none of these things will hurt you, but they rather kindle a fire of holy ambition, because the scripture says, "Blessed are they which are persecuted for righteousness' sake: for theirs is the kingdom of heaven" (Matthew 5:10). To be persecuted for Christ's sake is to be joined up with a blessed, blessed people, with those chosen to cry under the altar, "How long?" Oh, to know that we may be cooperated with Jesus on these lines: if, may be, we suffer persecution, rejoice in that day. Beloved, God wants witnesses, witnesses of truth, witnesses to the full truth, witnesses to the fulness of redemption, witnesses to the deliverance from sin, from disease, the power of sin and disease, witnesses that can claim their territory, because of the eternal power working in them, eternal life beautifully, gloriously filling the body, till the body is filled with life of the Spirit. God wants us to believe that we may be ministers of that kind, of glorious facts wrought in us by the Holy Ghost.

Look at the position. I want you to keep this in mind tonight. I beseeched the Lord that I should speak to you people. I knew I would be speaking to people baptized by the Holy Ghost, I knew I would be speaking to people in this meeting who are hungering to be filled with the Holy Ghost and I knew that I would be preaching tonight to a needy people, and if you notice, this blessed Gospel that we have got tonight, deals with so many things. Let us turn to the first, it will help us. See how Paul was lost in the zeal of his ministry, and see how the people — those disciples — gathered together on the first day of the week to break bread, see their need for breaking bread. As they were gathered together they were caught up with the ministry.

In Switzerland the people said to me, "How long can you preach to us?" I said, "When the Holy Ghost is upon us we can preach forever!"

If it was man's ability, and college training, we may be crack-brained before we began the piece, but if it is the Holy Ghost ministry, we shall be ripe through and through, all soundly ringing, as sound as a bell which has no flaw in it. It will be the Holy Ghost at the first, in the middle, and at the end. I want to know nothing amongst the preaching, and the preaching to know nothing save, "Thus saith the Lord." The preaching of Jesus, that blessed incarnation, that glorious loosing of the bondage, that blessed power that liberates from sin and the powers of darkness, that glorious salvation that saves you from death to life, and from the power of Satan to God. I see that Paul was lost in this glorious theme. In the middle it seems that a young man was too drowsy to be wakened up to the circumstances, and down he got, lower and lower, till he toppled over. I have often offered a pound note to anyone who fell asleep in my meetings — you have got the chance if you want it.

> For nothing really matters if the Lord loves me,
>
> And He does, He does.

I want you to notice in this meeting that he went on from evening to midnight, and night in the midst of it, this thing happened. If you turn to Philippians you will see a wonderful truth there. I may give you a message on it some night. If you notice there is a wonderful word there where Paul says, "...I might attain unto the resurrection..." (Philippians 3:11). Hear the word spoken to Martha and Mary — that wonderful saying where He said unto them, "I am the resurrection, and the life" (John 11:25). Here is Paul desiring to attain unto it, and it is remarkable evidence to me that you never attain to anything till opportunity comes, and on the activity of faith you will find that God will bring so many things before your notice that you will have no time to think over it, and you jump into it and bring authority by the power of the Spirit. If you took time to think, you would miss the case. I was in San Francisco — the first place after I left here — and driving down the main street one day, came across a group in the street, so the driver stopped and I jumped out of the car, and rushed across to where the tumult was. I found, as I broke the crowd, a body laid on the ground apparently in a tremendous seizure of death. I got down and asked, "What is amiss?" He replied in a whisper, "Cramp." I put my hand underneath his back and said, "Come out in the name of Jesus," and the boy jumped up and ran away, and never even said, "Thank you." (Laughter)

So you will find out that with the baptism of the Holy Ghost you will be in a position where you must act, because you have no time to think. The Holy Ghost works on the power of divine origin. It is the supernatural, God filling till it becomes an emancipation power by the authority of almightiness, and it sees things come to pass that could not come to pass in any other way. I had the same things happen on the ship as I came across. I want to come to Paul's position — midnight, death comes through a fall from a window. The first thing you notice he does is the most absurd thing to do, and yet it is the most practical thing to do in the Holy Ghost — he fell on him. Yes, fell upon him and embraced him, and left him alive — some would say he fell on him and crushed life into him and brought him back. It is activity by almightiness, so we must see that the power of the Holy Ghost in any meeting can bring divine operation till we have realized we are in the presence of God.

I want you to understand in these meetings we have — in this meeting tonight — that it is a meeting in the Holy Ghost. It is a meeting where all can be saved in the meeting, it is a meeting where all can be healed in the meeting, it is a meeting where the power of the resurrection of Jesus Christ is made manifest, it is a meeting where we see nought of things, but we see *Jesus* and we are here for the importance of impressing on you tonight that this same Jesus is in the midst — this same Jesus.

I wish every meeting was a breaking of bread service — I would not mind if it was scriptural. I would love to see every meeting, the saints gather together that they may remember His death, His resurrection, and His ascension. Oh, what a thought that Jesus Himself instituted this glorious presence for us. Oh, that God tonight would let us see that it is "as oft" as ye do it. It is not weekly, not monthly, not quarterly, but "as oft as ye do it," and in remembrance of Him. What a blessed remembrance it is tonight to know that He took our sins, what a blessed remembrance to me to know that He took my sins, what a blessed remembrance to me that He took my diseases, what a blessed remembrance it is tonight to know that He ever liveth to make intercession for the saints — not for sinners. He has left us to do that. "I pray not for the world, but I pray for you." He has left us to pray for the world. He is there interceding for us to keep right, holy, ready, mighty, filled with Himself that we might bring the fragrance of heaven to the world's needs. Can we do it? Yes, we can, we can do it.

I return to my thought, let me read you this. My heart is filled with the possibility of coming into this place where Paul was. I think I will read just one or two verses that we might get our minds perfectly fortified with this blessed truth that God has for us.

Acts 20:19 — "Serving the Lord with all humility of mind...." There is none of us (I believe it is best to say "us") going to be able to be ministers of this new covenant of promise in the unction or power of the Holy Ghost without humility. It seems to me that the way to get up is to get down. It is clear to me that if the dying of the Lord be in me, in the measure the death of the Lord is in me, the life of the Lord shall abound in me, and to me truly, the baptism of the Holy Ghost is not a goal, it is an inflow to reach the highest level, the holiest position that it is possible for human nature to reach. The baptism of the Holy Ghost comes to reveal Him Who is filled with all the fulness of God, so I see to be baptized with the Holy Ghost is to be baptized into death, into life, into power, into fellowship with Trinity, where we cease to be and God takes us forever. No man can live after seeing God, and God wants us all to see Him — when we shall live no more. Paul said, "Now I know that I live not, but another liveth" and I believe that God wants to so put His hand upon us tonight that we may reach ideal definitions of humility, ideals of human helplessness, ideals of human insufficiency, till we shall rest no more upon human plans, but have God's thoughts, God's voice, and God the Holy Ghost to speak to us.

Now here is a word for us, let us read it.

Acts 20:22 — "And now, behold, I go bound in the spirit...." There is the Word. Is that a possibility? Is there a possibility for the human to come so into the divine will of God?

Let me give you two verses of Scripture. Jesus was a man, flesh and blood like ourselves, while He was incarnation of divine authority and power and majesty of the glory of heaven, but still bore about in His body our flesh, our human weaknesses, tempted in all points like as we are and yet without sin. He was so lovely, such a perfect Savior — Oh, that I could shout "Jesus" tonight in such a way that the world would hear. There is salvation, life, power, and deliverance through that name, but beloved, I see that body, in Mark was driven by the Spirit, in the fourth chapter of Luke, "led" by the Spirit, and here comes Paul "bound" in the Spirit.

Oh, what an ideal condescension of heaven that God should lay hold of humanity and possess him so with His holiness, with His righteousness, with His truth, with His faith, that he could say, "I am bound, I have no choice" — the only choice is for God. The only desire, ambition, is God's — I am bound with God. Is it possible, beloved?

If you look into Galatians, first chapter, you will see how wonderfully he rose into this state of bliss. If you look at the third chapter of Ephesians, you see how he became less than the least of all saints. If you look in the twenty-sixth chapter of the Acts of the apostles you will hear him say this, "I have never lost the vision, King Agrippa, I have never lost it." If you look in Galatians you will see that in order to keep the vision he yielded not to flesh and blood, and God laid hold of him, God bound him, God preserved him. I ought to say, however, that it is a wonderful position to be preserved by almightiness, and we ought to see to it in our Christian experience that we leave ourselves to God, the consequences will be all right. He that seeketh to save his life shall lose it, but he that shall lose his life for My sake shall keep it unto the end. You say, what is it — bound by almightiness, preserved with infiniteness. There is no end to its resources, it reaches right into glory, it never finishes on earth — no climax with human arrangements. God lays hold of a man in the baptism of the Holy Ghost as he yields himself to God, till he may be taken whoever is left. Do you believe it? There is a possibility of being taken and yet left — taken charge of by God and left in the world to carry it out. That is one of God's possibilities for humanity, to be so taken over by the power of God, and left in the world to be the salt — in such a way as the Scripture gives.

Now, beloved, I am out for men, it is my business to be out for men, it is my business to make everybody hungry, dissatisfied, it is my business to make people either mad or glad. I must have every man filled with the Holy Ghost, must have a message from heaven that will not leave people as I found them. Something must happen if we are filled with the Holy Ghost, something must happen at every place. Men must know that a man filled with the Holy Ghost is no longer a man. I told you when I was here last year that God has no room for ordinary men. A man can be swept by the power of God in his first stage of revelation of Christ, and from that moment has to be an extraordinary man, but to be filled with the Holy Ghost he has to become a free, free body for God to dwell in, and no man can have Trinity abiding in him and be as he was before, so I appeal to you tonight, you people who have been filled with the Holy Ghost, I appeal to you whatever is the cost, let God have His way, and I appeal to you people who have got to move on, who cannot rest till God does something for you, I appeal to you as I could never have appealed to you without God had been speaking to me since I left this place. God has been speaking to me — let me tell you what He has been saying to me. God has been revealing to me that any man if he does not sin, if he remains in the same place for a week he is a back-slider. You say, "How is it possible?" Because of God's revelation for the man who will jump in.

Two days the same would almost be that you had *lost the vision*. The child of God must have a fresh vision every day, the child of God must be more active by the Holy Ghost every day. The child of God must come into line with the power of heaven, where He knows that God has put His hand upon him.

> I know the Lord, I know the Lord,
> I know the Lord has laid His hand on me,
> He filled me with the Holy Ghost.
> How do I know? Oh, the Spirit spoke through me.
> I know the Lord has laid His hand on me,
> I know the Lord has laid His hand on me — Glory.
> He healed the sick, and He raised the dead,
> I know the Lord has laid His hand on me.

It is the same Jesus, it is the very same Jesus. He went about doing good — God anointed Him, He went about doing good, casting out evil spirits, for God was with Him. Beloved, is not that the ministry that God would have us see we become heir to? Why? Because the Holy Ghost has to bring us a revelation of Jesus, and the purpose of the Holy Ghost filling our bodies is to give us a revelation of Jesus, and to make the Word of God just the same life as was given by the Son, as new, as fresh, as effective, and just so as if the Lord Himself were speaking. I wonder how many there are of the bride in the meeting? The bride loves to hear the Bridegroom's voice! Here it is, the blessed Word of God, the whole Word, not part of it, No, No, *No!* We believe in the whole thing. We really have such an effectiveness worked in us by the Word of life, that day by day we are finding out that the Word itself giveth life, and so the Spirit of the Lord breathing through, revealing by, giving so fresh to us, makes the whole Word alive today (Amen). So I have within my hands, within my heart, within my mind, this blessed reservoir of promises that is able to do so many marvelous things in this meeting. Now that is all I need to say apart from this, I believe that the Lord would deliver some of the people in this meeting tonight. Some of you people have most likely been suffering because you have a limited revelation of Jesus, a limited revelation of the fulness of Jesus, and there may be some in this meeting who need to be delivered. I can see tonight that we are surrounded in a great way differently from other places, by faith. Nevertheless, the Lord has been wonderfully manifesting Himself. Since I left you last year I have seen wonderful things, God has indeed been manifesting Himself.

I must tell you one of those cases which is worth telling in this meeting. In Oakland, near San Francisco, I had a theater. I want to tell you, to the glory of God only, that Oakland was in a very serious state, there was very little Pentecostal work there, and so a large theater was taken, and God wrought specially there in filling the place till we had to have overflow meetings. In these meetings we had a rising tide of people getting saved in the meetings by rising up voluntarily, up and down the place, and getting saved the moment they rose, and then we had a rising tide of people who needed help in their bodies, rising up in faith and being healed. One of them was an old man 95 years of age, he had been suffering three years gradually till he got to a place that for three weeks he was taking liquids, he was in a terrible state, but this man was different from the others, and I got him to stand while I prayed for him, and he came back and told us with such a radiant face that new life had come into his body. He said, "I am 95 years old, when I came into the meeting

I was full of pain with cancer in the stomach, and have been so healed that I have been eating perfectly, and have no pain." Lots of people in a similar way were healed.

I believe that God tonight, would have me help some of you people in the midst of this meeting. I want a manifestation to the glory of God. Anybody in this meeting who has pain in the head, in the feet, shoulders, legs, if you want deliverance rise up and I will pray for you, and you will find that God will so manifest His power that you will go out of this meeting free. If there is anyone in this meeting, in pain, from the head to the feet, anywhere, if you will rise I will pray for you and the Lord will deliver you. I hope you are expecting big things.

(A lady with rheumatism in the left leg rose, and after being prayed for, ran the full length of hall several times, then testified to partial healing. A young man with pain in the head was instantly healed. Another man with pain in the shoulder, was also instantly healed.)

If you look in the second chapter of Acts you will find that the Holy Ghost came and there was a manifestation of the divine power of God, and drunk as they seemed to be, there was such a manifestation that it brought conviction as the Word was spoken in the Holy Ghost.

In the third chapter of Acts, we see there a man was healed at the Beautiful Gate, through the power of the Spirit, as we see that it was so much so a miraculous, wonderful, evidence by the power of the Spirit that 5,000 men, women, and don't know how many children saved by the power of God. God makes a manifestation of His divine power, beloved, to prove that God is with us.

Now, how many would like to give their hearts to God tonight? How many would like to be saved?

Message given in Wellington, New Zealand

"To another discerning of spirits..." (1 Corinthians 12:10). There is a vast difference between natural discernment and spiritual. When it comes to natural discernment you will find many people loaded with it, and they can see so many faults in others. To such the words of Christ in the sixth chapter of Luke surely apply,

THE DISCERNING OF SPIRITS

December 8, 1923

> *...why beholdest thou the mote that is in thy brother's eye, but perceivest not the beam that is in thine own eye?*
>
> *Luke 6:41*

If you want to manifest natural discernment, focus the same on yourself for at least twelve months and you will see so many faults in yourself that you will never want to fuss about the faults of another. In the sixth chapter of Isaiah we read of the prophet being in the presence of God and he found that even his lips were unclean and everything was unclean. But praise God, there is the same live coal for us today, the baptism of fire, the perfecting of the heart, the purifying of the mind, the regeneration of the spirit. How important it is that the fire of God shall touch our tongues.

In 1 John 4:1 we are told,

> *Beloved, believe not every spirit, but try the spirits whether they are of God....*

We are further told, "And every spirit that confesseth not that Jesus Christ is come in the flesh is not of God: and this is that spirit of antichrist, whereof ye have heard that it should come; and even now already is it in the world" (v. 3). From time to time as I have seen a person under a power of evil, or having a fit, I have said to the power of evil, or satanic force that is within the possessed person, "Did Jesus Christ come in the flesh?" and straightway they have answered, "No." They either say, "No," or hold their tongues, refusing altogether to acknowledge that the Lord Jesus Christ came in the flesh. It is then, remembering that further statement of John's, "...greater is he that is in you, than he that is in the world," (1 John 4:4) that you can in the name of the

Lord Jesus Christ deal with the evil powers and command them to come out. We as Pentecostal people must know the tactics of the evil one and must be able to displace and dislodge him from his position.

I was preaching in Doncaster, England, at one time on the line of faith and a number of people were delivered. There was a man present who was greatly interested and moved by what he saw. He was suffering himself with a stiff knee and had yards and yards of flannel wound around it. After he got home he said to his wife, "I have taken in Wigglesworth's message and now I am going to act on it and get deliverance. Wife, I want you to be the audience." He took hold of his knee and said, "Come out, you devil, in the name of Jesus." Then he said, "It is all right, wife." He took the yards and yards of flannel off and found he was all right without the bandage. The next night he went to the little primitive Methodist church where he worshiped. There were a lot of young people who were in bad plight there and Jack had a tremendous business delivering his friends through the name of Jesus. He had been given to see that a great many ills to which flesh is heir are nothing else but the operation of the enemy, but his faith had risen and he saw that in the name of Jesus there was a power that was more than a match for the enemy.

I arrived one night at Gottenberg in Sweden and was asked to hold a meeting there. In the midst of the meeting a man fell full length in the doorway. The evil spirit threw him down, manifesting itself and disturbing the whole meeting. I rushed to the door and laid hold of this man and cried out to the evil spirit within him, "Come out, you devil! In the name of Jesus we cast you out as an evil spirit." I lifted him up and said, "Stand on your feet and walk in the name of Jesus." I don't know whether anybody in the meeting understood me except the interpreter, but the devils knew what I said. I talked in English, but these devils in Sweden cleared out. A similar thing happened in Christiania.

The devil will endeavor to fascinate through the eyes and through the mind. At one time there was brought to me a beautiful young woman who had been fascinated with some preacher, and just because he had not given her satisfaction on the line of courtship and marriage, the devil took advantage and made her fanatical and mad. They brought her 250 miles in that condition. She had previously received the baptism in the Spirit. You ask, "Is there any place for the enemy in one that has been baptized in the Holy Ghost?" Our only safety is in going on with God and in being constantly being filled with the Holy Ghost. You must not forget Demas. He must have been baptized with the Holy Ghost for he appears to have been a right-hand worker with Paul, but the enemy got him to the place where he loved this present world and he dropped off. When they brought this young woman to me, the evil power was immediately discerned and immediately I cast the thing out in the name of Jesus. It was a great joy to present her before all the people in her right mind again.

There is a life of perfect deliverance, and this is where God wants you to be. If I find my peace is disturbed on any line, I know it is the enemy who is trying to work. How do I know this? Because the Lord has promised to keep your mind in perfect peace when it is stayed on Him (Isaiah 26:3). Paul tells us to present our bodies a living sacrifice, holy, acceptable unto God, which is our reasonable service. The Holy Spirit breathes through him,

> *And be not conformed to this world: but be ye transformed by the renewing of your mind, that ye may prove what is that good, and acceptable, and perfect, will of God.*
>
> *Romans 12:2*

He further tells us in Philippians 4,

> *Finally, brethren, whatsoever things are true, whatsoever things are honest, whatsoever things are just, whatsoever things are pure, whatsoever things are lovely, whatsoever things are of good report; if there be any virtue, and if there be any praise, think on these things.*
>
> *Philippians 4:8*

As we think about that which is pure, we become pure. As we think about what which is holy, we become holy. And as we think about our Lord Jesus Christ, we become like Him. We are changed into the likeness of the object on which our gaze is fixed.

To discern spirits we must dwell with Him who is holy, and He will give the revelation and unveil the mask of satanic power on all lines. In Australia I went to one place where there were disrupted and broken homes. The people were so deluded by the evil power of Satan that men had left their wives, and wives had left their husbands, and had gotten into spiritual affinity with one another. That is the devil! May God deliver us from such evils in these days. There is no one better than the companion God has given you. I have seen so many broken hearts and so many homes that have been wrecked. We need a real revelation of these evil seducing spirits which come in and fascinate by the eye and destroy lives, and bring the work of God into disrepute. But there is always flesh behind it. It is never clean; it is unholy, impure, satanic, devilish, and hell is behind it. If the enemy comes in to tempt you on any line like this, I beseech you to look instantly to the Lord Jesus. He can deliver you from any such satanic power. You must be separated on all lines if you are going to have faith.

The Holy Ghost will give us this gift of discerning of spirits if we desire it so that we may perceive by revelation this evil power which comes in to destroy. We can reach out and get this unction of the Spirit that will reveal these things unto us.

You will have people come to meetings who are spiritists. You must be able to deal with spiritist conditions. You can so deal with them that they will not have any power in the meetings. If you ever have Theosophists or Christian Scientists, you must be able to discern them and settle them. Never play with them; always clear them out. They are better with their own company always, unless they are willing to be delivered from the delusion they are in. Remember the warning of the Lord Jesus, "The thief cometh not, but for to steal, and to kill, and to destroy..." (John 10:10).

Before Satan can bring his evil spirits, there has to be an open door. Hear what the Scriptures say, "...that wicked one toucheth him not" (1 John 5:18). "The Lord shall preserve thee from all evil: he shall preserve thy soul" (Psalm 121:7). How does Satan get an opening? When the saint ceases to seek after holiness, purity, righteousness, truth; when he ceases to pray, stops reading the Word and gives way to carnal appetites. Then it is that Satan comes. So often sickness comes as a result of disobedience. David said, "Before I was afflicted I went astray..." (Psalm 119:67). Seek the Lord and He will sanctify every thought, every act, till your whole being is ablaze with holy purity and your one desire will be for Him who has created you in holiness. Oh, this holiness! Can we be made pure? We can. Every inbred sin must go. God can cleanse away every evil thought. Can we have a hatred for sin and a love for righteousness? Yes, God will create within thee a pure heart. He will take away the stony heart out of the flesh. He will sprinkle thee with clean water and thou shalt be cleansed from all thy filthiness. When will He do it? When you seek Him for such inward purity.

Published in *The Pentecostal Evangel*

Divine Life Brings Divine Health

1925

 ark 1 - See from this Scripture how Jesus was quickened by the power of the Spirit of God, and how He was driven of the Spirit into the wilderness, and how John also was so filled with the Spirit of God that he had a "cry" within him, and the cry moved all Israel; showing that when God gets hold of a man in the Spirit he can have a new "cry" — something that should be in God's order.

BE FILLED WITH GOD

A man may cry for fifty years without the Spirit of the Lord, and the more he cries the less notice people would take of it; but if he were filled with the Holy Ghost and cried once, the people would feel the effects of it; so there is a necessity for every one of us to be filled with God. It is not sufficient to have just a "touch," or to be filled with a "desire." There is only one thing that will meet the needs of the people, and that is for you to be immersed in the life of God — God taking you, and making you so filled with His Spirit, till you live right in God; so that whether you eat or drink, or whatever you do, it may be all for the glory of God, and in that place you will find that all your strength and all your mind and all your soul are filled with a zeal, not only for worship, but for proclamation; proclamation accompanied by all the power of God, which must move satanic power, disturb the world, and make it feel upset.

The reason the world is not seeing Jesus is because Christian people are not filled with Jesus. They are satisfied with weekly meetings, and occasionally reading the Bible, and sometimes praying. Beloved, if God lays hold of you by the Spirit, you will find that there is an end of everything and a beginning of God, so that your whole body becomes seasoned with a divine likeness of God. He has begun not only to use you, but He has taken you in hand, so that you might be a vessel unto honor. And our lives are not to be for ourselves, for if we live unto ourselves we shall die; but if we, through the Spirit, do mortify the deeds of the body, we shall live. In this place we are subject to the powers of God; but he that liveth to himself shall die. The man in the former place lives a life of freedom and joy and blessing and service, and a life which brings blessing to others. God would have us to see that we must live in the Spirit.

In this Scripture, we have two important factors in the Spirit. One is Jesus filled with the Holy Ghost, driven by the Spirit's power, and the other is John the Baptist, who was so filled with the Spirit of God that his one aim was to go out preaching. We find him in the wilderness. What a strange place to be in! Beloved, it was quite natural for Jesus after He had served a whole day amongst the multitudes to want to go to His Father and pray all night. Why? He wanted a source of strength and power, and an association with His Father which would bring everything else to a place of submission; and when Jesus came from the mountain after communion with His Father, and after being clothed with His Holy presence and Spirit, when He met the demon power it had to go out. When He met sickness, it had to leave. He came from the mountain with power to meet the needs of the people, whatever they were. I do not know what your state of grace is — whether you are saved or not; but it is an awful thing for me to see people, who profess to be Christian, lifeless and powerless, and in a place where their lives are so parallel with the world's that it is difficult to discriminate which place they are in, whether in the flesh or in the Spirit. Many people live in the place which is described to us by Paul in Romans 7:25:

> *...with the mind I myself serve the law of God; but with the flesh the law of sin.*

That is the place where sin is in the ascendancy, but when the power of God comes to you, it is to separate you from yourself.

I want to talk till you are shaken and disturbed, and see where you are. If I can get you to search the Scriptures after I leave this place and see if I have been preaching according to the Word of God, then I shall be pleased. Wake up to see that the Scriptures have life for you — they have liberty and freedom, and nothing less than to make you sons of God, free in the Holy Ghost.

Now Jesus came to bring us back what was forfeited in the Garden. Adam and Eve were there — free from sin and disease and first sin came, then disease, and then death came after, and people want to say it is not so! But I tell you, "Get the devil out of you, and you will have a different body. Get disease out, and you will get the devil out."

Jesus rebuked sickness, and it went, and so this morning, I want to bring you to a place where you will see that you are healed. You must give God your life: you must see that sickness has to go and God has to come in; that your lives have to be clean, and God will keep you holy; that you have to walk before God, and He will make you perfect, for God says, "Without holiness no man shall see Him," and as we walk in the light, as He is in the light, we have fellowship one with another, and the blood of Jesus Christ, God's Son, cleanseth us from all sin.

FROM BONDAGE TO VICTORY

I want to say to you believers that there is a very blessed place for you to attain to, and the place where God wants you is a place of victory. When the Spirit of the Lord comes into your life it must be victory. The disciples, before they received the Holy Ghost, were always in bondage. Jesus said to them one day, just before the crucifixion, "One of you shall betray Me," and they were so conscious of their inability and their human depravity and helplessness that they said one to another, "Is it I?" And then Peter was ashamed that he had taken that stand, and he rose up and said, "Though all men deny Thee, yet will not I." And likewise the others rose and declared that neither would they; but they — every one — did leave Him.

But, beloved, after they received the power of the inducement of the Holy Ghost upon them, if you remember, they were made like lions to meet any difficulty. They were made to stand any test, and these men that failed before the crucifixion, when the power of God fell upon them in the upper room, they came out in front of all those people who were gathered together and accused them of crucifying the Lord of glory. They were bold. What had made them so? I will tell you. Purity is bold. Take, for instance, a little child. It will gaze straight into your eyes for as long as you like, without winking once. The more pure, the more bold; and I tell you, God wants to bring us into that divine purity of heart and life — that holy boldness. Not officiousness; not swelled-headness; not self-righteousness; but a pure, holy, divine appointment by One Who will come in and live with you, defying the powers of Satan, and standing you in a place of victory — overcoming the world.

You never inherited that from the flesh. That is a gift of God, by the Spirit, to all who obey. And so, none can say they wish they were over-comers, but that they have failed and failed until they have no hope. Brother, God can make *you* an overcomer. When the Spirit of God comes into your body He will transform you, He will quicken you. Oh, there is a life in the Spirit which makes you free from the law of sin and death, and there is an audacity about it — also, there is a personality about it. It is the personality of the Deity. It is God in you.

I tell you this morning that God is able to so transform and change and bring you into order by the Spirit that you can become a new creation after God's order. There is no such thing as defeat for the believer. Without the cross, without Christ's righteousness, without the new birth, without the indwelling Christ, without this divine incoming of God, I see myself a failure. But God, the Holy Ghost, can come in and take our place till we are renewed in righteousness — made the children of God. Nay, verily, the sons of God.

Do you think that God would make you to be a failure? God has never made man to be a failure. He made man to be a "son"; to walk about the earth in power; and so when I look at you I know that there is a capabil-ity that can be put into you which has the capacity of controlling and bringing everything into subjection. Yes, there is the capacity of the power of Christ to dwell in you, to bring every evil thing under you till you can put your feet upon it, and be master over the flesh and the devil; till within you there is nothing rises except that which will magnify and glorify the Lord; and this morning God wants me to show you these disciples, who were so frail, like you and me, that we, too, may now be filled with God, and become pioneers of this wonderful truth I am preaching. Here we see Peter frail, helpless, and, at every turn of the tide, a failure. And God filled that man with the Spirit of His righteousness, till he went up and down, bold as a lion, and when he came to death — even crucifixion — he counted himself unworthy of being crucified like his Lord, and asked that his murderers would put him head downwards on the tree. There was a deep submissiveness, and a power that was greater than all flesh. Peter had changed into the power of God.

The Scriptures do not tell two stories. They tell the truth. I want you to know the truth, and the truth will set you free. What is truth? Jesus said, "I am the Way, the Truth, and the Life." "He that believeth on me, as the Scriptures have said, out of his innermost being shall flow forth rivers of living water." This He spake of the Spirit that should be given them after Jesus was glorified.

I do not find anything in the Bible but holiness, and nothing in the world but worldliness. Therefore, if I live in the world I shall become worldly; but, on the other hand, if I live in the Bible, I shall become holy. This is the truth, and the truth will set you free. The power of God can remodel you. He can make you hate sin and love righteousness. He can take away bitterness and hatred and covetousness and malice, and can so consecrate you by His power, through His blood, that you are made pure — every bit holy. Pure in mind, heart and actions — pure right through. God has given me the way of life, and I want to give it to you, as though this were the last day I had to live. Jesus is the best there is for you, and you can each take Him away with you this morning. God gave His Son to be the propitiation for your sins, and not only so, but also for the sins of the whole world.

Jesus came to make us free from sin — free from disease and pain. When I see a person diseased and in pain I have great compassion for them, and when I lay my hands upon them, I know God means men to be so filled with Him that the power of sin shall have no effect upon them, and they shall go forth, as I am doing, to help the needy, sick, and afflicted. But what is the main thing? To preach the Kingdom of God and His righteousness. Jesus came to do this. John came preaching repentance. The disciples began by preaching repentance towards God, and faith in the Lord Jesus Christ, and I tell you, beloved, if you have really been changed by God, there is a repentance in your heart never to be repented of.

Through the revelation of the Word of God we find that divine healing is solely for the glory of God, and salvation is to make you to know that now you have to be inhabited by another, even God, and you have to walk with God in newness of life.

Originally published by Victory Press
North Melbourne, Australia

o another the word of knowledge by the same Spirit; To another faith by the same Spirit....

1 Corinthians 12:8,9

THE WORD OF KNOWLEDGE AND OF FAITH

January-March 1924

We have not passed this way hitherto. I believe that Satan has many devices and that they are worse today than ever before; but I also believe that there is to be a full manifestation on the earth of the power and glory of God to defeat every device of Satan.

In Ephesians 4 we are told to endeavor to keep the unity of the Spirit in the bond of peace, for there is one body, and one Spirit, one Lord, one faith, one baptism, and one God and Father of all (vv. 3-6). The baptism of the Spirit is to make us all one. Paul tells us that "...by one Spirit we are all baptized into one body...and have been all made to drink into one Spirit" (1 Corinthians 12:13). It is God's thought that we speak the same thing. If we all have the full revelation of the Spirit of God we shall all see the same thing. Paul asked these Corinthians, "Is Christ divided?" When the Holy Ghost has full control, Christ is never divided, His body is not divided, there is no division. Schism and division are the products of the carnal mind.

How important it is that we shall have the manifestation of "the word of knowledge" in our midst. It is the same Spirit who brings forth the word of wisdom that brings forth the word of knowledge. The revelation of the mysteries of God comes by the Spirit, and we must have a supernatural word of knowledge in order to convey to others the things which the Spirit of God has revealed. The Spirit of God reveals Christ in all His wonderful fulness, and He shows Him to us from the beginning to the end of the Scriptures. It is the Scriptures that make us wise unto salvation, that open to us the depths of the kingdom of heaven which reveal all the divine mind to us.

There are thousands of people who read and study the Word of God. But it is not quickened to them. The Bible is a dead letter except by the Spirit. The words that Christ spoke were not just dead words, but they were spirit and life. And so it is the thought of God that a living word, a word of truth, the Word of God, a supernatural word of knowledge, shall come forth from us through the power of the Spirit of God. It is the Holy Ghost who will bring forth utterances from our lips and a divine revelation of all the mind of God.

The child of God ought to thirst for the Word. He should know nothing else but the Word, and should know nothing among men save Jesus. "...Man shall not live by bread alone, but by every word that proceedeth out of the mouth of God" (Matthew 4:4). It is as we feed on the Word and

MEDITATE ON THE MESSAGE

it contains, that the Spirit of God can vitalize that which we have received, and bring forth through us the word of knowledge that will be as full of power and life as when He, the Spirit of God, moved upon holy men of old and gave them these inspired Scriptures. They were all inbreathed of God as they came forth at the beginning, and through the same Spirit they should come forth from us vitalized, living, powerful, and sharper than any two-edged sword.

With the gifts of the Spirit should come the fruit of the Spirit. With wisdom we should have love, with knowledge we should have joy, and with the third gift, faith, we should have the fruit of peace. Faith is always accompanied by peace. Faith always rests. Faith laughs at impossibilities. Salvation is by faith, through grace, and it is the gift of God. We are kept by the power of God through faith. God gives faith and nothing can take it away. By faith we have power to enter into the wonderful things of God. There are three positions of faith: saving faith, which is the gift of God; the faith of the Lord Jesus; and the gift of faith. You will remember the word of the Lord Jesus Christ given to Paul, to which he refers in Acts 26, where the Lord commissioned him to go to the Gentiles, "To open their eyes, and to turn them from darkness to light, and from the power of Satan unto God, that they may receive forgiveness of sins, and inheritance among them *which are sanctified by faith that is in me*" (Acts 26:18).

Oh, this wonderful faith of the Lord Jesus. Your faith comes to an end. How many times I have been to the place where I have had to tell the Lord, "I have used all the faith I have," and then He has placed His own faith within me.

One of our workers said to me at Christmas time, "Wigglesworth, I never was so near the end of my purse in my life." I replied, "Thank God, you are just at the opening of God's treasures." It is when we are at the end of our own that we can enter into the riches of God's resources. It is when we possess nothing that we can possess all things.

The Lord will always meet you when you are on the line of living. I was

IN IRELAND

at one time, and went to a house and said to the lady who came to the door, "Is Brother Wallace here?" She replied, "Oh, he has gone to Bangor, but God has sent you here for me. I need you. Come in." She told me her husband was a deacon of the Presbyterian church. She had herself received the baptism while she was a member of the Presbyterian church, but they did not accept it as from God. The people of the church said to her husband, "This thing cannot go on. We don't want you to be deacon any longer, and your wife is not wanted in the church." The man was very enraged and he became incensed against his wife. It seemed as though an evil spirit possessed him, and the home that had once been peaceful became very terrible. At last he left home and left no money behind him, and the woman asked me what should she do.

We went to prayer, and before we had prayed five minutes the woman was mightily filled with the Holy Ghost. I said to her, "Sit down and let me talk to you. Are you often in the Spirit like this?" She said, "Yes, and what could I do without the Holy Ghost now?" I said to her, "The situation is yours. The Word of God says that you have power to sanctify your husband. Dare to believe the Word of God. Now the first thing we must do is to pray that your husband comes back tonight." She said, "I know he won't." I said, "If we agree together, it is done." She said, "I will agree." I said to her, "When he comes home show him all possible love, lavish everything upon him. If he won't hear what you have to say, let him go to bed. The situation is yours. Get down before God and claim him for the Lord. Get into the glory just as you have got in today, and as the Spirit of God prays through you, you will find that God will grant all the desires of your heart."

A month later I saw this sister at a convention. She told how her husband came home that night and that he went to bed, but she prayed right through to victory and then laid hands upon him. He cried out for mercy. The Lord saved him and baptized him in the Holy Spirit. The power of God is beyond all our conception. The trouble is that we do not have the power of God in a full manifestation because of our finite thoughts, but as we go on and let God have His way, there is no limit to what our limitless God will do in response to a limitless faith. But you will never get anywhere except you are in constant pursuit of all the power of God.

One day when I came home from our open-air meeting at eleven o'clock I found that my wife was out. I asked, "Where is she?" I was told that she was down at Mitchell's. I had seen Mitchell that day and knew that he was at the point of death. I knew that it was impossible for him to survive the day unless the Lord undertook.

There are many who let down in sickness and do not take hold of the life of the Lord Jesus Christ that is provided for them. I was taken to see

A Woman Who Was Dying

and said to her, "How are things with you?" She answered, "I have faith, I believe." I said, "You know that you have not faith, you know that you are dying. It is not faith that you have, it is language." There is a difference between language and faith. I saw that she was in the hands of the devil. There was no possibility of life until he was removed from the premises. I hate the devil, and I laid hold of the woman and shouted, "Come out, you devil of death. I command you to come out in the name of Jesus." In one minute she stood on her feet in victory.

But to return to the case of Brother Mitchell, I hurried down to the house, and as I got near I heard terrible screams. I knew that something had happened. I passed Mrs. Mitchell on the staircase and asked, "What is up?" She replied, "He is gone! He is gone!" I just passed her and went into the room, and immediately I saw that Mitchell had gone. I could not understand it, but I began to pray. My wife was always afraid that I would go too far, and she laid hold of me and said, "Don't, Dad! Don't you see that he is dead?" I continued to pray and my wife continued to cry out to me, "Don't Dad. Don't you see that he is dead?" But I continued praying. I got as far as I could with my own faith, and then God laid hold of me. Oh, it was such a laying hold that I could believe for anything. The faith of the Lord Jesus laid hold of me, and a solid peace came into my heart. I shouted, "He lives! He lives! He lives!" And he is living today.

There is a difference between our faith and the faith of the Lord Jesus. The faith of the Lord Jesus is needed. We must change faith from time to time. Your faith may get to a place where it wavers. The faith of Christ never wavers. When you have that faith the thing is finished. When you have that faith you will never look at things as they are, you will see the things of nature give way to the things of the Spirit, you will see the temporal swallowed up in the eternal.

I was at a camp meeting in

CAZADERO, CALIFORNIA,

about eight years ago, and a remarkable thing happened. A man came there who was stone deaf. I prayed for him and I knew that God had healed him. Then came the test. He would always move his chair up to the platform, and every time I got up to speak he would get up as close as he could and strain his ears to catch what I had to say. The devil said, "It isn't done." I declared, "It is done." This went on for three weeks and then the manifestation came and he could hear distinctly 60 yards away. When his ears were opened he thought it was so great that he had to stop the meeting and tell everybody about it. I met him in Oakland recently and he was hearing perfectly. As we remain steadfast and unmoveable on the ground of faith, we shall see what we believe for in perfect manifestation.

People say to me, "Have you not the gift of faith?" I say that it is an important gift, but what is still more important is for us every moment to be making an advancement in God. Looking at the Word of God today I find that its realities are greater to me today than they were yesterday. It is the most sublime, joyful truth that God brings an enlargement. Always an enlargement. There is nothing dead, dry, or barren in this life of the Spirit; God is always moving us on to something higher, and as we move on in the Spirit of faith, it will always rise to the occasion as different circumstances arise.

This is how the gift of faith is manifested. You see an object and you know that your own faith is nothing in the case. The other day I was in San Francisco. I sat on a car and saw a boy in great agonies on the street. I said, "Let me get out." I rushed to where the boy was. He was in agony through cramp of the stomach. I put my hand on his stomach in the name of Jesus. The boy jumped, and stared at me with astonishment. He found himself instantly free. The gift of faith dared in the face of everything. It is as we are in the Spirit that the Spirit of God will operate this gift anywhere and at any time.

When the Spirit of God is operating this gift within a man, He causes him to know what God is going to do. When the man with the withered hand was in the synagogue, Jesus got all the people to look to see what would happen. The gift of faith always knows the results. He said to the man, "Stretch forth thine hand." His word had creative force. He was not living on the line of speculation. He spoke and something happened. He spake at the beginning and the world came into being. He speaks today and these things have to come to pass. He is the Son of God and came to bring us into sonship. He was the firstfruit of the resurrection, and He calls us to be firstfruits, to be the same kind of fruit like to Himself.

There is an important point here. You cannot have the gifts by mere human desire. The Spirit of God distributes them severally as He wills. God cannot trust some with the gift, but some who have a lowly, broken, contrite heart He can trust. One day I was in a meeting where there were a lot of doctors and eminent men, and many ministers. It was at a convention, and the power of God fell on the meeting.

ONE HUMBLE LITTLE GIRL

that waited at table opened her being to the Lord and was immediately filled with the Holy Ghost and began to speak in tongues. All these big men stretched their necks and looked up to see what was happening and were saying, "Who is it?" Then they learned it was "the servant!" Nobody received but "the servant!" These things are hidden and kept back from the wise and prudent, but the little children, the lowly ones, are the ones who receive. We cannot have faith if we have honor one of another. A man who is going on with God won't accept honor from his fellow beings. God honors the man of a broken, contrite spirit. How shall I get there?

So many people want to do great things, and to be seen doing them, but the one who God will use is the one who is willing to be bidden. My Lord Jesus never said He could do things, but He did them. When that funeral procession was coming up from Nain with the widow's son carried upon the bier, He made them lay it down. He spoke the word, "Arise!" and gave the son back to the widow. He had compassion for her. And you and I will never do anything except on the line of compassion. We will never be able to remove the cancer until we are immersed so deeply into the power of the Holy Ghost, that the compassion of Christ is moving through us.

I find that, in all my Lord did, He said that He did not do it, but that another in Him did the work. What a holy submission! He was just an instrument for the glory of God. Have we reached a place where we dare to be trusted with the gift? I see in 1 Corinthians 13 that if I have faith to remove mountains and have not charity, all is a failure. When my love is so deepened in God that I only move for the glory of God, then the gifts can be made manifest. God wants to be manifested, and to manifest His glory to humble spirits.

A faint heart can never have a gift. There are two things essential: first, love; and second, determination — a boldness of faith that will cause God to fulfil His Word. When I was baptized I had a wonderful time and had utterances in the Spirit, but for some time afterwards I did not again speak in tongues. But one day as I was helping another, the Lord again gave me utterances in the Spirit. I was one day going down the road and speaking in tongues a long while. There were some gardeners doing their work, and they stuck their heads out to see what was going on. I said, "Lord, You have something new for me. You said that when a man speaks in tongues, he should ask for the interpretation. I ask for the interpretation, and I'll stay right here till I get it." And from that hour the Lord gave me interpretation.

At one time I was in Lincolnshire in England and came in touch with the old

RECTOR OF THE CHURCH.

He became very interested and asked me into his library. I never heard anything sweeter than the prayer the old man uttered as he got down to pray. He began to pray, "Lord, make me holy. Lord, sanctify me." I called out, "Wake up! Wake up now! Get up and sit in your chair." He sat up and looked at me. I said to him, "I thought you were holy." He answered, "Yes." "Then what makes you ask God to do what He has done for you?" He began to laugh and then to speak in tongues. Let us move into the realm of faith, and live in the realm of faith, and let God have His way.

Published in *Confidence*

POSSESSION OF THE REST

January 14, 1924

 ebrews 4:1-16 — I believe this morning that it is in the perfect will of God that I read you some verses out of Hebrews 4:1-16.

Now we have here one of those divine truths which is so forceful in all of its bearings to us in this morning meeting.

God wants us all to see that we must not come short of that blessed rest which is spoken to us here this morning. I am not speaking about the rest there is through being saved, although it is a very blessed rest. I am not speaking about the rest we have in the body because pains have passed away, nor of the rest because of no sin, when sanctification has worked in a wonderful way by the blood, but God wants me to speak about the rest where you cease from your own works, and where the Holy Ghost begins to work in you and where you know that you are not your own, but absolutely possessed by God.

Beloved, I ask you to diligently follow me on these lines this morning, because there are so many people who are at unrest, they have no rest — unrested on so many lines. I believe that God can bring us into places of rest this day where we will cease from our own works, that we will cease from our own planning, that we will cease from our own human individuality which so interferes with God's power within us. God wants to fill the body with Himself, yes, to fill the bodies so full of Himself, that we are not; for God shall take us into His plan, His pavilion, His wisdom, and the government shall be upon His shoulders. Remember that wonderful word Jesus said to Peter, "...When thou wast young, thou girdest thyself, and walkedst whither thou wouldest: but when thou shalt be old, thou shalt stretch forth thy hands, and another shall gird thee, and carry thee whither thou wouldest not" (John 21:18).

In the twentieth chapter of Acts, Paul says, "I go bound in the Spirit," and now all that had to be done was not done by him, because the Holy Ghost was doing it. I want to take you for a moment into the sixteenth chapter of Acts where, in the power of the Holy Ghost, remember it was only in the power of the Holy Ghost, Paul, Silas, Barnabas, Mark, John, and Peter, learned a great plan in their lives, and that plan was that there had to be another mightier than them, holding them, choosing for them, even their words, their thoughts, for their lives had to be so divinely in the Holy Ghost that they would know exactly what to do and do it at the right time.

Turn for a moment only to that wonderful chapter, the sixteenth chapter of Acts, that we may have some idea as to what it means to have the Holy Ghost leading us all the time. I turn you for a moment to the sixth verse.

> *Now when they had gone throughout Phrygia and the region of Galatia, and were forbidden of the Holy Ghost to preach the word in Asia.*

Now you would say, "Had not Asia as much need for the Holy Ghost as anywhere else?" Certainly! Exactly so, but the Holy Ghost knows who is ready to receive the Holy Ghost. There may be a need, but they may not be ready. You may need lots of things, but if you are not ready for them, you will not get them. What is it to be ready and needy? To be ready and *hungry*, to be so hungry that you cannot rest unless you get everything God has for you. God can bring you there.

> *After they were come to Mysia, they assayed to go into Bithynia:*
> *but the Spirit suffered them not. And they passing by Mysia came*
> *down to Troas. And a vision appeared to Paul in the night; There*
> *stood a man of Macedonia, and prayed him, saying, Come over*
> *into Macedonia, and help us.*
>
> Acts 16:7-9

Ah, that was the place where they wanted help, that was the place where there was a cry for God. You need, beloved, to pray through that Wellington requires help, then she will get the blessing. Beloved, there is such a thing as people thinking they are full and rich, and knowing not that they are hungry, poor, and blind. The worst thing that can come to anyone, to a child of God, is to be satisfied — it is an awful position. Oh, what a startling truth we have in Revelation 3:15.

> *I know thy works, that thou art neither cold nor hot: I would thou*
> *wert cold or hot.*

Beloved, I want to preach to you by the grace of God this morning to move you so that you cannot rest till God gets you so for Himself that you will become bread for the people, water for the thirsty ground. There is no one in the place, either young or old, but God can meet you. God has grace for us all. God does not want any dwarfs. God is looking for a hungry people, a thirsty land.

Then, beloved, I notice here that many people fall short of coming into line with this divine blessing because of unbelief. Last time I was in Wellington I met people who had been Christians, breaking bread for years, but filled with unbelief. They will not have the right way of the Lord. They break bread, but they won't tow the line. God, save us from such a position. Now it is unbelief, nothing else, but when the Holy Ghost comes then unbelief is moved away, and they are humble, brokenhearted, thirsty, and they want God. May God keep us humble and hungry for the Living Bread. God is showing me that you cannot have this blessed power upon you without you become hungry.

Now, we have in the scriptures some very clear truths, so full of life and power that you need never be ashamed of the Gospel, it is so full of life and power. May God give us grace this morning to enter in.

I want you to notice that the Word of God is so clear. If you turn to the scriptures, you will find that the whole of Israel is a plan for us to see that God would have taken them on to many victories, but could not because of unbelief. They were eligible for all the fulness of God, but there was not a single person entered in but Joshua and Caleb. The reason they went in was because they had another Spirit. Have you never read it? Joshua and Caleb had another Spirit. The Spirit was so mighty upon Joshua and Caleb that they had no fear, the Holy Spirit upon them had such a dignity of reverence to God that these two people brought the bunches of grapes and presented them before the people. There were ten other people sent out, they had not received the Spirit and came back murmuring. If you get filled with the Spirit, you will never murmur anymore. I am speaking about the people who get the Holy Ghost and go on, not the people who remain stationary, but those who go right forward.

When these ten people came they were murmuring. What was it? They had no rest. "There remaineth therefore a rest to the children of God. For he that is entered into his rest, he also hath ceased from his own works..." (Hebrews 4:9,10), and God begins to work. These ten people said, "We shall become prey to them, and our children shall be slain by them," and God said through Moses, "Your children shall go in and you shall be shut out." It was only unbelief.

I pray God the Holy Ghost that you will search your hearts, and the Word, and see if you have received this Spirit. What is it? The Holy Spirit. It is to be filled with the Holy Spirit, filled with the life of the Spirit, that which we call unction, revelation, force. What do I call force? Force is that position in the power of the Spirit where instead of wavering you go through, instead of judgment you receive truth. May God help us.

I want to give you a very important point about the Holy Ghost this morning. The Holy Ghost is the only power Who manifests the Word in the body.

> *For the word of God is quick, and powerful, and sharper than any twoedged sword, piercing even to the dividing asunder of soul and spirit, and of the joints and marrow, and is a discerner of the thoughts and intents of the heart.*
>
> *Hebrews 4:12*

Investigate what I have said and when I give you a chance to ask questions bearing on the Word, God will be able to help me to help you to rest concerning these deep truths. Read that verse again. Quick and powerful.

> *Neither is there any creature that is not manifest in his sight: but all things are naked and opened unto the eyes of him with whom we have to do.*
>
> Hebrews 4:13

I want to deal now with the breath of the Spirit on the Word of God, that will give you rest. There is not a person in this place who understands, or gets into revelation on this Word, who would be deaf, there is not a person who would suffer indigestion, not a person who would have rheumatism, there is not such a thing as any evil power being in you if you understand it.

Concerning the breath of the Holy Ghost, we have in the second chapter of Acts one of the most divine elementary revelations. When the Holy Ghost came like a mighty rushing wind and filled the place where they were, cloven tongues of fire sat upon each of them, and they were filled with — this wind? Breath? Power? Person? — filled with God, the third person, the Holy Ghost filled their bodies.

I can declare to you this morning that not one of the 120 had the slightest defect in their bodies when they came out. I have seen people filled with the Holy Ghost, who used to be absolutely helpless, and when the power of God took their bodies they became like young men instead of old withered people, the power of the Holy Ghost, but now I am going to show you the reason.

The Word of God is quick and powerful. Paul said, "You hath He quickened." Powerful to the pulling down of the strongholds of Satan. I would like you to read 2 Corinthians 10:4-5:

> *For the weapons of our warfare are not carnal, but mighty through God to the pulling down of strong holds; Casting down imaginations, and every high thing that exalteth itself against the knowledge of God, and bringing into captivity every thought to the obedience of Christ.*

Now the Holy Ghost will take the Word, making it powerful in you till every evil thing that presents itself against the obedience and fulness of Christ would absolutely wither away. I want to show you this morning the need of the baptism of the Holy Ghost, by which you know there is such a thing as perfect rest, a perfect Sabbath coming to your life when you are filled with the Holy Ghost, and I want you to see perfect rest in this place. I want you to see Jesus — He was filled with the Holy Ghost, He lay asleep, filled with the Holy Ghost, and the storm began so terribly and filled the ship with water, till they cried, "Master, we perish," and He rose (filled with the Holy Ghost) and rebuked the wind. He asked, "Why are ye so fearful?"

I want you to see, beloved, that when the Holy Ghost comes in your life, if the house caught on fire you would be at rest, but I will tell you something better, the house would not be on fire for the Lord protects His own, that is better. Come a little nearer, I want you to see this Holy Ghost, this divine person, has to get so deep into us that He has to destroy every evil thing. Quick, powerful, sharper than any two-edged sword, piercing even to the dividing asunder of soul and spirit, and of the joints and marrow.

Some people got pain in their life after being saved, because of soulishness. Any amount of saved people are soulish, like Romans 7. They want to do good but they find evil, and they continue to do the thing they hate to do. What is up? They need the baptism of the Holy Ghost. Why? The baptism of the Holy Ghost is necessary, for then the Holy Ghost will so reveal the Word in the body that it will be like a sword, it will cut between the soul and the spirit, cut it right out till the soulishness cannot anymore long for indulgence in things contrary to the mind of God, and the will of God. Don't you want rest? How long are you going to be before you enter into that rest.

> *For he that entered into his rest, he also hath ceased from his own works, as God did from his. Let us labour therefore to enter into that rest, lest any man fall after the same example of unbelief.*
>
> *Hebrews 4:10,11*

Enter into rest, get filled with the Holy Ghost and unbelief will depart. Where they entered in they were safe from unbelief, and unbelief is sin. It is the greatest sin, because it hinders you from all blessings. There is another word that would be helpful to us this morning and I want you to take notice of it because it is so important.

> *For the word of God is quick, and powerful, and sharper than any twoedged sword, piercing even to the dividing asunder of soul and spirit, and of the joints and marrow, and is a discerner of the thoughts and intents of the heart.*
>
> *Hebrews 4:12*

You can see here (working his limbs) that there is an elbow working, a knee working, a shoulder working, and these could not work properly if the marrow should become congested, but hear about this salvation. God says this Holy Ghost power shall make the Word, this Christ of God, move in your marrow, till there would not be a stiff joint amongst us. How we need the Holy Ghost. Now probably when you go outside you will say, "He preached more about the Holy Ghost than anything." It is not so. My heart is so full of this matter, that Jesus is the Word, and it takes the Holy Ghost to make the Word act. Jesus is the Word that is mighty by the power of the Spirit to the pulling down of the strongholds, moving upon us so mightily that the power of God is upon us.

TONGUES AND INTERPRETATION: "God hath designed the fulness of the Gospel in its perfection and entirety that where the breath of heaven breathes upon it, the Gospel which is the power of God unto salvation, makes everything form in perfect union with divine trinity power till the whole man becomes a lively hope, filled with life, with fidelity, filled with God."

Remember Jesus is trinity, remember that Jesus is all fulness, remember Jesus was the fulness of the Godhead, and the Holy Ghost makes Him so precious that —

> It's all right now, it's all right now,
> For Jesus is my Savior,
> And it's all right now.

I don't want it to be like when they brought the grapes, they did not get the Spirit of Joshua and Caleb — I want you all to have a share. Oh, for the Holy Ghost to come with freshness upon us, then you could all sing, "It's all right now." If it is not, it may be, and God intends that it should be, and we are preaching in faith to you that it - *shall* be.

> It's all right now,
> It's all right now,
> For Jesus is *my* Savior, and
> It's all right now.

Let me encourage you. God is a God of encouragement. Now I want to take you to the thirteenth verse.

> *Neither is there any creature that is not manifest in his sight: but all things are naked and opened unto the eyes of him with whom we have to do.*
>
> *Hebrews 4:13*

No creature is hid from His sight, all are naked before Him. Now when God speaks of nakedness, He does not mean that He looks at flesh without clothing. God said, "That ye may be clothed that your nakedness may not appear." It is not your body, it is Christ clothing upon within, and you have no spot. He looks at your nakedness, at your weaknesses, at your sorrow of heart. He is looking into you right now, and what does He see?

> *Seeing then that we have a great high priest, that is passed into the heavens, Jesus the Son of God, let us hold fast our profession.*
>
> *Hebrews 4:14*

What is our profession? I have heard so many people testifying about their profession, some said, "Thank God, I am healed," "Thank God He has saved me," "Thank God He has cleansed me," "Thank God He has baptized me with the Holy Ghost." That is my profession — is it yours? That is the profession of the Bible, and God wants to make it your profession. You have to have a *whole* Christ, a *full* redemption, you have to be filled with the Holy Ghost, just a channel for Him to flow through. Oh, the glorious liberty of the Gospel of God's power.

> Heaven has begun with me,
> I am happy, now, and free.

> Since the Comforter has come,
> Since the Comforter has come.

It's all there. I know that God has designed this fulness, this rest, this perfect rest, I know He has designed it, and there ought not to be a wrinkle, a spot, a blemish, the Word of God says, "blameless and faultless." Praise the Lord for such a wonderful, glorious inheritance, through Him who loved us. Hallelujah!

Beloved, you must come in, every one of you. This morning meeting is to open the door of your heart to God to move in, till if you were to go away and live in some solitary place, you would be full there the same as in the Wellington assembly, it would make no difference.

When I think of John, as the legend says, how they tried to destroy him by boiling him in oil, and tried other things to destroy him, they took him to the Isle of Patmos, and he was in the Spirit — on the island in the Spirit. Yes. It is possible to be in the Spirit at the washtub, in the Spirit scrubbing floors, in the Spirit under all circumstances.

> Nothing really matters if the Lord loves me,
> And He does, He does,
> For nothing really matters if the Lord loves me,
> And He does, He does.

For we have not an high priest which cannot be touched with the feeling of our infirmities; but was in all points tempted like as we are, yet without sin.

Hebrews 4:15

There He is, there is the pattern, there is the Lord, and you say, "Tell me something very wonderful about Him." Yes, I will tell you this — He loved us to the end, He had faith in us right to the end, Jesus never let go the confidence that every soul would come right into the full tide line. There it is for us this morning.

There remaineth therefore a rest to the people of God.

Hebrews 4:9

Some people say, "Oh, yes, it is a rest up there." No, no, no. This is a rest where we cease from our works, there are no works up there —

where you cease from your own works, this day. I came to this meeting this morning entirely shut in with God, and if ever God spoke in a meeting He has spoken this morning. I may have been straight and plain on some lines. I had such a presentation of Wellington when I was here last time, I saw clearly people were resisting the Holy Ghost, as much as when Stephen said, "Ye stiffnecked and uncircumcised in heart and ears, ye do always resist the Holy Ghost: as your fathers did, so do ye" (Acts 7:51). Resisting the Holy Ghost.

Oh, if you won't resist the Holy Ghost, the power of God will melt you down, the Holy Ghost will so take charge of you that you will be filled to the uttermost with the overflowing of His grace.

Out of this subject this morning, if there is anything arisen in your heart that you need some further revelation on, I will help you.

Address given at Town Hall
Wellington, New Zealand

HOW TO UNDERSTAND VOICES

January 15, 1924

eloved, believe not every spirit, but try the spirits whether they are of God: because many false prophets are gone out into the world. Hereby know ye the Spirit of God: Every spirit that confesseth that Jesus Christ is come in the flesh is of God: And every spirit that confesseth not that Jesus Christ is come in the flesh is not of God: and this is that spirit of antichrist, whereof ye have heard that it should come; and even now already is it in the world. Ye are of God, little children, and have overcome them: because greater is he that is in you, than he that is in the world. They are of the world: therefore speak they of the world, and the world heareth them. We are of God: he that knoweth God heareth us; he that is not of God heareth not us. Hereby know we the spirit of truth, and the spirit of error. Beloved, let us love one another: for love is of God; and every one that loveth is born of God, and knoweth God. He that loveth not knoweth not God; for God is love. In this was manifested the love of God toward us, because that God sent his only begotten Son into the world, that we might live through him.

1 John 4:1-9

MANY VOICES

There are many voices in the world, we read it in 1 Corinthians 14. I want you to be able to understand voices, to understand spirit voices, to understand exactly what the Scripture means about these things.

Now I know there are a good many people who are great on Conan Doyle, who, you will find, is trying to delve into mysteries. Now there is nothing mystic about our business, and I want to tell everybody who comes to this place, you will have no share with us if you have anything to do with spiritism: we denounce it as being of the devil, and we don't want fellowship with you. If you want to join up with two things, the devil will get you at the finish.

Now, what is the difference between the spirit that now worketh, the spirit of disobedience, and the spirit of lawlessness? It is antichrist, and it is right in the midst of things — spiritism, Russellism, Christian Science, they are all akin, they have no room for the blood, and you cannot get near God but by the blood, it is impossible. The blood is the only power that can make a clear road into the Kingdom for you, the blood of Jesus.

Beloved, you have to be in a position to try the spirits whether they are of God. Why should we try them? You can always try the spirits whether they are of God for this reason, you will be able to tell the true revelation, and the true revelation which will come to you will always sanctify the heart, it will never have an "if" in it. When the devil came to Jesus, he had an "if." *If* thou be the Son of God, *if* thou wilt worship me. The Holy Ghost never comes with an *if*. The Holy Ghost is the divine orator of this wonderful Word, but the mystic Conan Doyle, etc. position, is satanic. Let me tell you a story.

One day I was walking along the street in Bradford, and I met one of my friends; he was a man who lived in the Spirit. I said to him, "Friend, where are you going?"

He replied, "I have a big job on tonight."

"What is it?"

"Oh, there is a spiritualistic seance tonight, and I'm going."

"Don't you think it is dangerous? I don't think it wise for believers to go to these places," I said.

"I am led to go to test it according to Scripture" he replied.

Now beloved, I advise none of you to go to these places.

My friend went, and sat down in the midst of the meeting, and the medium began to take control. This man did not speak, but just kept himself under the blood, whispering the preciousness of the blood of Jesus. After trying for some time to get under control, the leader said, "We can do nothing tonight, there is somebody believes in the blood."

Hallelujah! Do you all believe in the blood, beloved? I have often dealt with people under evil powers, people in fits and other things, and sometimes I have come across people so much controlled by evil powers that every time they want to speak the evil powers speak. It is a very dangerous position, but it is true, people get possessed with the devil.

The man in the tomb was terribly afflicted with these evil powers, and cut himself with stones, and strong cords, night and day, there he was in the tombs crying out. Jesus came on the scene, and these evil powers caused the man to run. Now it was all in the power of the devil, and as soon as the man got in front of Jesus the evil spirit said, "Why art thou come to torment us?" This man had no power to get free, but these evil spirits were so troubled in the presence of Jesus, that they cried out, "Why art thou come to torment us?"

Oh, thank God for Jesus. I want you to notice that Jesus wants you to be so under His power, so controlled by, and filled with the Holy Ghost, that the power of authority in you will resent all evil.

This is an important meeting for believers, because there are so many believers not on their guard. I want to impress you with this fact that every believer should reach a place in the Holy Ghost where he has no desire except the desire of God. The Holy Ghost has to possess us till we are filled, led, yes, divinely led by the Holy Ghost. It is a mighty thing to be filled with the Holy Ghost.

TONGUES AND INTERPRETATION: "The Lord, He is the mighty power of government, for the Scripture says, 'The government shall be upon His shoulders,' and now He has taken us on His shoulders; therefore let Him lead you where He will."

Don't you want to lead Jesus: if He leads you, He will lead you into truth; into nothingness, but when you are in nothingness you will be in power; into weakness, but when you are in weakness God will be with you in might, and everything that would seem of weakness on the human side would be under control of divine power.

WHERE TWO WAYS MEET

Now I want to deal with a very important thing. I have people by the hundreds, who are continually pressing on me with their difficulties, with their strange and yet holy and noble desires, but nevertheless strange, where two ways meet and they do not know which one to take. Some have impressions, but I would show you what becomes of impressions.

A person came to me one day and said, "Oh, you know the Spirit of the Lord was mighty upon me this morning."

I said, "Good!"

"Oh, I want to tell you about it. I want you to tell me if there is such a place as Ingerow anywhere near here."

I answered, "Yes, there is."

"Well, that place has been upon me, I have to go and preach there. There is nothing wrong with that, is there?"

But I asked, "What is the message?"

"I don't exactly know."

"Now come, what is the message?" I asked.

"Oh, I have to speak to someone about their soul."

"And you don't know there is such a place. The place is toward Skipton," I replied.

"But I have to go."

"How come?" I said, "I want you to think. You are working, are you not? Do you think anybody in the mill will commend you going to a place you don't know, to speak to someone you don't know?"

Was it of God? That is the first thing. It was an impression, of a desire to be something. That's the danger. My daughter tried to stop her, but she went the first chance she got. She got to the station, there was nobody there. The result was that she was soon in an asylum.

What was it? An impression. How shall we know this? There was a lady came to me yesterday and said, "Don't you know, the Spirit of the Lord is upon me, I have to preach the Gospel."

I said, "There is nothing wrong in that."

"I want to know where I have to go to, so I have come to you to see if the Lord has told you where I have to go to."

"Yes, you have to begin at home. Begin at Jerusalem, and if you are successful go to Judea, then if you are successful God will send you to the uttermost parts of the world." God is not going to send you to the uttermost parts of the world till you have been successful round about Jerusalem. This morning we have a tremendous big job, it is well worth doing, and I want to do it well. I want to tell you the difference between the right and the wrong way.

You have the Scriptures and you have the Holy Ghost, and the Holy Ghost has wisdom, and does not expect you to be foolish: the Holy Ghost having perfect insight into knowledge and wisdom, and truth always gives you balance.

You always have to have one thing removed and that is being terribly afraid, but fear moves and power and confidence come in its place. You always have to have another thing which must remain, and that is love. Love to obey God rather than obey you inclinations to be something, but if God wants to make you someone, that is different.

My wife tried her best to make me someone: she could not do it. Her heart was right, her love was right, she did her best to make me a preacher. She used to say, "Now, Father, you could do it if you would, and I want you to preach next Sunday."

I did everything to get ready, I tried everything, I don't know what I did not try — it would be best not to tell you what I did try. As many notes as would suit a parson for a week.

Her heart, her love, her desires were all right, but when I got up to preach I would give out my text, and then say, "If anybody can preach now is your chance, for I am done." That did not take place once, but many times. She was determined, and I was willing. When I got to the row of the penitent form I could take them right in: I could nurse the children while my wife preached, and pleased to do it. But don't you know when the Holy Ghost came, then I was ready. Then the preaching abilities were not mine but the Lord's. To be filled with the Holy Ghost is to be filled with divine equipment. It must be *all* for Jesus.

Oh, I tell you whatever you think about it, there is nothing good without Jesus is the whole thing.

Anyone could jump on this platform and say, "I am right." But when you have no confidence, then Jesus is all the confidence you require. God must have out of this audience men and women on fire for God. God will mightily send you forth in the unction of the Spirit, and sinners will feel condemned, but it will never be accomplished if you have anything in your mind that you are going to be something. The baptism is a baptism of death, and you live only unto God.

THE LIGHT OF TRUTH

I want to tell you an important thing about one of the most trying things I have had to deal with. I have had many trying things to deal with, people coming asking me all kinds of things, and to examine the position carefully and see what God has for them in that position.

I will relate a story which cannot help but help you. Is there anything wrong in wanting to be the best missionary in the world? Is there anything wrong about it? Not at all! Two young women worked at a place, they were telegraph operators. One of them had offered herself for the mission field. She was a beautiful girl, full of purity, truth, and righteousness; she had a lovely countenance, her expression almost would do wonderful things for God. A voice came to her. Oh, beloved, try the voices, try the spirits.

This voice came to her, "I will make you the mightiest missionary in the world." Exactly what she wanted, it was her heart's desire, you see, and she was so moved on.

"And I will find you all the money you want." She became so excited in this thing: her sister saw there was something just out of place so she went to the head person and said, "Could I and my sister have an hour off work?" She got her sister and herself free.

The voice came with such tremendous force that she could not let it go. Try the spirits, God will never do anything like that. He will never send you an unreasonable, unmanageable message. The devil said, "Don't tell anybody." That's the devil. Anything that is holy can be told on the housetops, there is no secret we have. All the secrets worth having are worth telling. If you cannot tell it, it is not worth having. God wants you to be able to tell all.

Then the voice came, "You might take your sister with you. I want you at the station tonight, you will find a train will come into the station at 32 minutes past 7:00, and after you have bought your ticket, you will have 6d. left, and in that train you will see a woman wearing a nurse's bonnet; and on the other side will be a man who has the money you want. When you get out at Glasgow, you can deposit the money in a certain bank at a certain place."

Here was lack of presentation of thought. There are no banks open at half past 7:00 P.M. and after investigation there was no such bank in that place. What did it? It got her ear, and I will tell you what is the danger. If I had but five minutes to go I would say this to you. If you cannot be reasoned with, you are wrong; if you are right and everybody else is wrong, I don't care who you are, if you cannot bear examination, if what you hold cannot bear the light of the truth, you are wrong. It will save a lot of you if you will just think.

But you say, "Oh, I know, *I know.*" It is a very serious thing when nobody else knows but you. May God deliver us from such a condition. If you think you have some specialty, it can be rehearsed.

We tried to console them, but nothing could be done, she knew it was the voice of the Lord.

There are two workings, and if it is to be the working of the Spirit, the workings of the Spirit are always contrary to the workings of the flesh.

Now the train came in at exactly 32 minutes past 7:00 p.m. She said to her sister, "Now we know it is right."

The change was exactly 6d. That was right.

Now the next thing was not right. The train came in, that was in order, but there were no such characters. Those voices went on. Ah, those evil voices. How shall we know whether they are of God? When God speaks He will speak on the lines of wisdom. When the devil came to Jesus he said, "*if* thou be the Son of God." The devil knew, and Jesus knew, and answered, "It is written, 'Thou shalt worship the Lord thy God, and Him only shalt thou serve.'"

Now with these two young women, was there anything wrong with it? The wrong was that she ought to have judged the spirits. If the young women had asked, "Did Jesus come in the flesh?" the voice would have answered *no*. There is no satanic voice in the world, and no spiritualistic medium will acknowledge that Jesus came in the flesh. The devil never will, and he is the father of those spiritualistic mediums, Conan Doyle included. Was she delivered? Certainly, but when these evil spirits knew she believed and would do anything they wanted, they said, "We will make you the biggest missionary in the world, and get you all the money." I never knew it to come true, and you never will as long as you live.

A man came to me and said, "I have got in my hands a certain food for invalids, which will bring in millions of pounds for the missionaries."

I said to him, "I will not have anything to do with it." These things are not a success. God does not work that way. If God wanted you to have gold, He could rain it in your houses while you were away. He has all the gold, and the cattle on a thousand hills are His.

Beloved, I want you to see that Jesus was the meekest man in the world, He had power to make bread, gold, and yet He never made it, only for somebody else.

When anybody preaches for the Kingdom's sake, He will provide. Seek to be filled with the Holy Ghost for the people's sake. Seek only for God, the rain will fall, the enduement of power will be made manifest in your mortal bodies if you are really in the Spirit.

Were these two young women delivered? Yes, and used in China for the last ten years — thank God there is a way out.

This is an important word, and I am saying everything I can by the grace of God and the revelation of the Spirit, to make you people careful, and yet careless. Careful of satanic powers, and careless when the power of God is upon you with unction force, so that He Himself shall be manifested, and not you.

HUMILITY IS ESSENTIAL

Is there anything wrong with the story I am going to tell you? I want you to see.

Quite a lot of people at York had been saved in the marketplace, and one of the young men that had been gathered in had the abilities of being a wonderful teacher, leading the people forth triumphantly in the morning meetings. He had teaching and preaching abilities, and everybody was lifted up in joy.

Now I am sure this is a word in season.

When I went there the power of the Spirit fell upon us, and straight away many people were under the power of God. When they saw this young man laid out under the power of the Spirit they said, "Oh, Brother Wigglesworth, we have got one of the finest young men, and for him to be filled with the Holy Ghost, we will have the greatest teacher in the world."

The leaders came and said they were overjoyed at the fact. I said, "Be still, the Lord will do His own work."

In a short time he was through in the Spirit, and everybody was rejoicing and applauding. They fell into great error there. Now what happened?

Oh, I do pray God will save you from that. I hope nobody in this Town Hall would say, "Oh, you did preach well tonight." It's as surely of the devil as anything that ever came to anybody. God has never yet allowed any human body to be applauded. This young man was in the power of the Holy Ghost — it was lovely.

They came round him, shaking him by the hand, saying, "Now we have got the greatest teacher there is." Was it wrong? Perfectly right, and yet it was the most wrong thing they could do: in their hearts they could have been thankful. I want to tell you the devil never knows your thoughts, and if you won't let your thoughts out in public you will be safe. He can suggest a thought, and thoughts of evil but that is not sin, all these things are from without. The devil can suggest evil things for you to receive, but if you are pure, it is like water on a duck's back.

What happened? They said, "I should not wonder if you were a second John the Baptist." They were really elated with him. The young man tried to throw it off and keep well balanced when he saw what was coming to him — but the devil came with a voice as loud as a cannon, "Don't you know, you are 'John the Baptist'" and still he threw it off.

Listen, it was the believers who did it, and the devil never let him alone. "You are surely John the Baptist, there is no person in the world like you. Arise, John the Baptist."

And I want to tell you that at eight o'clock in the morning that young man went down the street crying out "I am John the Baptist."

What was wrong? The saints applauded him, and I tell you that is the work of the devil.

Lord, bring us to a place of humility and brokenheartedness where we will see the danger of satanic powers. Don't you believe the devil is a big ugly monster; he comes as an angel of light, and he comes at a time when you have done well, and tells you about it. He comes to make you feel you are somebody, the devil is an exalted demon.

Oh, look at the Master; if you could see Him as I see Him sometimes: rich, and yet He became poor; in the glory, yet took upon Him the form of a servant, yes, a servant, that is the Lord. God give us these beatitudes where we will be broken and humble, and in the dust, and God will raise us and place us in a high place.

I don't suppose there is a person in this place believes it is 12:00 o'clock—I know you don't but it is, all the same. I propose we continue this service tomorrow morning, because we must have a quarter of an hour for questions, that I might help you with any difficult problems you have in your minds.

Address given at Town Hall
Wellington, New Zealand

Peter 1 — I want to read to you a few verses from 1 Peter 1. I believe that God wants to speak to us to strengthen our position in faith and grace. If I had my way I would have liked to

RISING INTO THE HEAVENLIES

January 24, 1924

close up with the gifts of the Spirit, and seeing I am going to give you another week, that week will be very much on those lines, so this morning I pray God that it will be just as the Spirit is moving, that we may be able to accept His truth.

Beloved, I want you to understand that you will get more than you came for. There is not a person in this place will get what he came for, God gives you more. No man gets his answers to his prayers, he never does, for God answers his prayers abundantly above what he asks or thinks. Don't you say, "I got nothing." You got as much as you came for, and more, but if your minds are not willing to be yielded, and your heart not sufficiently consecrated, you will find that you are limited on that line, because the heart is the place of reception. God wants you to have receptive hearts, to take in the mind of God. These wonderful scriptures are full of life-giving power. Let us read the first and second verses, I believe there are some words there I ought to lay emphasis on.

> *Peter, an apostle of Jesus Christ, to the strangers scattered throughout Pontus, Galatia, Cappadocia, Asia, and Bithynia,*
>
> *Elect according to the foreknowledge of God the Father, through sanctification of the Spirit, unto obedience and sprinkling of the blood of Jesus Christ: Grace unto you, and peace, be multiplied.*
>
> *1 Peter 1:1,2*

THE ELECT

I want you to notice that in all times, in all histories of the world, whenever there has been a divine rising, revelation, God coming forth with new dispensational orders of the Spirit, you will find there have been persecutions all over. You take the case of the three Hebrew children, and also Daniel, and Jeremiah. With any person in the old dispensation, as much as in the new, when the Spirit of the Lord has been moving mightily, there has arisen trouble and difficulty. What for? Because of three things very much against revelations of God and the Spirit of God. First, humanity, flesh, natural things are against divine things. Evil powers work upon this position of the human life, and especially when the will is unyielded to God, then the powers of darkness arise up against the powers of divine order, but they never defeat them. Divine order is very often in minority, but always in majority. Did I say that right? Yes, and I meant it. Wickedness may increase and abound, but when the Lord raises His flag over the saint, it is victory, though it is in minority and always triumphs. I want you to notice the first verse because it says "scattered," meaning to say they did not get much liberty in allowing them to meet together, driven from place to place. Even in the days of John Knox the people who served God had to be in very close quarters, because the Roman church set out to destroy them, nailed them to judgment seats, and destroyed them in all sorts of ways. They were in minority but swept through in victory and the Roman power was crushed and defeated. You take care that it does not rise again, the Roman power is always bloodshed and murder, and always against the Holy Ghost, so may God bring us into perfect order that we may understand these days that we may be in Wellington in minority, but in majority.

The Holy Ghost wants us to understand our privileges — elect according to the foreknowledge of God through sanctification of the Spirit. Now this word *sanctification* of the Spirit is not on the lines of sin cleansing. It is a higher order than the redemption work. The blood of Jesus is rich unto all powerful cleansing, also takes away other powers and transforms us by the mighty power of God. But when sin is gone, yes, when we are clean and when we know we have the Word of God right in us and the power of the Spirit is bringing everything to a place where we triumph, then comes revelation by the power of the Spirit, lifting you into higher ground, into all the fulness of God, which unveils the Christ in such a way. It is called our sanctification of the Spirit. Sanctification of the Spirit, elect according to the foreknowledge of God. I don't want you to stumble at the word *elect* — it is a most blessed word. You might say you are all elect: everyone in this place could say you are elected. God has designed that all men should be saved. This is the election, but whether you accept and come into your election, whether you prove yourself worthy of your election, whether

"A preacher should preach only what he is sure of;
everybody can think, the preacher should say
what he knows."

you have so allowed the Spirit to fortify you, whether you have done this I don't know, but this is your election, your sanctification, to be seated at the right hand of God.

This word *election* is a very precious word to me, foreordained, predestinated, these are words that God has designed before the world was, to bring us into triumph and victory in Christ. Some people play round about it and make it a goal. They say, "Oh, well, you see, we are elected, we are all right." I know many of them who believe in that condition of election and they say they are quite all right, they are elected to be saved, and I believe these people are so diplomatic that they believe others can be elected to be damned. It is not true! Everybody is elected to be saved, but whether they come into it, that is another thing.

Many don't come into salvation because the god of this world hath blinded their eyes lest the light of this glorious Gospel should shine unto them. What does it mean? It means this, that Satan has got mastery over their minds, and they have an ear to listen to corruptible things, you see? Corruptible things, the satanic side of it, where they say, "Oh, the pictures are the place for me, the theatre is the place for me, the race course is the place for me." Pictures, race courses, etc, are the downward way to hell, and no believer will darken their door. Perhaps the last thing the devil brought out is the picture show, and I find people can wait out in streams and great crowds, so I said, "This is my opportunity" and I shouted for all I was worth about Jesus, because I know there is no Jesus inside there, so they ought to have a little bit outside.

Beloved, I want you to see this election I am speaking about, to catch a glimpse of heaven, with your heart always on the wing, where you grasp everything spiritual, when everything divine makes you hungry, everything seasonable in spiritual fidelity will make you long after it.

If I came here in a year's time I should see this kind of election gone right forward, always full, never having a bad report, where you see Christ in some vision, in some way in your lives every day, growing in the knowledge of God every day but I cannot dwell there, for we have much to get through. It is through sanctification of the Spirit unto obedience and sprinkling of the blood of Jesus Christ. There is no sanctification if it is not sanctification unto obedience. There would be no trouble with any of us if we would come definitely to a place where we understood that word where Jesus said, "For their sakes I sanctify myself that they also might be sanctified through the truth." Thy Word is truth, sanctify them through Thy Word, which is truth (John 17:17).

No child of God ever asks a question about the Word of God. What do I mean? The Word of God is clear on breaking of bread, the Word of God is clear on water baptism, the Word of God is clear on all these things, and no person that was going on to the obedience and sanctification of the Spirit by election, will pray over that Word. The Word of God is to be swallowed, not to be prayed over.

If ever you pray over the Word of God there is some disobedience; you are not willing to obey. If you come into obedience on the Word of God, and it says anything about water baptism you will obey, if it says anything about speaking in tongues you will obey, if it says anything about breaking of bread and assembling ourselves together, you will obey. If you come into the election of the sanctification of the Spirit, you will be obedient in everything revealed in that Word; and in the measure you are not obedient, you have not come into the sanctification of the Spirit.

A little thing spoils many good things. People say, "Mr. So-and-so is very good, but...." "Mrs. So-and-so is excellent, but...." "Oh, you know that young man is progressing tremendously, *but*...." There are no "buts" in sanctification of the Spirit. "But" and "if" are gone, and it is "shall" and "I will" all the way through.

Beloved, if there are any *buts* in your attitude toward the Word of *truth* there is something unyielded to the Spirit. I do pray God the Holy Ghost that we may be willing to yield ourselves to the sanctification of the Spirit, that we may be in the mind of God in the election that we may have the mind of God in the possession of it. Perhaps to encourage you people it would be helpful to show to you what election is, because there is no difficulty in proving whether you are elected or not.

A STRANGE INWARD LONGING

You are here in this morning meeting (I am speaking about believers) and maybe if you had to search your own heart why you have been attending the meetings, you would not have to say "because it was Wigglesworth," it would be a mistake. But if there was in you that holy calling, or strange inward, longing desire for more of God, you could say it was the sanctification of the Spirit which was drawing you. Who could do that, but He who has elected you for that?

There are people in this place, say from 20 years — 30, 40 — we can even begin at 15 years — 20, 25, 30, 35, 40, and so on — and if I were to say to you, "Stand up you who never remember the time when the Spirit did not strive with you," it would be a marvelous thing how many people would stand. What do you call it? God bring you in, moving upon you. Strange? Very strange!

When I think of my own case, I recall that on my mother's side and on my father's side there was no desire for God, and yet in my very infancy I was strangely moved upon by the Spirit. At eight years I was definitely saved, and at nine years I felt the Spirit come upon me, just as when I spoke in tongues — elect according to the foreknowledge of God, and there are people in this place who have the same experience. You might say, "When I was in sin I was troubled." And there is a direct line of election between God and the human man, moving it, being wholly prepared for God.

It is a most blessed thought that we have a God of love, compassion, and grace, who willeth not the death of one sinner. God has made it possible for all men to be saved, and caused Jesus, His well beloved Son, to die for the sins of the people. It is true He took our sins; it is true He paid the price for the whole world; it is true He gave Himself a ransom for many; it is true, beloved. And you say, "For who?" "...whosoever will, let him take the water of life freely" (Revelation 22:17).

"What about the others?" It would be a direct refusal of the blood of Jesus; it would have to be a refusal to have Christ to reign over them, that's it. It is whosoever will, on this side and whosoever won't, on the other side; and there are people living in the world that won't. What is up with them? "...the god of this world hath blinded the minds of them which believe not, lest the light of the glorious gospel of Christ, who is the image of God, should shine unto them" (2 Corinthians 4:4).

Elect according to the foreknowledge of God the Father, through sanctification of the Spirit, unto obedience and sprinkling of the blood of Jesus Christ: Grace unto you, and peace, be multiplied.

1 Peter 1:2

Yes, but I cannot pass over it, and yet I must not stop at that because there are other important words here for us this morning.

Through sanctification of the Spirit, according to the election, you will get to a place where you are not disturbed. There is a peace in sanctification of the Spirit, because it is a place of revelation, taking you into heavenly places. It has a place where God comes and speaks and makes Himself known to you; and when you are face to face with God you get a peace which passeth all understanding, lifting you from state to state of inexpressible wonderment. It is really wonderful.

> Oh, this is like heaven to me,
> This is like heaven to me,
> I've stepped over Jordan to Canaan's fair land;
> And this is like heaven to me.

Oh, it is wonderful.

> *Blessed be the God and Father of our Lord Jesus Christ, which according to his abundant mercy hath begotten us again unto a lively hope by the resurrection of Jesus Christ from the dead.*
>
> *1 Peter 1:3*

We cannot pass that, because this sanctification of the Spirit brings us into definite line with this wonderful position of the glory of God. I want to keep before us the glory, the joy of a lively hope. Now a lively hope is exactly opposite to dead, exactly opposite to normal.

> Lively hope is movement.
> Lively hope is looking into.
> Lively hope is pressing into.
> Lively hope is leaving everything behind you.
> Lively hope is keeping the vision.
> Lively hope sees Him coming!

And you live in it, the lively hope. You are not trying to make yourself feel that you are believing, but the lively hope is ready, waiting, lively hope is filled with joy of expectation of the King. Praise the Lord!

I want you to know that God has this in his mind for you. Do you know what will move them? The real joy in expectation that will come forth with manifestation and then realization. Don't you know?

Well, I pray God the Holy Ghost that He will move you that way. Come now, beloved, I want to raise your hopes into such activity, into such a joyful experience, that when you go away from this meeting you will have such joy that you would only walk if you could not run, and you would not run if you could jump in a motor car, where you would go at head speed if you knew you could be there.

Now I trust that you will be so reconciled to God that there is not one thing which would interfere with you having this lively hope. If you had any love for the world it could not be, for Jesus is not coming to the world, Jesus is coming to the heavenlies and all the heavenlies are going to Him, so you cannot have anything but joy with it. The pride of life you could not have, all these things are contrary to the lively hope because of the greatness and the multimagnitudinous glories of the regions of eternity, which are placed before him in joyful expectation.

TONGUES AND INTERPRETATION: "The joy of the Lord is everything. The soul lifteth up like the golden grain ready to be ingathered for the great sheaf. All ready, waiting, rejoicing, longing for Him, till they say, 'Lord Jesus, we cannot stop longer.'"

What a wonderful expression of the Holy Ghost to the soul in interpretation. How He loves us, hovers over us, rejoiceth in us, how the Lord by the Holy Ghost takes a great drink with us and our cup is full and running over.

The joy of the Lord is your strength; you have to be right in these glorious places, it is the purpose of God for your soul. I hope you won't forget the lively hope. Do not have to be living on "tomorrow" because you did not catch it today. Oh, it is wonderful. Hallelujah!

GLORIES OF THE NEW CREATION

To an inheritance incorruptible, and undefiled, and that fadeth not away, reserved in heaven for you.

1 Peter 1:4

First, incorruptible. Second, undefiled. Third, fadeth not away. Fourth, reserved in heaven for you. Glory to God! I tell you it is great, it is very great. May the Lord help you to thirst after this glorious life of Jesus. Oh, brother, it is more than new wine, the Holy Ghost is more than new wine, the Holy Ghost is the manifestation of the glories of the new creation. An inheritance incorruptible. *Incorruptible* is one of those delightful words which God wants all the saints to grasp — everything corruptible fades away, everything seen cannot remain. Jesus said, "...where neither moth nor rust doth corrupt, and where thieves do not break through nor steal" (Matthew 6:20). None of these things are joined up with incorruptible. Incorruptible is that which is eternal, everlasting, divine, and therefore everything spiritual, divine, reaches a place where God truly is, what shall I say? Where God is truly in the midst of it. He is in existence from ever-lasting to everlasting. Holy, pure, divine, incorruptible.

This is one part of our inheritance in the Spirit, one part only. Hallelu-jah. An inheritance incorruptible and undefiled. Oh, how beautiful, per-fected forever, no spot, no wrinkle, holy, absolutely pure, all traces of sin withered, everything which is mortal has been scattered, and come into a place so purified that God is in the midst of it. Hallelujah. It is so lovely to think of that great and wonderful city, we read about it in Revelation.

"And I John saw the holy city, new Jerusalem, coming down from God out of heaven, prepared as a bride adorned for her husband" (Revelation 21:2). Think about it, the marriage. Oh, it is glorious. I saw the holy city as a bride adorned for her husband, undefiled, pure, glorious, all white, all pure. Who were they? They were once in the world, once corruptible, once defiled, now made by the blood holy, spiritual, now lifted from corruptible to incorruptible, and now undefiled in the presence of God. Hallelujah!

Oh, beloved, God means it for us this morning, every soul in this place must reach out to this ideal perfection. God has ten thousand more thoughts for you than you have for yourself. The grace of God is going to move us on, you will never sorrow anymore as long as you live, never weep anymore, but you will weep for joy. Undefiled, fadeth not away. Glory!

(The evangelist sang in tongues.)

Fadeth not away! What a heaven of bliss, what a joy of delight, what a foretaste of heaven on earth. Oh, the counting house lit up with can-dles, with oil, with electric light, it does not matter, it would fade away in the splendor of that glorious day, it all withers when you get in the Spirit. You would cheerfully do the work you have to do because of tomorrow in the presence of the King. Oh, brother, what a hope, what a joyous possibility, within a short time to be in that mighty multitude.

But you say, "My burden is more than I can bear." Cheerfully bear the burden, tomorrow you will be there. No sin would entice you, no evil spirit would be able to trip you, no, no, *no*, because of tomorrow with the Lord. With the Lord forever, an inheritance that fadeth not away. Now come a little further.

SALVATION AND PURIFICATION

Who are kept by the power of God through faith unto salvation ready to be revealed in the last time.

1 Peter 1:5

I would like to have a word here on the lines of salvation, because salvation is very much misunderstood; salvation which comes to you in a moment of time, believing unto salvation, this is only the beginning. Salvation is so tremendous, mighty, and wonderful, as the early apostles said, "Being saved every day." You begin with God and go right on to being saved day by day, forgetting the things which are behind, and pressing forward, through the power of the blood you go on unto salvation.

Salvation is like sanctification of the Spirit, it is not a goal, no, no, no. It is only a goal as you limit yourself. There is no limitation as we see the great preservation of the Master. We should never stand still for a moment, but mightily move on in God.

Wherein ye greatly rejoice, though now for a season, if need be, ye are in heaviness through manifold temptations.

1 Peter 1:6

Ah, what a blessing, you have no idea what God will mean to you in trials and temptations — it is purification of the Spirit.

That the trial of your faith, being much more precious than of gold that perisheth, though it be tried with fire, might be found unto praise and honour and glory at the appearing of Jesus Christ.

1 Peter 1:7

Gold perisheth, faith never perisheth — it is more precious than gold, though it be tried with fire. I went into a place one day and a gentleman said to me, "Would you like to see purification of gold this morning?"

I replied, "Yes."

He got some gold and put it in a crucible and put a blast of heat on it. First, it became blood red, and then changed and changed. Then I found this man took an instrument, passed it over the gold, which drew something off, something which the gold was foreign to. He did this several times until every part was taken away, and then at last he put it over again and said, "Look," and there we both saw our faces in the gold. It was wonderful.

My brother, the trial of your faith is much more precious than gold that perisheth. When God so purifies you through trials, misunderstandings, persecution, suffering because you are wrongfully judged, because you have not believed any amount of voices, Jesus has given you the keynote, *rejoice* in that day.

Beloved, as you are tested in the fire, the Master is cleaning away all that cannot bring out the image, cleaning away all the dross from your life, and every evil power, till He sees His face right in the life, till He sees His face right in your life.

Always bearing about in the body the dying of the Lord Jesus, that the life also of Jesus might be made manifest in our body. It may not seem to any of us to be very joyous — it is not acceptable to the flesh, but I have told you so often your flesh is against the Spirit; your flesh and all your human powers have to be perfectly submitted to the mighty power of God inwardly, to express and manifest His glory outwardly, but you must be willing for the process, and say "Amen" to God — it may be very hard but God will help you.

It is lovely to know that in the chastening times, in the times of misunderstanding, and hard tests when you are in the right and you are treated as though you were in the wrong, God is meeting you, blessing you. People say it is the devil. Never mind, let the fire burn, it will do you good. Don't you get rasping, but endure it joyfully. It is so sweet to understand this, love suffereth long and is kind. How lovely to get to a place where you think no evil, not easily provoked, and where you can bear all things, endure all things. Praise the Lord. Oh, the glory of it, the joy of it.

I understand what it means to jump for joy. I could jump for joy this morning. Why? Because of the Lord.

I know the Lord, I know the Lord
I know the Lord has laid His hand on me.

Whom having not seen, ye love; in whom, though now ye see him not, yet believing, ye rejoice with joy unspeakable and full of glory.

1 Peter 1:8

Whom having not seen we love. Oh, how sweet, there is no voice so gentle, so soft, so full of tenderness to me, there is no voice like His, and no touch. Whom having not seen we love. Is that possible? God will make it possible to all. Though now we see Him not, yet believing we rejoice with joy unspeakable and full of glory.

Rejoice? Oh, what a salvation God has procured for us and for nothing, all for worthlessness and all for nothingness, all for helplessness. I entreat you from the Lord to be so reconciled to Him that there will be no division between you and Him. When He would laugh, you would laugh, and when He saw you in tears His compassion would be all you need forever. Will you give Him preference? Will you give Him preeminence in all things? Shall He not have His right place and decide for you the way and plan of your life?

Brother, when you allow Him to decide for you, when you want nothing but His blessed will, when He has to be Lord and Governor over all, heaven will be there all the time. The Lord bless you with grace this morning to leave all and say, "I will follow You, Lord Jesus."

All you people who are longing to get nearer Jesus this morning (I would like a four-hour altar call where the fire would fall, but seeing it cannot be), I ask you in the name of Jesus to surrender yourself to Him, but you say, "Wigglesworth, I did it yesterday." I know, but this morning you want to do it more, I know I want to get nearer my Lord. Let us rise and get near to Him for a few minutes.

Address given at Town Hall
Wellington, New Zealand

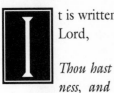

It is written of our blessed Lord,

Thou hast loved righteousness, and hated iniquity; therefore God, even thy God, hath anointed thee with the oil of gladness above thy fellows.

Hebrews 1:9

RIGHTEOUSNESS

February 9, 1924

It is the purpose of God that we, as we are indwelt by the Spirit of His Son, should likewise love righteousness and hate iniquity. I see that there is a place for us in Christ Jesus where we are no longer under condemnation but where the heavens are always open to us. I see that God has a realm of divine life opening up to us where there are boundless possibilities, where there is limitless power, where there are untold resources, where we have victory over all the power of the devil. I believe that, as we are filled with the desire to press on into this life of true holiness, desiring only the glory of God, there is nothing that can hinder our true advancement.

Peter commences his second epistle with these words,

> *Simon Peter, a servant and an apostle of Jesus Christ, to them that have obtained like precious faith with us through the righteousness of God and our Saviour Jesus Christ.*

It is through faith that we realize that we have a blessed and glorious union with our risen Lord. When He was on earth Jesus told us, "...I am in the Father, and the Father in me..." (John 14:11). "...the Father that dwelleth in me, he doeth the works" (John 14:10). And He prayed to His Father, not only for His disciples, but for those who should believe on Him through their word, "That they all may be one; as thou, Father, art in me, and I in thee, that they also may be one in us: that the world may believe that thou hast sent me" (John 17:21). Oh, what an inheritance is ours when the very nature, the very righteousness, the very power of the Father and the Son are made real in us. This is God's purpose, and as we by faith lay hold on the purpose we shall be ever conscious of the fact that greater is He that is in us than he that is in the world. The purpose of all scripture is to move us on to this wonderful and blessed elevation of faith where our constant experience is the manifestation of God's life and power through us.

Peter goes on writing to these who have obtained like precious faith, saying, "Grace and peace be multiplied unto you through the knowledge of God, and of Jesus our Lord" (2 Peter 1:2). We can have the multiplication of this grace and peace only as we live in the realm of faith. Abraham attained to the place where he became a friend of God, on no other line than that of believing God. He believed God and God counted that to him for righteousness. Righteousness was imputed to him on no other ground than that he believed God. Can this be true of anybody else? Yes, every person in the whole wide world who is saved by faith is blessed with faithful Abraham. The promise which came to him because he believed God was that in him all the families of the earth should be blessed. When we believe God there is no knowing where the blessing of our faith will end.

Some are tied up because, when they are prayed for, the thing that they are expecting does not come off the same night. They say they believe, but you can see that they are really in turmoil of unbelief. Abraham believed God. You can hear him saying to Sarah, "Sarah, there is no life in you and there is nothing in me, but God has promised us a son and I believe God." And that kind of faith is a joy to our Father in heaven.

One day I was having a meeting in Bury, in Lancashire, England. A young woman was present who came from a place called Ramsbottom, to be healed of goiter. Before she came she said, "I am going to be healed of this goiter, Mother." After one meeting she came forward and was prayed for. The next meeting she got up and testified that she had been wonderfully healed, and she said, "I shall be so happy to go and tell Mother that I have been wonderfully healed." She went to her home and testified how wonderfully she had been healed, and the next year when we were having the convention she came again. To the natural view it looked as though the goiter was just as big as ever; but that young woman was believing God and she was soon on her feet giving her testimony, and saying, "I was here last year and the Lord wonderfully healed me. I want to tell you that this has been the best year of my life." She seemed to be greatly blessed in that meeting and she went home to testify more strongly than ever that the Lord had healed her.

She believed God. The third year she was at the meeting again, and some people who looked at her said, "How big that goiter has become." But when the time came for testimony she was up on her feet and testified, "Two years ago the Lord gloriously healed me of goiter. Oh, I had a most wonderful healing. It is grand to be healed by the power of God." That day someone remonstrated with her and said, "People will think there is something the matter with you. Why don't you look in the glass? You will see your goiter is bigger than ever." That good woman went to the Lord about it and said, "Lord, You so wonderfully healed me two years ago. Won't You show all the people that You healed me?" She went to sleep peacefully that night still believing God and when she came down the next day there was not a trace or a mark of that goiter.

God's Word is from everlasting to everlasting. His Word cannot fail. God's Word is true and when we rest in the fact of its truth, what mighty results we can get. Faith never looks in the glass. Faith has a glass into which it can look. It is the glass of the perfect law of liberty.

> *...whoso looketh into the perfect law of liberty, and continueth therein, he being not a forgetful hearer, but a doer of the work, this man shall be blessed in his deed.*
>
> *James 1:25*

To the man who looks into this perfect law of God, all darkness is removed and he sees his completeness in Christ. There is no darkness in faith. There is only darkness in nature. Darkness only exists when the natural is put in the place of the divine.

Not only is grace multiplied to us through knowledge of God and of Jesus Christ, but peace also. As we really know our God and Jesus Christ whom He has sent, we will have peace multiplied to us even in the multiplied fires of ten thousand Nebuchadnezzars. It will be multiplied to us even though we are put into the den of lions, and we will live with joy in the midst of the whole thing. What was the difference between Daniel and the king that night when Daniel was put into the den of lions? Daniel knew, but the king was experimenting. The king came around the next morning and cried, "...O Daniel, servant of the living God, is thy God, whom thou servest continually, able to deliver thee from the lions?" (Daniel 6:20). Daniel answered, "My God hath sent his angel, and hath shut the lions' mouths..." (v. 22). The thing was done. It was done when Daniel prayed with his windows open toward heaven. All our victories are won before we go into the fight. Prayer links us on to our lovely God, our abounding God, our multiplying God. Oh, I love Him! He is so wonderful!

You will note, as you read these first two verses of the first chapter of the second epistle of Peter, that this grace and peace are multiplied through the knowledge of God, but that first our faith comes through the righteousness of God. Note that righteousness comes first and knowledge afterwards. It cannot be otherwise. If you expect any revelation of God apart from holiness, you will have only a mixture. Holiness opens the door to all the treasures of God. He must first bring us to the place where we, like our Lord, love righteousness and hate iniquity, before He opens up to us these good treasures. When we regard iniquity in our hearts the Lord will not hear us, and it is only as we are made righteous and pure and holy through the precious blood of God's Son that we can enter into this life of holiness and righteousness in the Son. It is the righteousness of our Lord Himself made real in us as our faith is stayed in Him.

After I was baptized with the Holy Ghost, the Lord gave me a blessed revelation. I saw Adam and Eve turned out of the garden for their disobedience and unable to partake of the tree of life, for the cherubim with flaming sword kept them away from this tree. When I was baptized I saw that I had begun to eat of this tree of life and I saw that the flaming sword was all round about. It was there to keep the devil away. Oh, what privileges are ours when we are born of God. How marvelously He keeps us so that the wicked one touches us not. I see a place in God where Satan dare not come. Hidden in God. And He invites us all to come and share this wonderful hidden place where our lives are hid with Christ in God, where we dwell in the secret place of the Most High and abide under the shadow of the Almighty. God has this place for you in this blessed realm of grace.

Peter goes on to say, "According as his divine power hath given unto us all things that pertain unto life and godliness, through the knowledge of him that hath called us to glory and virtue" (2 Peter 1:3). God is calling us to this realm of glory and virtue where, as we feed on His exceeding great and precious promises, we are made partakers of the divine nature.

Faith is the substance of things hoped for right here in this life. It is right here that God would have us partake of His divine nature. It is nothing less than the life of the Lord Himself imparted and flowing into our whole beings, so that our very body is quickened, so that every tissue and every drop of blood and our bones and joints and marrow receive this divine life. I believe that the Lord wants this divine life to flow right into our natural bodies, this law of the Spirit of life in Christ Jesus that makes us free from the law of sin and death. God wants to establish our faith that we will lay hold on this divine life, this divine nature of the Son of God, so that our spirit and soul and body will be sanctified wholly and preserved unto the coming of the Lord Jesus Christ.

When that woman was healed of the issue of blood, Jesus perceived that power had gone out of Him. The woman's faith laid hold and this power was imparted and immediately the woman's being was surcharged with life and her weakness departed. The impartation of this power produces everything you need; but it comes only as our faith moves out for its impartation. Faith is the victory. If thou canst believe, it is thine.

I suffered for many years from piles, till my whole body was thoroughly weak; the blood used to gush from me. One day I got desperate and I took a bottle of oil and anointed myself. I said to the Lord, "Do what You want to, quickly." I was healed at that very moment. God wants us to have an activity of faith that dares to believe God. There is what seems like faith, an appearance of faith, but real faith believes God right to the end.

What was the difference between Zacharias and Mary? The angel came to Zacharias and told him, "...thy wife Elisabeth shall bear thee a son..." (Luke 1:13). Zacharias was there in the holy place, but he began to question this message, saying, "...I am an old man and my wife well stricken in years" (v. 18). Gabriel rebuked him for his unbelief and told him, "...thou shalt be dumb, and not able to speak, until the day that these things shall be performed, because thou believest not my words..." (v. 20). But note the contrast when the angel came to Mary. She said, "Behold the handmaid of the Lord; be it unto me according to thy word..." (Luke 1:38). And Elisabeth greeted Mary with the words, "blessed is she that believed: for there shall be a performance of those things which were told her from the Lord" (v. 45). God would have us to lay hold on His Word in like manner. He would have us to come with boldness of faith declaring, "You have promised it, Lord. Now do it." God rejoices when we manifest a faith that holds Him to His Word. Can we get there?

The Lord has called us to this glory and virtue: and, as our faith lays hold on Him, we shall see this in manifestation. I remember one day I was holding an open-air meeting. My uncle came to that meeting and said, "Aunt Mary would like to see Smith before she dies." I went to see her and she was assuredly dying. I said, "Lord, can't You do something?" All I did was this, to stretch out my hands and lay them on her. It seemed as though there was an immediate impartation of the glory and virtue of the Lord. Aunt Mary cried, "It is going all over my body." And that day she was made perfectly whole.

One day I was preaching and a man brought a boy who was done up in bandages. The boy was in irons and it was impossible for him to walk and it was difficult for them to get him to the platform. They passed him over about six seats. The power of the Lord was present to heal, and it entered right into the child as I placed my hands on him. The child cried, "Daddy, it is going all over me." They stripped the boy and found nothing imperfect in him.

The Lord would have us to be walking epistles of His Word. Jesus is the Word and is the power in us, and it is His desire to work in and through us His own good pleasure. We must believe that He is in us. There are boundless possibilities for us if we dare to act in God and dare to believe that the wonderful virtue of our living Christ shall be made manifest through us as we lay our hands on the sick in His name.

The exceeding great and precious promises of the Word are given to us that we might be partakers of the divine nature. I feel the Holy Ghost is grieved with us because, when we know these things, we do not do greater exploits for God. Does not the Holy Ghost show us wide-open doors of opportunity? Shall we not let God take us on to greater things? Shall we not believe God to take us on to greater manifestations of His power? His call for us is to forget the things that are behind, and reach forth unto the things which are before and to press toward the mark for the prize of the high calling of God in Christ Jesus.

Published in *The Pentecostal Evangel*

PAUL'S CONVERSION AND HIS BAPTISM

April 26, 1924

ead Acts 9:1-22. Saul was probably the greatest persecutor that the early Christian had. We read that he made havoc of the church, entering into every house, and hating men and women, committed them to prison. At this time we find him breathing out threatenings and slaughter against the disciples of the Lord. He was on his way to Damascus for the purpose of destroying the church there. How did God deal with such a one? We should have dealt with him in judgment. God dealt with him in mercy. Oh, the wondrous love of God! He loved the saints at Damascus and the way He preserved them was through the salvation of the man who purposed to scatter and destroy them. Our God delights to be merciful and His grace is vouchsafed daily to both sinner and saint. He shows mercy to all. If we would but realize it, we are only alive today through the grace of our God.

More and more I see that it is through the grace of God that I am preserved every day. It is when we realize the goodness of God that we are brought to repentance. Here was Saul, with letters from the high priest, hastening to Damascus. He was struck down and there came to his vision a light, a light that was brighter than the sun. As he fell speechless to the ground he heard a voice saying to him, "Saul, Saul, why persecutest thou Me?" He answered, "Who art thou, Lord?" And the answer came back, "I am Jesus whom thou persecutest." And he cried, "Lord, what wilt thou have me to do?" (Acts 9:4-6).

I do not want to bring any word of condemnation to anyone, but I know that there are many who have felt very much as Saul felt against the children of God, especially those who have received the Pentecostal baptism. I know that many people tell us "You are mad"; but the truth is that the children of God are the only people who are really glad. We are glad inside and we are glad outside. Our gladness flows from the inside. God has filled us with joy unspeakable and full of glory. We are so happy about what we have received that if it were not for the desire to keep a little decent, we might be doing awful things. This is probably how Paul himself felt when he refers to being "beside ourselves" in the Lord. This joy in the Holy Ghost is beyond anything else. And this joy of the Lord is our strength.

As Saul went down to Damascus he thought he would do wonderful things with that bunch of letters he had from the high priest. But I think he dropped them all on the road, and if he ever wanted to pick them up he was not able for he lost his sight. And the men that were with him lost their speech — they were speechless — but they led him to Damascus.

There are some people who have an idea that it is only preachers who can know the will of God. But the Lord had a disciple in Damascus, a man behind the scenes, who lived in a place where God could talk to him. His ears were open. He was one who listened in to the things from heaven. Oh, this is so much more marvelous than anything you can hear on earth. It was to this man that the Lord appeared in a vision. He told him to go down to the street called Straight and inquire for Saul. And He told him that Saul had seen in a vision a man named Ananias coming in and putting his hand on him that he might receive his sight. Ananias protested, "...Lord, I have heard by many of this man, how much evil he hath done to thy saints at Jerusalem: And here he hath authority from the chief priests to bind all that call on thy name" (Acts 9:13,14). But the Lord reassured Ananias that Saul was a chosen vessel, and Ananias, nothing doubting, went on his errand of mercy.

The Lord had told Ananias concerning Saul, "...behold, he prayeth" (Acts 9:11). Repentant prayer is always heard in heaven. The Lord never despises a broken and contrite heart. And to Saul was given this vision that was soon to be a reality, the vision of Ananias coming to pray for him that he might receive his sight.

I was at one time in the city of Belfast. I had been preaching there and had a free day. I had received a number of letters and I was looking through them. There were about twenty needy cases in that city, cases that I was asked to visit. As I was looking through my letters a man came up to me and said, "Are you visiting the sick?" He pointed me to a certain house and told me to go to it and there I would see a very sick woman. I went to the house and I saw a very helpless woman propped up in bed. I knew that humanly speaking she was beyond all help. She was breathing with short, sharp breaths as if every breath would be her last. I cried to the Lord and said, "Lord, tell me what to do." The Lord said to me, "Read the fifty-third chapter of Isaiah." I opened my Bible and did as I was told. I read down to the fifth verse of this chapter, when all of a sudden the woman shouted, "I am healed! I am healed!" I was amazed at this sudden exclamation and asked her to tell me what had happened. She said, "Two weeks ago I was cleaning house and I strained my heart very badly. Two physicians have been to see me, but they both told me there was no help. But last night the Lord gave me a vision. I saw you come right into my bedroom. I saw you praying. I saw you open your Bible at the fifty-third chapter of Isaiah. When you got down to the fifth verse and read the words, 'With His stripes we are healed.' I saw myself wonderfully healed. That was a vision, now it is a fact."

I do thank God that visions have not ceased. The Holy Ghost can give visions, and we may expect them in these last days. God willeth not the death of any sinner, and He will use all kinds of means for their salvation. I do praise God for this Gospel. It is always so entreating. That is such a wooing message, "Look unto Me, and be ye saved, all ye ends of the earth." Oh, what a Gospel! Whatever people say about it, it is surely a message of love.

Ananias went down to the house on Straight Street, and he laid his hands on the one who had before been a blasphemer and a persecutor and he said to him, "Brother Saul, the Lord, even Jesus, that appeared unto thee in the way as thou camest, hath sent me, that thou mightest receive thy sight, and be filled with the Holy Ghost" (Acts 9:17). He recognized him as a brother that already his soul had been saved and that had come into relationship with the Father and with all the family of God, but there was something necessary beyond this. The Lord had not forgotten his physical condition and there was healing for him. But there was something beyond this. It was the filling with the Holy Ghost. Oh, it always seems to me that the Gospel is robbed of its divine glory when we overlook this marvelous truth of the baptism of the Holy Ghost. To be saved is wonderful, to be a new creature, to have passed from death unto life, to have the witness of the Spirit that you are born of God, all this is unspeakably precious. But whereas we have the well of salvation bubbling up, we need to go on to a place where from within us shall flow rivers of living water. The Lord Jesus showed us very plainly that, if we believe on Him, from within us should flow rivers of living water. And this He spake of the Spirit. The Lord wants us to be filled with the Spirit, to have the manifestation of the presence of His Spirit, the manifestation that is indeed given to profit withal, and for us to be His mouthpiece and speak as the very oracles of God.

God chose Saul. What was he? A blasphemer. A persecutor. That is grace. Our God is gracious and He loves to show His mercy to the vilest and worst of men. There was a notable character in the town in which I lived who was known as the worst man in the town. He was so vile, and his language was so horrible, that even wicked men could not stand it. In England they have what is known as the public hangman who has to perform all the executions. This man held that appointment and he told me later that he believed that when he performed the execution of men who had committed murder, that the demon power that was in them would come upon him and that in consequence he was possessed with a legion of demons. His life was so miserable that he purposed to make an end of life. He went down to a certain depot and purchased a ticket. The English trains are much different to the American. In every coach there are a number of small compartments and it is easy for anyone who wants to commit suicide to open the door of his compartment and throw himself out of the train. This man purposed to throw himself out of the train in a certain tunnel just as the train coming from an opposite direction would be about to dash past and he thought this would be a quick end to his life.

There was a young man at the depot that night who had been saved the night before. He was all on fire to get others saved and purposed in his heart that every day of his life he would get someone saved. He saw this dejected hangsman and began to speak to him about his soul. He brought him down to our mission and there he came under a mighty conviction of sin. For two and a half hours he was literally sweating under conviction and you could see a vapor rising up from him. At the end of two and a half hours he was graciously saved.

I said, "Lord, tell me what to do." The Lord said, "Don't leave him, go home with him." I went to his house. When he saw his wife he said, "God has saved me." The wife broke down and she too was graciously saved. I tell you there was a difference in that home. Even the cat knew the difference. Previous to this that cat would always run away when that hangsman came into the door. But that night that he was saved the cat jumped on to his knee and went to sleep.

There were two sons in that house and one of them said to his mother, "Mother, what is up in our house? It was never like this before. It is so peaceful. What is it?" She told him, "Father has got saved." The other son was struck with the same thing.

I took this man to many special services and the power of God was on him for many days. He would give his testimony and as he grew in grace he desired to preach the Gospel. He became an evangelist and hundreds and hundreds were brought to a saving knowledge of the Lord Jesus Christ through his ministry. The grace of God is sufficient for the vilest, and He can take the wickedest of men and make them monuments of His grace. He did this with Saul of Tarsus at the very time he was breathing out threatenings and slaughter against the disciples of the Lord. He did it with Berry the hangsman. He will do it for hundreds more in response to our cries.

You will notice that when Ananias came into that house he called the one-time enemy of the Gospel, "Brother Saul." He recognized that in those three days a blessed work had been wrought and that he had been brought into relationship with the Father and with the Lord Jesus Christ. Was not this enough? No, there was something further, and for this purpose the Lord had sent him to that house. The Lord Jesus had sent him to that house to put his hands upon this newly saved brother that he might receive his sight and be filled with the Holy Ghost. You say, "But it does not say that he spoke in tongues." We know that Paul did speak in tongues; that he spoke in tongues more than all the Corinthians. In those early days they were so near the time of that first Pentecostal outpouring that they would never have been satisfied with anyone receiving the baptism unless they received it according to the original pattern given on the day of Pentecost. When Peter was relating what took place in the house of Cornelius at Caesarea he said, "And as I began to speak, the Holy Ghost fell on them, as on us at the beginning" (Acts 11:15). Later, speaking of this incident, he said, "...God, which knoweth the hearts, bare them witness, giving them the Holy Ghost, even as he did unto us; And put no difference between us and them, purifying their hearts by faith" (Acts 15:8,9). And we know from the account of what took place at Cornelius' household that when the Holy Ghost fell "...they heard them speak with tongues, and magnify God" (Acts 10:46). Many people think that God does make a difference between us and those at the beginning. But they have no Scripture for this. When anyone receives the gift of the Holy Ghost, there will assuredly be no difference between his experience today and that which was given on the day of Pentecost. And I cannot believe that, when Saul was filled with the Holy Ghost the Lord made any difference in the experience that He gave him from the experience that He had given to Peter and the rest a short while before.

It was about sixteen years ago that a man came to me and said, "Wigglesworth, do you know what is happening in Sunderland? People are being baptized in the Holy Ghost exactly the same way as the disciples were on the day of Pentecost." I said, "I would like to go." I immediately took a train and went to Sunderland. I went to the meetings and said, "I want to hear these tongues." I was told, "When you receive the baptism in the Holy Ghost, you will speak in tongues." One man said, "Brother, when I received the baptism I spoke in tongues." I said, "Let's hear you." He could not speak in tongues to order, he could only speak as the Spirit gave him utterance and so my curiosity was not satisfied.

I saw these people were very earnest and I became quite hungry. I was anxious to see this new manifestation of the Spirit and I would be questioning all the time and spoiling a lot of the meetings. One man said to me, "I am a missionary and I have come here to seek the baptism in the Holy Ghost, I am waiting on the Lord, but you have come in and are spoiling everything with your questions." I began to argue with him and our love became so hot that when we walked home he walked on one side of the road and I the other.

That night there was to be a tarrying meeting and I purposed to go. I changed my clothes and left my key in the clothes I had taken off. As we came from the meeting in the middle of the night I found I did not have my key upon me and this missionary brother said, "You will have to come and sleep with me." But do you think we went to bed that night? Oh, no, we spent the night in prayer. We received a precious shower from above. The breakfast bell rang, but that was nothing to me. For four days I wanted nothing but God. If you only knew the unspeakable wonderful blessing of being filled with the Third Person of the Trinity, you would set aside everything else to tarry for this infilling.

I was about to leave Sunderland. This revival was taking place in the vestry of an Episcopal church. I went to the Vicarage that day to say goodby and I said to Sister Boddy, the vicar's wife, "I am going away, but I have not received the tongues yet." She said, "It isn't tongues you need, but the baptism." I said, "I have the baptism, Sister, but I would like to have you lay hands on me before I leave." She laid her hands on me and then had to go out of the room. The fire fell. It was a wonderful time as I was there with God alone. It seemed as though God bathed me in power. I was given a wonderful vision. I was conscious of the cleaning of the precious blood and cried out, "Clean! Clean! Clean!" I was filled with the joy of the consciousness of the cleansing. I saw the Lord Jesus Christ. I saw the empty cross and I saw Him exalted at the right hand of God the Father. As I was extolling, magnifying, and praising Him I was speaking in tongues as the Spirit of God gave me utterance. I knew now that I had received the real baptism in the Holy Ghost.

And so Saul was filled with the Holy Ghost and in the later chapters of the Acts of the apostles we see the result of this infilling. Oh, what a difference it makes. When I got home my wife said to me, "So you think you have received the baptism of the Holy Ghost. Why, I am as much baptized in the Holy Ghost as you are." We had sat on the platform together for twenty years but that night she said, "Tonight you will go by yourself." I said, "All right." As I went up to the platform that night the Lord gave me the first few verses of the sixty-first chapter of Isaiah, "The Spirit of the Lord God is upon me; because the Lord hath anointed me to preach good tidings unto the meek; he hath sent me to bind up the brokenhearted, to proclaim liberty to the captives, and the opening of the prison to them that are bound" (v. 1). My wife went back to one of the furthermost seats in the hall and she said to herself, "I will watch it." I preached that night on the subject the Lord had given me and I told what the Lord had done for me. I told the people that I was going to have God in my life and I would gladly suffer a thousand deaths rather than forfeit this wonderful infilling that had come to me. My wife was very restless, just as if she were sitting on a red-hot poker. She was moved in a new way and said, "That is not my Smith that is preaching. Lord, You have done something for him." As soon as I had finished, the secretary of the mission got up and said, "Brethren, I want what the leader of our mission has got." He tried to sit down but missed his seat and fell on the floor. There were soon fourteen of them on the floor, my own wife included. We did not know what to do, but the Holy Ghost got hold of the situation and the fire fell. A revival started and the crowds came. It was only the beginning of the flood-tide of blessing. We had touched the reservoir of the Lord's life and power. Since that time the Lord has taken me to many different lands and I have witnessed many blessed outpourings of God's Holy Spirit.

The grace of God that was given to the persecuting Saul is available for you. The same Holy Ghost infilling he received is likewise available. Do not rest satisfied with any lesser experience than the baptism that the disciples received on the day of Pentecost, then move on to a life of continuous receiving of more and more of the blessed Spirit of God.

Published in *The Pentecostal Evangel*

THE POWER TO BIND AND TO LOOSE

May 1924

Bible reading, Matthew 16.

The Pharisees and Sadducees had been tempting Jesus to show them a sign from heaven. He showed them that they could discern the signs that appeared on the face of the sky, and yet they could not discern the signs of the times. He would give them no sign to satisfy their unbelieving curiosity, remarking that a wicked and adulterous generation sought after a sign and that no sign should be given to them but the sign of the prophet Jonah. A wicked and adulterous generation stumbles over the story of Jonah, but faith can see in that story a wonderful picture of the death, burial and resurrection of our Lord Jesus Christ.

After Jesus had departed from the Pharisees, and had come to the other side of the lake, He said to His disciples, "Take heed and beware of the leaven of the Pharisees and of the Sadducees" (Matthew 16:6). The disciples began to reason among themselves, and all they could think of was that they had taken no bread. What were they to do? Then Jesus uttered these words, "O ye of little faith..." (v. 8). He had been so long with them, and yet they were still a great disappointment to Him because of their lack of comprehension and of faith. They could not grasp the profound spiritual truth He was bringing to them and could only think about having brought no bread. "O ye of little faith...Do ye not yet understand, neither remember the five loaves of the five thousand, and how many baskets ye took up? Neither the seven loaves of the four thousand, and how many baskets ye took up?" (Matthew 16:8,9).

Do you keep in memory how God has been gracious in the past? God has done wonderful things for all of us. If we keep these things in memory we shall become strong in faith. We should be able to defy Satan in everything. Remember all the way the Lord has led. When Joshua passed over Jordan on dry land he told the people to pick up twelve stones and pitch them in Gilgal, and these were to keep the children of Israel in constant memory that they came over Jordan on dry land. How many times had Jesus shown to His disciples the mightiness of His power, and yet failed in faith right here?

At one time Jesus said to Peter, "What thinkest thou, Simon? of whom do the kings of the earth take custom or tribute? of their own children, or of strangers?" (Matthew 17:25). Peter said, "Of strangers" (v. 26). Then Jesus said, "Then are the children free. Notwithstanding, lest we should offend them, go thou to the sea, and cast an hook, and take up the fish that first cometh up; and when thou has opened his mouth, thou shalt find a piece of money: that take, and give unto them for me and thee" (vv. 26,27). Peter had been at the fishing business all his life but he never had caught a fish with any silver in its mouth. But the Master does not want us to reason things out — for carnal reasoning will always land us in a bog of unbelief — but just to obey. "This is a hard job," Peter must have said, as he put the bait on his hook, "but since You told me to do it, I'll try," and he cast his line into the sea. There were millions of fish in the sea, but every fish had to stand aside and leave that bait alone, and let that fish with the piece of money in his mouth come up and take it.

Do you not see that the words of the Master are the instruction of faith? It is impossible for anything to miss that Jesus says. All His words are spirit and life. If you will only have faith in Him you will find that every word that God gives is life. You cannot be in close touch with Him, and you cannot receive His Word in simple faith without feeling the effect of it in your body as well as in your spirit and soul.

A woman came to me in Cardiff, Wales, who was filled with ulceration. She had fallen in the streets twice through this trouble. She came to the meeting and it seemed as if the evil power within her purposed to kill her right there, for she fell and the power of the devil was rending her sore. She was helpless and it seemed as if she had expired. I cried, "Oh, God, help this woman." Then I rebuked the evil power in the name of Jesus, and instantly the Lord healed her. She rose up and made a great to-do. She felt the power of God in her body and wanted to testify all the time. After three days she went to another place and began to testify about the Lord's power to heal. She came to me and said, "I want to tell everyone about the Lord's healing power. Have you no tracts on this subject?" I handed her my Bible and said, "Matthew, Mark, Luke, and John — they are the best tracts on healing. They are full of incidents about the working and power of Jesus. They will never fail to accomplish the work of God if people will but read and believe them."

That is where men lack. All lack of faith is due to not feeding on God's Word. You need it every day. How can you enter into a life of faith? Feed on the living Christ of whom this Word is full. As you get taken up with the glorious fact and the wondrous presence of the living Christ, the faith of God will spring up within you. "...faith cometh by hearing, and hearing by the word of God" (Romans 10:17).

Jesus asked His disciples what men were saying about Him. They told Him, "Some say that thou art John the Baptist: some, Elias; and others, Jeremias, or one of the prophets" (Matthew 16:14). Then He put the question to see what they thought about it, "But whom say ye that I am?" (v. 15). Peter answered, "Thou art the Christ, the Son of the living God" (v. 16). And Jesus said to him, "Blessed art thou, Simon Barjona: for flesh and blood hath not revealed it unto thee, but my Father which is in heaven" (v. 17).

It is so simple. Whom do you say He is? Who is He? Do you say with Peter, "Thou art the Christ, the Son of the living God"? (v. 16). How can you know this. He is to be revealed. Flesh and blood does not reveal this. It is an inward revelation. God wants to reveal His Son within us and make us conscious of an inward presence. Then you can cry, "I know He's mine. He is mine! He is mine!" "...neither knoweth any man the Father, save the Son, and he to whomsoever the Son will reveal Him" (Matthew 11:27). Seek God until you get from Him a mighty revelation of the Son, until that inward revelation moves you on to the place where you are always steadfast, unmovable, and always abounding in the work of the Lord.

There is a wonderful power in this revelation. "...upon this rock I will build my church; and the gates of hell shall not prevail against it. And I will give unto thee the keys of the kingdom of heaven: and whatsoever thou shalt bind on earth shall be bound in heaven: and whatsoever thou shalt loose on earth shall be loosed in heaven" (Matthew 16:18,19). Was Peter the rock? No. A few minutes later he was so full of the devil that Christ had to say to him, "Get thee behind me, Satan: thou art an offence unto me..." (v. 23). This rock was Christ. He is the Rock and there are many scriptures to confirm this. And to every one that knows that He is the Christ He gives the key of faith, the power to bind and the power to loose. Stablish your hearts with this fact. God wants you to have the inward revelation of this truth and of all the power contained in it.

> *...upon this rock I will build my church; and the gates of hell shall not prevail against it.*
>
> *Matthew 16:18*

God is pleased when we stand upon this Rock and believe that He is unchangeable. If you will dare to believe God, you can defy all the powers of evil. There have been times in my experience when I have dared to believe Him, and I have had the most remarkable experiences.

One day I was traveling in a railway train, and there were two people in the car that were very sick, a mother and her daughter. I said to them, "Look, I've something in this bag that will cure every case in the world. It has never been known to fail." They became very much interested, and I went on telling them more and more about this remedy that never failed to remove disease and sickness. At last they summoned up courage to ask for a dose. So I opened my bag, took out my Bible, and read them that verse, "...I am the Lord that healeth thee" (Exodus 15:26). It never fails.

He will always heal you if you dare believe Him. Men are searching everywhere today for things with which they can heal themselves, and they ignore the fact that the balm of Gilead is within easy reach. As I talked about this wonderful Physician, the faith of both mother and daughter went out toward Him, and He healed them both right in the train.

God has made His Word so precious that, if I could not get another copy, I would not part with my Bible for all the world. There is life in the Word. There is virtue in it. I find Christ in it; and He is the One I need for spirit, soul, and body. It tells me of the power of His name and of the power of His blood for cleansing. The lions may lack and suffer hunger, "…but they that seek the Lord shall not want any good thing" (Psalm 34:10).

A man came to me at one time, brought by a little woman. I said, "What's up with him?" She said, "He gets situations, but he fails every time. He is a slave to alcohol and nicotine poison. He is a bright, intelligent man in most things, but he goes under to these two things." I was reminded of the words of the Master, giving us power to bind and to loose, and I told him to put out his tongue. In the name of the Lord Jesus Christ, I cast out the evil powers that gave him the taste for these things. I said to him, "Man, you are free today." He was unsaved, but when he realized the power of the Lord in delivering him, he came to the services, publicly acknowledged that he was a sinner, and the Lord saved and baptized him. A few days later I asked, "How are things with you?" He said, "I'm delivered." God has given us the power to bind and the power to loose.

Another person came and said, "What can you do for me? I have had sixteen operations and have had my eardrums taken out." I said, "God has not forgotten how to make eardrums." I anointed her and prayed, asking the Lord that the eardrums should be replaced. She was so deaf that I do not think she would have heard if a cannon had gone off. She was as deaf as it was possible to be afterwards. But she saw other people getting healed and rejoicing. Had God forgotten to be gracious? Was His power just the same? She came the next night and said, "I have come to believe God tonight." Take care you do not come any other way. I prayed for her again and commanded her ears to be loosed in the name of Jesus. She believed, and the moment she believed she heard. She ran and jumped upon a chair and began to preach. Later I let a pin drop and she heard it fall. God can give drums to ears. All things are possible with God. God can save the worst.

Discouraged one, cast your burden on the Lord. He will sustain you. Look unto Him and be lightened. Look unto Him now.

Published in *Triumphs of Faith*

FAITH IS THE VICTORY
June 1924

I am pleased to be with you this morning. It is a great joy to be with the saints of God, especially those who have come into "like precious faith" to believe that God is Almighty. Beloved, we may be in a very low ebb of the tide but it is good to be in a place where the tide can rise. I pray that the Holy Ghost shall so have His right of way that there will not be one person in the test who shall not be moved upon by the Spirit of God. Everything depends upon our being filled with the Holy Ghost. And there is nothing you can come short of if the Holy Ghost is the prime mover in your thoughts and life, for He has a plan greater than ours and if He can only get us in readiness for His plan to be worked out, it will be wonderful.

Read Hebrews 11:1-10. This is a very remarkable Word to us, "Faith." Everything depends upon our believing God. If we are saved, it is only because God's Word says so. We cannot rest upon our feelings. We cannot do anything without a living faith. It is surely God Himself who comes to us in the person of His beloved Son and so strengthens us that we realize that our body is surrounded by the power of God, lifting us into the almightiness of His power. All things are possible to us in God. The purpose of God for us is that we might be in the earth for a manifestation of His glory, that every time satanic power is confronted, God might be able to say of us as He did of Job, "What do you think about him?" God wants us so manifested in His divine plan in the earth that Satan shall have to hear God. The joy of the Lord can be so manifested in us in this meeting that we shall be so filled with God that we shall be able to rebuke the power of the devil.

God has showed me in the night watches that everything that is not of faith is sin. I have seen this in the Word so many times. God wants so to bring us in harmony with His will that we will see that if we do not come right up to the Word of God, to believe it all, there is something in us that is not purely sanctified to accept the fulness of His Word. Many people are putting their human wisdom right in the place of God and God is not able to give the best because the human is so confronting God. God is not able to get the best through us until the human is dissolved.

"...faith is the substance of things hoped for..." (Hebrews 11:1). I want to speak about "substance," it is a remarkable word. Many people come to me and say, "I want things tangible. I want something to appeal to my human reasoning." Brother, everything that you cannot see is eternal. Everything you can see is natural and fadeth away. Everything you see in this tent will fade away and will be consumed but that which you cannot see, which is more real than you, is the substance of all things, which is God in the human soul, mightier than you by a million times. Beloved, we have to go out and be faced with all evil powers. Even your own heart, if it is not entirely immersed in the Spirit, will deceive you. So I am praying that there shall not be a vestige of your human nature that shall not be clothed upon with the power of the Spirit. I pray that the Spirit of the living God may be so imparted to your heart that nothing shall in any way be able to move you after this meeting. "...faith is the substance of things hoped for, the evidence of things not seen" (Hebrews 11:1).

God has mightily blessed to me First Peter 1:23:

> *Being born again, not of corruptible seed, but of incorruptible, by the word of God, which liveth and abideth for ever.*

We read, "In the beginning was the Word, and the Word was with God, and the Word was God" (John 1:1). Then we read that "...the Word was made flesh, and dwelt among us, (and we beheld his glory, the glory as of the only begotten of the Father,) full of grace and truth (John 1:14). And He is in the midst of us manifested. His disciples went out and manifested that they had seen and handled Him, the Word of life.

If you turn to Second Peter 1:4, you will find that we have received His divine nature which is infinite power, infinite knowledge, infinite pleasure, infinite revelation. But people are missing it because we have failed to apply it. But God is making up a people who will have to be a "firstfruits." By simple faith you entered in and claimed your rights and became Christians, being born again because you believed. But there is something different in knowing God, in having fellowship with Him; there are heights and depths in this wonderful blessing in the knowledge of Him. Human weakness, helplessness, impossibility. Everybody can see Jacob, but do not forget, beloved, that God changed Jacob into Israel. The Holy Ghost wants everybody to see the unveiling of Jesus. The unveiling of Jesus is to take away yourself and to place Himself in us; to take away all your human weakness and put within you that wonderful Word of eternal power, of eternal life, which makes you believe that all things are possible.

A man travelled with me from Montreal to Vancouver and then on ship to New Zealand. He was a dealer of race horses. It seemed he could not leave me. He was frivolous and talked about races, but he could not keep his end up. I did not struggle to keep up my end because mine is a living power. No person who has Jesus as the inward power of his body needs to be trembling when Satan comes around. All he has to do is to stand still and see the salvation of the Lord.

This man entered into a good deal of frivolity and talk of this world. Touching a certain island of the Fiji group, we all went out and God gave me wonderful liberty in preaching. The man came back afterwards; he did not go to his racing and card-playing chums. He came stealing back to the ship and with tears in his eyes, he said, "I am dying. I have been bitten by a reptile." His skin had turned to a dark green and his leg was swollen. "Can you help me?" he asked. If we only knew the power of God! If we are in a place of substance, of reality, of ideal purpose, it is not human; we are dealing with almightiness. I have a present God, I have a living faith, and the living faith is the Word and the Word is life, and the Word is equipment, and the Lord is just the same yesterday, and today, and forever (Hebrews 13:8). Placing my hand upon the serpent bite, I said, "In the name of Jesus, come out!" He looked at me and the tears came. The swelling went down before his eyes and he was perfect in a moment.

Yes, "Faith is the substance of things hoped for, the evidence of things not seen." Faith is that which came into me when I believed. I was born of the incorruptible Word by the living virtue, life and personality of God. I was instantly changed from nature to grace. I became a servant of God, and I became an enemy of unrighteousness.

The Holy Ghost would have us clearly understand that we are a million times bigger than we know. Every Christian in this place has no conception of what you are. My heart is so big that I want to look in your faces and tell you if you only knew what you had, your body would scarcely be able to contain you. Oh, that God shall so bring us into divine attractiveness by His almightiness that the whole of our bodies shall wake up to resurrection force, to the divine, inward flow of eternal power coursing through the human frame.

Let us read Ephesians 4:7,8,11-13:

> But unto every one of us is given grace according to the measure of the gift of Christ. Wherefore he saith, When he ascended up on high, he led captivity captive, and gave gifts unto men...And he gave some, apostles; and some, prophets; and some, evangelists; and some, pastors and teachers; For the perfecting of the saints, for the work of the ministry, for the edifying of the body of Christ: Till we all come in the unity of the faith, and of the knowledge of the Son of God, unto a perfect man, unto the measure of the stature of the fulness of Christ.

God took you into His pavilion and began to clothe upon you and give you the gifts of the Spirit that in that ministry by the power of God you should bring all the Church into the perfect possession of the fulness of Christ. Oh, the wonder of it! Oh, the adaptability of His equipment!

TONGUES AND INTERPRETATION: "God has designed it. In the pavilion of His splendor, with the majesty of His glory He comes, and touching human weakness, beautifies it in the Spirit of holiness till the effectiveness of this wonderful sonship is made manifest in us, till we all become the edification of the fulness of Christ."

I believe God wants something to be in you this morning that could never be unless you cease to be for yourself. God wants that you should be for God, to be for everybody. But, oh, to have the touch of God! Beloved, the Holy Ghost is the Comforter. The Holy Ghost came not to speak of Himself, but He came to unveil Him who said, "Take my yoke upon you, and learn of me; for I am meek and lowly in heart: and ye shall find rest unto your souls" (Matthew 11:29). The Holy Ghost came to thrill thee with resurrection power and that thou shouldest be anointed with fresh oil running over in the splendor of His almightiness. Then right through thee shall come forth a river of divine unction that shall sustain thee in the bitterest place, and quicken the deadest formality and say to the weak, "Be strong" and to them that have no might, "The Lord of hosts is here to comfort thee." God would have us to be like the rising of the sun, filled with the rays of heaven, all the time beaming forth the gladness of the Spirit of the Almighty. Possibility is the greatest thing of your life.

I came in the tent yesterday afternoon. No one but myself could understand my feelings. Was it emotion? No, it was an inward inspiration to find hearts that God had touched and [that had] met me with such love it was almost more than I could bear. I have to thank God for it and take courage that He has been with me in the past, and He will be with me in the future. Brother and sister, I am satisfied that love is the essential. Love is of God; nay, love is God. Love is the Trinity working in the human to break it up that it may be displaced with God's fulness.

When I was ministering to the sick, there came a man amongst the crowd. If you had seen him, your heart would have ached for him. He was shrivelled, weakened, his cheek bones sticking out; eyes sunk, neck all shrivelled — just a form. His coat hung on him as you would put it on some stick. He whispered, for he could only speak with a breath of voice, "Can you help me?" I asked "What is it?" He said that he had had a cancer on his stomach and on the operation table they had taken away the cancer but in the operation they moved the "swallow," so the man could not swallow. He said, "I have tried to take the juice of a cherry today but it would not go down." Then he pulled out a tube about nine inches long, which had a cup at the top. He whispered, "I have a hole in my stomach. As I pour liquid in, my stomach receives that. I have been living three months in that way."

You could call it a shadow of life he was living. Could I help him? Look! This Book can help anybody. This Book is the essence of life. God moves as you believe. This Book is the Word of God. Could I help him? I said,

"On the authority of this Word, this night you shall have a big supper." But he said he could not eat. "Do as I tell you," I answered. "How could it be?" "It is time," I said, "to go and eat a good supper." He went home and told his wife. She could not understand it. She said, "You cannot eat. You cannot swallow." But he whispered, "The man said I had to do it." He got hungry and more hungry and ventured. "I will try it." His wife got it ready. He got a mouth full and it went down just as easy as possible and he went on taking food until he was filled up. Then he and his wife had one of the biggest times of their lives. The next morning he was so full of joy because he had eaten again. He looked down in curiosity to see the hole and found that God had closed it up!

But you ask, "Can He do it for me?" "Yes, if you believe it." Brother, faith is the victory. Here I am, so thankful this morning. Thirty years ago this body you see was sick and helpless and dying. God, in an instant, healed me. I am now sixty-five years within a day or two and so free and healthy; oh, it is wonderful! There are people in this place who ought to be healed in a moment. People who ought to receive the Holy Ghost in a moment. The power of possibility is in the reach of every man. The Holy Ghost is full of the rising tide. Every one of us can be filled to overflowing. God is here with His divine purpose to change our weakness into mighty strength and faith. The Word of God! Oh, brother, sister, have you got it? It is marrow to your bones. It is unction. It is resurrection from every weakness, it is life from the dead.

If there is anything I want to shake you loose from, it is having a word of faith without the power of it. What are we here for? Surely we are not to hear only, we are to obey. Obedience is better than sacrifice. God the Holy Ghost would give us such a revelation of Christ that we would go away as men who had seen the king. We would go away with our faces lit up with the brilliancy of heaven.

How many in this place are willing to believe? The people who would like God to know they are in sincerity and they will do whatever His Spirit tells them, rise up and walk to the front and cry to God until you have all you want. Let God have His way. Touch God this morning. Faith is the victory.

Message at Pentecostal Camp Meeting
Berkeley, California

et us read this morning the third chapter of the First Epistle of John.

SONSHIP

June 2, 1924

This is one of those remarkable passages which is exhaustless. So whatever time the Lord may permit us to be together this morning we shall find that we are still in a place of more hunger for this divine proposition of God. God wants all His believers to understand these words which have been written.

INHERITING THE SCRIPTURES

It is the believer's attitude, his inspiration, his divine ability, a place where he rests in faith, a place where God has done something marvelous for him. He has taken him out of the world. It is a remarkable word that Jesus said, "I pray not that thou shouldest take them out of the world...They are not of the world..." (John 17:15,16). It is a great truth for us to understand. And in this glorious position of God's own we come to a place where we know with confidence, we say it without fear of contradiction of our own heart or even the contradiction of outside voices, "Beloved, now are we the sons of God."

Beloved, I want us to examine ourselves as the Word comes forth as there are any amount of Scriptures which are definitely purposed of God that we should inherit them but we do not come into line to claim them. Remember this, there are any amount of things you may quote without having the essential of the reality of the fact of the production of them. I want us to have something more than the literal word. Words are of no importance without they have unction of the assurance of the abiding of those words.

Let me say a few things which are contained in the Scriptures that ought to be ours. Here is one: "Beloved, now are we the sons of God..." (1 John 3:2). That is Scripture. That is divine. That is for us, but it is another thing altogether to have it. Here is another word: "...he that doeth righteousness is righteous, even as he is righteous" (1 John 3:7). There is also another word I want to give you. It is also a word which is used by most believers: "...greater is he that is in you, than he that is in the world" (1 John 4:4). That is quoted by many people, but may God reveal unto us the meaning is something more than saying it. You can quote these words and you know all the time you are failures without being in the place of victory.

Any person that has come to the place of this word, "...greater is he that is in you, than he that is in the world," which is a divine proposition, is mightier than all the powers of darkness, is mightier than the power of disease, mightier than his own self. There is something reigning supremely great in him more than in the world when he is in that place. But beloved, we must come to the place of a knowledge. It is not sufficient for you to quote the Word of God. You never come to a place of righteousness, of truth, until you are in possession of these things which I am giving you by the Word.

TONGUES AND INTERPRETATION: "God, who has divinely brought forth the Word by the power of His might through His Son, gave it displacement in the human soul that the human may be dried up, withered by God, coming in by the force of living power."

Beloved, God wants us to be something more than ordinary people. Remember this, whosoever you are, if you are ordinary you have not touched the ideal principles of God. The only thing that God has for a man is to be extraordinary. God has no room for an ordinary man. There are millions of ordinary people in the world. They are only counted as nations, as people. But when God lays hold of a man He makes him extraordinary in personality, power, unction, thought and activity.

"Beloved, now are we the sons of God." It is a divine plan. It is a divine will in the plan. God has not anything He does not mean us to possess. God means us to possess all these things. "Beloved, now are we the sons of God." God has such purposes to perform in us that He has a great desire to utter these words in our heart that we may rise, that we may claim, that we may be ambitious, that we may be covetous, that there may be something in us that nothing can satisfy us without we not only tow the line but live in the line and claim the whole thing as ours. God must have it to be so.

You will never reach ideal purposes on any line without that Word becomes the epistle. You become the living epistle by the power of the Holy Ghost — nay, you become the living force of the epistle of the revelation of God, the incarnation of the personality of His presence in the human soul till you know you are sons. Son-likeness, son-desires, son-expressions, son-activities. Look at Him! See Him! He is the most beautiful of all. He is the most glorious, God-impassionated, a body filled with all the fulness of God, coming forth in the glory of the majesty of His Father, and He stands in the earth, flesh.

Ah, but look! Read with me Romans 8:3. It is a good word to concentrate on for a moment.

> *For what the law could not do, in that it was weak through the flesh, God sending his own Son in the likeness of sinful flesh, and for sin, condemned sin in the flesh.*

There is our very image, natural weakness. Jesus made of a woman, flesh after our flesh.

Look at Hebrews 2:14, for there will be an expression of beatitude for you. Hearken!

> *Forasmuch then as the children are partakers of flesh and blood, he also himself likewise took part of the same; that through death he might destroy him that had the power of death, that is, the devil.*

Oh, I like that thought! The manifestation of the power of God. God came and indwelt that flesh, that weakness, that law for you. He came in, chanted it, lived in it, moved in it and they beheld Him as the Son of God.

TONGUES AND INTERPRETATION: "Yes, it was the purpose of almightiness to swing through weakness and just quicken it by His mighty power till flesh became the habitation of God in the Spirit."

Beloved, there is the principle, there is the remarkable position of every soul in this place to be so inhabited by Jesus that you become a living personality of God's ideal Son. It is very remarkable, it is very beautiful. God has these divine plans for us because so many people believe because they are natural they are always to be in the place of weakness. Beloved, your weaknesses have to be swallowed up with the ideal of Him who never failed.

Every time He was tried He came out victorious. Every time He was oppressed — never mind, it did not matter what happened. He "...was in all points tempted like as we are, yet without sin" (Hebrews 4:15). A purpose there that He might be able to succor all who were tempted and tried and oppressed in any way. He was the great embodiment of personality from God to the human life to unveil us in our weaknesses to behold His mightiness through us that we might be strong in the Lord. Praise the Lord!

> It's all right now, it's all right now,
> For Jesus is my Savior and it's all right now.

Beloved, there is something very definitely appropriate for this morning's address in that. It is always all right when He is almighty. Then we are all right. The Word of God says:

> *Therefore being justified by faith, we have peace with God through our Lord Jesus Christ: By whom also we have access by faith into this grace wherein we stand, and rejoice in hope of the glory of God.*
>
> *Romans 5:1-2*

It is a great position. It is to be saved by this immensity of power, this great inflow of life, this great fulness of God. This wonderful inhabiting of the Spirit to come right into the human soul and shake the husks away, shake the mind!

DIVINELY ADJUSTED

Oh, how many people have lost out because the mind and the head are too big! If only God could cut our heads off and get to the heart! The head is too big, the mind is too active, and the whole thing is too natural, therefore God cannot get His way. May God sweep through us today and show us that the only thing that is ever going to help us is the heart. "For with the heart man believeth unto righteousness..." (Romans 10:10). It is the heart where we believe in faith. It is the heart that is inhabited by the Spirit. It is the heart that is moved by God. The mind is always secondary.

The tongue is the third position. The heart conceives, the mind reflects, and the mouth is operated. But you must not try to reverse the order. Some people are all tongue, neither head nor heart. But when He comes in, there is perfect order. It is as right as rain. Look how it comes! The heart, the conception; the heart, the inflowing; the heart, the great place of ventilating till it flows through and quickens the members of the mind, till the reflection is wonderful. And then the operation of the tongue brings out the glory of the Lord.

TONGUES AND INTERPRETATION: "Oh, it was the love that flowed from Calvary that moved with compassion for the mighty need of the world's cry. It entered the heart of the Father and unveiled His love to the world, gave us His Son in affection and the work was done."

Praise the Lord! Then it is done. It is perfectly done. The Scriptures are perfect, the sacrifice is perfect, the revelation is perfect, and everything is so divinely adjusted by almightiness that every person who comes into infinite revelation touched of God sees that the whole canon of Scripture is perfect from the beginning to the end. There is not a single thing in the Scriptures that clashes or comes up against the Spirit and makes trouble.

When the whole life is surged by the power of God, the Word becomes the personality of the subject. We become the subjects of the Spirit of the living God, and we are moved by the almightiness of God till we live and move and have our being with this flow of God's integrity. What a wonderful adjustment for weaknesses! Do you believe it is possible?

"...God is able to make all grace abound..." (2 Corinthians 9:8). God is able to so shake us through, to send a wind and blow the chaff away till it will never be seen anymore. God is so able to refine us that everybody in the place will shout today. Oh, if something would happen to cause you all to shout!

> It is better to shout than to doubt,
> It is better to rise than to fail,
> It is better to let the glory out,
> Than to have no glory at all.

"Beloved, now are we the sons of God." I don't want to leave the subject till I feel God has given you a rising tide of expectancy or adaptability within your soul which will bring you into the very place God has made for you. It is as easy as possible if you can touch it by faith this morning.

I am the last man to say anything about fasting, or about praying, or about anything that has been a source of blessing to others. But I have learned by personal experience that I can get more out of one moment's faith than I can get out of a month's yelling. I can get more by believing God a moment than I can get by screaming for a month. Also I am positive that blessing comes out of fasting when the fasting is done in the right way. But I find so many people that make up their mind to fast and they finish off with a thick head, and troubled bones, and sleepy conditions. I am as satisfied as possible that that is no way to fast. But there is a way to fast and I find it in so many Scriptures.

Praying and fasting, the Spirit leading you to pray. The Spirit lays hold of you till you forget even the hour or the day, and you are so caught up by the power of the Spirit that you want nothing, not even meat or drink. Absolutely Holy Ghost fasting. Nay, praying and fasting. Then God gets His plan through because He has you through. So the Lord of hosts, I trust, will so encamp round about us with songs of deliverance, and give us inward revelations till the whole of our being shall be absolutely on the rising tide.

I can understand now clearer than ever the 24th Psalm: "Lift up your heads, O ye gate!..." (v. 7). Human gates, human hindrances, human thoughts, human trying. "Lift up your heads, O ye gates; and be ye lift up, ye everlasting doors; and the King of glory shall come in." Let Him in! Oh, if He comes in, what a wonderful Jesus! Ah, you say, He is in. My word! I believe that if God could only get right in, you would be so far out you would never get in anymore. The difficulty is, some people are on the edge waiting to see which way to go. Brother, you will get blown off. May God the Holy Ghost wake us up to see we must rise with the tide.

Who dares [to] believe God this morning? Who dares claim his rights? What are the rights? "Now are we the sons of God." Absolutely the position of rest, the position of faith. Perfect trust, perfect habitation, no disturbance, peace like a river. Look at the face of God. Hallelujah! The very Word itself that comes to judge comes to help.

Look! The law came as a judgment, but when the Spirit comes and breathes through the law He comes to lift us higher and higher. Oh, Hallelujah! We must go a little further. God comes to us and says, "I will make it all right if you dare believe it." It is so in everything.

All the great things of God that come to us with such revelation, only can come in as we are unclothed and then clothed upon that our nakedness disappears. Nakedness is everything that is coinciding with worldly evil. If you can be attracted by anything earthly, you have missed the greatest association that God has for you. If it is your ranch, your bank, your associations, any human thing, if it can attract you from God, you are not a son in this respect. I will prove it by the next words:

> *Beloved, now are we the sons of God, and it doth not yet appear what we shall be: but we know that, when he shall appear, we shall be like him; for we shall see him as he is. And every man that hath this hope in him purifieth himself....*
>
> 1 John 3:2,3

Hallelujah! So you see, beloved, the importance of coming into line with God's Word. Let us confront the Word, let us confront God and see if this thing really is so.

ASSOCIATION WITH GOD

"Beloved, now are we the sons of God." Sonship! What is the reality of it? God gives it as clear as anything. If sonship, heirship; if heirship, joint heirship. But look at the tremendous, gigantic power of almightiness behind sonship. Son, power, joint power, all power. There you come into it. Will you shiver on the edge of it like the boys do at the bath? Or will you take a plunge into omnipotence and find the waters are not as cold as people told you? Dare you let the warmth of the power of God make you see your inheritance in the Spirit? Nay, nay, something better than that! Oh, the joyfulness, the expressiveness, the inward motion, the divine inflow, the habitation of the Spirit. God in the soul making the whole body cry out for the living God! Glory! Glory! Glory!

Wanting God! Wanting fellowship in the Spirit! Wanting the walk with Him! Wanting communion with Him! Everything else is no good. You want the association with God, and God says, "I will come and walk with you. I will sup with you and you with Me, and I will live in you." A joyful hallelujah! Attaining to a spiritual majority, a fulness of Christ, a place where God becomes the perfect Father and the Holy Ghost has a rightful place now as never before.

The Holy Ghost breathes through and says, "You are My Father, You are My Father." The Spirit crieth, "Abba Father, My Father." Oh, it is wonderful! And God the Holy Ghost grant to us this morning that richness of His pleasure, that unfolding of His will, that consciousness of the beaming of His countenance upon us. There is no condemnation; the law of the Spirit of life making us free from the law of sin and death. Glory!

The Spirit is having perfect way because if we see it as clear as God intends us to see it, we will all be made so much riper, looking forward to the Blessed One who is coming again. Here we are face to face with facts. God has shown us different aspects of the Spirit, He has shown us the pavilion of splendor, He has unfolded to us the power of the relationship of sonship. He has shown us that they that are sons of God have likeness unto it, they have activity in it, they are claiming the rights by it. They speak and it is done. They are binding the things that are loose and loosing the things that are bound. And the perfection of sonship is being so manifested there is absolutely a rising tide of the sons of God.

> I know the Lord, I know the Lord,
> I know the Lord's laid His hands on me,
> Oh, I know the Lord, I know the Lord,
> I know the Lord's laid His hands on me.

Do you believe it? Let us see you act it. Beloved, God the Holy Ghost has a perfect plan for us to make us a movement. There is a difference between a movement and a monument. A movement is something that is always active. A monument is something that is fixed at a corner and neither speaks nor moves, but there is a tremendous lot of humbug and nonsense to get it there. It is silent and does nothing. A movement is where God has come into the very being of a person, where he becomes active for God. He is God's property, God's mouthpiece, God's eyes, God's hands.

We read, "And the very God of peace sanctify you wholly; and I pray God your whole spirit and soul and body be preserved blameless unto the coming of our Lord Jesus Christ" (1 Thessalonians 5:23). The sanctification of the eyes, of the hands, of the mouth, of the ears; to be so operated that you live only for the habitation of the Spirit, a wonderful place for God to bring us to.

"Beloved, now are we the sons of God, and it doth not yet appear what we shall be..." (1 John 3:2). There is the greatest thought in the Scriptures. On what lines? Heirs, joint heirs, revelations, dispensation of God in the man till the man becomes the habitation of God, and He walks up and down in the world as God. He is filled, moved, intensified till he is on the wing. It would not take a trumpet for he is already on the wing and he will land very soon. He would hear the voice no matter how many street cars were passing.

We read in 1 Corinthians 2:9:

But as it is written, Eye hath not seen, nor ear heard, neither have entered into the heart of man, the things which God hath prepared for them that love him.

Everything that is going to help you, you have to make yours. "God hath prepared for them." He has laid it up already. You don't want a stepladder to get it. It is laid up to be handed out to you when you become joined with Him. When you walk with Him He will either drop everything He has on you or take you where you are to remain forever. Enoch could not understand all the weights of glory so He stripped him and took him into it as soon as He could.

Beloved, it is impossible to estimate the loving-kindness of God or the measureless mind of God in our finite condition. When we come into like-mindedness with the Word, instead of looking at the Word we begin to see what God has for us in the Word. This is a very exhaustless subject but I pray God He will make us an exhaustless people. I want something to happen on the line of this verse:

> Me with a quenchless thirst inspire,
> A longing, infinite desire
> Fill my craving heart.
> Less than Thyself You do not give,
> Thy might within me now to live.
> Come, all Thou hast.

God, just come and make me so that there is not a possibility for me to ever be satisfied but to have a quenchless thirst for the living God! And then I shall not be overtaken. Then I shall be ready. Then I shall have eyes which beam, filled with the extremity of delight looking at the Master.

THE SON OF GOD REVEALED

You ask, "What, we see the Master?" Here, look at Him! His Word is Spirit — and life-giving. This is the breath, the Word of Jesus. Through the Holy Ghost men have written and spoken. Here is the life, here is the witness, here is the truth, here is the Son of God revealed from faith to faith, from heart to heart, from vision to vision, till we all come into perfect unity of fellowship into the fulness of Christ.

There it is, beloved. Look! "Now are we the sons of God." If you are there we can take a step further. But if you are not there you may hear but not cross over. But there is something about the Word of God which says that if there is a hearing of faith it shall profit, but if there is a hearing not mixed with faith it shall not profit.

You can hear this Word on the lines of faith.

> *Beloved, now are we the sons of God, and it doth not yet appear what we shall be: but we know that, when he shall appear, we shall be like him; for we shall see him as he is.*
>
> 1 John 3:2

The future is what you are today. The future is not what you are going to be tomorrow. This is the day when God makes the future possible. When God can get something through you today, tomorrow is filled with further illumination of God's possibility for you.

Dare you come into the place of omnipotence? of wonderment? Dare you step into line with God's possibility and say, "I am ready for all Thou hast for me"? It will mean a clean life. It will mean a holy life. It will mean a separated life. It will disjoin you from everything. It will mean your heart is so perfect, your prospects are so divinely separated that you say to the world, "Goodbye!" Hear what Paul said, "I conferred not with flesh and blood," that he might inherit this great possession that God has laid up for us.

TONGUES AND INTERPRETATION: "Holiness is the habitation of Thy house. Purity, righteousness and truth are God's glorified position in the Spirit. The great desire of the Master is to make sons of God, for many sons He will gather into glory."

Listen to what God has to say. Everything must be absolutely the Word, so I only speak to you by the Word. Let us read Hebrews 2:6-10.

> *But one in a certain place testified, saying, What is man, that thou art mindful of him? or the son of man, that thou visitest him? Thou madest him a little lower than the angels; thou crownedst him with glory and honour, and didst set him over the works of thy hands: Thou hast put all things in subjection under*

his feet. For in that he put all in subjection under him, he left nothing that is not put under him. But now we see not yet all things put under him. But we see Jesus, who was made a little lower than the angels for the suffering of death, crowned with glory and honour; that he by the grace of God should taste death for every man. For it became him, for whom are all things, and by whom are all things, in bringing many sons unto glory, to make the captain of their salvation perfect through sufferings.

Oh, this second chapter of Hebrews is one of the mighty, glorified positions for the children of God! God would have me herald, like a great trumpet call, my voice to sound in every heart. Brother, the design is to bring you as a son clothed with the power of the gifts and graces, ministries and operations; to bring you into glory clothed upon with a majesty of heaven for He shall bring many sons unto glory, son-likeness, son perfection. Oh, this is like heaven to me! My very body is filled with heaven this morning.

Oh, what an exhaustless position we are in! Therefore, seeing these things are so, what manner of persons ought we to be. How? In looking, in hasting, and keeping our eyes upon Him that we may be ready for the rapture. Oh, brothers, sisters, what immensity of pleasure God has for us in these meetings! What unbounded conditions of sobermindedness God is bringing us to that we may be able to apprehend that for which God has apprehended us in the Spirit. Oh, that we may look not on the things that are, but with eyes of chaste virgin purity seeing only the invisible Son! And so having our whole bodies illuminated by the power of the Holy Spirit we grow in grace, from grace to grace, in faith, from faith to faith, in personality of son-likeness till there is not any difference between us and Him.

Let me give you the Word if you can receive it: "As He is, so are we in this world." What a word! Who dare believe it? God only can take us on to such heights and depths and lengths and breadths in the Spirit. Brother, sister, are you prepared to go all the way? Are you willing for heights and depths and lengths and breadths? Are you willing for your heart to have only one attraction? Are you willing to have only one lover? Are you willing for Him to become the very perfect Bridegroom?

For I understand the more bride-like we are, the more we love to hear the Bridegroom's voice, and the less bride-like we are, the less we long for His Word. If you cannot rest without it, if it becomes your meat day and night, if you eat and drink of it, His life will be in you and when He appears you will go. Help us, Jesus!

How many are prepared to be unmantled before the King? Prepared to yield to His call, yield to His will, yield to His desires? Keep your hands up. Everybody knows in this meeting just how far you have missed the plan. The Word has gone forth, the Spirit has been quickening you. How many are going to say, "At all costs I will go through!" Who says so? Who means it? Are you determined? Is your soul on the wing? Come forward and make a full consecration to God right in this sawdust here, every one of you. It is between you and God this morning. It is nothing to do with your next door neighbor. You are going now to get in the presence of God. Make a full breast of everything in the presence of God!

Message given at Pentecostal Camp Meeting
Berkeley, California

OVERCOMING
June 3, 1924

 I think it will please God if I read to you the fifth chapter of the first epistle of John. This is one of those wonderful and divine truths of God which bring to the life, heart affection, which verifies in every condition of life that they are of God. This is one of those essential truths that shall give to us a clear discernment of our position in Christ. God wants us all to be so built up in truth, righteousness, and the life of God that every person we come in contact with may know of a truth that we are of God. And we who are of God can assure our hearts before Him, and we can have perfect confidence.

There is something more in the believer than words. Words are of little effect without they have a personal manifestation of God. We must not look at the Word as only a written Word. The Word is a live fact to work in the human body living truths, changing it, moving it till the person is a living fact of God's inheritance, till He is in the body reigning, in the world, over it. In conversation or activity he is a production of God. It is truly a human plan first, but it is covered with God's inheritance.

I want to come to the Word itself, and by the grace of God bring us into a place where it would be impossible, whatever happened, to move us from our plan.

REGENERATED POSITION

Let us look at the first verse:

> *Whosoever believeth that Jesus is the Christ is born of God: and every one that loveth him that begat loveth him also that is begotten of him.*
>
> *1 John 5:1*

There are hundreds of "religions," so called, crowded everywhere. But look! All these differences of opinions wither away, and there is to be a perfect oneness and divine union, and it will surely have to come to pass. You ask, "How is it possible?" This is truth, it is the Word of God, it is God Himself portrayed in Word. You see God in the Word. God can manifest Himself through that Word till we become a living factor of that truth because God is light and in Him is no darkness. God is life. God is revelation. God is manifestation, and God is operation. So God wants to bring us truly into a place where we have the clearest revelation — there may be many convictions through it — but the clearest revelation of where we stand.

"Whosoever believeth that Jesus is the Christ is born of God." What is the outcome of being born of God? God's life, God's truth, God's walk, God's communion, fellowship, oneness, like-mindedness. All that pertaineth to holiness, righteousness and truth comes forth out of this new birth unto righteousness. And in it, through it, and by it we have a perfect regenerated position just as we have come into light through this.

Again, it is an impartation of love, an expression of Himself, for God is love. The first breathing or revelation of light of the new creation within the soul is so pure, so unadulterated, so perfect and so righteous that if we go back to when you were first enlightened and had the revelation, when you first believed in your heart, you felt so holy, you felt you loved so much you were in a paradise of wonderment. You had no desire for sin and sin had lost its desire.

There you were with a new birth unto righteousness, filled with the first love of purity and truth. You felt everybody was going to be saved and that the world was going to be turned upside down because you had got it. That was the first touch. It was a remarkable revelation to me when I first saw that God had purposed that every newborn babe in Christ was called to be a saint; called from the darkness to light, from the power of Satan unto God; separated at the revelation that Jesus was the Son of God.

Another fact was this: that for days and days there was something so remarkable come over your life that you neither had desire nor did sin. How many have a recollection of those moments? Praise God! God had designed the plan for you before the world was. I believe that God wants to open your heart and mind to a predestined condition of why you are here.

We want to be so established with facts that there won't be a thing in the world able to move us from our perfect position. How many people are there who, though sin is striving with them, though evil forces are round about them, yet never remember a day when God did not strive with them? It is impossible to be in the world without satanic forces trying to bid very loudly for your lives. But how many are here who from their very infancy have always remembered that the good hand of God was with them? If you knew the Scriptures you could say like Paul, that from your mother's womb God had called you.

Beloved, God has predestined. There are two great words in the Scriptures: "Whosoever will," and "Whosoever won't." God has covered the world with His blood, and every man is redeemed whether he will have it or not. But there are some people whom God has wonderfully chosen before the foundation of the world. And as surely as we are here, we can say that God has predestined us even to this day. Though you have been defeated, the tendency, and the longings, and the cryings, and the desires of your whole life have been, you wanted God.

See how much God has for you in the Word! God wants people who are mighty in the Spirit, who are full of power. God has no such thing as small measures for man. God has great designs for man. God has determined by His power and His grace through the Son to bring many sons unto glory, clothed upon with the holy One from heaven.

TONGUES AND INTERPRETATION: "The Lord of life and glory, who has begotten us to a lively hope, hath chosen us before the foundation of the world that He may manifest His Son in us, and get the glory over the powers of darkness and the devil, and every evil thing, that we may reign over the powers of the devil."

The Holy Ghost is jealous over us this morning. How He longs for us to catch the breath of His Spirit! How He longs for us to be moved in union with Himself that there may not be a thought in heaven but that the Holy Ghost could breathe through the natural and so chasten it by His divine plan, so that you should have a new faith or a revelation of God. You would be so perfect before Him that there would not be a thing that Satan could say contrary to His child.

DIVINE HEDGE

Hear what Satan says to God: "Hast not thou made an hedge about him...?" (Job 1:10). God said, "...all that he hath is in thy power; only upon himself put not forth thine hand..." (Job 1:12). We see that God put a hedge about His child. Oh, that we would believe! Hearken to what Jesus says: "How is it that ye do not understand?... Do ye not yet understand, neither remember the five loaves of the five thousand, and how many baskets ye took up? Neither the seven loaves of the four thousand, and how many baskets ye took up." Oh, if we had not forgotten the blessings and the pressed out measures, everything would be moved by the manifestation of the children of God who would stand by the power of the righteousness of heaven and move the world.

"Who is he that overcometh the world, but he that believeth that Jesus is the Son of God?" (1 John 5:5). It is most beautiful! "For whatsoever is born of God overcometh the world: and this is the victory that overcometh the world, even our faith" (1 John 5:4). We shall have to come into divine measurement, divine revelation. The possibilities are ours.

One day I was in Belfast, Ireland. I had a friend there they called Morris. He had been with us at Bradford, and I wanted to see him, so I went to his house and said, "Is Brother Morris here?" The woman answered, "It is not Morris you want. God sent you for me. I am a broken-hearted woman. I am going through death, having the greatest trial of my life.

Come in." I went in. She continued, "My husband is a deacon in the Presbyterian Church, and you know when you were here, God filled me with the Holy Ghost. As a deacon's wife, I sat in a prominent place in the Church. The Spirit of the Lord came upon me and I was so filled with joy that I broke out in tongues. The whole Church turned round to look at me for making such a disturbance."

At the close of the meeting the deacons and the pastor came to her husband saying, "You cannot be a deacon in this church because of your wife's behavior." It nearly broke his heart. When he saw all his influence was to go, he came home in bitterness. He and his wife had lived together many years and had never known a discord. After causing much trouble he left his wife with the words, "I will never come near you again as long as I live."

After she told me the story we prayed, and the power of God shook her. God showed me that He would give to her all she required. "Mrs., wake up," I exclaimed. "Look, the situation is yours. God has given you the situation. It is according to the Word of God: 'For the unbelieving husband is sanctified by the wife, and the unbelieving wife is sanctified by the husband...For what knowest thou, Oh, wife, whether thou shalt save thy husband, or how knowest thou, Oh, man, whether thou shalt save thy wife? You will be the means of your husband being saved and baptized." "Yes," she replied, "if I could believe he would ever come back, but he will never come back."

"Look," I said, "The Word of God says, 'That if two of you shall agree on earth as touching any thing that they shall ask, it shall be done for them of My Father which is in heaven.' We will agree that he comes home tonight."

TONGUES AND INTERPRETATION: "God has designed a purpose for His people. And the Word of truth comes to us by interpretation: 'Whatsoever thou shalt bind on earth shall be bound in heaven. And whosoever thou shalt loose on earth shall be loosed in heaven.'"

I advised her, "When he comes home you show him you love him. It is possible that he won't have it. As soon as he retires you get down before God and get filled just as you were here. Then touch him in God."

Her husband was obliged to come home. Whatsoever you desire, if you believe God, comes to pass. He marched up and down in the house as though he never saw her, then retired to his room. Then she got down before God. Oh, the place of all places where God comes to the soul! The Spirit came upon her till her whole being was filled with the flame of heaven. Then she touched him. He screamed and rolled off onto the floor and cried for mercy. She never left him till he was filled with the Holy Ghost.

Nothing happens to the believer but what is good for him. "All things work together for good to them that love God." But we must not forget this injunction, "to them who are the called according to His purpose." Remember, you are called "according to His purpose" in the working out of the power of God within you for the salvation of others. God has you for a purpose.

Look, beloved, I want you without carefulness. How many people are bound and helpless, and their testimony is naught because of carefulness. Hear what the Scripture says: "...thou hast hid these things from the wise and prudent, and hast revealed them unto babes. Even so, Father: for so it seemed good in thy sight" (Matthew 11:25,26).

LIKE A CHILD

The first thing that God really does with a newborn child is to keep him as a child. There are wonderful things for children. The difference between a child and the wise and prudent is this: the prudent man is too careful. The wise man knows too much. But the babies! We have had babies and sometimes have had to pull the bottle back lest they take the bottle with the milk — so ravenous. The child cannot dress itself but God clothes it. He has a special raiment for children, white and beautiful. God says there is no spot on the child, "Thou art pure, thou art altogether lovely." The babe cannot talk. But it is lovely to know that you will take no thought what you shall say, the Holy Ghost can speak through you. If you are a child, if you give all over to God, He can speak through you. He loves His children. Oh, how beautifully He sees to His children! How kind and good He is!

"Who is he that overcometh the world, but he that believeth that Jesus is the Son of God?" (1 John 5:5). That pure, that holy, that devoted Person who made the world submits His will to Almighty God, and God uses His will and God indwells Him in fulness. He meets the world's need. He comes in at the dry time when there is no wine and

He makes the wine. Glory to God. When there is no bread He comes and makes the bread.

He that believes that Jesus is the Son of God overcomes the world. You ask, "How can a man overcome the world because he believes that Jesus is the Son of God?" Because Jesus is so holy and you become His habitation. Jesus is so sweet, His love passeth all understanding. His wisdom passeth all knowledge, and therefore He comes to you with the wisdom of God and not of this world. He comes to you with peace not as this world giveth. He comes to you with boundless blessing, with a measure pressed down and running over. You do not require the world, for you have meat to eat that the world knows not of. God is a rewarder of all them that diligently seek Him, for they that seek Him shall lack no good thing.

Brother, where are your bounds this morning? There are heights and depths and lengths and breadths to the love of God. Beloved, the Word of God contains the principles of life. I live not but another mightier than I liveth. The desires have gone into the desires of God. It is lovely! It is so perfected in the Holy Ghost that God is continually bringing forth things new and old.

"Who is he that overcometh the world, but he that believeth that Jesus is the Son of God?" How do we overcome? We may come into this great inheritance of the Spirit. We long that there shall not be anything in us which Satan could use in overcoming us. Remember the words of Jesus, "...the prince of this world cometh, and hath nothing in me" (John 14:30). We desire to reach such a place as this. Is it possible? Brother, it is the design of the Master. Without holiness, no man shall see the Lord. "...he that is begotten of God keepeth himself, and that wicked one toucheth him not" (1 John 5:18).

Surely the Lord is not going to send you away empty. He wants to satisfy your longing soul with good things. "...whatsoever is born of God overcometh the world: and this is the victory that overcometh the world, even our faith" (1 John 5:4). Let me speak about three classes of faith. There is a good and there is a better and there is a best. God has the best. In Pentecost I find some people are satisfied with "tongues." That would never satisfy me. I want the Person who gives them. I am the hungriest man that ever you saw. I want all He has. Without God gives me, I am a perfectly spoiled baby. "Father," I say, "You will have to give me."

When I was a little boy I would go to my father and say, "Father, will you give me some bird lime?" "No, no," he would answer. I knew just what he meant from the way he said it. I would plead, "Father, father, father, father." I would follow him as he walked out. "Father, father, father." Mother would ask, "Why don't you give the lad what he wants?"

I got to the place where I believed my father liked me to say it. If you only knew how God likes to hear us say, "Father, my Father!" Oh, how He loves His children! I never forget when we had our first baby. He was asleep in the cradle. We both went to him and my wife said, "I cannot bear to have him sleep any longer. I want him!" And I remember waking the baby because she wanted him. "If ye then, being evil, know how to give good gifts unto your children: how much more shall your heavenly Father give the Holy Spirit to them that ask him?" (Luke 11:13). Ah, He is such a lovely Father!

"But" you say, "sometimes I give in." Never mind, I am going to bring you to a point where you need never give in. Praise God! If I did not know the almighty power of God I would jump off this platform. Because we are quickened and made alive we move into the new spirit, the spirit of fellowship that was lost in the garden. Oh, hallelujah, new birth, new life, new person!

Human faith works and then waits for the wages. That is not saving faith. Then there is the gift of faith. "For by grace are ye saved through faith; and that not of yourselves: it is the gift of God" (Ephesians 2:8). Faith is that which God gave you to believe. "Whosoever believeth that Jesus is the Christ is born of God..." (1 John 5:1). The sacrifice is complete, and God has kept you because you could not keep yourself.

I want to tell you of something that does not fail. Let us read Acts 26:16-18:

> *But rise, and stand upon thy feet: for I have appeared unto thee for this purpose, to make thee a minister and a witness both of these things which thou hast seen, and of those things in the which I will appear unto thee; Delivering thee from the people, and from the Gentiles, unto whom now I send thee, To open*

their eyes, and to turn them from darkness to light, and from the power of Satan unto God, that they may receive forgiveness of sins, and inheritance among them which are sanctified by faith that is in me.

That is another faith.

In 1 Corinthians 12:9 we read, "To another faith by the same Spirit...." When my faith fails, then another faith lays hold of me. One day I called at a home where a woman had not slept for seven weeks. She was rolling from one side of the bed to the other. In came a young man with a baby in his arms. He stooped down over the mother to try to kiss her. Instantly she rolled to the other side of the bed. Going around to her, the young man touched the lips of the mother with the baby to bring consciousness again. But she switched to the other side. I could see that the young man was broken-hearted.

"What have you done for this woman?" I asked. "Everything," they replied. "We have had doctors here, injected morphine, etc." The sister said, "We must put her in an asylum. I am tired and worn out." I asked, "Have you tried God?" The husband answered, "Do you think we believe in God here? We have no confidence in anything. If you call anything like this God, we have no fellowship with it."

Oh, I was done then! A young woman then grinned in my face and slammed the door. The compassion in me was so moved I did not know what to do. I began to cry and my faith took me right up. Thank God for faith that lifted. I felt another grip me like the Son of God. The Spirit of the Lord came upon me and I said, "In the Name of Jesus, come out of her!" She fell asleep and did not wake for fourteen hours. She wakened perfectly sane. Brother, there is a place to know the Son of God that absolutely overcomes the world.

OVERTAKEN BY GOD

One time I thought I had the Holy Ghost. Now I know the Holy Ghost has got me. There is a difference between our hanging on to God and God lifting us up. There is a difference between my having a desire and God's desire filling my soul. There is a difference between natural compassion and the compassion of Jesus that never fails. Human faith fails but the faith of Jesus never fails.

Oh, beloved, I see through glorious truths a new dawning, assemblies loving one another, all of one accord. Until that time comes, there will be deficiencies. Hear what the Scripture says: "...every one that loveth him that begat loveth him also that is begotten of him" (1 John 5:1). "By this shall all men know that ye are my disciples, if ye have love one to another" (John 13:35). Love is the secret and center of the divine position. Build upon God.

You ask, "What is the gift of faith?" It is where God moves you to pray. Here is a man called Elijah with like passions as we have. The sins of the people were grieving the heart of God, and the whole house of Ahab was in an evil state. But God moved upon this man and gave him an inward cry. "...There shall not be dew nor rain these years, but according to my word. ...and it rained not on the earth by the space of three years and six months" (1 Kings 17:1, James 5:17). Oh, if we dared believe God! A man of like passions as we are stirred with almightiness! "And he prayed again, and the heaven gave rain, and the earth brought forth her fruit" (James 5:18).

Brother, sister, you are now in the robing room. God is adding another day for you to come into line, for you to lay aside everything that has hindered you, for you to forget the past. And I ask you, "How many want to touch God for a faith that cannot be denied?" I have learned this that if I dare put up my hands in faith, God will fill them. Come on, beloved, seek God and let us get a real touch of heaven this morning. God is moving.

This day is the beginning of days, a day when the Lord will not forsake His own but He will meet us. Come near to God! Jesus, Jesus, bless us! We are so needy, Lord. Jesus, my Lord! Oh, Jesus, Jesus, Jesus! Oh, my Savior, my Savior! Oh, such love! Thou mighty God! Oh, loving Master! Blessed, blessed Jesus! None like Jesus! None so good as He! None so sweet as He! Oh, Thou blessed Christ of reality, come! Hallelujah!

Message given at Pentecostal Camp Meeting
Berkeley, California

Bible reading, Matthew 8:1-17. Here we have a wonderful word. All the Word is wonderful. This blessed Book brings such life and health and peace, and such an abundance that we should never be poor anymore. This Book is my heavenly bank. I find everything I want in it. I want to show you how rich you may be, that in every-

HIMSELF TOOK OUR INFIRMITIES

October 1924

thing you can be enriched in Christ Jesus. He has abundance of grace for you and the gift of righteousness, and through His abundant grace all things are possible. I want to show you that you can be a living branch of the living Vine, Christ Jesus, and that it is your privilege to be right here in this world what He is. John tells us, "...as he is, so are we in this world" (1 John 4:17). Not that we are anything in ourselves, but Christ within us is our all in all.

The Lord Jesus is always wanting to show forth His grace and love in order to draw us to Himself. God is willing to do things, to manifest His Word, and let us know in measure the mind of our God in this day and hour. There are many needy ones, many afflicted ones, but I do not think any present are half as bad as this first case that we read of in Matthew 8. This man was a leper. You may be suffering with consumption or cancers or other things, but God will show forth His perfect cleansing, His perfect healing, if you have a living faith in Christ. He is a wonderful Jesus.

This leper must have been told about Jesus. How much is missed because people are not constantly telling what Jesus will do in this our day. Probably someone had come to that leper and said, "Jesus can heal you." And so he was filled with expectation as he saw the Lord coming down the mountainside. Lepers were not allowed to come within reach of people, they were shut out as unclean. And so in the ordinary way it would have been very difficult for him to get near because of the crowd that surrounded Jesus. But as He came down from the mount, He met, He came to the leper. Oh, this terrible disease! There was no help for him humanly speaking, but nothing is too hard for Jesus. The man cried, "...Lord, if thou wilt, thou canst make me clean" (Matthew 8:2). Was Jesus willing?

You will never find Jesus missing an opportunity of doing good. You will find that He is always more willing to work than we are to give Him an opportunity to work. The trouble is, we do not come to Him, we do not ask Him for what He is more than willing to give.

And Jesus put forth His hand, and touched him, saying, "...I will; be thou clean. And immediately his leprosy was cleansed" (Matthew 8:3). I like that. If you are definite with Him, you will never go away disappointed. The divine life will flow into you and instantaneously you will be delivered. This Jesus is just the same today, and He says to you, "I will; be thou clean." He has an overflowing cup for thee, a fulness of life. He will meet you in your absolute helplessness. All things are possible if you will only believe. God has a real plan. It is so simple. Just come to Jesus. You will find Him just the same as He was in days of old.

The next case we have in this chapter is that of the centurion coming and beseeching Jesus on behalf of his servant who was sick of the palsy and grievously tormented. This man was so in earnest that he came seeking for Jesus. Notice this, that there is one thing certain, there is no such thing as seeking without finding. He that seeketh findeth. Listen to the gracious words of Jesus, "...I will come and heal him" (Matthew 8:7). Most places that we go to, there are so many people that we cannot pray for. In some places there are 200 or 300 who would like us to visit them, but we are not able to do so. But I am so glad that the Lord Jesus is always willing to come and heal. He longs to meet the sick ones. He loves to heal them of their afflictions. The Lord is healing many people today by means of handkerchiefs as you read that He healed people in the days of Paul. You can read of this in Acts 19:12.

A woman came to me in the city of Liverpool and said, "I would like you to help me. I wish you would join me in prayer. My husband is a drunkard and every night comes into the home under the influence of drink. Won't you join me in prayer for him?" I said to the woman, "Have you a handkerchief?" She took out a handkerchief and I prayed over it and told her to lay it on the pillow of the drunken man. He came home that night and laid his head on the pillow in which this handkerchief was tucked. He laid his head on more than the pillow that night. He laid his head on the promise of God. In Mark 11:24, we read:

...What things soever ye desire, when ye pray, believe that ye receive them, and ye shall have them.

The next morning the man got up and called at the first saloon that he had to pass on his way to work and ordered some beer. He tasted it and said to the bartender, "You have put some poison in this beer." He could not drink it, and went on to the next saloon and ordered some more beer. He tasted it and said to the man behind the counter, "You put some poison in this beer; I believe you folks have agreed to poison me." The bartender was indignant at being thus charged. The man said, "I will go somewhere else." He went to another saloon and the same thing happened as in the two previous saloons. He made such a fuss that they turned him out. After he came out from work he went to another saloon to get some beer, and again he thought he had been poisoned and he made such a disturbance that he was thrown out. He went to his home and told his wife what had happened and said, "It seems as though all the fellows have agreed to poison me." His wife said to him, "Can't you see the hand of the Lord in this, that He is making you dislike the stuff that has been your ruin?" This word brought conviction to the man's heart and he came to the meeting and got saved. The Lord has still power to set the captives free.

Jesus was willing to go and heal the sick one, but the centurion said, "Lord, I am not worthy that thou shouldst come under my roof: but speak the word only, and my servant shall be healed" (Matthew 8:8). Jesus was delighted with this expression and said to the man, "...Go thy way; and as thou hast believed, so be it done unto thee. And his servant was healed in the selfsame hour" (Matthew 8:13).

I received a telegram once urging me to visit a case about 200 miles from my home. As I went to this place I met the father and mother and found them brokenhearted. They led me up a staircase to a room, and I saw a young woman on the floor and five people were holding her down. She was a frail young woman, but the power in her was greater than all those young men. As I went into the room, the evil powers looked out of her eyes and they used her lips saying, "We are many, you can't cast us out." I said, "Jesus can." He is equal to every occasion. He is waiting for an opportunity to bless. He is ready for every opportunity to deliver souls. When we receive Jesus it is true of us, "...greater is he that is in you, than he that is in the world" (1 John 4:4). He is greater than all the powers of darkness. No man can meet the devil in his own strength, but any man filled with the knowledge of Jesus, filled with His presence, filled with His power, is more than a match for the powers of darkness. God has called us to be more than conquerors through Him that loved us.

The living Word is able to destroy satanic forces. There is power in the name of Jesus. I would that every window in the street had the name of Jesus written upon it. His name, through faith in His name, brought deliverance to this poor, bound soul, and thirty-seven demons came out giving their names as they came forth. The dear woman was completely delivered and they were able to give her back her child. That night there was heaven in that home and the father and mother and son and his wife were all united in glorifying Christ for His infinite grace. The next morning we had a gracious time in the breaking of bread. All things are wonderful with our wonderful Jesus. If you would dare rest your all upon Him, things would take place and He would change the whole situation. In a moment, through the name of Jesus, a new order of things can be brought in.

In the world they are always having new diseases and the doctors cannot locate them. A doctor said to me, "The science of medicine is in its infancy, and really we doctors have no confidence in our medicine. We are always experimenting." But the man of God does not experiment. He knows, or ought to know, redemption in its fulness. He knows, or ought to know, the mightiness of the Lord Jesus Christ. He is not, or should not, be moved by outward observation, but should get divine revelation of the mightiness of the name of Jesus and the power of His blood. If we exercise our faith in the Lord Jesus Christ, He will come forth and get glory over all the powers of darkness.

> *When the even was come, they brought unto him many that were possessed with devils: and he cast out the spirits with his word, and healed all that were sick: That it might be fulfilled which was spoken by Esaias the prophet, saying, Himself took our infirmities, and bare our sicknesses.*
>
> Matthew 8:16,17

The work is done if you only believe it. It is done. Himself took our infirmities and bare our sickness. If you can only see the Lamb of God as He went to Calvary! He took our flesh that He might take upon Himself the full burden of all our sin and all the consequence of sin. There on the cross of Calvary the results of sin were also dealt with.

> *...as the children are partakers of flesh and blood, he also him-*
> *self likewise took part of the same; that through death he might*
> *destroy him that had the power of death, that is, the devil; And*
> *deliver them who through fear of death were all their lifetime*
> *subject to bondage.*
>
> *Hebrews 2:14,15*

Through His death there is deliverance for you today.

Published in *Triumphs of Faith*

THE SUBSTANCE OF THINGS HOPED FOR

October 25, 1924

Read Hebrews 11. This is a wonderful passage, in fact all the Word of God is wonderful. It is not only wonderful, but it has power to change conditions. Any natural condition can be changed by the Word of God, which is a supernatural power. In the Word of God is the breath, the nature, and the power of the living God, and His power works in every person who dares to believe His Word. There is life though the power of it; and as we receive the Word of faith we receive the nature of God Himself. It is as we lay hold of God's promises in simple faith that we become partakers of the divine nature. As we receive the Word of God we come right into touch with a living force, a power which changes nature into grace, a power that makes dead things live, a power which is of God, which will be manifested in our flesh. This power has come forth with its glory to transform us by divine act into sons of God, to make us like unto *the*

Son of God, by the Spirit of God who moves us on from grace to grace and from glory to glory as our faith rests in this living Word.

It is important that we have a foundation truth, something greater than ourselves, on which to rest. In Hebrews 12 we read, "Looking unto Jesus the author and finisher of our faith" (v. 2). Jesus is our life and He is the power of our life. We see in the fifth chapter of Acts that as soon as Peter was let out of prison the Word of God came, "Go...speak...all the words of this life" (v. 20). There is only one Book that has life. In this Word we find Him who came that we might have life and have it more abundantly, and by faith this life is imparted to us. When we come into this life by divine faith (and we must realize that is by grace we are saved through faith, and that it is not of ourselves, but is the gift of God), we become partakers of this life. This Word is greater than anything else. There is no darkness at all in it. Anyone who dwells in this Word is able under all circumstances to say that he is willing to come to the light that his deeds may be made manifest. But outside of the Word is darkness, and the manifestations of darkness will never come to the light because their deeds are evil. But the moment we are saved by the power of the Word of God we love the light, the truth. The inexpressible divine power, force, passion, and fire that we receive is of God. Drink, my beloved, drink deeply of this Source of life.

Faith is the substance of things hoped for. Someone said to me one day, "I would not believe in anything I could not handle and see." Everything you can handle and see is temporary and will perish with the using. But the things not seen are eternal and will not fade away. Are you dealing with tangible things or with the things which are eternal, the things that are facts, that are made real to faith? Thank God that through the knowledge of the truth of the Son of God I have within me a greater power, a mightier working, an inward impact of life, of power, of vision and of truth more real than anyone can know who lives in the realm of the tangible. God manifests Himself to the person who dares to believe.

But there is something more beautiful than that. As we receive divine life in the new birth we receive a nature that delights to do the will of God. As we believe the Word of God a well of water springs up within our heart. A spring is always better than a pump. But I know that a spring is apt to be outclassed when we get to the baptism of the Holy

Ghost. It was a spring to the woman at the well, but with the person who has the Holy Ghost it is flowing rivers. Have you these flowing rivers? To be filled with the Holy Ghost is to be filled with the Executive of the Godhead, who brings to us all the Father has and all the Son desires; and we should be so in the Spirit that God can cause us to move with His authority and reign by His divine ability.

I thank God He baptizes with the Holy Ghost. I know He did it for me because they heard me speak in tongues and then I heard myself. That was a scriptural work and I don't want anything else, because I must be the epistle of God. There must be emanating through my body a whole epistle of the life, of the power, and of the resurrection of my Lord Jesus. There are wonderful things happening through this divine union with God Himself.

"[God]...hath in these last days spoken unto us by his Son, whom he hath appointed heir of all things, by whom also he made the worlds" (Hebrews 1:2). By this divine Person, this Word, this Son, God made all things. Notice that it says that He made the worlds by this Person and made them out of the things that were not there. Everything we see was made by this divine Son. I want you to see that as you receive the Son of God, and as Christ dwells in your heart by faith, there is a divine force, the power of limitless possibilities, within you, and that as a result of this incoming Christ God wants to do great things through you. By faith, if we receive and accept His Son, God brings us into sonship, and not only into sonship but into joint-heirship, into sharing together with Him all that the Son possesses.

I am more and more convinced every day I live that very few who are saved by the grace of God have a right conception of how great is their authority over darkness, demons, death, and every power of the enemy. It is a real joy when we realize our inheritance on this line.

I was speaking like this one day and someone said, "I have never heard anything like this before. How many months did it take you to get up that sermon?" I said, "My brother, God pressed my wife from time to time to get me to preach and I promised her I would preach. I used to labor hard for a week to get something up, then give out the text and sit down and say, 'I am done.' Oh brother, I have given up getting things up. They all come down. And the sermons that come down stop down, then go back, because the Word of God says His Word shall not return unto Him void. But if you get anything up it will not stop up very long, and when it goes down it takes you down with it."

The sons of God are made manifest in this present earth to destroy the power of the devil. To be saved by the power of God is to be brought from the realm of the ordinary into the extraordinary, from the natural into the divine.

Do you remember the day when the Lord laid His hands on you? You say, "I could not do anything but praise the Lord." Well, that was only the beginning. Where are you today? The divine plan is that you increase until you receive the measureless fulness of God. You do not have to say, "I tell you it was wonderful when I was baptized with the Holy Ghost." If you have to look back to the past to make me know you are baptized, then you are backslidden. If the beginning was good, it ought to be better day by day, till everybody is fully convinced that you are filled with the might of God in the Spirit. Filled with all the fulness of God! "...be not drunk with wine, wherein is excess; but be filled with the Spirit" (Ephesians 5:18). I don't want anything else than being full, and fuller, and fuller, until I am overflowing like a great big vat. Do you realize that if you have been created anew and begotten again by the Word of God that there is within you the word of power and the same light and life as the Son of God Himself had.

God wants to flow through you with measureless power of divine utterance and grace till your whole body is a flame of fire. God intends each soul in Pentecost to be a live wire. Not a monument, but a movement. So many people have been baptized with the Holy Ghost; there was a movement but they have become monuments and you cannot move them. God, wake us out of sleep lest we should become indifferent to the glorious truth and the breath of the almighty power of God. We must be the light and salt of the earth, with the whole armor of God upon us. It would be a serious thing if the enemies were about and we had to go back and get our sandals. It would be a serious thing if we had on no breastplate. How can we be furnished with the armor? Take it by faith. Jump in, stop in, and never come out, for this is a baptism to be lost in, where you only know one thing and that is the desire of God at all times. The baptism in the Spirit should be an ever-increasing endowment of power, an ever-increasing enlargement of grace. Oh, Father, grant unto us a real look into the glorious liberty Thou hast designed for the children of God, who are delivered from this present world, separated, sanctified, and made meet for Thy use, whom Thou hast designed to be filled with all Thy fulness.

Nothing has hurt me so much as this, to see so-called believers have so much unbelief in them that it is hard to move them. There is no difficulty in praying for a sinner to be healed. But with the "believer," when you touch him he comes back and says, "You did not pray for my legs." I say you are healed all over if you believe. Everything is possible to them that believe. God will not fail His Word whatever you are. Suppose that all the people in the world did not believe, that would make no difference to God's Word, it would be the same. You cannot alter God's Word. It is from everlasting to everlasting, and they who believe in it shall be like Mount Zion which cannot be moved.

I was preaching on faith one time and there was in the audience a man who said three times, "I won't believe." I kept right on preaching because that made no difference to me. I am prepared for a fight any day, the fight of faith. We must keep the faith which has been committed unto us. I went on preaching and the man shouted out, "I won't believe." As he passed out of the door he cried out again, "I won't believe." Next day a message came saying there was a man in the meeting the night before who said out loud three times, "I won't believe," and as soon as he got outside the Spirit said to him, "Because thou wouldst not believe thou shalt be dumb." It was the same Spirit that came to Zacharias and said, "...thou shalt be dumb, and not able to speak, until the day that these things shall be performed, because thou believest not my words..." (Luke 1:20). I believe in a hell. Who is in hell? The unbeliever. If you want to go to hell, all you need to do is to disbelieve the Word of God. The unbelievers are there. Thank God they are there for they are no good for any society. I said to the leader of that meeting, "You go and see this man and find out if these things are so." He went to the house and the first to greet him was the man's wife. He said, "Is it true that your husband three times in the meeting declared that he would not believe, and now he cannot speak?" She burst into tears and said, "Go and see." He went into the room and saw the man's mouth in a terrible state. The man got a piece of paper and wrote, "I had an opportunity to believe. I refused to believe, and now I cannot believe and I cannot speak." The greatest sin in the world is to disbelieve God's Word. We are not of those who draw back, but we are of those who believe, for God's Word is a living Word and it always acts.

One day a stylishly dressed lady came to our meeting and on up to the platform. Under her arm, going down underneath her dress, was a concealed crutch that nobody could see. She had been helpless in one leg for twenty years, had heard of what God was doing, and wanted to be prayed for. As soon as we prayed for her, she exclaimed, "What have you done with my leg?" Three times she said it, and then we saw that the crutch was loose and hanging, and that she was standing straight up. The lady that was interpreting for me said to her, "We have done nothing with your leg. If anything has been done it is God who has done it." She answered, "I have been lame and used a crutch for twenty years, but my leg is perfect now." We did not suggest that she get down at the altar and thank God; she fell down among the others and cried for mercy. I find when God touches us it is a divine touch, life, power, and it thrills and quickens the body so that people know it is God and conviction comes and they cry for mercy. Praise God for anything that brings people to the throne of grace.

God heals by the power of His Word. But the most important thing is: are you saved, do you know the Lord, are you prepared to meet God? You may be an invalid as long as you live, but you may be saved by the power of God. You may have a strong, healthy body but may go straight to hell because you know nothing of the grace of God and salvation. Thank God I was saved in a moment, the moment I believed, and God will do the same for you. God means by this divine power within you to make you follow after the mind of the Spirit by the Word of God, till you are entirely changed by the power of it. You might come on this platform and say, "Wigglesworth, is there anything you can look up to God and ask Him for in your body?" I will say now that I have a body in perfect condition and have nothing to ask for, and I am sixty-five. It was not always so. This body was a frail, helpless body, but God fulfilled His Word to me according to Isaiah and Matthew — Himself took my infirmities and my diseases, my sicknesses, and by His stripes I am healed. It is fine to go up and down and not know you have a body. He took our infirmities. He bore our sickness, He came to heal our brokenheartedness. Jesus would have us to come forth in divine likeness, in resurrection force, in the power of the Spirit, to walk in faith and understand His Word, what He meant when He said He would give us power over all the power of the enemy. He will subdue all things till everything comes into perfect harmony with His will. Is He reigning over your affections, desires, will? If so, when He reigns you will be subject to His reigning power. He will be authority over the whole situation. When He reigns, everything must be subservient to His divine plan and will for us.

See what the Word of God says: "No man can say that Jesus is the Lord, but by the Holy Ghost." "Lord!" Bless God forever. Oh, for Him to be Lord and Master! For Him to rule and control! For Him to be filling your whole body with the plan of truth! Because you are in Christ Jesus all things are subject to Him. It is lovely, and God wants to make it so to you. When you get there you will find divine power continually working. I absolutely believe that no man comes into the place of revelation and activity of the gifts of the Spirit but by this fulfilled promise of Jesus that He will baptize us in the Holy Ghost.

I was taken to see a beautiful nine-year-old boy who was lying on a bed. The mother and father were distracted because he had been lying there for months. They had to lift and feed him; he was like a statue with flashing eyes. As soon as I entered the place the Lord revealed to me the cause of the trouble, so I said to the mother, "The Lord shows me there is something wrong with his stomach." She said, "Oh no, we have had two physicians and they say it is paralysis of the mind." I said, "God reveals to me it is his stomach." "Oh, no, it isn't. These physicians ought to know, they have X-rayed him." The gentleman who brought me there said to the mother, "You have sent for this man, you have been the means of his coming, now don't you stand out against him. This man knows what he has got to do." But Dr. Jesus knows more than that. He knows everything. You have no need to ring the bell for doctors. All you have to do is ring your bell for Jesus and He will come down. You should never turn to human things, because divine things are so much better and just at your call. Who shall interfere with the divine mind of the Spirit which has all revelation, who understands the whole condition of life? For the Word of God declares He knoweth all things, is well acquainted with the manifestation of thy body, for everything is naked and open before Him with whom we have to do. Having the mind of the Spirit we understand what is the will of God. I prayed over this boy and laid my hands on his stomach. He became sick and vomited a worm thirteen inches long and was perfectly restored. Who knows? God knows. When shall we come into the knowledge of God? When we cease from our own mind and allow ourselves to become clothed with the mind and authority of the mighty God.

The Spirit of God would have us understand there is nothing that can interfere with our coming into perfect blessing except unbelief. Unbelief is a terrible hindrance. As soon as we are willing to allow the Holy Ghost to have His way, we will find great things will happen all the time. But oh, how much of our own human reason we have to get rid of, how much human planning we have to become divorced from. What would happen right now if everybody believed God? I love the thought that God the Holy Ghost wants to emphasize the truth that if we will only yield ourselves to the divine plan, He is right there to bring forth the mystery of truth.

How many of us believe the Word? It is easy to quote it, but it is more important to have it than to quote it. It is very easy for me to quote, "Now are we the sons of God," but it is more important for me to know whether I am a son of God. When the Son was on the earth He was recognized by the people who heard Him. Never man spake like Him. His word was with power, and that word came to pass. Sometimes you have quoted, "Greater is he that is in you than he that is in the world," and you could tell just where to find it. But brother, is it so? Can demons remain in your presence? You have to be greater than demons. Can disease lodge in the body that you touch? You have to be greater than the disease. Can anything in the world stand against you and hold its place if it is a fact that greater is He that is in you than he that is in the world? Dare we stand on the line with the Word of God and face the facts of the difficulties before us?

I can never forget the face of a man that came to me one time. His clothes hung from him, his whole frame was shrivelled, his eyes were glaring and glassy, his jawbones stuck out, his whole being was a manifestation of death. He said to me, "Can you help me?" Could I help him? Just as we believe the Word of God can we help anybody, but we must be sure we are on the Word of God. If we are on the Word of God it must take place. As I looked at him I thought I had never seen anybody alive that looked like him. I said, "What is it?" He answered with a breath voice, "I had a cancer on my chest. I was operated on and in removing the cancer they removed my swallower; so now I can breathe but cannot swallow." He pulled out a tube about nine inches long with a cup at the top and an opening at the bottom to go into a hole. He showed me that he pressed one part of that into his stomach and poured liquid into the top; and for three months had been keeping himself alive that way. It was a living death. Could I help him? See what the Word of God says: "...whosoever...shall not doubt in his heart, but shall believe that those things which he saith shall come to pass; he shall have whatsoever he saith" (Mark 11:23). God wants to move us on scriptural lines. On those lines I said, "You shall have a good supper tonight." "But," he said, "I cannot swallow." I said, "You shall have a good supper tonight." "But I cannot swallow." "You shall have a good supper; go and eat."

When he got home he told his wife that the preacher said he could have a good supper that night. He said, "If you will get something ready I'll see if I can swallow." His wife got a good supper ready and he took a mouthful. He had had mouthfuls before but they would not go down. But the Word of God said "whatsoever," and this mouthful went down, and more and more went down until he was full up. Then what happened? He went to bed with joy of the knowledge that he could again swallow, and he wakened next morning with that same joy. He looked for a hole in his stomach, but God had shut that up when he opened the other.

Faith is the substance of things hoped for. Faith is the Word. You were begotten of the Word, the Word is in you, the life of the Son is in you, and God wants you to believe.

Published in *The Pentecostal Evangel*

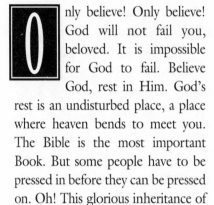

THE CLOTHING OF THE SPIRIT FOR THE WORLD'S NEED

1925

Only believe! Only believe! God will not fail you, beloved. It is impossible for God to fail. Believe God, rest in Him. God's rest is an undisturbed place, a place where heaven bends to meet you. The Bible is the most important Book. But some people have to be pressed in before they can be pressed on. Oh! This glorious inheritance of joy and Holy Faith — this glorious baptism in the Holy Ghost — a perfected place. All things are new, for ye are Christ's and Christ is God.

> *...ye shall receive power, after that the Holy Ghost is come upon you: and ye shall be witnesses unto me both in Jerusalem, and in all Judaea, and in Samaria, and unto the uttermost part of the earth.*
>
> *Acts 1:8*

God means us to be in this royal way — when God opens a door, no man can shut it. John made a royal way and Jesus went in and left it for us to let Him bring forth through us the greater works. Jesus left His disciples with a revelation which meant much to them and much more to be added, something lasting until God receives us in that day, when we receive power we must stir up ourselves to the truth that we are responsible for the need around us. God will supply all our need that the need of the needy may be met through us — a great indwelling force of power. If we do not step into our privileges it is a tragedy.

TONGUES AND INTERPRETATION: "God who ravishes thee, brings forth within the heart new revelation, never the same again, changed by the Spirit from vision to vision, from light to light, from glory to glory."

POWER AND ACTION

There is no standing still in this blessed life. It is a fearful thing to fall into the hands of the living God. Oh, that blessed concession of God to fill us with the Holy Ghost. He will lead us into all truth and show us things to come. As He is, so are we in this world. The offspring of God with impulse divine. We must get into line. The life of the Son of God to make the whole body a flame of fire. After ye have received ye shall have power. God has given me a blessed ministry to help to stir others up — our gatherings must be for increase. I am jealous to come into the divine plan. If I wait further for power I have mistaken the position. If I could only feel the power! Ah! We have been too much on that line. When the Holy Ghost came He came to abide — what are you waiting for? God is waiting for you to act. Jesus was perfect activity. He began to do and to teach. He lived in the realm of divine appointment making the act come forth. God never separates power from holiness — the pure in heart see God. The Holy Ghost reveals Him. He that believes that Jesus is the Christ overcomes the world. He is the source of revelation. The fulness of God dwells in Him.

> Christ liveth in me — Christ liveth in me.
> Oh, what a salvation this
> That Christ dwelleth in me.

After the Holy Ghost came, with the revelation of the purity of Jesus we saw things which were unseen before. The Holy Ghost came in as the breath of the moving of the mighty wind. Is the Holy Spirit a person? Yes! Wind! Breath! Fire! Our God is a consuming fire.

You never know what you have until you begin. God wants you to begin on the authority of the Word tonight, as you stand upon the Word of God you will be amazed at the outcome.

On going along in a car I saw a crowd of people 'round a boy. I asked the driver to stop. I said, "Boy, what is it?" "Cramp." I said, "In the name of Jesus, come out!" The boy got up free. Faith in the operation of God. Wind! Fire! Breath! Life — a ministry of life. Gripping death with life.

The word was in. I laid hold "...for the Word is nigh thee, in thy mouth and in thine heart." Thus the boy, by the operation of God, was free. We are baptized into one Spirit. We are tomorrow what we design to be today. This is a rising tide — a changing.

TONGUES AND INTERPRETATION: "God, who is the wealth of our inheritance, hath for us greater things. After ye have received ye shall believe."

POWER AND PROGRESS

This is the confidence we have in Him. If we ask anything according to His will He heareth us — and we have the petition we have desired of

Him; when the Holy Ghost comes in it is to crown Jesus King. We must dare and press on to that place where God will come forth with mighty power. Men of faith always have a good report. God has given us a large open door and will bless the people as we dare to believe His Word. The opportunity is all around — the needy are everywhere, begin. Ye shall receive power, the Holy Ghost coming upon you. The stones will cry out against us if we do not press on. May God give us the hearing of faith that the power may come down like a cloud. Once I saw it mighty at Stavenger in Norway — it was a great crowded place. God said to me: Ask! And I will give you every soul. It seemed too much. The voice came again. Ask! And I will give you every soul. I dared to ask. The power of God swept the meeting like a mighty wind. I had never seen anything like it up to that time. We look for this in London. Go — speak all the words of this life. Begin from tonight. Press on until Jesus is glorified and multitudes gathered in. Let us all stand and offer ourselves unto God.

Receive! Receive! Receive! Ye shall receive power.

Message given at Sion College, London

FLOODTIDE THE INCREASE OF GOD

1925

Wherever Jesus went, the multitudes followed Him, because He lived, moved, breathed, was swallowed up, clothed and filled with God. He was God and as Son of man the Spirit of God rested upon Him, the Spirit of creative holiness. It is lovely to be holy. Jesus came to impart to us the spirit of holiness.

We are only at the edge of things, the almighty plan is marvelous for the future. God must do something to increase. A revival to revive within and without all we touch. A floodtide with a cloudburst behind it. Jesus left 120 men to turn the world upside down. The Spirit is upon us to change the situation. We must move on to let God increase in us for the deliverance of multitudes and we must travail through until souls are born and quickened into new relationship with heaven. Jesus had divine authority with power, and He left it for us. We must preach truth, holiness and purity in the inward parts.

> *Thou hast loved righteousness, and hated iniquity; therefore God, even thy God, hath anointed thee with the oil of gladness above thy fellows.*
>
> Hebrews 1:9

I am thirsty for more of God. He was not only holy, but He loved holiness.

TONGUES AND INTERPRETATION: "It is the depths that God gets into that we may reflect Him and manifest a life having Christ enthroned in the heart, drinking into a new fulness, new intuition, for as He is, so are we in this world."

He trod the winepress alone, despising the cross and the shame. He bore it all alone that we might be partakers of the divine nature, sharers in the divine plan of living, holiness. That's revival — Jesus manifesting divine authority. He was without sin. They saw the Lamb of God in a new way. Hallelujah! Let us live holy and revival will come down and God will enable us to do the work to which we are appointed. All Jesus said came to pass. Signs, wonders, mighty deeds. Only believe, and yield and yield, until all the vision is fulfilled.

God has a design, a purpose, a rest of faith. We are saved by faith, and kept by faith. Faith is substance, it is also evidence. God is! He is!!! And He is a rewarder of them that diligently seek Him. We are to testify, to bear witness to what we know. To know that we know is a wonderful position.

TONGUES AND INTERPRETATION: "The Lord is the great promoter of divine possibility, pressing you into the attitude of daring to believe all the Word says. We are to be living words, epistles of Christ, known and read of all men. The revelation of Christ, past and future, in Him all things consist. He is in us."

We are living in the inheritance of faith because of the grace of God, saved for eternity by the operation of the Spirit bringing forth unto God. A substance of divine proposition and attainment, bringing heaven to earth until God quickens all things into beauty, manifesting His power in living witnesses. God in us for a world, that the world may be blessed. Power to lay hold of omnipotence and impart to others the Word of life. This is a new epoch, new vision, new power. Christ in us is greater than we know. All things are possible if you dare believe. The treasure is in earthen vessels that Jesus may be glorified.

Let us go forth bringing glory to God. Faith is substance, a mightiness of reality, a deposit of divine nature, God creative within. The moment you believe you are mantled with a new power to lay hold of possibility and make it reality. They said, "Lord, evermore give us this bread, for he that eateth Me shall live by Me." Have the faith of God. The man who comes into great association with God needs a heavenly measure. Faith is the greatest of all. Saved by a new life, the Word of God, an association with the living Christ. A new creation continually taking us into new revelation.

> *In the beginning was the Word, and the Word was with God,*
> *and the Word was God....All things were made by him; and*
> *without him was not any thing made that was made.*
>
> *John 1:1,3*

All was made by the Word. I am begotten by His Word. Within me there is a substance that has almighty power in it if I dare believe. Faith going on to be an act, a reality, a deposit of God, an almighty flame moving you to act, so that signs and wonders are manifest. A living faith within the earthen casket. Are you begotten? Is it an act within you? Some need a touch, liberty to captives. As many as He touched were made perfectly whole. Faith takes you to the place where God reigns imbibing God's bountiful store. Unbelief is sin, for Jesus went to death to bring us the light of life.

Jesus said, "Are ye able to drink of the cup that I drink of and be baptized with the baptism I am baptized with?" The cup and the baptism, a joined position. You cannot live if you want to bring everything into life. His life is manifested power overflowing. Human must decrease if the life of God is to be manifested. There is not room for two kinds of life in one body. Death for life, the price to pay for the manifested power of God through you. As you die to human desire there comes a fellowship within, perfected cooperation, you ceasing, God increasing. God in you a living substance, a spiritual nature. You live by another life, the faith of the Son of God.

TONGUES AND INTERPRETATION: "The Spirit, He breathed through and quickeneth until the body is a temple exhibiting Jesus, His life, His freshness, a new life divine. Paul said, 'Christ liveth in me and the life I live in the flesh I live by faith.'"

As the Holy Ghost reveals Jesus, He is real — the living Word, effective, acting, speaking, thinking, praying, singing. Oh, it is a wonderful life, this substance of the Word of God, including possibility and opportunity, and confronting you, bringing you to a place undaunted. Greater is He that is in you. Paul said, "...when I am weak, then am I strong" (2 Corinthians 12:10).

Jesus walked in supremacy, He lived in the Kingdom, and God will take us through because of Calvary. He has given us power over all the power of the enemy. He won it for us at Calvary. All must be subject. What shall we do to work the works? This is the work of God that ye believe. Whatsoever He saith shall come to pass. That is God's Word.

A man, frail, weak, with eyes shrunk, and neck shriveled, said, "Can you help me?" Beloved, there is not one that cannot be helped. God has opened the doors for us to let Him manifest signs and wonders. The authority is inside, not outside. Could I help him? He had been on liquid food three months, fed through a tube. I said, "Go home and eat a good supper." He did, and woke up to find the tube hole closed up. God knew he did not want two holes. We must keep in a strong resolute resting on the authority of God's Word. One great desire and purpose to do what He saith. To live in this holy Word, rejoicing in the manifestation of the life of God on behalf of the sick and perishing multitudes. Amen.

REVIVAL – IT'S COMING . . . THE PRICE – MARTYRDOM

1925

Revival is coming. God's heart is in the place of intense passion. Let us bend or break, for God is determined to bless us. Oh, the joy of service and the joy of suffering to be utterly cast upon Jesus. God is coming forth with power. The latter rain is appearing.

YIELDED WILL

There must be no coming down from the cross but a going on from faith to faith and from glory to glory with an increasing diligence to be found in Him without spot and blameless (2 Peter 3:14). A divine plan is outworking. Behold, the husbandman waiteth for the precious fruit of the earth until he receive the early and the latter rain (James 5:7). Jesus is waiting to do all. Worship is higher than fellowship.

Oh, the calmness of meeting with Jesus. All fears are gone. His tender mercy and indescribable peace is ours. I have all if I have Jesus. Pruning the tree. All God's plans for us are to the end of a yielded will. God is waiting for the precious fruit of the earth. The outcome of a sown life diviner, lovelier. The seed has to die. Great is the day of Jezreel (whom God sows) (Hosea 1:11). One head. I will break the bow of Israel in the valley of Jezreel (whom God sows or the seed of God) (Hosea 1:5). I will break the battleaxe out of the earth — and I will betroth thee unto me forever in righteousness, judgment, lovingkindness, in mercies, even betroth thee unto me in faithfulness and thou shalt know the Lord. I will hear the heavens (sit with me). They shall hear the earth (this company hear the groaning of the people, and the earth shall hear the corn and the new wine and the oil and they shall hear Jezreel (the seed of God). Amen.

Let them hear — Let God do it — He commands it. God says, "Let there be light! Let your light shine!" God awaits the death of the seed. It springs into life. How do you know the seed is dead? Why, the green shoots appear. God awaits the evidence of death, for Isaiah 11 to appear. A place of profound rest. Jesus said, "I will pray the Father and He shall give you another Comforter."

> Not a sound invades the stillness
> Not a form invades the scene
> Save the voice of my Beloved
> and the person of my King.
>
> Precious, gentle, Holy Jesus
> Blessed Bridegroom of my heart
> In thy secret inner chamber
> Thou wilt whisper what Thou art.

And within those heavenly places
Calmly hushed in sweet repose
There I drink with joy absorbing
All the love thou wouldst disclose.

Wrapt in deep adoring silence
Jesus Lord, I dare not move
Lest I lose the smallest saying
Meant to catch the ear of love.

Rest then, oh my soul, contented
Thou hast reached that happy place
In the bosom of thy Savior
Gazing up in His dear face.

AN OUTPOURING

The early and the latter rain appears. The early rain is to make the seed die. To come to an end, ashes. And out of the ashes the great fire of consummation that shall burn in the heart of the people, the Word of the living God producing the Christ by the breath of the Spirit. Ashes, then the latter rain appears a surging of life. The old finished. Now shall come forth on those that know the Father a surging life and the effects of the latter rain and universal outpouring of the Holy Spirit. The coming of the Lord is at hand. The judge is standing at the door — Has He come? (John 16:8) When He comes He will convict the world, convincing men of sin. Has He come! Of judgement, the prince of this world has been judged (v. 11). If I go I will send Him unto you. Has He come!

God awaits to move and shake all that can be shaken (Mark 16), the signs following those that believe, an outpouring, mighty and glorious. The early rain has been to get us ready for that which is to come. Be killed. Be prepared — a vessel to pour out torrents. The baptism of the Holy Spirit is for the death of the seed. The Holy Ghost wakes up every passion, permits every trial. His object is to make the vessel pure. All must die before a manifestation of God unthought of, undreamt of. It's a call to martyrdom, to the death of spirit, soul, and body. To the death. The choice is before you, decide, accept, the path for death to life. Absolute abandonment for a divine equipment for the early and the latter rain appears.

Isaiah 11 is God's equipment for the understanding of the worldwide purposes of God, for the loveliness of Jesus and the glory of God. Revelation to a perishing world — where there is no vision the people perish. Wake up — the air is full of revival, but we look for a mighty outpouring, shaking all that can be shaken. Take all, but give me vision and revelation of the purposes of God and a wonderful burning love. It is difficult to tell of the freedom of the Holy Ghost in revealing the love of Jesus a fulcrum (2 Samuel 22). And David spoke this song and said, "My cry did enter into His ears."

Oh, yes, it must come, this surging life — this uttermost death for uttermost life. The early and the latter rain appears — we count those happy that endure. Count it not strange beloved — for the fiery breath of revival is coming. There is a ripple on the lake, a murmur in the air. The price is tremendous, it's martyrdom. We must seal the testimony with our blood. There must be the outworked cross. Dying — searching — crucifixions — no resistance. Trust me, it is finished.

Yes, be sown first, then comes the revelation of God with eternal issues for multitudes. The latter rain appears. All moves before the men God has moved, and millions are ingathered and the heart of God is satisfied.

> Since thou art come to that holy room
> Where with the choirs of saints forevermore
> Thou art made my music.
> Thine the instrument here at the door
> And what Thou must do then think here before.

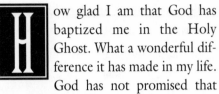

THE BAPTISM OF THE HOLY SPIRIT

June 1925

How glad I am that God has baptized me in the Holy Ghost. What a wonderful difference it has made in my life. God has not promised that we should feel very wonderful, but He has promised that if we stand on His Word, He would make His Word real. It is faith first; then it becomes a fact. There are plenty of feelings in the fact, I assure you. God fills us with His own precious joy.

Samson has his name recorded in the eleventh chapter of Hebrews as being a man of faith. He was a man who was chosen of God from his mother's womb, but he only had the power of God coming upon him on certain occasions; whereas now we who have received the fulness of the Holy Ghost, the Comforter, may have the unction which abides forever. The Lord has promised that we shall have life and have it abundantly. Look at the fifth chapter of Romans and see how many times the expression "much more" is used. Oh, that we might take this grace of God and revel in the Word of God and be so full of expectancy, that we might have these "much mores" coming out as fruit in our lives.

Maybe some people here realize that they have had the power of the Lord upon them and yet they have lost out. Friends, what about you? God in His love and kindness has put Samson in Hebrews 11. There came a time when because of Samson's sin, his eyes were put out. His hair had been shorn and he lost his strength. He tried to break the cords but the Philistines got him. But his hair grew again and the Philistines wanted him to make sport for them, but he prayed a prayer and God answered. Oh, that we might turn to God and pray this prayer: "Oh, Lord God, remember me, I pray Thee and strengthen me, I pray Thee, only this once, oh God." If you will turn to God with true repentance, He is plenteous in mercy and He will forgive you. Repentance means getting back to God. When Samson took hold of the pillars upon which the house stood, he pulled the walls down. God can give you strength and you can get hold of the posts and He will work through you. No matter what kind of a backslider you have been, there is power in the blood. "...the blood of Jesus Christ his Son cleanseth us from all sin" (1 John 1:7). Oh, if I could only tell you how God so wonderfully restored me! And I had my "first love" again and He has filled me with the Holy Ghost.

Let me read a few verses to you from the second chapter of the Acts of the apostles:

> *And when the day of Pentecost was fully come, they were all with one accord in one place. And suddenly there came a sound from heaven as of a rushing mighty wind, and it filled all the house where they were sitting. And there appeared unto them cloven tongues like as of fire, and it sat upon each of them. And they were all filled with the Holy Ghost, and began to speak with other tongues, as the Spirit gave them utterance.*
>
> *Acts 2:1-4*

What a wonderful divine position God means us all to have, to be filled with the Holy Ghost. There is something so remarkable, so divine, as it were, a great open door into all the treasury of the Most High. As the Spirit comes like rain upon the mown grass, He turns the barrenness into greenness and freshness and life. Oh, Hallelujah! God would have you know that there is a place where you are dispensed with and where God comes to be thy assurance and sustaining power spiritually, till thy dryness is turned into springs; till thy barrenness begins to be floods, till thine whole life becomes vitalized by heaven, till heaven sweeps through you and dwells within and turns everything inside out, till you are absolutely so filled with divine possibilities that you begin to live in a new creation. The Spirit of the living God sweeps through all weaknesses.

Beloved, God the Holy Ghost wants to bring us to a great revelation of life. He wants us to be filled with all the fulness of God. One of the most beautiful pictures we have in the Scriptures is of the Trinity. I want you to see how God unfolded heaven, and heaven and earth became the habitation of Trinity. Right on the banks of Jordan, Trinity was made manifest: the voice of God in the heavens looking at His well-beloved Son coming out of the waters, and there the Spirit was manifested in the shape of a dove. The dove is the only bird without gall, so timid a creature that at the least thing it moves and is afraid. No person can be baptized with the Holy Spirit and have bitterness — gall.

My brother, it is the double cure you want. It is saving and cleansing and the baptism of the Holy Ghost till the old man shall never rise anymore; till you are absolutely dead unto sin, and alive unto God by His Spirit, and know that old things have passed away. When the Holy Ghost gets possession, there is a new man entirely — the whole being becomes saturated with divine power. We become a habitation of Him who is all light, all revelation, all power, and all love. Yea, God the Holy Ghost is so manifested within us that it is glorious.

There was a certain rich man in London whose business flourished. He used to get hold of his bank book and checks, then scratched his head — he didn't know what to do. Walking about his great building he came to a boy keeping the door. He found the boy whistling. Looking at him he took the full size of the whole situation and went back to his office again and scratched his head. Back to business he went but he could get no peace. His bank could not help him; his checks, his success could not help him. He had an aching void. He was helpless within. My brother, a whited sepulchre is to have the world without God.

When he could get no rest he exclaimed, "I will go and see what the boy is doing." Again he went and found him, whistling. "I want you to come into my office," he said. On entering the office he said, "Tell me, what makes you so happy and cheerful?" "Oh," replied the boy, "I used to be so miserable until I went to a little Mission and heard about Jesus. Then I was saved and filled with the Holy Ghost. It is always whistling inside: if it is not whistling, it sings. I am just full!"

This rich man secured the address of the Mission from the boy, went to the services and sat beside the door. But the power of God so moved that when the altar call was given he responded and God saved him, and a few days afterwards filled him with the Holy Ghost. He found himself at his desk shouting, Oh, hallelujah!

> I know the Lord, I know the Lord,
> I know the Lord's laid His hand on me.
> I know the Lord, I know the Lord.
> I know the Lord's laid His hand on me.

Oh, this blessed Son of God wants to fill us with such glory till our whole body is aflame with the power of the Holy Ghost. I see there is "much more." Glory to God! My daughter asked some African boys to tell us the difference between being saved and being filled with the Holy Ghost. "Ah," they said, "when we were saved it was very good, but when we received the Holy Ghost it was 'more so.'" Many of you have never received the "more so."

After the Holy Ghost comes upon you, you shall have power; God mightily moving within the human life; the power of the Holy Ghost overshadowing, inwardly moving you till you know there is a divine plan different from anything that you had in your life before. Has He come? He is going to come tonight. I am expecting that God shall so manifest His presence and power that He will show you the necessity of receiving the Holy Ghost; also God will heal the people who have need of healing. Everything is to be had now: salvation, sanctification, and the fulness of the Holy Ghost and healing. God is working mightily by the power of His Spirit, bringing into our meeting a fulness of His perfect redemption until every soul may know that God has all power.

Published in *Triumphs of Faith*

DIVINE REVELATION

June 4, 1925

Praise the Lord. Praise the Lord. Praise the Lord. Only believe! Only believe! All things are possible, only believe. There is something very remarkable about that chorus. God wants to impress it so deeply on our hearts tonight that we may in our corners, rooms, private places, get so engrossed in the fact with this divine truth that if we *will!* only believe! He can get in us and out of us for others what otherwise would never be possible. Oh, for this to lay hold of us tonight that God comes to us afresh and says, "Only believe." Beloved, let me tell you, the tune will help you, especially if you sing it in time. Everything ought to be in time, because it means so much to be in time; but beloved! The Lord, I trust tonight, will give me something to make you ready for everything, that you will not be behind time but in the place God has designed for you.

The possibilities are within the reach of all. Let us read from Matthew 16:13, "...Whom do men say that I...am?...Thou art the Christ, the Son of the living God" (Matthew 16:13,16).

This is a blessed truth. Lord, help me tonight. I am deeply convinced that there is such a marvelous work done in the revelation to the heart of the incoming One; of the new life of God. There is a tremendous, a divine treasure, within the human soul that comes into line with this truth, that they are in a place where God intends that they shall not only bind and loose, but that they shall be in the position by the grace of God to so stand in the lot of their day that the gates of hell shall not be able to prevail against them. I know the Roman Catholics have made a great to-do about this, but beloved, what I am desiring above all, is that I shall be emblematic in every way in this truth that this word shall be in me a light, a flame of fire, burning in my bones, presenting to me, within my being a fact because God's Word declares such and such and such things.

I would like someone to read to me John 1:12,13. They are wonderful words. To "...as many as received him, gave he power to become the sons of God." Born of God. His nature. Born of God. This divine nature we have received came to us with the reception of the Word of God. And he said to them, "Whom do ye say that I...am?" Peter answered, "...Thou art the Christ" (Matthew 16:13,16). Wonderful. Wonderful. Whom do you say that He is tonight? Oh, glory to God, whom do you say He is? The Christ, the Son of the living God. And the truth comes to us — blessed are ye; flesh and blood hath not revealed this but He alone; to have this revelation that He is the Son of God is a revelation that He was manifested to destroy the works of the devil. Sometimes it is important that we stir one another up with these divine relationships. The baptism in the Holy Ghost gives us not only a plan of the operations of God, but also unfolds to us the position we have, by the Holy Ghost, in this world.

THE ROCK — THE KEY

My message is to the believer tonight in every sense, and I know the Lord is going to bless this word to us. Now it is a perfect revelation to me tonight and to you; I know the fact that God declares it to us by His own Son is this, that the new birth is a perfect place of royalty, reigning over the powers of darkness, bringing everything to perfect submission to the rightful owner, and that is the Lord. He it is who rules within and reigns there, and our bodies have become temples of the Holy Ghost.

He said to Peter, "Upon this rock will I build my church." What rock was it? The rock is the living Word. Upon this rock will I build my church. What is the rock? The Son of the living God. He is the rock. But what are the keys? The keys are the divine working by faith in the things of God. And I will give thee the keys of unlocking. Remember this. It is the key which has life within it. It is the key which has power to enter in. It is life divine, that verse opens and unlocks all the dark things and brings life and liberty to the captive. Upon this rock will I build my church, and the gates of hell shall not prevail.

Now let us see how it works. It works, it always works, it never fails to work. Now let me bring before you the truth, because you know you cannot depend upon yourself in this, so I want to help you. You will never be able to get anything by your own initiative. You cannot do it. It is divine life flowing through you that empowers you to act and the vessel is in the position where the glory of the new life brings the thing into action.

OPPORTUNITY — ACTION

On the ship one day they said to me, "We are going to have an entertainment." They said, "Would you be in the entertainment?" "Oh," I said, "Yes, I will be in anything that is going to be helpful," and I believe God was in it. So they said to me, "What can you do? What place will you take in the entertainment?" I said, "I can sing." So they said to me, "Where would you like to be put down in the entertainment?" They said, "We are going to have a dance." I said, "Put me down just before the dance," and so my turn came.

If you knew how I was longing for my turn to come, because there had been a clerical man there trying to sing and entertain them, and it seemed so out of place. My turn came on, and I sang: "If I could only tell Him as I know Him." I went through, and when I got through the people said, "You have spoilt the dance." Well, I was there for that purpose to spoil the dance, and a preacher came to me afterwards and said, "How dare you sing that?" Why, I said, how dare I not sing it, it was my opportunity, and he was going to India, and when he got to India he wrote in his periodical, and sent it over to England. He said, "I did not seem to have any chance to preach the Gospel," but "there was a plumber on board who seemed to have plenty of opportunities to preach to everybody, and he said things to me that remain. He told me that the Acts of the Apostles was only written because they acted; you see I was in the drama of life acting in the Name of Jesus.

TONGUES AND INTERPRETATION: "Out of the depths I cried and the Lord heard my cry and brought me into a large place on sea, on land, in a large place."

Glory to God.

And so that opened the door, and got me in the place that I could speak all the time, the door was open in every way. Next morning a young man and his wife came to me and said, "We are in a terrible state, we are looking after a gentleman and lady in the first-class; she is a Christian Scientist, and a great teacher of Christian Science; she has been taken seriously ill, and the doctor gives her little hope. We have told her about you, and she said she would like to see you." I said, "All right." That was my opportunity. Opportunity is a wonderful thing. Opportunity is the great thing of the day. And so when I went into the first-class room of the lady, I saw she was very sick. I said, "I am not going to speak to you about anything, neither about your sickness nor anything, I am simply going to lay my hands upon you in the Name of Jesus, and the moment I do, you will be healed."

As soon as I laid my hands upon her, the fever left her, and she was perfectly healed. She was terribly troubled, and for three days she was worse, troubled in her mind and heart. I knew it would have been as easy as possible to break to her the Bread of Life and bring her into liberty, but God would not have it. Just before she got saved she felt she would be lost forever, and then God saved her. Hallelujah. Yes, and she said, "What shall I do?" I said, "What do you mean?" "Oh," she said, "for three years I have been preaching all over England; we live in a great house in India, and we have a great house in London. I have been preaching Christian Science, and now what can I do?" She said, "You know it is all so real, I am a new woman altogether, and then she was filled with joy." She said, "Shall I be able to continue smoking cigarettes?" I said, "Yes, smoke as many as ever you can, smoke night and day if you can." Then she said to me, "You know we play cards; bridge and other things. Can I play?" I said, "Yes, play all night through, go on playing." And she said, "You know we have a little wine, just a little with our friends in the first-class. Shall I give it up?" "No," I said, "drink all you want."

When she got to Aden she called a maid to her, and said, "I want you to take this telegram, and stop that thousand cigarettes." She called her husband, and said, "I cannot go into all these things again."

We have not to go down to bring Him up nor up to bring Him down. He is nigh thee, He is in thy heart. The word of faith which we preach, and this is a living word, and God wants you all to know in this meeting tonight that if you only dare to act upon the divine principle that is written there the gates of hell shall not prevail. Praise the Lord.

REIGNING IN LIFE

And so, beloved, it is all for us tonight. Do not forget this. Every one of you can know this union, this divine relationship, this uttermost power which will be within keeping you alive to the fact that God has come to make you know that everything is subject to you. You have to reign in that body by one Christ Jesus. It is a lovely word, reigning in life by one Jesus.

Now I must keep to this, the Lord is welling up in my heart. You know that we have continual power; in the sixteenth chapter of Mark's gospel we read these words. There are two ways to enter into these divine relationships. I am here tonight to say it does not matter how many times we have failed, there is one key note in Pentecost, "Holiness unto the Lord." I find the association with my Lord brings purity, and makes my whole being cry out after God, after holiness. Holiness is power. Holiness unto the Lord. Why do I know this, because I see Jesus my Lord, I see Him, He is so beautiful. When the whole of that place was filled with unbelief Jesus wept, he wept because of their unbelief. He could not weep because Lazarus was dead, He was the resurrection life.

But their unbelief moved Him to groan in His spirit and He wept, and the sequel to that glorious triumph was the great union with His Father. He said to His Father, "I know that Thou hearest Me always, but because of these that stand around." Oh, the blessedness of the truth.

That word moves me tremendously. "If I know that He heareth me." "If I know He heareth me, then I know that I have the petition that I desired." Glory to God. Knowing there is not a power in the world can take that away from you. Every soul in the place is privileged to go into the Holiest of Holies, through the blood of the Lamb.

Address given at Whitsuntide
Convention, Kingsway Hall

cts 1:1-8 — God means us to be in this way where Jesus went and all His disciples, He has left this place open. "Greater works than these shall ye do; because I go to my Father." Jesus left nothing less than this, a power which was for them and to which more was to be added if we believe.

POWER
June 9, 1925

We have recently had seven years of earthly power, and are feeling the effects of it today, how it has broken hearts, homes and in fact the whole world, and filled it with such distressing effects and made it an awful place, that we never want it again.

This power is so much different; it restores the fallen, it heals the brokenhearted, it lifts, it lives, it brings life into existence in your own hearts. All the time there is something that is round about you, something that you know is lasting and will be forever, until the Lord will receive us unto Himself.

God, help me to speak tonight, I came not to speak only but to stir us up to our privilege to make men feel they are responsible for the state of things round about.

POWER AND PROGRESS

It thrills my soul and makes me think that I must step into line where God has called me. Sometimes I speak like this, some of you know what a tragedy is, you have heard of such things, and some of you know what a calamity is. I speak to every baptized soul here tonight, if you have not made any progress, you are a backslider in the sight of God; because of the privilege of the revelation of the Spirit within you, privilege and more power of entering into more light.

It is a wonderful thing to get into touch with the living God, it is a glorious thing, a blessed condescension of God to fill us with the Holy Ghost. But the responsibility after that, for the Spirit of God, for Jesus to be so pleased with His child that He fills His child with the Holy Ghost; that the child may now have the full revelation of Himself, for the Holy Ghost shall not speak of Himself, but He shall take of the truth and reveal it unto us. As He is we have to be, and just as righteous as He is we have to be, we are truly the offspring of God, actuating with divine impulse, and God is proving us to see that we must step into line, and see that the truth is still the same.

"...Ye shall receive power..." (Acts 1:8). Brothers, it is so real, His life for me the life of the Son of God within, characteristics to make the whole body a flame of fire, after that ye shall receive power. I am clearly coming to understand this in my ministry, God has given me a gracious ministry and I thank God for it. God has given me a ministry which I prize because it helps me to stir people, especially leaders. I am here tonight to stir you, I could not think that God would have me leave you as I found you. If I thought I was entrusted to speak for half an hour, and leave you as I found you. So my desire is that this half hour shall be so full of divine purpose, that everyone shall come into line with the plan of God tonight.

POWER AND PURITY

I am as satisfied as anything that if I wait further, I have mistaken the position. On this line I so want to say things to prove the situation. There is a great deal too much on the lines of, "If I can only feel the power." Our young brother said distinctly that the Holy Ghost came to abide. What are we waiting for? What is God waiting for? For you to get into the place. What do I mean? I mean this: that Jesus was a perfect activity, a life in activity. The Scripture declares it. He began to do, and then to teach. It is as clear as possible, in a realm of divine appointment, where He was able to make the act conform.

So I am truly on the Word of God tonight, if we have received the power the power is there. I am not going to say, that there has not to be an unbroken fellowship with Him, He never separates power from holiness, the pure in heart shall see God. But I believe that if He has come to reveal unto us Him, you cannot lack it, because he that believes that Jesus is the Christ, overcomes the world.

He is the purifier, He is the abiding presence, the one great source of righteousness, then all the fulness of the Godhead bodily dwells in Him, there is the situation.

(Chorus: Christ liveth in me.)

And you know that after the Spirit gave the revelation of the purity of Christ by the Word of the Lord, He made you see things as you never saw them before.

I would like to speak for a few moments on the breath of the Spirit, because I see the Holy Spirit came as a breath, or as the moving of a mighty wind. I see so much divine appointment in this for humanity, this great thought, the Holy Spirit fills the life by the breath. It is wonderful — this prophetic position. Who did you hear speak? Yes, I hear Mr. Wigglesworth and Mr. Carter. Yes, that is the term. Behind it all you will find that language is breath.

When you are filled with the breath of the Spirit, the breath of God, the holy fire and the Word, it is Christ within you.

Life is given, he that heareth my words and believeth on Him that sent me hath everlasting life. We need the Spirit, to be filled with prophetic power to bring forth to the needs of the people, life. This is life, I am perceiving that I must be so in this order. Let me give you one or two positions.

POWER IN ACTION

God wants everybody, without exception, to begin on the Word of God, and to act. It will be the most surprising thing that ever came. As you stand on the Word it will be an amazing thing.

One day as I was going down the streets of San Francisco in a car, when looking through the window I saw a great crowd of people at the corner of the street. "Stop," I said, "there is something amiss," so I rushed as fast as possible to the edge of the crowd. I was so eager I pressed myself into the crowd, and I saw a boy laid on the ground who was held in a death-like grip.

The Word is in thee. I put my ear to his mouth as the boy lay there struggling. "Tell me, boy, what it is"; and the boy said, "It is cramp," so I put my hands around him, and said, "Come out in the Name of

Jesus." The boy immediately jumped up, ran off and had no time to say thank you. It is for everyone. After that you have received you are in the place. I am not saying that glibly, my thoughts are too serious for that. **I cannot be any more after tonight what I was today, and tomorrow is mightier than today.** This is the reason the tide is changing with God, this is the reality.

It is no little thing to be baptized, it is the promise of the Father, Jesus must be there, and the Holy Ghost also bringing us to the place where we can be baptized. Are you going to treat it as a great thing? What do you really believe it is? I believe when the Holy Ghost comes that He comes to crown the King.

And the King from that day gets His rightful place, and we don't have to claim anything, and He becomes King of all the situations.

I only say this to help you. It is a need, that I am speaking about, that I cannot get away from the fact, because where I look I see growth. I see you people, I see the growth, I have been away from England three years, and I see changes, and even though we see there is growth, life and blessing, there is much more ground to be possessed, and we shall have to dare before God can work.

God has given me an open door. Nothing moves me, only this, except I see men and women coming into line with this.

I want the people of Pentecost to rise as the heart of one man, God has us for a purpose in these last days, and in the meeting God helps me.

At a certain meeting, I said, "There is a man in this meeting suffering, and shall I preach before I help this man, or would you like to see this person free before I commence?" This man was a stranger and did not know who I was speaking about. There he was, with cancer on the face and full of pain, and I said, "Is it right to preach, or shall I heal this man?"

I saw what was the right thing, and I went down off the platform and placed my hand on him in the Name of Jesus.

This was because of what the Word said, that man knew nothing of healing, but in a moment he was able to stand up, and said, "I have been twelve years in pain, something has happened to me," and that night he gave himself to God, and testified night after night, that he was completely cured. What was it? God ministered through daring to believe

His Word. There are cases round about you, and what a story you would have to tell next year if only people took a stand on the Word of God from tonight.

A woman brought her husband to me and said, "I want you to help my husband." I said, "Well, I will." She said, "He has too many complaints to tell you of."

[I said,] "There is a man here so full of pains and weakness that I am going to pray for him on the authority of God's Word, and tomorrow night I am going to ask him to come back and tell you what God has done for him." And I placed my hand on him in the Name of Jesus. The next night this man came walking straight, and he said, "Will you let me speak to these people tonight? For forty years I have had ulcers and running sores, and today is the first day that my clothes have been dry, and now I am a new man." Brothers and sisters, this is declared in the Word, and wonderful things happen.

I had been speaking about divine healing, and six seats from the rear was a man with a boy and he lifted him up when I had finished. The boy was held together with irons, and his head, loins and shoulders were bandaged. The father handed him over to me.

There he put the irons down with the boy standing in them. I have never known what there is in the laying on of hands, let me give you a description of it. This boy was about nine years of age, and laying hands on him in the Name of Jesus, there was a perfect silence, when suddenly this boy cried out. "Dad, it is going all over me," and I said, "Take the irons off." You say that is our power. No, it is His power; no, it is the Father you have received. Dare we be still and be quiet, the stones would cry out if we did.

Sometimes I go in for what they call wholesale healings. My son and daughter are here, and they can declare that they have seen 100 healed without the touch a hand. I believe there is to be wholesale baptisms of the Holy Ghost. One day God told me something, at a place called Staranga in Norway.

I said to my interpreter, "We are both very tired; We will rest today until 4:00 P.M." I can never forget the sight; this story has just occurred to me. May God bend your ears down. There is a hearing of faith, a much higher faith. May the Lord bend our ears.

We had been out for a short time, and coming back into the street I shall never forget the sight. The street was filled with all kinds of wheel-chairs, we went along up to the house, and the house was filled with people, and the woman said, "What can we do?"

"The house is filled, what are we to do?" So I pulled off my coat and I got to business. My brothers, you ought to have been there, the power of God came like a cloud and people were healed on every side.

God healed all the people. This is what I have to tell you. We were sat down for a little refresher before the meeting, and the telephone bell rang. And the pastor went to the telephone, and they said, "What can we do? The great Town Hall is packed. Come down as soon as you can." And this is what I mean by the hearing of faith: I declare that the people could not have fallen down if they had wanted to. I never saw a place so packed, and I began to preach, and when I was preaching the voice came from the Lord.

"Ask and I will give thee every soul." The voice came again, "Ask and I will give you every soul," and I dared to ask, "Give me every soul," and there was a breath came like the rushing of a mighty wind, and it shook everybody and fell on everyone. I have never seen anything like it.

I am hoping to see this in London. Is there anything too hard for God? Cannot God begin to do these things? Will we let Him?

I know it might be a difficult thing. Is it not possible to have a conse-cration tonight? Who is there who will begin tonight and begin to act in the power of the Holy Ghost?

Address given at Second Annual Convention of the Assemblies of God
Kingsway Hall

"My brethren, count it all joy when ye fall into divers temptations" (James 1:2). This letter was addressed "...to the twelve tribes which are scattered abroad..." (James 1:1). Only one like the Master could stand and say to the people, "Count it all joy" when they were scattered everywhere, driven to their wits' end and persecuted. The Scriptures say that "...they wandered in deserts, and in mountains, and in dens and caves of the earth" (Hebrews 11:38). These people were scattered abroad but God was with them.

It does not matter where you are if God is with you. He that is for you is a million times more than all who can be against you. Oh, if we could by the grace of God see that the beatitudes of God's divine power come to us with such sweetness, whispering to us, "Be still, My child. All is well." Only be still and see the salvation of the Lord. Oh, what would happen if we learned the secret to only ask once and believe? What an advantage it would be if we could only come to a place where we know that everything is within reach of us. God wants us to see that every obstacle can be moved away. God brings us into a place where the difficulties are, where the pressure is, where the hard corner is, where everything is so difficult that you know there are no possibilities on the human side — God must do it. All these places are of God's ordering. God allows trials, difficulties, temptations and perplexities to come right along our path, but there is not a temptation or trial which can come to man but God has a way out. You have not the way out; it is God who can bring you through.

A lot of saints come to me and want me to pray for their nervous system. I guarantee there is not a person in the whole world who could be nervous if they understood the fourth chapter of first epistle of John. Let us read verses 16-18:

> *And we have known and believed the love that God hath to us. God is love; and he that dwelleth in love dwelleth in God, and God in him. Herein is our love made perfect, that we may have boldness in the day of judgment: because as he is, so are we in this world. There is no fear in love; but perfect love casteth out fear: because fear hath torment. He that feareth is not made perfect in love.*

Let me tell you what perfect love is. He that believeth that Jesus is the Son of God, overcometh the world. What is the evidence and assurance of salvation? He that believeth in his heart on the Lord Jesus. Every expression of love is in the heart. When you begin to breathe out your heart to God in affection, the very being of you, the whole self of you, desires Him. Perfect love means that Jesus has gotten a grip of your intentions, desires and thoughts and purified everything. Perfect love cannot fear.

What God wants is to impregnate us with His Word. His Word is a living truth. I would pity one who has gone a whole week without temptation. Why? Because God only tries the people that are worthy. If you are passing through difficulties, and trials are rising and darkness is appearing and everything becomes so dense you cannot see through, Hallelujah! God is seeing through. He is a God of deliverance, a God of power. Oh, He is nigh unto thee if thou wilt only believe. He can anoint you with fresh oil; He can make your cup run over. Jesus is the balm of Gilead; yes, the Rose of Sharon.

I believe that God, the Holy Ghost, wants to bring us into line with such perfection of beatitude, of beauty, that we shall say, "Lord, Lord, though thou slay me, yet will I trust thee" (Job 13:15). When the hand of God is upon you and the clay is afresh in the Potter's hands, the vessel will be made perfect as you are pliable in the almightiness of God. Only melted gold is minted; only moistened clay is molded; only softened wax receives the seal; only broken, contrite hearts receive the mark as the Potter turns us on His wheel, shapen and burnt to take and keep the mark, the mould, the stamp of God's pure gold. He can put the stamp on this morning. He can mould you afresh. He can change the vision. He can move the difficulty. The Lord of Hosts is in the midst of thee and is waiting for thy affection. Remember His question, "...Simon, son of Jonas, lovest thou me more than these?..." (John 21:15). He never lets the chastening rod fall upon anything except that which is marring the vessel. If there is anything in you which is not yielded and bent to the plan of the Almighty, you cannot preserve that which is spiritual only in part. When the Spirit of the Lord gets perfect control, then we begin to be changed from glory to glory by the expression of God's light in our human frame and the whole of the body begins to have the fulness of His life manifested until God so has us that we believe all things.

Brother, Sister, if God brings you into oneness and the fellowship with the most High God, your nature will quiver in His presence, but God can chase away all the defects, all the unrest, all the unfaithfulness, all the wavering and He can establish you with such strong consolation of almightiness that you just rest there in the Holy Ghost by the power of God ready to be revealed. God invites us to higher heights and deeper depths.

> Make me better, make me purer,
> By the fire which refines,
> Where the breath of God is sweeter,
> Where the brightest glory shines.
> Bring me higher up the mountain
> Into fellowship with Thee,
> In Thy light I'll see the fountain,
> And the blood that cleanseth me.

I am realizing very truly these days that there is a sanctification of the Spirit where the thoughts are holy, where the life is beautiful, with no blemish. As you come closer into the presence of God, the Spirit wafts revelations of His holiness till He shows us a new plan for the present and the future. The heights and depths, the breadth, the lengths of God's inheritance for us are truly wonderful.

We read in Romans 8:10, "And if Christ be in you, the body is dead because of sin; but the Spirit is life because of righteousness." Oh, what a vision, beloved! "The body is dead" because sin is being judged, is being destroyed. The whole body is absolutely put to death and because of that position there is His righteousness, His beauty; and the Spirit is life, freedom, joy. The Spirit lifts the soul into the presence of heaven. Ah, this is glorious.

"...Count it all joy when ye fall into divers temptations" (James 1:2). Perhaps you have been counting it all sadness until now. Never mind, you turn the scale and you will get a lot out of it, more than ever you had before. Tell it to Jesus now. Express thine inward heart throbbings to Him.

> He knows it all, He knows it all,
> My Father knows, He knows it all,
> The bitter tears, how fast they fall,
> He knows, My Father knows it all.

Sometimes I change it. And I would like to sing it as I change it because there are two sides to it:

> "The joy He gives that overflows,
> He knows, my Father knows it all."

Ah yes, the bitterness may come at night, but joy will come in the morning, Hallelujah! So many believers never look up. Jesus lifted up His eyes and said, "...Father, I thank thee that thou hast heard me" (John 11:41). He cried with a loud voice, "...Lazarus, come forth" (v. 43). Beloved, God wants us to have some resurrection touch about us. We may enter into things that will bring us sorrow and trouble, but through them God will bring us to a deeper knowledge of Himself. Never use your human plan when God speaks His Word. You have your cue from an Almighty source which has all the resources, which never fades away. His coffers are past measuring, abounding with extravagances of abundance, waiting to be poured out upon us.

Hear what the Scripture says, "...God...giveth to all men liberally, and upbraideth not..." (James 1:5). The almighty hand of God comes to our weakness and says, "If thou dare to trust Me and will not waver, I will abundantly satisfy thee out of the treasure house of the Most High." "And upbraideth not." What does it mean? He forgives, He supplies, He opens the door into His fulness and makes us know that He has done it all. When you come to Him again, He gives you another overflow without measure, an expression of a Father's love.

Who wants anything from God? He can satisfy every need. He satisfieth the hungry with good things. I believe a real weeping would be good for us. You are in a poor way if you cannot weep. I do thank God for my tears. They help me so that I do like to weep in the presence of God. I ask you in the name of Jesus, will you cast all your care upon Him? "...For he careth for you" (1 Peter 5:7). I am in great need this morning; I do want an overflow. Come on, beloved, let us weep together. God will help us. Glory to God. How He meets the need of the hungry.

Message delivered at Pentecostal Camp Meeting
Berkeley, California

John 1. I am "the voice of one crying in the wilderness, Prepare ye the way of the Lord, said the prophet Isaiah" (Matthew 3:2). "...Repent ye: for the kingdom of heaven is at hand." "Then went out to him Jerusalem, and all Judaea, and all the region round about Jordan, And were baptized of him in Jordan, confessing their sins" (vv. 5,6). His raiment was camel's hair, his girdle leather, his meat locusts and wild honey.

THE CRY OF THE SPIRIT

August 1925

JOHN'S EXAMPLE

John was without the food and clothing of his earthly father's priestly home. Only a groan, a cry, the cry of the Spirit. No angels or shepherds or wise men or stars heralded his immediate coming. But the heavenly messenger Gabriel (God is mighty), who spoke to Daniel and to Mary spoke also to his father Zachariah. Yet from his place in the wilderness, he moved the whole land. God, through him, cried. The cry of the Spirit — oh, that awful cry. All the land was moved by that piercing cry. Some are ashamed to cry. There is a loneliness in a cry. God is with a person with only a cry. So God speaks to him and tells him a new thing — water baptism.

> *And John bare record, saying, I saw the Spirit descending from heaven like a dove, and it abode upon him. And I knew him not: but he that sent me to baptize with water, the same said unto me, Upon whom thou shalt see the Spirit descending, and remaining on him, the same is he which baptizeth with the Holy Ghost. And I saw, and bare record that this is the Son of God.*
>
> *John 1:32-34*

God spoke to John in the wilderness about water baptism. It was a clean cut, new way. He had been with circumcism, lineage. Now he was an outcast. It was the breaking down of the old plan. When they heard him cry — oh, when they heard that cry, the awful cry of the Spirit — and the message he said, "Repent! For the kingdom of heaven is at hand. Make straight paths — no treading down of others or exacting undue rights. Make straight paths for your feet." All were startled! Awakened! Thinking the Messiah had come. The searching was tremendous! Is this He? Who can it be? He said I am a voice, crying, crying, making a way for Messiah to come. "...this is the record of John, when the Jews sent priests and Levites from Jerusalem to ask him, Who are thou? And he confessed, and denied not; but confessed, I am not the Christ. And they asked him, What then? Art thou Elias? And he saith, I am not. Art thou that prophet? And he answered, No.... I am the voice of one crying in the wilderness, Make straight the way of the Lord, as said the prophet Esaias" (John 1:19-21,23).

Individual purging purposing. God pressing through his life. God through him moved multitudes and changed the situation. The banks of Jordan were covered — filled. The conviction was tremendous. They cried out. The rough place "shall be made smooth; And all flesh shall see the salvation of God. Then said he to the multitude that came forth to be baptized of him, O generation of vipers, who hath warned you to flee from the wrath to come? Bring forth...fruits worthy of repentance, and begin not to say within yourselves, We have Abraham to our father...God is able of these stones to raise up children unto Abraham. And now also the axe is laid unto the root of the trees: every tree therefore which bringeth not forth good fruit is hewn down, and cast into the fire. And the people asked him, saying, What shall we do then? And he said unto them, Exact no more than that which is appointed you. And the soldiers likewise demanded of him...what shall we do? And he said unto them, Do violence to no man, neither accuse any falsely; and be content with your wages" (see Luke 3:5-14).

The people, the multitude, cried out and were baptized of John in Jordan confessing their sins.

Oh, to be alone with God.

IN THE WILDERNESS

...the word of God came unto John the son of Zacharias in the wilderness. And he came...preaching the baptism of repentance for the remission of sins.

Luke 3:2,3

Alone! Alone!
Jesus bore it all alone!
He gave Himself to save His own.
He suffered — bled and died alone — alone.

To be alone with God, to get His mind and thought. God's impression and revelation of the need of the people.

The Word of God came to him in the wilderness. There was nothing ordinary about John — all was extraordinary (v. 19). Herod was reproved by him for Herodias, his brother Philip's wife, and for all the evils which Herod had done. Her daughter danced before Herod who promised her (up) to half his kingdom. She asked for John the Baptist's head. This holy man was alone. God had John in such a way that he could express that cry — the burden for the whole land. He could cry for the sins of the people.

God is holy. We are the children of Abraham — the children of faith. Awful judgment is coming. Cry! Cry! He could not help it because of their sin. John was filled with the Holy Ghost from his mother's womb. He had the burden. He was stern, but the land was open to Jesus. Jesus walked in the way. He came a new way. John came neither eating nor drinking — John came crying. The only place he could breathe and be free was in the wilderness — the atmosphere of heaven — until he turned with a message to declare the preparation needed. Repentance before Jesus came to open out the place of redemption.

First a working of the Spirit in you; then God working through you for others.

His father and mother left behind. His heart bleeding at the altar. Bearing the burden, the cry. The need of the people.

TONGUES AND INTERPRETATION: Give way unto the Lord even to the operation of the Spirit. A people known of God, doing exploits, gripped by God. Continue in the things revealed unto thee. The enemy put to flight. Even those around thee shall acknowledge the Lord has blessed.

Family Prayers
Lluelly Wales

DIVINE CHARGING
Changing Others
August 1925

If thou will believe, thou shalt see the salvation of God. "Only believe." Something to bring us into the Kingdom of God — out of a natural order, into a divine order with divine power for promotion charged by the power of God by another greater than us, a divine order. He came unto His own, but His own received Him not, but as many as received Him He gave power to become sons of God. Only believe. A man is in a great place when he has no one to turn to but God. With only God to help, we are in a great place, God shall change the situation. Not I, but Christ. A new divine order for us to come into, that divine place where God works the miracle. God waits for us to act. Some boilers are made to go off at a ten-pound pressure, some 250, some 350-pound pressure. What pressure do you want to blow off tonight? Only believe. All things are possible. "Only believe."

CHARGED

"...Ye shall receive power, after that the Holy Ghost is come upon you..." (Acts 1:8). What there is for us in this mighty baptism of the Holy Ghost. So moved by the power until (city) Llarelly and the whole South Wales feels again the power of God. Their great inheritance in Christ Jesus, that all shall know we have been with Jesus — is changing. A meeting — it was so as they met with Jesus, and we are bone of His bone, flesh of His flesh and He has given us of His Spirit — grace for grace. Baptized into the same Spirit, partakers of the divine nature, living in a divine changing with our whole being aflame with the same passion that Jesus had, for Acts 1:8 says, "Ye shall receive power, the Holy Ghost coming upon you." Decked with grace, lost moments, so filled with the power of the Spirit. He, through the Holy Ghost, gave to man grace. In Him Trinity so manifest, promising a like power Himself. He was in agony, but the work had to continue. Those He left were to be so clothed, so charged with divine power by the divine working of the Spirit. Some have thought this wonderful baptism in the Spirit would quiet them down. It reminds me of the first engine.

When Stephenson got it all ready he was [sure] that his sister Mary should see it. When Mary saw it, she said, "John, it will never go. It will never go!" Stephenson said to his sister, "Get in!" and pressing a button the engine went. She said, "Oh, John. Oh, John, it will never stop, it will never stop!" We know as we waited and prayed — it looked as if the baptism would never come, but it did come and now we know that it will never stop. But we had the sense to wait until it did come. When I see people seeking the Holy Ghost, do you know, beloved, I believe it is wrong to wait for the Holy Ghost; the Holy Ghost is waiting for us. The Holy Ghost has come and He will not return until the church goes to be with her Lord for evermore. So when I see people waiting, I know something is wrong. The Holy Ghost begins to reveal uncleanness, judging, hardness of heart, all impurity, and until the process of cleansing is complete, the Holy Ghost cannot come but when the body is clean, sanctified. Jesus delights to fill us with His Holy Spirit. I know it will never stop, we are wholly God's in the process of cleansing, the Holy Ghost preparing our bodies a temple for the Spirit to be made like unto Him.

TONGUES AND INTERPRETATION: "It is the will of God, even your sanctification, that you should be filled into all the fulness of God like a bannered army clothed upon with Him. Dynamite flowing through, Trinity working in holy, mighty power within the human frame. God in divine order, meaning us to be swallowed up in Him — a new body, a new mind, a new tongue. No man can tame the tongue, but God can change by the Holy Ghost the whole body to a perfect position. The Christ enthroned within, from that a divine order, a divine cooperation. Ye shall receive power..., the Holy Ghost coming upon you in His perfect operative divine adjustment, the Word of God causing, unfolding the divine plan by the sanctification of the Spirit."

THIS POWER DIVINE

Here is the hallmark of the mystery of divine ability — which must come in our day in its fulness. Jesus went about doing good. God was in Him bodily, in all fulness. I see, I know the divine order, we must press in to the fulness of it. We speak that which we do know and testify of that which we have seen, the Holy Ghost being our witness. I see with the Master in His royal robe of holiness, an impregnation of love moving and acting in the present tense of divine power, an association to be imparted. Ye shall receive power. The Master was in it. In Acts 1:8, the disciples had to come into it. We are in it, of it, into it. You cannot get rid of it, once it is in you, this power divine. It is a tremendous thing to be born into by God. It is a serious thing, once engrafted it is a serious thing to grieve the Holy Ghost. The baptism of the Holy Ghost is a fearful place if we are not going on with God. Great is our conviction of sin. The Holy Ghost comes to abide. God must awaken us to our responsibility, an inbreathed life of power. We can never be the same after that the Holy Ghost has come upon us (Acts 1:8). We must be instant in season and out of season, full of the Spirit, always abounding, always full of the life of God. Ready for every emergency. This is preliminary now for my subject.

> I know the Lord laid His hand on me.
> I know the Lord laid His hand on me.
> He filled me with the Holy Ghost.
> I know the Lord laid His hand on me.

I am always, always in the place greater than the position and the need of the place. The baptism of the Holy Ghost is to prepare us for acting when two ways meet where only God can give decision and bring off the victory and you stand still and see the salvation of God. It's a great place, to reach such a place of dignity, able to shout when the walls are up, when it looks as if all would fail. Shout! Shout! The victory is yours! The victory is yours! Not to come at some future time. The victory is yours. Just as you shout, the ensign will arise and the walls will dry and you will walk in and possess the city. It's a designed position. It is not of our making, it's a rising position, honoring the cry of the Master. "It is finished," not, "to be finished." "It is finished" — God can make manifest that position as I am in loyalty with His divine purposes.

It is no little thing to be baptized with the Holy Ghost, and to be saved from the power of Satan unto God. It is a greater thing than moving Mount Sinai to change a nature from an earthly position, to a heavenly desire. In the first place Jesus was in perfect order. He began to do and to teach, He began to be. He lived in a know. It must be God through the personality. God has declared it, we must be living epistles of Christ, known and read of all men. To be known, knowledge. His Word abiding

"A man is in a great place when he has no one
to turn to but God."

in our hearts, a word of activity, a word of power. The power we have received — the Holy Ghost coming upon us, making us witnesses in Jerusalem, Judaea, Samaria and to the uttermost parts of the earth.

DIVINE COMPASSION

One morning very early, I was traveling in Sweden — there came into the carriage an old lady leaning on her daughter's arm. I saw her sit down, her face so full of anguish, I was disturbed. I could not rest. I am pursuing a course: how to get into the kingdom of the Master, compassion that faileth not, that sees when no other sees, that feels when no other feels. It's a divine compassion. It comes by the Word, for He is the Word of God. We are balanced upon God's side according to our faith, as our faith is embodied in the Master. Who is he that overcomes the world, but he that believeth that Jesus is the Christ. Our life in another, the association with another. He taking the lead through me. You living only for Him to extend Himself through you.

I said to my interpreter, "What is the cause of that woman's trouble? Get to know."

The dear old lady said, "I am over seventy; I had hoped to carry my body through but gangrene has set in my legs and I am on my way to the hospital to have my legs off and the pain is terrible. I do not want to have my legs off at my age." I was bound to tell her Jesus could heal. Her face lit up; her eyes sparkled; she became radiant with hope. Then the train stopped; the carriage filled up with a workman who stood between me and the woman. It looked hopeless for further talk. A big man stood between us. The devil said, "Now you are done." Jesus knew how to answer the devil. He answered him with the Word of God. The devil may leave a dead fish but not a live one. The devil said, "Now you are done." I said, "No! My Lord will make a way." Just then the big man stretched his legs out. I put my hand on the woman and said, "In the Name of Jesus, I bind and loose this woman." The man did not know why, but God knew. That moment she was healed.

What is my object in telling this story? "...ye shall receive power, after that the Holy Ghost is come upon you..." (Acts 1:8). Jesus was clothed upon with power and with a ministry of imparting the power emblemistic of divinity with an installation that never failed. Power to breathe in life and scatter the power of the enemy and nothing shall by any means hurt you! When the train stopped, the old lady began to get out of the carriage. The daughter said, "Why, Mother!" She said, "I'm going back home. I am healed." As long as the train stood, she walked up and down past the carriage window. She said to the interpreter, "I am going home, I am healed."

> He'll never forget to keep me.
> He'll never forget to keep me.
> My Father has many dear children.
> But He'll never forget to keep me.

God will not allow those who trust in Him to become failures in the straightened place. God does the work. Yes. He can, this Word is a living Word of divine activity with momentum. Power to change the nature by the power of the Spirit. All disease and weakness must go at the rebuke of the Master. God enables us to bind the enemy and set free the captive. Beloved, arise, the glory of the Lord is risen upon thee, pouring life into thy weakness, God making thee not the tail, but the head. This is a wonderful day, filled with the Spirit. The breath of the Almighty, God the Holy Ghost can take the Word of Jesus and inbreathe into the hearers a quickened Spirit. Jesus began to do, then to teach. You are in a divine process with revelation and divine power in the place of manifestation. If I only come to impart the life which has brought revelation God will be with me and blessing flows.

One day in New York on a busy car route, I saw a great crowd. I asked the driver to stop. I saw a boy lying in the agony of death. I said, "What is it, boy?" He answered in a weak voice, "Cramp." There was no time to pray. Only to act! I see Acts 1:8, "...ye shall receive power...." It's the divine order. Fire burning, power flowing, divine glory, getting my hand around the boy, I said, "Come out!" The boy jumped up and ran off — never even saying, "Thank you!"

Another day on board ship — I had risen early and was on deck. I saw my table steward, he did not see me. He seemed in great pain. I heard him say, "Oh, I cannot bear it. What shall I do?" I jumped up. I said, "Come out!" He said, "What is it?" I said, "It's God." He had hurt his back lifting a heavy weight.

Yes, beloved. We have an almighty God. Able to help, able to comfort — the God of all comfort.

With power of impartation to a needy world, acting, for ye have renewed power. The power of changing. The Holy Ghost coming upon you. Then God is glorified and the needy — the need of the needy — met. Power received. The unction goes forth and God is glorified.

Receiving the Power (Acts 1:8) the rivers flow (John 7:37). Amen.

Sermon preached at South Wales Convention

FAITH
Hebrews 11:6
August 1925

Hebrews 11:6 — Here is the substance of all things, I think, no I am sure, because a preacher should preach only what he is sure of; everybody can think, the preacher should say what he knows. I am going to preach what I know. That is a wonderful position to be in, so we have a great subject this morning. We must understand nothing less than this, we have to be the epistle of Christ, a living word, a living faith, equipped with the revelation of the plan of the future, all things consist of Him (v. 1).

FAITH: A LIVING POWER

Faith is a reality, not something that you can handle, but something that handles you to handle others. I am living in the inheritance of it because of the faith of God. It is a gift of God (Ephesians 2:8).

Through faith the eternal Word by the operation of His Spirit brings forth life in our hearts, and we realize we are living in a divine order, where God is manifesting His power and living with us. This is the plan of God for us, our inheritance, that the world should receive a blessing through us.

God has come in us, living in us with a life divine. Everyone without exception shall go away with a new vision, a new book, that we may go forth because of the Word.

The Lord has one great plan in the meeting, to reveal to us that we are so much greater than we know, a thousand times greater than you have any conception of. The Word of the Lord will reveal that all things are possible, if you dare believe, and signs and wonders are within reach of all of us. The Lord wishes me to make it known this morning, you have not to go up nor down to find Him. He is in your hearts. The Word of life. I am perceiving that the Lord has this treasure within us, that the excellency of the power shall bring glory of God.

We have become partakers of the divine nature, the moment you believe you are begotten with a new power, a lively hope, the power to lay hold of impossibilities and make them actual. Do you like it? Evermore give us this Bread, they were enamored with Him, live forever, real life, eternal life, the man that comes into this association with the Lord, it [is] his beyond all his earthly measurement. You will need a heavenly measure to measure this.

I am very hungry for you today. I have seen the possibilities of every man in Christ. I must show you that by the grace of God, it is impossible under all circumstances to fail. This knowledge of the Truth you have within you is so remarkable, it will put you in a place where failure is not to be, you will see the power of God manifest in your midst. If I speak with any less Truth than this it would be of no importance, this is the greatest truth of all, I am saved by a new life, by the Word of the Lord, by the living Christ. I become associated with a new creation, and He is continually taking me into new revelations.

FAITH AND THE WORD OF GOD

Compare Hebrews 11:3 and John 1:1-3.

There is nothing made without the Word of God. Peter says, "I am begotten with this Word." There is something within me which has Almighty power within it, if I dare believe it; it is heavenly treasure, and is called the substance of faith.

Praise the Lord, it is from this meeting that you have to go away realizing that God is within you as a mighty power, to act. That signs and wonders may be made manifest; this is the great purpose. Have I believed just to get to heaven? We must be in the world for signs and wonders, for the manifestation of the mighty power of God.

(Chorus: It's All Right Now.)

The great secret of everything is this, are you begotten? If so, it is all right. It is an act within you. There are people here who are in need of a touch, the well is at the side of you this morning, life and liberty for captives. God can make this manifest. You must understand this: while faith is a great assurance and takes in God's bountiful provision; yet unbelief is sin. You have to see the contrast.

I am positive there has to be in human life possibilities of divine life, and so there has to be a death. In my true knowledge of truth, it is the depth of death which brings life, association with Jesus. With Him it was real.

He said to the disciples: Are you able to drink of this cup? And they said, "We are able." He replied, "Ye shall drink." The cup and the baptism perfectly join together. "You" cannot live if you want to bring everything into life, it is only His life that brings forth manifestations of His power. It is not in the human, it is foreign to the human. The human must decrease if the power of the life of God shall be made manifest by His Spirit.

There is not room for two lives in one body. Death to you is the way to the life of the Christ of God being manifested through you. Your human desires are a tremendous hindrance and curse to your life. Human supremacy, wanting to be someone, wanting to do something special; and not until you can cease can God increase.

Unbelief would then be foreign to your spiritual nature, for you would then say, "I live by the faith of the Son of God."

The Holy Spirit is the only One to reveal Jesus, and the revelation He gives makes Jesus so real. I want to prove to you that this Word is so effective, that we live it, we speak it, we act it, and we think it. Do you find Him in the streets, in the room, are you occupied there speaking and thinking in the Holy Ghost, praying and singing in the Holy Ghost? It is the most wonderful thing in life. It is wonderful how God works along these lines. Character is that which is within you. Realize the importance of that Word, it will be helpful for all time. Paul said when I am weak, then am I strong. Who is weak, and I am not weak. Just in the measure of your weakness, so is your strength.

FAITH—KNOWLEDGE—SUPREMACY

When you have nothing you can possess all things. If you rely upon anything else, you cannot possess the greater things. The infinite God is behind the man who has no trust in earthly things, you are in a place where you are trusting in nothing but God. I have never yet condemned anyone of taking means, or using means, but I see the difference between having a whole Bible, a rich inheritance in God, and a part. I see the plan of God is so much greater than all else, if I have Him, I have life in me, I have an abundance of this life. Jesus walked about in the knowledge of supremacy, He was so living in the knowledge of the fulness of God in Him that when He met this people, they were bound to believe that He was in the place where He was in the supremacy. That is a wonderful thing, that God the Holy Ghost can take us to where we know we have the supremacy in the power of the Name. It is a great word, how every moment you are so safe that you receive nothing less than the divine life of Him Who has all power.

I am saved by the living Word which is Christ, where the living substance is Christ. And everything was subject to Him so that I understand. Really, everything must be subject unto me because of the knowledge that He has there manifested His divine authority.

How shall I know? On the authority of the Word. What shall we do? He says believe. God wants to bring us there this morning, He intends us to know this Word. "Whatsoever He saith shall come to pass." On the authority of the Word of God, let me prove it.

A certain man who was very weak, and frail in every way, his eyes were sunk, cheekbones were sticking out, and his neck was shrunken, he came to me and said, "Can you help me?" Could I help him? You will find there will not be a person in the place that cannot be helped. Whatsoever you are suffering from can be cured, and that pain from suffering can be cured, and that pain can cease. If there are any persons suffering they may be healed at once, when God is manifesting His power. There must be signs and wonders. This man told me that he had a cancer, and that the physician, in removing some of the matter, had taken away his swallow, and now he could not swallow. When he spoke to me he spoke with his breath.

He pulled out a tubing, and showed me a piece of tubing about nine inches long. This left an opening in his stomach through which he had been feeding himself for three months with liquid. He was a living skeleton, but I could help him on the Word of God. "It shall come to pass whatsoever He saith, if ye believe," I began in the name of the Lord to saith. "Go home and eat a good supper." He went home and told his wife that the preacher said he had to have a good supper. She prepared a supper, and when it was ready he began to take it and chew it over and over. But the Word of God must come to pass. I saith he should have a good supper, and it went down, until he was full up, and he went to bed full up. He had a new experience, life had come, but this joy was not all. Waking next morning with a knowledge of this, out of curiosity, he looked down to his stomach, and he found that God had healed him; the opening in his stomach having been closed.

All this is divine revelation. We must not measure ourselves by ourselves, if we do we shall always be small. Measure yourself by the Word of God, the great measurement that God brings to you. Don't be fearful, He wants to make us strong, powerful, stalwart, resolute, resting upon the authority of God. It is on this line that I can only speak, and shall we not equip ourselves like men? We are those who have seen the King, we have been quickened from the death. God has wrought special miracles in us all; we are made with one great design and purpose.

A man stood in the doorway of a building, and he had not slept much for three years, until he got in such a state that when he was shaving, an evil spirit would say, "Life is not worth living," and at times it had almost been done. Then when he went to the water's edge the evil spirit would say, "Jump in, jump in, and finish with it, it is not worth it." He came and heard that he could be delivered, and he says, "I came up to the man that had been preaching, and said to him, I cannot sleep." According to the Word of God, I said, "Go home and sleep in the Name of Jesus." Now he says, "I can sleep anywhere. I sleep, sleep, sleep, and God saved me." This was on the Word of God. I must live on nothing else, it must be more than my meat, more than my associations, to live in this Holy Word. We have been preaching faith this morning, and I want you that are suffering from pain in the body to stand. I must deal with someone that is conspicuous. We must deal with you on the Word of God. There is no one here that will be overlooked, we have come here for that purpose, nobody shall be overlooked.

This meeting finished at 1:40 P.M., the congregation singing:

> Only believe, only believe,
> All things are possible,
> Only believe.

Several having divers diseases and infirmities were prayed for at the close of the foregoing address at the Monday morning meeting, and at the evening meeting the same day the following testified that God had healed them.

THE MOVING BREATH OF THE SPIRIT

Monday P.M., August 1925

T he Word is God Himself (see John 1:1).

In the beginning was the Word, and the Word was with God, and the Word was God.

John 1:1

Here is our attitude of rest. All our hope is in the Word of the living God. The Word of God abideth forever. Oh, the glorious truths found therein. Never compare this Book with other books. This is from heaven; it does not contain the Word of God, it is the Word of God. Supernatural in origin, eternal in duration, value, infinite in scope, divine in authorship. Read it through, pray it in, write it down. The fear of the Lord is the beginning of wisdom. The knowledge of our weakness brought the greatness of redemption — knowledge is coupled with joy. You cannot have the knowledge of the Lord without joy. Joy in the knowledge of Him. Faith, grace is peace. Not long petitions, but faith is peace. Where faith is undisturbed is peace. Eternal faith, daring to believe what God has said. If I dare but trust Him, I find it always comes to pass — no wavering. "...let not that man think...he shall receive any thing of the Lord" (James 1:7). Only believe.

THE PROMISE HAD COME

Luke 4: "...Jesus being full of the Holy Ghost returned from Jordan...."
Jesus, I'll go through with Thee. What did it really mean when He said, "Be filled with the Holy Ghost"? Oh, the difference when we understand

Acts 2 and know the flow of the life of the Spirit and we leap for joy beyond all that had gone before, and the holy laughter. Bringing out of the shadow the reality of the substance, that which had been promised had come. He our glorious Lord who could speak as no other, had come to help the oppressed. The King unfolds His will covering His child, flooding the soul with open vision, untiring zeal. Fire! Fire! Fire! Burning intensity in the human soul, until he becomes an expression of the King.

I know the Lord laid His hand on me. He filled me with the Holy Ghost. I know the Lord laid His hand on me. This Jesus, this wonder-working Jesus. He came to be King! Is He King? He must reign — oh, so to yield that He always has the first place. Glory be to God. He has come to abide forever, flooding our souls. For Jesus said, "When I go, I will send Him unto You."

> Has He come to you?
> Has He come to you?
> Has the Comforter come to you?

The Lord will reprove the world of sin, when the Comforter comes to you. In Him God has given us an enrichment, a perfection of revelation. He came to fill the Body and to bring forth that which all the prophets had spoken of: taking of the things of Jesus and showing them unto us.

The woman had a well, but after the Holy Ghost had come, it was a river, rivers of living water, grows life from birth, prophetic utterance — a divine incoming, filled into all the fulness of God. Like a flash of lightning, opening up divine revelation, that we can dance and sing in the Spirit enjoying sweeter music, rarity of character — Christ in you the hope of glory. A vision of the glory of God in the face of Jesus Christ. This the baptism of the Holy Spirit brings to us — "...Jesus being full of the Holy Ghost..." (Luke 4:1). He is the Spirit of truth unveiling, making manifest, breathing through in such a way, burning, quickening, until men cry out, "What must we do to be saved?" The breath of life burning with intensity until the world feels the warmth and cries, "What must we do?" Oh, the joy of being filled with the Holy Ghost, with the divine purpose! Activity! In season and out of season with the sense of the divine approval. As the apostles were in their day, we are to be in our day. Filled — filled into all the fulness of God. This same Holy Ghost. This same warmth. This same life, this same heaven in the soul. The Holy Ghost brings heaven to us as He reveals Jesus, who is the King of heaven. Oh, the perfection of belonging to Him, a preparation for every need. He has us in the divine moments. No need to groan, cry, travail, or sigh. The Spirit of the Lord is upon me. The sense of the Holy Ghost. Experience, the wonder of His breath, lifting the Word, making all new, meeting the present need. These are the last days. Very wonderful are they and blessed with signs. The breath of the Spirit unfolding, helping.

REVEALED PRESENCE

I believe in the Holy Ghost. I believe in the Holy Ghost. God gave us the Holy Ghost for true Son-likeness, Son-expressiveness, with enforcement of expression. In Sweden in a park a large platform was erected for meetings, on the condition that the Englishman did not put his hands on the people. I said, "Lord, You know all about this. You can work." And there the Lord revealed His presence and healed and saved the people. I said, "Who here is in need? Put your hands up." Hands went up all over. I saw a large woman. I said, "Tell your trouble!" She said pains were all over her body. She was in terrible distress. I said, "Lift up your hands in Jesus Name!" (He came to heal the sick, to unbind, to set free — He said greater works than these shall we do. He that believeth on me.) I said, "In the Name of Jesus, I set you free in His name. Are you free?" She replied, "Yes, perfectly free!"

God put His hands on the people. God, His wonderful ways of meeting the need. I believe to see the glory of God, setting free from all weakness.

Jesus said, "The Spirit of the Lord is upon me to make disciples of all nations."

In New Zealand when I first preached this glorious truth, I saw hundreds baptized. In Sweden the church was not pleased — a woman in the king's household was healed but I had to leave the country. On one occasion there, I stayed in a side street. I arrived at 9:30 — the meeting was at 4:30 — so I went to the coast for a few hours' rest. When I came up, the street was full from end to end with wheelchairs and cars filled with the helpless and needy. The conveners said, "What shall we do?" I said, "The Holy Ghost came to abide, to reign in supreme royal dignity.

Live in unction, freedom, inspiration. Like a river flowing. Nothing less. That God may be glorified."

God loosed the people and brought deliverance to the captives. Was that all? No! Only the beginning! The house was packed too! Oh, the joy of being ready — God must set us all on fire — there is much land to be possessed. The fields are white unto harvest.

Oh, the cry of the people — talk about weeping — oh, the joy of weeping. Awful place when you cannot weep with the breath of God upon you.

I went on helping the people. Oh, the breath of the Spirit.

Jesus said, "The Spirit of the Lord is upon me." God spoke to me as clearly as possible, "Ask me! I will give you all in the place." (I thought it was too big.) He whispered again, "Ask, I will give you all in the house." I said, "Oh my God, say it again." "Ask of me — I will give you all in the house." I said, "I ask! I ask in faith! I believe it." The breath of heaven filled the place — the people continued to fall down, weeping, crying, repenting. There is something wonderful in this breath.

"The Spirit of the Lord is upon me," Jesus said.

Upon me! Upon me!

May God move in our hearts to act in it. Do you want God to have you in His splendid palace? Is it the longing cry of your heart to come to this place? God can only choose those filled to the uttermost. How many long to step into line — filled to the uttermost, hungering and thirsting after God's fulness? Stand in a living experience as Jesus, saying, "The Spirit of the Lord is upon me." God, grant it to every one of you. Amen.

Sermon preached at L'Velly Convention

HIGHER LIFE

September 5, 1925

I want you to get an Artesian well today. Something full of joy. If you have to cause it, there is something wrong. If God causes it there is something right all the time. We must be careful to see that God intends, that He means something greater than ever we have touched yet.

I have thought a great deal about momentive position. I find there is such a thing as to trust upon past tenses.

If a car has got to a certain place, some people get out, but some go on to the terminus. Let us go far enough. There is only one thing: to keep in full rank, to be always connected to the switch. It will not do to trust to the past tense. Let us go forward.

Momentive power. Past tense won't do. We must have an inflow of the life of God manifested, because we are in that place of manifestation. I want you to sing today what I sing in all my meetings. "Only believe."

> Only believe, only believe,
> All things are possible, only believe,
> Only believe, only believe,
> All things are possible, only believe.

The importance of that chorus is that right there in the midst of that chorus is that word *only*. If I can get you to see today that when you can get rid of yourself and your human help and everything else and only have God behind you, you have got to a place of great reinforcement and you have got to a place of continual success. If you help yourself — in the measure you help yourself, you will find that the limitations of the life of God and the power of God are diminished. I find so many people trying to help themselves. What God wants is an absolute entire cling to Him — only one grand plan which God has got for us, "only believe." Absolute rest, perfect submission. Entirety, where God has taken charge of the situation, and you are absolutely brought into everything that God has, because you dare "only believe" what He says. Conditions on God's side are always beyond your asking or thinking. The conditions on your side cannot reach the other side without you come into a place that as you see that as you rest on the omnipotent plan of God, it cannot fail to be successful. God would have me to press into your heart a living truth — only to believe, absolute rest, perfect tranquility, where God is absolutely taking charge of the whole situation, and you say, "God has said it, and it cannot fail." All His promises are yea and amen to those who believe. Are you ready to sing it now? Let us see how far you get on with it now. Only believe, only believe, all things are possible, only believe....

THE LIFE CONTRARY TO THIS LIFE

Romans 8:1-17 — We have got a tremendous big subject today, but it will be one that will be helpful because it is in the realm of spiritual vitality, and I want today to speak to you on life, because I find that there is nothing going to help you in this higher life, of reaching it, of pressing in or living by unction, only this divine life, which shall always, if we yield ourselves absolutely to it. We get not only exercised by it, but kept in perfect rest, where God is giving us rest. And it is needed in this day, for this is a day when people everywhere are getting self-contented on the natural lines and there is not that definite cry or prayer within the soul that is making them cease from everything and crying out for God and the coming of the Son. So I am intensely anxious and full of desire today that I may by some means quicken or move you on to a place where you shall see what is for you in the Spirit.

Life. Life is one of those positions in Christ which is absolutely different from death. Life has everything in it to make people long for. Death has everything in it that makes people shudder from. And this light of the life of the Spirit that God wants me to bring before you today is an absolute position where God has designed for us to live free from the law of sin and death. So you can see I have a great subject after the divine mind of the Master. You remember what the Master said. He said, "He that lived to himself would die. He that seeketh to live would die, but he that is willing to die will live." God wants us to see that there is a life that is contrary to this life.

The Spirit of the Lord reveals to us in the Word of God — He that believeth on the Son hath life, he that believeth not shall not see life, and yet he is living and walking about, and yet he is not seeing life. There is a life which is always brought into condemnation, which is living in death. There is a life which is free from condemnation — living in the *life*.

TONGUES AND INTERPRETATION: "God, the Author, the Finisher, the bringing into, the expression in the human life, changing it from that downward grade and lifting it and bringing it into a place of revelation to see that God has designed me to be greater than anything in the world."

I want you all to understand today that the design of God's Son for us is to be so much greater in this world than we have ever comprehended. The design is not where I was when I came into the room, it is what the spiritual revelation shall bring me into touch with — a divine harmony until I touch ideals today, until it is something more. My eyes are looking up, my heart is surrendered. My heart is big and enlarged in the presence of God, for I want to hear one word from God, "Come up higher" and God will give us that. Higher into a holy association.

There is a word of helpfulness in the first verse. "There is therefore *now* no condemnation." The most important thing in all the world — there is nothing to be compared to it. It is beyond all you can think — the person who has the heavens opened above him, the person who has come into the realm of faith and joy to know, for I know that he hears me when I pray, I know I have the petition. So God the Holy Ghost today would have us to understand that there is a place in the Holy Ghost order where there is no condemnation. Holiness, purity, righteousness, higher ground, perfection, and being more perfected in the presence of God. This higher ground state, it is holy desire, it is perfectness where God is bringing us to live in, that He may smile through and act upon until our bodies become a flame of light ignited by omnipotence. This is God's plan for us in the inheritance. It is an inheritance in the race that God wants us today in, this race, this divine race, this crowned race, this divine place is for us today.

No condemnation. The great secret of the plan of God for us this afternoon is to see our covering. To those which are *in*. Oh, the covering, oh, the enfolding, oh, those eyes, those lovely eyes, that lovely Jesus, that blessed assurance of entrenchment, that knowledge of the Rock of Ages cleft for me, that place where I know I am in. And that joy unbounding where I know there are neither devils nor angels nor principalities nor powers to interfere with that life in Christ. Wonderful! No weapon that is formed against thee shall prosper — evil report or good report — God makes us devil-proof, so that power of the Most High

God has put us in. If we had put ourselves in, it would have been different. We were in the world, but God took us out of the world and put us into Christ, so God today by His Spirit wants us to see how this regenerative power, this glorious principle of God's high thoughtfulness is for us. I can see if I will leave myself in His sweetness — oh, there is a sweetness about the Lord, oh, there is a glorious power behind us when God is behind. There is a wonderful going before when He goes before, and He said, "I will go before and I will be thy reward," and so I see that God the Holy Ghost wants me today to penetrate or bring forth or show forth the glorious joy there is in this wonderful incarnation of the Spirit for us all in Christ Jesus. Glory to God!

> It reaches me, it reaches me,
> Wondrous grace it reaches me,
> Pure exhaustless, ever flowing,
> Wondrous grace it reaches me.

I can see this order of life that God has for us today, it is to make me free from the law of sin and the law of death. Praise the Lord! And I find that all sin is down-grade and gravity, and I find that all faith is a lifting place into the admiration of God. So God wants to spread forth His wings and show that He is able, He is almightiness, and He is able to preserve that which we have committed unto Him, because He is our Lord. Not only Creator, but Preservator.

Not only redeemed me, but now He is preserving me. I see I cannot do any of these things of myself, but He has made it possible, if I believe, He will do it. So I absolutely believe that the Word I am preaching unto you is sent forth by the power of the Spirit. I find out that God has strengthened your hands and is preparing you for the race, the race that is set before you. It is the divine plan I see to ask in my life that I may be absolutely in the place where I am preserved from all evil. These are days when Satan is very great, oh yes, he is tremendously busy seeking whom he may devour, but I am finding out this: that God has blessed me and has blessed us that we will be in a place where we are more than overcomers. It is to have a shout at the end of the fight — to not only overcome, but to be able to stand when we have overcome, not fallen down. I count it a great privilege that God has opened my eyes to see that this great plan of His has been arranged for us before the foundation of the world and we may all just come into line with God to believe that these things which He has promised must come to pass to him that believeth. Turn back once more to the thought. No man, whoever he is, will ever make progress without he learns that he is greater than the adversary. If you don't learn, if you don't understand, if you don't come into line today with the thought that you are greater than the adversary, you will find out that you have a struggle in your life. I want to breathe through you today a word which is in the Scripture, which is, "He that is with you." I don't want to take anybody out of their bearings, I want to be so simple that everyone who is here and hears this truth shall so know that they have a fortification, that they have the oracles of God behind them in truth, that they have the power of God with them to overcome him through the blood of the Lamb. Who is he that overcomes, but he that believeth that Jesus is the Christ, for it is he that overcomes the world, even through this your faith. Now faith is the supreme, divine character-istic position where God is entrenched, not only in the life, but through the life, the mind, the body. You will never find you are anything equal against the power of the enemy only on the authority that within you, you have an authority laid down. He that believeth in His heart is able to move the mountain, but you do not believe in your heart, till your heart is made perfect in the presence of God, for as you think in your heart, so are you. So if your great thoughts are on the Holy One, if you are seeing God...blessed are the pure in heart, for they shall see God. These are the people that see this truth that I am presenting to you today and it is in them, that makes them more than conquerors. Life over sin, life over death, life over the diseases, life over the devil. Praise the Lord!

TONGUES AND INTERPRETATION: "God is not the Author of confusion but the Author of peace and bringeth to life and focuses the eye till it sees God only and when you come there you shall stand."

Oh, the thought, the standing, the pure hands, the clean heart, so God the Holy Ghost has designed for us within the plan of this realm of grace, hidden, lost, completely lost to the devil, not able to come near. He covereth; He hideth; we are sealed. Bless the Lord! Sealed until the day of redemption. We so believe in the authority of the Almighty that we triumph in this glorious realm. Oh, this divine touch of God to the human soul brings us all to say "all things are possible."

Praise the Lord 'tis so, praise the Lord 'tis so,
Once I was blind but now I see,
Once I was bound but now I am free,
Through faith I have got the victory,
Praise the Lord 'tis so.

And so the Lord has a great plan for us today to see, or rather bring us to, our wealth in Christ; our wealth, how rich, beyond all comparison. Deep calleth unto deep. The Lord hath prepared for us not only a son-ship, but an heirship, not only an heirship, but a joint-heirship, not only feeling the breath of God, but the breath of God moving us, not only touching fire, but fire burning everything that cannot stand fire, and so in this holy sea of life, this divine inheritance for us I see the truth so full of joy unspeakable today and I see it and I read it to you. There is there-fore now no condemnation to them which are *in* Christ Jesus. Oh, hal-lelujah! Then I notice clearly that we must see and we must get always the facts of these truths. It is a law. Well, there is a law of gravitation and there is a law of life and we must see the difference and we must live in life which ceases to die, we must live in a life which continues to die and to die daily, because when you die you receive life, and in that life, the baptism of the Holy Ghost is a baptism into a death, to a likeness unto death, to the Son of Man in His likeness. The baptism of the Holy Ghost is the purifying, energizing, and bringing the soul where it touches ideal immensity. God wants us to have no other plan in our mind but this.

FLOODTIDE OF REFRESHING

Now come along with me for the Lord has many things to say to us. I see that the devil wants to destroy. Now listen, you will find that John 10:10 is more real than ever. It says that the devil or the thief cometh to steal because he is a thief and then if he can steal, he will destroy, he will kill and then he will destroy. I also find that Jesus comes along with a floodtide of refreshing and says, "I have come with life, with life and abundance of life." *Abundance of life* means that you live in an activity of divine inspiration, that you never touch the other thing, you are above it, you are only in association with it to pray it through or cause the salt to be more salty or the light to be more bright till they can see the way like the city that cannot be moved. It is a foundation of God's principle and everyone that knows it says that is God. I will go a little further to help you. I find out this, that whatever you learn in this meeting or these meetings today, I say it fearlessly, fearless of any contradiction. God has given you another chance of seeing light and life. If you fail to seize the opportunity, you will find you will be worse tomorrow.

God speaks through me to tens of thousands all over. God is sending me forth to stir the people to diligence. Mine is not an ordinary message. You will never find I have an ordinary message. The past tense is ordinary message. I must be on fire, the day is too late for me to stop. I must be catching fire, and in the wing. I am intensely in earnest and mean all I say in this meeting. Within are the thoughts to impregnate you today with a desire from heaven to let you see that you have not to give place to the devil, neither in thought nor word, and I pray God the Holy Ghost you will be so stirred that you will have a conviction come over your soul that you dare disbelieve any of that truth, but rather the whole body shall be aflame with the epistle of truth. He that hath seen me hath seen the Father. Is that so? Oh, He said, "Me and My Father will come and dwell in you." Yes, and when He comes to dwell in us, it is to be the epistle, it is to be the manifestation, the power, it is to be the Son of God working miracles, destroying the power of the devil, casting out evil spirits, laying hands on the people. They shall live that were dying under the power of the devil. This is life divine and this is God's thought for you in this meeting: if you will not fail to recognize the good hand of God coming to us this afternoon, God speaking to us of these deep things of Himself, that means so much for us.

Oh, bless God that I am entrusted with such a Gospel, with such a message, but in me first it burns. You cannot bring anything to anybody else before you have reached it first yourself. You cannot talk beyond your wisdom. God brings you to test these things. Then because you desire to handle, and because you chance to eat these things, and out of the eating and digesting of these things, it shall come as the refining fire and floodtide upon the dry ground, because we shall be a flame of fire for God. Divine inspiration, catching the vision all the time and walking in the Holy Ghost. Oh, bless the Lord!

> I know the Lord, I know the Lord,
> I know the Lord has laid His hands on me.

Glory to Jesus! That Good hand of God. On me only? No! No! No! God has come to more than me in this place, but the important thing is that we recognize the hand of God and the voice of God and that we recognize the power of God, how to be careful and gentle and how to have wisdom to abide in the anointing and to keep in the place where God is not only consuming fire, but also purifying fire. Glory to God! Oh, for this holy, intense zeal or this zealous position for God to give us today, that shall absolutely put us in a place where we know *this day* has God spoken to me, once more this day has God brought before me another opportunity. This day. Thank God in His grace and kindness opened the way, beloved. The Lord speaks once, yea twice. God unfolds the Kingdom to you, but He expects you to jump in and go through.

THE JUST PLACE

There is therefore now no condemnation. I would not take a million of all the banks possess for this. What does it mean? There is condemnation comes to us if we know that we ought to be further on in the race than we are. Something has stopped us. It does not mean to say because there is no sin in your life — that is not it — it may be that — it will have some demarcation on all lines. It means so much to me. I know I was baptized with the Holy Ghost. The Holy Ghost was not the life — Jesus is the life, but the Holy Ghost came to reveal the life. The Holy Ghost is not truth — Jesus is the truth, but the Holy Ghost is the Spirit of that truth. So I must see this, that God means so much for me today.

I notice and am noticing that to be without condemnation I must be in the just place with God. It is a wonderful thing to be justified by faith, but I find there is a greater place of justification than this. I find this, because Abraham believed God He accounted it to him for righteousness. That was more than the other. God accounted it to him for righteousness because Abraham believed God. He imputed no sin and therefore He gives him wings. When he imputed no sin, he lifted him into the righteousness of God, lifted him out of himself into a place of rest and God covered him there. Abraham has not received anything of the Lord that He is not willing to give to anyone in this place. I am seeing today whatever I have reached I am only on the rippling of the wave of the bosom of God's intense zeal of love and compassion. He is always saying, nothing less than this, "*Come on,*" so I am going forward. I am here this afternoon with a whole heart to say, "Come with me, for the Lord has spoken good concerning His people, and He will give them the land of promise and no good thing will He withhold." So I know that God is in the place to bless today, but I want you to catch the fire, I want you to come out of all your natural propensities, for I tell you nothing is detrimental to your spiritual rising as your natural mind and your body, which is a thought that is thought over before it has been coming out in thought. Nothing will destroy your spiritual life but your own self. He knew that did Paul and therefore he said, "I count myself but dung." Anything else? Yes! He says, "Therefore I conferred not with flesh and blood." He was getting very near this. I tell you there is a good many things, natural associations. As a Jew he came over to the plan of redemption where everything was absolutely foolishness in their estimation and rank hypocrisy. Anything else? Certainly! If I can only win Him. Oh, what apprehension there was in him, what beautiful positions of his character. He had revealed to him about this Nazarene King who was worthy of him to come into line to see. I can understand today that God breathes upon him absolutely, it is the breath of divine order, it is the breath of desire. God breathes on, and as He breathes on him I see this.

Oh, to know! My word, to know that so many years since, God baptized me and I can say without a shadow of a doubt, God has swept me on. You know it! How I have always longed to go. I tell you, if you come there, you will have to say "no" to a thousand things in your natural order, for your own hearts will deceive you. Be careful of your friends and relations, they are always a damp rag or a wet blanket. God wants us to lean on Him, and go on with Him and dare to believe Him. No condemnation. Oh, how sweet the thought. Never mind, brothers, I am not here today to crush any here, to bruise. I am here in the Holy Ghost order I know, to make you long to come on, long to obey, long to say to everything that is not the high order of holiness, that makes me say, "Whoever misses, I will go through."

> I'm going through, Jesus, I'm going through,
> I'll pay the price whatever others do,
> I'll take the way of the Lord's despised few,
> I'm going through, Jesus, I'm going through.

DAILY OFFERING

It is worth it all. Praise the Lord! Worth it all. Since last time I was with you before, thank God, quickened by the Spirit, I have covered over 44,000 miles. You cannot think about it in your mind: it is too vast. At all places God in His Spirit has been moving me. My, I have seen the glory of God moving. I have had the pleasure of seeing 2,000 people in the morning and in the evening over 5,000 to hear me preach. What opportunities! What times of refreshing! What wonderful things one sees, and I realize this that nothing would do — you could not rely upon anything of the past, and so I am realizing the truth now, it is this, I see it is a whole burnt offering, I see it is an offering in righteousness, and I see, it is an offering that is accepted, and I see it is a daily offering. No past sanctification is good enough for today, and I find that this life leads you on to see that it is a sanctification with an inward desire of being more perfected every day. And while I know I was wonderfully saved, yet I find, it is being saved — while I see it has designs within it for the coming of the King, I see it enriches me with a ceaseless warmth that I cannot get out of it. Nothing will do without I am absolutely heated up with this life, because I must see the King.

Pentecost, since it came, has been spoken against, and if there is not someone rising up against you, if there is not a war on, it is a bad job for you. I tell you this in sincerity, if you are not making the people mad or glad, there is something amiss with your ministry. If you leave people as you found them, God is not speaking by you. So, there must be an intensity of enlargement of this divine personality, of God in the soul, so absolutely bringing to a place where you know it would be awful to remain two days in the same place.

I do not know how it sounds, but I tell you, it is intense zeal. Come a little nearer now...opportunities possible. God has right of way to the heart and life to bring them to a place where opportunities are made for the possibility to be accomplished. There is a place in God where God has need and the need is the opportunity, but He must have someone to jump in the place to meet the need so the opportunity is the place that God has met and the fulfilling of the place is where God has you in hand for the place. I am realizing this that God must impress upon your heart right 'round about you wherever you are God has for you today an opportunity. It will stand erect before you and by that means you will be brought into a place where you will convince the people because God is there. The Word of God is without shadow or doubt effective, destroying. And bringing about perfect life.

Notice further, let me give you an instance. God has a place, a way in this remarkable....I came across, (God had to reveal to me these things), came across a man in my last trip. He travelled with me. I saw he was a man that [was] absolutely eaten up with natural life, natural positions in life, he was a man that bred race horses. He was a man eaten up with the world's ambitions. He had a lot of race horses, and as I spoke to this man he was in a terrible state. He wept, he was in such a state about this thing, as I spoke to him he did everything he could to try to shake off, and I held to it that God had me there for that place to shake that man through and by some means to bring him to a right place where deliverance would come. While the Word of God pressed through me, he shook it off and shook it off and came before me from time to time bringing others with him to laugh the thing through, but I knew God had me in the right place.

And then we stopped at a place called Fiji Islands. It is remarkable that people get to know that I am on the ship, there is generally a wireless to know if I will stop and preach at this place. Whilst I was preaching the Lord blessed me amongst these people.

This man went out along with a lot more in a car and when they got out in the bush wood, he was bitten with a snake, and I saw it as clear as anything. I saw that God's hand was in the whole thing, but he came to me and as he looked at me his face was as pale almost as my handkerchief. As he looked at my face he said, "I am dying, I know I am dying," he says, "I have been bitten with a snake." He pulled up his trousers, there his leg was changed. He said, "It is going over my body, I am poisoned through," he says, "Can you help me?"

I have been going up and down the world twice all over the world on a world round trip and besides the islands of the sea, God has had me and I have never yet found a position that I could not help...or...on the authority on that word, and there is not a person in this place this afternoon, I do not care what you are or what is amiss but what God can help you. As I said this last week at a large place, I said to the whole place, "I am a perfect stranger, this meeting has been got up for this time." I said, "I stand here and in the Name of Jesus," I said, "There is not a person in this meeting that if you are in pain would be in pain if you would let me pray for you. And [God] healed the people even before I touched them. Oh, we have a wonderful God, we must know Him and we must let nothing come between us that we do not get to know Him more. and looking at me again he said, "Can you help me?"..."Yes," I says, "I can."

Now how could I help him? What did Jesus say, did He say, is His Word true, "Greater things than these shall ye do." The authority of this Word is right before us. Anything else? "I will give you power over all the power of the enemy and nothing shall by any means hurt you," and taking my hand and placing it on that bitten place of the serpent, I said, "In the Name of Jesus I command this to leave," and he stamped his foot and stamped his foot and he said, "I know I am healed, there is not an atom of pain and my whole body is different." He pulled up his trouser's leg and the swelling and everything went right down before the eye.

Oh, this same Jesus, this igniting power. What do you say it is? I say it is life! You cannot explain it by any other, it is the law of the life of the Spirit of Christ making manifest in your heart everything contrary to sin and death and disease and so awakening within you the living principle of divine order till erect in the authority of God you stand, till you know that He who has given you power will give you power for His glory to be exhibited in the world. I am here to invite you to a wonderful full apprehension, to a fuller life in Christ.

SWALLOWED UP IN LIFE

I am going to close with one word, because of the importance of the word — I want to give you one word more of life. Turn with me to the fifth chapter of the Second Corinthians, it will have something to do with this important treasure. I am seeing this, if I preach anything less than these three things, I find I miss the whole opportunity of my life. I must have a ministry of faith and I must have clothing this ministry of faith, I must have the Spirit of life to make manifest this ministry of faith and then I must have a convincing evidence through the power of the Spirit of imparting that to the lives of the people. I pray that you shall lay hold of this truth.

We have here in this fifth chapter one of the best things that God has given me now for some time is this, this ministry of life.

> *For we that are in this tabernacle do groan, being burdened: not for that we would be unclothed, but clothed upon, that mortality might be swallowed up of life.*
>
> 2 Corinthians 5:4

Here is one of the greatest truths that was in this Pentecostal evidence, or life in evidence or the evidence in the life. I find that Jesus is not coming to fetch the body — that is perfectly in order, we cannot get away from the fact, but Jesus is coming for the life in the body. The body may mortify, but that body will not be in the glory. God will give it a body, and the only thing He is going to give is life, and the life is not your life, but His life in you. Your life is quickened by that which is in association with the life. You cannot define the position, it is so complete this. He that dwelleth in God dwelleth in Him and He in him. Jesus came to give us His life. Paul says, "Now I live, yet not I but He lives — His life." In Colossians we read this that when He appears, who is our life, then shall we appear.

Now lest we should miss this great awakening of these last days to be ready to be caught up, which is as you are in the activity of a holy ascendancy of life, you will find your whole desire is to see Him because He gives the desire and you will find you have not a desire outside the desire of pleasing Him. Between you there is a joy or fulness of expression all the joy that you have come into oneness where you see it is His life being manifest in your mortal body that is making you so free from the natural life and you are joined up to the supernatural.

Paul said He wanted to go, not to be unclothed but clothed upon — there is a thought. Do we want to go? No! No! That is not the order of the body, that is not the order of the natural man, that is not the order of the human — what does he want? He wants to be so clothed upon, that is the first thing, clothed upon. When? Now! Anything else? Yes! And the life clothed upon and the life within the body eating up every mortality, every sense, every human desire, everything that has caused grief, sorrow, brokenness of heart, interfering with our rest, stopping the shining of our face, making us feel how sorry we were. God wants to have His way with us, live in us to eat up everything, till the body shall only be a body filled with the Spirit life, the body only to be an existence only for the temple as the temple for the Spirit — and then what?

No! No! But preserved blameless, the body, the soul, the spirit — in the world blameless, and the coming of the King, taking the life and changing it to present it with Him — God bring us there. As sure as you leave here today, as sure as I have had this fellowship with you in the Spirit, as sure as your heart has been warmed in this holy place, I look at you today and I say never mind the past. You may have a thousand things that spoils you — forget them. Count that God has overcome for you in order that you shall overcome and present you faultless, yea spotless, in the presence of the King — this life eating up mortality. Hallelujah! The law of the life of the Spirit of Christ making you free from the law of sin and death.

Can I attain today? This is a problem. "I have failed a thousand times," you say. Never mind, brother. Is your heart warmed? Do you love to be beaten, or do you love to come into line with Him? Will you pay the price for it? What is the desire of your heart? You may be sorry for the past, but let God have you for the future. You would not like to remain as you were before you came in this meeting, I know you would not, you feel exactly the position. You say, "Lord, forgive everything of the past but help me, Lord, today to offer an offering in righteousness before Thee, today I give myself afresh.

Message given at Bethany Pentecostal Mission Room
Pudsey

RIGHTEOUSNES, SUFFERING, DEATH

September 1925

Philippians 3:1-14 — I believe the Lord's will is that I read this, it is the most blessed truth, God is revealing Himself so as to give us a vision of the Master. Paul had many visions of the Master, but there were many things that had to be told him because he was not amongst the disciples who walked with the Master, nor connected with those plans of the Master, he was born as one out of due season. There were many things that were rehearsed to him. Picture his life and the various manifestations, there was always something about the Master told to him.

Now he gets to a place where he desires all that the Master has. As far as keeping the law he was blameless, and he had a zeal which went so far as to persecute the Church. In the midst of it all he sees what the Master had. I want by the grace of God this morning to help you. Christ is the great principle, not only the great teacher.

There is something in the new birth of the divine character, that makes us long all the time that we may be like Him. Not so much an impression, but something in our life, words, acts, which makes people know we have been with the Master, and that we have learned of Him. Paul was there, we are the circumcision which worship God in the Spirit, and are righteous in Jesus Christ, and have no confidence in the flesh. I am perceiving by the Spirit of the living God that there is no good thing in me. That in Him there is not only energizing power, but the Spirit moves me to see that in the act there was divine character. The presence of the ideal character that kept Him all the time, calm, collected, and within Him also there was something of that compassion, that knowledge of the needy. This is the place for me to reach, yes I feel after that, the character of the Lord. I want to emphasize the word.

WIN CHRIST

Yea doubtless, and I count all things but loss for the excellency of the knowledge of Christ Jesus my Lord: for whom I have suffered the loss of all things, and do count them but dung, that I may win Christ.

Philippians 3:8

Paul was not seeking the knowledge of salvation, there was something which salvation brought as a spring into his soul, all the life which was within the life, which had within itself divine resources, a longing after Him. Oh, that I might win Him, all of us *must* reach the state of the crucifixion. Paul had heard about it, how before the judgment seat, he uttered not a word, and how with the rod they smote Him, and gave

Him vinegar and how in the midst of the crucifixion, He had love for His enemies, "Father, forgive them, for they know not what they do."

To win Him in persecution and in trial, to turn the soft answer, when reviled not to revile again.

Is this the true picture within our hearts this morning, is it the reality, have we felt like this? Is there no help for us? We are apprehended to be made perfect, even though we have had a thousand failures God has apprehended us, it does not matter. For the perfection, the ideal perfection, nothing less than sonship, nothing less than purity. "Be ye therefore perfect..." (Matthew 5:48).

The security of our position, the importance is to win Him, though we fail, don't give in. The excellency of the character is before us, the divine purpose is working right through.

We are not to be in the Convention to be entertained, but these days are days of quickening, reviving, stirring, and moving us. Oh, yes, the Master is before us in many revelations as we hear the speakers, the Lord opens the door so that we can have a new vision and enter into the divine character of the Lord.

RIGHTEOUSNESS

Verse 9 — "And be found in him, not having mine own righteousness...." I am continually confronted with this; am I prepared and willing, God comes to me over and over again. Oh, for this faith to be always realizing what happens. God is my plan for the purpose of making me know the righteousness which is by faith. That I may be found in Him, undisturbed whatever it is. There is something in the righteousness which is of faith, which helps you to graduate.

It lives, this rock is so real to be upon, and yet from that position, you find the Word of God lives, and your own position fails. God says he will hold them with the righteousness which is by faith. This "found in Him" is so remarkable, it is right for every emergency.

Philip. What shall we do for this great multitude today? Look at John 6. What a picture of the Master, who was at rest in the knowledge, they have been with Him now for very many days, and they will be fainting by the way. He was proving Philip, for He Himself knew. That is the wonderful thing, in Him.

Can we reach the place, where we can be in the Master's will, where we can absolutely see where God can plan for us? I like the righteousness which is of faith.

Are you at your wit's end, or in a tried place, do you think you have committed the unpardonable sin? Brothers and sisters, there is a place where God puts you in a place, where you are in Him, however severe the storm or strain may come.

Philip says, "200d. worth of bread is not sufficient for these people, and it is a desert place, but there is a lad here with a few loaves and fishes." This was a striking evidence of foresight, and quite easy to the Master.

Some have said it was quite easy to feed with these loaves, they were so big, but they do not say the boy carried them.

The Master handled them, and when the Master handles us, my word, the Lord can enlarge us if we are ready, He has a wonderful way of enlarging things. He Himself knew what He would do. And Paul said, "If only I can get there, the principle of the righteousness of this Christ, the place where nothing was too big, he could meet the need of all." There is something God wants us to handle this morning, not only to win Him and His principles, He was always in the restful place, in Him, Praise God.

My soul is warm this morning, it is the principle of the Master, where nothing is too much for me to do if only I can reach the state where Christ was living in me. He moves in this great scene, he has another plan here, the Lord wants to bring us a little further.

RESURRECTION

Verse 10 — "That I may know him, and the power of his resurrection...." There is something prior to the great resurrection, these are principles. Only to know the power of His resurrection with a divine revelation of the principles, to make us see that while Jesus was in the earth, He had the power of the resurrection.

It is lovely for me to hear how God is establishing the truth I said in the gifts. Greater works than these shall ye do, and He was raising from the dead. Lord, give us grace not to stumble.

May He bring us to the place, where we count all but loss that we may gain Him. There is to be a new man made within the man to manifest the divine plan for the people in our day. It is glorious to read of the prophets, Isaiah, Ezekiel, and also of Enoch and Lot, but this is our day. God's plan for me is the outpouring of the Holy Ghost, and there is within this great plan a rising of our minds that we may be associated with this great principle of faith.

When Dorcas died they sent for Peter, and he came, and they brought out the things she had made. This woman had lived in benevolence, and gave her life for the people. The eagerness and the longings of the people brought Peter to a place where he sat by the corpse. What was it that moved him? It was the longings of the cry of the people, her ministry to them had been the ministry of Christ.

Her spirit drew, and manifested itself, and laid hold of Peter, and he sat down by this corpse.

Realizing the need of a presence, he said, "Dorcas," and she opened her eyes, it was the principle, it must come to a place of helplessness on every line.

"Look Peter, James and John, I will show you, stand on one side, I am the resurrection and the life." The presentation before them was death, they had just brought within the gates of Nain a young man dead, did He say I will show you how to do it? Oh, no, that is not the way of the Master.

Jesus had compassion on the widow, and the compassion for the widow was greater than death. May I be found in Him not having mine own righteousness, the truth that is hidden in me, is greater than me, manifesting the power of God. It is not in human nature, but in the power of God.

SUFFERINGS

Verse 10 — Does God want me to suffer for another, one man has suffered. There is something about the fellowship of His sufferings, can we reach the agony of the depressed, and broken? This fellowship is only to be reached in one way, that is to bear with them. "If He knew what manner of woman this was," the disciples said. We know they all knew her, and that she was a woman of the city, but nobody knew her as well as Him, that is the fellowship of suffering. She had seen the Master, and she knelt at the feet of Jesus and got what she wanted, and she was among them in the upper room that spoke with tongues.

DEATH

Conformable to His death. Is it the death of His cross? No, but death-likeness. What would happen if the trumpet blew for you to be a King? That night He went to pray although He was a King.

There was a death there, it was the very clamour of human justice. And God can make His death to save us from where the flesh rises to be something, to keep us where we can be for God, He has a perfect way of doing it.

God can grant you the desires of your heart, because He hath laid hold of you, apprehended you. You are in the meeting that you may see your apprehension, and be apprehended of Him. Whatsoever is in your hearts this morning, God is greater than your hearts, greater than all things, let us rise and give ourselves to God.

Message given at Second Annual Convention of the Assemblies of God
Kingsway Hall

THE FAVOURED PLACE

October 1925

Are you in? *Oh, be IN! In Christ in God.* Ready for action, moved by the breath of the Spirit — to pray through, to preach through, manifesting the glory of the Lord, having a double portion of the Spirit, bathed in ecstasy, delight, and joy. Thy will be done — each a perfect son.

To have union with God is worth all. To have direct communion with God — no power interfering. Transmitting power, an ascent and descent of communication, charged by the divine operation of the Spirit — God intending our view as we eat His flesh and drink His blood — to whom can we go — Thou only has the Word of eternal life.

You are in a favoured place, a priceless position — if you have no way out but God, the closest revelation of what He is — they still cling around

Him as He spoke of that spiritual bread. They were so fed from the depths — they knew they had never had that before — They said, "Lord, evermore give us this bread." It is not an earthly conception, it has no earth roots — all divine, perfect, no human oratory. God wants such a people that He can feed with the finest wheat. For the harvest is fully ripe and ready to be gathered in. First the blade, then the ear — now the full corn in the ear. Ready to be ingathered, into the golden grainery forever.

TONGUES AND INTERPRETATION: "And this bread is that which cometh down. God gave the life of His Son, bestowing the true bread. He — the Lamb slain from the foundation of the world."

> *I beseech you therefore, brethren, by the mercies of God, that ye present your bodies a living sacrifice, holy, acceptable unto God, which is your reasonable service. And be not conformed to this world: but be ye transformed by the renewing of your mind, that ye may prove what is that good, and acceptable, and perfect, will of God.*
>
> Romans 12:1,2

The breathing through of the Spirit. The divine character, priceless, no bounds — enlarging and enlarging in our hand as the bread in the Master's hand — as He fed the 5,000 men so today the bread is enlarging — The child of God who can enter into this life-given truth held! held! held! He no longer holds God — God has hold of him! The Son has hold of him. The Holy Ghost has hold of him — has him — born into by God — all things swing out victoriously — a movement — off — manifesting the moving of God changing you. You see the necessity that God is glorified and you get rid of yourself. It is not an easy path. Some seem born good — goody, goody — I am of a different order.

I speak from a human standpoint — weak, deprived humanity with a touch of heaven in the body to change it all sufficient. His blood — His touch, His grace. Not abundance of revelation, but the revelation of our own weaknesses — the grace that comes in a time of extremity, meeting our need — a real messenger of possibility. God taking all, making us from today channels of holiness — righteousness, purity — wholly swallowed up in the life of the Spirit inexpressible! Life divine — joy — full. Yesterday I was interested in cycles — I was at the motor show. I never was so in the midst of it and out of it — never — I shouted, "Hallelu-jah!" and "Glory!" and all kinds of talk to God. I could not fellowship with what was there. I was in it — but not of it. There is a new order above nature's plan and it is the order of God. How beautiful God spoke to me this verse, "I beseech you brethren by the mercies of God — that you present your bodies a holy sacrifice."

It is not the end of sanctification — that has no end. It is not the end of the cleaning of the blood. It is wholly a life proven. We are not saved — but we are out of fellowship many times. Salvation is a being saved, a readiness to meet Jesus any moment — a plan of increasing, a decreas-ing with an increasing — an enlarging to revelation to display Him, making every time a progress in sanctification — purification our whole body, our set purpose to be by the Holy Ghost. This is the great order — a daily changing. I am seeing the altar the sacrifice — It is according to the mercies of God. The sacrifice was holy — it came to the place of acceptance with God — not finished, but God occupying it — God took the will, the whole desire and put them into his coffers of love and said, "I will accept it," and He did. Oh, the joy of the knowledge of the completing — the more helpless — ashes — the *dependance more*, the bliss of the breath — every human power and human program fails — every divine inflow of the power of the Spirit is to an enlarging, bring-ing the soul into separation, into divine revelation when God bends over and sweetly smiles it is all right — only further on! on! on!

Oh, the joy of the knowledge, Paul spoke out of offering. You cannot speak out of anything else. All God's choice positions are out of an offering — because Jesus offered Himself for us, God gave Him a Name above every Name — present your bodies a living sacrifice — a whole offering — not perfect, but God began a new plan of His great purpose.

So, He will rest in His love and joy over us with singing. The precious fruit. He prepared it for flood time of the early and now the latter rain for He is coming.

> *...be not conformed to this world: but be ye transformed by the renewing of your mind, that ye may prove what is that good, and acceptable, and perfect, will of God.*
>
> *Romans 12:2*

The baptism of the Holy Ghost is perfected — coming into the helpless, investing with a force mightier than the human. Moving — knowing that the greatest of all is there. The Holy Ghost gets the great position, focusing all on the Son — the Holy Ghost reveals the Son in you — you decreasing — He must increase. How? On the line of the revelation of the Spirit — There is no experience like the second chapter of Acts. The greatest opportunity God has afforded to man — submit to Almighty God. The human spirit may be in great activity in a person who has offered — Your "I" must be knocked out and your personality be fully surrendered to God. God moves me to see that there is no good thing in me. No! You can polish up the old man — but he is still the old creation and worthless. Rise to the higher order of revelation with God. Jesus is the greatest of all — fulfilling, revealing, divine activity.

He lives and moves in the world — and He learned obedience by the things that He suffered. He came not to do His own will. He lived freely and the Father could act His will through Him. There was nothing in the flesh, it was weak — But God sent His Son in the likeness of sinful flesh and for sin condemned sin in the flesh. This grown Son speaking, acting — divine revelation coming to us on this breath. Be not conformed — transformed, proven, seeing, knowing the perfect will of God.

TONGUES AND INTERPRETATION: "Forever the King reigneth when the body is yielded, the will is conformed by the power of the Son of God through the Spirit."

He lives and reigns forever and by His grace we shall reign forever with Him — It is worth a thousand deaths to come into one life — even if we have failed a thousand times God can fan and fan and fan until the smoking floss is ablaze — with divine equipment and a divine association, living with the King.

> I know the Lord
> I know the Lord
> He laid His hand on me.
> He filled me with the Holy Ghost.
> I know the Lord laid His hand on me.

Praise the Lord. Beloved God had more in His mind than the necessity of changing us. Full of the Holy Ghost. Gifts prove the rarities of heaven dawning upon you — wholly separated unto God forever — All spiritual revelation and power come within the body. The joy and help to others work through without I have travailed. I know nothing about birth. The travailing with God and labour until God brings forth the process of His inward working — All heaven's rays focus until the body seems too small to contain what is coming in — understanding the breath of the Spirit — the breath of God — born to yield — knowing when to begin and when to stop. To be at all times a perfect channel for the breath of the Spirit of God.

Send — fly — flee — all a perfect blending of Trinity divine to keep us in the place where God has us all the time a mind of reflection. The reflection of the mind always makes the operation of the tongue — The sanctity of the spirit, not conformed but transformed — not your mind on earth, but shorn of earthly desire. But a supernatural order filled with illumination for Acts 1:8. Ye shall receive power — not power by the Holy Ghost, but the illumination of the Holy Ghost on the power — all power is given unto Him. The Holy Ghost reveals Him — all power and floodtide are through Him. The Holy Ghost conveys to the mind all the fulness in Him — The blood of Jesus purified the position — after the blood — a perfect offering.

The Holy Ghost then takes the position of sanctifying the whole of your actions that all is for the glory of the Son. The human is never in it. The human exists for the purpose of manifesting the glory of God — the channel never robbing the glory. The Spirit so sanctifying the activity all the time. Not conformed but transformed, raising the mind through the sanctifying of the will and desires — sanctifying every thought — robbing us of all pride and exaltation, so sanctified by the Spirit, nothing hindering the manifestation of the glory of God, being included in the perfection of the will of God.

The epistles of Saint Paul were all written to people baptized with the Holy Ghost — here you touch deep water, the Holy Spirit must be in control, so that you are able to read and to understand what God means you to be. In Ephesians we read, "according to the purpose of God and according to the will of God." — The simplicity of the truth, the sincere milk of the Word. "Learn from Me, for I am meek and lowly in heart and the anointing that you have received abideth and shall teach you all things."

The sanctification of the Spirit. The Holy Ghost alone giving the utterance after the cleansing by the blood comes the sanctification of the Spirit. Not any human desire, but your mind more and more purified for the glory of God — When we get into the Spirit, time has gone. In the Spirit and the glory a thousand years are as one day. If I live in the Spirit, I have no dreary days. Some days the sun shines more, but it makes no difference.

We are not in Egypt's sand — Oh, you must not look for me down in Egypt's sand — the Holy Ghost wants to perfect in us what He has begun. It was God who sought and drew our hearts until we pray in the Spirit — that is how we began and how we just continue. This is that — and if you think it out that is God. God's work in us. God has been pouring out His spirit, waking us up to a new order in the Spirit. The Spirit has begun to breathe through the land.

There must be something happening — We pay a big price to go — much weeping, travail, groaning and we cannot get out of it. But God is going before us.

We need no questions — it is a poor people who cannot praise the Lord. Suppression of praise never disturbs the devil. God wants firebrands — lives aflame by the power of God. God has made me so hungry. I never was so hungry and thirsty after God. We are at a place not it will be, but it must be. If we will pay the price — God will open the heavens. All I know I am doing to meet the will and mind of God — that God may bring us a deluge of the latter rain. God the Holy Ghost, a perfect blending for God's glory. Jesus manifesting the glory of the Father — full of the Holy Ghost — The Holy Ghost revealing the Son, reflecting the Son, the King of glory — to bring millions out of darkness into light — for the glory of the King of glory — and God shall be revealed, God bringing us to a place wholly separated unto Himself — sanctified in spirit, soul and body. Separated — going in and out finding pasture and able to feed the multitude with the bread of life. Abundance of peace — debtors to God who has chosen us and brought us to a desired place — inspiring us — We never know how weak we are until we are covered by His mighty strength — not to fail — but to stand for God and having done all to stand, Jesus will carry us through.

Surrender all — a fresh consecration — will be saved tonight than when we began — more knowledge of God, causing us to triumph in Him, more holiness — deeper abasement.

Believe God! Give yourself wholly to Jesus — a large heart, a whole heart, perfectly yielding to God, controlling every thought. "Oh, Lord have me for Thy glory!"

Have I obtained it? Yes! For he that asketh receiveth. Now don't fail God. Believe, and it shall come to pass! Whatsoever ye desire when ye pray, God will grant it. This day can God fill me with His Spirit now? Yes, when I ask:

> Will He fill me? Yes! Yes! If I ask in faith.
> Yes filled with God,
> Yes filled with God,
> Pardoned and cleansed,
> And filled with God.
> An end of self and filled with God.
> Stand with God for the new day.
> Self out, the curse away.
> Filled with God and Jesus glorified! Amen.

Message given in London, England

FAITH
Mark 5
November 1925

Beloved, I believe that God would be pleased for me to read to you from the fifth chapter of St. Mark's gospel, from verse 21 to the end of the chapter. This is a wonderful passage; in fact, all of God's Word is wonderful. It is the Word of life, and it is the impartation of the life of the Savior. Jesus came to give eternal life and He also came to make our bodies whole. I believe that God, the Holy Ghost, wants to reveal the fulness of redemption through the power of Christ's atonement on Calvary until every soul shall get a new sight of Jesus, the Lamb of God. He is lovely. He is altogether lovely. Oh, He is so beautiful! You talk about being decked with the rarest garments, but oh, brother, He could weep with those who weep. He could have compassion on all. There were none that missed His eye.

When He was at the pool, He knew the impotent man and understood his case altogether. Yes, brother, and when He was at Nain, the compassion of the Master was so manifested that it was victorious over death. Do you know that love and compassion are stronger than death? If we touch God, the Holy Spirit, He is the ideal principle of divine life for weaknesses; He is health; He is joy.

God would have us know that He is waiting to impart life. Oh, if thou wouldest believe! Oh, you need not wait another moment. Just now as I preach, receive the impartation of the life by the power of the Word. Do you now know that the Holy Ghost is the breath of heaven, the breath of God, the divine impartation of power that moves in the human and which raises from the dead and quickeneth all things. One of the things that happened on the day of Pentecost in the manifestation of the Spirit was a mighty, rushing wind. The Third Person was manifested in wind, power, mighty, revelation, glory and emancipation. Glory to God! This is why I am on this platform — because of this holy, divine Person who is breath, life, revelation. His power moved me, transformed me, sent me, revised the whole of my position. This wind was the life of God coming and filling the whole place where they were sitting. And when I say to you, "Breathe in," I do not mean merely breathe; I mean breathe in God's life, God's power, the personality of God. Hallelujah!

In the Scripture which we read, we see a man and woman in great trouble. They have a little daughter lying at the point of death. Everything has failed, but they know if they find Jesus, she shall be made whole. Is it possible to seek for Jesus and not find Him? Never! There is not one person in this place who has truly sought for Jesus and has not found Him. As you seek, you will find; as you knock, the door will swing open; as you ask, you will receive. Yes, if you can find Jesus, your little daughter will live. As the Father goes along the road, there is great commotion. He sees the dust rising a long time before he reaches the great company of people who surround Jesus. Hearken to the children's voices and the people shouting. All are delighted because Jesus is in the company. Oh, this camp meeting will rise to a tremendous pitch as we look for Jesus.

Yes, the Father met Him; glory to God! "And besought him greatly, saying, My little daughter lieth at the point of death: I pray thee, come and lay thy hands on her, that she may be healed; and she shall live. And Jesus went with him..." (Mark 5:23,24). I want you to know that this same Jesus is in the midst of His people today. He is right here with His ministry of power and blessing.

But as Jesus went with the man, something happened. "...a certain woman, which had an issue of blood twelve years...came in the press behind, and touched his garment" (vv. 25,27). This poor woman was in an awful state. She had spent all her money on physicians and was "...nothing bettered, but rather grew worse." This poor woman said, "...If I may touch but His clothes...I shall be whole." No doubt she thought of her weakness, but faith is never weak. She may have been very weary, but faith is never weary. The opportunity had come for her to touch Him and "...straightway the fountain of her blood was dried up; and she felt in her body that she was healed of that plague" (v. 29).

The opportunity comes to you now to be healed. Will you believe? Will you touch Him? There is something in a living faith that is different from anything else. I have seen marvelous things accomplished just because people said, "Lord, I believe." Jesus knew that virtue had gone out of Him and He said, "Who touched me?" The woman was fearful and trembling, but she fell down before the Lord and told Him all the truth. "And he said unto her, Daughter, thy faith hath made thee whole; go in peace, and be whole of thy plague" (v. 34).

"While he yet spake, there came from the ruler of the synagogue's house certain which said, Thy daughter is dead: why troublest thou the Master any further?" (v. 35). But Jesus encouraged the ruler of the synagogue and said, "...Be not afraid, only believe" (v. 36). Ah, what things God does for us when we only believe. He is so rich to all that call upon Him. What possibilities there are in this meeting if we would only believe in the divine presence, for God is here. The power of the Spirit is here. How many of you dare rise and claim your healing? Who will dare rise and claim your rights of perfect health? All things are possible to him that believeth. Jesus is the living substance of faith. You can be perfectly adjusted by the blood of Jesus. We must believe in the revelation of the Spirit's power and see our blessed position in the risen Christ.

Only believe! Only believe! All things are possible, Only believe!

"For as the lightning cometh out of the east, and shineth even unto the west; so shall also the coming of the Son of man be" (Matthew 24:27).

Portion of message delivered at Camp Meeting
Berkley, California

THE HEARING OF FAITH

December 1925

Praise the Lord. Praise the Lord. Only believe. All things are possible, only believe. Absolute dependency. God only. His grand will. Only believe.

What Abraham our father as pertaining to the flesh hath found. What hath Abraham found as pertaining to the flesh? (Romans 4:1) Something wonderful through God the Holy Ghost. Also seeing that all flesh is as grass, and that in me, that is in my flesh dwelleth no good thing, what hath Abraham our father found pertaining to the flesh? Only this, for the believer God has some One that can live in the flesh, hold the flesh by the power of God above sin and judgment. Jesus Christ, the center of the life where the body, the flesh, has come to the place of being inhabited by God, where God, dwelling in these earthly temples, can live and reign supreme.

He hath quickened that which was dead, bringing life and immortality to light through the Gospel, and the Son of God is manifested there.

God has for us wonderful things. Many days in the past have been wonderful, but no day is like the present. The Holy Ghost lifting us into His presence, the power flowing, our whole being flaming with the glory of God. Here is God's divine plan for humanity when the Holy Ghost has come. Today we are nearer the goal, the vision is clearer, the Holy Ghost bringing us into the treasure of the Most High. What hath our father Abraham pertaining to the flesh? I depend upon the Holy Ghost to bring us into revelation. There is no room for weakness if we see this mighty incoming life through the Spirit.

OBEY GOD

What hath our father Abraham found pertaining to the flesh? He found that as he heard the voice of God and obeyed it, it not only judged him but wonderful things were manifested. One day away there God said to Abraham, Come out. God has wonderful things to say to you if you come to the hearing of faith, not the natural order, taste, desire, affection. Oh yes, if God gets your ear you will come out.

One day God said to me, Come out. I had not been in long. I was in the Wesleyan Church. Was there anything wrong? No. Only God said, Come out. He had something further. The Salvation Army was in full swing. I was very anxious to get the best. Revival was at full, but they turned to other things. So God said, Come out. We need to have the hearing of faith, always soaring higher, understanding the leading of the Spirit. Oh, the breath of God. Then I went to the brethren, they had the Word, but so much of the letter with it, and splitting of hairs. God said, Come out. Oh, they said, he has gone again, there is no satisfying him. Then came the baptism of the Holy Ghost, with signs following according to Acts 2. God alone speaking. Faith bringing us to a place of revelation to cover us, God coming in and manifesting His power.

What had our father Abraham found pertaining to the flesh? Two things — (1) A righteousness by law; (2) a righteousness by faith. Believing what God says, and daring on the authority of God's Word to act. God will meet us there, within that blessed place, making for us opportunities of blessing. Love, truth, revelation, manifestation. God and you in activity, bringing divine ability and activity into action.

> Oh it's all right now, it's all right now,
> For Jesus is my Savior,
> So it's all right now.

The way into the treasure house of the Most High is the authority of the living Word. The kingdom of heaven is open to all believers.

He has called us, bringing us into divine association with heaven, if we will dare to believe, for all things are possible to him that believeth.

When we believe, we shall find, like Abraham who believed God, tremendous ability, changing weakness into strength, character, power, association within, making all things new. A life yielded, absorbed by divine authority. Standing on the principles of God.

In Wellington, New Zealand, there was a crowd of needy people come for help, among them a heavy built woman. God revealed to me the presence of the enemy within the body. She cried out, "You are killing me," and fell down in the aisle. I said, "Lift her up. God has not done yet." The onlookers in judgment didn't know, but three yards off she was loosed from a cancer. It is wise to believe God. God has a place for the man or woman who dares to believe. The man God has His hand on is not subject to the opinions of others. This our father Abraham found pertaining to the flesh. May God increase the number who dare to believe under all circumstances. To dare to believe God on the authority of the Word.

I came across a peculiar case. A man bent double, he was in agony, cancer on the bladder, he cried and cried. I said, "Do you believe God?" He said, "No, I have nothing in common with God." I tried to bring him to the place of believing, but his mental capacity was affected. I said, "I see you don't understand, it may be God wants me to help you." I said the Name of Jesus. What is it? It is the One that met us at Calvary, come with new life divine.

Before all the message, God means us to be an extraordinary people with this wonderful life of faith in the body. Abraham found, when he believed God, that he was bound to Almighty power, equipped for service, by faith.

Laying my hands on the sick man in the Name, I didn't have to say, "Are you whole?" He knew he was whole. He couldn't tell what he had got. This man had been interested in yachts, he was a member of a yacht club. His friends went as usual to see him and began talking about yachts. He said, Yachts! Yachts! Talk to me about Jesus! Oh yes, there is something in the Name. Our father Abraham pertaining to the flesh found it. The Word of God the link, the key, the personality of divine equipment. There is something mighty in believing God. Have you found it? A faith that believes God apprehends what God said. What did God say? God said that because Abraham believed Him He would cover him with His righteousness, holiness, integrity of faith. God loves to see His children when they believe Him. He covers them. It is a lovely covering, the covering of the Almighty. Blessed is the man to whom God imputeth righteousness. Is it to be?

God has for us a perfect work, a hearing of faith, that has within the sound of His voice, hearing Him speak, our speech betraying us. Epistles of the divine character, having His life, passion, compassion. Beloved, there must be this divine fellowship between us and God.

The disciples said: What shall we do to do the works of God? Jesus said: This is the work of God that ye believe on Him Whom He hath sent.

CHRIST DWELLING WITHIN BY FAITH

This is what our father Abraham pertaining to the flesh hath found. A written epistle, known and read of all men. Paul was enamored of it, he followed this divine fire with all that are in the faith with Abraham. When Paul speaks in Ephesians and Colossians we see what he with Abraham had received pertaining to the flesh, Christ in you the hope of glory. It's all embedded there, all we need, filled unto all the fulness of God.

The baptism in the Holy Ghost crowns Jesus King in His royal palace. When the King is crowned what tremendous things we find pertaining to the flesh. Perpetual divine motion. The power of God sweeping through the regions of weakness. What have we got pertaining to the flesh? New life flowing through. All the Word of God is yea and amen to faith. Divine actions in the human frame mighty, so full of operation till we see God working. For these young men and women I see such possibilities in coming into line with God, nothing can interfere with the progress of God, the Author of life and finisher of faith. Never be afraid of your voice when the Spirit is upon you, nor living for yourself but with a ministry of freedom.

First Corinthians 12 — No man can call Jesus Lord but in the Holy Ghost. I see the dew of the Spirit, the order of blessing, ability to crown Jesus King, set apart for God.

Then there is the sealing of the Spirit, the great adjusting, giving us the knowledge in the revelation of Jesus as King over all, affections, desires, wishes; all His.

His compassion, His meekness, His dynamic — the power to move the devil away. A big plan — a force of unity, a divine capacity — making things move.

A man and his wife came to me troubled about things taking place in their meeting. I said: You two can be so perfectly joined in unity, as to take victory for every meeting, not a thing could stand against you, a perfect fellowship, which the devil is not able to break, if any two of you agree. Dare on the authority of God's Word to bind every spirit in the meeting.

A faith pertaining to our flesh manifested in human bodies, circumcision for home affairs, financial difficulties, more than conquerors in this operation of faith.

Romans 4:16 — It is of faith that it might be of grace, that the promise might be sure to all the seed. Nothing is so large, inhabited by this operation of faith, that is brought to us through Calvary. Mighty revival, I feel it coming, my whole being moves towards it. I dare to believe in simplicity of faith.

Once in Norway, the halls were packed and the streets thronged to hear God's Word, we want it in London. God has given us a divine plan to operate with Him. The deluge can come, a Pentecostal outpouring for the glory of God.

There is now a way into the kingdom of heaven by faith. No reserve on God's side, only believe, to see the mighty power of God fall, we are here to awake you.

Abraham was tested. God is greater than the testing and opens a door of deliverance. Faith! God never changes. What had Abraham received? Testing. But called, chosen and faithful, faithful to God in the trial; twenty-five years Abraham waited — he believed against hope, giving glory to God. Not one thing will fail if you dare believe. All fulness in manifestation arising in faith, all needs of the body met in a moment on the word of faith, give God the glory, stammering tongue, consumption, neurasthenia, need of salvation, all needs met if we dare believe. We are in the place of receiving all our father Abraham did, pertaining to the flesh. Let us put in our claim, letting the deluge come, that God wants to send.

Romans 4:20,21 — Giving glory to God, becoming strong in faith, being fully persuaded that what He has promised He is able also to perform. That God may be glorified in us and we in Him, having found as Abraham did, the hearing of faith. The righteousness that is ours through faith. Amen.

Published in *Redemption Tidings*

JOHN **7:37-39**

1926

ow here we have our Lord in a present tense position He is in the activity and the actual workings of the power of God, and He knows that He is empowered or driven or led by a power that has to be the world's share. The believers have to reach this blessed attitude and be clothed upon within with the rays of heaven's light that they may be exactly as He was with a clear conception of the knowledge of satanic forces; of the powers of God; or the limitations of Satan, and the powerfulness of the Almighty.

SUCH A CRY

Here He is speaking of what may be the position of every believer now that the Holy Ghost has been given. At that time He was speaking of a future tense, and therefore He knew that everybody that received what He was waiting to give they would be the people that were ready for the power when it came.

So they had been to Jerusalem to worship, and were returning dry and barren and needing blessing. Beloved, I believe that God has a great plan in this for us to see. Those that were thirsty could have something that morning. Those that were hungry could have something that morning. They that had been to Jerusalem making the offerings; they that were going away dry and helpless; and He was the only One that could cry out this message:

> *...If any man thirst, let him come unto me, and drink... out of his belly shall flow rivers of living water.*
>
> *John 7:37,38*

This spake He of the Spirit that should be given after Jesus was glorified. Now keep before you this morning the facts that I want you to see. First, you must know that there is a dry condition existing everywhere today. I find it all over. People are longing for a fulness. There never was such a cry, and beloved, it is because the Scriptures are being fulfilled. The former rain fell in a very blessed way, clothing the apostles with power, and the Acts of the Apostles came forth because they dared to act. We see the deliverance of the captives; the mightiness flowing through like a river till thousands and tens of thousands were saved by the power of the former rain which was by the Spirit; but in these last days God will pour out upon all flesh the Latter Rain, and I believe all flesh will feel the effects of it. It will not be possible for anyone to miss it. They may refuse it; but it will be there for the taking, and I believe God would have us to see that the Latter Rain has begun to fall. I do not say we are anywhere near the fulness of it; but I do see a great thirst after the fulness, and I believe that that thirst is not brought about by visible man. You cannot love righteousness and hate iniquity — neither can you desire purity on any line through the flesh. Flesh was never subject to the law neither indeed can it be so. The flesh has to come into regeneration and the regenerated heart is becoming hungry.

God is creating a hunger and thirst. I see it all over. There are people who begin waiting on God and they do not know what they are waiting for — they have no idea. I believe that God is making the thing so that you cannot get out of it. You may refuse it and you may come within its reach and come outside the boundaries of it; but it is for you. It is a personal baptism — it is not a church baptism. It is for the body of the believers which is to be clothed with the power and unction of the Spirit by this glorious waiting. What do I mean by saying the Church? Why, because people get their minds on a building when I say churches. You see, it is the believers who compose the 'body' — believers in the Lord Jesus Christ — whatever sect or creed or denomination they are, and I tell you also that Paul goes so far as to say that some people have very strange ideas of who will be ready for the coming of the Kingdom. All in Christ will be ready, and you have got to decide whether you are in that or not. The Scripture says in the first verse of Romans eighth chapter:

> *There is therefore now no condemnation to them which are in Christ Jesus, who walk not after the flesh, but after the Spirit.*

If you are there — Praise the Lord! That is a good position. I pray the Lord that He will bring us all into that place — what a wonder it will be.

LIKE A RIVER

I want you to see this morning that the Master had no less idea than a river through every one. Whatever you think about it — Jesus would have your salvation to be as a river and I am sure that Jesus was the ideal for us all. The lack today is the lack of apprehension of that blessed fulness of Christ. He came to do nothing less than embody us with the same manifestation as He had "*to do.*" Just moving for a moment to His attitude in the Holy Ghost I would like you to see a plan there. Acts 1: We find that Jesus began to "do" and "teach," and the believer should always be so full of the Holy Ghost that he begins to "do," and then He can "teach." He must be ready for the man in the street. He must be right ready — flowing like a river. He must have three things: ministration, operation and manifestation, and those three things must always be forthcoming. We ought to be so full of the manifestation of the power of God that in the Name of Jesus we can absolutely destroy the power of Satan. We are in the world — not of it. He overcame it and to subdue it unto God we are in the world — overcomers. We are nothing but in Christ we are more than conquerors through the blood — more than a match for satanic powers on every line and may the Lord so let us see that we must be loosed from ourselves, for if you examine yourself you will be natural; but if you look at God, you will be supernatural. If you have a great God, you will have a little devil; if you have a big devil, you will have a little God, so may the Lord let us see that we must be so full of the order of the Spirit of life that we are always overcoming him which had the power of death — even the devil.

Jesus was only laying a foundation which is the new birth unto righteousness. It is the drink at the well; it is receiving Him and by receiving Him you may have power to become sons of God, for to as many as receive Him, they become the sons of God. So here He was — the great throngs of people which had thronged the place returning from the feast were dissatisfied and there He stood and cried:

If any man athirst, let him come unto Me and drink, and out of that drink that flow the rivers of living water, now who does not want them? Now this He spake of the Spirit that should be given after He was glorified, for the Holy Ghost was not yet given (John 7:37-39).

Let me by the grace of God just put us into the place of where to expect and receive. Now we know as well as anything that the day of Pentecost came; we know that He was received up into glory, and that the angel spoke as He was going away and said, "This same Jesus would come again." We know that the disciples tarried at Jerusalem till they were endued with power from on High, and we know the Holy Ghost came, and so while we know the Holy Ghost came, it is wrong now to wait for the Holy Ghost. I know it was personally right; it was divinely right for those apostles to hear what Jesus said and to tarry for the Holy Ghost, but it is not right now to tarry for the Holy Ghost. Then why do we not all receive the Holy Ghost, you ask? Because the bodies are not ready for it; the temples are not cleansed. When the temples are purified and the minds put in order so that carnalities and fleshly desires and everything has [have] gone, then the Holy Ghost can take full charge. The Holy Ghost is not a manifestation of carnality. There are any amount of people which never read the Word of God who could not be led away by the powers of Satan. The power of the Holy Ghost is most lovely divine in all its construction. It is a great refiner. It is full of life but it is always divine — never natural. If you touch flesh after you are baptized in the Holy Ghost, you cease to go on.

Beloved, I want to speak about something greater, something to lift your minds; elevate your thoughts; bring you into divine lines; something that elevates you out of yourself into God; out of the world into a place where you know you have rest for your feet; where you cease from your own works where God worketh in you mightily to will and to do of His good pleasure.

THE INRUSH

When I think about a river, a pure, holy, divine river, I say — what can stand against its inrush? Wherever it is — in a railway carriage, or in the street, or in a meeting, its power and flow will always be felt; it will always do its work. Jesus spoke about the Holy Ghost which was to be given. I want you to think how God gave it, and how its coming was manifested; its reception and its outflow after it had come.

In Acts 8 we find three positions on the Holy Ghost. The first is a rushing mighty wind and I want you to keep that in your mind. The second — cloven tongues of fire — keep that in your mind, and then the fact of the incoming of the manifestations. Now keep your mind for a moment on the rushing mighty wind, and then see the cloven tongues of fire over every one; then see the incoming and outflow through it. I am glad that the Holy Ghost is manifested to us as wind, person and fire. I am also glad that the Holy Ghost is a manifestation to us of fire, for it is wonderful, is fire. Then I want you to know that the Holy Ghost is power — those three things.

Can we be filled with a river? How is it possible for out of us to flow a river? A river of water is always an emblem of the Word of God — the Water of life, and so when the Holy Ghost comes, He clothes and anoints the Christ which is already within the believer; who will be just the same only so much different, because the power of the Spirit of the life of Christ is now being manifested in a new way — for it is the plan of God. You should be filled with the matter of the Word, for that is the life. You will never get to know God better by testimony — testimony should always come through the Word. You will not get to know God better by prayer — prayer has to come out of the Word. The Word is the only thing that reveals God and is going to be helpful in the world through you in that when the breath and the presence of God come — the executive of God the Father and the Son — the Holy Ghost speaks expressively according to the mind of the Father and the Son and so when you are filled with the Holy Ghost, then the breath — the power — the unction; the fire takes hold of the Word of life which is Christ, and out of you flow the rivers, and God wants to fill us with that divine power, that out of us shall flow rivers.

The preparation is the place where Paul had reached when he said he had become the least of all; where he counted everything was dung and that in his body there was no good thing. Then he was in a place of denunciation. If there is anything in you that likes to be seen and heard, it will have to die — for Jesus must have all the glory in a body. It is not possible for you and God to dwell in the same body in fulness. (As you come to an end of yourself, then is the beginning of an almightiness of God — a little thing may stop the flow.)

I have never seen a man keep the unction of the baptism of the Holy Ghost who took intoxicating liquors; I have never seen a man manifest and carry forth the order of the baptism of the Holy Ghost that smoked, and if these outward things which can be seen hinder God from holding sway in our lives; what about the inward things?

It was perfectly right for Jesus to say that a man that looked on a woman to lust had committed adultery already in his heart, because James says that when you are drawn aside and tempted it is because of your own lust; then before the Holy Ghost can have His way within you, you must be cleansed from your own evil appetites and there must be a body prepared for the Holy Ghost. Can it be so? Yes.

TONGUES AND INTERPRETATION: "It is the divine plan which is the inward movement of the Spirit, which is the divine order of Trinity taking hold of nature and transforming it into power and bringing it into a place where out of it flows rivers of living water; light, revelation, open door — intercession, making a way into all darkness; bringing to God the things that are so manifestly declared that day by day we are the sons of God."

YIELD TO HIM

And this river flows without an effort. When the Holy Ghost takes hold of you, you will have no more cracked brains and sleepless nights through preparing your addresses — God will do it. Another thing, you will be able to dispense with and lock up your libraries forever. You will have a contained library in the Holy Ghost. He has the last thoughts of heaven — the first thoughts for earth. He has everything He wants you to have, and if you have anything that He doesn't want you to have, it is worthless. If you have to be the oracles of God — the apostles of Christ; and as those quickened from the dead, enlarged by the Spirit; intensified with the zeal of the Almighty and made a river. You will have to be on fire, for nothing but fire will make the water boil. Oh, it is lovely.

You see, beloved, the grace of God is so full that He makes you know that you have ceased to be and if I could only impregnate that into your heart this morning. Is it possible? Yes — this is the great plan of God for you. It is the sole purpose of God — a greater purpose than you can conceive and it is God's thought for you — He has no less plan for you than to make you a son of God with power according to the resurrection. I tell you that the incarnation of God by the Spirit is to unveil the glory; let in a cloudburst and make inroads into you till there are new rivers. Oh, for your old rivers to be dried up and the new river by the cloudburst of heaven to make a new plan for you for all time for He is able to do these things in the Spirit.

God is able to do this for any one of us who will yield to Him. You will find that there is Abraham, Isaac, and Jacob. Abraham was the father of all; Isaac was the seed of all; Jacob was the failure of all; but you never find God mentioning Abraham and Isaac but he brings in Jacob. Can Jacobs be changed? There are plenty of them. Yes. That is the plan of God to make the Jacobs into Israels; He takes the waywardness and the supplanting of Jacob and changes them so that they will no longer follow those conditions, and when his sons were going into Egypt to see him; when they brought all the money back he said take double and take a present and take this and that. What a difference! When he was with Laban, he took the lot; but God had changed him. Oh, beloved, I tell you when we get to see that God Almighty would always bring in the weaknesses with His power; when we see that when He has a plan for us, and when I know that God can take my weakness and make it power; when He can take our weakness and depravity and make us holy, then I know I have a God of immensity. He takes the first, establishes the second and the first is not again mentioned. The last man is from heaven; the first man is of the earth. God wants us to know this morning the power of the Christ of God is to make the first man heavenly. Oh, hallelujah!

TONGUES AND INTERPRETATION: "It is He that created all things for Himself that has come in to create us for Himself that we may be no longer of the outward but inward perfection with Him Who hath created us in power and might and revelation — gods in the earth. Hallelujah—clothed with power!"

Beloved, listen: "Philip saith to Jesus: I would like you to show me the Father." Hear the answer: "If thou hast seen Me thou hast seen the Father." O brother, the time had to come that when they looked at Philip they had to see Jesus. The world has not to see us; it has to see Jesus. It can only be convinced that Jesus has been formed in the hearts and lives of the people in this way. Then again, the same Word must come to us in power this morning. Hear what it says: "The works that I do, I do not but He that dwelleth in Me." Brother, when that comes to our lost state — what a transformation. When the Holy Ghost comes, He doeth the work. You are only the instrument, you are the vessel; but glory to God, He condescended to dwell in us — Praise the Lamb! "The works that I do, I do not; but He doeth them." How lovely to be filled with such incarnation of God's order that the power of the Spirit of the life of Jesus should flow through you and you should be a new creation of the Spirit under the mighty power of God. "If thou hast seen Me, thou hast seen the Father."

Directly after the baptism of the Holy Ghost came, those crooked, indifferent and peculiar disciples were transformed till one day Peter and John came down and mixed with the people who said: "They are unlearned and ignorant but we see that they have been with Him." Can they say that about us? Have we been with Jesus? Do not think you will comfort people by singing wonderful hymns — they are lovely. Do not think you will comfort people any other way but by the Word of God being made manifest in that you have been with Jesus. There must be the law of the Spirit of life in Christ Jesus that shall put to death every other thing.

It is one thing to read the Word of God, another thing to believe it. It is possible to be real and earnest and have zeal and fastings and yet not to have faith. And do you not know that one little bit of faith which can only come through the Word of God is worth more than all your cryings — all your rolling on the floor — all your screaming and everything; but beloved, God is better than anything.

May the Holy Ghost give us today an inward knowledge of what it is to believe. It is God's purpose to make every believer to subdue everything and to make you perfect and entire and overcoming.

THE INCARNATION OF MAN

January 1926

Romans 8. For a short time I want especially to speak to those in this meeting who are saved. God wants them to be holy. He wants them to be filled with the power that will keep them holy. He wants us to have a revelation of what sin and death are, and what the Spirit and life of the Spirit are. Look at the first two verses: It is full of matter.

> *There is therefore now no condemnation to them which are in Christ Jesus, who walk not after the flesh, but after the Spirit. For the law of the Spirit of life in Christ Jesus hath made me free from the law of sin and death.*
>
> *Romans 8:1,2*

"No condemnation!" This is the primary word for me tonight, because it means so much; it has everything within it. If you are without condemnation, you are in a place where you can pray through; where you have a revelation of Christ; for, for Him to be in you brings you to a place where you cannot, if you follow the definite leadings of the Spirit of Christ, have any fellowship with the world; and I want you to see that the Spirit of the Lord would reveal unto us this fact tonight. If you love the world, you cannot love God, and the love of God cannot be in you; so God wants a straight cut tonight, because if you are in Christ Jesus, you are of a new creation order; you are in Him and, therefore, you walk in the Spirit and are free from condemnation.

TONGUES AND INTERPRETATION: "It is the Spirit alone that, by revelation, brings the whole truth, visiting the Son in your hearts and revealing unto you the capabilities of sonship that are in you after you are created after the image of Him."

So the Spirit of the Lord tonight would bring you into revelation. He wants you without condemnation. What will that mean? Much every way, because God wants all His people to be targets. More than that, He wants them to be salted; to be lights; to be like cities set on a hill which cannot be hid; so "in God for the world's redemption" that the world may know that ye belong to God. That is the law of the Spirit. What will it do? The law of the Spirit of life in Christ Jesus will make you free from the law of sin. Sin will have no dominion over you. You will have no desire to sin, and it will be as true of you as it was of Jesus when He said, "Satan cometh, but findeth nothing in Me." He cannot draw; he has no power. His power is destroyed in the tenth verse:

> ...the body is dead because of sin; but the Spirit is life because of righteousness.
>
> Romans 8:10

To be filled with God means that you are free! Filled with joy, peace, blessing, enduement, strength of character in God, and transformed by His mighty power.

Notice there are two laws: The law of the Spirit of life in Christ Jesus making you free from the law of sin and death. The same law is in you as was in you before, but it is dead; the same flesh, only it is dead; you are just the same, only quickened into spiritual life; you are a new creation, a new creature, created in God afresh after the image of Christ. Now, beloved, some people who come into line with this do not understand their inheritance, and they go down; and instead of making you weak, and inclined to go under, you have to rise triumphantly over it. You say, "Show us this law!" I will, God helping me.

Romans, seventh chapter, last verse, reads:

> *I thank God through Jesus Christ our Lord. So then with the mind*
> *I myself serve the law of God; but with the flesh the law of sin.*
> *Romans 7:25*

God wants to show you that there is a place where we can live in the Spirit and not be subject to the flesh. Live in the Spirit till sin has no dominion; till we reign in life and see the clothing of God over us in the Spirit. Sin reigned unto death, but Christ reigned over sin and death, and so we reign with Him in life.

There is not a sick person here who could be said to be reigning in life: satanic power reigns there, and God wants you to know that you have to reign. God made you like Himself, and Jesus brought back for you in the Garden of Gethsemane everything that was lost in the Garden of Eden, through that agony which He suffered. He bought that blessed redemption. When I think of redemption! People say, "Could anything be greater than the fellowship which prevailed in the Garden of Eden, when God walked and talked and had fellowship with men?" Yes, redemption is greater. Nothing but that which was local was in the garden, but the moment a man is born again he is free from the world, and lives in heavenly places. He has no destination except "in the glory."

Redemption is, therefore, greater than the Garden, and God wants you to know that you may come into this glorious redemption not for salvation only, but also for your bodies; to know that they are redeemed from the curse of the law; to know you have been made free, and to know that all praise and glory are due to the Son of God. Hallelujah! No more Egypt places! No more sandy deserts! Praise the Lord! Free from the law of sin and death! How was it accomplished? The third verse tells us. It is the master verse.

For what the law could not do, in that it was weak through the flesh, God sending his own Son in the likeness of sinful flesh, and for sin, condemned sin in the flesh: That the righteousness of the law might be fulfilled in us, who walk not after the flesh, but after the Spirit.

Romans 8:3,4

Righteousness was fulfilled in us! Brother, sister, I tell you there is a redemption, there is an atonement in Christ, a personality of Christ to dwell in you; there is a Godlikeness for you to attain unto; a blessed resemblance of Christ, of "God in you" that shall not fail **if you believe the Word of God**.

TONGUES AND INTERPRETATION: "The living Word is sufficient for thee. Eat it. Devour it. It is the *Word of God*."

Jesus was manifested to destroy the works of the devil. God was manifested **in Him**; the fulness of God came into Jesus, and He walked about glorified, filled with God. Incarnate! Is it to be mine? May I be filled with Incarnation? Yes. How can I be so filled with God that all my movements, all my desires, my mind and will are so moved upon by a new power that "I am not," for God has taken me? Praise the Lord! **Certainly it can be so.** Did you ever examine the condition of your new birth unto righteousness? Did you ever investigate it? Did you ever try to see what there was in it? Were you ever able to fathom the fulness of that redemption plan that came to you through believing in Jesus?

In the first place, He was "of God." He was called "The Word." In the second place, He and God became so one in their operation that they said it was "God," and then the cooperation of oneness, the deity, the strength of power! And you have to see that **before the foundation of the world this redemption was all completed** and set in order before the fall; and then notice that this redemption had to be so mighty and had to redeem us all so perfectly, that there should be no lack in the whole of redemption! Let us see how it comes about. **He became flesh!** Then **He was filled with the Holy Ghost.** Then, **He became the "operation" or "voice";** and **the operation of the Word,** by the power of God through the Holy Ghost, became **"the Authority."** Now, let me go further with you.

You are born (see note at end of sermon) of an incorruptible power of God; born of the Word, who has the personality, the nature of God. You were begotten (see note at end) of God, and you are not your own. You are now incarnated, so you can believe that you have passed from death unto life, and have become an heir of God and a joint heir of Christ **in the measure in which you believe His Word**. The natural flesh, **the first order**, has been changed into a **new order**, for the **first order** was Adam, the natural, and the **last order** was Christ, the heavenly; and now you become changed by a heavenly power existing in an earthly body and **that power can never die**. I want you to see that you are born of a power, and have existing in you a power, of which God took and made the world that you are in. It is the law of the Spirit of life in Christ Jesus that makes you free from the law of sin and death.

Now, let us look at the law without the Spirit, the law of sin and death. Here is a man who has never come into the new law. He is still in the law of Adam; never having been regenerated; never having been born again. He is led captive by the devil at his will. There is no power that can convert a man except the power of the blood of Jesus. Brother, the carnal life is not subject to the will of God, neither indeed can be. Carnality is selfishness and uncleanness. It cannot be subject to God; it interferes with you; it binds and keeps you in bondage; but, beloved, God destroys carnality by a new life, which is so much better, and fills you with joy unspeakable and full of glory. The half can never be told. Everything that God does is too big to tell. His grace, His love, His mercy, His salvation, are all too big to understand.

Do you not know that ours is an abundant God, who is able to do for us far exceeding and abundantly above all that we can ask or think? We are illuminated and quickened by the Spirit, looking forward to a day of rapture when we will be caught up and lifted into the presence of God. **God's lines are magnitude** — wonderful and glorious!

Now, let me touch another important point, eleventh verse: Can you think about Jesus being dead in the grave? Do you think that God could do anything for us if Jesus were still there? After His crucifixion and until He was laid in the grave, everything had to be done for Him, and I want you to see that a dead Christ can do nothing for you. He carried the cross — so don't you carry it. The cross covered everything, and the resurrection brought everything to life. When He was in the grave, the Word of God says that He was raised from the grave by the operation of God through the Spirit, and this Jesus was quickened by the Spirit in the grave, and **this same Spirit dwells in your mortal bodies**. Jesus rose by the quickening power of the Holy Ghost.

> *But if the Spirit of him that raised up Jesus from the dead dwell in you, he that raised up Christ from the dead shall also quicken your mortal bodies by his Spirit that dwelleth in you.*
> *Romans 8:11*

If you will allow Jesus to have charge of your bodies, you will find that this Spirit will quicken you, will loose you. Talk about divine healing! You cannot get it out of the Scriptures. They are full of it. You will find, also, that all who are healed by the power of God — especially believers — will find their healing an incentive to make them purer and holier. If divine healing was merely to make the body whole, it would be worth very little. Divine healing is the divine act of the providence of God coming into your mortal bodies, and after being touched by almightiness, can you ever remain the same? No. Like me, you will come out to worship and serve God.

Note: *Begotten* and *born* are both translations of the Greek word *genao*, meaning "generate"; but Mr. Wigglesworth is giving deep teaching concerning the reality of the new birth, and if the reader will uniformly use the word *begotten* throughout the paragraph he will more readily grasp the author's thought, for *begotten* covers the new birth right from its inception to its culminating point, of which the word *born* is rightly used. St. Paul also describes this culmination of the new birth process as "the manifestation" (Romans 8:19), "our adoption," or "redemption" (v. 23), and "clothing upon" (2 Corinthians 5:4); that glorious time when we shall be like Him, for we shall see Him as He is (1 John 3:2) — editor

Published in *Redemption Tidings*

aith is an act, a changing. If we dare believe God's Word, He moves and changes the situation. *Our purpose is to let the Holy Ghost glorify God through us.* Only believe! It shall be to you as you believe.

A NEW EPOCH, A DIVINE VOCATION

March 1926

Hebrews 11 — A bundle of treasure of divine purpose, God unfolds His truth to us and through us to others. Dare to believe God, He will not fail. Faith is the greatest subject; power to lay hold of the Word of God.

It is God that bringeth us into victory through the blood of the slain Lamb. Faith quickens into a divine order, a living new source, a holy nature, having divine rights through Jesus. A new epoch, a new vocation, white hot!! For eye hath not seen, nor ear heard, neither hath it entered into the heart of man the things God hath prepared for them that love Him, but unto us it hath been revealed through the Spirit.

We must be ablaze with passion for souls that someone may catch a new ray to bring in a new day, for the end is not yet. Praise the Lord! Glory!

Faith is the substance, bigger than we know. Power to express the new creation and bring forth the glory of God. Faith is always at peace, undisturbed whatever happens. The waves may be terrible, the wind contrary. He was asleep — "Carest Thou not that we perish?" He spoke! There was a great calm. Jesus Christ, the author and finisher of faith, the divine authority with inspiration. This word of faith which we preach to bring forth to the world, the touch of heaven.

The Lord is in this place, He is here to revive, to fill, to change, to express, to give power over all the power of the enemy.

> *There is therefore now no condemnation to them that are in Christ Jesus, who walk not after the flesh, but after the Spirit. For the law of the Spirit of life in Christ Jesus hath made me free from the law of sin and death.*
>
> *Romans 8:1,2*

Life came out of death because of the cross, then resurrection, a manifestation of the operation of God. I was dead in trespasses and sins and now I am alive unto God. Eternal life.

He openeth the prison doors to all who believe, by faith we enter in. He is made unto us righteousness, we are one with Him forever. Heirship and joint-heirship made possible unto us by His death and ascension.

There is no condemnation to them that are in Christ Jesus — no cloud — nothing between — oh the thrill of it. Hidden with Christ in God — immersed, covered — nothing can break through. It is the grace of God to be here, and as sure as we are here we shall be there. Receiving a Kingdom which cannot be moved, for our God is a consuming fire. There is something very beautiful about being in Christ in God, ready for everything — ready!

He hath begotten us unto a lively hope — to make us like unto Himself. The radiance of the divine to break through makes a new creation. The law of the Spirit of life making us free from the law of sin and death.

The quickening Spirit, fellow-heirs, a divine flow — white heat — full! Holy! Inflammable — causing others to catch fire — quickening — no condemnation. Do you know it? Glory! A large conception of our eternal relationship — catching the rays of divine glory — a changing all the time. Ready! Because of the intensity of the fire within. Jesus manifested in the flesh, ruling — reigning — until the rivers flow and floodtide is here. Bringing life — life to all —

> Filled with the Holy Ghost,
> Has He come?
> Does He abide?
> (Chorus)
> I know the Lord laid His hand on me,
> He fills me with the Holy Ghost,
> I know the Lord laid His hand on me.
> Filled! A flowing, quickening, moving flame of God.

Not drunk with wine, but filled with the Spirit, more and more filled with this life, this great expansiveness of God's gifts, graces, and beatitudes — changing us all the time — moving us on to greater enlargement in the Spirit.

God is with thee. The Spirit of the Lord is upon thee. Count on Him. Be a chosen vessel in fellowship with God for this day. If you in any way fail to be filled some need will be unmet. God makes the opportunity for the man that is ready. The Bible is our all. There God reveals His plan and feeds us. Those who trust in Him shall never be confounded.

We cannot be ordinary people; God must be glorified in us. Some say: If I could only feel the power! Do not mind what you feel, if in the needy place you are moved to an act. The authority of the power. God makes the occasion when we are in the place — hidden in God — with Christ in God. The law of the Spirit of life is opposed to death, disease; opposite to that which is earthly, for within us is a heavenly production. Fresh desire for God's glory makes us ready for the place of opportunity. Our God is a consuming fire. The cross empty and Jesus glorified through us. Risen — rivers flowing — white heat.

Multitudes — multitudes in the valley of determination, the day of the Lord is near in the valley of determination.

Decide and the floods appear.

Faith is the victory — for faith is substance and evidence.

Published in *Redemption Tidings*

FLAMES OF FIRE

May 24, 1926

Praise the Lord! I am sure anyone would have great liberty in preaching in this Convention! I believe God the Holy Ghost can so bring into our hearts these truths that we shall live in the top place of expectation. There may be much variation in these meetings, but I believe God will give us the desire of our hearts. I am so glad to be here — my heart is full on so many lines.

The message to me this morning was very fine. I know that only *God* can satisfy my thirst. I know this — that the man who is to be possessed with a zeal of God's work can only possess it as he is thirsty after God. Jesus had a great longing — a great passion. It was the zeal of the house of God. I believe this morning God wants to bring us to a place where we shall realize there is revolution coming in our lives.

Oh, beloved, it seems to me that we shall never be anywhere for God until there has been a perfect revolution in our whole being.

It was a tremendous thought for me to know that I had received the Holy Ghost, but I am coming to a great wonderment of splendor to know that the Holy Ghost has at last got me! And the revolution has had such an effect upon my life that everything is of a new order — a reviving process — a divine mark right within the inner heart. It is certainly an incision without a mark, but God puts His stamp into the hidden desires and cravings, and the whole thing is a great plan of a divine creation — the thirst of *God* after the image of the one He first created. It was forfeited, but it is now being brought back to its beginning. It may only be in its infancy, but oh! The development since last year of God's incarnation in my whole soul. Nothing less will please the Lord, only a constant, full burnt offering for God, where He is in absolute and utter authority over my whole being, until I am living, thinking, acting in the power of the Holy Ghost. Praise the Lord!

It is worthy of thought this morning, to allow God to bring a powerful might to so burst upon all our natural desires and longings that we may at last come on to a plane of the divine plan where God breathes His own breath and makes His own food and eats and drinks with us and lives within us — an overflowing measure that shall never be taken away.

There is something in this Pentecostal work for God that it seems a continual decreasing with an increasing measure that seems to press you beyond measure to take over the measureless measure! I am satisfied in my heart this morning that the hand of God is upon us. If we could only believe — if we could only believe to see the glory of the salvation that God has got for us in the Person of Jesus!

A FLAME OF FIRE

Shall we read the first chapter of Hebrews — it is full of holy vision. The word that I have for you this morning is in the 7th verse.

> *And of the angels he saith, Who maketh his angels spirits, and his ministers a flame of fire.*

His ministers are to be flames of fire! This means so much for us this morning. It seems to me that no man with a vision, especially a vision by the Spirit's power, can read that wonderful verse — that divine truth — without being kindled to such a flame of fire for his Lord that it seems as if it would burn up everything that would interfere with his progress. A flame of fire! A perpetual fire; a constant fire; a constant burning; a holy inward flame which is exactly that which God's Son was in the world manifesting for us all. I can see this — that *God has nothing less for us than to be flames!*

It seems to me that if Pentecost is to rise and be effective it must have a living faith, personated and changed into life, until we live, increasingly live, so in His great might and power which flows through us until the life becomes energized, moved and causes us to be aflame for God.

TONGUES AND INTERPRETATION: "It is the flame of God's love flashing through the human nature, changing it, until the place shall know it no more forever. It shall see the face of God and die and never live again. Only love — a wave of His life to send forth till others shall feel His love and be kindled into a flame of grace!"

The import of our message is that the Holy Ghost has come to make Jesus King. It seems to me that the seed, which is an eternal seed, that life which was given to us when we believed was of such a nature of resurrection power that I see a new creation rising with a kingly position, and I see that when the Holy Ghost comes, He comes to crown Jesus King. So, beloved, it is not only the King within, but all the glories of the kingly manifestations which are brought forth. So I see this, that even that alone would cause you to feel a burning after Jesus; a longing, a passion after Him. Oh, for Him to so work in us, melting us until a new order rises, moved with compassion!

There is something about the message that I want you to catch this morning. It does not seem to me that God can in any way ever make us to be anything, but I do see that we can so come into a place in the order of God that He sets us up where the vision becomes so much brighter and where the Lord is in His glory with all His beatitudes and gifts and all His glory seems to fill the soul who is absolutely dead and alive to Him. There is so much talk about death, but I do see that there is a death which is so deep in God that out of that death God brings the splendor of His life and all His glory.

On Fire — Always

A remarkable evidence of being a flame of fire for God came when I was traveling from Egypt to Italy. It is quite true when I tell you on the ship and everywhere God has been with me. A man on the ship suddenly collapsed; his wife was in a terrible state and everybody else seemed to be. Some said that it had come to the end, but oh, to be a flame — to be indwelt by the living Christ! We are a back number if we have to pray for power, if we have to wait until we feel a sense of His presence. The baptism of the Holy Ghost should empower you for any emergency. "Ye shall have power after that the Holy Ghost is come upon you." Within you there is a greater power than there is in the world. Oh, to be awakened out of our unbelief into a place of daring for God! On the authority of the blessed Book! So in the Name of Jesus I rebuked the devil, and to the astonishment of the man's wife and himself, he was able to stand. He said, "What is this? It is going all over me. I have never felt anything like this before." For from the crown of his head to the soles of his feet the power of God shook him.

"In season and out of season." God has for us an authority over the powers of the devil — over all the power of the enemy. Oh, that we may live in the place where the glory excelleth! I would that we could all see *Him* this morning. God says to us through this lovely Word in Hebrews 1:3, "Who being the brightness of his glory, and the express image of his person, and upholding *all things* by the word of his power, when he had by himself purged our sins, sat down on the right hand of the Majesty on high."

It would make anyone a flame of fire. Praise God, it is a fact! Jesus is in our body, and He is the express image of God, and He has come to our human weaknesses to change them and us into a divine substance so that by the power of His might we may not only overcome, but rejoice in the fact that we are more than overcomers. God wants you to have the last part — more than overcomers! Beloved, all I speak this morning is burning in my soul. The baptism of the Spirit has come for nothing less than to eat the whole of my life. It set up Jesus as King, and nothing can stand in His holy presence when He is made King. Everything will wither before Him. I am realizing this.

I feel I come to a convention like this to stir you up and to help you to know that this inheritance of the Spirit is given to every man to profit withal. Praise the Lord! And in the Holy Ghost order, we have to come behind with no gift, but I love the thought that all the gifts are of no qualification or service to us if the Giver does not work the gift. If He is working the gift, and it is there in operation, and you are there only as an instrument or a voice or a temple, *He* fills the bill! Oh, it is lovely! He dwells inside! He lives; He moves; He reveals. He causes us to forget our sorrow and rejoice with joy unspeakable and full of glory. "The brightness of His glory and the express image of God."

We must not forget that we must make this a personal thing. When God made the angels, He made them sing. All that were in the heavens did obedience to this wonderful royal King, and, beloved, we must see that this Word this morning is a personal experience. I look at the Scriptures, and I say, "Oh, Lord, it *must* be mine if you give it to me — You must make it mine." This is how I talk to Him, so He knows my language well! And I am the thirstiest man in the world, and He has a reservoir specially for me and for us all. We sometimes get to a place where we say, "Lord, it is no good, nothing You have shown me yet has moved me sufficiently. You will have to do something that will make the people marvel." "I will yet do things that ye may marvel."

This same Jesus has come for one purpose, that He might so be made manifest in us that the world shall see Him, and we must be burning and shining lights to reflect such a holy Jesus. We cannot do it with cold, indifferent experiences, and we never shall. I come across those people at times who always "have a good report," but *oh* for a Pentecostal ring in our hearts all the time! Oh, what have you got, brother-sister?

A FLAME OF FIRE — "NOW"

Oh, there is so much difference between these things and the past times. There was a good deal of looking through the lattice, but now — within the veil! This is a "Now" experience. A taking now. I must be filled with the might of the Spirit. John was a burning and a shining light, and I come to you this morning, and I see that the angels are to be ministering spirits, but His servants are to be *flames* — the very essence of the Word — the life of Jesus. Jesus is life and the Holy Ghost is the breath, and He breathes through us the life of the Son of God, and we give it to others and it giveth life everywhere.

We have to launch out. The Word of God says you shall not drown if you pass through the waters, and you shall not burn if you pass through the fire. You should have been with me in Ceylon! It was in a Wesleyan Chapel.

You have to be ready for anything — a good bather does not wait, he goes right out into the water. God wants us to be unhinged and yet bound together. Unloosed for anything and tightened up for everything! That's good! In this Wesleyan Chapel they said, "You know, four days is not much to give us." "No," I said, "but it is a good share!" They said, "We have never seen anything like this. What are we going to do because we are not touching the people at all?" I said, "Can you have a meeting early in the morning — at eight o'clock? They said they would, so I said, "We will tell all the mothers who want their babies to be healed to come, and all the old people over seventy to come, and then after that we will have an address to the people to make them ready for the Holy Ghost."

Oh, it would have done you all good to see 400 mothers with their babies! It was fine! And then to see 150 black people with their white hair come to be healed. I believe you need to have something more than smoke to touch people. You need to be a burning light for that. His ministers must be flames of fire. There were thousands outside to hear the Word of God. There were about 3,000 people crying for mercy at once. I tell you it was a sight. From then the meetings rose to such an extent that every night 5,000 to 6,000 gathered there after you had preached in a temperature of 110°. Then you had to minister to these people. But I tell you, a flame of fire can do anything! Things change in the fire. It was an experience of the people in the eleventh chapter of Hebrews. This is Pentecost! It must go *up*. If ever it goes down it will never go up again. The prospects are so wonderful — up there that you will say, "Lord — *higher!*" What about your feet? Never mind them, get your head in the right place! And whatever you do, don't let your heart get in the wrong place, for it is there where all the illumination comes, and you are made a flame by the igniting of His power inside.

It will come, as sure as anything. But what moved me more than anything was this — and I say it this morning with thought and with a broken spirit because I would not like to mislead anything — there were hundreds who tried to touch me, they were so impressed with the power of God that was present, and they testified everywhere that with a touch they were healed. And it was not the virtue of Wigglesworth — it was the same faith in the Son of God that was with those at Jerusalem when they said that Peter's shadow would heal them.

TONGUES AND INTERPRETATION: "God, Who is beginning to breathe, will not stop breathing until the breath touches all into glory, for it is the Holy Ghost which came like a rushing mighty wind. It will increase — till a nation shall be born in a day and the latter rain will increase, and *God* is *now* sending the latter rain."

Praise the Lord. Brothers and sisters — you say "Wigglesworth, I want it. I am longing for it." Do you know I am never satisfied with what comes to me, and Jesus is coming to us all in greater fulness. Only you must stop your earnest cry. You must believe that God the Holy Ghost is touching you. For this is not your own human desire — it is a divine inclination, a heavenly call, that has caused you to begin to crave after God, and He will never cease until He has accomplished every purpose of His in your heart.

It is His purpose to take you into the promised land. What an inward burning — what an inward craving God can give! It is a taste of the heavenlies! And we want more! More of these wonderful joys, until God has absolutely put His stamp upon everyone by the power of His presence.

Now, beloved, my time is coming to a close, but you can have something in three minutes that you can carry with you into the glory. What do you want? Is anything too hard for God? God can meet you now. God sees you inwardly, He knows all about you, nothing is hidden from Him, and He can satisfy the soul and give you a spring of eternal blessing that will carry you right through. My soul is so thirsty — I am the thirstiest person here!

There are two things that you must have in a Pentecostal meeting. You must have an offering — never be ashamed to take an offering, even if you have three meetings a day. And you must have a broken spirit. The nearer I get to God the more broken I am in spirit.

How many want more of God? Offer yourselves to Him, and reach heaven.

Address given at Kingsway Convention

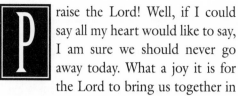

GREATER, GREATER, GREATER

May 1926

Praise the Lord! Well, if I could say all my heart would like to say, I am sure we should never go away today. What a joy it is for the Lord to bring us together in this way, where we hear the words that are so precious and convincing of all that Jesus said. For there was never One who came to the world with such a loving compassion, and who entered into all the needs of the people as Jesus did. Now we see Jesus at the right hand of the Father today, interceding with God for the needs of the people, and there is something about His last message to the world which is so wonderful. Because He was going to the Father, the Father cooperates with Him for the redemption of the world, and because of this, the Father will grant us all that we need. Jesus said, "If I go to the Father, I will send the Comforter," and He kept His word, and the Father kept His word, and that promise was made real on the day of Pentecost! He had ascended with the purpose of giving new power, new blessing, new vision, and a living faith to all those who should follow, that the great work should be carried on. We have today, and for many days, been drinking at this measureless measure, that makes our hearts swell over with such rapture and delight, and we know we are living and moving in the power of the Holy Ghost! What wonderful things are held out to us. Now the vision is clear.

Many of you know as long back as twelve or fourteen years ago, how we used to gather with small companies of people, and divine healing was a small thing in those days, but as we lived and moved among the people they were healed and they are healed today. God meant to work out His purpose, that we should loose people who were bound with graveclothes, and that they should be set free by the power of God. We should be so filled with the power of God, that we should not know what it is to have a body. Hallelujah!

All over the world I tell the people that since the Lord healed me over thirty years ago, I don't know what it is to have a body. Hallelujah! It is redemption in all its fulness, no neuralgia, no stomach trouble, no kidney disease, no dyspepsia, no rheumatism. Hallelujah! No lumbago, no corns, absolutely and entirely a new order of things. This is the inheritance of all that seek Him, this is the inheritance there is in Jesus. Jesus said to the woman, "Shall I give the children's bread to dogs?" But hallelujah! There is bread, there is life, there is perfect healing from the Son of God. There was power in Him that moved every evil thing. It changes our circumstances, and makes you know that the new creation is a living vital thing. My word to you this afternoon is a special word, because it is the word of the Master.

He is moved with compassion as He sees us here today. Many people are around us that want a new vision of Jesus, that they may go away from this Convention to carry on the work, for we are here to make disciples of the Nazarene. It is His will that we should do the works that Jesus declared we should do.

There are two things in faith. There is a faith which acts, there is a faith which needs to be accompanied with works, and we believe today that Jesus meant all He said. Now let us look at what He said. There are three very important verses, and I trust you will not forget them, whatever else you forget. What is the word? It is in the 14th chapter of John, verses 12-14. Looking at them we are filled with joy. How I love, how I cherish the words of Jesus, truly they are lovely. When I think of the infinite wisdom of God in this measure, why did not God come to us and make Himself openly manifested to us? Why not? Because our finite beings could not stand His glory. You remember that as Saul went into Damascus, the light of the Son just flashed on the road, and those with him fell to the earth, and he was turned blind at the same time. We could not stand God's glory, because we are only finite beings, but God did the very best for us. When He could not present Himself to us, He gave us His Word. His Word has a quickening power. David knew it, he says that Word has quickened him. This Word is the divine revelation, it is the Word of life, of healing, of power. God has given us His own Word. I would that all who can hear me would give themselves carefully over to reading more of the Word of God, if you only knew how I love it. There is something about the Word which is so wonderful. It brings new life into you, until you realize you are a new creature. Hallelujah!

GOD IS GREATER THAN ALL

Listen to this word today.

Verily, verily, I say unto you, He that believeth on me, the works that I do shall he do also; and greater works than these shall he do; because I go unto my Father.

John 14:12

Oh, glory to God! God says, "Not one word shall fail, of all that I have promised." Sometimes we fail, but God never does. Hallelujah. What do I mean? Well, I am here today to get you to a place of resting upon the Word of God. If I could get you there, you can say in faith, "It is done." If I can speak to you today by the grace of God, it can be finished in your seat. The Word of God cannot fail, because it is the living Word. Listen to the words of Jesus as He says, "Greater works than these shall ye do." I know as truly as I stand upon this platform that we shall see the rising tide of blessing and divine healing go forth with greater power, but Satan will always try to hinder the real work of God. Whenever the power of God is being manifested, Satan will be there trying to upset it.

Satanic forces will be there, but God is greater. When we were baptized in the Holy Ghost, the spiritualist people got to know of it and they came to one of our meetings. They heard that we were speaking in tongues and they came, and they filled two seats. Then I began speaking in tongues, (that was natural to me), and then these muttering devils began also. I went to these two seats and I said "Go out, you devils, go out," and they came out like a flock of sheep! They went right outside, and when they got outside they cursed, and cursed, but they were outside. So I know that the devil will have manifestations, but in the Name of Jesus his power is gone.

What I want to impress upon you is that we must see these greater works that the Lord promised we should see. Listen, "Greater works than these shall ye do, because I go to My Father." "And whatsoever ye shall ask in My name, that will I do, that the Father may be glorified in the Son." What is it that you want? "Whatsoever ye shall ask in My Name, that will I do." Glory to God. Is there any purpose in it? Yes, "that the Father may be glorified in the Son."

If you want God to be glorified in the Son. If you want God to be glorified in Jesus, you must live in the position where these things are being done. Praise God, He has been delivering people in these meetings. Now you people that have been delivered this morning put up your hands. Now we will have some testimonies of the deliverances. The power of God is here to deliver the people, but I am not satisfied. You think that I am satisfied? I have never seen anything yet to satisfy me. I am the hungriest person there is in this place!

GREATER POWER

There is something very remarkable and forceful in this verse. It says, "Verily, verily, I say unto you...greater works than these shall ye do." In the power of His Name there is power against the devil, and all his hosts. It is a marvelous force against all these things. Glory to God. I will give you an illustration of this. In the course of my travels I went to Sweden, and while going along one day I saw a man fall into a doorway. People came along and said he was dead. I could not speak Swiss, but I could speak English, and the devil knew I could speak English, (he knows all the languages), and I used the power and authority of the Name of Jesus, and instantly he was delivered. The man had been troubled like this for years. The Lord told me to make him a public example, so I got him to come to the meeting, and he came and told us of his deliverance. He told us the most awful things that the devil had been telling him, and then he told us how the devil had gone right out of him. Praise God.

While I was in Ceylon, I was sent for to go to a certain place to pray for someone. I said "what is the case?" It was a woman dying of cancer. I said, "Take this handkerchief in the Name of the Lord." But nothing happened. They said to me, "You must go this time." I went and looked at the woman. She was in a terrible condition, with cancer in the womb, and nearly dead. The house was full of people, and I preached Jesus to them, and how precious He became to me as I did so. I said to them, "I know this woman will be healed," but I want you to know the power of my Lord. This case can be delivered, but I want you to know Him who can deliver. Jesus said, "Greater works," what did He mean? Standing on the authority of the Word of God. Hallelujah! The deliverance was so marvelous, and had such an effect upon the home that they went to the papers themselves and published it, and the woman herself came to the meeting and stood up and told the people what great things the Lord had done for her. Hallelujah! "Greater works than these shall ye do." You say, "How"? Only believe. What is it to believe? It is to have such confidence in what the Lord said that we take Him at His Word because He said it. Glory to God.

> Yes, I know this book is true,
> Yes, I know this book is true,
> I'm acquainted with the Author,
> And I know this book is true.

WHATSOEVER

Let us look at the last part of this verse, it is very important. It says, "And whatsoever ye shall ask in My Name, that will I do, that the Father may be glorified in the Son." Tell me, what does *whatsoever* mean? It means everything. You say there is a difference between everything and anything. *Everything* means the world, *anything* means you, so it is you that I am dealing with, I am not dealing with people in America today but you. Redemption is so complete that the person who believes it is made complete. Look at our Master as He calls the man who had the withered hand to stand before Him. Jesus looked upon that withered hand, and at His command the hand is restored. He gave the living Word, "Stretch forth thy arm," and the arm was healed. People today are waiting for the manifestation of the sons of God. The world is crying out for something after the new creation order.

I remember one day a man came to see me about a woman who was dying, and asked me to visit her. When I got into the room I saw there was no hope, as far as human aid was concerned. The woman was suffering from a tumor and it had sapped her life away. I looked at her, and I knew there was no possibility of help, except a divine possibility. Thank God I knew He was able. I never say it cannot be. I find God is able to do everything. I said to her, "I know you are beyond everything now, but if you cannot lift your arm, or raise it at all, it might be possible that you could raise your finger as an indication that you desire to get better. Her hand lay upon the bed, but she lifted her finger just a little. I said to my friend, "We will pray with her, and anoint her," and after anointing her, her chin dropped, death came on, and my friend said, "She is dead." He was scared, I have never seen a man so frightened in my life. He said, "What shall I do?"

You may think what I did was one of the most absurd things to do, but I did it. I reached over into the bed and pulled her out, and carried her across the room, and stood her against the wall and held her up, as she was absolutely dead. I looked into her face and said, "In the Name of Jesus I rebuke this death," and from the crown of her head to the sole of her foot her whole body began to tremble, and then her feet stood on the floor, and I said, "In the Name of Jesus I command you to walk," and she began to walk. I repeated, "In the Name of Jesus, in the Name of Jesus, walk," and she walked back to the wardrobe, and back into bed.

My friend went out and told the people that he had seen a woman raised from the dead! One of the elders of the mission where she attended said he was not going to have this kind of thing, and tried to stop it. The doctor heard of it and went to see the woman. He said, "I have heard from Mr. Fisher, the elder, that you have been brought back to life, and I want you to tell me if it is so." She told him it was so. He said, "Dare you come and give your testimony at a certain hall, if I take you in my car?" She said, "I will go anywhere to give it."

She came to the hall, looking so white, but there was a lovely brightness on her face. She was dressed in white, and I thought how beautiful she looked. This is what she said. "For many months I have been going down to death, now I want to live for my children. I came to the place where it seemed there was no hope. I remember a man came to pray with me, and said to me, 'If you cannot speak, or cannot lift your hands, if you want to live, move one of your fingers.' I remember moving my finger, but from that moment I knew nothing else until I was in the glory. I feel I must try and tell you what the glory is like. I saw countless numbers of people, and oh! The joy, and the singing, it was lovely, but the face of Jesus lit up everything, and just when I was having a beautiful time, the Lord suddenly pointed to me, without speaking, and I knew I had to go, and the next moment I heard a man say, "Walk, walk, in the Name of Jesus! If the doctor is here, I would like to hear what he has to say."

The doctor rose. He had a white beard, and I cannot forget the color of his waistcoat, it was a canary colored pattern. When he stood up, he began to speak, but he could not at first, his lips quivered and then his eyes looked like a fountain of waters, and I thought whatever is going to happen? Then he said that for months he had been praying, and at last he felt there was no more hope, and he told them at the house that the woman would not live much longer, in fact it was only a matter of days. Never live? Hallelujah. But this is where "the greater works" come in.

Thank God, if we believe all things are possible. It can be done now, this moment as you sit in your seat, if you believe it shall be done for the glory of God. I ask you, while I preach today to believe God's Word, and it shall come to pass. Glory to God. Now I want a wholesale healing this afternoon. I believe it may be possible for some to have that divine, inward, moving of living faith that will make you absolutely whole. If you deny yourself, and believe God's Word, you will be healed at the touch of the Lord. Now I want you to live in the sunshine.

I went to Dover to preach, and we had twenty people instantly healed at once. I have seen a hundred people healed in the meeting instantly, as they believed. People have been healed as they have risen from their seats. I want you to get to such a place of faith, that you will not know you have a body. Mr. Stephen Jeffreys will be telling you tonight, that there is a perfect redemption for all our needs. We want this meeting to go away with the knowledge of a full redemption. If you believe on the authority of God's Word you are healed, you will have perfect health from your finger's ends to your whole body. We will sing that chorus —

> I do believe, I will believe that Jesus heals me now,
> I do believe, I will believe that Jesus heals me now.

Amen.

Address given at Kingsway Hall
London

I want to read to you a few verses from the first chapter of the Acts of the Apostles, verses 1 to 11.

THE BAPTISM IN THE HOLY GHOST

May-June 1926

I have been perplexed this afternoon as to what the message should be. I have had distinctly three messages on my mind, but none of them has come forth. It appears God has a plan for this afternoon's meeting, and I believe the plan for you and for me is to know more about the baptism of the Holy Ghost. And I believe that God wants us so to know the truth that we may all go away from this meeting with a clear knowledge of what God means for all His people to receive the Holy Ghost.

When Jesus, our Mediator and Advocate, was so filled with the Holy Ghost, He gave commandment concerning these days we are in, and gave commandment of the time through the Holy Ghost. I can see that if we are going to accomplish anything we are going to have it because we are under the power of the Holy Ghost.

During my life I have seen lots of satanic forces, spiritists, and all other "ists." And I tell you that there is a power which is satanic, and there is a power which is the Holy Ghost. I remember after we received the Holy Ghost, and when people were speaking in tongues as the Spirit gave utterance — we don't know the Holy Ghost any other way — the spiritists heard about it, and came to the meeting in good time to fill two rows of seats.

When the power of God fell upon us, these imitators began their shaking, and moving with utterances of the satanic forces. The Spirit of the Lord was mighty upon me. I went to them and said, "Now you demons, clear out of this!" And out they went. I followed them right out in the street, and then they turned round and cursed me. It made no difference, they were out.

Beloved, God would have us to know in these days that there is a fulness of God where all other powers must cease to be. And I beseech you this afternoon to hear that the baptism in the Holy Ghost is to possess us so that we are, and may be continually, so full of the Holy Ghost that utterances, and revelations, and eye-sight and everything, may be so remarkably controlled by the Spirit of God that we live and move in this glorious sphere of usefulness for the glory of God.

And I believe that God wants to help us to see that every child in the meeting ought to receive the Holy Ghost. Beloved, God wants us to understand that there is no difficulty when we are in the right order. And I want you to see what there is in seeking the Holy Ghost.

THE PURPOSE OF THE BAPTISM

If we go into John's gospel we could see that Jesus predicted all that we are getting today when the Holy Ghost came. He said He should take of the things of His Word and reveal them unto us when the Holy Ghost came. He should just live out in us all the life of Jesus.

And if we could only think what it really means! It is one of the ideals. Talk about graduation! My word! Come into the graduation of the Holy Ghost by the Spirit, and you will simply strip out everything they have in any college there ever was. You would leave them all behind just as I see the sun leave the mist behind in San Francisco. You would leave that which is as cold as ice, and go into the sunshine.

God the Holy Ghost wants us to have such an ideal of this fulness of the Spirit that we would neither be ignorant, neither would we have mystic conceptions, but we would have a clear, unmistakable revelation of all the mind of God for these days.

TONGUES AND INTERPRETATION: "The Spirit of the living God comes with such divine revelation, such unveiling about Him, such a clearness of what He was to the people, and brings within us the breath of that eternal power that makes us know we are right here this very hour to carry out His plan for now, and what God shall have for the future, for there is no limitation but rather an enforcement of character, of clearness of vision, of an openness of countenance till we behold Him in every divine light."

Glory! Oh, it is grand! Thank God for that interpretation.

I beseech you, beloved, in the Name of Jesus, that you should see that you come right into all the mind of God. Jesus verily said, "But ye shall receive power, after that the Holy Ghost is come upon you." And I want you to know that "He showed Himself alive after His passion by many infallible proofs, being seen of them forty days." He is all the time unfolding to everyone of us the power of resurrection.

Remember the baptism of the Holy Ghost is resurrection. If you can touch this ideal of God with its resurrection power, you will see that nothing earthly can remain; you will see that all disease will clear out. If you get so full of the Holy Ghost, all satanic forces of fit-taking, all these lame legs, all these corn afflictions, and all these nervous, fearful things, all these kidney troubles will go. Resurrection is the word for it. Resurrection is to shake away death to breathe in you life, to let you know that you are from the dead quickened by the Spirit, made like unto Jesus. Glory to God!

Oh, the word resurrection! I wish I could say it just on parallel lines with the word Jesus. They very harmoniously go together. Jesus is resurrection, and to know Jesus in this resurrection power is simply to see that you have no more to be dead but alive unto God by the Spirit.

THE NECESSITY OF THE BAPTISM

There is a necessity of being baptized in the Holy Ghost for a businessman. For any kind of business we need to know the power of the Holy Ghost, because if you are not baptized with the Holy Ghost Satan has a tremendous power to interfere with the power of your life. If you come into the baptism of the Holy Ghost there is a new plane for your business.

I remember one day being in London at a meeting. About eleven o'clock they said to me, "We shall have to close down, we are not allowed to have this place any longer than eleven o'clock." There were several under the power of the Spirit. A man rose up, looked at me, saying, "Oh, don't leave me, please. I feel I dare not be left. I must come through. Will you go home with us?" "Yes," I said, "I will go." His wife was there as well. They were two hungry people just being wakened up by the power of the Spirit to know they were lacking in their life, and they needed the power of God.

In about an hour's time we arrived at their big, beautiful house in the country. It was winter time. He began stirring the fire up, and putting coal on, and said, "We will soon have a tremendous fire, so we will get warmed. Then we will have a big supper." And I suppose the next thing would have been going to bed.

"No, thank you," I said. "I have not come here for your supper, nor for your bed. I thought you wanted me to come with you that you might receive the Holy Ghost." "Oh," he replied. "Will you stop with us and pray?" "I have come for nothing else." I knew I could keep myself warm in a prayer meeting without a fire.

About half-past three in the morning his wife was as full as could be, speaking in tongues. It was a lovely day. I went to the end of the table. There he was having a terrible groan. So I said, "Your wife is through." "Oh," he said, "this is going to be a big night for me." Yes, I tell you, they are big nights for you whether you come through or not, if you seek with all your heart.

I often say there is more done in the seeking than any other way. If we knew the Scriptures there is no such thing as seeking for the Holy Ghost, but a place where we need to know that without we meet face to face with God, and get all crooked places out of our lives, there would be no room for the Holy Ghost, for the indwelling presence of God. But when God gets a chance at us, and by the vision of the blood we see ourselves as God sees us, then we have a revelation. Without its accomplishment we are undone and helpless.

At five o'clock in the morning, this man stood up and said, "I am through." He was not baptized. "I am settled," he continued. "God has settled me. Now I must have a few hours' rest before I go to business at eight o'clock." My word! That was a day at his business. In many years he never lived a day like that. He was going around about his business amongst all his men. They said, "What is up with the man? What is up with the governor? What has taken place? Oh, what a change!"

The whole place was electrified. God had turned the lion into the lamb. Oh, he was like a great big lion prowling about under the old conditions, but God had touched him. The touch of omnipotence had broken down this man till right there in the business the men were broken up in his presence. Oh, I tell you, there is something in pursuit, there is something in waiting. What is it? Oh, it is this, God slays a man that he may begin on a new plane in his life. We shall have to be slain utterly if we want to know that resurrection power of Jesus.

A short time afterwards when I was passing through the grounds towards this man's house, his two sons rushed out to where I was, threw their arms round me and kissed me, saying, "You have sent us a new father." The same night in which he went to work, he had been baptized about ten o'clock in a meeting. Oh, the power of the Holy Ghost is to create new men and new women. It is to take away the stony heart out of your flesh, and give you a heart of flesh by the Spirit. And when God gets a way like that there is a tremendous shaking amongst the dry bones, for God gets His way with the people.

We must see that we are no good without God takes charge of us. But when He gets real charge of us what a plan for the future! What a wonderful open door for God! Oh, brethren, we must see this ideal by the Spirit! What shall we do? Do? You dare not do anything but go through. Submit to the power of God. If you yield other people are saved. You will die without you have a power of resurrection, a touch for others. But if you live only for God, then other people will be raised out of death, and all kinds of evil into a blessed life through the Spirit.

THE BAPTISM IS ESSENTIAL

Beloved, we must see that this baptism of the Spirit is greater than all. You can talk as you like, say what you like, do as you like, but until you have the Holy Ghost, you won't know what the resurrection touch is. Resurrection is by the power of the Spirit. And remember, when I talk about resurrection I talk about one of the greatest things in the Scriptures, because resurrection is an evidence that we have waked up with a new line of truth that cannot cease to be but will always go on with a greater force of an increasing power with God.

TONGUES AND INTERPRETATION: "Hallelujah! The Spirit breathes, the Spirit lifts, the Spirit renews, the Spirit quickens."

The man that is baptized in the Holy Ghost is baptized in a new order altogether. It cannot be that you shall ever be ordinary after that. You are on an extraordinary plane, you are brought into line with the mind of God. You have come into touch with ideals on every line.

If you want oratory, there it is in the baptism of the Spirit. If you want the touch of quickened sense that moves your body till you know that you are all renewed, it is the Holy Ghost. And while I say so much about the Holy Ghost today, I withdraw everything that doesn't put Jesus in the ordered place He belongs, for when I speak about the Holy Ghost it is always with reference to revelations of Jesus. The Holy Ghost is only the revealer of the mighty Christ who has all for us that we may never know any weakness but all limitations are gone. And you are now in a place where God has taken the ideal, and moved you on with His own velocity which has a speed beyond all human mind and thought. Glory to God!

TONGUES AND INTERPRETATION: "Wake thou that sleepest, and allow the Lord to wake thee into righteousness. The liberty wherewith God has set thee free — God hath made thee free to enlarge others which are bound."

So the Spirit of the Lord must have His way on every line today. What will happen if we all loosen ourselves up! Sometimes I think it is necessary almost to give an address to baptized souls, because I feel just like the Corinthian Church, we may have, as it were, gifts and graces, and use them all, but sit in them and not go on beyond.

I maintain that all gifts and graces are only for one thing, to make you go in for gifts and graces. Don't miss what I say. Every touch of the divine life by the Spirit is only for one purpose, to make your life go on to a higher height than where you are. Beloved, if anybody has to rise up in the meeting to tell me how they were baptized with the Holy Ghost in order for me to know they are baptized, I say, "You have fallen from grace. You ought to have such a baptism that everybody can tell you are baptized without your telling how you were baptized. That would make a new day. That would be a sermon of itself to everybody not only in here but outside. Then people would follow you to get to know where you have come from, and where you are going. You say, "I want that, I won't settle till I get that." God will surely give it to you.

The Holy Ghost can only come when bodies are ready, for the Holy Ghost dwells in temples not made with hands, but in the fleshy tables of the heart. So it doesn't matter what kind of a building you get, you cannot count on the building being a substitute for the Holy Ghost. You will all have to be temples of the Holy Ghost to have the building anything like Holy Ghost order.

THE BAPTISM AND THE COMING OF THE LORD

The Holy Ghost could not come till the apostles and those that were in the upper room, were all of one mind and heart, all with one accord with themselves and with God. Suppose I read one verse to help you, because I am on this definite principle of what it means, the fulness of the latter rain, and the taking away of the Church. James 5:7, is a beautiful verse on that line:

> *Be patient therefore, brethren, unto the coming of the Lord. Behold,*
> *the husbandman waiteth for the precious fruit of the earth....*

What is precious fruit of the earth? Is it cabbages? Is it grapes? The precious fruit of the earth is the Church, it is the Body of Christ. And God has no thought for other things. He causes the others to grow, and the glory of the flower. He looks into the beauty of it because He knows it will please us. But when speaking about the precious fruit of the earth our Lord has His mind upon you today, and He says:

> *...Behold, the husbandman waiteth for the precious fruit of the*
> *earth, and hath long patience for it, until he receive the early*
> *and latter rain. Be ye also patient; stablish your hearts: for the*
> *coming of the Lord draweth nigh.*
>
> *James 5:7,8*

So if you want the coming of the Lord you must certainly advocate every believer being filled with the Holy Ghost. The more a man is filled with the Holy Ghost, the more he will be ready to forecast and send forth this glorious truth.

Some people have an idea, I don't know how they get it...but the Holy Ghost cannot come till the church is ready. And you say, "When will the church be ready?" If the believers were in the attitude God could send the breath this afternoon to make the church ready in ten minutes, and less than that.

So we can clearly say the coming of the Lord is nigh unto us but it will be more high unto us as we are ready for receiving a fuller and greater manifestation. What will be the manifestation of the coming of the Lord? If we were ready, and if the power of God was pressing that truth today we should be rushing up against one another saying, "He is coming, I know He is coming." "He is coming!" "Yes, I know He is." Every person round about would be saying, "He is coming," and you would know He is coming.

That is the only hope of the looking forward, and there is nothing but the Holy Ghost can prepare the hearts of the people to rush up and down and say, "He is coming," and will come soon. Praise God, He will come as surely as we are in this place, He is coming!

How To Receive

There are things I have had to learn about the baptism.

One day in England a lady wrote to ask if I would go down and help her. She said she was blind, having two blood clots behind the eye. And I sent a letter like this, not knowing who it was. I had only been in London lately and I didn't feel I wanted to go, but I said if she was willing to go into a room with me, and shut the door, and never come out till she had perfect sight, I would come.

"Oh," she sent word, "Come!" And the moment I reached the house, they brought in this blind woman. After shaking hands this blind woman made the way to the room, opened the door, allowed me to go in, then she came in and shut the door. "Now," she said, "we are with God." Have you ever been there? It is a lovely place.

In a hour and a half the power of God fell upon us, and rushing to the window she exclaimed, "I can see! Oh, I can see! The blood is gone, I can see!" Sitting down in a chair she asked, "Could I receive the Holy Ghost?" "Yes," I replied, "if all is square." "You don't know me," she continued, "but for ten years I have been fighting your position. These tongues I couldn't bear but God settled it today. I want the baptism of the Holy Ghost."

After she had prayed and repented of what she had said about "tongues" she was filled with the Holy Ghost, and was speaking in tongues.

When you put your hands upon people, you can tell when the Holy Ghost is in. And if you will only let go, my word! What would happen.

And I wonder how many people there are today who are prepared to be baptized? Oh, you couldn't be baptized? You have been a man too long. Do you know there is a difference between being a baby and anything else in the world. Many people have been waiting for years for the baptism, and what has been up? We are told in the Scriptures,

> *At that time Jesus answered and said, I thank thee, O Father,*
> *Lord of heaven and earth, because thou hast hid these things*
> *from the wise and prudent, and hast revealed them unto babes.*
> Matthew 11:25

What is there up with the wise man? A wise man is too careful. And while he is in the operation of the Spirit, he wants to know what he is saying. No man can know what he is saying when the Spirit is upon him. His own mind is inactive. If you get into that near place your mind is entirely obliterated and the mind of Christ comes by the power of the Spirit, and in that condition He prays and speaks in the Spirit as the Spirit gives utterance.

This is the mind and plan of God for us to receive the Holy Ghost. What is the difference between the wise and prudent man, and a baby? If you get baby-enough this afternoon we shall have at least fifty people baptized in the Holy Ghost. If you will only yield to God and let the Spirit have His way God will fill you with the Holy Ghost.

At Sweden, the power of God was upon us, and in a quarter of an hour I believe more than a hundred received the Holy Ghost. May God grant it this afternoon. Beloved, it shall be so for God is with us.

The natural man cannot receive the Spirit of God, but when you get into a supernatural place, then you receive the mind of God. The difference between a wise and prudent man and a baby, what is it? The baby swallows it all, and the mother has to hold the bottle or some of that will go down. The baby cannot walk. That is how God wants it to be in the Spirit. But God walks in the baby. The baby cannot talk, but God talks through the baby. The baby cannot dress himself, but God dresses it and clothes it with His righteousness.

Oh, beloved, if we can only be babes today great things will take place in the line and thought of the Spirit of God. The Lord wants us all to be so in like-mindedness with Him that He puts His seal upon us.

There are some in the meeting who have no doubt never been saved. Where the saints are seeking, and leaving themselves to the operation of the Spirit there are newborn children in the midst. God will save in our midst. God will use this means of blessing if we only let ourselves go. You say, What can I do? The fiddler will drop his fiddle, the drummer his drum. If there is anybody here who has anything hanging round about him it will drop off. If you get baby-enough today everything else will drop off and you will be free. You will be able to run and skip in the street, and you will be happy.

Does the baby ever lose its brilliancy? Does he ever lose his common sense position? Does the baby that comes in the will of God lose its reason, or its credentials on any line? No, God will increase your abilities and help you on all lines.

It isn't what I am speaking about, to be a baby. It is a baby in the Spirit. Paul says in 1 Corinthians 14:20, "...in malice be ye children, but in understanding be men." And I believe the Spirit would breathe through all these attributes of the Spirit that we may understand what the mind of the Lord is concerning us in the Holy Ghost.

Oh, this blessed thought. I want to help all that are being baptized to help others. If ever you have spoken in tongues in your life, this afternoon let yourself go and God will speak through you. You must have a day you have never had before. This must be an ideal day in the Spirit, a day with the unction of the Spirit, a day with the mind of God in the Spirit.

Published in *Redemption Tidings*

WE MEAN BUSINESS WITH GOD

June 4, 1926

Acts 5 — Only believe. Only believe. There is a power in God's Word which brings life where death is. Jesus said the time should come when the dead should hear the voice of the Son of man and live. He that believeth this Word, all things are possible to him that believeth. The life of the Son is in the Word, all that are saved can preach this Word. This Word frees from death and corruption, it is life in the natural. Jesus brought life and immortality to life through the Gospel.

We can never exhaust the Word, it is so abundant. There is a river the streams of which make glad the city of God, its source is in the glory.

The essence of its life is God. The life of Jesus embodied is its manifested power.

TONGUES AND INTERPRETATION: "Jesus Himself has come into death and has given us the victory, the victorious Son of God in humanity overcometh, who succoreth the needy. Immortality produced in mortality has changed the situation for us. This is life indeed and the end of death. Christ having brought life and immortality to life through the Gospel."

THE CHURCH ESTABLISHED

We have a wonderful subject tonight because of its church manifestation, for in God's first church no lie could live. The new church the Holy Ghost is building has no lie, but purity and holiness unto the Lord. I see the new Church established in the breath of the [Lord]. God is working in a supernatural way making faces shine with His glory. Men so in likeness with God, loving right, hating iniquity, evil fearing before Him, a lie unable to remain in the midst, no condemnation, no man can condemn you. Many may try. But God's Word says, "Who is he that condemneth Christ that died?" Will Jesus condemn the sheep for whom he died? He died to save men and He saves all who believe.

God is purifying our hearts by faith. God has come forth clothing us with His Spirit's might, living in the blaze of this glorious day — for there is nothing greater than the Gospel.

Ananias and Sapphira were moved to bring an offering. The day will come when we shall count nothing our own. We shall be so taken up with the Lord the church ripened into coming glory. The first day was a measure, the latter day was to be more glorious. They sold a possession, it was their own, but when it was sold it looked so much. They reasoned, "The Pentecostal order was new, it might dry up." So they agreed to give a part and reserve the other.

Satan is very subtle, many miss the greatest things by drawing aside. Let us pay our vows unto the Lord. Peter said, "...Ananias, why hath Satan filled thine heart to lie to the Holy Ghost?..." (Acts 5:3). The moment Ananias lied to the Holy Ghost he was smitten.

God has shown us in this Holy Ghost baptism a new order of the Spirit. One day when I came into my house, my wife said, "Did you come in at the front door?" I said, "No, I came in at the back." "Oh," she said.

"At the front you would have seen a crowd and a man with little clothing on, crying out, 'I have committed the unpardonable sin.'" As I went to the door, God whispered to me, "This is what I baptized you in the Spirit for." The man came in crying, "I have committed the unpardonable sin." I said, "You lying devil, come out in Jesus' Name." He said, "What is it? I am free. Thank God I never did it."

Not a man living has committed the unpardonable sin, for the good and evil are preserved until the Holy Ghost is withdrawn from the world. We are all in a good place, kept by the power of God.

ONENESS OF ACCORD

Great fear came upon the church, the love that fears to grieve Him. Why, they could ask and get anything. One accord, perfect fidelity love, oneness, consolation. God lifting the Church into a place of manifested reconciliation, oneness of accord, until the devil has no power in our midst. God smiling on us all the time. "And by the hands of the apostles were many signs and wonders wrought among the people..." (Acts 5:12). A purity of life before God — a manifested power among men with multitudes gathered into the Kingdom. God has mightily blessed Elim work. Those of you who are still lingering outside the Kingdom, yield to God tonight. Get clean hands and a right purpose and join that which is holy and on fire and mean business for God (v. 14).

Oh, for this kind of revival, God breaking forth everywhere and London swept by the power of God. There must be a great moving among us, a oneness of heart and soul, and it is sure to be as God moves upon the people.

Insomuch as they brought the sick into the streets, and laid them on beds and couches, that at the least the shadow of Peter passing by might overshadow some of them. There came a multitude out of the cities round about unto Jerusalem...and they were healed every one (see vv. 15,16). Oneness of accord has the effect of working the oracle every time. Glory to God, it is so lovely. The people had such a living faith, one heart, one mind. Oh, if only Peter's shadow passed over them God will do it.

Have faith. God will heal the land. Oneness of heart and mind on the part of the church means signs and wonders in all lands. Whatsoever things ye desire when ye pray — only believe. I see, beloved, we need to get more love and the Lord will do it. How the Master can move among the needy and perishing when He has the right of way in the church.

The finest thing is persecution — we must have a ministry which makes the people glad and the devil mad. Never mind if they run out, for conviction is in and God has got them. And if the people are glad, the Lord has them, so it works both ways. Don't be disturbed at anything. Remember it was written of the Master, "The zeal of thine house hath eaten me up." A melting, moving, broken condition. Poor making many rich, having nothing and yet possessing all things. Let us be in harmony with the divine plan, having knowledge cemented with love. Death to the old, having perfect place in us, so that the life-power can be manifested.

I once went for weekend meetings and when I arrived on Saturday night, it was snowing hard and a man stood at the door of the hall laden with parcels. As we walked home, at the first lamppost, I said, "Brother, are you baptized in the Holy Ghost?" I said, "Say you will be tonight." As we went along at every lamppost (nearly a hundred) I repeated the question, "Say you will be baptized tonight." So he began wishing I was not staying at his house. At last we reached the gate — I jumped over and said, "Now you don't come in here unless you say you will be baptized with the Holy Ghost tonight." "Oh," he said. "I feel so funny but I will say it." We went in. I asked his wife, "Are you baptized in the Holy Ghost?" She said, "Oh, I want to be — but supper is ready, come in." I said, "No supper until you are both baptized in the Holy Ghost."

Did God answer? Oh yes, soon they were both speaking in tongues. Now I believe tonight God will baptize you — put up your hands and ask Him to. Move into the other hall — also those seeking healing and salvation and God will meet you every one. Amen.

Sermon preached at Elim Tabernacle

"Only believe! Only believe! All things are possible, only believe!" Praise God, He has made all things possible. There is liberty for everyone, whatever the trouble. Our Lord Jesus says, "Only believe." He has obtained complete victory over

FULL! FULL! FULL!

June 12, 1926

every difficulty, over every power of evil, over every depravity. Every sin is covered by Calvary.

Who are of the tribe of Abraham? All who believe in Jesus Christ are the seed of faith, Abraham's seed. If we dare come believing, God will heal, God will restore, will lift the burden and wake us up to real overcoming faith. Look up! Take courage! Jesus has shaken the foundations of death and darkness. He figheth for you and there is none like Him. He is the great *I Am*. His name is above every name. As we believe we are lifted into a place of rest, a place of conformity to Him. He says to us as He did to Abraham, "...I will bless thee... and thou shalt be a blessing" (Genesis 12:2). He says to us as He did to His people of old, "With lovingkindness have I drawn thee." Hallelujah! "He'll never forget to keep me, He'll never forget to keep me; my Father has many dear children, but He'll never forget to keep me." Believe it. He will never forget.

In the sixth chapter of Acts we read of the appointment of seven deacons. The disciples desired to give themselves wholly to prayer and to the ministry of the Word, and they said to the brethren, "...look ye out among you seven men of honest report, full of the Holy Ghost and wisdom, whom we may appoint over this business" (Acts 6:3). And they chose Stephen, "...a man full of faith and of the Holy Ghost..." (v.5), and six others. We read that Stephen, full of faith and power, did great wonders and miracles among the people, and his opponents were not able to resist the wisdom and the spirit by which he spake. When his opponents brought him before the Sanhedrin, all that sat in the Council looked steadfastly on him, and they "...saw his face as it had been the face of an angel..." (Acts 6:15).

I see many remarkable things in the life of Stephen. One thing moves me, and that is the truth that I must at all costs live by the power of the Spirit. God wants us to be like Stephen, full of faith and full of the Holy Ghost. You can never be the same again after you have received this wonderful baptism in the Holy Spirit. It is important that day by day we should be full of wisdom and faith, and full of the Holy Ghost, acting by the power of the Holy Ghost. God has set us here in the last days, these of apostasy, and would have us be burning and shining lights in the midst of an untoward generation. God is longing for us to come into such a fruitful position as the sons of God, with the marks of heaven upon us, His divinity bursting through our humanity, so that He can express Himself through our lips of clay. He can take clay lips, weak humanity, and make of such an oracle for Himself. He can take frail human nature and by His divine power make our bodies meet to be His holy temple, washing our hearts whiter than snow.

Our Lord Jesus says, "...All power is given unto me in heaven and in earth" (Matthew 28:18). He longs that we should be filled with faith and with the Holy Ghost and declares to us, "...He that believeth on me, the works that I do shall he do also; and greater works than these shall he do; because I go unto my Father" (John 14:12). He has gone to the Father. He is in the place of power and he exercises His power not only in heaven but on earth, for He has all power on earth as well as in heaven. Hallelujah! What an open door to us if we will but believe Him.

The disciples were men after our standard on the line of the flesh. God sent them forth, joined to the Lord and identified with Him. Peter, John and Thomas, how diverse they were! Impulsive Peter, ever ready to go forth without a stop! John, the beloved, leaning on the Master's breast, how different! Thomas, with hard nature and defiant spirit. "I won't believe, unless I put my finger into the print of the nails and my hands into His side." What strange flesh! How peculiar! But the Master could mold them. There was no touch like His. Under His touch even stony-hearted Thomas believed. Ah, my God, how Thou hast had to manage some of us. Have we not been strange and very peculiar? But oh, when God's hand comes upon us, He can speak to us in such a way — a word, a look, and we are broken. Has He spoken to you? I thank God for His speaking. Back of all His dealings we see the love of God for us. It is not what we are that counts, but what we can be as He disciplines and chastens us and transforms us by His all skillful hands. He sees our bitter tears and our weeping night after night. There is none like Him. He knows. He forgives. We cannot forgive ourselves; we oftentimes would give the world to forget, but we cannot. The devil won't let us forget. But God has forgiven and forgotten. Do you believe self, or the devil, or God? Which are you going to believe? Believe God. I know the past is under the blood and that God has forgiven and forgotten, for when He forgives He forgets. Praise the Lord! Hallelujah! We are baptized to believe and to receive.

In making provision for the serving of tables and the daily ministration, the disciples knew who were baptized with the Holy Ghost. In the early days of the church all who touched the work had to be men full of the Holy Ghost. I am hungry that I may be more full, that God may make choice of me for His service. And I know that the greatest qualification is to be filled with the Spirit. The Holy Spirit has the divine commission from heaven to impart revelation to every son of God concerning the Lord Jesus, to unfold to us the gifts and the fruit of the Spirit. He will take of the things of Christ and show them unto us.

Stephen was a man full of faith and of the Holy Ghost. God declares it. God so manifested Himself in Stephen's body that he became an epistle of truth, known and read of all. Full of faith! Such men never talk doubt. You never hear them say, "I wish it could be so; or if it is God's will." No if's. They *know*. You never hear them say, "Well, it does not always act." They say, "It is sure to be." They laugh at impossibliites and cry, "It shall be done!" A man full of faith hopes against hope. He shouts while the walls are up and they come down while he shouts! God has this faith for us in Christ. We must be careful that no unbelief is found in us, no wavering.

"...Stephen, full of faith and power, did great wonders and miracles among the people" (Acts 6:8). The Holy Ghost could do mighty things through him because he believed God, and God is with the man who dares to believe His Word. All things were possible because of the Holy Ghost's position in Stephen's body. He was full of the Holy Ghost so God could fulfill His purposes through him. When a child of God is filled with the Holy Ghost, the Spirit maketh intercession through him for the saints according to the will of God. He fills us with longings and desires until we are in a place of fervency as of a molten fire. What to do we know not. When we are in this place the Holy Ghost begins to do. When the Holy Ghost has liberty in the body He wafts all utterance into the presence of God according to the will of God. Such prayers are always heard. Such praying is always answered; it is never bare of result. When we are praying in the Holy Ghost, faith is in evidence and as a result the power of God can be manifested in our midst.

When there arose certain of the various synagogues to dispute with Stephen they were not able to resist the wisdom and the Spirit by which He spake. When we are filled with the Holy Ghost we will have wisdom.

Praise God! One night I was entrusted with a meeting and I was jealous of my position before God. I wanted approval from the Lord. I see that God wants men full of the Holy Ghost, with divine ability, filled with life, a flaming fire. In the meeting a young man stood up, a pitiful object, with a face full of sorrow. I said, "What is it, young man?" He said he was unable to work, he could scarcely walk. He said, "I am so helpless. I have consumption and a weak heart, and my body is full of pain." I said, "I will pray for you." I said to the people, "As I pray for this young man, you look at his face and see it change." As I prayed his face changed and he was in a strange way. I said to him, "Go out and run a mile and come back to the meeting." He came back and said, "I can now breathe freely." The meetings were continuing and I missed him. After a few days I saw him again in the meeting. I said, "Young man, tell the people what God has done for you." "Oh," he said, "I have been to work. I bought some papers and I have made $4.50." Praise God, this wonderful stream of salvation never runs dry. You can take a drink, it is close to you. It is a river that is running deep and there is plenty for all.

In a meeting a man rose and said, "Will you touch me, I am in a terrible way. I have a family of children, and through an accident in the pit I have had no work for two years. I cannot open my hands." I was full of sorrow for this poor man and something happened which had never come before. We are in the infancy of this wonderful outpouring of the Holy Spirit and there is so much more for us. I put out my hand, and before my hands reached his, he was loosed and made perfectly free. I see that Stephen, full of faith and of power, did great wonders and miracles among the people. This same Holy Ghost filling is for us, and right things will be accomplished if we are filled with His Spirit. God will grant it. He declares that the desires of the righteous shall be granted. Stephen was an ordinary man made extraordinary in God. We may be very ordinary, but God wants to make us extraordinary in the Holy Ghost. God is ready to touch and to transform you right now. Once a woman rose in the meeting asking for prayer. I prayed for her and she was healed. She cried out, "It is a miracle! It is a miracle! It is a miracle!" That is what God wants to do for us all the time. As sure as we get free in the Holy Ghost something will happen. Let us pursue the best things and let God have His right of way.

All that sat in the council looked steadfastly on Stephen and saw his face as it had been the face of an angel. It was worth being filled with the

Holy Ghost for that. The Spirit breaking through. There is a touch of the Spirit where the light of God will verily radiate from our faces.

The seventh chapter of Acts is the profound prophetic utterance that the Spirit spoke through this holy man. The Word of God flowed through the lips of Stephen in the form of divine prophecy so that they who heard these things were cut to the heart. But he, being full of the Holy Ghost, looked up steadfastly into heaven, and saw the glory of God, and Jesus standing on the right hand of God, and said, "...Behold, I see the heavens opened, and the Son of man standing on the right hand of God" (Acts 7:56). Right to the last Stephen was full of the Holy Ghost. He saw Jesus standing. In another part we read of Him seated at the right hand of God. That is His place of authority. But here we see that He arose. He was so keenly interested in that martyr Stephen. May the Lord open our eyes to see Him and to know that He is deeply interested in all that concerns us. He is touched with the feeling of our infirmities.

All things are naked and open unto the eyes of Him with whom we have to do. That asthma, He knows. That rheumatism, He knows. That pain in the back, that head, those feet, He knows. He wants to loose every captive and to set you free just as He has set me free. I do not know that I have a body today. I am free of every human ailment, absolutely free. Christ has redeemed us. He has power over all the power of the enemy and has wrought out our great victory. Will you have it? It is yours — a perfect redemption.

And they stoned Stephen, who called upon God and said, "...Lord Jesus, receive my spirit. And he kneeled down, and cried with a loud voice, Lord, lay not this sin to their charge. And when he had said this, he fell asleep" (Acts 7:59,60). Stephen was not only filled with faith, but he was also filled with love as he prayed just as his Master prayed, "Father, forgive them."

It is God's thought to make us a new creation, with all the old things passed away and all things within us truly of God, to bring in a new, divine order, a perfect love and an unlimited faith. Will you have it? Redemption is free. Arise in the activity of faith and God will heal you as you rise. Only believe and receive in faith. Stephen, full of faith and of the Holy Ghost, did great signs and wonders. May God bless to us this word and fill us full of His Holy Spirit, and through the power of the Holy Ghost more and more reveal Christ in us.

The Spirit of God will always reveal the Lord Jesus Christ. Serve Him, love Him, be filled with Him. It is lovely to hear Him as He makes Himself known to us. He is the same yesterday; today and forever. He is willing to fill us with the Holy Ghost and faith just as He filled Stephen.

Published in *The Pentecostal Evangel*

WAY, MANIFESTATION, MINISTRY
July 1926

Corinthians 3. Three things have been pressing through this morning. 1. The way of faith. 2. The manifestation of the power of the Spirit. 3. The ministry of the Spirit. Now is entrusted to us the ministry of the Spirit. The word may be in letter or in power, we must be in the place of edifying the Church. Law is not liberty, but if there is a moving of God within you, God has written His laws in our hearts that we may delight in Him.

PLACE OF DELIGHT

God desires to set forth in us a perfect blending between His life and our life, that we may have abounding inward joy, a place of reigning over all things, not of endeavor. Ours is not an endeavor society, but a delight to run in the will of God. There is a great difference between an endeavor and a delight. "...Be ye holy; for I am holy" (1 Peter 1:16). Trying will never reach it, but there is an attitude where God puts you in faith in resting on His Word, a delighting inwardly over everything. I delight to do Thy will. There is a place of great joy. Do we want condemnation?

We know there is something within that has been wrought by the power of God, something greater than there could be in the natural order of the flesh. We are the representatives of Jesus, He was eaten up with zeal. This intense zeal so changing us by the operation of the Word, we rest not in the letter, but allow the blessed Holy Spirit to lift us by His power. Ye are our epistle, such a beautiful order prevailed in this church, a place of holiness and power in Christ, perfect love, the sweetness of association with Christ.

The disciples were with Jesus three years, He spoke out of the abundance of His heart towards them. John said, "...which we have seen with our eyes, which we have looked upon, and our hands have handled..." (1 John 1:1). Did Jesus know about Judas? Yes. Did He ever tell? No. They said one to another, "Is it I?" And Peter said to John who was close to Jesus, "Get to know." The essence of divine order to bring the Church together, so that there is no schism in the Body, but a perfect blending of heart to heart. The letter killeth. The sword cut off Malchus' ear, but the Spirit healed it again.

Our ministry has to be in the Spirit, free from the law of sin and death. When we live in the ministry of the Spirit we are free, in the letter we are bound. If it is an eye for an eye, we have lost the principle. If we are to come to a place of great liberty the law must be at an end. Yet we love the law of God, we love to do it and not put one thing aside.

TONGUES AND INTERPRETATION: "The way is made into the treasure house of the Most High as God unfolds the Word. Hearts are blended, an incision being made by the Spirit of the living God, that we may move, live, act, think, and pray in the Holy Ghost, a new order, life in the Holy Ghost, ministry in the Spirit."

"...manifestly declared to be the epistle of Christ ministered...with the Spirit of the living God...in fleshy tables of the heart" (2 Corinthians 3:3). It's heart worship when God has made the incision, the Spirit has come to blend with humanity.

There is something beautiful about a baby. Jesus said, "Whosoever therefore shall humble himself as this little child, the same is greatest in the kingdom of heaven" (Matthew 18:4).

There was a house with ten children and only ten chairs. What was to happen for the baby? When the baby came, every chair was a seat for the baby. It is a great joy to us to dedicate children, but we believe when they are old enough they should be buried in water baptism. Of such is the kingdom of heaven. A baby is a beautiful thing, and God looks on His people, at the possibility. The child is lent to us to be brought up in the fear of God.

> I know He's mine, this Friend so dear
> He lives in me, He's always near.

I want to refer to the word *incision*. God's Word, our life written on the fleshy tables of the heart. I have been in Rome. I saw thousands of pilgrims kissing the steps there. It made me sorrowful. How I thank God for His Word. There are many Pentecostal Assemblies in Italy, and I saw on the people there a great hunger and thirst after God. God moved mightily among them and people were saved and baptized in the Holy Ghost in the same meeting.

We must keep in the spiritual tide, God supreme, the altar within the body. God in the Spirit, faith the evidence, the power, the principle, keeping us in rest, having the Spirit in unction, intercession, revelation, and great power of ministry. To be baptized in the Holy Ghost is to be in God's plan, the Spirit preeminent, revealing the Christ of God, making the Word of God alive, something divine, able to minister the Spirit.

PLACE OF REFINING

"...Our sufficiency is of God; Who also hath made us able ministers of the...spirit giveth life (2 Corinthians 3:5,6). I knew a brother who carried out bags of coal. He had been in bed three weeks away from his work. I showed him a verse in Romans 7:25. "I thank God through Jesus Christ our Lord. So then with the mind I myself serve the law of God; but with the flesh the law of sin." I said, "Keep your mind on God and go to work, shout victory." He did, and the first day he was able to carry a hundred bags, his mind stayed on God and kept in peace.

If your peace is disturbed, there is something wrong. If you are not free in the Spirit, your mind is in the wrong place.

Apply the blood of Jesus and keep your mind stayed upon Jehovah. Their hearts are fully blessed, finding as He promised, perfect peace and rest. Keeping the mind on God, gaining strength in Him day by day.

"...The law was given by Moses, but grace and truth came by Jesus Christ" (John 1:17). This new dispensation, this divine place, Christ in you, the hope and evidence of glory.

TONGUES AND INTERPRETATION: "Let thine eyes be stayed upon Him, thy heart moved by the Spirit, thy whole being in a place of refining to come forth as gold. Behold, see the glory. God covereth thee with a mantle of power."

"For the Lord delighteth in thee, to serve Him with all thy heart and strength. Take in all the land, worldwide. Oh, the rest of faith. Ask largely of Him. Hitherto ye have asked nothing."

May God so gird you with truth. I commend you to Him in the Name of Jesus. Amen.

Message given at Clarence Place Mall
Belfast

APPREHENDED FOR APPREHENSION
August 1926

Philippians 3. What a wonderful word — to be filled into all the fulness of God. God's Word is our food; if we leak out here we miss the association and meeting the need. Let us preach by life, act, presence and glory, being always living epistles of Christ, bringing forth the knowledge of the truth; known and read of all men in apostolic order.

Buy the truth and sell it not, ever alert with divine inspiration. If we went all the way with God, what would happen? Seeking the honor which cometh from God only. Paul is on the line of desiring to attain, there is no standing still, we move on in the regeneration of the Spirit, never satisfied, yet born to be satisfied always.

Abraham came out. We never get into a new place until we come out of the old one. We must be monuments of God's personality. We never can be satisfied, for the truth rises and rises in majesty. We must move on, or we shall perish; rising all the time from possibility to possibility after the Holy Ghost order; then God will arise.

Paul was a man who had kept the law — blameless — it was an ideal standard. There was an issue which caused him to see what he did see. He saw something (Acts 9) — a light from heaven! He was new. Are you new? He was one born out of due time. He was not with the other apostles, but he had been told of the Word of life (1 John 1); wonderful things, ideal principles — he had not yet attained. But he had zeal, and before him was a possibility (vv. 3-6). The present was nothing to him; he was something beyond (for the excellency). Something that made people move — a thirst, not only for the present creation, but the creation — the new creation that is moved by the Word. I count all things loss for the excellency of the knowledge of Jesus Christ my Lord. That I may win Christ. This endless living person, speaking, breathing forth such words that shall awaken men in the trying hour. In the garden He spoke — the men fell backward. He, the Creator submitted Himself to men. Yet He said, "Let these go their way." Paul perceived these principles, power to use the power of the Christ for the lifting up of humanity even in us. And when they reviled, He reviled not again.

Beloved — a definite life within the life. God in the man — a presentation. They sought to make Him a King. Jesus retired to pray. Paul said, "Oh, if I could only win that. To win Christ and be found in Him." Is he less than authority to make human character? Oh, can I win Him? Is it possible to change and change, having His apprehension, His dispensing, His love? Peter said, "They shall not take you," and cuts Malchus's ear off. Jesus puts it on again. Oh, if I could only win Christ? Oh, the dignity of Christ who comes to create a new order of life. Emblematic that can say, "Clean! Clean! Clean! Through the blood shed on Calvary!" Oh, to win Him and to be found in Him, the righteousness which is of God by faith. Jesus identified Himself with us. — He came to be a firstfruit. How zealous is the farmer as he watches his crops to see the first shoots and blades he sees the harvest. This same Jesus was a firstfruit, and God will have a harvest! Sons of God, perfectly adjusted in the presence of God and in place (found in Him), a lovely position. You say, "It is a trying morning," or "I am in a needy place." — He is just the same. For three days the multitude had had nothing to eat! He knew they were faint. He said to Philip, "What shall we do?" Did you ever walk a while on the way to Emmaus? — the things! What things? Art thou a stranger? Oh, believe, if we only knew. He walked with them. Their hearts burned both ways. All so full of telling the story. He made Himself known to them in the breaking of the bread. He appeared again, just in the morning. Oh, to be found in the place where He is — always there, never out of order, ripe. How did He get there? He was there all the time. We need to have our eyes open. Always there, to bring us to the place where we are confident; the Lord is with us.

There is such a place; Abraham touched it. Jesus lived in it. Paul desired to have it. Have you got it?

Him! Him! Found in Him! The righteousness which is of God by faith. Abraham touched it. God did two things. He gave him righteousness because he believed. God imputes righteousness. He adds to take away. Takes away hindrances and imputes the biggest blessing — the rest of faith. I will keep in perfect peace whose mind is stayed on *Me*. The rest of faith. Jesus had that which Paul coveted. Paul knew Jesus by revelation as we do. Not in human ministry as the other apostles. Paul saw Jesus lived in resurrection power, in the act with power to give. Paul wanted to gain the rest, so he refused all hindrances and pressed through. To know Him — denying all interference. "Stop while I go yonder," Jesus said — in order to go into the place of apprehension to attain. To know Him and the power of His resurrection — manifestations of power, a manifestation of the presence of Jesus in resurrection order.

Here is the widow's only son on the way to burial. The fact of life, the fact to win Him, knowing how to act in the trying hour, with the rest of what brought manifestation. Faith for divine leadings. God bringing us to a living faith with a dare to act on the know. The widow's son: when Jesus saw him, it was not compassion on the boy. His great heart had such compassion for the widow, that death had no power — could not hold him. Oh, compassion is greater than death, greater than the suffering. Oh, God give it to us! Because of compassion the other must come forth! "Put him down!" "Young man, I say unto you, 'Arise.'"

He that was dead sat up.

When they told Paul, he said, "Oh, to know His compassion." What is the object? That I may apprehend the quickening power — that God may lay hold of me.

He said, "I will not stop until I lay hold of what God laid hold of me for." The righteousness of a living faith. The Word of the Son of God manifested through you and to you. Oh, God, help me to manifest that faith!

One day at eleven o'clock, I saw a woman with tumors — she could not live out that day. I said, "Do you want to live?" She could not speak; she just moved her finger. I said, "In the Name of Jesus," and poured on the oil. (Mr. Fisher was with me. It was in Canada.) He said, "She's gone!"

Oh, the place of the rest of faith. There is a place in it beyond all. One dare not think — The righteousness which is of God by faith, stands with God. The righteousness of faith has resurrection in it and moves on resurrection lines.

A little blind girl led me to the bedside. Compassion broke me up for the child's sake. I had said, "Lift your finger."

Carrying the mother across the room, I put her up against the wardrobe. I held her there. I said, "In the Name of Jesus, death, come out."

Like a fallen tree, leaf after leaf, her body began moving. Upright instead of lifeless, her feet touched the floor. "In Jesus Name, walk," I said. She did, back to bed. I told this story in the assembly — there was a doctor there. He said, "I'll prove that." He saw her. She said, "It is all true. I was in heaven, I saw countless numbers all like Jesus. He pointed and I knew I had to go. Then I heard a voice saying, 'Walk, in the Name of Jesus.'"

The power of His resurrection — The righteousness which is of God by faith. Are we apprehended for it? Can we have it?

It is His love. It is His life in us. It is His compassion.

See that apprehension is apprehended. Miss it not! Oh, miss Him not! It is the righteousness which is of God by faith - the rest of faith.

Love will break the hardest thing. There is nothing love will not break. Amen.

Address given in Buford, Ireland

nly believe. To so hear the Word of God by the Spirit's power. Changed by the grace of God. Changed by the revelation of God. Only believe. Other refuge have I none.

THE ROCK FAITH

November 1926

If thou wilt believe. Awake to the fact, knowing the Scriptures, resting unconditionally, absolutely upon the Word of God. God has never failed anyone relying upon His Word.

Some human plan or your mind may come between, but rest upon what God's Word says. Only believe. Oh the charm of the truth, making you rich forever, taking away all weariness. Those who put their trust in God are like Mount Zion, they cannot be moved. Rock of Ages cleft for me. Oh, the almightiness of God's plan for us, tremendous. We are only weak and helpless when we forget the visitation of the Lord. From the uttermost to the uttermost. Ask and ye shall receive, seek and ye shall find, knock and it shall be opened unto you.

HIS ROCK — THIS ROCK

When Jesus came into the coasts of Caesarea Phillippi, he asked his disciples, saying, Whom do men say that I the Son of man am?... And Simon Peter answered and said, Thou art the Christ, the Son of the living God. And Jesus answered and said unto him, Blessed art thou, Simon Bar-jona: for flesh and blood hath not revealed it unto thee, but my Father which is in heaven. And I say also unto thee, That thou art Peter, and upon this rock I will build my church; and the gates of hell shall not prevail against it. And I will give unto thee the keys of the kingdom of heaven: and whatsoever thou shalt bind on earth shall be bound in heaven: and whatsoever thou shalt loose on earth shall be loosed in heaven.

Matthew 16:13,16-19

Jesus was full of ideals, perfect in those He was dealing with. Jesus came with a perfect purpose that many might hear and live and come into apostolic conditions, divine life. Jesus was a firstfruit to bring to the disciples a knowledge that they were in a divine act to supersede every last power in the world. Holiness is the keynote. Saving grace is a revelation from heaven. Christ within sets up the heavenly standard, the heavenly mind, so that we live, act and think in a new world.

Whom do men say that I, the Son of man, am? Then Peter, with eyes and heart aflame said, "You are the Christ, the Son of the living God." Jesus perceiving in a moment that the revelation had come from heaven said, "Blessed art thou Simon Bar-jona, for flesh and blood hath not revealed it unto thee, but My Father in heaven." *God's great plan is that*

His children should be salt for a world diseased. Ye are the salt of the earth, ye are the light of the world. To be saved is to have the revelation of the glory of Christ, it is our inheritance to have the evidence of the Holy Ghost coming upon us. Sons with power, manifestations of the Son, built upon the faith of the Son of God. Upon this Rock will I build My Church, and the gates of hell shall not prevail against it.

God is visiting the earth with His resplendent glory. His coming is to revive, to heal, to deliver from the power of the pit. The ransom is the Lord, and He comes to save the oppressed, whose eyes, ears, and heart shall see, hear, and feel with a new beauty.

IMPREGNABLE FAITH

In the innermost soul of the Holy Ghost abiding in power, for the King has come to fill and rule the body, and transform the life. A new creature, a perfect preservation and manifestation over all the powers of evil, pure and holy. He is so sweet, He is the most lovely of all. The bruised reed He will not break nor quench the smoking flax. God has designed, by the Holy Ghost, to bring forth character divine. As He is, so are we in this world. God has saved and chosen and equipped that those bound by Satan may go free. Jesus is speaking to the disciples on a plan of ministry. "Verily, verily, I say unto you, He that believeth on me, the works that I do shall he do also; and greater works than these shall he do; because I go unto my Father" (John 14:12), laying emphasis on the fact of this truth, faith, and Christ's Rock are one and the same structure, rock! Upon this Rock I will build My Church, and the gates of hell shall not prevail against it. Rock! Emblematic of a living faith, a divine principle, what God the Holy Ghost has to create and bring forth within us. No devil or evil power should be allowed to remain where we are. Jesus was teaching His disciples that as they believed greater things would be accomplished because He was going. Upon this Rock! Upon this living faith will I build My Church. Whatsoever ye bind or loose on earth shall be bound or loosed in heaven, (Matthew 16:19). Keep in mind this word, Satan has tremendous power in the world, and people suffer as they never would if they only knew the truth, which cannot be gainsaid. Upon this Rock will I build My Church. The Kingdom, the new birth come with power, upon this Rock, this living faith. This awful responsibility, that unless I believe and act on this Word, it will not be operative in others. Ninety percent and more diseases are satanic power. How many here received a touch from Jesus this afternoon, and were loosed from their pains? How was this accomplished? By binding and destroying the evil power in the Name of Jesus. Not only are we given power to loose and bind, but Jesus says the gates of hell shall not prevail against His Church. There must be the fellowship of Christ's sufferings. He has suffered for the people, there must be an entering in, a compassion, we are to be moved in union with needy sufferers. Jesus was moved with compassion. Oh, the compassion of Jesus! We must be moved, the compassion taking us to the place of delivering the people. God knows all about this meeting, and we have power to bind or loose in the Name of Jesus. Who would believe? Have ye received the Holy Ghost since ye believed? After God has saved you by His power He wants you to be illuminators of the King, new creations. The King is already on the throne, the Holy Ghost has come to reveal the fulness of power of His ministry. To be filled with the Holy Ghost is to be filled with prophetic illumination. The baptism in the Holy Ghost brings divine utterance, the divine bringing out pure prophecy. Then it becomes a condition. God is our foundation, the Word of God is our standing. We are here to glorify God. I know how weak I am. Struggle, are we to struggle? No, no! Believe what God has said. We must be in our place ready for the opportunity. God wants to give us divine life from heaven. The gates of hell shall not prevail against it. The rock of deliverance by the key of faith. You shall open the kingdom of heaven and shut the gates of hell. You shall bind and loose in Jesus' Name.

He cometh with the truth. Know His strength for the broken and the helpless. He revealeth His strength. A great tide of revival spirit. Clothed with His Spirit, the Lord shall give thee light. Fall down and worship Him.

Ask what ye will. Whatsoever things ye desire when ye pray, believe! Believe! Ye shall have them!

"Only as men become godlike and holy do they
become real men."

Wherever Jesus went, the multitudes followed Him because He lived, moved, breathed, was penetrated, clothed and filled with God. He was God and as Son of man the Spirit of God rested upon Him, the Spirit of creative holiness. It is lovely to be holy. Jesus came to impart to us the Spirit of holiness, a flame of holy, intense desire after God likeness.

THE CHRISTIAN PATHWAY FOR WORLD FLOODTIDE

December 1926

TONGUES AND INTERPRETATION: "God — Who quickeneth and bringeth into like-mindedness the human by His power, divine sons with power — created after the image of the new man. The Spirit of holiness and truth. Jesus was the Truth."

We are only at the edge of things, the Almighty plan is marvelous for the future. God must do something to increase. A revival to revive within and without all we touch. A floodtide with a cloudburst behind it. Jesus left 120 men to turn the world upside down. The Spirit is upon us to change the situation. We must move on to let God increase in us for the deliverance of others. We must travail through until souls are born and quickened into new relationship with heaven. Jesus had divine authority with power, and He left it for us. We must preach truth, holiness and purity in the inward parts.

> *Thou hast loved righteousness, and hated iniquity; therefore God, even thy God, hath anointed thee with the oil of gladness above thy fellows.*
>
> *Hebrews 1:9*

I am thirsty for more of God. He was not only holy, but He loved holiness.

TONGUES AND INTERPRETATION: "It is the depths that God gets into that we may reflect Him and manifest a life having Christ enthroned in the heart, drinking into a new fulness, new intuition, for as He is, so are we in this world."

HOLINESS AND REVIVAL

He trod the winepress alone. He despised the cross and the shame. He bore it all alone that we might be partakers of the divine nature, sharers in the divine plan of living, desiring holiness. That's a revival. Jesus manifested divine authority. He was without sin. They saw the Lamb of God in a new way. Hallelujah! Let us live holiness, and revival will come down. God will enable us to do the work to which we are appointed. All Jesus said came to pass. Signs, wonders. Amen. Only believe, and yield and yield, until all the vision is fulfilled.

God has a design, a purpose, a rest of faith. We are saved by faith, kept by faith. Faith is substance, it is also evidence. God is! He is! And He is a rewarder of them that diligently seek Him. I am sure of this. We have to testify, to bear witness to what we know. To know that we know is a wonderful position.

TONGUES AND INTERPRETATION: "The Lord is the great promoter of divine possibility, pressing you into the attitude of daring to believe all the Word says. We are to be living words, epistles of Christ, known and read of all men. The revelation of Christ, past and future. In Him all things consist. He is in us."

We are living in the inheritance of faith because of the grace of God, saved for eternity by the operation of the Spirit bringing forth purity unto God. A substance of divine proposition and attainment, bringing heaven to earth until God quickens all things into beauty, manifesting His power in living witnesses. God in us for a world, that the world may be blessed. Power to lay hold of omnipotence and impart to others the Word of life. This is to be a new epoch, new vision, new power. Christ in us is a thousand times greater than we know. All things are possible if you dare believe. The treasure is in earthen vessels that Jesus may be glorified.

Let us go forth ringing glory to God. Faith is substance, a mightiness of reality, a deposit of divine nature; God creative within. The moment you believe, you are mantled with a new power to lay hold of possibility and make it reality. They said, "Lord, evermore give us this bread, for he that eateth Me shall live by Me." Have the faith of God. The man that comes into great association with God needs a heavenly measure. Faith is the greatest of all. Saved by a new life, the Word of God, an association with the living Christ. A new creation continually taking us into new revelation.

PERSONAL REVIVAL PREPARATION

In the beginning was the Word, and the Word was with God, and the Word was God... All things were made by him; and without him was not any thing made that was made.

John 1:1,3

All was made by the Word. I am begotten by His Word, within me there is a substance that has almighty power in it if I dare believe. Faith going on to be an act, a reality, a deposit of God, an almighty flame to move you to act, so that signs and wonders are done. A living faith in the earthen casket. Are you begotten? Is it an act within you? Some need a touch, liberty to captives. Faith takes you to the place where God reigns and imbibes God's bountiful store. Unbelief is sin, for Jesus went to death to bring us the light of life.

Jesus said, "Are ye able to drink of the cup that I drink of and be baptized with the baptism I am baptized with?" The cup and the baptism, a joined position. You cannot live if you want to bring everything into life. His life is manifested power overflowing. Human must decrease if the life of God is to be manifested. There is not room for two kinds of life in one body. Death for life, the price to pay for the manifested power of God through you. As you die to human desire there comes a fellowship within, perfected cooperation, you ceasing, God increasing, you decreasing. God in you a living substance, a spiritual nature, you live by another life, the faith of the Son of God.

TONGUES AND INTERPRETATION: "The Spirit, He breatheth through and quickeneth until the body is a temple exhibiting Jesus — His life, His freshness, a new life divine. Paul said, "Christ liveth in me and the life I live in the flesh I live by faith."

As the Holy Ghost reveals Jesus, He is so real, the living Word — effective, acting, speaking, thinking, praying, singing. Oh, it is a wonderful life, this substance of the Word of God, including possibility and opportunity, and confronting you, bringing you to a place undaunted. Greater is He that is in you. Paul said, "When I am weak, then am I strong."

Jesus walked in supremacy, He lived in the Kingdom, and God will take us through because of Calvary. He has given us power over all the power of the enemy. He won it for us at Calvary. All in us must be subject.

What shall we do to work the works? This is the work of God that ye believe. Whatsoever He saith shall come to pass. That is God's Word.

A man, frail, weak, with eyes shrunk, and neck shriveled, said, "Can you help me?" Beloved, there is not one that cannot be helped. God has opened the doors for us to let Him manifest signs and wonders. The authority is inside, not outside. Could I help him? He had been on liquid food three months, fed through a tube. I said, "Go home and eat a good supper." He did, and woke up to find the tube hole closed up. God knew he did not want two holes. We must keep in a strong resolute resting on the authority of God's Word. One great desire and purpose to do what He saith. The Word is more to live in this holy Word, rejoicing to manifest the life of God on behalf of the sick and perishing multitudes. Amen.

Published in *Redemption Tidings*

AUTHOR AND FINISHER OF OUR FAITH

February 1927

Praise the Lord! I remember coming to London for the first Convention many years ago, and at that time I was in a very strange place, but there were people who were very kind to me. The kindness of the people of God at that time was wonderful.

HOLY LAND

You probably don't know, but I have had a month or six weeks in Canaan. I have crossed the river of Jordan, been on the lake of Galilee, bathed in the Dead Sea, drunk at Jacob's well, had a drink at Elijah's fountain, preached on the top of Mount Olives, stood with tears running down my face just opposite Mount Calvary, with hands lifted up, seen the place of sacrifice, passed by the spot where the holy inn stood of Bethlehem, and as I thought of all the holy associations connected with that land, my heart was melted. God has been very good to me.

HEBREWS 12

One of my favorite texts tonight, is in the 12th chapter of Hebrews. I want to read a few verses there. What a wonderful revelation the Hebrews is to us. I will read the first two verses.

> *Wherefore seeing we also are compassed about with so great a cloud of witnesses, let us lay aside every weight, and the sin which doth so easily beset us, and let us run with patience the race that is set before us, Looking unto Jesus, the author and finisher of our faith....*
>
> *Hebrews 12:1,2*

The thought here is Jesus as the Author and Finisher of our faith. Glory to God. What a sight to see our Lord Jesus Christ come forth robed in His own majesty and glory, as no man was ever robed. He is clothed in majesty. What compassion He had when He saw the heaving multitude, when He saw the crowds in need, His heart yearned with compassion. How He handled the bread. Never any man handled bread like Jesus. I can almost look into His face, and see His eyes glisten as He sees the multitude. He said to Philip, "I would like to feed these people, how much would it take to feed them?" Philip said, "Two hundred penny-worth of bread is not sufficient, and besides, this is a desert place." If you had been to Palestine and seen the sights I have seen, you would understand what is meant by a desert place. I have looked for many things in the Scriptures as I was over there, and God has spoken to me through it. They have the early and the latter rain there, and the land is a beautiful land. Praise the Lord! It was lovely to be there, and see these things, but, beloved, it made me cherish the Bible as I have never cherished it before. Why? Because God has given us the assurance that makes our hearts know it is true. If you never see the Holy Land, you can live in the Holy Land, and see all the wonderful things, and read of them in your Bible. Beloved, I want to speak tonight on the Author and the Finisher of our faith, and I want us to remember that Abraham, and Daniel, and all the prophets, were men of faith. We must not look at the things that have been done in the past, we must look at Jesus the Author and the Finisher of our faith. We must "run with patience the race that is set before us, looking unto Jesus." We must so look at the Author and the Finisher of our faith that the same glory and power shall be resting upon us as was upon Him, we must have such grace, such holiness that we shall be landmarks showing His power is upon us. Praise the Lord. Don't stumble at what I am going to say, but I praise God we not only have the abiding presence of the Spirit's power in our midst, but we have the living Word, the living Christ. He is the Author and the Finisher of our faith. He has given to us eternal life, that is, if we have His Word and believe.

My dear wife has now entered the glory, but during her lifetime she was a great revivalist. She was the preacher. I have seen the mighty power of God fall upon her, and seen her face light up with a heavenly light as she preached, and many are the ministers of the Gospel today through her preaching and her faithfulness, and others are missionaries and working for God. We shall never know the extent of her work, until the last day. You see, beloved, as we are faithful to God, and come into line with Him and labor for Him, our work will be rewarded. A great crowd is looking on. God is doing a work in these days, and these are:

DAYS OF OPPORTUNITY

God has been blessing in New Zealand, and you must hear all about that land, and in Australia 400 people were baptized in the Holy Ghost. Everywhere the Holy Ghost is being poured out, and the tide of blessing is rising. The power of the Holy Ghost is greater than we have ever conceived. The ring of the Pentecostal testimony should be — holiness. What is the strength of our position today? Holiness. I say to you and to everyone in this meeting tonight, if you fall a thousand times in a week, strive to be holy. It does not matter how many times you fall, do not give in because you fall.

I was staying in a house, and the lady of the house prepared a room and a bed for me to rest upon, as I had just got off the train and was very tired. When I awoke she said, "I want you to lay in my son's bed, I should like him to know you have laid in the bed." I slept in that bed for three nights, and two people slept in the same bed and both got baptized in the Spirit. Hallelujah! I would that everyone who is seeking would get baptized in the same way. That lady had such a sense of the presence of God that she said, "Lay in my son's bed." As soon as I opened my eyes, I looked across the room, and saw these words, "A man does not fall because he makes a blunder, he falls because he makes a blunder the second time." But God does not want us to fall but to be kept by His grace from falling, and to strive for holiness. I see the Word of God is the living Word, and Jesus is the Author of the Word. The Holy Ghost is the enlightener of the Word. If you look at the 1st of Acts, you will see these words, "He gave commandment by the Holy Ghost." This is the Word we have tonight. We shall find as we go on that the Lord Jesus Christ is:

THE AUTHOR OF OUR LIFE

He is the source of our life, our spiritual life, and He is producing holiness.

I am going to stop soon, for I have such respect for my brother who is going to speak. I love him so. I want to leave this word with you. I had intended to speak about the vision, but as my time is short, I cannot speak about it now. I want you to see what David said in the 63rd Psalm, "To see thy power and thy glory, so as I have seen thee in the sanctuary" (v. 2). Jesus said, "Father, glorify Thou Me with Thine own self, with the glory which I had with Thee before the world was." The greatest glory that was ever seen was manifested on the cross. The glory was manifested when Jesus offered Himself "through the eternal Spirit, on the cross." He said to Judas, "What thou doest, do quickly, and now is the Son of Man glorified." So we see that God was glorified in Jesus, He was reconciling the world unto Himself.

Everyone who has desires tonight for God, believe the Word of God, take Jesus as the Author and the Finisher of your faith. All the desires and purposes of your heart shall be accomplished, because God is faithful. God cannot fail, His Word is true. But what is real Pentecost? It is the manifestation of the power of God, the manifestation of the power of the Holy Ghost. Real Pentecost is the manifestation of the signs and wonders. Real Pentecost is manifested in those who are determined to know "nothing among men, save Jesus Christ, and Him crucified." I say tonight, as I have said before, "Whom have I in heaven but Thee, and there is none upon earth that I desire besides Thee." He is my all in all. Amen.

Published in *Redemption Tidings*

I believe the Lord would be pleased for us to read from the third chapter of Philippians this morning:

THAT I MAY KNOW HIM

March 1927

For we are the circumcision, which worship God in the spirit, and rejoice in Christ Jesus, and have no confidence in the flesh...But what things were gain to me, those I counted loss for Christ. Yea doubtless, and I count all things but loss for the excellency of the knowledge of Christ Jesus my Lord: for whom I have suffered the loss of all things, and do count them but dung, that I may win Christ. And be found in him, not having mine own righteousness, which is of the law, but that which is through the faith of Christ, the righteousness which is of God by faith: That I may know him, and the power of his resurrection, and the fellowship of his sufferings, being made conformable unto his death; If by any means I might attain unto the resurrection of the dead. Not as though I had already attained, either were already perfect: but I follow after, if that I may apprehend that for which also I am apprehended of Christ Jesus. Brethren, I count not myself to have apprehended: but this one thing I do, forgetting those things which are behind, and reaching forth unto those things which are before, I press toward the mark for the prize of the high calling of God in Christ Jesus.

Philippians 3:3,7-14

One can only pray for God to enlarge these visions today. I believe that God will, by His power, bring us into like-minded precious faith to believe all the Scriptures say. The Scriptures are at such depths that one can never be able to enter into those things without being enlarged in God. Beloved, one thing is certain this morning, God can do it. "All things that pertain unto life and godliness" are in the pursuit, with a faith that will not have a dim sight, but clears everything and claims all that God puts before it. And so this morning I pray God to so unfold to us the depths of His righteousness that we may no longer be poor, but very rich in God by His Spirit. Beloved, it is God's thought to make us all very rich in grace, and in the knowledge of God through our Lord Jesus Christ.

We have before us this morning a message which is full of heights and depths, and lengths, and breadths; a message which came out of brokenness of spirit, the loss of all things, enduring all things; a message where flesh and all that pertains to this world had to come to nothing. We can never worship God only in the Spirit. God can take us into this spiritual plane with Himself that we may be grounded in all knowledge, and so settled on all spiritual lines till from that place we will always be lifted by God. Men try to lift themselves, but there is no inspiration in that. But when you are lifted by the Spirit, when you are taken on with God, things all come into perfect harmony and you go forth right on to victory. That is a grand place to come to where we "rejoice in Christ Jesus and have no confidence in the flesh." Paul adds, "Though I might also have confidence in the flesh." Paul had kept the law blameless, but I find Another holds him in the same place.

Oh, that is the greatest of all, when the Lord Jesus has the reins. Then we have no longer anything to boast about because we see all our perfection according to law-keeping; and law-abiding ceases. Oh, it is beautiful as we gaze upon the perfect Jesus! Jesus so outstrips everything else. For this reason Paul felt that everything must become as dross, whatever he was, whatever he had been. There was no help for anything in him.

There is no help for us only on the lines of helplessness and nothingness. I know nothing like a travail in the Spirit. Oh, it is a burden till you are relieved. I have had those days, and I have had it this morning; but now God is lifting. And I say, brother, sister, unless God brings us into a place of brokenness of spirit, unless God remolds us in the great plan of His will for us, the best of us shall utterly fail. But when we are absolutely taken in hand by the Almighty God, God makes even weakness strength. He makes even that barren, helpless, groaning cry come forth, so that men and women are born in the travail. There is a place where the helplessness is touched by the almightiness of God and where you come out shining as gold tried in the fire.

Oh, brother, I see there is no hope for Pentecost only on broken conditions. It was there on the cross that our Lord died with a broken heart. Pentecost came out of jeering and sneering, and a sip of vinegar, and a smite with a rod, and a judgment that was passed away from Him, and a cross that He had to bear. But, glory to God, Pentecost rings out this morning through the Word, "It is finished," for you! And now because it is finished, we can take the same place that He took, and rise out of that death in majestic glory with the resurrection touch of heaven that shall make people know, after this day, that God has done something for us.

BE MADE NEW

Every day there must be a revival touch in our hearts. Every day must change us after His fashion. We are to be made new all the time. There is no such thing as having all grace and knowledge — there is a beginning, and God would have us begin in all these beatitudes of power this morning, and never cease, but rise and rise and go on to perfection. There are some beatitudes here God must have us reach this day! "But what things were gain to me, those I counted loss for Christ. Yea doubtless, and I count all things but loss for the excellency of the knowledge of Christ Jesus my Lord: for whom I have suffered the loss of all things, and do count them but dung, that I may win Christ." Also we will turn to Hebrews 10:32, "But call to remembrance the former days, in which, after ye were illuminated, ye endured a great fight of afflictions." I am positive that no man can attain like-mindedness on these lines only by the illumination of the Spirit.

God has been speaking to me over and over again that I must press all the people in to receive the baptism of the Holy Ghost, because I see in the baptism of the Holy Ghost unlimited grace, and the endurance in that revelation by the Spirit. I see the excellency of Christ can never be understood, only by illumination. And I find the Holy Ghost is that great Illuminator who makes me understand all the depths of Him. I must witness Christ. Jesus said to Thomas, "...Thomas, because thou hast seen me, thou hast believed: blessed are they that have not seen, and yet have believed" (John 20:29).

So I can see there is a revelation which brings me into touch with Him where we get all, and see right into the fulness of our Head, even Christ, and I can see that Paul, as he saw the depths and heights of the grandeur, longed that he might win Him. Before his conversion, in his passion and zeal, Paul would do anything to bring Christians to death. And that passion that was in him raged like a mighty lion. As he was going on the way to Damascus, he heard the voice of Jesus saying, "Saul, Saul, why persecutest thou me?" (Acts 9:4). What broke him up was the tenderness of God.

Brother, it is always God's tenderness over our weakness and over our depravity that has broken us all the time. If somebody came along to thwart us we would stand in our corner, but when we come to One who forgives us all, we know not what to do. Oh, to win Him, my brother! There are a thousand things in the nucleus of a human heart which need softening a thousand times a day. There are things in us that unless God shows us the excellency of the knowledge of Him, will never be broken and brought to ashes. But God will do it. Not merely to be saved, but to be saved a thousand times over! Oh, this transforming, reregeneration by the power of the Spirit of the living God makes me see there is a place to win Him, that I may stand complete there. As He was, so am I to be. The Scriptures declare it, it shall be.

"And be found in him, not having mine own righteousness, which is of the law, but that which is through the faith of Christ, the righteousness which is of God by faith" (Philippians 3:9). Not depending upon my works, but upon the faithfulness of God, being able under all circumstances to be hidden in Him, covered by the Almighty presence of God! The Scriptures declare unto us that we are in Christ and Christ is in God. What is able to move you from the place of omnipotent power? Shall tribulation, or persecution, or nakedness, or peril, or sword? Ah, no! Shall life, or death, or principalities, or powers? No, we are more than conquerors through Him that loved us.

FOUND IN HIM

Oh, but I must be found in Him! There is a place of seclusion, a place of rest and faith in Jesus where there is nothing else like it. Jesus came to them on the water and they were terrified, but He said, "It is I; be not afraid." My brother, He is always there. He is there in the storm as well as in the peace; He is there in the adversity. When shall we know He is there? When we are "found in Him," not having our own work, our own plan, but resting in the omnipotent plan of God. Oh, is it possible for the child of God to fail? It is not possible. "He that keepeth Israel shall never slumber." He shall watch over thee continually. Oh, but we must be found *in Him*. I know there is a covert place in Jesus which opens to us this morning. My brother, my sister, you have been nearly weighed down with troubles. They have almost crushed you. Sometimes you thought you would never get out of this place of difficulty but you have no idea that behind the whole thing God has been working a plan greater than all.

"That I may know Him, and the power of His resurrection." Jesus said to Martha, "I am the resurrection, and the life." Today is a resurrection day. We must know the resurrection of His power in brokenness of spirit. Oh, to know this power of resurrection, to know the rest of faith! To know the supplanting of His power in thee this morning! To make thee see that any one of us, without exception, can reach these beatitudes in the Spirit. Ah, there is something different between saying you have faith and then being pressed into a tight corner and proving that you have faith. If you dare believe, it shall be done according to your faith. "...What things soever ye desire, when ye pray, believe that ye receive them, and ye shall have them" (Mark 11:24). Jesus is the resurrection and the life, and I say, we must attain to it. God, help us to attain. We attain to it in that knowledge that He that came forth is to make us white as snow, pure and holy as He, that we may go with boldness unto the Throne of grace. Boldness is in His holiness. Boldness is in His righteousness. Boldness is in His truth. You cannot have the boldness of faith if you are not pure. What a blessed word follows, "The fellowship of His sufferings." Remember, except that fellowship touches us we shall never have much power.

What helped Him at all times when He saw the withered hand, when He saw the woman bowed together and could in no wise help herself? When the Spirit of the Lord blows upon you, you will be broken down and then built up. Jesus came forth in the glory of the Father, filled with all the fulness of God. It was the thought of God before the foundation of the world, with such love over all the fearful, helpless human race, with all its blackness and hideousness of sin, and God loved and God brought redemption. May God give us this morning such fellowship of his sufferings that when we see the person afflicted with cancer, we will pray right through until the roots are struck dead. When we see the crooked and helpless woman and man, so infirm, God gives a compassion, God gives a fellowship with them that shall undo their heavy burdens and set them free. How often we have missed the victory because we did not have the Lord's compassion at the needed moment. We failed to go through with a broken heart.

Is there anything more? Oh, yes, we must see the next thing. "Being made conformable unto His death." "...Except a corn of wheat fall into the ground and die, it abideth alone: but if it die, it bringeth forth much fruit" (John 12:24). God wants you to see that unless you are dead indeed, unless you come to a perfect crucifixion, unless you die with Him, you are not in the fellowship of His suffering. May God move upon us in this life to bring us into an absolute death, not merely to talk about it, not assuming it, but a death through which His life may indeed be made manifest. Paul said, "I count not myself to have apprehended: but this one thing I do, forgetting those things which are behind, and reaching forth unto those things which are before, I press toward the mark for the prize of the high calling of God in Christ Jesus." He had just said that he was following after in order to apprehend that for which he had been apprehended of Christ Jesus.

And I believe God wants us to come this morning in like-mindedness that we may be able to say, "I know I am apprehended." The Lord wants us to understand that we must come to a place where our natural life ceases, and by the power of God we rise into a life where God rules, where He reigns. Do you long to know Him? Do you long to be found in Him? Thy longing shall be satisfied this day. This is a day of putting on and being clothed upon in God. I ask you to fall in the presence of God; all you that want to know God, yield to His mighty power and obey the Spirit.

Published in *Triumphs of Faith*

A True Prophet

March 1927

The prophet's message is a word of the Lord that has become a burden upon the soul or a fire shut up in the bones, a burden, a pent-up fire, and anguish and a travail. The word of the Lord is a living flame — The symbol of Pentecost is a tongue of fire. Jeremiah had spoken his message, he felt that God had let him down and exposed him to ridicule and mockery. He would speak no more, but in the silence the fire burnt in his bones. He was full of the fury of the Lord until he was prostrate with holding himself in. The fire consumed him until he could no longer hold, until one day the fire suddenly lept forth in forked lightning, or a flaming sword.

The moment comes when the prophet is full of power by the Spirit of the Lord or to declare unto Jacob his transgression and Israel his sin. The fire constrains and consumes him and his generation persecute and despise his word.

The Lord came to bring fire. He was straightened in Spirit but it was accomplished. So is every man who brings fire. There is a brooding — questioning, reasoning, excusing — hoping foreboding. The whole being is consumed. The very marrow burns. Speech may not or must not or will not come. Then in a moment suddenly it flames out. He becomes a voice through which another speaks. Fire compels attention, it announced itself and you don't have to advertise a fire. When the fire comes, the multitude come.

Life is given, he that heareth my words and believeth on Him that sent me hath everlasting life. We need the Spirit, to be filled with prophetic power to bring forth to the needs of the people, life. This is life, I am perceiving that I must be so in this order. Let me give you one or two positions.

POWER IN ACTION

God wants everybody without exception, to begin on the Word of God, and to act it will be the most surprising thing that ever came, as you stand on the word it will be an amazing thing.

One day as I was going down the streets of San Francisco in a car, when looking through the window I saw a great crowd of people at the corner of the street. "Stop," I said, "There is something amiss." So I rushed as fast as possible to the edge of the crowd. I was so eager, I pressed myself into the crowd, and I saw a boy laid on the ground who was held in a death like grip.

The Word is in thee, Romans 10. I put my ear to his mouth as the boy lay there struggling, tell me boy what it is; and the boy said, "It is cramp," so I put my hands around him, and said, "Come out in the name of Jesus." The boy immediately jumped up, ran off and had no time to say thank you. It is for everyone. After that you have received you are in the place. I am not saying that glibly, my thoughts are too serious for that. **I cannot be any more after tonight what I was today, and tomorrow is mightier than today.** This is the reason the tide is changing with God, this is the reality.

It is no little thing to be baptized, it is the promise of the Father, Jesus must be there, and the Holy Ghost also bringing us to the place where we can be baptized. Are you going to treat it as a great thing, what do you really believe it is? I believe when the Holy Ghost comes that He comes to crown the King.

And the King from that day gets His rightful place, and we don't have to claim anything, and He becomes King of all the situations.

I only say this to help you. It is a need, that I am speaking about, that I cannot get away from the fact, because where I look I see growth. I see you people, I see the growth, I have been away from England three years, and I see changes, and even though we see there is growth, life and blessing there is much more ground to be possessed, and we shall have to dare before God can work.

God has given me an open door, nothing moves me, only this except I see men and women coming into line with this.

I want the people of Pentecost to rise as the heart of one man, God has us for a purpose in these last days, and in the meeting God helps me.

At a certain meeting, I said there is a man in this meeting suffering, and shall I preach before I help this man, or would you like to see this person free before I commence. This man was a stranger and did not know who I was speaking about, there he was, with cancer on the face and full of pain, and I said, "Is it right to preach, or shall I heal this man."

I saw what was the right thing, and I went down off the platform and placed my hand on him in the name of Jesus.

This was because of what the Word said, that man knew nothing of healing but in a moment he was able to stand up, and said I have been twelve years in pain, something has happened to me, and that night he gave himself to God, and testified night after night, that he was completely cured, what was it? God ministered through daring to believe His Word. There are cases round about you, and what a story you would have to tell next year if only people took a stand on the Word of God from tonight.

A woman brought her husband to me and said, "I want you to help my husband." I said, "I will." She said, "He has too many complaints to tell you of."

There is a man here so full of pain and weakness that I am going to pray for him on the authority of God's Word, and tomorrow night I am going to ask him to come back and tell you what God has done for him, and I placed my hand on him in the name of Jesus. The next night this man came walking straight, and he said, "Will you let me speak to these people tonight?"

"For 40 years I have had ulcers and running sores, and today is the first time that my clothes have been dry, and now I am a new man brothers and sisters, this is declared in the Word and wonderful things happen."

I had been speaking about divine healing, and six seats from the rear was a man with a boy and he lifted him up when I had finished, the boy was held together with irons, and his head, loins and shoulders were bandaged, the father handed him over to me.

There he put the irons down with the boy standing in them. I have never known what there is in the laying on of hands, let me give you a description of it. This boy was about nine years of age, and laying hands on him in the name of Jesus, there was perfect silence, when suddenly this boy cried out. "Dad it is going all over me," and I said, "Take the irons off." You say that is our power. No it is His power, no it is the Father you have received. Dare we be still and be quiet, the stones would cry out if we did.

Sometimes I go in for what they call wholesale healings. My son and daughter are here, and they can declare that they have seen 100 healed without the touch of a hand. I believe there is to be wholesale baptisms of the Holy Ghost. One day God told me something, at a place called Staranga in Norway.

I said to my interpreter, we are both very tired, we will rest today until 4 P.M., I can never forget the sight, this story has just occurred to me. May God bend your ears down, there is a hearing of Faith, a much higher Faith, may the Lord bend our ears.

We had been out for a short time, and coming back into the street I shall never forget the sight, the street was filled with all kinds of wheeled chairs, we went along up to the house, and the house was filled with people, and the woman said, "What can we do. The house is filled what are we to do?" So I pulled off my coat and I got to business. My brothers you ought to have been there, the power of God came like a cloud and people were healed on every side.

God healed all the people, this is what I have to tell you, we were sat down for a little refresher before the meeting, and the telephone bell rang. And the Pastor went to the telephone, and they said, "What can we do the great Town Hall is packed, come down as soon as you can," and this is what I mean by the hearing of Faith, I declare that the people could not have fallen down if they had wanted to, I never saw a place so packed, and I began to preach, and when I was preaching the voice came from the Lord. "Ask and I will give thee every soul." The voice came again, "Ask and I will give you every soul," and I dared to ask, "Give me every soul," and there was a breath came like the rushing of a mighty wind, and it shook everybody and fell on everyone. I have never seen anything like it.

I am hoping to see this in London, is there anything too hard for God, cannot God begin to do these things, will we let Him?

I know it might be a difficult thing, is it not possible to have a consecration tonight, who is there who will begin tonight and begin to act in the power of the Holy Ghost.

Published in *Redemption Tidings*

DARE TO BELIEVE GOD, THEN COMMAND!

May 1927

erily, verily, I say unto you, He that believeth on me, the works that I do shall he do also; and greater works than these shall he do; because I go unto my Father. And whatsoever ye shall ask in my name, that will I do, that the Father may be glorified in the Son. If ye shall ask any thing in my name, I will do it.

John 14:12-14

"He that believeth." What a word! God's Word changes us and we enter into fellowship and communion, into faith assurance and Godlikeness, for we saw the truth and believed. Faith is an operative power; God opens the understanding and reveals Himself. "Therefore it is of faith, that it might be by grace..." (Romans 4:16). Grace is God's benediction coming down to you. You open the door to God, which is an act of faith, and God does all you want.

Jesus drew the hearts of the people to Himself; they came to Him with all of their needs and He relieved them all. He talked to men, He healed the sick, relieved the oppressed, and cast out demons. "The works that I do shall he do also." "He that believeth on Me...." The essence of divine life is in us by faith. He that believeth — it will come to pass; we become supernatural by the power of God. If you believe, the power of the enemy cannot stand, for God's Word is against him. Jesus gives us His Word to make faith effectual. Whatsoever ye desire, if you can believe in your heart you begin to say; whatever you dare to say shall be done. He shall have whatsoever he saith after he believes in his heart (Mark 11:23,24). Dare to believe and then dare to speak, for you shall have whatsoever you say if you doubt not.

Some time ago in England, the power of God was on the meeting, and I was telling the people they could be healed. If they would rise up I would pray for them and the Lord would heal them. There was a man with broken ribs healed. Then a little girl fourteen years old said, "Will you pray for me?" "Mother," she said, "I am being healed." She had straps on her feet three and one-half inches deep. These were removed and God healed her right away. Dare to believe God, and it shall be as you believe. Amen.

Published in *Triumphs of Faith*

HEALING TESTIMONIES
May 1927

The healings at the meetings have been blessed. At every meeting the sick were invited to remain, but in many of the meetings Brother Wigglesworth would pray for all who would stand up and believe that the Lord would heal them. At other times he would ask any who had pain to stand up and he prayed for them from the platform.

A lady stood saying she had pain in her head, and gallstones causing suffering. When Brother Wigglesworth prayed, the power of the Spirit came upon her.

Healed of a tumor in hospital. Handkerchief taken from the evangelist and laid on the sick.

Mrs. Ingram writes of a visit to a hospital, taking a handkerchief with her. Her friend was to be operated on on Monday. On Wednesday when she visited her, her friend told her that she had been on the operating table and the ether had been administered. When she came to herself she discovered they had not operated because they said there was no need now for the operation. She was able to get up and the swelling was all gone.

High blood pressure. Mrs. A. Lavery, of Collingwood writes, "I thank God for the blessed healing power. Hands were laid on my head; I had blood pressure pains in my head for one year and six months night and day. I know I am healed."

Displaced kidneys, running ear. Mrs. Green, 23 Hardy Street, East Brunswick, testifies, "I had mastoid trouble in my ear, and general weakness through my body, both of my kidneys have dropped an inch. I suffered terribly, but had relief when prayed for. My ear was discharging, now I am free."

Broken ribs, broken collar bone, pierced lungs. Mr. R. Eddison, 155 Hoddle Street, West Richmond, was injured in a car accident in 1926. He had his ribs broken, lungs pierced, and collar bone broken. He was in the hospital three weeks; had suffered much pain for three months, until prayed for in the meeting.

A woman who had been ill in bed sixteen weeks, was raised up by the Lord, baptized in water later, and the day following received the baptism of the Holy Spirit.

A dying baby was healed.

A woman who had suffered pain in her legs for eleven years was set free.

Mrs. Rose Jesule writes, "The Lord touched my body in the audience, and I am free."

Another writes, "I have received the second handkerchief which you prayed over, and the Lord is blessing. This cancer is slowly drying up. I have had no more hemorrhages and the terrible odor is leaving. Praise the Lord."

Meetings in Richmond Temple, Melbourne, Australia
Published in *Triumphs of Faith*

 "Be not afraid, only believe" (Mark 5:36).

This is one of those marvelous truths of the Scriptures that is written for our help, that we may believe as we see the almightiness of God and also our privilege, not only to enter in by faith, but to become partakers of the blessing He

BE NOT AFRAID, ONLY BELIEVE

July 16, 1927

wants to give us. My message is on the lines of faith. Because some do not hear in faith, it profits them nothing. There is a hearing of faith and a hearing which means nothing more than listening to words. I beseech you to see to it that everything done may bring not only blessing to you but strength and character, and that you may be able to see the goodness of God in this meeting.

I want to impress upon you the importance of believing what the Scripture says, and I may have many things to relate about people who dared to believe God until it came to pass. This is a wonderful Word. In fact, all of the Word of God is wonderful. It is an everlasting Word, a Word of power, a Word of health, a Word of substance, a Word of life. It gives life into the very nature, to everyone that lays hold of it, if he believes. I want you to understand that there is a need for the Word of God. But it is a need, many times, that brings us the blessing. What am I here for? Because God delivered me when no other hand could do it. I stand before you as one who was given up by everybody, when no one could help. I was earnest and zealous for the salvation of souls. If you were in Bradford (England), you would know. We had police protection for nearly twenty years in the best thoroughfare in the city, and in my humble way with my dear wife, who was all on fire for God, we were ministering in the open air. Full of zeal? Yes. But one night, thirty years ago, I was carried home helpless. We knew very little about divine healing, but we prayed through. It is thirty years and more since God healed me. I am sixty-eight years old and fresher, in better health, and more fit for work than I was at that time. It is a most wonderful experience when the life of God becomes the life of man. The divine power that sweeps through the organism, cleaning the blood, makes the man fresh every day. The life of God is resurrection power.

When they brought me home helpless we prayed all night. We did all we knew. At ten o'clock the next morning I said to my wife, "This must be my last roll call." We had five children around us. I tell you it was not an easy thing to face our circumstances. I told my wife to do as she thought best but the poor thing didn't know what to do. She called a physician who examined me, shook his head and said, "It is impossible for anything to be done for your husband; I am absolutely helpless. He has appendicitis and you have waited too long. His system will not stand an operation. A few hours, at best, will finish him."

What the doctor said was true. He left her and said he would come back again but he couldn't give her any hope. When he was nicely out of the house an old lady and a young man who knew how to pray came in. The young man put his knees on the bed and said: "Come out, you devil, in the name of Jesus." It was a good job, we had no time for argument, and instantly I was free. Oh, hallelujah! I was as free as I am now. I never believed that any person ought to be in bed in the daytime and I jumped up and went downstairs. My wife said: "Oh, are you up?" "I'm all right, wife; it is all right now," I said. I had some men working for me and she said none of them had turned up that morning, so I picked up my tools and went to work. Then the doctor came. He walked up the stairs and my wife called, "Doctor, doctor, he is out!" "What?" he said. "Yes," she said, "He is out at work." "Oh," he said, "you will never see him alive again. They will bring him in a corpse." Am I a corpse? Oh, when God does anything it is done forever! And God wants you to know that He wants to do something in you forever. I have laid my hands on people with appendicitis when the doctors were in the place, and God has healed them.

I will tell you one incident before I pass on. It will stir up your faith. I am not here to be on exhibition. I am here to impart divine truth to you concerning the Word of God that after I leave you can do the same thing. I went to Switzerland and after I had been there for some weeks, a brother said, "Will you not go to meeting tonight?" "No," I said, "I have been at it all this time, you can take charge tonight." "What shall we do?" he asked. "Do?" I said, "Paul the apostle, left people to do the work and passed on to another place — I have been here long enough now, you do the work." So he went to the meeting. When he came back he said, "We have had a wonderful time." "What happened?" He said: "I invited them all out, took off my coat, and rolled up my sleeves, and prayed and they were all healed. I did just like you did." Jesus says, "I give unto you power over all the power of the enemy" (Luke 10:19). They entered into the houses and healed the sick that were therein. The ministry of divine operation in us is wonderful, but who would take upon himself to say, "I can do this or that?" If it is God, it is all right, but if it is yourself, it is all wrong. When you are weak, then you are strong. When you are strong in your own strength, you are weak. You must realize this and live only in the place where the power of God rests upon you, and where the Spirit moves within you. Then God will mightily manifest His power and you will know as Jesus said, "The Spirit of the Lord is upon me."

God brings a remarkable, glorious fact to our minds tonight, the healing of a little helpless girl. The physicians had failed. The mother said to the father: "There is only one hope — if you can see Jesus! As sure as you can meet Jesus our daughter will live." Do you think it is possible for anybody anywhere to go looking for Jesus without seeing Him? Is it possible to think about Jesus without Jesus drawing near? No. This man knew the power there was in the name of Jesus: "...In my name shall they cast out devils..." (Mark 16:17). But we must be sure we know that name, for in Acts 19 the seven sons of Sceva said to the man possessed with devils, "We adjure you by Jesus whom Paul preached to come out" (v. 13). The evil spirit said, "I know Paul and I know Jesus, but who are you?" (v. 15). Yes, the devil knows every believer — and the seven sons of Sceva nearly lost their lives. The evil powers came upon them and they barely escaped. It is more than repeating the name; it is the nature of the name in you; it is more than that; it is the divine personality within the human life which has come to take up His abode in you, and when He becomes all in all then God works through you. It is the life, the power of God. God works through the life.

The Lord is that life, and the ministry of it and the power in the ministry, but the Holy Spirit brings everybody in such a place of divine relationship that He mightily lives in us and enables us to overcome the powers of the enemy. The Lord healed that child as they got a vision of Jesus. The word of the Lord came not with observation but with divine, mighty power, working in them until by the power of the Spirit, men and women were created anew by this new life divine. We have to see that when this divine Word comes to us by the power of the Holy Ghost, it is according to the will of God that we speak, not with men's wisdom, but with divine minds operated by the Word of God; not channels only, but as oracles of the Spirit.

As the ruler of the synagogue sought Jesus he worshiped Him. How they gathered around Him! How everybody listened to what He had to say! He spoke not as a scribe, but with authority and power, decked with divine glory. A young man was preaching in a marketplace. At the close of the address some atheist came and said, "There have been five Christs. Tell us which one it is that you preach." He answered, **"The Christ that rose from the dead."** There is only One that rose from the dead. There is only one Jesus who lives. And as He lives, we live also. Glory to God! We are risen with Him, are living with Him, and will reign with Him.

This ruler, as he drew near the crowd, went up to Him and said, "Jesus, my daughter lieth at the point of death. Come and lay thy hands upon her, and she will be healed." [And Jesus went with him.] (See Mark 5:23,24.) What a beautiful assurance. But as they were coming along the road, a woman met them who had an issue of blood for twelve years. When she began with this trouble she sought many physicians. She had some money, but the physicians took it all, and left her worse than they found her. Have you any that do the same thing around here? When I was a plumber I had to finish my work before I got the money, and I didn't always get it then. I think that if there was an arrangement whereby no doctor got his fee until he cured the patient, there wouldn't be so many people die. Twelve years of sickness this woman had. She needed someone now who could heal without money, for she was bankrupt and helpless. Jesus comes to people that are withered up, diseased, lame, crippled in all kinds of ways, and when He comes there is liberty to the captive, opening of eyes to the blind, and the opening of ears to the deaf. Many had said to this woman, "If you had only been with us today. We saw the most marvelous things, the crooked made straight, the lame to walk, the blind to see" — and the woman twelve years sick said, "Oh, you make me feel that if I could only see Him I should be healed." It strengthened her faith and it became firm. She had a purpose within her. Faith is a mighty power. Faith will reach at everything. When real faith comes into operation you will not say, "I don't feel much better." Faith says, "I am whole." Faith doesn't say, "It's a lame leg." Faith says, "My leg is all right." Faith never sees a goiter.

A young woman with a goiter came to be prayed for. In a testimony meeting she said, "I do praise the Lord for healing my goiter." She went home and said to her mother, "Oh Mother, when the man prayed for me, God healed my goiter." For twelve months she went about telling everybody how God healed her goiter. Twelve months afterward I was in the same place and people said, "How big that lady's goiter is!" There came a time for testimony. She jumped up and said, "I was here twelve months ago and God healed me of my goiter. Such a marvelous twelve months!" when she went home her folks said, "You should have seen the people today when you testified that God had healed your goiter. They think there is something wrong with you. If you go upstairs and look in the glass you will see the goiter is bigger than ever it was." She went upstairs, but she didn't look in the glass. She got down on her knees and said, "O Lord, let all the people know just as You have let me know, how wonderfully You have healed me." The next morning her neck was as perfect as any neck you ever saw. Faith never looks. Faith praises God — it is done!

This poor, helpless woman who had been growing weaker and weaker for twelve years pushed into the crowded thoroughfare when she knew Jesus was in the midst. She was stirred to the depths, and she pushed through and touched Him. If you will believe God and touch Him, you will be healed at once. Jesus is the Healer!

Now listen! Some people put the touch of the Lord in the place of faith. The Lord would not have that woman believe that the touch had done it. She felt as soon as she touched Him that virtue had gone through her, which is true. When the people were bitten by fiery serpents in the wilderness, God's Word said through Moses, "He that looketh shall be healed." The look made it possible for God to do it. Did the touch heal the woman? No. The touch meant something more — it was a living faith. Jesus said, "...thy faith hath made thee whole..." (Mark 5:34). If God would just move on us to believe, there wouldn't be a sick person who could not receive healing. As soon as this woman in the street, with all the crowd about her, began to testify, the devil came. The devil is always in a testimony meeting. When the sons of God gathered together in the time of Job, he was there.

While this was happening in the street, [a] person came rushing from the house of Jairus and said, "There is no use now, your daughter is dead. This Jesus can do nothing for a dead daughter. Your wife needs you at home." But Jesus said, "Be not afraid, only believe" (Mark 5:36). He speaks the word just in time! Jesus is never behind time. When the tumult is the worst, the pain the most severe, the cancer gripping the body, then the word comes, "Only believe." When everything seems as though it will fail, and is practically hopeless, the Word of God comes to us, "Only believe."

When Jesus came to that house there were a lot of people weeping and wailing. I have taken my last wreath to the cemetery. To be absent from the body is to be present with the Lord, and if you believe that, you will never take another wreath to the cemetery. It is unbelief that mourns. If you have faith that they are with the Lord, you will never take another flower to the grave. They are not there. Hallelujah!

These people were round about, weeping, wailing, and howling. He says, "Why make you this to-do? The maid is not dead, but sleepeth" (Mark 5:39). There is a wonderful word that God wants you to hear. Jesus said, "I am the resurrection, and the life..." (John 11:25). The believer may fall asleep, but the believer doesn't die. Oh, that people would understand the deep things of God — it would change the whole situation. It makes you look out with a glorious hope to the day when the Lord shall come. What does it say? "They that sleep will God bring with Him." Jesus knew that. "The maid is not dead, but sleepeth; and they laughed him to scorn" (vv. 39,40). To show the insincerity of these wailers, they could turn from wailing to laughing. Jesus took the father and the mother of the maid and, going into the room where she was, took her hand and said, "Daughter, arise." And the child sat up. Praise the Lord! And He said, "Give her something to eat."

Oh, the remarkableness of our Lord Jesus! I want to impress upon you the importance of realizing that He is in the midst. No person need be without the knowledge that they are not only saved, but that God can live in these bodies. You are begotten the moment you believe, unto a lively hope. "He that believeth **hath eternal life**." You have eternal life the moment you believe. The first life is temporal, natural, material, but in the new birth you exist as long as God — forever — we are begotten by an incorruptible power, by the Word of God. The new birth is unto righteousness, begotten by God the moment that you believe. God always saves through the heart. He that believeth in the heart and confesseth with his mouth shall be saved.

Jesus is here tonight to loose them that are bound. If you are suffering in your body. He will heal you now as we pray. He is saying to every sin-sick soul, to every disease-smitten one. "Be not afraid, only believe."

Published in *The Pentecostal Evangel*

ut I tell you of a truth, there be some stand-ing here, which shall not taste of death, till they see the kingdom of God.

Luke 9:27

ABIDING

August 1927

How God fascinates me with His Word. I read and read and read, and there is always something new, and as I get deeper into the knowledge of the Bridegroom, I hear the voice of Jesus saying, "The bride rejoices to hear the Bridegroom's voice." The Word is His voice, and the nearer we are to Jesus, the more we understand the principles of His mission. He came to take for Himself a people for His bride, He came to find a body.

God's message to us tonight is that Jesus is going to take out a bride unto Himself. So while we are here to talk about salvation, there are deeper truths God wants to show us. It is not only to be saved, but there is an eternal destiny in the plan of God for us. The wonders of His glory, that in the ages to come we may share with Him. God has given us this blessed revelation, how He lived and loved and said these words. "Some of you shall not see death until you have seen the kingdom of God come in power."

Jesus, who could pray until He was transfigured, until His face did shine as the sun and His raiment became white and glistening. Praise God, He also said, "I have power to lay down My life, I have power to take it again" (John 10:18). By wicked hands He was taken and crucified, but He was willing, for He had all power, and could have called on legions of angels to deliver Him. But His purpose was to save us and bring us into fellowship and oneness with Himself, that the same life principles might be ours. Jesus never looked back, He never withheld. He went through death that His life might be our portion in time and in eternity. Our Lord Jesus Christ, the at-one-ment for the whole world, the Son of God, the sinner's friend. He was wounded for our transgressions. He lived to manifest, to bring forth the glory of God on earth. He gives His disciples the glory He had with the Father before the world was. He said, "I have given them the glory that Thou gavest Me" (John 17:22).

So God today is giving grace and glory, no good thing will He withhold from them that walk uprightly. Health, peace, joy in the Holy Ghost, a life in Christ Jesus. In! In! In! Are you in? It is wonderful, lovely, shall we ever go back to Egypt? Shall we look back? Never! Oh, you need not look for me down in Egypt's sand, for I have pitched my tent far up in Beulah land.

There is redemption for all through the blood of Jesus, which is heaven on earth, joy and peace in the Holy Ghost. A change from darkness to light, from the power of Satan unto God. To be made sons, heirs and joint heirs with Christ. Three times God rent the heavens with the Word. This is My beloved Son in Whom I am well pleased. Yes, it is true He was born in Bethlehem, that He worked as a carpenter, He took upon Himself flesh and God indwelt that flesh and manifested His glory, so that He was a perfect overcomer. He kept the law and fulfilled His commission, so that He could redeem us by laying down His life. Jesus was manifested in the flesh to destroy the power of the devil. God's specimen to show us that what He had done for and in Jesus, He could do for and in us.

He can make us overcomers, destroying the power of sin and indwelling us by His mighty power, transforming us until we love righteousness and hate iniquity, so that we can be holy. We receive sonship because of His obedience. He learned obedience by the things He suffered. His family said He was beside Himself. The scribes said, "He hath a devil and casts out devils by Beelzebub the prince of devils." In the synagogue they reviled Him and would have thrown Him over the cliff, but He, passing through their midst, seeing a blind man, He healed him.

Jesus is God's speciality, meditate on the beatitudes, the attributes and divine position Jesus manifested. It is a new creation, a birth unto righteousness by faith in the Atonement, transforming and changing you till you are controlled, dominated, and filled with the Spirit of Jesus. Still in the body, governed by the Spirit, with fruit unto holiness and the end eternal life. He was a firstfruits for us. Oh, Lord, reveal Thyself unto this people, and give them unfeigned love and faith. Then you will stand persecution, ridicule, slander.

Christ loved you when you were yet sinners, and He seeks your love in return, imparting to you an inwrought love by the Holy Ghost, changing you from faith to faith, from glory to glory, for He shall see His seed, He shall prolong His days and the pleasure of the Lord shall prosper in His hand.

TONGUES AND INTERPRETATION: "Glory to God, the living shall praise Him, for out of the dust of the earth He has brought forth a harvest of souls, to praise Him for all eternity. He is seeing His seed, and the pleasure of the Lord is already prospering in His hand."

Yea, beloved, this is the day of the visitation of the Lord again in Adelaide. Look at Him tonight, you needy ones. As you gaze upon Him you will be changed, a strength will come to you, you will exchange strength. He is the God of Jacob, the God of the helpless and undone. The devil had a big play with Jacob, but there was one thing Jacob knew. *knew*. He knew that God would fulfil His promise. God had at Bethel, let him see the ladder, where the angels began at bottom and went to the top. Bethel, the place of prayer, the place of changing conditions, earthly entering heaven. God had promised him and He brought him back to Bethel, but the same old Jacob was left, and as long as God allowed him to wrestle he wrestled. That is a type of holding on to this world. And God touched him. God has a way to touch us. Jacob cried, "Don't go till you have blessed me." God will bless you there. A place of helplessness and brokenness, there God will meet *you*. Have you been there?

Jesus came down from the mount of transfiguration and set right forward to fulfil His commission for you and me. From the glory to the cross. At the foot of the mount the man cried, "Here is my son, I brought him to thy disciples." Oh, God, take away unbelief! "Oh, faithless generation, how long must I suffer you. Bring him to Me." Jesus cast out the evil spirit. Even in the Master's presence the evil spirit tore the boy and left him as one dead. Satanic power. May God keep us in Himself where Satan has no power or victory. Has He come to you, has the Comforter come to you? The Lord will rebuke the world of sin when the Comforter comes to you. Be ye transformed. Let Jesus come aboard. He that has received Christ and the power of the Spirit, healing will abide, life will abide. No man can keep himself, the weak is capable if he is in Christ Jesus. Are you willing to surrender yourselves to Christ, that Satan shall have no dominion over you, in Jesus' name I ask you? Let us pray.

> The power of God is just the same today,
> It does not matter what the people say,
> Whatever God has promised He is able to perform,
> For the power of God is just the same today. Amen.

Address given at Adelaide, Australia

ow exhaustless is the treasure house of the Most High! How near God is to us when we are willing to draw nigh! And how He comes with refreshings to us when our hearts are attuned and desire Him only, for the desires of the righteous shall be granted.

GOD'S TREASURE HOUSE

August 1927

God has for us today a stimulation of divine acquaintance, a life divine to flow through our being that shall be sufficient for us in all times of need. When God is for you, who can be against you? What a blessed assurance this is to the hungry heart. How it thrills one to the very depths of their soul.

My heart's desire is that I bring you again to a banquet. That wonderful reserve, that great blessed day of appointment for us with the King, that we may believe that all the precious promises are yea and amen to us as we dare believe.

Oh, to believe God! Oh, to rest upon what He says, for there is not one jot or tittle of the Word which shall fail till all is fulfilled! Has He not promised and will He not also perform? Our blessed Lord of life and glory impressed upon us before He left that He would send the Comforter and when He came He should take the words of Jesus and He would pray through us and whatsoever we would ask, the Lord would hear us.

So I want you to get in a definite place, daring to ask God for something that shall be the means of stimulating your life forever.

Are you ready? You say, "What for?" To have some of the promises fulfilled.

Are you ready? "What for?" That God shall this day so clothe you with the Spirit that there shall be nothing within that shall war against the Spirit. Are you ready? Search your heart diligently.

Are you ready? "What for?" That you may know the Word of God, that they that dwell and live in the Spirit of God are kept in perfect condition of no condemnation.

I am so desirous that you should get so stimulated with prospective condition, then come into a realizing condition, because that is what God wants you to have; to get so moved by the power of God to believe that the things that you hear shall be yours.

So many people miss a great many things because they are always on the line of thinking it was for someone else. I want you to know that God's Word is for you, and you are to make a personal application for all there is in the Scriptures.

I do not believe the Scriptures are for pastors, teachers, evangelists, prophets, apostles; but they are for the whole body of Christ, for it is the Body that has to be the epistle of Christ. So the Word of God has to abound in you till you are absolutely built and fixed upon the living Word.

ALL GIFTS FOR EDIFICATION

I am going to read again the fourteenth chapter of First Corinthians, the twelfth verse, because I want to make it the keynote of all that is spoken.

> *Even so ye, forasmuch as ye are zealous of spiritual gifts, seek that*
> *ye may excel to the edifying of the church.*

Keep that definitely before your mind, because whatever happens in a service it means nothing to me without it is to edification or comfort or consolation.

God wants to make you worthy of His wonderful name; only you must always understand that all the gifts and graces of the Spirit are most helpful to you as you are a blessing to others. *The Holy Ghost came not to exalt you, but that you should exalt the Lord.*

Before these services are over I shall be able to tell you definitely how to receive a gift, then how to use a gift or how to be in a place where the gift can be used. We should cover much ground because the Spirit is going to speak. If I use my own reasoning, you won't be edified. There is only one edification that is going to last, and it is the spiritual, inward revelation of Christ. *Mind matter is no good without it is spiritually quickened through the heart affections.* So let us remember it is more important that we should be filled with the Holy Ghost, that the Spirit should have its perfect control and way, than that we should be filled with knowledge to no profit. "Knowledge puffeth up, a little knowledge is dangerous" — in fact, all knowledge is in very great danger without it is balanced in a perfect place where God has the controlling position.

BE NOT IGNORANT

Reviewing the first few verses of the twelfth chapter of First Corinthians, we find the Holy Ghost is speaking. He would not have you ignorant concerning spiritual gifts, he says. *You are not to be ignorant of the best gift God has arranged for you.* You are to come into possession. It is a will that has been left by God's Son. He rose to carry it out, and He is on the throne to carry out His own will. His will is that you should be filled with all the fulness of God. Wonderful will!

The next thought is that because we are Gentiles God has entrusted to us the proclamation of the Gospel in the power and demonstration of the Spirit, that we may not speak with man's wisdom, but by the oracles of the operation of God.

So the Holy Ghost is to make us ready for every perfect work, and so ready that opportunities are taken advantage of. Just as much as if He were in the world, we must be in the world, ready for the glorious, blessed anointing and equipment for service, that the power of hell shall not prevail but we may bind the powers of Satan. We are in a great position to be occupied with him.

SPIRITUAL INTERPRETATION

The Spirit Himself bringeth forth light and truth to edify and build up the Church in the most holy faith, that we might be ready for all activity in God. For the Spirit of the Lord is upon us to bring forth that which God has declared and ordained, that we should go forth bearing precious fruit, and come forth rejoicing, singing, and harvesting together.

Oh, to keep in the covenant place where you are hidden in Christ, where He alone is superseding, controlling, leading, directing, and causing you to live only for the glory of God!

WORD OF GOD UNCHANGEABLE

We pass on to the third verse, "No man can call Jesus accursed by the Holy Ghost."

Don't forget that you are entrusted with the Word of life, which speaks to you as the truth. Jesus was the Way, the Truth, and the Life, and He declared eternal life by the operation of the Gospel; for we receive immortality and life by the Gospel. Seeing these things are so, you can understand that for them that receive the life of Christ, they pass out of condemnation into eternal life.

But what about those that do not? Still under condemnation, without hope and without God in the world, and in danger of eternal destruction. God save them!

Don't get away from the fact, Jesus is the personality of eternal death and of eternal life. Hell fire will never be changed by what men say about it. Hell fire will be the same forever. You will never change the Word of God by men's opinions. The Word of God is fixed forever.

The Lord wants you to be in a great place, the Holy Ghost having such control of your inner eyes to reveal the fulness of the Lord of life, till Jesus is magnified tremendously by the revelation of the Holy Ghost, till He becomes Lord over all things, over your affections, your will, your purposes, your plans, and your wishes forever. Let Him be Lord.

SPIRITUAL INTERPRETATION

For when the Lord changes the situation, then thou dost come out of the hiding of captivity into the fulness of the revelation of the blaze of His glory, for when He has molded thee then He can build thee and change thee till He is having His way.

CHANGED FROM GLORY TO GLORY

It is a great purpose that God has for us that we can be changed, and you are in a great place when you are willing to have this change take place. You are in a greater place when you are willing to drop everything that has brought you to where you thought you could not be changed, and when you have dropped all things that have hindered you, you have leaped forth and been tremendously changed.

If you have held anything on a human plane, no matter how it has come, if it is not according to the biblical standard of the Word of God let it be weeded out. If you do not get it weeded out, there is a time coming that wood, hay, and stubble will be burned and the gold, the silver, and the precious stones will stand the fire.

Lots of people would like to know what kind of crown they will have when they get to glory. Well, the Lord will take everything that could not be burnt by the fire and make your own crown; so everybody is forming his own crown. Now you be careful not to be all wood, hay, and stubble. Have something left for the crown. There is a crown of life that fadeth not away that I am trying to help you to build for today.

God Particularizes

God has a particularizing way of meeting particular people of today. We all so vary, in our faces, in our make-up, so God has a way to particularize a gift that would fit you perfectly so that you will not be lopsided. I am trusting the Lord to help me to build you without having lop sides.

Be Not Lopsided

Lots of people have good things — but. Lots of people might be very remarkably used — but. Lots of people might soar into wonderful places of divine positions with God — but. And it is the "but" that spoils it.

Some people have a very good gift — all the gifts of God are good — but because the gift has been made a blessing they transgress with the same gift and speak in tongues longer than they ought to. So it is the "but" in the way that is spoiling the best.

Some people have prophecy, very wonderful prophecy, but there is a "but." They have prophesied and the Lord has been with them in the prophecy, but because the people have applauded them in the prophecy they have gone beyond divine prophecy and used their own human mind, and the "but" has spoiled them till they do not want the hidden prophecy.

Mrs. So-and-so has a wonderful testimony and we all like to hear her for three minutes, but we are all sick of it if she goes on five minutes. Why so? There is a "but" about it.

Brother So-and-so kindles fire in every prayer meeting he begins in, but after about five minutes all the people say, "I wish he would stop," and there is a "but" there.

It is because of the lopsidedness of people I want to speak advisedly that you do not transgress. Do not use divine liberty to spoil God's position; but be wise and the Lord will make you to understand what it means. Be wise.

When you say that you have been baptized with the Holy Ghost people look and say, "Well, if that be so, there ought to be something very beautiful."

Yes, it is true, and if there is something which is shady, something uncanny, not expressing the glory or grace, the meekness or the love of Christ, there is a "but" about it and the "but" is that you have not really got your own human spirit under control by the divine Spirit, the human is mingled and it is spoiling the divine.

Now, a word for the wise is sufficient, and if you are not wise after you have heard, it shows that you are foolish. Do not be foolish: be wise!

"Let not your goodness be evil spoken of." God wants people in these days who are so fortified, so built in Christ that they need not be ashamed.

SPIRITUAL INTERPRETATION

For it is God who hath called thee for His own purpose. It is Christ who ordained thee, and being ordained by Christ we go forth to bring forth much fruit, and God is being glorified when our anointing or our covenant with Christ is being reserved for God only and we live and move for the glory of the exhibition of Christ. Then that is the place where Jesus is highly honored, and when you pray God is glorified in the Son, and when you preach the unction abideth and the Lord bringeth forth blessing upon the hearers.

DIVERSITIES OF GIFTS

In the fourth to seventh verses of the twelfth chapter of First Corinthians you notice very remarkable words. In these verses we are dealing with the Spirit, with the Lord, and with God, every one of them in cooperation with this position.

> *Now there are diversities of gifts, but the same Spirit. And there are differences of administrations, but the same Lord. And there are diversities of operations, but it is the same God which worketh all in all. But the manifestation of the Spirit is given to every man to profit withal.*
>
> *1 Corinthians 12:4-7*

There are diversities, varieties of gifts which truly are to be in the believer. There are nine gifts and I would like you to notice that they never interfere with the gifts that Jesus gave. If you turn to Ephesians 4, you will find there that Jesus has gifts, but you won't find them in the twelfth chapter of First Corinthians. They are not there, because when we are dealing with the twelfth chapter of First Corinthians we are dealing with the gifts the Holy Ghost has; but when we read Ephesians 4, we are dealing with the gifts Jesus has.

Let us look at them. How beautifully He arranges the thing.

> *...When he ascended up on high, he led captivity captive, and gave gifts unto men.*
>
> *Ephesians 4:8*

Paul was in captivity. How do we know? Because Paul describes his position as the chief of sinners — and as long as we know the chief of sinners has been saved, every man that ever lives can be saved. The chief of sinners, and he was led captive when he was mad with indignation against the disciples when he was rushing everywhere to apprehend them and put them in prison and make them blaspheme that same name.

Paul was in captivity, Jesus took him out of captivity and took him into captivity, and gave him gifts.

Jesus has already made disciples, has gone up on high leading captivity captive, then He is giving gifts.

> *And he gave some, apostles; and some, prophets; and some, evangelists; and some, pastors and teachers; For the perfecting of the saints, for the work of the ministry, for the edifying of the body of Christ.*
>
> *Ephesians 4:11,12*

This is the divine position of our Lord, giving gifts to those He has in captivity.

Now who do you think is likely most to be in captivity in this meeting? The people who are lost in God, hidden.

Baptizing in water is an emblem of death and the moment a person is immersed in the water, he is lifted out. But not so with the baptism with the Holy Spirit. To be baptized in the Holy Ghost is every day to be deeper in, never lifted out, never coming out; in captivity, ready for gifts.

Now, is a person made a prophet or an apostle or a teacher before the baptism or after? I want to speak to you very definitely and I want you to keep in mind what the Spirit shall say to us at this time.

EPISTLES ARE ONLY FOR BAPTIZED CHRISTIANS

When I went to New Zealand, the power of God was very present and God did wonderfully work miracles and wonders there, and the gift that laid hold of the whole place was the gift of tongues and interpretation. It moved the whole of that city till the place which held 3,500 often was overcrowded and we had 2,000 and 3,000 people who could not get in.

Now when the Plymouth Brethren, who knew the Word of God, saw the grace of God upon me they wanted to have some conversation with me; so I gave them an audience and eighteen of them came.

As soon as they began they said, "Well, we know God is with you; it is a clear proof."

(In ten days we had 2,000 people saved and we had 1,500 of those young converts sit down to breaking bread; and it was the Plymouth Brethren who served us the wine and the bread.)

"Now," they said, "we want to examine the truth with you to see where things stand."

I said, "All right, brethren."

In a moment or two they were quoting to me the Ephesians.

"But," I said, "Beloved, you know better than anybody that the man that climbs up some other way is a thief and a robber, don't you? How many times have you preached that? Jesus is the door, and everyone entering that way shall be saved. What does it mean? Jesus is Truth."

They continued quoting to me the Ephesians.

"But, Brethren," said I, "you have no right to Ephesians; you have no right to the epistles. The epistles are not for you. You are climbing up some other way."

Without fear of contradiction, on the authority of God, I say today, there is no person in this place who has a right to the epistles until they have gone through the Acts of the Apostles and received the Holy Ghost.

They said I could not prove it. I said, "I can prove it very easily."

And I read,

> *For he that speaketh in an unknown tongue speaketh not unto men, but unto God: for no man understandeth him; howbeit in the spirit he speaketh mysteries.*

1 Corinthians 14:2

"Now," I said, "Brethren, tell me if you understand that."

They said, "No."

"Simply because you have never received the Holy Ghost. Every person who receives the Holy Ghost receives that, speaking unto God by the Spirit.

"The gospels are the Gospel of the Kingdom. The Acts of the Apostles are where people see water baptism, sanctification, and also see the fulfilled receiving of the Holy Ghost. *So the moment you pass through the Acts of the Apostles you are ready for the epistles, for the epistles are written to baptized believers.*"

"I will prove it another way," I said, and read Romans 8:26-27:

> *Likewise the Spirit also helpeth our infirmities: for we know not what we should pray for as we ought: but the Spirit itself maketh intercession for us with groanings which cannot be uttered. And he that searcheth the hearts knoweth what is the mind of the Spirit, because he maketh intercession for the saints according to the will of God.*
>
> Romans 8:26,27

Here is another distinct position of a man filled with the Holy Ghost. That is not the Spirit of Christ, that is the Holy Spirit. There is quite a difference between the Spirit of Christ and the Holy Spirit.

SPIRITUAL INTERPRETATION

For the Lord Himself is the chief director of all truth, for He is the Way and the Truth; and therefore the Spirit taketh the Word, which is Christ, and reveals it unto us, for He is the life by the Word. "He that heareth my word and believeth on him that sent me hath everlasting life." Jesus is the Way, Jesus is the Truth, Jesus is the Life.

GRACES AND BEATITUDES OF THE SPIRIT

The Holy Spirit is jealous over you. The Holy Spirit has a godly jealousy over you. Why? Lest you should turn to yourself. He wants you entirely to exhibit the Lord.

So He girds you, sees to you in every way that you will not be drawn aside by human desires but Jesus shall become the Alpha and Omega in all your desires.

Now to this end the Spirit knoweth the great hunger of the heart. What for? Gifts, graces, beatitudes.

Oh, it is lovely when we can be so we can only pray in the Holy Ghost!

Praying in the Spirit

I am going to give you a very important word about what is the use of praying in the Spirit. Lots of people are still without an understanding as to what it is to pray in the Spirit. In First Corinthians the fourteenth chapter and the fifteenth verse we read:

> ...*I will pray with the spirit, and I will pray with the understanding also: I will sing with the spirit, and I will sing with the understanding also.*

I am going to tell you a story that will help you to see how necessary it is that you should be so lost in the Holy Ghost order that you should pray in the Holy Ghost.

Our work in the center of Africa was opened by Brothers Burton and Salter, the latter my daughter's husband. He is now there in Congo. When they went there, there were four of them, an old man wanting to go to help them build, a young man was led believing it was a call. The old man died on the road and the young man turned back, so there were only two left.

They worked and labored; God was with them in a wonderful way. But Burton took sick and all hopes were gone.

Fevers are tremendous there, mosquitoes swarm, great evils are there.

There he was, laid out; there was no hope. They covered him over, went outside very sorrowful because he truly was a pioneer missionary. They were in great distress and uttered words like this: "He has preached his last sermon."

When they were in that position, without any provocation whatever, Brother Burton stood right in the midst of them. He had arisen from his bed and walked outside and stood in the midst of them. They were astonished and asked how and what had happened.

All he could say was that he was awakened out of deep sleep with a warm thrill over his head right down his body and out of [his] toes.

"I feel so well," he said. "I don't know anything about my sickness." But the mystery still held. Later when he was over in England visiting, a lady said to him: "Brother Burton, do you keep a diary?"

He said, "Yes."

"Don't open the diary," she said, "until I talk with you."

"All right."

This is the story she told.

"On a certain time on a certain day the Spirit of the Lord moved upon me. I was so moved by the power of the Spirit that I went into a place alone to pray. As I went there, believing that just as usual I was going to open my mouth and pray, the Spirit lay hold of me and I was praying in the Spirit — not with understanding, but praying in the Spirit.

"As I prayed, I saw right into Africa, and I saw you laid out helpless, and to all appearances apparently dead. I prayed on, until the Spirit lifted me and I knew I was in victory, and I saw you had risen up from that bed.

"Look at your diary, will you?"

He looked in the diary and found it exactly the same day.

So there are revivals to come, there are wonderful things to be done when we can be lost till the Spirit prays through.

SPIRITUAL INTERPRETATION

It is only He, it is He who rolls away the cloud. He alone is the One who lifts the fallen, cheers the faint, brings fresh oil, and changes the countenance. It is the Lord thy God. He has seen thy misery, He has known thy heart brokenness, and He has known how near you seem to be to despair....

Oh, beloved, God is in the midst of us to help us into these wonderful divine places of appointment!

Are you ready? You say, "What for?" To let all differences cease and to have the same evidence they had in the Upper Room.

Are you ready? "What for?" To so be in the place for God's Son to be pleased that He gives you all the desire of your heart.

Are you ready? "What for?" That God can fill you with new life, stimulate you with new fire. He can inflame you with great desire. We are in the midst of blessing; I want you to be blessed.

Faith is the greatest positioner that brings us evidence.

Faith is that which will lift you into every place, if you do not interfere with it.

Don't forget you are in the presence of God. This day has to be covered with a greater day. It is not what you are, it is what you are intending to be.

If any person has spoken in tongues, believe it is your right and your privilege to have anything in the Bible. *Don't let your human mind interfere with the great plan of God. Submit yourself to God.*

May the divine likeness of Him who is the express image of the Father dwell in you richly, abounding through all, supplying every need, bringing you into a place where you know the hand of God is leading you from treasure to treasure, from grace to grace, from victory to victory, from glory unto glory, by the Spirit of the Lord.

Published in *The Bridal Call Foursquare*

f you do not let your heart be examined when the Lord comes with blessing or correction, if you do not make it a stepping stone, then you are receiving the grace of God in vain.

WORTHY SAYINGS

September 1927

People could be built far greater in the Lord and be more wonderfully established if they would move out sometimes and think over the grace of the Lord.

When you are in prayer, remember how near you are to the Lord. It is a time that God wants you to change strength there and He wants you to remember He is with you.

You must every day make higher ground. You must deny yourself to get on with God. You must refuse everything that is not pure and holy and separate. God wants you pure in heart. He wants your intense desire after holiness.

There is always a blessing where there is harmony. "One accord" is the keynote of the victory that is going to come to us all the time.

Remember this: you never lose so much as when you lose your peace.

There is no person ever able to talk about the victory over temptation without he goes through it. All the victories are won in battles.

Nothing but libraries make swelled heads, and nothing but the Library makes swelled hearts. You are to have swelled hearts, because out of the heart full of the fragrance of the love of God there issues forth the living life of the Lord.

od can so reserve you for Himself that the whole of your body shall be in operation of the Spirit.

* * *

The way into all the treasures of God's omnipotent portal is through the living Word of the Father.

* * *

WORTHY WORDS FROM WIGGLESWORTH
1927

The people who are the most sanguine about their salvation are those who have witnessed to it the most.

* * *

As soon as you reach a standard where you hate sin, victory is right over you.

* * *

There is one great plan the Lord is seeking thee for: it is to make thee like Himself that thee might be in the world as He was.

* * *

Put thyself into the Almighty Treasury, let Him save thee; God can make thee another person.

* * *

God can change even the most unlikely thing.

* * *

It is impossible for us to touch God on God's line of thought and not bring to pass.

* * *

We may have God's Spirit moving upon us till it is more than our meat and drink to see people saved by the power of God.

* * *

To ask anything for yourself as many as five times is unbelief. Get to the place where you ask and believe, that your joy might be full.

* * *

When we have nothing, we possess all things. It is absolutely at the end of us that God begins. When you come to a place where He alone girds you with strength, then all the promises are yours.

* * *

Be not afraid to ask, because God is on the throne waiting to answer your request.

* * *

Nothing will spoil your life like jealousy. It is cruel as the grave. It mars your spiritual vision.

* * *

It is the divine plan, and the divine will that we should live in the world triumphant over it, so the lust of the flesh and the pride of life will not control.

* * *

Only as men become Godlike and holy do they become real men.

* * *

I would rather be five minutes clothed upon with the Holy Ghost than have all the money there is in Los Angeles.

* * *

Sin has death in its sting; righteousness has heaven in its illumination.

* * *

We are in a lifting place. It is not what we are now: it is what God has designed for us.

* * *

I pray God that you may not lose the divine inheritance that God has chosen for you, greater than you could choose if you have all your mind ten times more largely exercised.

* * *

It is worth the world to be under the power of the Holy Ghost.

Quotes from sermons preached at Angelus Temple in Los Angeles, California

WILT THOU BE MADE WHOLE?

September 1927

I believe the Word of God is so powerful that it can transform any and every life. There is power in God's Word to make that which does not appear to appear. There is executive power in the Word that proceeds from His lips. The psalmist tells us, "He sent His word, and healed them..." (Psalm 107:20). And do you think that Word has diminished in its power? I tell you nay, but God's Word can bring things to pass today as of old.

The psalmist said, "Before I was afflicted I went astray: but now have I kept thy word" (Psalm 119:67). And again, "It is good for me that I have been afflicted; that I might learn thy statutes" (Psalm 119:71). And if our afflictions will bring us to the place where we see that we cannot live by bread alone, but must partake of every word that proceedeth out of the mouth of God, they will have served a blessed purpose.

REST ASSURED

But I want you to realize that there is a life of purity, a life made clean through the Word He has spoken, in which, through faith, you can glorify God with a body that is free from sickness, as well as with a spirit set free from the bondage of Satan.

Here they lay, a great multitude of impotent folk, of blind, halt, withered, around that pool, waiting for the moving of the water. Did Jesus heal everybody? He left many around that pool unhealed. There were doubtless many who had their eyes on the pool and who had no eyes for Jesus. There are many today who have their confidence all the time in things seen. If they would only get their eyes on God instead of on natural things, how quickly they would be helped.

The question arises, Is salvation and healing for all? It is for all who will press right in and get their portion. You remember the case of that Syrophenician woman who wanted the devil cast out of her daughter. Jesus said to her, "Let the children first be filled: for it is not meet to take the children's bread, and to cast it unto the dogs" (Mark 7:27). Note, healing and deliverance are here spoken of by the Master as "the children's bread;" so, if you are a child of God, you can surely press in for your portion.

The Syrophenician woman purposed to get from the Lord what she was after, and she said, "Yes, Lord: yet the dogs under the table eat of the children's crumbs" (Mark 7:28). Jesus was stirred as He saw the faith of this woman, and He told her, "For this saying go thy way; the devil is gone out of thy daughter" (Mark 7:29). Today there are many children of God refusing their blood-purchased portion of health in Christ and are throwing it away, while sinners are pressing through and picking it up from under the table, as it were, and are finding the cure not only for their bodies, but for their spirits and souls as well. The Syrophenician woman went home and found that the devil had indeed gone out of her daughter. Today there is bread, there is life, there is health for every child of God through His all-powerful Word.

> *Is any sick among you? let him call for the elders of the church;*
> *and let them pray over him, anointing him with oil in the*
> *name of the Lord: And the prayer of faith shall save the sick,*

> *and the Lord shall raise him up; and if he have committed sins, they shall be forgiven him.*
>
> *James 5:14,15*

We have in this precious Word a real basis for the truth of healing. In this scripture God gives very definite instructions to the sick. If you are sick, your part is to call for the elders of the church; it is their part to anoint and pray for you in faith, and then the whole situation rests with the Lord. When you have been anointed and prayed for, you can rest assured that the Lord will raise you up. It is the Word of God.

I believe that we all can see that the church cannot play with this business. If any turn away from these clear instructions they are in a place of tremendous danger. Those who refuse to obey, do so to their unspeakable loss.

James tells us in connection with this,

> *...if any of you do err from the truth, and one convert him; Let him know, that he which converteth the sinner from the error of his way shall save a soul from death....*
>
> *James 5:19,20*

Many turn away from the Lord, as did King Asa, who sought the physicians in his sickness and consequently died; and I take it that this passage means that if one induces another to turn back to the Lord, he will save such from death and God will forgive a multitude of sins that they have committed. This scripture can also have a large application on the line of salvation. If you turn away from any part of God's truth, the enemy will certainly get an advantage over you.

Does the Lord meet those who look to Him for healing and obey the instructions set forth in James? Most assuredly. Let me tell you a story to show how He will undertake for the most extreme case.

The Word can drive every disease away from you body. It is your portion in Christ who Himself is our bread, our life, our health, our all in all. And though you may be deep in sin, you can come to Him in repentance, and He will forgive and cleanse and heal you. His words are spirit and life to those who will receive them. There is a promise in the last verse in Joel, "...I will cleanse their blood that I have not cleansed..." (Joel 3:21). This is as much as to say He will provide new life within.

The life of Jesus Christ, God's Son, can so purify men's hearts and minds that they become entirely transformed, spirit, soul, and body.

WILT THOU BE MADE WHOLE?

There they are round the pool; and this man had been there a long time. His infirmity was of thirty-eight years' standing. Now and again an opportunity would come, as the angel stirred the waters, but his heart would be made sick as he saw another step in and be healed before him. But one day Jesus was passing that way, and seeing him lying there in that sad condition, enquired, "Wilt thou be made whole?" Jesus said it, and His Word is from everlasting to everlasting. This is His Word to you, poor, tried, and tested one today. You may say, like this poor impotent man, "I have missed every opportunity up till now." Never mind about that — *Wilt thou be made whole?*

I visited a woman who had been suffering for many years. She was all twisted up with rheumatism and had been two years in bed. I said to her, "What makes you lie here?" She said, "I've come to the conclusion that I have a thorn in the flesh." I said, "To what wonderful degree of righteousness have you attained that you have to have a thorn in the flesh? Have you had such an abundance of divine revelations that there is danger of your being exalted above measure?" She said, "I believe it is the Lord who is causing me to suffer." I said, "You believe it is the Lord's will for you to suffer, and you are trying to get out of it as quickly as you can. There are doctor's bottles all over the place. Get out of your hiding place and confess that you are a sinner. If you'll get rid of your self-righteousness, God will do something for you. Drop the idea that you are so holy that God has got to afflict you. Sin is the cause of your sickness and not righteousness. Disease is not caused by righteousness, but by sin.

There is healing through the blood of Christ and deliverance for every captive. God never intended His children to live in misery because of some affliction that comes directly from the devil. A perfect atonement was made at Calvary. I believe that Jesus bore my sins, and I am free from them all. I am justified from all things if I dare believe. He Himself took our infirmities and bare our sicknesses; and if I dare believe, I can be healed.

See this poor, helpless man at the pool. "Wilt thou be made whole?" But there is a difficulty in the way. The man has one eye on the pool and one on Jesus. There are many people getting cross-eyed this way these days; they have one eye on the doctor and one on Jesus. If you will only look to Christ and put both your eyes on Him you can be made every whit whole, spirit, soul, and body. It is the Word of the living God that they that believe should be justified, made free from all things. And whom the Son sets free is free indeed.

You say, "Oh, if I only could believe!" He understands. Jesus knew he had been a long time in that case. He is full of compassion. He knows that kidney trouble, He knows those corns, He knows that neuralgia. There is nothing He does not know. He only wants a chance to show Himself merciful and gracious to you. But He wants to encourage you to believe Him. If thou canst only believe, thou canst be saved and healed. Dare to believe that Jesus was wounded for your transgressions, was bruised for your iniquities, was chastised that you might have peace, and that by His stripes there is healing for you right here and now. You have failed because you have not believed Him. Cry out to Him even now, "Lord, I believe, help Thou mine unbelief."

Testimonies

I was in Long Beach, California, one day, and with a friend, was passing a hotel. He told me of a doctor there who had a diseased leg; that he had been suffering from it for six years, and could not get out. We went up to his room and found four doctors there. I said, "Well, doctor, I see you have plenty on, I'll call again another day." I was passing another time, and the Spirit said, "Go join thyself to him." Poor doctor! He surely was in a bad condition. He said, "I have been like this for six years, and nothing human can help me." I said, "You need God Almighty." People are trying to patch up their lives; but you cannot do anything without God. I talked to him for awhile about the Lord, and then prayed for him. I cried, "Come out of him, in the name of Jesus." The doctor cried, "It's all gone!"

Oh, if we only knew Jesus! One touch of His mightiness meets the need of every crooked thing. The trouble is to get people to believe Him. The simplicity of this salvation is so wonderful. One touch of living faith in Him is all that is required, and wholeness is your portion.

I was in Long Beach about six weeks later, and the sick were coming for prayer. Among those filling up the aisle was the doctor. I said, "What is the trouble?" He said, "Diabetes, but it will be all right tonight. I know it will be all right." There is no such thing as the Lord not meeting your need. There are no "ifs" or "mays;" His promises are all "shalls." All things are possible to him that believeth. Oh, the name of Jesus! There is power in that name to meet every condition of human need.

At that meeting there was an old man helping his son to the altar. He said, "He has fits — many every day." Then there was a woman with a cancer. Oh, what sin has done! We read that, when God brought forth His people from Egypt, "...there was not one feeble person among their tribes" (Psalm 105:37). No disease! All healed by the power of God! I believe that God wants a people like that today.

I prayed for the sister who had the cancer and she said, "I know I'm free and that God has delivered me." Then they brought the boy with the fits, and I commanded the evil spirits to leave, in the name of Jesus. Then I prayed for the doctor. At the next night's meeting the house was full. I called out, "Now, doctor, what about the diabetes?" He said, "It has gone." Then I said to the old man, "What about your son?" He said, "He hasn't had any fits since." We have a God who answers prayer.

Jesus meant this man at the pool to be a testimony forever. When he had both eyes on Jesus, He said to him, "Do the impossible thing. Rise, take up thy bed, and walk." Jesus called on the man with the withered hand to do the impossible — to stretch forth his hand, the man did the impossible thing — he stretched out his hand, and it was made every whit whole. And so with this impotent man — he began to rise, and he found the power of God moving within. He wrapped up his bed and began to walk off. It was the Sabbath day, and there were some of those folks around who think much more of a day than they do of the Lord; and they began to make a fuss. When the power of God is in manifestation, a protest will always come from some hypocrites. Jesus knew all about what the man was going through, and met him again; and this time He said to him, "Behold, thou are made whole: sin no more, lest a worse thing come unto thee" (John 5:14).

There is a close relationship between sin and sickness. How many know that their sickness is a direct result of sin? I hope that no one will come to be prayed for who is living in sin. But if you will obey God and repent of your sin and quit it, God will meet you, and neither your sickness nor your sin will remain. "...the prayer of faith shall save the sick, and the

Lord shall raise him up; and if he have committed sins, they shall be forgiven him" (James 5:15).

Faith is just the open door through which the Lord comes. Do not say, "I was healed by faith." Faith does not save. God saves through that open door. Healing comes the same way. You believe, and the virtue of Christ comes. Healing is for the glory of God. I am here because God healed me when I was dying; and I have been all round the world preaching this full redemption, doing all I can to bring glory to the wonderful name of Jesus, through whom I was healed.

"Sin no more, lest a worse thing come upon thee." The Lord told us in one place about an evil spirit going out from a man. The house that he left got all swept and garnished, but it received no new occupant. And that evil spirit, with seven other spirits more wicked than himself, went back to that unoccupied house, and the last stage of the man was worse than the first. The Lord does not heal you to go to a baseball game or a race meeting. He heals you for His glory and that from henceforth your life shall glorify Him. But this man remained stationary. He did not magnify God. He did not seek to be filled with the Spirit. And his last state became worse than the first.

The Lord would so cleanse the motives and desires of our hearts that we will seek but one thing only and that is, His glory. I went to a certain place one day and the Lord said, "This is for My glory." A young man had been sick for a long time confined to his bed in an utterly hopeless condition. He was fed only with a spoon, and was never dressed. The weather was damp, and so I said to the people of the house, "I wish you would put the young man's clothes by the fire to air." At first they would not take any notice of my request, but because I was persistent, they at last got out his clothes, and, when they were aired, I took them into his room.

The Lord said to me, "You will have nothing to do with this;" and I just lay out prostrate on the floor. The Lord showed me that He was going to shake the place with His glory. The very bed shook. I laid my hands on the young man in the name of Jesus, and the power fell in such a way that I fell with my face to the floor. In about a quarter of an hour the young man got up and walked up and down praising God. He dressed himself and then went out to the room where his father and mother were. He said, "God has healed me." Both the father and mother fell prostrate to the floor as the power of God surged through that room. There was a woman in that house who had been in an asylum for lunacy, and her condition was so bad that they were about to take her back. But the power of God healed her, too.

The power of God is just the same today as of old. Men need to be taken back to the old paths, to the old-time faith, to believe God's Word and every "thus saith the Lord" therein. The Spirit of the Lord is moving in these days. God is coming forth. If you want to be in the rising tide, you must accept all God has said.

"Wilt thou be made whole?" It is Jesus who says it. Give Him your answer. He will hear and He will answer.

Published in *The Bridal Call Foursquare*

FAITH: THE SUBSTANCE
October 1927

e will read from Hebrews 11. This is one of the greatest subjects there is from Genesis to Revelation. It is impossible to bring to you anything greater than the nature of God. We have now entered not in the covenant but the very nature of God, the divine nature, through faith. God has all thoughts and all knowledge, and we may have glimpses of His divine life. The Word of God is life, Jesus was made flesh, He came in the flesh for this very purpose to move people. Yes, beloved, the Creator was in the midst of creation. He opened blind eyes, unstopped deaf ears, made the lame walk; but He had all knowledge.

It is a new birth, just as we allow natural things to cease; then He comes in, in all His fulness. But you say, can we be in and out. Yes, if He comes in, the old man goes out; we can become out and out. Now I believe this morning's plan is for us all, but we must get into the real spirit of it. Beloved, do not stumble if you cannot move mountains; oh no, there may be some molehills need moving first. "Greater is He that is in you, than he that is in the world" (1 John 4:4). God has no need of a man who is hot today and cold tomorrow; He needs men who are hot today and hotter tomorrow and still hotter the next day — that is the man who is going to touch the glory. The Lord never changes, He is just the same; if you change it does not mean to say God has changed. I am amazed all the while at what God is doing — it is from glory to glory. Now, it is no good unless we have a foundation; but, glory to God, our foundation is the most powerful and unmovable foundation — it is the very Word of God. When we are born again we are born of a substance — the Word of God — no corruption in it, the incorruptible Word of God. I believe when a man is born again he gets knowledge how to sow the Word of God in such a way that will bring another into the same knowledge. Everyone who is born again can sow. Now, when Jesus said God so loved the world, it was an unmeasurable sow — it's a fact that is worked in and has to come out; but it is the plan of God, and you are all in it this morning, and I believe that there can be such an enlargement in us that will swallow us up, and if you are not in that place, then you must be a back number. But remember this, we have all more than we are using.

Now I want to dwell a little on this word substance. We must build ourselves up in the most holy faith; do not stop running in the race — it is an awful thing for a person to run and then stop, and someone else get the prize. Paul speaks on this line in 1 Corinthians 9:24.

> *Know ye not that they which run in a race run all... So run, that ye may obtain.*

Also he says in Philippians 3:12:

> *Not as though I had already attained, either were already perfect: but I follow after, if that I may apprehend that for which also I am apprehended of Christ Jesus.*

So he cries out, I *press* toward the mark. It is a disgrace to God for a person just to keep pace. We must press on; if you are making no headway, you must be a backslider, because you have had such opportunities. Now, substance is the evidence of things not seen.

Right in every born-again person there is that power which is greater than the natural force. God says twice in one chapter "...lay hold on eternal life," (1 Timothy 6:12,19) a thing you cannot see, and yet we have to lay hold of it.

Now, beloved, we must pass more than anything we have passed before. I really mean all I say. I am not speaking from the abundance of my mind, but my heart. The abundance of the mind makes swelled heads, but we want swelled hearts. I want to make you all drunk with new wine. We can have this treasure in earthen vessels. God does not want you to be nat- ural people. He wants you to be people who will cut through anything. Born into God's life, the new birth is life, the life of God. Christ in you, the hope of glory. No person can go on in this way and stand still. Love the Word of God. "In the beginning was the Word, and the Word was with God, and the Word was God" (John 1:1). Jesus was the only begot- ten of the Father, full of grace and truth. Perhaps you have never known before what God wants you to possess. Now take these words:

> *Through faith we understand that the worlds were framed by the word of God, so that things which are seen were not made of things which do appear.*
>
> *Hebrews 11:3*

My word if you do not all become big today — I do not mean in your own estimation. Now when you first came into the world you were made, but when you were born again you were begotten. Now read John 1:1-3:

> *In the beginning was the Word, and the Word was with God, and the Word was God. The same was in the beginning with God. All things were made by him; and without him was not any thing made that was made.*
>
> *John 1:1-3*

So you see, all things were made by Him. Oh, beloved, He will act if you will let Him have a chance. What do I mean? Well, listen! A man came to me and said, "Can you help me, I cannot sleep, and my nerves are terrible."

Now Jesus put a principle in the Word of God, He said, "Ask anything in My name and I will do it," so I prayed for the man, and said, "Now go home and sleep in the name of Jesus"; he said, "But I can't sleep"; I said "Go home and sleep," and gave him a push. So he went, and according to the Word of God, he went home and slept, and he slept so long his wife went to wake him up, but, thinking he was tired, let him sleep on; but he slept all Saturday, and the poor wife did not know what to do; but the man awoke, and was so changed he got up and went about shouting, "I am a new man, praise the Lord."

What had done it? Why, it was the Word of God, and we have the Word in us, the faith of the Son of God. Now we can all have from God this morning what we believe for. If you want anything, put your hands up. If you are in earnest, walk out to the front. And if you are really desperate, run out. Amen.

Published in *Redemption Tidings*

THE PENTECOSTAL POWER

November 12, 1927

Bible Reading: Acts 19:1-20

This is a wonderful reading. It has many things in it which indicate to us that there was something more marvelous about it than human power, and when I think about Pentecost I am astonished from day to day because of its mightiness, of its wonderfulness and how the glory overshadows it. I think sometimes about these things and they make me feel we have only just touched it. Truly it is so, but we must thank God that we have touched it. We must not give in because we have only touched. Whatever God has done in the past, His name is still the same. When hearts are burdened and they come face to face with the need of the day, they look into God's Word and it brings in a propeller of power or an anointing that makes you know He has truly visited. It was a wonderful day when Jesus left the glory. I can imagine all the angels and God the Father and all heaven so wonderfully stirred that day when the angels were sent to tell that wonderful story: "Peace on earth and good will to men." It was a glorious day when they beheld the Babe for the first time and God was looking on. What happened after that day and until He was thirty years old I suppose it would take a big book to put it all in. It was a working up to a great climax.

I know that Pentecost in my life is a working up to a climax, it is not all done in a day. There are many waters and all kinds of times until we get to the real summit of everything. The power of God is here to prevail. God is with us. The mother of Jesus hid a lot of things in her heart. The time came when it was made manifest at Jordan that Jesus was the Son of God. Oh, how beautifully it was made known! It had to be made known first to one that was full of the vision of God. The vision comes to those who are full. Did it ever strike you we cannot be too full for a vision, we cannot have too much of God? The more of God, then the visions begin. When God has you in His own plan, what a change, how things operate. You wonder, you see things in a new light. And how God is being glorified as you yield from day to day, and the Spirit seems to lay hold of you and bring you on. Yes, it is pressing on, and then He gives us touches of His wonderful power, manifestations of the glory of these things and indications of great things to follow, and these days which we are living in now speak of better days. How wonderful!

Where should we have been today if we had stopped short, if we had not fulfilled the vision which God gave us? I am thinking about that time when Christ sent the Spirit; and Paul did not know much about that, his heart was stirred, his eyes were dim, he was going to put the whole thing to an end in a short time, and Jesus was looking on. We can scarcely understand the whole process only as God seems to show us, when He gets us into His plan and works with us little by little. We are all amazed that we are amongst the "tongues people," it is altogether out of order according to the natural. Some of us would have never been in this Pentecostal movement had we not been drawn, but God has a wonderful way of drawing us. Paul never intended to be among the disciples, Paul never intended to have anything to do with this Man called Jesus, but God was working. God has been working with us and has brought us to this place. It is marvelous! Oh! the vision of God, the wonderful manifestation which God has for Israel.

I have one purpose in my heart, and it is surely God's plan for me, that I want you to see that Jesus Christ is the greatest manifestation in all the world, and His power is unequaled, but there is only one way to minister it. I want you to notice that these people, after they had seen Paul working wonders by this power, began on a natural line. I see it is necessary for me if I want to do anything for God, I must get the knowledge of God,

I must get the vision of God, I cannot work on my own. It must be a divine revelation of the Son of God. It must be that. I can see as clearly as anything that Paul in his mad pursuit had to be stopped in the way, and after he was stopped in the way and had the vision from heaven and that light from heaven, instantly he realized that he had been working the wrong way. And as soon as ever the power of the Holy Ghost fell upon him, he began in the way in which God wanted him to go. And it was wonderful how he had to suffer to come into the way. It is broken spirits, it is tried lives, and it is being driven into a corner as if some strange thing had happened, that is, surely the way to get to know the way of God.

Paul had not any power to use the name of Jesus as he did use it, only as he had to go through the privations and the difficulties, and even when all things seemed as though shipwrecked, God stood by him and made him know that there was something behind all the time that was with him, and able to carry him through, and bring out that for which his heart was all the time longing. Unconsciously he seemed to be so filled with the Holy Ghost that all that was needed was just the bringing of the aprons and the handkerchiefs and sending them forth. I can imagine these people looking on and seeing him and saying, "But it is all in the name, don't you notice that when he sends the handkerchiefs and the aprons he says, 'In the name of the Lord Jesus I command that evil to come out'?"

These people had been looking round and watching, and they thought, "It is only the name, that is all that is needed," and so these men said, "We will do the same." These vagabond Jews, those seven sons of Sceva, were determined to make this thing answer, and they came to the place where that man had been for years possessed with an evil power, and as they entered in they said, "We adjure thee in the name of Jesus to come out." The demons said, "Jesus we know, and Paul we know, but who are ye?" and this evil power leaped upon them and tore their things off their backs, and they went out naked and wounded. (See Acts 19:13-17.) It was the name, only they did not understand it. Oh, that God should help us to understand the name! It is the name, oh, it is still the name. But you must understand there is the ministry of the name, there is something in the name that makes the whole world charmed. It is the Holy Spirit back of the ministry, it is the knowledge of Him, it is the ministry of the knowledge of Him, and I can understand it is only that.

I want to speak about the ministry of the knowledge; it is important. God, help us to see. I am satisfied with two things; one is this, I am satisfied it is the knowledge of the blood of Jesus Christ today, and the knowledge of His perfect holiness. I am perfectly cleansed from all sin and made holy in the knowledge of His holiness. I am satisfied today that as I know Him, and the knowledge of His power, and the Christ that is manifested, and the power that worketh in me to minister as I am ministering only in the knowledge of it, it is effective, so that it brings out the very thing which the Word of God says it will do, in the ministry of which, as I know it, it has power over all evil powers by its effectual working in that way. I minister today in the power of the knowledge of the ministry of it, and beyond that there is a certain sense that I overcome the world according to my faith in Him, and I am more than a conqueror over everything just in the knowledge that I have of Him being over everything, as crowned by the Father to bring everything into subjection. Shouting won't do it, but there is a lubrication about it which is gloriously felt within and brings it into perfect harmony with the will of God, but it is not in the shout, and yet we cannot help but shout, but it is in the ministry of the knowledge that He is Lord over all demons, all powers of wickedness.

TONGUES AND INTERPRETATION: "The Holy One which anointed Jesus is so abiding by the Spirit in the one that is clothed upon to use the name till the glory is manifested and the demons flee, they cannot stand the glory of the manifestation of the Spirit which is manifest."

So I am realizing that Paul went about clothed in the Spirit. This was wonderful, His body was full of virtue? No!! He sent forth handkerchiefs from his body and aprons from his body, and when they touched the needy, they were healed and demons were cast out. Virtue in his body? No! Virtue in Jesus, by the ministry of faith in the name of Jesus through the power of the unction of the Holy Ghost in Paul.

TONGUES AND INTERPRETATION: "The liberty of the Spirit bringeth the office."

It is an office, it is a position, it is a place of rest, of faith. Sometimes the demon powers are dealt with very differently, not all the same way: but the ministry of the Spirit by which it is ministered by the power of the word "Jesus" never fails to accomplish the purpose for which the one in charge has wisdom or discernment to see, because along with the Spirit of ministry there comes the revelation of the need of the needy one that is bound.

So differently the Spirit ministers the name of Jesus. I see it continually happening. I see those things answer and all the time the Lord is building up a structure of His own power by a living faith in the knowledge of the sovereignty of the name of Jesus. If I turn to John's gospel I get the whole thing practically in a nutshell. To know Thee, O God, and Jesus Christ whom Thou hast sent, is eternal life. We must have the knowledge and power of God and the knowledge of Jesus Christ, the embodiment of God, to be clothed upon with God, God in human flesh. I see there are those who have come into line, they are possessed with the blessed Christ, and the power of the baptism which is the revelation of the Christ of God within, and it is so evidently in the person who is baptized and the Christ is so plainly abiding that the moment he is confronted with evil, instantly he is sensitive of the position of this confronting, and he is able to deal accordingly.

The difference between the sons of Sceva and Paul is this: They said, "It is only using the word." How many people only use the word, how many times people are defeated because they think it is just the word, how many people have been brokenhearted because it did not answer when they used the word? If I read into my text this afternoon this, "He that believeth shall speak in tongues, he that believeth shall cast out devils, he that believeth shall lay hands on the sick," if I read this into my text, on the surface of it, it seems exactly easy, but you must understand this, there are volumes to be applied to the word *believe*. To believe is to believe in the need of the majesty of the glory of the power, which is all power, which brings all other powers into subjection.

And what is belief? Sum it up in a few sentences. To believe is to have the knowledge of Him in whom you believe, it is not to believe in the word *Jesus*, but to believe in the nature, to believe in the vision, for all power is given unto Him, and greater is He that is within thee in the revelation of faith than he that is in the world, and so I say to you, do not be discouraged if every demon has not gone out. The very moment you have gone, do not think there is an end of it. What we have to do is to see this, that if it had only been using the name, those evil powers would have gone out in that name by the sons of Sceva. It is not that. It is the virtue of the power of the Holy Ghost, with the revelation of the deity of our Christ of glory, where all power is given unto Him, and in the knowledge of Christ, in the faith of what He is, demons must surrender, demons must go out, and I say it reverently, these bodies of ours are so constructed by God that we may be filled with that divine revelation of the Son of God till it is manifest to the devils you go to and they have to go. The Master is in, they see the Master. Jesus I know, and Paul I know. The ministry of the Master! How we need to get to know Him till within us we are full of the manifestation of the King over all demons.

Brothers and sisters, my heart is full. The depths of my yearnings are for the Pentecostal people. My cry is that we will not miss the opportunity of the baptism of the Holy Ghost, that Christ may be manifested in the human till every power of evil will be subject to the Christ which is manifested in you. The devils know. Two important things are before me. To master the situation of myself. You are not going to meet devils if you cannot master yourself, because you soon find the devil bigger than yourself, and it is only when you are subdued that Christ is enthroned and the embodiment of the Spirit is so gloriously covering the human life that Jesus is glorified to the full. So first it is the losing of ourself and then it is the incoming of Another; it is the glorifying of Him which is to fulfill all things and when He gets lives He can do it. When He gets lives that will so yield themselves to God, God will be delighted to allow the Christ to be so manifested in you, that it will be no difficulty for the devil to know who you are.

I am satisfied that Pentecost is to reestablish God in human flesh. Do I need to say it again? The power of the Holy Ghost has to come to be enthroned in the human life so it does not matter what state we are in. Christ is manifested in the place where devils are, the place where religious devils are, the place where a false religion and unbelief are, the place where a formal religion has taken the place of holiness and righteousness. You have need to have holiness, the righteousness and Spirit of the Master, so that in every walk of life everything that is not like our Lord Jesus will have to depart and that is what is needed today. I ask you in the Holy Ghost to seek the place where He is in power. "Jesus I know, Paul I know but who are ye?" May God stamp it upon us for the devil is not afraid of you. May the Holy Ghost make us today terrors of evildoers, for the Holy Ghost came into us to judge the world of sin, of unbelief, of righteousness, and that is the purpose of the Holy Ghost. The devils will know us, and Jesus will know us.

Published in *The Pentecostal Evangel*

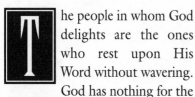

EXTRAORDINARY
December 1927

The people in whom God delights are the ones who rest upon His Word without wavering. God has nothing for the man who wavers, for "let him that wavereth expect nothing from God." Therefore I would like us to get this verse deep down into our hearts, until it penetrates every fiber of our being:

"Only believe! Only believe! All things are possible — *only believe.*"

God has a plan for this meeting, beyond anything that we have ever known before. He has a plan for every individual life, and if we have any other plan in view, *we miss the grandest plan of all!* Nothing of the past is equal to the present, and nothing of the present can equal the things of tomorrow, for "tomorrow" should be so filled with holy expectations that we will be "living flames" for Him. God never intended His people to be ordinary, or common-place; His intentions were that they should be on fire for Him, conscious of His divine power, realizing the glory of the cross that foreshadows the crown.

SANCTIFIED UNTO GOD

God has given us a very special Scripture for this service:

> *And in those days, when the number of the disciples was multiplied, there arose a murmuring of the Grecians against the Hebrews, because their widows were neglected in the daily ministration. Then the twelve called the multitude of the disciples unto them, and said, It is not reason that we should leave the word of God, and serve tables. Wherefore, brethren, look ye out among you seven men of honest report, full of the Holy Ghost and wisdom, whom we may appoint over this business...And the*

> *saying pleased the whole multitude: and they chose Stephen, a*
> *man full of faith and of the Holy Ghost, and Philip....*
>
> *Acts 6:1-3,5*

During the time of the inauguration of the Church the disciples were hard pressed on all lines; the things of natural order could not be attended to, and many were complaining concerning the neglect of their widows. The disciples therefore decided upon a plan, which was to choose seven men to do the work — men who were "full of the Holy Ghost." What a divine thought! No matter what kind of work was to be done, however menial it may have been, the person chosen must be *filled with the Holy Ghost*. The plan of the Church was that everything, even of natural order, *must be sanctified unto God*, for the Church had to be a "Holy Ghost" Church. Beloved, *God has never ordained anything less!*

ENDUED WITH POWER

There is one thing that I want to stress in these meetings; that is, no matter what else may happen, first and foremost I would emphasize the question:

"Have you received the Holy Ghost since you believed?" "Are you filled with divine power?"

This is the heritage of the Church, to be so endued with power that God can lay His hand upon any member at any time to do His perfect will. There is no "stop" in the Spirit-filled life: we begin at the cross, the place of ignominy, shame, and death, and that very death brings the power of resurrection life; and, being filled with the Holy Spirit, we go on "from glory to glory." Let us not forget that possessing the baptism in the Holy Spirit means there must be an "ever-increasing " holiness. How the Church needs divine unction — God's presence and power so manifest that the world will know it. The people know when the tide is flowing; they also know when it is ebbing.

The necessity that seven men be chosen for the position of "serving tables" was very evident. The disciples knew that these seven men were *men ready for active service*, and so they chose them. In the fifth verse, we read: "And the saying pleased the whole multitude: and they chose Stephen, a man full of faith and of the Holy Ghost, and Philip...." There were others but Stephen and Philip stand out most prominently in the Scriptures. Philip was a man so filled with the Holy Ghost that a revival always followed wherever he went. Stephen was a man so filled with divine power, that although "serving tables" might have been all right in the minds of the other disciples, yet, God had a greater vision for him — *a baptism of fire*, of power and divine unction, that took him on and on to the climax of his life, until he saw right into the "open heavens."

Had we been there with the disciples at that time, I believe we would have heard them saying to each other, "Look here! Neither Stephen nor Philip are doing the work we called them to. If they do not attend to business, we will have to get someone else!" That was the *natural* way of thinking, but divine order is far above our finite planning. When we please God in our daily ministration, we will always find in operation the fact "that everyone who is faithful in little, God will make faithful in much." We have such [an] example here — a man chosen to "serve tables," having such a revelation of the mind of Christ and of the depth and height of God, that there was no "stop" in his experience, but a going forward with leaps and bounds. Beloved, there is a race to be run, there is a crown to be won; *we cannot stand still!* I say unto you, be vigilant! *Be vigilant! "Let no man take thy crown!"*

ABOVE THE ORDINARY

God has privileged us in Christ Jesus to live above the ordinary human plane of life. Those who want to be "ordinary" and live on a lower plan, can do so; but as for me, *I will not!* For the same unction, the same zeal, the same Holy Ghost power is at our command as was at the command of Stephen and the apostles. We have the same God that Abraham had, that Elijah had, and *we need not come behind in any gift or grace.* We may not possess the gifts, as abiding gifts, but as we are full of the Holy Ghost and divine unction, it is possible, when there is need, for God to *manifest every gift of the Spirit* through us, but a *manifestation of the gifts* as God may choose to use us.

This *ordinary* man Stephen became mighty under the Holy Ghost anointing, until he stands supreme, in many ways, among the apostles — "And Stephen full of faith and power, did great wonders and miracles among the people." As we go deeper in God, He enlarges our conception and places before us a wide-open door; and I am not surprised that this man, chosen to "serve tables," was afterwards called to a higher plane. "What do you mean?" you may ask. "Did he 'quit' this service?" "No! but he was 'lost' in the power of God." He lost sight of everything in the natural, and steadfastly fixed his gaze upon Jesus, the Author and Finisher of our faith, until he was transformed into a "shining light" in the Kingdom of God. Oh, that we might be awakened to believe His Word, to understand the mind of the Spirit, for there is an inner place of whiteness and purity where we can "see God." *Stephen was just as ordinary a man as you and me, but he was in the place where God could so move upon him that he, in turn, could move all before him.* He began in a most humble place, and ended in a blaze of glory. Beloved, *dare to believe Christ!*

As you go on in this life of the Spirit, you will find that the devil will begin to get restless and there will be a "stir" in the synagogue; it was so with Stephen. Any amount of people may be found in the "synagogue," who are very proper in a world sense — always correctly dressed, the "elite" of the land, welcoming everything into the church but the power of God. Let us read what God says about them:

> *Then there arose certain of the synagogue, which is called the synagogue of the Libertines, and Cyrenians, and Alexandrians...disputing with Stephen. And they were not able to resist the wisdom and the spirit by which he spake.*
>
> *Acts 6:9,10*

"The Libertines" could not stand the truth of God. With these opponents, Stephen found himself in the same predicament as the blind man whom Jesus healed. As soon as the blind man's eyes were opened they shut him out of the synagogue. *They will not have anybody in the "synagogue" with their eyes open;* as soon as you receive "spiritual eyesight," *out you go!* These Libertines, Cyrenians, and Alexandrians, rose up full of wrath in the very place where they should have been full of the power of God, full of love divine, and reverence for the Holy Ghost; they *rose up against* Stephen, this man "full of the Holy Ghost." Beloved, if there is anything in your life that in any way *resists* the power of the Holy Ghost and the entrance of His Word into your heart and life, *drop on your knees and CRY ALOUD for mercy!* When the Spirit of God is "brooding" over your heart's door, do not resist Him, but open your heart to the touch of God. There is a "resisting unto blood" striving *against sin*, and there is a "resisting of the Holy Ghost" that will drive you into sin.

MIGHTY FOR GOD

Stephen spoke with marked wisdom; where he was, things began to move. You will find that there is always a "moving" when the Holy Spirit has control. These people were brought under conviction by the message of Stephen, but they "resisted," they lied, they did anything and everything to stifle that conviction. Not only did they lie, but they got others to lie against this man, who would have laid down his life for any one of them. Stephen was used to heal the sick, perform miracles, and yet they brought "false accusations" against him. What effect did it have on Stephen?

> *And all that sat in the council, looking stedfastly on him, saw his face as it had been the face of an angel.*
>
> *Acts 6:15*

Something had happened in the life of this man, chosen for menial service, and he became *mighty for God*. How was it accomplished in him? It was because *his aim was high;* faithful in little, God brought him to full fruition. Under the inspiration of divine power by which he spoke, they could not help but listen — even the "angels" listened, as with holy prophetic utterance he spoke before the Council. Beginning with Abraham and Moses, he continued unfolding the truth. What a marvelous exhortation! Take your Bible and read it, "listen in" as the angels listened in. As light upon light, truth upon truth, revelation upon revelation, found its way into their hearts, they gazed at him in astonishment; their hearts perhaps became warm at times, and they may have said, "Truly, this man is sent of God" — but then he hurled at them the truth:

> *Ye stiffnecked and uncircumcised in heart and ears, ye do always resist the Holy Ghost: as your fathers did, so do ye. Which of the prophets have not your fathers persecuted? and they have slain them which shewed before of the coming of the Just One; of whom ye have been now the betrayers and murderers: Who have received the law by the disposition of angels, and have not kept it.*
>
> *Acts 7:51-53*

Then what happened? These men were *moved*; they were "...cut to the heart, and they gnashed upon him with their teeth" (Acts 7:54).

There are two occasions in the Scriptures where the people were "pricked to the heart." In the second chapter of the Acts of the Apostles, verse 37, after Peter had delivered that inspired sermon on the Day of Pentecost, the people were "pricked to the heart" with conviction, and there were added to the Church 3,000 souls. Here is Stephen, speaking under the inspiration of the Holy Ghost, and the men of this Council being "pricked to the heart" rise up as one man to slay him. As you go down through this chapter, from verse 55, what a picture you have before you. As I close my eyes, I have a vision of this scene in every detail — the howling mob with their vengeful, murderous spirit, ready to devour this holy man, and he "being full of the Holy Ghost, gazing stedfastly into heaven." What does he see there? From his place of helplessness, he looked up and said:

> *...Behold, I see the heavens opened, and the Son of man standing on the right hand of God.*
>
> Acts 7:56

Is that the position that Jesus went to take? No! He went to "sit" at the right hand of the Father; but in behalf of the "first martyr" in behalf of the man with that burning flame of Holy Ghost power, God's Son "stood up" in honorary testimony of him who, called to serve tables, was faithful unto death. But is that all? No, I am so glad that it is not all. As the stones came flying at him, pounding his body, crashing into his bones, striking his temple, mangling his beautiful face, what happened? How did this scene end? With that sublime, upward look, this man chosen for an ordinary task but filled with the Holy Ghost, was so moved upon by God that he finished his earthly work in a blaze of glory, magnifying God with his latest breath. Looking up into the face of the Master, he said, "Lord Jesus, *forgive them!* 'Lay not this sin to their charge.' And when he had said this, he fell asleep" (Acts 7:60).

Friends, it is worth all to gain that spirit. My God! What a divine ending to the life and testimony of a man who was "chosen to serve tables." *Amen!*

A message given in New York

Matthew 11 - The Lord wishes to bring before us a living fact which shall by faith bring into action a principle within

NOT OFFENDED!
April 1928

us, so that Christ can destroy every power of Satan. We need to stir ourselves so that we understand the mighty power God has for us. Not a dormant position, but a power, a revelation, a life. The possibility of man in the hands of God.

John the Baptist had a wonderful revelation and a mighty anointing. The power of God rested upon him, and God through John moved Israel to repentance. Now when John heard in prison of the works of Jesus he sent two disciples, and they said unto Him, "Art Thou He that should come, or look we for another?" I come across men who might be giants in faith, leaders who might subdue kingdoms, but they go down because they allow Satan to dethrone their better knowledge of the power of God. Jesus sent these men back with a personal, effective knowledge that they had met Him whom the prophets had spoken of. Jesus answered and said to them, "...Go and shew John again those things which ye do hear and see: The blind receive their sight, and the lame walk, the lepers are cleansed, and the deaf hear, the dead are raised up, and the poor have the gospel preached to them" (Matthew 11:4,5). And when they saw the miracles and wonders and heard the gracious words that He spoke as the power of God rested upon Him, they were ready. You shall hear the truth, and the truth shall make you free.

As they departed, Jesus began to say unto the multitude concerning John: "What went ye out in the wilderness to see, a reed shaken by the wind?" No, God wants to make men flames of fire; strong in the Lord and in the strength of His might powerful.

The Spirit of the Lord breathes upon the slain and upon dry bones, and upon the things that are not, and changes them in a moment of time and makes the weak strong. He is among us tonight to quicken the dead and make alive.

"...from the days of John the Baptist until now the kingdom of heaven suffereth violence, and the violent take it by force" (Matthew 11:12). Every believer has the life of the Lord in him. If Jesus were to come into our life, our life would go out to meet His life. "Your life is hid with Christ in God" (Colossians 3:3) The kingdom of heaven suffereth violence. Every suffering one, every needy one, every paralyzed condition, every weakness means that the kingdom of heaven is suffering violence at the hand of the adversary.

Could the kingdom of heaven bring weaknesses? Beloved, the kingdom of heaven is within you. The kingdom of heaven is the life of Jesus, the power of the Highest; no disease, no imperfection. It is as holy as God is. Satan comes to steal, to kill, and to destroy. Every ailment is of satanic origin; there is no purification in disease. I have seen blindness and idiocy and possession as a result of vaccination. There may be some here still asleep concerning the deep things of God. I want God to give you a revelation, an awakening, an audacity, a flowing indignation against the powers of Satan. Lot had a righteous indignation against Satan, but it was too late. He should have had it when he went into Sodom. There is something you must wake up to where you will never allow disease to have you, or a weak heart, or pain in the back. You will never allow anything but perfect life. The power of God brings glory. If some were as sorry for their sickness as their sin, they would be out of it tonight. Satan has tremendous power over certain functions of the body. Satan will make the pain and weakness so distracting that it will always bring down your mind to where the pain is. Anything that takes me from an attitude of worship is of Satan; if only a finger or a toothache, the kingdom of heaven suffereth violence, and blessed is he who shall not be offended in Me. Oh, again the blind receive their sight, the lame walk, the lepers are cleansed, and the poor have the Gospel preached unto them.

> Just the same, just the same,
> He is just the same today.
> Praise the Lord. Amen.

Published in *Redemption Tidings*

God has a plan for us in this life of the Spirit, this abundant life. Jesus came that we might have life. Satan comes to steal and kill and destroy, but God has for us abundance, full measure, pressed down, shaken together, overflowing, abundant measure. God filling us with His own personality, presence, making us salt and light and giving us revelation of Himself. God with us in all circumstances and afflictions, persecutions, in every trial, girding us with truth. Christ the initiative, the Triune God in control, our every thought, word, action must be in line with Him, with no weakness or failure. Our God is a God of might, light, revelation, preparing us for heaven. Our life is hid with Christ in God; when He Who is our life shall be manifested, we also shall appear with Him in glory (Colossians 3:3,4).

CLOTHED WITH THE SPIRIT

June 1928

THE EARNEST OF THE SPIRIT

For we know that if our earthly house of this tabernacle were dissolved, we have a building of God, an house not made with hands, eternal in the heavens. For in this we groan, earnestly desiring to be clothed upon with our house which is from heaven: If so be that being clothed we shall not be found naked. For we that are in this tabernacle do groan, being burdened: not for that we would be unclothed, but clothed upon, that mortality might be swallowed up of life. Now he that hath wrought us for the selfsame thing is God, who also hath given unto us the earnest of the Spirit. Therefore we are always confident, knowing that, whilst we are at home in the body, we are absent from the Lord.

2 Corinthians 5:1-6

God's Word is a tremendous Word, a productive Word, producing what it is — power. Producing God-likeness. We get to heaven through the Word of God, we have peace through the blood of His cross. Redemption is ours through the knowledge of the Word. I am saved because God's Word says so.

> *...if thou shalt confess with thy mouth the Lord Jesus, and shalt believe in thine heart that God hath raised him from the dead, thou shalt be saved.*
>
> Romans 10:9

If I am baptized with the Holy Spirit it is because Jesus said, "Ye shall receive power, the Holy Ghost coming upon you." We must all have one idea — to be filled with the Holy Ghost, to be filled with God.

TONGUES AND INTERPRETATION: "God hath sent His Word to free us from the law of sin and death. Except we die, we cannot live; except we cease to be, God cannot be."

The Holy Ghost has a royal plan, a heavenly plan. He came to unveil the King, to show the character of God, to unveil the precious blood. As I have the Holy Spirit within me, I see Jesus clothed for humanity; He was moved by the Spirit, led by the Spirit. We read of some who heard the Word of God but were not profited, because faith was lacking in them. We must have a living faith in God's Word, quickened by the Spirit. A man may be saved and still have a human spirit; with many who are spoken to about the baptism of the Holy Ghost, the human spirit at once arises against the Holy Spirit. The human spirit is not subject to the law of God, neither can it be. The disciples at one time wanted to call down fire from heaven. Jesus said, "Ye know not what spirit ye are of."

"Now he that hath wrought us for the selfsame thing is God, who also hath given us the earnest of the Spirit" (v. 5). The clothing upon of the Spirit, human depravity covered, all contrary to the mind of God destroyed. God must have bodies for Himself, perfectly prepared by the Holy Ghost, for the day of the Lord. "For in this we groan, earnestly desiring to be clothed upon with our house which is from heaven" (v. 2). Is Paul speaking here of the coming of the Lord? No; yet it is in conjunction, this condition of preparedness. The Holy Ghost is coming to take out a church and a perfect bride; He must find in us perfect yieldedness, every desire subjected to Him. He has come to reveal Christ in us, that the glorious flow of the life of God may outflow, rivers of living water to the thirsty land.

> *...if Christ be in you, the body is dead because of sin; but the Spirit is life because of righteousness.*
>
> Romans 8:10

THE PLAN OF THE SPIRIT

TONGUES AND INTERPRETATION: "This is that which God hath declared: freedom from the law. If we love the world, the love of the Father is not in us."

> *For all that is in the world, the lust of the flesh, the lust of the eyes, and the pride of life, is not of the Father, but is of the world.*
>
> 1 John 2:16

The Spirit has to breathe in a new tenancy, a new order. He came to give the vision of a life in which Jesus is perfected.

> *Who hath saved us, and called us with an holy calling, not according to our works, but according to his own purpose and grace, which was given us in Christ Jesus before the world began, But is now made manifest by the appearing of our Saviour Jesus Christ, who hath abolished death, and hath brought life and immortality to light through the gospel.*
>
> 2 Timothy 1:9,10

Saved, called to be saints, called with a holy calling, holy, pure, Godlike, sons with power. It is a long time now since it was settled and death abolished. Death has no more power; mortality is a hindrance; sin has no more dominion; you reign in Christ, you appropriate His finished work. Don't groan and travail for a week if you are in need, only believe. Don't fight to get some special thing, *only believe.* It is according to your faith. God blesses you with faith. Have faith in God. If you are free in God, *believe*, and it shall be.

"If ye then be risen with Christ, seek the things that are above, where Christ is seated at the right hand of God" (Colossians 3:1). Stir yourselves up, beloved; where are you? I am risen with Christ, planted. It was a beautiful planting. Seated. God gives me credit and I believe Him; why should I doubt?

TONGUES AND INTERPRETATION: "Wherefore do you doubt? Faith reigns. God makes it possible. How many receive the Holy Ghost and Satan gets a doubt in? Don't doubt; believe. There is power and strength in Him; who dares believe God?"

Quit Doubting Street; live in Faith-Victory Street. Jesus sent seventy away, and they came back in victory. It takes God to make it real. Dare to believe till there is not a sick person, no sickness, everything withered, and the life of Jesus implanted within.

Redemption Tidings

BE WIDE AWAKE

September 1928

Matthew 11:1-12 - Faith brings into action a principle within our hearts, so that Christ can dethrone every power of Satan. God's accomplishment for us can be proved in our experience, not a dormant position, but a power, a revelation, a life; oh, the greatness of it. The possibilities of man in the hand of God, brought out in revelation and force.

John [the]Baptist had a wonderful revelation, a mighty anointing; how the power of God rested upon him. All Israel was moved. Jesus said, "...there hath not risen a greater than John the Baptist: notwithstanding he that is least in the kingdom of heaven is greater than he" (Matthew 11:11). We see how satanic power can blind the mind unless we are filled or insulated by the power of God. Satan suggests to John, "Don't you think you have made a mistake"?

I find men who might be used by God to subdue kingdoms go down through, allowing suggestions of Satan to dethrone their better knowledge of the power of God. So John sent two of his disciples to Jesus, "Art Thou He that should come or look we for another?" Jesus said, "Go and show John the things ye do hear and see." And when they saw the miracles and wonders they were ready. Jesus said, "What went ye out to see, a reed shaken with the wind?" No; God wants men flames of fire, strong in the Lord and in the power of His might. Let us live as those that have seen the King, having a resurrection touch. We know we are sons of God as we believe His Word and stand in the truth of it.

TONGUES AND INTERPRETATION: "The Spirit of the Lord breathes upon the bones and upon the things that are not and changes them in a moment, making the weak strong, quickening that which is dead into life."

The kingdom of heaven is within us, the Christ, the Word of God. The kingdom of heaven suffereth violence. How? Every suffering one, every paralyzed condition, if you feel distress in any way, it means that the kingdom is suffering violence at the hands of the adversary. Could the kingdom of heaven bring weakness, disease, consumption, cancers, tumors? The kingdom of God is within you, it is the life of Jesus, the power of the Highest, pure, holy; it has no disease or imperfection. But Satan cometh to steal and kill and destroy.

Scientists and doctors of the last days tell us a child can be helped by putting impure matter in vaccination. I have seen blindness, idiocy, and all kinds of evil come from this hideous science. I have in my mind a beautiful girl nine years old; from the day of her vaccination an evil spirit possessed her, she screamed and moaned for years. The neighbors complained. The father said, "These hands shall work, but my child shall never go to an asylum."

One day I went to this home; the Spirit of the Lord came upon me; I took hold of the child, looked right into her eyes and said, "You evil spirit, come out in the name of Jesus." She went to a couch and fell asleep, and from that day she was perfect. I know deliverance came, but I want you to see the wiles of Satan and in the name of Jesus, dethronement. The almightiness of God against the might of Satan.

Oh! Be not asleep concerning the deep things of God. Have a flaming indignation against the power of Satan. Lot had a righteous indignation, but too late; he should have had it when he went into Sodom. Be thankful you are alive to hear, and that God can change the situation. We all have a greater audacity of faith and fact to reach. Fools because of their iniquity are afflicted; they draw near to death, then they cry to the Lord in their trouble and He healeth them out of their distresses. Catch faith by the grace of God and be delivered. Anything that takes me from an attitude of worship, peace, and joy, of consciousness of God's presence, has a satanic source. Greater is He that is in you.

Is there anyone here suffering? (A young man steps out.) Are you saved? "I am." Do you believe that the kingdom of God is within you? "I do." Now, young man, say, "In Jesus' name, come out of my leg, thou evil power!" Are you free? "Yes." Oh! People, put the Bible into practice and claim your blood-bought rights! Every step of my way since I received the baptism of the Holy Ghost I have paid the price for others, letting God take me through that I might show people how to get free. Some say, "I am seeking the baptism; I am having such a struggle, is it not strange?" No; God is preparing you to help somebody else.

Why I am so rigid on the necessity of receiving the baptism of the Spirit is, I fought it out myself. I could have asked anybody, but God was preparing me to help others. The power of God fell on me. I could not satisfy or express the joy within as the Spirit spoke through me in tongues. I had anointings before, but when the fulness came with a high tide I knew it was the baptism, but God had to show me.

There is a difference between having the gift of tongues and speaking as the Spirit giveth utterance; the Holy Ghost uses the gift. If I could make every person who has a bad leg so vexed with the devil that he would kick the other leg, we should get through with something. I only use extravagance to wake you up. Many times I have been shut up with insane people praying for their deliverance; the demon power would come and bite, but I never gave in. It would dethrone a higher principle if I gave in. It is the inward presence of God suffereth violence at the hands of Satan, and the violent take it by force. By the grace of God we are to see tonight we are to keep authority over the body, making the body subject to the higher power — God's mighty provision for sinful humanity.

> Jesus paid it all,
> All to Him I owe;
> Sin had left a crimson stain,
> He washed it white as snow.

Address given at Adelaide, Australia.

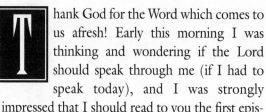

LOVE AND GIFTS

August 1928

T hank God for the Word which comes to us afresh! Early this morning I was thinking and wondering if the Lord should speak through me (if I had to speak today), and I was strongly impressed that I should read to you the first epistle of the Corinthians, and the thirteenth chapter.

I am so thankful to God that He has dovetailed this thirteenth chapter of Corinthians between the twelfth and the fourteenth, because the twelfth chapter deals expressly with the gifts of the Spirit, and the fourteenth is on the lines of the manifestations and the gifts of the Spirit, and the thirteenth of Corinthians is the governor balls over the engine. If ever you see an engine working, you will find right over the main valve that lets in the steam, there are two little balls going round as fast as they can, and sometimes they go slowly. They open and shut the valve that sends in the steam to the pistons. These are constructed so that the engine does not run away.

I find that God the Holy Ghost in His remarkable wisdom has placed the thirteenth chapter right between these wonderful chapters that we love to dwell upon so much, the gifts. How wonderful, how magnificent they are, how God has given them to us that we may be useful, not ornamental, to prove in every case and under every circumstance we might be there right at the time with these gifts. They are enduement for power, they are expressive of His love, they are to edification and comfort to so many weary souls. We find that God brings these gifts in perfect order that the church may receive blessings, but how many people, how many of us have failed to come to the summit of perfection because the governor balls did not work well, because we were more taken up with the gift than the power that moved the gift, because we were more delighted frequently in the gift than the giver of the gift! Then it became fruitless and helpless and we were sorry, and it brought on rebuke sometimes, and sometimes we suffered, suffered much or suffered less.

TONGUES AND INTERPRETATION: "The love that constraineth, the grace that adorns, the power that sustains, the gift that remaineth may be in excellence, when He is the Governor, the controller, the worker."

How I do thank God for the tongues and interpretation, because they introduce new vision, they open the larger avenue. "Let it please Thee today, Lord, to show us how to work, and how to walk and not stumble."

THE GIFTS

Now beloved, the subject is far too big for anything like half an hour, but we will do all we can by the grace of God that we may say things that will live after we have gone away, for it is of such a necessity that we should receive the Holy Ghost in the first place, and then after receiving the Holy Ghost, we must be covetous for the gifts, and then, after receiving the gifts, may we never lose the fact that the gift is entrusted to us for bringing out favors of God to the people. For instance, divine healing is a gift for ministering to the needs of the people, the gift of wisdom — a word in season at the moment to show you just what to do; the gift of knowledge, or the word of knowledge is to inspire you because of the consecutiveness of the Word of God, to bring you life and joy; this is what God intends.

Then the gift of discernment. We are not to discern one another, but to discern evil powers and deal with them, and command them back to the pit from whence they came. The gift of miracles: God intends us to come to the place where we shall see miracles wrought. So God would have us understand that tongues are profitable only when they exalt and glorify the Lord. Then when interpretation is given. Oh, that we might really know what it means — it is not to have beautiful sensations merely and think that is interpretation, but such that the man who has it does not know what is coming, for if he did, it would not be interpretation. Interpretation is not knowing what you are going to say, but it is being in the place where you say exactly what God says. So when I have to interpret a message, I purposely keep my mind from anything that would hinder, and say sometimes, "Praise the Lord," and "Hallelujah," that everything shall be a word through the Spirit, and not my word, but the word of the Lord!

Now I understand that we can have these divine gifts so perfectly balanced by divine love that they shall be a blessing all the time, but there is such a desire sometimes in the human to do something. How the people listen and long for divine prophecy, just as interpretation comes forth; how it thrills! There is nothing wrong with it; it is beautiful. We thank God for the office and the purpose that has caused it to come, but let us be careful to finish when through, and not continue on your own. That is why prophecy is [spoiled]. At the end of the unction you use strange fire, at the end of the message you try to continue. Don't fail, beloved, because the people know the difference, they know that which is full of life, that which is the real thing.

Then again, it is the same with a person praying. We love people to pray in the Holy Ghost; how we love to hear them pray even the first sentences because the fire is there, but what spoils the most holy person in prayer is that after the spirit of prayer has gone forth, they continue on, and people say, "I wish they would stop," and the church becomes silent. They say, "I wish that brother would stop; how beautifully he began, now he is dry!" He won't stop. A preacher once was having a wonderful time, and the people enjoyed it, but when he was through he continued. A man came outside and said to someone at the door, "Has he finished?" "Yes," said the man, "long since, but he won't stop!" May God save us this morning from that. People know when you are praying in the Spirit, why should you take time and spoil everything because the natural side has come to it? God never intended that. God has a supernatural side, and that is the true side, and how beautiful it is! People know sometimes better than us, and we would know if we were more careful. The Lord grant us this morning revelation; we need discernment, we need intuition. It is the life inside, it is the inside salvation, cleansing, filling, it is all inside. Revelation is inside, it is for exhibition outside, but always remember this. God's Son said so much when He said this, "The pure in heart shall see God." There is an inward sight of God, and it is the pure in heart that see God. "Lord keep us pure, so that we shall never block the way."

THE LOVE

Love is always in the place of revelation, but "Though I speak with the tongues of men and of angels, and have not charity, I am become as sounding brass, or a tinkling cymbal. And though I have the gift of prophecy, and understand all mysteries, and all knowledge; and though I have all faith, so that I could remove mountains, and have not charity, I am nothing." Now it is a remarkable fact that God intends us to be examples of the truth. These are divine truths, and God means that we should be examples of these truths. Now beloved, it is lovely to be in the will of God. How many people would like to be nothing this morning? I absolutely refuse to be nothing. You notice I did not put my hand up, but I know you mean the same, and your heart is the same exactly. Now then, how may we be something? By just being nothing, by receiving the Holy Ghost, by being in the place where you can be operated by God and be filled with the power to operate. What it really means to have a language, a beautiful language as so many men have. There are men who are wonderful in language. I used to like to read Talmadge when he was alive; how his messages used to inspire me. Oh, this divine power! It is wonderful to have the tongue of an angel so that all the people who hear you are moved by the language, but how I should weep, how my heart would be broken if I came to speak before you in beautiful language without the power! If I had an angel's language and the people were all taken up with what I should say, and then Jesus was not glorified at all, it would be all hopeless, barren and unfruitful; I should be nothing, but if I speak and say, "Lord, let them hear Thy voice, Lord, let them be compelled to hear Thy truth, Lord, anyhow, anyway hide me today," then He becomes glorious, and all the people say, "We have seen Jesus!"

When I was in California I spent many days with our dear Brother Montgomery when I had a chance. There was a man who lived in Fraser Valley. He had been saved, but he had lost his joy, he lost all he had. He wrote to Brother Montgomery and said, "I am through with everything. I am not going to touch this thing again, I am through." Mr. Montgomery wrote to him and said, "I will never try to persuade you again if you will hear once. There is a man from England, and if you will only just hear him once, I will pay all expenses." So he came. He listened, and at the end of the time he said to me, "This is the truth I am telling you. I have seen the Lord standing beside you, and I heard His voice. I never saw you even.

"I have a lot of money and I have a valley 500 miles long. If you speak the Word to me, I will go on your word, and I will begin and open that valley for the Lord." I have preached in several of his places and God used him wonderfully to speak right through that valley. What I should have missed when he came, the first day, if I had been trying to say something of my own instead of the Lord being there and speaking His words through me. Never let us do anything to lose this divine love, this close affection in our hearts that says, "Not I, but Christ, not I, but Christ!" I want to say forget yourself and get lost in Him. Lose all your identification in the Son of God, let Him become all in all, seek only the Lord and let Him be glorified. You will have gifts, you will have grace, and wisdom. God is waiting for the man that will lay all on the altar, fifty-two weeks in the year, three hundred and sixty-five days in the year, and then continue perpetually in the Holy Ghost.

Now beloved, I must stop; I would like to have gone on. I have such joy in this. I have had the joy of taking this chapter three times in my meetings, one hour every morning, and then giving out questions and answers. I would like something like that this morning, but beloved, go on for every blessing from the Lord that the Lord shall be large in you, that the wood and the hay and the stubble shall be burnt up and the Lord shall bring you to a great harvest time. Now beloved, shall we not present ourselves this morning to the Lord, that He may put His hand upon us and say, "My child, my child be obedient to the message, hear what the Spirit saith to thee that thou mayest go on and possess the land," and the Lord shall give thee a great inheritance.

Published in *Redemption Tidings*
An address given at the Kingsway Hall Whitsuntide Convention, London, May, 1928

UTTERMOST SALVATION

October 1928

cripture reading: Matthew 5:3-7. Many people say that this fifth chapter of St. Matthew's gospel is for the millennial age, that people cannot live it now. Consequently, many drop this chapter and do not carefully investigate it. But for those who have come on with God and received the Holy Ghost, there is a little heaven on earth. They reach a place where they have no fellowship with darkness and the world knoweth them not.

After I was baptized in the Holy Ghost I saw distinctly that God had given me to eat of that tree of life, which Adam and Eve were not able to eat of, and I saw that when the Holy Ghost came in, He so revealed the Christ of God that I was feeding on Him in my heart and having great joy through the strength given by His life. I know that the baptism of the Holy Ghost brings us into possession of all the fulness of God. The people often sing, "Oh, that will be glory for me," but I could see that God had changed that for me and I can sing this morning,

> Oh, now it is glory for me,
> Now it is glory for me,
> For as by His grace,
> I look on His face,
> Now it is glory for me.

Let me come to this wonderful chapter God has given. I will begin with the third verse,

> *Blessed are the poor in spirit: for theirs is the kingdom of heaven.*
> *Matthew 5:3*

The people who have touched this idea, and have identified themselves with the Lord Jesus Christ have come to a place where they now see that all things are possible with God. We have come to a place of an unlimited supply in God and in this poverty of spirit we are entitled to all that God has, "...for theirs is the kingdom of heaven." All that God has is mine, as I come into meekness, into humility, into helplessness in myself.

You will remember that when Jesus came to a city of Samaria, "...being wearied with his journey, sat thus on the well...his disciples were gone away unto the city to buy meat" (John 4:6,8). When they returned they saw Him at peace. He was not looking for food, but was quite at ease. "Therefore said the disciples one to another, Hath any man brought him aught to eat?" (John 4:33). This portrays to us the possibility for man to live in God, to be absorbed in God, with no consciousness of the world under any circumstances, except as we bring help to it. And He said unto them, "...behold, I say unto you, Lift up your eyes, and look on the fields; for they are white already to harvest" (John 4:35). That is the meat; the spiritual life in God, which is joy in the Holy Ghost. He comes to ravish our souls, to break every bond of mere human affection and replace in us the divine instead of the earthly, the pure instead of the unholy, the eye of faith that sees God instead of human feelings. The divine Son of God is to be in us, mightily moving through us, as we cease to be; and nothing helps us, in the human place but this poverty of spirit, which is spoken of in this beatitude.

We must live in such a pure atmosphere that God will shine in and through our souls. Oh, this uttermost salvation! I am satisfied that as we get to know the Son of God, we will never be weak anymore, the tide will be so turned. Let us look at the next verse,

> *Blessed are they that mourn: for they shall be comforted.*
> *Matthew 5:4*

Did Jesus mean mourning over death? No, He meant mourning over the sons and daughters belonging to us, who have not yet touched heaven, who know nothing about the things of the Spirit of life. When God gets within us a mourning cry to move the powers of God, then He will send a revival in every home. Another thing, it is impossible to get this spiritual mourning over lost souls without having the very next thing that God says, "Ye shall be comforted." As though God could give you a spirit of mourning over a needy soul, then not give you victory! Beloved, it is the mighty power of God in us. And when the Spirit brings us to this mourning attitude over lost souls, and over all the failures that we see in professing Christians, till we can go into the presence of God with that mourning spirit, nothing will happen. But when that happens, rejoice; God shall bring you through.

Brothers, sisters, God wants us to rejoice this morning. He has brought us into this blessed place that we may mourn and then rejoice. Let us go on with the chapter because much depends on the next verse:

> *Blessed are the meek: for they shall inherit the earth.*
> *Matthew 5:5*

You say, "Don't talk to me about being meek; I shall never reach that." Take the case of Moses — He surely was not meek, when he slew the Egyptian. But when God got Moses into His hand in the land of Midian, He so molded him that he became the meekest man in all the earth. I do not care what side your temper is on — if you only get a flash light of heaven, God can so mold you and bring you down that you can be the meekest people of all the earth.

Such a bad temper I used to have, it made me tremble all over and it would make me furious with its evil power. A man came around preaching. I saw that this temper had to be destroyed, it could not be patched up. One day the power of God fell upon me. I came out to the meeting and fell down before the Lord. The people began asking, "What sin has Wigglesworth been committing?" This went on for a fortnight. Every time I came to the altar God used to sweep through me with such a manifestation of my helplessness, that I would go down before God and weep right through. Then the preacher or the leader was broken up and came alongside of me. God made a revival begin in that. God had broken me up and revival began through His revival in me. Oh, it was lovely! At last my wife said, "Since my husband had that touch, I have never been able to cook anything that he was not pleased with. It is never too cold and never too hot."

Only God can make people right. Only melted gold is minted. Only moistened clay receives the mold. Only softened wax receives the seal. Only broken, contrite hearts receive the mark as the Potter turns us on His wheel. Oh, Lord give us that blessed state where we are perfectly and wholly made meek.

Ah, a wonderful chapter is this! The beatitudes of the Spirit are truly lovely.

> *Blessed are they which do hunger and thirst after righteousness: for they shall be filled.*
>
> *Matthew 5:6*

"They shall be filled." Oh yes, praise the Lord! We must emphasize the fact that God will not fail to fill us. No man can hunger and thirst after righteousness, without God has put the thirst in him. And I want you to notice what kind of a righteousness this is. This righteousness is the righteousness of Jesus.

In the [first] epistle of John we find in the fifth chapter, fourth and fifth verses, "...this is the victory that overcometh the world, even our faith. Who is he that overcometh the world, but he that believeth that Jesus is the Son of God?" Righteousness is more than paying our way. We hear someone say, "Oh, I never do anything wrong to anybody. I always pay my way." This is simple life in the natural, but there is a higher law of the Spirit of life in Christ Jesus. I must see that Jesus is my perfect righteousness. He came by the power of God. "For what the law could not do, in that it was weak through the flesh, God sending his own Son in the likeness of sinful flesh, and for sin, condemned sin in the flesh" (Romans 8:3). We must see that if we get this righteousness of God, sin is destroyed. These are beautiful words in the ninth verse of the first chapter of Hebrews:

> *"Thou hast loved righteousness, and hated iniquity; therefore God, even thy God, hath anointed thee with the oil of gladness above thy fellows."*

But the climax of divine touches of heaven is never to leave you stationary but rather to increase the thirst and the appetite for greater things. There is something within that makes you press on till you have everything else out that you may have that which God is pressing in. This righteousness is a walk with God, it is a divine inheritance, it is seeing the face of Jesus, till you cannot be satisfied without drinking of His Spirit and being overflowed continually with His blessings. I cannot be satisfied without Christ's righteousness. He gives us thirst for the immensity of God's power. It is a divine problem which is solved in only one way: having *Him*. And having Him, we have all things.

Beloved, I beseech you this morning, by the power of God that He will bring you into a death unto self, and a life unto righteousness, which shall please God in the Spirit. Thus we understand in some measure what God has for us in the next verse:

> *Blessed are the merciful: for they shall obtain mercy.*
>
> *Matthew 5:7*

I believe this is truly a spiritual condition, which is higher than the natural law. Sometimes when we talk about mercy, we think of being kind, or amiable, or philanthropic towards others. We think those are high positions. So they are, but the world has that. Beloved, we should have all that but we should have much more. Our Lord Jesus had something on the lines of mercy that we shall never know until He fills us with Himself. My blessed Lord! Can there ever be one like Him? Can you think of such rarity, such beauty, such self-sacrifice? "Blessed are the merciful." We must have heaven's riches to give to souls in poverty; the spiritual life of Christ to be poured in. You cannot be filled with the Lord and not be merciful. You cannot have the baptism with power without this supernatural mercy, this divine touch of heaven, that stops satanic forces, that turns captivity, loosing the oppressed, and that which strengthens the helpless. That is the spirit that God wants to give us this morning. Oh, for heaven to bend down upon us with this deep inward cry for a touch of Him, His majesty, His glory, His might, His power.

It is a very remarkable thing that the merciful always obtain mercy. Look at the measure of this spiritual life — first full, then pressed down, then shaken together, and then running over. This divine touch of heaven is lovely, the most charming thing on earth, sweeter than all. I am just running over with new wine this morning. God wants you to have this new wine. Oh, it thrills the human heart! How it mightily sweeps you right into heaven!

I ask you all this morning, needy souls, whatever you want, to come boldly to the throne of grace. Come, and the Lord bless you.

Triumphs of Faith

ABOUT THE GIFTS OF THE SPIRIT

October 27, 1928

 orasmuch as ye are zealous of spiritual gifts, seek that ye may excel to the edifying of the church.

1 Corinthians 14:12

This is the Word of God and it is most important that when we read it we do so with purpose of heart to obey its every precept. We have no right to open the Word of God carelessly or indifferently. I have no right to come to you with any message unless it is absolutely in the perfect order of God. I believe we are in order to consider further the subject so necessary to be informed about in these days when so many people are receiving the baptism of the Holy Ghost, and then do not know which way to go.

We have a great need today. It is that we may be supplied with revelation according to the mind of the Lord, that we may be instructed by the mind of the Spirit, that we may be able rightly to divide the Word of truth, that we may not be novices, seeing that the Spirit of the Lord has come to us in revelation. We ought to be alert to every touch of divine, spiritual illumination.

We should carefully consider what the apostle said to us, "...grieve not the Holy Spirit, whereby ye are sealed unto the day of redemption" (Ephesians 4:30). The sealing of the Spirit is very remarkable and *I pray God that not one person may lose the divine inheritance that God has chosen for you, greater than you could choose if you had your mind ten times more largely exercised.* God's mind is greater than yours. His thought is higher than the heavens over you, so that you need not be afraid.

I have great love for my boys in England, great love for my daughter here; but it is nothing in comparison to God's love toward us. God's love is desirous that we should walk up and down the earth as His son, clothed, filled, radiant, with fire beaming forth from the countenance, setting forth the power of the Spirit, so that the people jump into liberty.

But there is deplorable ignorance among those who have gifts. It is not right for you to think that because you have a gift you are to wave it before the people and try to get their minds upon that, because if you do you will be out of the will of God. Gifts and callings may be in the body without repentance, but remember that God calls you to account for the gifts being properly administered in a spiritual way after you have received it. It is not given to adorn you, but to sustain, build, edify, and bless the church. When the church receives this edification and God ministers through that member, then all the members will rejoice together. God moves upon us as His offspring, as His choice, and fruit of the earth. He wants us to be decked in wonderful raiment, even as our Master.

His operations upon us may be painful but the wise saint will remember that among those whom God chastens it is he who is exercised by that chastening to whom "...it yieldeth the peaceable fruit of righteousness..." (Hebrews 12:11). Therefore let Him do with you what seemeth Him good, for He has His hand upon you and He will not willingly take it off till He has performed the thing He knows you need. So if He comes with a fan, be ready for the fan. If He comes with chastisement, be ready for chastisement. If He comes with correction, be ready for correction. Whatever He wills to do, let Him do it and He will bring you to the land of plenty. Oh, *it is worth the world to be under the power of the Holy Ghost!*

If He chastens you not, if you sail placidly along without incident, without crosses, without persecutions, without trials, remember that "...if ye be without chastisement, whereof all are partakers, then are ye bastards, and not sons" (Hebrews 12:8). Therefore "Examine yourselves, whether ye be in the faith" (2 Corinthians 13:5). Never forget that Jesus said this word: "They that hear My voice, follow Me." Jesus wants you all to follow, wants you to have a clear ring in your testimony.

You are eternally saved by the power of God. Do not be led astray by anything, do not take your feelings for your salvation, do not take anybody's word for your salvation. Believe that God's Word is true. What does it say?

> *He that believeth on the Son hath everlasting life: and he that believeth not the Son shall not see life; but the wrath of God abideth on him.*
>
> John 3:36

When your will becomes entirely the will of God, then you are clearly in the place where the Holy Ghost can make Jesus Lord in your life, Lord over your purchases, Lord over your selling, Lord over your eating and your drinking, your clothing and your choice of companionship.

> *Now there are diversities of gifts, but the same Spirit. And there are differences of administrations, but the same Lord. And there are diversities of operations, but it is the same God which worketh all in all. But the manifestation of the Spirit is given to every man to profit withal.*
>
> 1 Corinthians 12:4-7

The variation of humanity is tremendous. Faces are different, so is physique. Your whole body may be so tempered that one particular gift would not suit you at all while it would suit another person.

So the Word of God deals here with varieties of gifts, meaning that these gifts perfectly meet the condition of people in this place. That is God's plan. Not one person, it may be, would be led out to claim all gifts. Nevertheless, do not be afraid; the Scriptures are definite. Paul said that you need not come behind in any gift. God has for you wonderful things beyond what you have ever known. The Holy Ghost is so full of prophetic operation of divine power, that it is marvelous what may happen after the Holy Ghost comes.

How He loosed me! I am no good without the Holy Ghost. The power of the Holy Ghost loosed my language. I was like my mother. She had no language. If she began to tell a story, she couldn't go through. My father would say, "Mother, you will have to begin again." I was like that. I couldn't tell a story. I was bound. Plenty of thought, but no language. But oh, after the Holy Ghost came!

When He came I had a great desire after gifts. So the Lord caused me to see that it is possible for every believer to live in such holy unction, such divine communion, such pressed-in measure by the power of the Spirit that every gift can be his.

But is there not a vast and appalling unconcern about possessing the gifts? Ask of a score of saints chosen at random from almost any assembly, "Have you any of the gifts of the Spirit?" and the answer will be, "No," and given in a tone and with a manner that conveys the thought that the saint is not surprised at not having the gifts, that he doesn't expect to have any of them, and does not expect to seek for them. Isn't this terrible when this living Word exhorts us specifically to "covet earnestly the best gifts"?

So in order that the gift might be everything and in evidence, we have to see that we cease to live excepting for His glory. He works with us, we work with Him, cooperative, working together. This is divine. Surely this is God's plan.

God has brought you to the banquet and He wants to send you away full. We are in a place where God wants to give us visions. We are in a place where His great love is being bent over us with kisses. Oh, how lovely the kiss of Jesus, the expression of His love!

Oh come, let us seek Him for the best gifts, and let us strive to be wise and rightly divide the Word of truth, giving it forth in power that the church may be edified and sinners may be saved.

Published in *The Pentecostal Evangel*

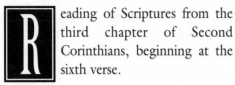

CHANGED FROM GLORY TO GLORY

April 1929

Reading of Scriptures from the third chapter of Second Corinthians, beginning at the sixth verse.

Notice especially the seventh verse, where we read that the glory that was on the face of Moses had to be "done away." For what reason was it to be done away? For something else that had exceeding glory.

> *For if the ministration of condemnation be glory, much more doth the ministration of righteousness exceed in glory. For even that which was made glorious had no glory in this respect, by reason of the glory that excelleth.*
>
> *2 Corinthians 3:9,10*

I am positive that we have no conception of the depths and heights of the liberty and blessing of the "ministration of the Spirit." We must attain to this position of godliness, and we must be partakers of the divine nature. The law was so glorious that Moses was filled with joy in the expectation of what it should mean. To us there is the excellence of Christ's glory in the ministration of the Holy Spirit. In Him we live and move, and reign over all things. It is no more "thou shalt not." It is God's will, revealed to us in Christ. "I delight to do Thy will, O God." And, beloved, in our hearts there is exceeding glory. Oh, the joy of this celestial touch this morning!

When Peter was rehearsing that wonderful day in the Mount, he says, "...there came such a voice to him from the excellent glory..." (2 Peter 1:17).

If I should come to you this morning, and say, "Whatever you do, you must try to be holy," I should miss it, I should be altogether outside of God's plan, but I take the words of the epistle this morning, which says by the Holy Ghost, "Be ye holy." (1 Peter 1:16). It is as easy as possible to be holy, but you can never be holy by your own efforts. When you lose your heart and Another takes your heart, and you lose your desires and He takes the desires, then you live in that sunshine of bliss which no mortal can ever touch. God wants us to be entirely eaten up by this holy zeal of God, so that every day we shall walk in the Spirit. It is lovely to walk in the Spirit, for He will cause you to dwell in safety, and rejoice inwardly and praise God reverently.

"...much more doth the ministration of righteousness exceed in glory" (2 Corinthians 3:9). I want to speak about righteousness now. You cannot touch this beatitude we are dwelling on this morning, without saying that the excellent glory exceeds in Christ. All excellent glory is in Him, all righteousness is in Him. Everything that pertains to holiness and godliness, everything that denounces and brings to death the natural, everything that makes you know that you have ceased to be forever, is always in an endless power in the risen Christ. Whenever you look at Jesus you can see so many different facts of His life. I see Him in those forty days before His ascension, with wonderful truth, infallible proofs of His ministry. What was the ministry of Christ? When you come to the very essence of His ministry it was the righteousness of His purpose. The excellence of His ministry was the glory that covered Him. His Word was convincing, inflexible, divine, with a personality of an eternal endurance. It never failed. He spake and it stood fast. It was an immovable condition with Him, and His righteousness abideth. God must bring us there: we must be people of our word, so that people will be able to depend upon our word. Jesus was true inwardly and outwardly. He is the Way, the Truth, and the Life (John 14:6), and on this foundation we can build.

When we know that our own heart condemns us not, we can say to the mountain, "Be removed." But when our own hearts condemn us, there is no power in prayer; no power in preaching. We are just sounding brass and tinkling cymbals. May the Holy Ghost show us that there must be a ministry of righteousness. Christ was righteousness through and through. He is lovely! Oh, truly, He is beautiful! God wants to fix it in our hearts that we are to be like Him; like Him in character. God wants righteousness in the inward parts, that we may be pure through and through. The Bible is the plumb line of everything, and unless we are plumbed right up with the Word of God, we will fail in righteousness.

"For even that which was made glorious had no glory in this respect, by reason of the glory that excelleth" (2 Corinthians 3:10). You have to get right behind this blessed Word and say it is of God. Here we come again to the law. I see that it was truly a schoolmaster that brought us to

Christ. Law is beautiful when law is established in the earth. As far as possible in every country and town, you will find that the law has something to do with keeping things straight, and in a measure the city has some kind of sobriety because of the law. But, beloved, we belong to a higher, nobler citizenship, not an earthly citizenship, for our citizenship is in heaven. If the natural law will keep an earthly city in somewhat moderate conditions, what will the excellent glory be in divine relationship to the citizenship to which we belong? What is meant by excellent glory is that it outshines. The earth is filled with broken hearts, but the excellent glory fills redeemed men and women so that they show forth the excellency of the grace of the glory of God.

> *Seeing then that we have such hope, we use great plainness of speech: And not as Moses, which put a veil over his face, that the children of Israel could not stedfastly look to the end of that which is abolished.*
>
> *2 Corinthians 3:12,13*

The man who is going on with God will have no mix-up in his oratory. He will be so plain and precise, and divine in his speech, that everything will have a lift towards the glory. He must use great plainness of speech, but he must be a man who knows his message. He must know what God has in His mind in the Spirit, not in the letter. He is there as a vessel for honor, God's mouthpiece: therefore he stands in the presence of God, and God speaks and uses him.

I always say that you cannot sing victory on a minor key. If your life is not in constant pitch, you will never ring the bells of heaven. You must always be in tune with God, and then the music will come out as sweet as possible. We must be the mouthpiece of God, not by letter but by the Spirit, and we must be so in the will of God that He will rejoice over us with singing. If we are in the Spirit, the Lord of life is the same Spirit. "Now the Lord is that Spirit: and where the Spirit of the Lord is, there is liberty" (2 Corinthians 3:17). There is no liberty that is going to help the people so much as testimony. I find people who do not know how to testify rightly. We must testify only as the Spirit gives utterance. You are not to use your liberty except for the glory of God.

So many meetings are spoiled by long prayers and long testimonies. If the speaker keeps in the Spirit, he will know when he should sit down. When you begin to rehearse yourself, the people get wearied, and they wish you would sit down, for the unction has then ceased. It is lovely to pray, and it is a joy to hear you pray when you are in the Spirit, but if you keep on after the Spirit has finished, all the people get tired of it. So God wants us to know that we are not to use liberty, because we have it to use, but we are to let the liberty of the Spirit use us, and then we shall know when to end. The meetings ought to be so free in the Spirit that people would always go away with the feeling. "Oh, I wish the meeting had gone on for another hour," or, "Was not that testimony meeting a revelation!"

The last verse is the most glorious of all for us:

> *But we all, with open face beholding as in a glass the glory of the Lord, are changed into the same image from glory to glory, even as by the Spirit of the Lord.*
>
> *2 Corinthians 3:18*

So there is glory upon glory, and joy upon joy, and a measureless measure of joy and glory. Beloved, we get God's Word so wonderfully in our hearts that it absolutely changes us in everything. And as we so feast on the Word of the Lord, so eat and digest the truth, inwardly eat of Christ — we are changed every day from one state of glory to another. You will never find anything else but the Word that takes you there, so you cannot afford to put aside that Word.

I beseech you, beloved, that you come short of none of these beatitudes we have been speaking of. These grand truths of the Word of God must be your testimony, must be your life, your pattern. "Ye are...the epistle of Christ" (2 Corinthians 3:2,3). God says this to you by the Spirit. When there is a standard which has not yet been reached in your life, God by His grace, by His mercy, and your yieldedness, can fit you for that place which you can never be prepared for only by a broken heart and a contrite spirit, and yielding to the will of God. But if you will come with a whole heart to the throne of grace, God will meet you and build you up on His spiritual plane.

Triumphs of Faith

MEN-CATCHERS . . . ASTONISHMENT!

April 1929

uke 5:1-8 — Every time I preach I am impressed with the fact that the Word of God is full of life and vitality — changing us. God's Word must come to pass in us. How can we get more faith? God's Word tells us, "Faith cometh by hearing and hearing by the Word of God."

Faith is a gift. We receive our inheritance by faith. A new order. Spiritual children. Sons — born a living fact. Sons of God without rebuke. May God manifest it in us by the power of His might. The people said, "Blessed is she that bare Thee"; but Jesus said, "Blessed are they who hear the Word of God and keep it." This blessed Christ of God they said never spake like this Man. We do not hear Him like scribes; we hear Him with authority. The living Son of God — the Son of His love came to us with open understanding, ministering the breath of His Father. We knew a quickening spirit. The moment we believed we knew we had a new nature, a new life. He had a wonderful word, a sweet influence; men saw love in those beautiful eyes and were convinced of sin in His presence. The people pressed upon Him — yet He said, "Foxes have holes and the birds of the air have nests, but the Son of Man hath not where to lay His head." Jesus said to Peter, "...Launch out into the deep, and let down your nets for a draught" (v. 4). Peter said, "...We have toiled all night, and have caught nothing...." Lord, You know nothing about fishing — daytime is the wrong time to fish — nevertheless, at Thy Word I will let down the net. I believe every fish in the lake tried to get into that net; they wanted to see Him. I must see Jesus. There was a banquet for cripples, and in the middle of it a father brought a boy on his shoulder; the father lifted the boy up. I said, "In the name of Jesus." The boy said, "Papa! Papa! It is going all over me." Jesus healed him. Peter filled one ship — then another. Oh, what would happen if you put down all the nets? Believe God! He says, "Look unto *Me* and be ye saved." He says, "Come unto Me all ye that are weary and heavy laden and I will give you rest." He says, "He that believeth on the Son hath everlasting life." Believe! Oh, believe. It's the Word of God.

There is a river that makes glad the city of God. Peter saw the ship sinking. He looked round and he saw Him. He fell down at Jesus' feet, saying, "Depart from me, for I am a sinful man, oh Lord," for he was astonished and all that were with him at the draught of the fishes which they had taken. That spotless Lamb stood there. They looked unto Him and were lightened, and their faces were not ashamed. To see Jesus is to see a new way, to see all things differently: new life, new plans; as we gaze at Him we are satisfied; there is none like Him. Sin moves off. Jesus was the express image of the Father. The Father could not be in the midst, so He clothed Jesus with a body — with eternal resources. Let us gather together unto Him. Oh, this moving unto Him. He has all we need. He will fulfil the desire of our hearts, granting all our petitions.

There was a man who had a cancer in the rectum; night and day he had morphine every ten minutes. I went to see him. He said, "I do not know how to believe God! Oh, if I could believe. Oh, if I could, if God would work a miracle." I placed my hand upon him in Jesus' name. I said to the nurse, "You go to the other room. God will work a miracle." The Spirit of God came upon me; in the name of Jesus I laid hold of the evil power, with hatred in my heart against the power of Satan; while I was praying it burst. I said to the nurse, "Come in." She did not understand, but the man knew God had done it. Now, previously, this man had a hobby; it was yachting. He was very fond of his yacht; it was all he wanted to talk about. Did he want to talk about yachting now? No! He said, "Tell me about Jesus — the sin bearer, the Lamb of God." He who made things happen, will you let Him in? One body. The bread and the wine is a presentation of Christ. His body broken for you — broken to meet every human need.

Hebrews 4:12. Quick and powerful. How it works in spirit, soul, and body, separating the desires, heart, thought, word, deed, intent, stiff knees. The Word enters into the joints and the marrows. The Word of the living God — one body, one bread — so conductive. He says, "Begin to do if you want the furniture of God's place put in order." I kneel down; I begin to pray. You begin in the Spirit; the Spirit leads you to pray by the Spirit. You begin — God will come in. God will lift you as you begin. We are here to help you to a place of beginnings. You must begin. Come in to a Person that has no end — Jesus by His Spirit. Feed upon Him;

believe Him. The day is a day of communion. One body, unbroken fellowship. Look at Him. Reign with Him, live in His presence.

Peace, Peace. Sweet peace;
Sweet peace, the gift of God's love.

God could give us many gifts, but the lovely gift of Him that suffered and died for us God is satisfied with Him. One bread, one body. *Keep the vision.* Bring your ships to land — forsake all and follow Him. For He was astonished, and all that were with him, at the draught of the fishes which they had taken...Fear not; from henceforth thou shalt catch men" (vv. 9,10).

Published in *Redemption Tidings*

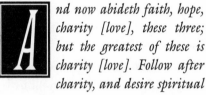

THE FULNESS OF THE SPIRIT

September 1929

nd now abideth faith, hope, charity [love], these three; but the greatest of these is charity [love]. Follow after charity, and desire spiritual gifts, but rather that ye may prophesy. For he that speaketh in an unknown tongue speaketh not unto men, but unto God: for no man understandeth him; howbeit in the spirit he speaketh mysteries. But he that prophesieth speaketh unto men to edification, and exhortation, and comfort.

1 Corinthians 13:13–14:3

It is quite easy to construct a building if the foundation is secure. It is not so easy to rise spiritually, unless you have a real spiritual power working within you. It will never do for us to be top heavy — the base must always be very firmly set. So I believe that while we might have gone on, we will have to consider the pit from whence we were dug. Except we rightly understand the spiritual leadings, according to the mind of God, we will never be able to stand when the winds blow, when the trials come, and when Satan appears as an angel of light. We shall never be able to stand unless we are firmly fixed in the Word of God.

There must be three things in our lives if we wish to go right through with God in the fulness of Pentecost. First we must be grounded and settled in love. We must have a real knowledge of what love is, and then we must have a clear understanding of the Word, for love must manifest the Word. Then we must understand clearly our own ground, because it is our own ground that needs to be looked after the most.

The Lord speaks at least twice of the good ground, into which seed is sown, which also bore fruit and brought forth some one hundred fold, and some sixty, and some thirty. It was in different portions of thirty, sixty, and one hundred fold even in the good ground. I maintain truly that there is no limitation to the abundance of a harvest when the ground is perfectly in the hand of the Lord. So we must clearly understand that the Word of God can never come forth with all its primary purposes unless our ground is right. But God will help us, I believe, to see that He can make the ground in perfect order as it is put into His hands.

Let me speak of the first verse, then I must pass on quickly. I want you to notice that the primary thought in the mind of the Spirit is, that when love is in perfect progress, all other things will work in harmony, for prophetic utterances are all of no value unless they are perfectly covered with divine love. Our Lord Jesus would never have accomplished His great plan in this world, only because He was so full of love to His Father, and love to us, that love never failed to accomplish its purpose. It worked in Him and through Him by the power of the Father's love in Him. I believe that love will have to come into our lives. Christ must be the summit, the desire, the plan of all things. All our sayings, doings, and workings must be in and unto Him well pleasing, and then our prophetic utterances will be a blessing through God, and they will never be side issues. There is no imitation in a man filled with the Holy Ghost. Imitation is lost in the great plan of Christ being the ideal of his life.

God wants you to be so balanced in spiritual unction that you will always be able to do what pleases Him, and not that which shall please other people, or yourself. The ideal must be that it shall all be to edification, and everything must go on to this end to please the Lord. "Follow after charity [love], and desire spiritual gifts, but rather that ye may prophesy" (1 Corinthians 14:1). When they came to Moses and said that there were two others in the camp prophesying, Moses said,

"...would God that all the Lord's people were prophets..." (Numbers 11:29). That is a clear revelation on this line that God would have us in such a spiritual, holy place, that He could take our words, and so fill them with divine power that we would speak only as the Spirit leads in prophetic utterances.

Beloved, there is spiritual language, and there is also human language, which always keeps on the human plane. There is a divine incoming into the same language so it is changed by spiritual power, and brings life to those who hear you speak. But this divine touch of prophecy will never come on any line except being filled with the Spirit. If you wish to be anything for God, do not miss His plan. God has no room for you on ordinary lines. You must realize that within you there is the power of the Holy Spirit, who is forming within you everything you require. I believe we have too much preaching, and too little testifying. You will never have a living Pentecostal church with a preacher every night preaching, preaching, preaching. The people get tired of this constant preaching, but they never get tired when the whole place is on fire: when twenty or more jump up at once, and will not sit down until they testify. So, remember you must awake out of your lethargy.

> *And it shall come to pass afterward, that I will pour out my spirit upon all flesh; and your sons and your daughters shall prophesy, your old men shall dream dreams, your young men shall see visions: And also upon the servants and upon the handmaids in those days will I pour out my spirit.*
>
> *Joel 2:28,29*

This is spoken by the prophet Joel, and we know that this is that which occurred on the day of Pentecost. This was the first outpouring of the Spirit, but what should it be now if we would only wake up to the words of our Master? "Greater works than these shall [ye] do" (John 14:12). Hear what the Scripture says to us:

> *Howbeit when he, the Spirit of truth, is come, he will guide you into all truth: for he shall not speak of himself; but whatsoever he shall hear, that shall he speak....*
>
> *John 16:13*

The Holy Ghost is inspiration, the Holy Ghost is revelation, the Holy Ghost is manifestation, the Holy Ghost is operation, and when a man comes into the fulness of the Holy Ghost he is in perfect order, and built up on scriptural foundations. I have failed to see any man who understood the 12th, 13th, and 14th chapters of First Corinthians unless he had been baptized with the Holy Ghost. He may talk about it, but it is all a surface condition. When he gets baptized with the Holy Ghost he speaks about a deep inward conviction by the power of the Spirit working in him, a revelation of that Scripture. On the other side, there is so much that a man receives when he is born again. He receives the first love, and has a revelation of Jesus.

> *But if we walk in the light, as he is in the light, we have fellowship one with another, and the blood of Jesus Christ his Son cleanseth us from all sin.*
>
> *1 John 1:7*

But God wants a man to be on fire so that he will always speak as an oracle of God. He wants to so build that man on the foundations of God that everyone who sees and hears him will say, "That is a new man after the order of the Spirit."

> *...old things are passed away; behold, all things are become new.*
> *2 Corinthians 5:17*

New things have come, and he is now in the divine order. When a man is filled with the Holy Ghost, he has a vital power that makes people know he has seen God. He ought to be in such a place that if he should go into a neighbor's house, or out amongst people, they will feel that God has come in their midst.

> *...he that prophesieth speaketh unto men to edification, and exhortation, and comfort. He that speaketh in an unknown tongue edifieth himself; but he that prophesieth edifieth the church.*
> *1 Corinthians 14:3,4*

So there are two edifications spoken of here. Which is the first? To edify yourself, because after you have been edified by the Spirit you are able to edify the Church through the Spirit. What we want is more of the

Holy Ghost. Oh, beloved. It is not merely a measure, it is a pressed down measure. It is not merely a pressed down measure, it is shaken together and running over. Anybody can hold a full cup, but you cannot hold an overflowing cup, and the baptism of the Holy Ghost is an overflowing cup. Praise the Lord!

Published in *Triumphs of Faith*

 Second Peter 1 — God has always had a person that He could illuminate, enlarge until there was nothing hindering the power of God flowing out to a world in need. This, like faith is the gift God is willing to

LIKE, LIKE, LIKE

September 1929

give us in order (if need be) that we may subdue kingdoms, work righteousness, and stop the mouths of lions; ability to triumph under all circumstances because our helper is Almighty God. Always strong, *faithful*. The faithful always have a good report — living in the divine order of victory — because God has taken His place in them. The divine author bringing to our minds "thus saith the Lord" every time. If any man speak, let him speak as an oracle of God. Having the Word of God as the standard for all need.

This "like" faith is the same faith that Abraham had. It counts the things that are not as though they were — and believes what God has is the essence of the substance of the power of eternal life.

Jesus is the Word, and if you have the Word, you have faith — *"like faith."* There is no way into the power and deep things of God without a broken spirit. We erasing from ourselves and God taking the reins and ruling. Faith in God, power with God, lies in the knowledge of the Word of God. We are no better than our faith. For whatsoever is born of God overcometh the world, and this is the victory that overcometh the world, even our faith. If you believe in Him, you are purified for He is pure. You are strengthened for He is strong. You are made whole because He is whole.

THE LIVING PRINCIPLE

You may receive all His fulness because of the revelation of Him. This like *(like)* faith is imparted in all the principles of the Word of God. Faith is the living principle of the Word of God. If we are led by God's Spirit we shall be definitely led into the deep things of God and His truth. The revelation of Him being so clear that we shall live by His life.

Now beloved — I cannot understand God except by His Word (not impressions, feelings, or sentiment). If I am going to know God I am going to know Him by His Word. Every man that is born of God — a divine act, when God comes in, working a personality of Himself — Christ formed in us.

God is almighty, no limitation. And His purpose is to bring many souls to glory. He speaks about His divine power, which has given us all things that pertain to life and godliness, through the knowledge of Him. God's Word is multiplication — yesterday, today, and forever the same.

God wants to give a great multiplication in the knowledge of Himself. Then faith will use, and we shall know the wonderful flow of the peace of God. If we open ourselves to God, God will flow through us.

If we know God hears us when we pray we know we have the petition we have desired.

THE LIVING WORD

For God's Word is:

1. Supernatural in origin.
2. Eternal in duration.
3. Inexpressible in valor.
4. Infinite in scope.
5. Regenerative in power.
6. Infallible in authority.
7. Universal in application.
8. Inspired in totality.

> 1. Read it through.
> 2. Write it down.
> 3. Pray it in.
> 4. Work it out.
> 5. Pass it on.

The Word of God changes a man until he becomes an epistle of God. Transforming the mind, changing the character from grace to grace, giving us an inheritance in the Spirit — until we are conformed — God coming in, dwelling in us, walking in us, talking through us, supping with us. There is no God like our God. *I believe in the Holy Ghost.* God is love. He that dwelleth in love dwelleth in God. God wants to take ordinary men and bring them out into extraordinary conditions.

God has room for the thirsty man, who is crying out for more of Himself.

It is not what we are, but it is what God wants us to be.

Blessed are the poor in spirit for Christ is the kingdom of heaven. Beloved! let us rededicate ourself afresh to God.

Every new revelation means a new dedication.

Let us seek His face and take away from this meeting the desire of our hearts. For God has promised to fulfill, *fill full,* the desire of those that fear Him.

> *Like, like faith,*
> *Like fulfillment. Amen.*

Published in *Redemption Tidings*

 es, *I believe!* Oh, that our hearts and minds this day might come to that place of understanding, where we realize that it is possible, if we "only believe," for God to take all our human weaknesses and failures and transform us by His mighty power into a new creation. What an inspiration to give God the supreme place in our lives; when we do He will so fill us with the Holy Spirit that the government will rest upon His shoulders. Oh, to believe, and come into the holy realm of the knowledge of what it means to yield our all to God. Just think of what would happen if we only *dared to believe God!* Oh, for a faith that *leaps* into the will of God and says, Amen!

THE HOUR IS COME

December 1929

COMMUNION PREPARATIONS

There is no service so wonderful to me as the service of partaking of the Lord's supper, the holy communion. The Scriptures say, *"As oft as ye do it, ye do it unto me"* — you do it in remembrance of Him. I am sure that every person in this place has a great desire to do something for Jesus; and that which He wants to do, is to keep in remembrance the cross, the grave, the resurrection, and the ascension, for the memory of these four events will always bring you into a place of great blessing. You do not need, however, to continually live on the cross, or even in remembrance of the cross, but what you need to remember about the cross is, *"It is finished."* You do not need to live in the grave, but only keep in remembrance that "He is risen" out of the grave, and that we are to be "seated with Him in glory."

> *Then came the day of unleavened bread, when the passover must be killed. And He sent Peter and John, saying, Go and prepare us the passover, that we may eat.*
>
> Luke 22:7-8

The institution of the holy communion is one of those settings in Scripture, a time in the history of our Lord Jesus Christ, when the mystery of the glories of Christ was being unveiled. As the Master trod this earth, how the multitudes would gather with eagerness and longing in their hearts to hear the words that dropped from His gracious lips; but there were also those who had missed the vision. They saw the Christ, heard His words, but those wonderful words were to them like idle tales. When we *miss the vision* and do not come into the fulness of the ministry of the Spirit, there is a cause. Beloved, there is a *deadness* in us that must have the resurrection touch. Today we have the unveiled truth, for the dispensation of the Holy Ghost has come to unfold the fulness of redemption, that we might be clothed with power; and that which brings us into the state where God can pour upon us His blessing, is a *broken spirit and a contrite heart.* We need to examine ourselves this morning to see what state we are in, whether we are just "religious" or whether we be truly "in Christ."

The human spirit, when perfectly united with the Holy Spirit, has but one place, and that is death, death, and deeper death. The human spirit will then cease to desire to have its own way, and instead of "my" will, the cry of the heart will be, "Thy will, oh, Lord, be done in me."

> *And he sent Peter and John, saying, Go and prepare us the passover, that we may eat. And they said unto him, Where wilt thou that we prepare? And he said unto them, Behold, when ye are entered into the city, there shall a man meet you, bearing a pitcher of water; follow him into the house where he entereth in. And ye shall say unto the goodman of the house, The Master saith unto thee, Where is the guestchamber, where I shall eat the passover with my disciples? And he shall shew you a large upper room furnished: there make ready.*
>
> Luke 22:8-12

It is one thing to handle the Word of God, but it is another thing to "believe" what God says. The great aim of the Spirit's power within us is to so bring us in line with His perfect will that we will unhesitatingly believe the Scriptures, daring to accept them as the authentic divine principle of God. When we do, we will find our feet so firmly fixed upon the plan of redemption that it will not matter from whence come trials or other things, for our whole nature will be so enlarged, that it will be no more I, but, "Lord, what wilt thou have me to do?"

Every believer should be a living epistle of the Word, one who is "read and known of all men." Your very presence should bring such a witness of the Spirit that every one with whom you come in contact would know that you are a "sent" one, a light in the world, a manifestation of the Christ; and last of all, that you are a "biblical" Christian.

Those disciples had to learn that whatever Jesus said must come to pass. Jesus said, very slowly, I believe, and thoughtfully, "When you go into the city, there shall a man meet you bearing a pitcher of water. Follow him into the house, and just when he has entered in, say, the Master hath need of a room where he may eat the passover with his disciples." That is the way that Jesus taught them. Beloved, let me say this: *There is no person in Palestine who has ever seen a "man" bearing a pitcher of water.* It is a thing unknown. Therefore, we find Jesus beginning with a prophecy which brought that inward knowledge to them that what He said must come to pass. This is the secret of the Master's life — *prophecy which never failed.* There is no power that can change the Word of God. Jesus was working out this great thought in the hearts of His disciples, that they might *know* that *"it shall come to pass."*

After Jesus had given that wonderful command to Peter and John, those disciples were walking into the city, no doubt in deep meditation, when suddenly they cried out in amazement, "Look! There He is! Just as the Master hath said."

When in Jerusalem I was preaching on Mount Olivet, and as I looked down, at my right hand I saw where the two ways met, where the ass was tied. I could see the Dead Sea, and all the time I was preaching I saw at least 150 women going down with vessels and then carrying them back on their heads full of water; but, *not one man.* However, Jesus said that it had to be a "man," and so it was, for no one could change His word. Some have said to me that He had it all arranged for a man to carry a pitcher of water. I want to tell you that God does not have to arrange with mortals to carry out His plans. If He has the power to hear the cry of some poor needy child of His who may be suffering, and that one may be in England, Africa, China, or anywhere else, saying, "Oh, God, Thou knowest my need," and here in New York, Germany, California, or some other place, there is a disciple of His on his knees, and the Lord will say unto that one, "Send help to that brother or sister, and do not delay it," — and the help comes. He did not need to get a man to help Him out by carrying a pitcher of water. *According to His Word He worketh,* and Jesus said a "man" should carry water.

What did those disciples do as they saw the man — go forward to meet him? No, they waited for the man, and when he came up they probably walked alongside of him, without a word, until he was about to enter the house; and then I can hear one saying to him, "Please, Sir! the Master wants the guestchamber!" "The guestchamber? Why, I was preparing it all day yesterday but did not know whom it was for." With man things are impossible, but God is the unfolder of the mysteries of life, and He holds the universe in the hollow of His hand. What we need to know this morning is that "The Lord in the midst of thee is mighty," and He works according to His Word.

And when the hour was come, he sat down, and the twelve apostles with him. And he said unto them, With desire I have desired to eat this passover with you before I suffer: For I say unto you, I will not any more eat thereof, until it be fulfilled in the kingdom of God. And he took the cup, and gave thanks, and said, Take this, and divide it among yourselves: For I say unto you, I will not drink of the fruit of the vine, until the kingdom of God shall come. And he took bread, and gave thanks, and brake it, and gave unto them, saying, This is my body which is given for you: this do in remembrance of me.

Luke 22:14-19

It takes the Master to bring the Word home to our hearts. His was a ministry that brought a new vision to mankind, for "never man spake as He spake." How I love to hear Him preach. How He says things. I have watched Him as He trod this earth. Enter into the Scriptures and watch the Lord, follow Him, take notice of His counsel, and you will have a story of wonders. The Book speaks today! It is life, and looms up full of glory. It reflects and unfolds with a new creative power. The words of Jesus are life — never think they are less. If you believe it you will feel quickened. The Word is powerful; it is full of faith. *The Word of God is vital!* Listen! "The word profited them nothing because it was not mixed with faith in them that heard it" (Hebrews 4:2). There has to be a "hearing" in order to have faith. Faith is established and made manifest as we "hear" the Word. Beloved, read the Word of God in quietude, and read it "loud," so that you can "hear" it — for "He that *heareth* my word," to them it giveth life.

Beloved, listen! "With desire" — the "hour is come!" He speaketh! From the beginning of time there has never been an hour like this. These words were among the greatest that He ever spoke: *"The hour is come!"* What an hour, for, the *end of time had come.* "What?" you ask. Yes, I repeat it, for the redemption of the cross, the shedding of the blood, brought in a "new" hour. Time was finished and eternity had begun for a soul that was covered with the blood. All people lived but to die until "that" hour, but the moment the sacrifice was made, it was not the end, but only the beginning. Time was finished and eternity had begun. The soul that is covered with the blood has moved from a natural to an eternal union with the Lord, and then the commandment, *"Thou shalt not,"* which had so

"The power of God will take you out of your own plans
and put you into the plan of God."

worried the people and brought them into such dissatisfaction because they could not keep the Law, was changed into a new commandment; and it was no more, "Thou shalt not," but, *"I delight to do thy will, oh, God."* "All in Adam died," but now the "hour is come" and "all in Christ shall be made alive." Not death, but the fulness of life divine.

"I have a desire to eat this passover with you before I suffer. I know that within a few moments the judgment hall awaits me." Beloved, do you think that I could be in Jerusalem and not want to pass through the gate that He went through? Do you think that I could be in Jerusalem and not want to pass over the Brook Kedron? Could you imagine me being in Jerusalem and not want to go into the Garden, or view the tomb where His body was laid? I knelt down at that holy place, for I felt that I must commune with my Lord there.

While in Jerusalem I preached many weeks outside the Damascus Gate, and God mightily blessed my ministry. It is wonderful to be in the place where God can use you. As I was leaving Jerusalem, some Jews who had heard me preach wanted to travel in the same compartment with me, and they wanted to stay at the same hotel where I was staying. Sitting around the table having food, they said, "What we cannot understand is, when you preach we feel such power; you 'move' us. There is something about it that we cannot help but feel that you have something different from what we have been used to hearing. Why is it?" I replied that it was because I *preached Jesus* in the power of the Holy Spirit, for He was the Messiah, and He causes a child of His to so live in the reality of a clear knowledge of Himself that others know and feel His power. It is this knowledge that the Church today is very much in need of.

Beloved, do not be satisfied with anything less than the knowledge of a real change in your nature, a knowledge of the indwelling presence and power of the Holy Ghost. Do not be satisfied with a life that is not wholly swallowed up in God.

There are many books written on the Word, and we love clear, definite teaching on it, but go yourself to the Book and listen to what the Master says, and you will lay a sure foundation, that cannot be moved; for we are "begotten by the incorruptible Word of God." How we need that simplicity, that rest of faith, that brings us to the place where we are steadfast and immovable. Oh, the living Word of God! Can you not see that the Master was so interested in you that He could despise the shame, despise the cross? The judgment hall was nothing to Him; all the rebukes and scorn could not take from Him the joy of saving you and me. It was that joy that caused Him to say, "I count nothing too vile for Wigglesworth, I count nothing too vile for Brown, for *soul is on the wing to save the world!* How beautiful! How it should thrill us! He knew that death was represented in that sacred cup, and yet He joyfully said, "With desire — *I have a desire* to eat this passover with you before I suffer. Take the bread, drink of the cup, and as oft as ye take it, remember." In other words, take the memory of what it means home with you; think on it, analyze its meaning.

Jesus brought in a new creation by the words of His ministry. "No man born of woman is greater than John the Baptist, but the least in the *kingdom of Heaven* is greater than he" (Matthew 11:11). He said, "...the kingdom of God is within you" (Luke 17:21), and that He would "no more drink of the fruit of the vine until the Kingdom of God shall come" (Mark 14:25) and every person who has the new nature, the new birth, has the kingdom of God within them. If you believe God's Word, it will make you so live that the kingdom of God will be ever increasing, and the whole creation of the kingdom of God will be crying, "Come, Lord Jesus, Come!" and He will come.

As we come to the time of the breaking of bread, the thought should be, "How shall I partake of it?" Beloved, if before His death He could take it and say, "With desire I eat this passover with you before I suffer," we should be able to say, "Lord, I desire to eat it to please Thee, for I want my whole life to be on the wing for Thee!" What grace! As the stream of the new life begins to flow through your being, allow yourself to be immersed, carried on and on, with an ever-increasing flow, until your life becomes a ceaseless flow of the River of Life, and then it will be "No more I but Christ in me."

Get ready for the breaking of bread, and in doing so, "remember." Get ready for partaking of the wine, and in doing it, "Remember Him."

Published in *Glad Tidings Herald*

Praise God! It is a great joy to see you all. There is something that brings us all here. What will it be when we get rid of this body of flesh, and when Jesus is the light of the city of God? Nevertheless, God means for us while here to put on the whole armour of God. He wants us to be covered with the covering of His Spirit, and to grow in grace and the knowledge of God. Oh, what God has laid up for us, and what we may receive through the name of Jesus! Oh, the value of the name, the power of the name; the very name of Jesus brings help from heaven, and the very name of Jesus can bind evil powers and subdue all things unto Himself. Thank God for victory through our Lord Jesus Christ.

A LIVING FAITH

January 1930

For the sake of saving us, He endured the cross, despising the shame. How beautiful it is to say with our whole will, "I will be obedient unto God." Oh, He is lovely, He is beautiful — I never remember coming to Him when He once denied me anything; He has never turned me away empty. He is such a wonderful Saviour, such a Friend that we can depend upon with assurance and rest and complete confidence. He can roll away every burden. This afternoon think of Him as the exhaustless Saviour, the everlasting Friend, One who knows all things, One who is able to help and deliver us. When we have such a Source as this, we can stretch out our hands and take all that we need from Him.

I will speak to you from the eleventh chapter of Mark's gospel.

> *And Jesus entered into Jerusalem, and into the temple: and when he had looked round about upon all things, and now the eventide was come, he went out unto Bethany with the twelve. And on the morrow, when they were come from Bethany, he was hungry: and seeing a fig tree afar off having leaves, he came, if haply he might find anything thereon: and when he came to it, he found nothing but leaves; for the time of figs was not yet. And Jesus answered and said unto it, No man eat fruit of thee hereafter for ever. And his disciples heard it.*
>
> *Mark 11:11-14*

The fig tree dried up from the roots. We may think we have faith in God, but we must not doubt in our hearts, "...What things soever ye desire, when ye pray, believe that ye receive them, and ye shall have them" (Mark 11:24). This is a very wonderful word.

You meet here every Monday, and the great theme of this meeting is the theme of faith, so I will talk about faith. Your inactivity must be brought to a place of victory. Inactivity — that which wavers, that which hesitates, that which fears instead of having faith; that closes up everything, because it doubts instead of believing God. What is faith? Faith is the living principle of the Word of God. It is life, it produces life, it changes life.

Oh, that God today might give us a real knowledge of the Book. What is there in it? There is life. God wants us to feed on the Book, the living Word, the precious Word of God. All the wonderful things that Jesus did were done that people might be changed and made like unto Himself. Oh, to be like Him in thought, act, and plan. He went about His Father's business and was eaten up with the zeal of His house. I am beginning to understand First John 3:2:

> *Beloved, now are we the sons of God, and it doth not yet appear what we shall be: but we know that, when he shall appear, we shall be like him; for we shall see him as he is.*
>
> *1 John 3:2*

As I feed on the Word of God, my whole body will be changed by the process of the power of the Son of God.

> *But if the Spirit of him that raised up Jesus from the dead dwell in you, he that raised up Christ from the dead shall also quicken your mortal bodies by his Spirit that dwelleth in you.*
>
> *Romans 8:11*

The Lord dwells in a humble and contrite heart, and makes His way into the dry places, so if you open up to Him, He will flood you with His life, but be sure to remember that a little bit of sin will spoil a whole life. You can never cleanse sin, you can never purify sin, you can never be strong if in sin, you will never have a vision while in sin. Revelation stops when sin comes in. The human spirit must come to an end, but the Spirit of Christ must be alive and active. You must die to the human spirit, and then God will quicken your mortal body and make it alive. "Without holiness no man shall see God" (Hebrews 12:14).

We have a wonderful subject. What is it? *Faith.* Faith is an inward operation of that divine power which dwells in the contrite heart, and which has power to lay hold of the things not seen. Faith is a divine act, faith is God in the soul. God operates by His Son, and transforms the natural into the supernatural. Faith is active, never dormant; faith lays hold, faith is the hand of God, faith is the power of God, faith never fears, faith lives amid the greatest conflict, faith is always active, faith moves even things that cannot be moved. God fills us with His divine power, and sin is dethroned. "The just shall live by faith" (Habakkuk 2:4; Romans 1:17; Galatians 3:11; Hebrews 10:38). You cannot live by faith until you are just (righteous). You cannot live by faith if you are unholy, or dishonest.

The Lord was looking for fruit on the tree. He found "nothing but leaves." There are thousands of people like that. They dress up like Christians, but it is all leaves. "Herein is my Father glorified, that ye bear much fruit..." (John 15:8). He has no way in which to get fruit, only through us. We have not to be ordinary people. To be saved is to be an extraordinary man, an exposition of God. When Jesus was talking about the new life He said, "...Except a man be born again [of God], he cannot see the kingdom of God...That which is born of the flesh is flesh; and that which is born of the Spirit is spirit" (John 3:3,6).

In order to understand His fulness we must be filled with the Holy Ghost. God has a measure for us that cannot be measured. I am invited into this measure; the measure of the Lord Jesus Christ in me. When you are in relationship, sin is dethroned, but you cannot purify yourself; it is by the blood of Jesus Christ, God's Son, that you are cleansed from all sin.

When Jesus saw nothing but leaves, He said to this tree: "No man eat fruit of thee hereafter for ever. And his disciples heard it" (Mark 11:14). The next morning as they passed the same place, they saw the fig tree dried up from the roots. You never see a tree dry from the roots. Even a little plant will dry from the top. But God's Son had spoken to the tree, and it could not live. He said to them, "Have faith in God" (Mark 11:22). We are His life, we are members of His body; the Spirit is in us, and there is no way to abide in the secret place of the Lord only by holiness.

Be filled with the Word of God. "For the word of God is quick, and powerful, and sharper than any twoedged sword, piercing even to the dividing asunder of soul and spirit..." (Hebrews 4:12). Listen, those of you who have stiff knees and stiff arms today, you can get a tonic by the Word of God that will loosen your joints, and that will divide asunder even your joints and marrow. You cannot move your knee if there is not any marrow there, but the Word of God can bring marrow into your bones.

Anything else? One of the greatest things in the Word of God is that it discerns the thoughts and intents of the heart. Oh, that you may all allow the Word of God to have perfect victory in your body, so that it may be tingling through and through with God's divine power. Divine life does not belong to this world but to the kingdom of heaven, and the kingdom of heaven is within you. God wants to purify our minds until we can bear all things, believe all things, hope all things, and endure all things. God dwells in you, but you cannot have this divine power until you live and walk in the Holy Ghost, until the power of the new life is greater than the old life.

Jesus said to His disciples, if ye will believe in your heart not only the tree will wither but the mountain shall be removed. God wants us to move mountains, anything that appears to be like a mountain can be moved. The mountains of difficulty, the mountains of perplexity, the mountains of depression or depravity. Things that bound you for years. Sometimes things appear as though they could not be moved, but you believe in your heart, stand on the Word of God, and God's Word will never be defeated.

Notice again this Scripture: "...What things soever ye desire, when ye pray, believe that ye receive them, and ye shall have them" (Mark 11:24). First, believe that you get them, and then you shall have them. That is the difficulty with people. They say: "Well, if I could feel I had it, I would know I had it," but you must believe it, and then the feeling will come; you must believe it because of the Word of God. God wants to work in you a real heart-faith.

I want you to know this afternoon that God has a real remedy for all your ailments. There is power in this meeting this afternoon to set everybody free.

Published in *Triumphs of Faith*

ohn 15 and 2 Peter 1:1 — "Like precious faith" — What would happen to us and to the need of world, if we would get to the place, where we could believe God? May God give the desire. Faith is a tremendous power, an inward mover. We have not seen yet all that God has for us.

AMBITION REALIZED — DESIRE FULFILLED

July 1930

When I was a little boy, I remember asking my father for a pennyworth of something. He did not give it to me. So I sat down by his side and every now and then I touched him ever so gently, saying, "Father, Father." My mother said to my father, "Why don't you answer the child?" My father replied, "I have done so." But still I sat on, "Father, Father, Father," ever so quietly, then if he went into the garden I followed him. I would just touch his sleeve and say, "Father, Father!" Did I ever go away without the accomplishment of my desire? No, not once. Let God have His way with us. Let God fulfil His great desire in us for heart purity, that Christ may dwell in our hearts by faith, that the might of God's Spirit may accompany our ministry. Filled with divine enthusiasm with rivers flowing.

PRECIOUS FAITH

"...to them that have obtained faith..." (2 Peter 1:1). Our foundation test in a time of strain — a faith of divine origin springing up in our hearts. But the outside must be as the inside. It is good to have the Holy Spirit, but the sun inside must give a brilliancy outside. Faith! Like precious faith, greater than the mind or body or any activity. Faith, a living power revealed in you the moment you believe, you have what you believe for. For faith is substance and evidence. You were not saved by feelings or experiences. You were saved by the power of God the moment you believed the Word of God. God came in by His Word and laid the foundation. Faith. Bursting up the old life-nature by the power of God...the old life by the Word of God. You must come to God's Book. His Word is our foundation. When we speak of the Word we speak of almighty power, a substance of rich dynamite diffusing through the human, displaying its might, and bringing all else into insignificance. The

Word of God formed within the temple, a living principle laid down of rock, *the Word of the living God formed in us — mighty in thought*, language, activity, movement, and unction, a fire mightier than dynamite and able to resist the mightiest pressure the devil can bring against it.

In these eventful days we must have nothing ordinary but extraordinary, allowing God by His wonderful revelations, to display His goods in your hearts for the deliverance of others. Peter said, "Like precious faith." The same kind that Abraham had, he could have said, "God!" Have the faith of God. Being born again, we are in the working of a supernatural power, the unique peace of God, working with a changed vision; we are more wonderful than we know. Peter and John said to the lame man, "Such as we have we give thee, in the name of Jesus," and there was operation and manifestation. Faith! Like precious faith, all of the same material: believe in God's Word. Noah had tried faith. Abraham had faith, and all the prophets had thus one fact — working faith!

No Limitation

They had limitation, but God has come to us with no limitation, exceeding abundantly above all we can ask or think. There have been memorable days when the Holy Ghost has come. At twenty-one years of age God flooded my life with His power, and there has not been a day since without happenings wonderful. God by His divine power flooding human vessels. God manifest in flesh, in our flesh, Christ being made manifest by the power of God. God has chosen us in a new way. He has made us kings and priests Himself, and the day is not far distant when we shall be with Him forever.

The Holy Ghost could not come without Jesus coming first. The Holy Ghost crowning Him King and all the power of His power is to be manifested through us. How?

TONGUES AND INTERPRETATION: "Rivers of living water. The man divinely operated, discerning the mind of Christ without measure. To live, to drink, to sup, to walk, to talk with Him."

> Oh, 'tis all right now,
> Oh, 'tis all right now,
> For Jesus is a friend of mine
> And 'tis all right now.

But He must come in first, all God's fulness is in Him. All God's revelation is in Him. The incoming life of God by faith. Like precious faith, an eternal process of working, no end, but a beginning. Faith cometh by hearing and hearing by the Word of God. Faith is a forming in our human nature, things of eternal forces. Faith, God's embrace, the grip of almightiness. What is faith? It is the eternal nature of God, it can never decay or fade away, it is with you all the way, to end in eternal day. Faith is the Word. Three things. Faith has so many springs. Forever, Thy Word is settled in heaven, a copy of things to come.

Be a man of desire, hungry and thirsty. Don't be satisfied. I cannot move on faith unless it is better than my mind, greater than me. None are made on trailing clouds of glory; we are made in hard places; at Wit's End Corner, with no way out. A man is made in adversity. David said, "In distress, God brought me to a large place, and I was enlarged, and He helped me" (Psalms 4:1; 18:36).

Eight years ago after a distressing voyage, going straight from the ship to the meeting, as I entered the building, a man fell down across the doorway in a fit. The Spirit of the Lord was upon me, and I commanded the devil to leave. In my visit this year, I ventured to ask, "Does anyone remember the incident?" I spoke in English. The man did not know a word of English, he stood up, I told him to come to the platform. He said he knew the binding power of the name of Jesus, and he had not had a fit since the stranger came. I had to know Acts 2:15, and then I began to do. Oh, my God, keep me there!

In Palestine at Damascus' Gate and on the Mount of Olives, I saw men baptized with the Holy Ghost as in Acts 2. Begin to do, and then to preach. God is always waiting to manifest His divine power. God intends us to begin.

COMMUNICATION

Be a communicator of divine life for others (2 Peter 1:3). His divine power has called us to glory and virtue. My wife used to say, "He giveth grace and glory too." Oh! Beloved receive virtue. Believe for the virtue of the Lord to be so manifested through your body that, as they touch they are healed. Then the illumination of the power of the life! Believe for the current to go through you to others. It is amazing in a necessity what can happen, and God can arrange for a necessity, no time to pray, only to act. The man that is filled with the Holy Ghost lives in an act. I come with the life of the risen Christ, my mouth enlarged, my mind operative to live and act in the power of the Holy Ghost. We must so live in God that we claim an enlarging in the wisdom of God.

At one place there were 6,000 people outside the building, poor things in chairs, and as I went laying my hands on them they were healed, as they touched they were whole. This faith means increase in the knowledge of God and the righteousness of Christ. Life filled with God! His mantle upon you with grace multiplied. God did for Abraham, and added blessing on blessing. "Blessed are they that hear the Word of God, and keep it." What shall we do to do the works of God? Believe on Him Whom He has sent. "Greater works than these shall you do." Faith sees the glory of another, and it is from faith to faith. You may increase wonderfully before I see you again.

When I was in Orebrö eight years ago I ministered to a girl twelve years old, blind, this time they told me she had perfect sight from that day. I never knew it, it is after I get away testimonies come.

> *...whosoever shall say unto this mountain, Be thou removed, and be thou cast into the sea; and shall not doubt in his heart, but shall believe that those things which he saith shall come to pass; he shall have whatsoever he saith. Therefore I say unto you, What things soever ye desire, when ye pray, believe that ye receive them, and ye shall have them.*
>
> *Mark 11:23,24*

Have faith in God! If I believe — what? What I wish, as I begin to say, God brings it to pass — not a fig tree — a mountain — what you saith.

In one place a man said, "You have helped all but me." I said, "What is the trouble?" He said, "I cannot sleep, I am losing my reason!" So I began to say, "No need to go anywhere; believe!"

There are nine fruits of the Spirit and nine gifts of the Spirit. Wisdom is coupled with love — knowledge with joy — faith with peace.

Examine yourselves — are you in peace? God is delighted when we are in peace, so I said to the brother, "Go home and sleep; and I will believe God," he went home. His wife said, "Well, did you see him?" He said, "He helped all but me." However, he fell asleep. His wife said, "I wonder if it is all right." Morning, noon, night he was still asleep, he awoke bright and happy, rested and restored.

What was it? Believe in God — then speaking, "He shall have whatsoever he says." Have you this like precious faith? Deal bountifully with the oppressed. "He that asketh receiveth." Ask — it is done. Live for God. Keep clean and holy. Live in unction, in God's desires and plans. Glorify Him in the establishment of blessing for the people — seeing God's glory manifested in the midst. Amen.

Published in *Redemption Tidings*

salm 126. "They that sow in tears shall reap in joy" (v. 5). The Lord hath set apart him that is godly for Himself. His enemies will

TRANSFORMED
August 1930

be at peace with him, and God will send him prosperity in hard times. A life on the altar for service. There, not a hoping to be there. Paul had reached a reserved place, separated. He was now in the place where the Holy Ghost can speak.

"I beseech thee, with all that see this truth, to present your bodies a living sacrifice" (Romans 12:1). Here is the mercy of God, the unfathomable, desirable will of God. The body presented a living sacrifice. It's a present, a living sacrifice, not a worn-out life. The body, soul, and spirit to be presented blameless at the coming of the Lord. The present life given with no choice but God's will. So on the altar. Oh, Lord, not mine. Thine now! Lord, use it for Thy glory. Through with kicks and won'ts. All! A living body, placed at God's disposal. A holy body, with the best mind. Without a thought outside holiness unto the Lord. God only asks for what you can give! Be not conformed to this world. Be not conformed — moved by it, not a hermit or careless — but transformed (Romans 12:2). Every hour more pure *transformed* to prove what God's will is for you. It's a holy acceptable will. No sourness or irritability, or that thing about you that nobody wants. It's an acceptable will. If you give, you give cheerfully; if you love, you love warmly; if you shake hands, people know you mean it. The whole life beautiful — cleaving unto God. Rejoicing in hope — *tribulation!* Meeting it with prayer. A blessing without a curse. This kind of life is received by men, and is acceptable in the sight of God — and at the closing-up day, it has a sure reward.

Let us pray and commit our whole way to God. Being not conformed, but transformed, proving God's good and acceptable and perfect will. Amen.

From an address given in London
Published in *Redemption Tidings*

FAITH'S LAUGHTER

November 1930

"My faith pure, my joy sure."
Romans 4.

In Isaac (laughter) shall thy seed be called. Faith is the great inheritance, for the just shall live by faith. Twenty-five years Abraham waited for God to fulfil His promise to give him a son. He looked to God Who never fails, and believed His Word. As we live in the Spirit, we live in the process of God's mind, and act according to His will.

Could a child be born? Yes!! On the law of faith in God who had promised. Here is no limitation (Romans 4:16). Therefore it is of faith, that it might be of grace. Grace is God's inheritance in the soul that believes.

Faith always brings a fact and a fact brings joy.

Faith! Faith! Making us know God is, and that He is a rewarder of those who diligently seek Him. God! Who quickeneth that which was dead, and calleth the things that are not as though they were. There is no want to those who trust God. He quickeneth the dead. The more Abraham was pressed, the more he rejoiced. Being not weak in faith. He considered not his own body. He staggered not through unbelief, but was strong in faith, giving glory to God, that what He had promised He was able to perform. Heir of the world through a righteousness by faith. God quickening that which is dead. The more there was no hope Abraham believed in hope. If we knew the value of trial we should praise God for it. It is in the furnace of affliction God gets us to the place where He can use us (Philippians 1:19). Paul says of difficulty, I do and will rejoice. For I know that this shall turn to my salvation through your prayers and the supply of the Spirit of Jesus Christ — that Christ shall be magnified in my body. Before God puts you in the furnace He knows you will go through. It is never above we are able to bear. If you know the baptism of the Holy Ghost is in the Scriptures, never rest until God gives it to you. If you know it is Scriptural to be healed of every weakness — to be holy, pure, to overcome amid all conditions — never rest until you are an overcomer.

If you have seen the face of God and have had vision and revelation, never rest until you attain to it. That ye may apprehend with all saints. Holy men spake as God gave them power and utterance. We must be blameless amid the crooked positions of the world. Jesus is the type of Sonship for our attainment. He was God's pattern, a firstfruit clothed with power. We must go in His name, that when you lay hands on the sick, Satan has no power, and when you command in Jesus' name he has to go.

> The walls are falling down,
> The walls are falling down;
> Oh praise the Lord. Praise ye His name,
> The walls are falling down.

Let us take God's Word and stand upon it, as our strength to resist the devil till he is forced to flee. Amen, amen.

Published in *Redemption Tidings*

olossians 4:1-6. "That God would open to us a door of utterance to speak the mystery of Christ that I may make it manifest as I ought to speak."

UTTERANCE

January 1931

NEED OF UTTERANCE

Paul felt as we do, the need of utterance. He had plenty of language, but he wanted utterance. We can have inspiration, operation, tongue, mind, heart — we need all these. God works thus! In this divine order to give forth the truth most needed for the time. But the supreme need of the hour is the need of prayer for utterance, "Praying that God would open to us a door, a door of utterance, that I may speak as I ought."

These men were sent forth by the power of the Holy Spirit. But they cannot without unction open the door or give forth the right word for the hour. Paul and his helpers are unequal to meet the need. Then was something out of order? No! For "except the Lord keepeth the house the watchman keepeth it in vain." *We are dependent upon the Holy Spirit to breathe through us.* Apart from this living breath of the Spirit, the message is ordinary and not extraordinary. The question is: how can we live in this place, thrown on omnipotent power? The Spirit of the Lord giving vent, speaking through us. It is not an easy thing. God said to David, "It is good that the desire is in thine heart." But that will not do for us, who live in the latter days, when God is pouring forth His Spirit and rivers are at our word. The need is Mark 11:22-23: "Have the faith of God...He shall have whatsoever he saith." In Genesis 1:3 God said: "Let there be light." Let God arise. Let God breathe His Holy Spirit through your caravan of nature, through your eye and tongue. The supernatural in the natural for the glory of God. God raised Paul for this ministry.

> *To open their eyes, and to turn them from darkness to light, and from the power of Satan unto God, that they may receive forgiveness of sins, and inheritance among them which are sanctified....*
>
> *Acts 26:18*

What was the means? Jesus said, "By the faith that is in Me." The faith of God.

The Lord God hath given me the tongue of the learned, that I should know how to speak a word in season to him that is weary: he wakeneth morning by morning, he wakeneth mine ear to hear as the learned. The Lord God hath opened mine ear, and I was not rebellious....

Isaiah 50:4,5

Do you believe it? Oh! For more to believe God that "the tongue of the dumb sing..." (Isaiah 35:6). When will they? When they believe and fulfil the conditions; oh, beloved, it is not easy. But Jesus died and rose again for the possibility. "Have the faith of God." "Have the tongue of a ready writer."

The whole man immersed in God that the Holy Spirit may operate and the dying world have the ministry of life for which it is famishing.

But if the Spirit of him that raised up Jesus from the dead dwell in you, he that raised up Christ from the dead shall also quicken your mortal bodies by his Spirit that dwelleth in you.

Romans 8:11

As the dead body of Christ was quickened and brought out by the Holy Spirit. For eyes to see and ears to hear, as well as speech speaking as the oracles of God. If any man speak, let him speak as the oracles of God. That's our orders: speaking that which no man knoweth, save the Holy Spirit as the Spirit giveth divine utterance — a language which would never come at all, except the Holy Spirit gave utterance, taking the things of Christ and revealing them.

"The mystery of Christ." "...praying also for us, that God would open unto us a door of utterance, to speak the mystery of Christ, for which I am also in bond: that I may make it manifest, as I ought to speak" (Colossians 4:3,4). Did God answer the prayer? Yes! "Through mighty signs and wonders, by the power of the Spirit of God; so that from Jerusalem, and round about unto Illyricum, I have fully preached the gospel of Christ" (Romans 15:19). It was the grace of our Lord Jesus Christ, that great Shepherd of the sheep that brought to us redemption. It was the grace of God, His favour and mercy — a lavished love, an undeserved favour God brought salvation — we did not deserve it.

SEASONED WITH SALT

"Let your speech be alway with grace, seasoned with salt..." (Colossians 4:6). Salt has three properties: 1. It smarts; 2. It is healing; and 3. It has preservation. So your words by the Spirit, filled with grace, yet, cut to the heart, and brings preservation. We must be very careful to be salty. His Word shall not return void, it shall accomplish and it shall prosper — but our mouths must be clean and our desire wholly for God. Jesus used straight words — He said: "Ye hypocrites, ye whitened sepulchres," to the elite of the holiness movement of His day. To others He said, "You are deceived, you have an idea that you are of the seed of Abraham, but you are of the seed of the devil and his works you do." His mouth was full of meekness and gentleness, yet so salty, because of their corruption. Without you knew the charm of Christ, you might think you were out of the wheel of the working of His eternal power. Hear the prophet again — "The bruised reed He shall not break"; to those for whom there is no lifting up, "He comes as balm of Gilead." "...that you may know how you ought to answer every man" (Colossians 4:6). This is not easy to learn. It is only learned in the absorbed (eaten up) place of God. When we are there we seek to glorify God, and can give a chastening word full of power, to waken up and to save.

Use the salt, beloved! Use conviction, use the healing for their preservation. How true we have to be! You are seasoned with salt. I love it! It is inspiring! Conviction! Thus the Holy Ghost writes upon the fleshy tables of the temple of the Spirit. Oh Lord, enlarge our conception of our sense of Thy presence in the temple, discerning the Lord's body in the midst.

> For He is so precious to me,
> For He is so precious to me;
> 'Tis heaven below
> My Redeemer to know.
> For He is so precious to me.

Our whole being so full of the life of our Lord, that the Holy Ghost can speak and act through us. Living always in Him. Oh, the charm of His divine plan. Living out on God for His omnipotent place for future ministry. Crying out for the inspiration of the God of power. Acting in the Holy Ghost. Breathing out life divine. The glory, miracles, wonders, working out the plan of the most High God. Eaten up — knowing nothing among men, save Jesus and Him crucified. Unto Thee, O God, be the glory and the honour and the power!

Can you wonder why it is I love Him so! A cry for a production of a cry until Acts 11:15: "And as I began to speak...."

> Oh, be on fire, oh, be on fire,
> Oh, be on fire for God.
> Oh be on fire, be all on fire,
> Be all on fire for God.
> Amen. Amen.

From an address given in Switzerland
Published in *Redemption Tidings*

THE GIVEN GLORY
February 1931

Then came to him the mother of Zebedee's children with her sons, worshipping him, and desiring a certain thing of him. And he said unto her, What wilt thou? She saith unto him, Grant that these my two sons may sit, the one on thy right hand, and the other on the left, in thy kingdom. But Jesus answered and said, Ye know not what ye ask. Are ye able to drink of the cup that I shall drink of, and to be baptized with the baptism that I am baptized with? They say unto him, We are able. And he saith unto them, Ye shall drink indeed of my cup, and be baptized with the baptism that I am baptized with: but to sit on my right hand, and on my left, is not mine to give, but it shall be given to them for whom it is prepared of my Father.

Matthew 20:20-23

We have here a wonderful subject — all God's Word is life-giving — it is life and light. If we are poor it is because we do not know the Word of God. God's Word is full of riches ever opening to us fresh avenues of divine life. It is the Spirit that quickeneth. Jesus said, "...the words that I speak unto you, they are spirit, and they are life" (John 6:63). It has a mighty changing power effectively working in us. We need not remain in the same place two days. It is the Word of God, and He giveth us richly all things to enjoy. This Book is the copy of the Word — the original is in the glory.

> *In the beginning was the Word, and the Word was with God, and the Word was God.*
>
> *John 1:1*

You will find the moment you reach the glory you will have the principle of the Word. The Author is there — the Author of faith is there. He is our life and fills us with illumination — the Holy Ghost unveiling unto us the Christ. A brother came to see me to ask about the Holy Ghost. He was so anxious that his ministry should be a success. I pointed out to him the words of Jesus to His disciples, "The Holy Ghost is with you and shall be in you." I said to him, "You see the sun this morning — how it pours into the room from the outside? But if the light was inside, how the light would shine forth outside illuminating the dark places."

When we receive the baptism in the Holy Ghost, we receive a new ministry with divine power and glory. The kingdom of God is not meat and drink, but righteousness, peace, and joy in the Holy Ghost. The Holy Ghost reveals the Christ Who reigns in every believer when Jesus is coronated, and Jesus is coronated when you receive the Holy Ghost. Have you received the Holy Ghost since you believed? Jesus is king over your desires — no man can call Jesus Lord but by the Holy Ghost. When the Holy Ghost comes in, Jesus is Lord — then His Word floods our souls, and the tide flows out to the needy, the vision increases. Hungrier than ever — nothing satisfies me but God. I like the word, "What wilt thou?...Grant that these my two sons may sit, the one on thy right hand, and the other on the left, in thy kingdom" (Matthew 20:21). I am sure James and John had this desire, and you can have the same desire. Jesus is the mighty worker of desire. He moves people to desire. He said, "Ye know not what ye ask." Did they know? No! Did Mary know? No! But she said, "...be it unto me according to thy word" (Luke 1:38). James and John said, "We are able." Would they have said it if they had known? On another occasion they asked, "What must we do to work the works of God?" Jesus said, "Believe on Him Whom He hath sent." I believe it is more than saying it. It is the life of God in the nature, that stretches out to believe and to receive. We can be so drawn into the love of the Spirit, the law of the Spirit of life making us free from the law of sin and death, and you know you are in that which will never pass away. Jesus said, "I am come to send fire on the earth. The father shall be divided against the son, and the son against the father, and a man's foes shall be they of his own household" (See Luke 12:49,53; Matthew 10:36).

I remember twenty-two years ago when I received the baptism of the Holy Ghost according to Acts 2:4. I sent home a wire (the post office was opposite my house), that I had received the baptism of the Holy Ghost and was speaking in other tongues. The news ran like fire — everybody seemed to know. When I arrived home my wife said to me, "So you have received the baptism of the Holy Ghost and are speaking in tongues?" She said, "I want you to know I am baptized as much as you." Right in my house the war begun. She said, "For twenty years I have been the preacher." (I could not preach; I have tried many a time.) Preachers are God-made men. Jesus was moved with compassion. My wife said, "Next Sunday you go on the platform by yourself — and I'll see if there is anything in it." I had been under great pressure what I was to speak about, and as I went on to the platform Jesus said to me, "The Spirit of the Lord is upon [thee]..." (Luke 4:18).

I don't know what I said — but my wife — she got up — she sat down — she got up — she sat down — she said, "That is not my husband." No man can be filled with the Holy Ghost and be the same man. He is turned into another man.

THE CUPS

Yes, Jesus speaks of the cups — the cup of blessing and the cup of suffering. They go together. It is always the hundredfold but with persecutions also — but it's going all the way. The cross is not greater than His grace. The cloud cannot hide His blessed face. I am satisfied to know that with Jesus here below I can conquer every foe. Did John know what it meant? No! Thank God there is something we cannot resist — saying Lord give me the baptism of the Holy Ghost, this luxury — this summit of perfection — making your whole being cry out for the living God — and you say, "Yes, Lord!" Never mind any cost! I saw one man in a waiting meeting seeking the baptism of the Holy

Ghost about to leave. I said, "Brother, why are you leaving?" "Oh," he said, "I must go home — I have something to do — I wrote a letter to my wife's brother, and I must say I am sorry." He told his wife what he was doing. She said, "You fool." The baptism of the Holy Ghost means a clean heart. The next night there he was at the meeting again. "Oh," he said, "It is too much this time." I said, "Brother, obey God at any cost. It does not matter how bitter the cup, God will give you grace." He was a farmer, and was accustomed to send a cheque regularly for corn, but one time he missed, and he had put off paying his account. The blessing of God came upon his life.

Oh, yes, we must be eligible for this wonderful place in the glory. We must drink the cup — but it will mean the baptism — the baptism of the Holy Ghost means the fulness of the divine anointing. Jesus returned in the power of the Spirit into Galilee. "This day," He said, "is this scripture fulfilled in your ears" (Luke 4:21). And there are days when the Spirit is mighty upon us and it's a "this day."

Once in a ship going from Alexandria to Venice, and again the other day at Liverpool, seeing the crowd, some thousand people, my heart was moved with compassion. I began. All was still as death — captain, crew, and passengers — as they listened to the message God gave me for them. There are times when you know the Spirit of God is mighty upon you and you act, though to the onlooker it may seem out of place, but you have got your orders, and you act, and the Holy Ghost bears witness to it.

THE FIRE

Another time in Jerusalem at the place of wailing, the Spirit of the Lord moved me. I saw young men, many of them in the prime of manhood, beating their breasts, weeping bitterly, saying, "Lord, how long, Lord, how long?" I preached unto them Jesus. On the next day ten came to see me, and with them a rabbi. They said, "Where did the fire come from? When you preached we felt the fire. We have no fire in our synagogues." Oh, brother, the baptism of the Holy Ghost is a fire of baptism.

...he shall baptize you with the Holy Ghost, and with fire.
Matthew 3:11

So I began to talk with them about God's promises of a Messiah, and how He was crucified at Calvary. God wants us so filled with the Holy Ghost that people feel the power — feel the fire. At Alexandria I got on the ship. I wanted to preach, but I could not. I had not the language, and no interpreter. I read Acts 1:1, "...Jesus began both to do and to teach." To do and then to teach. I wanted to do, but how? I was ready, but I had no opportunity. Men cannot make the opportunity. He has to be ready. It is God who makes the opportunity, and just where I stood a man fell on the deck. His wife cried out, "My husband is dead." One ran for the doctor, but before he arrived I began to do. I said, "In the name of Jesus," and the man revived. There was much excitement and pointing at me — all wanted to know what had happened. I could not speak to them, but I found five people who could interpret me. And all on the ship heard the old story of Jesus and His love. Don't forget, we have to begin to do, then to teach.

Nine years ago I went to Sweden. The people did not know me, but God led me there. We are as truly sent by God as ever the apostles were. I had a rough journey, and thought after landing I had some hours in the train, but a meeting was ready for me, and as I entered the building a man fell across the doorway in a fit. I rebuked the devil in Jesus' name, and the man got up. I said, "Give your testimony." He obeyed and said it was as if something had snapped from top to bottom of his body, and he was free. This incident was the key to many open doors of opportunity.

Seven years later I was again at that place. I asked if any remembered. A man rose in the gallery and said, "It was me, and I have been free since." Jesus began to do. There is no one that loves me like Jesus. There is no one can heal me like Him. He is acquainted with my weakness. He knows all my sorrows. There is no one can heal me like Him. Oh, yes, it's a real baptism of fire and a real baptism of suffering. The suffering keeps you in balance. Jesus did the most astounding things, making the people marvel. As He is we have to be. He fed five thousand. He healed the man born blind. Where Jesus was, the crowds came — the children came — He could not be hid — the crowds followed Him. Blind Bartimeus — he heard the noise. "Who is it? Who is it?" "It's Jesus!" He cried, "Jesus!" "Jesus! Jesus! Thou Son of David, have mercy upon me." He stopped, and He'll stop tonight. "Jesus, thou Son of David, have mercy upon me." They said, "Hold thy peace." But presently it changed to, "Be of good cheer — arise — He calleth for thee." Jesus said, "What wilt thou?" Bartimeus cried and Jesus stood still and commanded him to be called — and Jesus is here tonight. Yes, it is a cup of blessing and a cup of suffering and the place prepared in the glory. May we so yield to God that the Holy Ghost can prepare us for the place — and the glory (Acts 1:1-2), that we may begin to do and to teach until the day when we are taken up having the same testing as He had (Acts 1:1-2). It is finished! Ministering the cup of blessing which means the cup of suffering.

Published in *Redemption Tidings*

THE MINISTRY OF THE FLAMING SWORD
March 1931

This glorious in-working of Holy Ghost power is preparing us for rapture. Our greatest theme — the glory of the splendor of our Lord. His face! His tenderness! His sweetness! Making our hearts long to be forever with the Lord. Amen! So let it be!

> *What shall we then say to these things? If God be for us, who can be against us? Who shall separate us from the love of Christ? shall tribulation, or distress, or persecution, or famine, or nakedness, or peril, or sword? Nay, in all these things we are more than conquerors through him that loved us. For I am persuaded, that neither death, nor life, nor angels, nor principalities, nor powers, nor things present, nor things to come, Nor height, nor depth, nor any other creature, shall be able to separate us from the love of God, which is in Christ Jesus our Lord.*
>
> *Romans 8:31,35,37-39*

Oh, the joy of the thought of it! What shall separate us from the love of Christ? A place of confidence, assurance, and rest, where God has perfect control over all human weakness and you stand as on the mount of transfiguration manifested and glorified as in the presence of God, able to say, "I know all things are working together for good within me," silently destroying all that can be destroyed that He might have preeminence in the body. If God be for us, who can be against us?

God is bringing forth a new creation; the sons of God are to be manifested, and we must see our inheritance in the Holy Ghost. Nothing can separate us! What is it God wants us to know? Right in our earthly temple God has brought forth a son with power, with manifestation, with grace, crowned already in the earth, crowned *with glory*. "And the glory which thou gavest me I have given them; that they may be one, even as we are one" (John 17:22).

The Spirit of the Lord is showing me God must get a people who can see that from before the foundation of the world He has had them in His mind. God has been delivering us through all difficulty. Where sin abounded He has brought in His grace, where disease came in to steal our life, God raised up a standard and we are here having come through tribulation. God has been purifying us, strengthening us, equipping us with divine audacity by the power of almightiness — till we can say, "What shall we say then to these things?"

Shall we dethrone what we know up to the present time has equipped us and brought us through? Shall we allow our hearts to fail us in the day of adversity? No! That which God has already strengthened and perfected!! — weakness made strong! — corruption changed to purity! Knowing that in the tribulation and the fire of God has purified us, what shall we say to these things? These light afflictions are working for us a far more exceeding and eternal weight of glory.

THE NEW CREATION

People have been in meetings where the glory of God has fallen and the expression of God has been upon everything, and fortifications have been made in the body. The next morning the power of Satan has assailed — but the spiritual life, the Son manifested, the glory of the new creation is already in our mortal body — but the flesh is a battle-ground for the enemy and is tested, but that which God is forming is greater than the mortal body — the spirit which is awakening into the glorious liberty of a son of God is greater. From perfection to perfection, it is this knowledge of what He has done — what shall we say? How shall we compare this with that which is to come?

The flesh profiteth nothing, but the Spirit of the living God. Though worms destroy this body, I have another life greater than this life which shall look upon God — which shall see Him in His perfection, which shall behold Him in His glory — which shall be changed like unto Him and be formed into Him. By the presence of God, a new creation — a glorious celestial shall so clothe us that we shall be there in the presence of His likeness. Knowing this, shall I give place to the devil? Shall I fear? Shall I let my feelings change the experience of the Word of God? Shall I trust in my fears? No! A million times, no! There has never been any good thing in the flesh, but God has quickened the spirit till we live a new life divine over all time and are eternally shaped for God.

What shall we say? Are you going to let the past where God has wrought for you bring you to a place of distress, or are you standing to your testing — "Now are we the Sons of God" — remembering how God has answered our prayers, brought light into our home, delivered us from carnality and touched us when no power in the world could avail? What shall we say? Can anything be brought against the elect of God? I know in Whom I have believed and I am persuaded that He Who purposed us for God, will surely bring us to the place where we shall receive the crown of life through the faith that God has given us.

God is in you mightily, forming within you a new creation by the Spirit — to make you ready for the glory that shall be revealed in Him. One said to me the other day, "I am in terrible trouble; a man is cursing me all the time." If God be for us, who can be against us? God is never small in any of His blessings. He takes you into all He has. "He that spared not his own Son...how shall he not with him also freely give us all things?" (Romans 8:32). God has given us Jesus, the bosom of His love, the express image of His Person, so perfect in brilliance, purity, righteousness, and glory. I have seen Him many times, and it always changes me. Your struggle is one of the "all things." Many needs have broken my heart, but I could say to the troubled one, God is greater than your heart — greater than circumstances — greater than the thing that holds you. God will deliver you if you dare to believe Him, but we have to press it in and in and in before we can get the people to believe God.

A dear woman was marvelously delivered and saved, but she said, "I am so addicted to smoking, what shall I do?" "Oh," I said, "Smoke night and day," and she said, "In our circumstances we take a glass of wine and it has a hold on me." "Oh," I said, "Drink all you can." It brought some solace to her, but she was in misery. She said, "We play cards." I said, "Play on!" But after being saved she called her maid and said, "Wire to London and stop the shipment of those cigarettes." The new life does not want it. It has no desire. The old is dethroned.

A clergyman came. He said, "I have a terrible craving for tobacco." I said, "Is it the old man or the new?" He broke down. "I know it's the old," he said. Put off the old man with his deeds. One said, "I have an unlawful affection for another." I said, "You want revelation? Seeing God has given you Jesus, He will give you all things. He will give you power over the thing, and it will be broken," and God broke it. "Allow God to touch thy flesh." Now He has quickened thy spirit. Allow Him to reign, for He shall reign until all is subdued. He is preeminently King in thy life over thy affection, thy will, thy desire, thy plans. He rules as Lord of Hosts over thee, in thee, through thee, to chasten thee and bring thee to the perfection of thy desired haven. It is Christ in thee. It is the glory. "Who shall separate us from the love of Christ?" Once things could separate us, but they no more can. We have a vision. What is the vision? Those days when we have eaten of the hidden manna.

THE SWORD

When I was baptized in the Holy Ghost, God showed me when Adam and Eve transgressed and were turned out of the garden — at the gate was put a flaming sword — a sword of death if they entered in — but the baptism of the Holy Ghost put the tree of life right in me and a flaming sword outside to keep the devil from me — that I might eat all the time of the eternal bread. I am eating of this wonderful bread of life. It is the life in the body which has come to a perfect place to this life from which nothing can separate us. It is increasing tremendously — perpetually — rapture has something to do with it. In a moment this will clear out and leave the body. What is it? What shall separate us? Tribulations come, but they only press us in — press us nearer persecution, the finest thing that can come. There among the persecuted, you get the ripest, the holiest, the purest, the most intent, filled with divine order — all these things work for us — nothing comes but what is helpful — trials lift you — distresses give you a heave and sigh, but God causes us to triumph. Greater is He that is in you than all the powers of darkness.

Whatever befalls you as you abide in Him, is the good hand of God upon you, so that you won't lose your inheritance. Every trial is a lift — every burden a place of exchanging strength. God will work. "Who can lay anything to the charge of God's elect?" People do it, but it makes no difference. God is for us. "...Eye hath not seen, nor ear heard, neither have entered into the heart of man, the things which God hath prepared for those that love him" (1 Corinthians 2:9). But unto us it hath been revealed by the Spirit. Not a weapon that is formed against you can prosper. Know the wisdom and purpose of the great hand that is upon you. Glorify God in distresses and persecutions, for the Spirit of God is there made manifest. Be chastened! Be perfected! Press on to heights, lengths, depths, breadths. Faith is the victory. The hope is within you, the joy set before you. The peace which passeth all understanding. The knowledge that the flesh has withered in the presence of the purifying of the Word. He Who has brought you hitherto, will take you to the end. I have wept bitterly and mourned when I needed revelation of God, but I need not have done.

The Lord lifteth up and changeth and operateth, and makes body and soul till He can say, "There is no spot in thee." Yes it was persecution, tribulation, and distress that drew us near. Lifting places, changing places — the operation of God by the Spirit. Do not let us pass this way but let God have His way.

God stretched out His hand, covered us with the mantle of His love, and brought us nearer and nearer into the channel of His grace until our heart has moved and yielded, and so turned to the Lord that every moment has seen a divine place where God has met us and stretched out His arms and said, "Seek ye My face — look unto Me." Behold and see what great love the Master has for thee, to lead thee to the fountain of living water. Yield! Be led! And let God be glorified! Amen.

Published in *Redemption Tidings*

esus saith, "Be not afraid, only believe" (Mark 5:36). The people in whom God delights are the ones who rest upon His Word without wavering. God has nothing for the man who wavers, for "let him that wavereth expect nothing from God." Therefore I would like us to get this verse deep down into our hearts, until it penetrates every fibre of our being: "Only believe! All *things are possible — ONLY BELIEVE.*"

FULL OF THE HOLY GHOST

May 28, 1932

God has a plan for this meeting, beyond anything that we have ever known before. He has a plan for every individual life, and if we have any other plan in view, *we miss the grandest plan of all!* Nothing of the past is equal to the present, and nothing of the present can equal the things of tomorrow, for "tomorrow" should be so filled with holy expectations that we will be "living flames" for Him. God never intended His people to be ordinary, or commonplace; His intentions were that they should be on fire for Him, conscious of His divine power, realizing the glory of the cross that foreshadows the crown.

God has given us a very special Scripture for this service:

> *And in those days, when the number of the disciples was multiplied, there arose a murmuring of the Grecians against the Hebrews, because their widows were neglected in the daily ministration. Then the twelve called the multitude of the disciples unto them, and said, It is not reason that we should leave the word of God, and serve tables. Wherefore, brethren, look ye out among you seven men of honest report, full of the Holy Ghost and wisdom, whom we may appoint over this business...And the saying pleased the whole multitude: and they chose Stephen, a man full of faith and of the Holy Ghost, and Philip...."*
>
> *Acts 6:1-3,5*

During the time of the inauguration of the Church, the disciples were hard pressed on all lines; the things of natural order could not be attended to, and many were complaining concerning the neglect of their widows. The disciples therefore decided upon a plan, which was to choose seven men to do the work — men who were "full of the Holy Ghost." What a divine thought! No matter what kind of work was to be done, however menial it may have been, the person chosen must be *filled with the Holy Ghost*. The plan of the Church was that everything, even of natural order, *must be* sanctified unto God, *for the Church had to be a Holy Ghost church*. Beloved, *God has never ordained anything less!* There is one thing that I want to stress in these meetings; that is, no matter what else may happen, first and foremost I would emphasize the question —

"Have you received the Holy Ghost since you believed?" "Are you filled with divine power?"

This is the heritage of the Church to be so endued with power that God can lay His hand upon any member at any time to do His perfect will.

There is no stop in the Spirit-filled life: we begin at the cross, the place of ignominy, shame, and death, and that very death brings the power of resurrection life; and, being filled with Holy Spirit, we go on "from glory to glory." Let us not forget that possessing the baptism in the Holy Spirit means there must be an "ever-increasing" holiness. How the Church needs divine unction — God's presence and power so manifest that the world will know it. The people know when the tide is flowing; they also know when it is ebbing.

The necessity that seven men be chosen for the position of "serving tables" was very evident. The disciples knew that these seven men were *men ready for active service*, and so they chose them. In the fifth verse, we read: "And the saying pleased the whole multitude: and they chose Stephen, a man full of faith and of the Holy Ghost, and Philip...." There were others, of course, but Stephen and Philip stand out most prominently in the Scriptures. Philip was a man so filled with Holy Ghost that a revival always followed wherever he went. Stephen was a man so filled with divine power, that although serving tables might have been all right in the minds of the other disciples, yet, God had a greater vision for him — *a baptism of fire*, of power and divine unction, that took him on and on to the climax of his life, until he saw right into the open heavens.

Had we been there with the disciples at that time, I believe we should have heard them saying to each other, "Look here! Neither Stephen nor Philip are doing the work we called them to. If they do not attend to business, we shall have to get someone else!" That was the *natural* way of thinking, but divine order is far above our finite planning. When we please God in our daily ministration, we shall always find in operation the fact "that everyone who is faithful in little, God will make faithful in much." We have such an example right here — a man chosen to "serve tables," having such a revelation of the mind of Christ and of the depth and height of God, that there was no stop in his experience, but a going forward with leaps and bounds. Beloved, there is a race to be run, there is a crown to be won; we *cannot stand still!* I say unto you, be vigilant! *Be vigilant! "Let no man take thy crown!"*

God has privileged us in Christ Jesus to live above the ordinary human plane of life. Those who want to be ordinary, and live on a lower plane, can do so; but as for me, *I will not!* For the same unction, the same zeal, the same Holy Ghost power is at our command as was at the command of Stephen and the apostles. We have the same God that Abraham had, that Elijah had, and *we need not come behind in any gift or grace.* We may not possess the gifts, as abiding gifts, but as we are full of the Holy Ghost and divine unction, it is possible, when there is need, for God to *manifest every gift of the Spirit* through us. As I have already said, I do not mean by this that we should necessarily possess the gifts permanently, but there should be a *manifestation of the gifts* as God may choose to use us.

This *ordinary* man Stephen became mighty under the Holy Ghost anointing, until he stands supreme, in many ways, among the apostles — "And Stephen, full of faith and power, did great wonders and miracles among the people" (Acts 6:8). As we go deeper in God, He enlarges our conception and places before us a wide-open door; and I am not surprised that this man chosen to "serve tables" was afterwards called to a higher plane. "What do you mean?" you may ask. "Did he quit this service?" No! But he was lost in the power of God. He lost sight of everything in the natural, and steadfastly fixed his gaze upon Jesus, "the author and finisher of our faith," until he was transformed into a shining light in the kingdom of God. Oh, that we might be awakened to believe His Word, to understand the mind of the Spirit, for there is an *inner* place of whiteness and purity where we can "see God." Stephen was just as ordinary a man as you and me, but he was in the place where God could so move upon him that he, in turn, could move all before him. He began in a most humble place, and ended in a blaze of glory. Beloved, *dare to believe Christ!*

As you go on in this life of the Spirit, you will find that the devil will begin to get restless and there will be a stir in the synagogue; it was so with Stephen. Any amount of people may be found in the "synagogue," who are very proper in the worldly sense — always correctly dressed, the elite of the land, welcoming into the church everything but the power of God. Let us read what God says about them:

> *Then there arose certain of the synagogue, which is called the synagogue of the Libertines, and Cyrenians, and Alexandrians...disputing with Stephen. And they were not able to resist the wisdom and the spirit by which he spake.*
>
> Acts 6:9,10

"The Libertines" could not stand the truth of God. With these opponents, Stephen found himself in the same predicament as the blind man whom Jesus healed. As soon as the blind man's eyes were opened they shut him out of the synagogue. *They will not have anybody in the "synagogue" with their eyes open;* as soon as you receive spiritual eyesight, *out you go!* These Libertines, Cyrenians, and Alexandrians, rose up full of wrath in the very place where they should have been full of the power of God, full of love divine, and reverence for the Holy Ghost; they *rose up against* Stephen, this man "full of the Holy Ghost." Beloved, if there is anything in your life that in any way resists the power of the Holy Ghost and the entrance of His Word into your heart and life, *drop on your knees and CRY ALOUD for mercy!* When the Spirit of God is brooding over your heart's door, do not resist Him but open your heart to the touch of God. There is a resisting "unto blood" striving *against sin,* and there is a resisting of the Holy Ghost that will drive you *into sin.*

Stephen spoke with marked wisdom; where he was, things began to move. You will find that there is always a moving when the Holy Spirit has control. These people were brought under conviction by the message of Stephen, but they resisted, they did anything and everything to stifle that conviction. Not only did they lie, but they got others to lie against this man who would have laid down his life for any one of them. Stephen was used to heal the sick, perform miracles, and yet they brought false accusations against him. What effect did it have on Stephen?

> *And all that sat in the council, looking stedfastly on him, saw*
> *his face as it had been the face of an angel.*
>
> *Acts 6:15*

Something had happened in the life of this man, chosen for menial service, and he became *mighty for God.* How was it accomplished in him? It was because *his aim was high;* faithful in little, God brought him to full fruition. Under the inspiration of divine power by which he spoke, they could not but listen — even the angels listened, as with holy, prophetic utterance he spoke before that council. Beginning with Abraham and Moses, he continued unfolding the truth. What a marvelous exhortation! Take your Bibles and read it, "listen in" as the angels listened in. As light upon light, truth upon truth, revelation upon revelation, found its way into their calloused hearts, they gazed at him in astonishment; their hearts perhaps became warm at times, and they may have said, "Truly, this man is sent of God" — but when he hurled at them the truth...

> *Ye stiffnecked and uncircumcised in heart and ears, ye do always*
> *resist the Holy Ghost: as your fathers did, so do ye. Which of the*
> *prophets have not your fathers persecuted? and they have slain*
> *them which showed before of the coming of the Just One; of whom*
> *ye have been now the betrayers and murderers: Who have received*
> *the law by the disposition of angels, and have not kept it.*
>
> *Acts 7:51-53*

...then what happened? These men were moved; they were "...cut to the heart, and they gnashed on him with their teeth" (v. 54).

There are two marvelous occasions in the Scriptures where the people were "pricked to the heart." In the second chapter of the Acts of the apostles, thirty-seventh verse, after Peter had delivered that inspired sermon on the day of Pentecost, the people were "pricked to the heart" with conviction, and there were added to the church three thousand souls. Here is Stephen, speaking under the inspiration of the Holy Ghost, and the men of this council being "pricked to the heart" rise up as one man to slay him. As you go down through this chapter, from the 55th verse, what a picture you have before you. As I close my eyes, I can get a vision of this scene in every detail the howling mob with their revengeful, murderous spirit, ready to devour this holy man, and he "being full of the Holy Ghost," gazed steadfastly into heaven. What did he see there? From his place of helplessness, he looked up and said:

> *...behold, I see the heavens opened, and the Son of man standing on the right hand of God.*
>
> Acts 7:56

Is that the position that Jesus went to take? No! He went to "sit" at the right hand of the Father but in behalf of the *first martyr*, in behalf of the man with that burning flame of Holy Ghost power, God's Son *stood up* in honorary testimony of him who, called to serve tables, was faithful unto death. But is that all? No! I am so glad that it is not all. As the stones came flying at him, pounding his body, crashing into his bones, striking his temple, mangling his beautiful face, what happened? How did this scene end? With that sublime, upward look, this man chosen for an ordinary task but filled with the Holy Ghost, was so moved upon by God that he finished his earthly work in a blaze of glory, magnifying God with his last breath. Looking up into the face of the Master, he said: *Lord Jesus, forgive them!* "...lay not this sin to their charge. And when he had said this, he fell asleep" (Acts 7:60).

Friends, it is worth dying a thousand deaths to gain that spirit. My God! What a divine ending to the life and testimony of a man who was "chosen to serve tables."

Published in *The Pentocostal Evangel*

 ow faith is the substance of things hoped for, the evidence of things not seen. For by it the elders obtained a good report.
Hebrews 11:1-2

LIVING FAITH

February 1935

BLESSED REALITY

God has moved me tonight to speak on the marvelous, glorious reality of God's Word. How great should be our faith, for we cannot be *saved* except by faith, we cannot be *kept* but by faith; we can only be *baptized* by faith, and we will be *caught up* by faith; therefore, what a *blessed reality* is faith in the living God.

What is faith? It is the very nature of God. Faith is the Word of God. It is the personal inward flow of divine favor, which moves in every fiber of our being until our whole nature is so quickened that we *live* by faith, we *move* by faith, and we are going to be *caught up to glory* by faith, for *"Faith is the Victory!"* Faith is the glorious knowledge of a personal presence within you, changing you from strength to strength, from glory to glory, until you get to the place where you walk with God, and God thinks and speaks through you by the power of the Holy Ghost. Oh, it is *grand*, it is *glorious*!

God wants us to have far more than that which we can *handle* and *see*, and so He speaks of *the substance of things hoped for, the evidence of things not seen*; but, *with the eye of faith*, we may see it in all its beauty and grandeur. God's Word is from everlasting to everlasting, and "faith is the substance." If I should give some of you ladies a piece of cloth, scissors, needle, and thread, you could produce a garment. Why? Because you had the material. If I should provide some of you men with wood, saw, hammer, and nails, you could produce a box. Why? Because you had the material. But God, *without material*, spoke the Word and produced this world with all its beauty. There was no material there, but *the Word of God* called it into being by His creative force; and with the knowledge that you are begotten by this incorruptible Word, which liveth and abideth forever, you *know* that within you is this living, definite hope, greater than yourself, more powerful than any dynamic force in the world, *for faith worketh in you by the power of the new creation of God in Christ Jesus; therefore with the audacity of faith* we should throw ourselves into the omnipotence of God's divine plan, for God has said to you, "If thou canst believe, all things are possible to him that believeth" (Mark 9:23). It is possible for the power of God to be so manifest in your human life that you will never be as you were before; for you will be ever going forward, from victory to victory, for faith knows *no defeat*.

The Word of God will bring you into a wonderful place of rest in faith. God means you to have a clear conception of what faith *is*, how faith *came*, and how it *remains*. Faith is in the divine plan, for it brings you to the open door *that you might enter in*. You must have an open door, for you cannot open the door; it is *God* who does it, but He wants you *to be ready to step in and claim His promises to all the divine manifestation of power in the name of Christ Jesus*. It is only *thus* that you will be able to meet and conquer the enemy, for *"He that is within you is greater than he that is without."*

Living faith brings *glorious power* and *personality*, it gives *divine ability*, for it is by faith that Christ is manifested in your mortal flesh by the Word of God. I would not have you miss the knowledge that you have *heard from God*, and to realize that God has so changed you that all weakness, fear, inability — everything that has made you a failure, has passed away. Faith has power to make you what *God* wants you to be, only you must be *ready to step into the plan and believe* His Word.

The first manifestation of God's plan was the *cross of Calvary*. You may refuse it, you may resist it, but God, who loves you with an everlasting love, has followed you through life, and will follow you with His great grace, that He may bring you to a knowledge of *this great salvation*. God, in his own plan for your eternal good, may have brought something into your life that is distasteful; something that is causing you to feel *desperate*, that your life is *worthless*. What does it mean? It means that the Spirit of God is showing you *your own weakness* that you might *cry out unto Him*, and when you do He will show you the cross of redemption; then God will give you *faith to believe*, for faith is the gift of God.

BEYOND THE PLACE OF SALVATION

God, who has given us this faith, has a wonderful plan for our life. Do you remember when God brought you to this place of salvation, how the faith He gave you brought a great desire to do something for Him, and then He showed you that wonderful open door? I was saved over sixty-seven years ago, and I have never lost the witness of the Spirit. If you will not allow your human nature to crush your faith and interfere with God's plan in its wonderful divine setting, you will mount up like the eagles. Oh the wonderful effectiveness of God's perfect plan working in us, with the divine trinity flowing through humanity, changing our very nature to the extent that we cannot *disbelieve*, but *act faith, talk faith*, and in faith *sing praises unto the Lord*. There is no room for anything that is *not* faith, for we have passed beyond *the natural plane* into a *new* atmosphere — *God enclosed and enclosing us.*

Faith is an *increasing* position, always *triumphant.* It is not a place of *poverty* but of *wealth.* If you always live in fruitfulness you will always have plenty. What does it say in this scripture? *"The elders obtained a good report!"* The man who *lives in faith* always has a *good report.* The Acts of the Apostles were written because the lives of the apostles bore the fruit of *active faith.* To *them* faith was *an every-day-fact.* If your life is in the divine order, you will not only have living, active faith but you will always be building up someone else in faith.

What is the good of preaching without faith? God intends that we should so live in this glorious sphere of the power of God, that we will always be in a position to tell people of the act that brought the fact. You must act before you can see the fact. What is the good of praying for the sick without faith? You must *believe* that God will not deny Himself, *for the Word of God cannot be denied.* I believe this message is given in divine order, that you may no longer be in a place of *doubt* but will realize that "faith is the substance!" Beloved, even with all the faith we have, we are not even so much as touching the hem of God's plan for us. It is like going to the seashore and dipping your toe in the water, with the great vast ocean before you. God wants us to rise on the bosom of the tide, and not keep paddling along the shore. Oh to be connected with that sublime power, that human nature may know God and the glory of the manifestation of Christ!

The Word of God is *eternal* and *cannot be broken.* You cannot improve on the Word of God, for it is *life,* and it produces *life.* Listen! God has begotten you to a "lively hope." You are begotten of the Word that created worlds. If you dare to believe, it is powerful. God wants us to be powerful, a people of faith, a purified people, a people who will launch out in God and dare to trust Him in glorious faith which always takes you beyond that which is commonplace to an abiding place in God.

TESTING THE SPIRITS

May 1935

eloved, believe not every spirit, but try the spirits whether they are of God: because many false prophets are gone out into the world. Hereby know ye the Spirit of God: Every spirit that confesseth that Jesus Christ is come in the flesh is of God.

1 John 4:1-2

If this passage was honeycombed right through our own circumstances, there would be no room for fear. Dealing this morning with a subject that deals with satanic power, that we may be able to discern evil spirits.

We can so live in this divine communion with Christ that we can sense evil in any part of the world. In this present world, powers of evil are rampant. There are two battles going on all the time. The man who lives in God is afraid of nothing. The plan of God is that we might be so in Him that we will be equal to any occasion.

"TRY THE SPIRITS...

...whether they are of God." Be ready to challenge the devil. Don't be afraid, you will be delivered from fear if you believe. You can have ears to hear and not hear, which is the ear of faith, and your ears will be so open to that which is spiritual, that they will lay hold.

When the Word of God becomes the life and nature of you, you will find that the minute you open it, it becomes life to you — you have to be joined up with the Word. Ye are to be the epistles of Christ. This means the same Christ is the Word, and He will be known by the fruits. He is the life and the nature of you. It is a new nature. New life, new breath, new spiritual atmosphere, no limitation in this standard, but in everything else you are limited. "...greater is he that is in you, than he that is in the world" (1 John 4:4). When the Word of life is repeated because it is your life, then it is enacted and it beings forth that which God has desired. When we quote the Scriptures, we must be careful that it is ours. The Word of God has to abide in you, for the Word is life, and it brings forth life, and this is the life that makes you free from the law of sin and death.

HOW TO TRY THE SPIRITS

There are evil thoughts and there are thoughts of evil. Evil thoughts are suggestive of the evil one. We are to be able to understand what is the evil and how to deal with it. The Word of God makes us strong. All evil powers are weak. The devil has nothing strong, the weakest believer dethrones him when he mentions Jesus. "Young men, ye are strong because ye know the Word" (See 1 John 2:14).

There are evil thoughts and thoughts of evil. Where do thoughts of evil come from? They come from the unclean believer. The man that is not entirely sanctified. The devil does not know your thoughts, but God does; that is where the devil is held. God knoweth all things. Satan suggests an evil thought to try to arouse in you your carnal nature.

If you are disturbed, if you are weak, if you are troubled, depressed, then you are in a wonderful place. If you never tell anybody, and you are not disturbed, the carnal powers have never been destroyed in you. But if you tell anybody, then it is proof you are clean, it is because you are clean that you weep. If you are not disturbed, if you have no conviction, it is because of the uncleansed heart, you have let sin come in.

HOW SHALL THE BELIEVER BELIEVE...

...himself that he may not be tormented? How shall we be master of the situation is the question asked. Did Jesus come in the flesh? "...Every spirit that confesseth that Jesus Christ is come in the flesh is of God" (1 John 4:2). Mary produced a Son in the likeness of God, the same seed that came in us produces a life, a person, which is Christ in us which rose up in us till the reflection of the Son of God is in everything we do. She produced a son for redemption. God's seed in us produces a son of perfect redemption, until we live in Him, move by Him, and our whole nature comes to be a perfect Son of God in us. In the name of Jesus, cast self out and you will be instantly free.

The Holy Ghost has all power, has all language. If you won't tell anybody when these suggestive evil powers come, it is a proof that you are not sanctified. A spiritualistic person will never say that Jesus came in the flesh. The Lord would have us to understand that spiritualistic evidences, etc., are of the devil.

WE MUST BE IN A PLACE...

...where we can discern evil things, and evil spirits. There is a place where we can bind these evil powers and loosing the people set them free. Read Mark 9. There is an exchange of life, of power until it is absolutely as the Word says, "...greater is he that is in you, than he that is in the world" (1 John 4:4). God can change you until you will not be afraid of anything.

Life comes after you have been filled with the Holy Ghost, get down and pray for power. You ask, "What is the trouble that you come away from prayer with no changes?" Two reasons: when you go into your place lock the door. Should you pray silently? No — pray loud. The devil has never disturbed anybody who prayed aloud. There the Holy Ghost's power is a proof.

If you will, you can rebuke, cast out the satanic powers. Rebuke Satan. Never cast a devil out twice, or he will run about and laugh at you. He will know you did not believe it the first time. "Ask and you will receive." The moment you ask, believe you will receive and you will have it. Now I am going to pray, "Father, in the name of Jesus, increase my compassion." Thank You, Lord, I have it. I know I have it.

THE WAY OF FAITH

June 15, 1935

In Romans 4:16 we read, "...it is of faith, that it might be by grace," meaning that we can open the door and God will come in. What will happen if we really open the door by faith? God is greater than our thoughts. He puts it to us, "...exceeding abundantly above all that we ask or think..." (Ephesians 3:20). When we ask a lot, God says "more." Are we ready for the "more"? And then the "much more"? We may be, or we may miss it. We may be so endued by the Spirit of the Lord in the morning that it shall be a tonic for the whole day. God can so thrill us with new life that nothing ordinary or small will satisfy us after that. There is a great place for us in God where we won't be satisfied with small things. We won't have any satisfaction unless the fire falls, and whenever we pray we will have the assurance that what we have prayed for is going to follow the moment we open our mouth. Oh, this praying in the Spirit! This great plan of God for us! In a moment we can go right in. In where? Into His will. Then all things will be well.

You can't get anything asleep these days. The world is always awake, and we should always be awake to what God has for us. Awake to take! Awake to hold it after we get it! How much can you take? We know that God is more willing to give than we are to receive. How shall we dare to be asleep when the Spirit commands us to take everything on the table. It is the greatest banquet that ever was and ever will be — the table where all you take only leaves more behind. A fulness that cannot be exhausted! How many are prepared for a lot?

> *And Jesus entered into Jerusalem, and into the temple: and when he had looked round about upon all things, and now the eventide was come, he went out unto Bethany with the twelve. And on the morrow, when they were come from Bethany, he was hungry: And seeing a fig tree afar off having leaves; he came, if haply he might find any thing thereon: and when he came to it, he found nothing but leaves; for the time of figs was not yet. And Jesus answered and said unto it, No man eat fruit of thee hereafter for ever. And his disciples heard it.*
>
> *Mark 11:11-14*

Jesus was sent from God to meet the world's need. Jesus lived to minister life by the words He spoke, He said to Philip, "...he that hath seen me hath seen the Father...the words that I speak unto you I speak not of myself: but the Father that dwelleth in me..." (John 14:9,10). I am persuaded that if we are filled with His words of life and the Holy Ghost, and Christ is made manifest in our mortal flesh, then the Holy Ghost can really move us with His life, His words, till as He was, so are we in the world. We are receiving our life from God, and it is always kept in tremendous activity, working in our whole nature as we live in perfect contact with God.

Jesus spoke, and everything He said must come to pass. That is the great plan. When we are filled only with the Holy Spirit, and we won't allow the

Word of God to be detracted by what we hear or by what we read, then comes the inspiration, then the life, then the activity, then the glory! Oh, to live in it! To live in it is to be moved by it. To live in it is to be moved so that we will have God's life, God's personality in the human body.

By the grace of God I want to impart the Word, and bring you into a place where you will dare to act upon the plan of the Word, to so breathe life by the power of the Word that it is impossible for you to go on under any circumstances without His provision. The most difficult things that come to us are to our advantage from God's side. When we come to the place of impossibilities it is the grandest place for us to see the possibilities of God. Put this right in your mind and never forget it. You will never be of any importance to God till you venture in the impossible. God wants people on the daring line. I do not mean foolish daring. "Be filled with the Spirit," and when we are filled with the Spirit we are not so much concerned about the secondary thing. It is the first with God.

Everything of evil, everything unclean, everything satanic in any way, is an objectionable thing to God, and we are to live above it, destroy it, not to allow it to have any place. Jesus didn't let the devil answer back. We must reach the place where we will not allow anything to interfere with the plan of God.

Jesus and His disciples came to the tree. It looked beautiful. It had the appearance of fruit, but when He came to it He found nothing but leaves. He was very disappointed. Looking at the tree, He spoke to it. Here is shown forth His destructive power, "No man eat fruit of thee hereafter for ever" (Mark 11:14). The next day they were passing by the same way and the disciples saw the tree "...dried up from the roots" (v. 20). They said to Jesus, "...behold, the fig tree which thou cursedst is withered away" (v. 21). And Jesus said, "Have faith in God" (v. 22).

There isn't a person who has ever seen a tree dried from the root. Trees always show the first signs of death right at the top. But the Master had spoken. The Master dealt with a natural thing to reveal to these disciples a supernatural plan. If He spoke, it would have to obey. And God, the Holy Ghost, wants us to understand clearly that we are the mouthpiece of God and are here for His divine plan. We may allow the natural mind to dethrone that, but in the measure we do, we won't come into the treasure which God has for us. The Word of God must have first place. It must not have a second place. In any measure that we doubt the Word of God, from that moment we have ceased to thrive spiritually and actively. The Word of God is not only to be looked at and read, but received as the Word of God to become life right within our life. "Thy word have I hid in mine heart, that I might not sin against thee" (Psalms 119:11).

"...I give unto you power...over all the power of the enemy..." (Luke 10:19). There it is. We can accept or reject it. I accept and believe it. It is a word beyond all human calculation. "Have faith in God." These disciples were in the Master's school. They were the men who were to turn the world upside down. As we receive the Word we will never be the same; if we dare to act as the Word goes forth and not be afraid, then God will honor us. "The Lord of hosts is with us; the God of Jacob is our refuge" (Psalms 46:7). Jacob was the weakest of all, in any way you like to take it. He is the God of Jacob, and He is our God. So we may likewise have our names changed to Israel.

As the Lord Jesus injected this wonderful Word, "Have faith in God," into the disciples, He began to show how it was to be. Looking around about Him He saw the mountains, and He began to bring a practical application. A truth means nothing unless it moves us. We can have our minds filled a thousand times, but it must get into our hearts if there are to be any results. All inspiration is in the heart. All compassion is in the heart.

Looking at the mountains He said, "Shall not doubt in his heart." That is the barometer. You know exactly where you are. The man knows when he prays. If his heart is right how it leaps. No man is any good for God and never makes progress in God who does not hate sin. You are never safe. But there is a place in God where you can love righteousness and where you can hate iniquity till the Word of God is a light in your bosom, quickening every fiber of your body, thrilling your whole nature. The pure in heart see God. Believe in the heart! What a word! If I believe in my heart God says I can begin to speak, and "whatsoever" I say shall come to pass.

Here is an act of believing in the heart. I was called to Halifax, England, to pray for a lady missionary. I found it an urgent call. I could see there was an absence of faith, and I could see there was death. Death is a terrible thing, and God wants to keep us alive. I know it is appointed unto man once to die, but I believe in a rapturous death. I said to the woman, "How are you?" She said, "I have faith," in a very weak tone of voice. "Faith? Why you are dying? Brother Walshaw, is she dying?" "Yes." To a friend standing by, "Is she dying?" "Yes."

Now I believe there is something in a heart that is against defeat, and this is the faith which God hath given to us. I said to her, "In the name of Jesus, now believe and you'll live." She said, "I believe," and God sent life from her head to her feet. They dressed her and she lived.

"Have faith." It isn't *saying* you have faith. It is he that *believeth in his heart*. It is a grasping of the eternal God. Faith is God in the human vessel. "...this is the victory that overcometh the world, even our faith" (1 John 5:4). He that *believeth* overcomes the world. "...faith cometh by hearing, and hearing by the word of God" (Romans 10:17). He that believeth in his heart! Can you imagine anything easier than that? He that believeth in his heart! What is the process? Death! No one can live who believes in his heart. He dies to everything worldly. He that loves the world is not of God. You can measure the whole thing up, and examine yourself to see if you have faith. Faith is a life. Faith enables you to lay hold of that which is and get it out of the way for God to bring in something that is not.

Just before I left home I was in Norway. A woman wrote to me from England saying she had been operated on for cancer three years before, but that it was now coming back. She was living in constant dread of the whole thing as the operation was so painful. Would it be possible to see me when I returned to England? I wrote that I would be passing through London on the 20th of June last year. If she would like to meet me at the hotel I would pray for her. She replied that she would be going to London to be there to meet me. When I met this woman I saw she was in great pain, and I have great sympathy for people who have tried to get relief and have failed. If you preachers lose your compassion you can stop preaching, for it won't be any good. You will only be successful as a preacher as you let your heart become filled with the compassion of Jesus. As soon as I saw her I entered into the state of her mind. I saw how distressed she was. She came to me in a mournful spirit, and her whole face was downcast. I said to her, "There are two things going to happen today. One is that you are to know that you are saved." "Oh, if I could only know I was saved," she said. "There is another thing. You have to go out of this hotel without a pain, without a trace of the cancer."

Then I began with the Word. Oh, this wonderful Word! We do not have to go up to bring Him down; neither do we have to go down to bring Him up. "...the word is nigh thee, even in thy mouth, and in thy heart: that is, the word of faith, which we preach" (Romans 10:8). I said, "Believe that He took your sins when He died at the cross. Believe that when He was buried, it was for you. Believe that when He arose, it was for you. And now at God's right hand He is sitting for you. If you can believe in your heart and confess with your mouth, you shall be saved." She looked at me saying, "Oh, it is going all through my body. I know I am saved now. If He comes today, I'll go. How I have dreaded the thought of His coming all my life! But if He comes today, I know I shall be ready."

The first thing was finished. Now for the second. I laid my hands upon her in the name of Jesus, believing in my heart that I could say what I wanted and it should be done. I said, "In the name of Jesus, I cast this out." She jumped up. "Two things have happened," she said. "I am saved and now the cancer is gone."

> Faith will stand amid the wrecks of time,
> Faith unto eternal glories climb;
> Only count the promise true,
> And the Lord will stand by you.
> Faith will win the victory *every* time!

So many people have nervous trouble. I'll tell you how to get rid of your nervous trouble. I have something in my bag, one dose of which will cure you. "...I am the Lord that healeth thee" (Exodus 15:26). How this wonderful Word of God changes the situation. "...perfect love casteth out fear..." (1 John 4:18). "There is no fear in love..." (v. 18). I have tested that so often, casting out the whole condition of fear and the whole situation has been changed. We have a big God, only He has to be absolutely and only trusted. The people who really do believe God are strong, and "he that hath clean hands shall be stronger and stronger."

At the close of a certain meeting a man said to me, "You have helped everybody but me. I wish you would help me." "What's the trouble with you?" "I cannot sleep because of nervous trouble. My wife says she has not known me to have a full night's sleep for three years. I am just shattered." Anyone could tell he was. I put my hands upon him and said, "Brother, I believe in my heart. Go home and sleep in the name of Jesus." "I can't sleep." "Go home and sleep in the name of Jesus." "I can't sleep." The lights were being put out, and I took the man by the coat collar and said, "Don't talk to me anymore." That was sufficient. He went after that. When he got home his mother and wife said to him, "What has happened?" "Nothing. He helped everybody but me." "Surely he said something to you." "He told me to come home and sleep in the name of Jesus, but you know I can't sleep in anything."

His wife urged him to do what I had said, and he had scarcely got his head on the pillow before the Lord put him to sleep. The next morning he was still asleep. She began to make a noise in the bedroom to awaken him, but he did not waken. Sunday morning he was still asleep. She did what every good wife would do. She decided to make a good Sunday dinner, and then awaken him. After the dinner was prepared she went up to him and put her hand on his shoulder and shook him, saying, "Are you never going to wake up?" From that night that man never had any more nervousness.

A man came to me for whom I prayed. Then I asked, "Are you sure you are perfectly healed?" "Well," he said, "there is just a little pain in my shoulder." "Do you know what that is?" I asked him. "That is unbelief. Were you saved before you believed or after?" "After." "You will be healed after." "It is all right now," he said. It was all right before, but he hadn't believed.

The Word of God is for us. It is by faith that it might be by grace.

Published in *The Pentecostal Evangel*

MEN OF FAITH
The Life That Ventures on the Word of God

September 11, 1936

od has drawn us together and He has something to give us. He is not ordinary, but extraordinary, not measured, but immeasurable, abounding in everything. There is nothing small about our God, and when we understand God we will find out that there ought not to be anything small about us. We must have

AN ENLARGEMENT OF OUR CONCEPTION OF GOD,

then we will know that we have come to a place where all things are possible, for our God is an omnipotent God for impossible positions.

We are born into a family that never dies, and it is the plan of God to subdue all things that are natural to a supernatural order. Nothing about us has to be dwarfed. God comes in with His mighty power and so works in us that sin has no dominion; evil is subdued, and God's Son begins to reign on the throne of your heart, transforming that which was weak and helpless.

But there must be a revolution if we would have almighty God living in and controlling our mortal flesh. We must conclude that there is no good thing in the flesh, and then we must know that God can come in the flesh and subject it till every mighty thing can be manifested through the human order.

Now, beloved, have you come for a blessing? Turn to Hebrews, chapter 11.

The Christian life is a going on, a non-stop, until you reach the top. If you ever stop between Calvary and the glory, it is you who blocked the way. There is no stop between Calvary and the glory except by human failure, but if you allow God to have His way, He will surely transform us, for His plan is to change us from what we are to what He intends us to be, and never to lose the ideal of His great plan for us. God wants to shake us loose and take the cobwebs away, and remove all the husks from the wheat, that we may be pure grain for God to work upon. In order to do that we must be willing to let go; as long as you hold on to the natural, you cannot take hold of divine life.

The child of God has never to be on the line of speculation but on the line of faith, with audacity to prove that God is what He has promised to be. You will not get strong in faith until you

VENTURE ON THE IMPOSSIBLE.

If you ask for anything six times, five is unbelief. You are not heard for your much speaking, but because you believe. If you pray round the world, you will get into a whirlwind, and spoil every meeting you get into.

Now God does not want anybody in the world, under any circumstances, to be in a place where they live on eyesight and on feelings. Faith never feels and faith never looks. Faith is an act, and faith without an act is not faith, but doubt and disgrace. Every one of you has more faith than you are using.

Now this "substance" I am speaking about cannot be looked at nor handled. God wants us to have something greater than what we can see and handle. It is declared in the Scriptures that the earth is going to be melted with fervent heat and the heavens shall depart, but the Word will remain, and this is substance. So we must know whether we are living in substance that cannot be handled or living in the temporal, for everything you can see is going to be moved, and that which you cannot see is going to remain forever.

God gives us this remarkable substance that is called faith. It consists of the Word of God, of the personality of God, of the nature of God, and the acts of God, and those four things are all in faith. Faith is a deep reality caused by God's personality waking up our humanity to leap into eternal things and be lost forever in something a million times greater than yourself. To be possessed by and be the possessor of something a million times greater than you!

THERE IS ALWAYS A GOING ON WITH GOD.

There is a growing in faith after we are saved. Backsliding is knowing the way of holiness and shutting the door. So if you know to do good and you do not do it, that is backsliding. What standard is holiness? There is none. A person who is newborn is as holy as the aged while he walks according to the light he has, and the oldest saint with more light is not more holy than the person who is just saved and walking in the light.

You cannot make anything without material, but I want to read to you of something being made without material.

> *Through faith we understand that the worlds were framed by the word of God, so that things which are seen were not made of things which do appear.*
>
> Hebrews 11:3

God took the Word and made this world out of things that were not there. He caused it all to come by the word of faith. You were born of, created by, made anew by, the same word that made the world. God, in His infinite mercy, brings His infinite light and power right into our finite being so that we have revelations of the mighty God and of His wonderful power. That is the reason why I lay hands on the sick and know they will be healed.

God has taken all ranks and conditions of people to make the 11th chapter of Hebrews. Samson made terrible mistakes, but he is included. Then there is Barak who wouldn't go without Deborah. He couldn't have been a strong man when a woman had to go with him, but he is mentioned. Now why can you not believe that God will have you also included.

The Acts of the Apostles finishes abruptly. It is not finished, and all who are in this place tonight must add to the Acts of the Apostles. This is a record of an incompletion, because when you get there you will find you are among the Acts of the apostles.

WATCH THAT NOBODY TAKES YOUR CROWN.

You have to be zealous. You have not to let anybody stand in your way. Salvation is the beginning; sanctification is a continuation; the baptism in the Holy Ghost is the enlargement of capacity for the risen Christ. God comes along and inspires your thoughts and says, "Now go forward, My child; it will be all right. Do not give in."

The Lord may permit your tire to be punctured many a time, but you must not be discouraged because the wind has gone out. You must pump it up again. The life that He began cannot be taken away from you. If you have an inspiration to "go forth," you cannot be stopped. You know you are called to an eternal purpose and nothing shall stand in your way. It is His purpose that we shall be sanctified, purified, and renewed. We are a people who have been raised from the dead, and if Jesus comes, you go because you have resurrection in you.

The elders always had a good report because of faith, and if devastating winds blow, it does not matter. The men of faith are not moved by anything they see or hear. The man of faith does not live in time. He has begun in eternity. He does not count on the things that are;

HE RELIES ON THE THINGS THAT ARE NOT.

We must be in the place of buoyancy. The man of faith is subject to God, but never in subjection to the devil. He is not puffed up. No, he lives in meekness and grows in grace. If you ask God to give you power, you have fallen from grace. You *have* power after the Holy Ghost is come upon you. Act in faith. Act in wisdom, "For it is God which worketh in you both to will and to do of his good pleasure" (Philippians 2:13).

Published in *Redemption Tidings*

A LIVING SACRIFICE

April 23, 1937

I beseech *you therefore, brethren, by the mercies of God, that ye present your bodies a living sacrifice, holy, acceptable unto God, which is your reasonable service. And be not conformed to this world: but be ye transformed by the renewing of your mind, that ye may prove what is that good, and acceptable, and perfect, will of God.*

Romans 12:1-2

Here we have, by the breath of the Spirit, the words of a man who had come right out of the ashes of broken faith, speaking to all saints, saying: He has brought me to the place where everything has gone on the altar, only for God. Such a lovely place! Such a wealthy place! Such a rich place! And I want all the saints to come into the same place.

THE FLESH IS ALWAYS WEAKNESS

Flesh will interfere with us and stop our progress, but if the Spirit of the Lord is upon us, the flesh is brought to a place where we understand Romans 8:10:

> *And if Christ be in you, the body is dead because of sin; but the Spirit is life because of righteousness.*

The moment flesh is dealt with and judgment comes to it, we are brought to a place of helplessness. The flesh has gone — dead — but the Spirit is life within us. Then the body is helpless, but it is dominated by the power of the Spirit till it only longs to breathe and act in the Spirit. It is beautiful.

One of the greatest mercies that ever you will have as long as you live will be a revelation to your heart of how to get rid of yourself. It is one of the greatest revelations that can come to the human life, and there are many after that. There are boundless resources after the flesh has gone. The word to revel in is: "Blessed are they which do hunger and thirst after righteousness: for they shall be filled" (Matthew 5:6). You cannot hunger and thirst after righteousness if you have any tendency to the natural life. The righteousness of God is a perfect development in your life of inward heart sanctification, where no defilement can enter, and the pure in heart always see God. It is a deep death, and it is a great life. God makes it a holy sacrifice, and He accepts it as an offering, and then, when we have perfectly considered the whole thing and everything has gone, we come to the conclusion that it was

A REASONABLE THING TO DO,

and anything less than that is unreasonable, because God has claimed us. We are His by right, in every way.

You go straight away from this meeting, and you sit down at the tables, where God, in His great plan of provision, has so supplied that there is enough to satisfy our natural order, and, remember this, a man is more capable of doing the mighty works of God and the will of God with a strong body than with a weak body. Only the strong body is never so richly in the presence of God as it is when it knows its weakness, for then there comes a real presentation. Strong bodies, strong minds, strong physique, strong muscles, are wonderful, but no good until all is on the altar, and within the body God can flow through and vibrate, and give that man perfect life, and he receives the resurrection life of the Spirit. Then his whole body is spiritual, it is severed from the natural, and he gets the fulfillment of the promise, "...strong in the Lord, and in the power of his might" (Ephesians 6:10) and the natural body is in perfect harmony to show forth the glory of God.

There is a word in the Scriptures which we very seldom understand. It has taken me a long time to understand it. It is this: "So then death worketh in us, but life in you" (2 Corinthians 4:12). Only as death was manifested in them could life come to the saints. Death to us, life to you. Now that means absolutely nothing less than that everything you count life has to go, and in its going, it is transformed. Death worketh in us, and life in you.

WE DIE TO LIVE

And in what measure we keep dead, we live for evermore, and it is the law of the Spirit of life in Christ which has made us free.

"Transformed by the renewing of your mind." The mind of Christ being in you and your mind subservient to the mind of Christ. Jesus submitted Himself to present His mind, body, and will. Wonderful Jesus. He lived as no one else. He was beautiful. I am enamored of Him. I love the Word of God. Christ is in every verse, illuminating every chapter, and this is the breath of God, and it is life to you. It is eternal life. God, enable us always to breathe it in.

Address given at Preston Convention
Published in *Redemption Tidings*

THE FAITH THAT DELIVERS

August 13, 1937

The divine plan is so much greater than all human thought. When He can only have us in His hand, when we are willing to yield to His sovereign will, when we have no reserve, how wonderful

God is, always willing to open the door till our whole life is filled with the fragrance of heaven. Heaven is right here, for Jesus is the substance and fulness of the divine nature, and He dwells in our hearts. Oh this wonderful fascinating Jesus, eating into our hearts, burning in our bosom. What a wonderful Jesus we have. Something about Him kindles fire in the darkest place. Something about our Lord makes all darkness light. God's Son is for all our human nature, and when we have Him we have more than we can speak about and think about. God's Son can set the world ablaze and bring heaven right into the place where we live. I am going to read Hebrews 11:5.

> *By faith Enoch was translated that he should not see death; and was not found, because God had translated him: for before his translation he had this testimony, that he pleased God.*
>
> *Hebrews 11:5*

THE DISPENSATION OF THE HOLY GHOST

Without faith it is impossible to please God, and he that cometh to God must believe that God is, and that God is working, able to work out the plan, and is working though you if you believe that God is. Possibilities are within your reach if you dare to believe that God is.

Evil spirits have no more control, if I believe that God is, and I do, I do. I know I am free from all the powers of darkness, free from all the powers of evil, and it is a wonderful thing to be free, and because you are free you step into the liberty of freed men and claim the possessions of God.

This is the dispensation of the Holy Ghost. It is twenty-nine years ago since God filled me with the Holy Ghost, and it burned in my bosom and it is still burning, with more activity for God than twenty-nine years ago. The Holy Spirit is not played out.

HOW GOD MOVED

It will be ridiculous for me to begin to speak about myself in South Africa, but I think it is fair to say what they said and not Wigglesworth. At every place without exception the people said, "We have never seen anything like this before in our lives." When we arrived at Cape Town, people I had never seen before came running all around so, so glad to see us. One man threw his arms round me and kissed me, full of joy to see the man his heart had been longing for years. God is waiting for people who dare to believe, and when you believe all things are possible.

> Only believe, Only believe,
> All things are possible, only believe.
> Only believe, Only believe,
> All things are possible, only believe.

It is the breath of God. It is the Word of the Spirit. It is the revelation of the Most High. God wants to show you to sweep away everything else, and dare to believe that Word. If you allow anything to come in between you and that Word, it will poison your whole system, and you will have no hope. One bit of unbelief against that Word is poison. It is like the devil putting a spear into you. It is the Word of life. It is the breath of heaven. It is God and His breath of quickening power by which your very life is changed, and you begin to bear the image of the heavenly. The people said, "We are ready for you." We began the same night. A man was there whose deathly face was filled with the very devil's manifestation of cancer. I said to the people, "Here is a man in the place suffering with a tremendous thing. He does not know I am talking about him at all. You can have the choice, if you desire me to deliver that man, so as to enjoy the meeting, I will go down in the name of the Lord and deliver him, or I will preach." They said, "Come down." I went down and the people saw what God had done and saw that man shouting, raving, for he was like a man that was intoxicated. He was shouting, "I am free, I have been bound." They were getting all the cameras ready and there was flash after flash. It was a wonderful thing to see that man changed. It was wonderful how God sustained me in the heat, wet through. The people said at the end of the campaign that we ought to have some rest, and yet there we were fresh to go on, ready to make other people dare to believe God. You cannot measure our conditions, they are immeasurable. Divine association with God is more than ten regiments of soldiers. Jesus said, "I will pray the Father to send legions of angels." We must pray tonight that God will send us a deluge. It shall be unto you if you believe.

THE MANIFESTATION OF FAITH

One man after laying out £900 upon his dear wife for operation after operation, year by year, brought her helpless to the meeting. Now I knew for a fact that nothing could help that woman, only after seeing acts of faith. I went to her and said, "Look here, this is the greatest opportunity of your life. You will see that I will give an altar call tonight. There will be fifty people come up, and when you see them loosed, you believe, and you will be loosed like them, and then we will have a testimony from you." They came and my hands were laid upon them in the name of the Lord and I said "testify" and they testified. This woman saw their faces, and when all these people were through I said, "Do you believe?" and she said "I cannot help but believe." There is something in the manifestation of faith. I laid hands upon her in the name of Jesus and the power of God went right through her. I said, "In the name of Jesus, arise and walk." An impossibility! If you do not venture, you remain ordinary as long as you live. If you dare the impossible then God will abundantly do far above all you can ask or think. As if a cannon had blown her up, she rose and I thought her husband would go mad with joy and excitement because he saw his wife mightily moved by the power of God, made free, the first in the meeting afterwards to glorify God.

Heavenly Intoxication

My brethren, this is reality that I am talking about. It burns in my bones, it thrills my whole being. My whole being is blessed with the intoxication of heaven.

The first meeting the fire broke out. The people were standing out in the streets, and we went to the town hall and over a thousand people were saved by the power of God. They were so intoxicated by the thing that was shown that the first Sunday after we went, over 300 met together.

A young man read my book, who was dying of consumption, and he was saved and then God healed him. Then this young man so grew in the knowledge of God, he was made a pastor, and he came up to me like a son to a father. "If you like, I will go with you all the way over South Africa." He had had a wonderful education, and we said we will let him go all the way. He bought the best car for the job. If you go to South Africa you must have a car to go through the ploughed fields, one that will jump the hedges, jump in the river, and jump out again. That young man drove us 5,000 miles through all the territories, right amongst the Zulus, and rode in every place and God took us through everything. Talk about life, why this is overcoming life.

If there is anyone in this meeting who wants to be saved, this is your opportunity, and I will pray for you. There is a man who wants to be saved. Thank God. God will answer prayer for that man. There is a young man down there. God bless you. Who is the next? Here is a young woman who wants to be saved. Is there another now? Come now, do not fail to take this opportunity.

A sermon preached by Smith Wigglesworth at Sion College
on April 16th after his return from his South African Tour
Published in *Redemption Tidings*

DOMINANT FAITH

December 30, 1939

*N*ow faith is the substance of things hoped for, the evidence of things not seen. For by it the elders obtained a good report. Through faith we understand that the worlds were framed by the word of God, so that things which are seen were not made of things which do appear.

Hebrews 11:1-3

Faith is the substance and it is a reality, and God wants to bring us to the fact of it. He wants us to know that we have something greater than we can see or handle, because everything you can see and handle is going to pass away. The heavens are going to be wrapped up and the earth melt with fervent heat, but the Word of the Lord shall abide for ever.

> *Through faith we understand that the worlds were framed by the word of God, so that things which are seen were not made of things which do appear.*
>
> *Hebrews 11:3*

God spoke the Word and made the world, and I want to impress upon you this wonderful Word which made the world. I am saved by the incorruptible Word, the Word that made the world, and so my position by faith is to lay hold of the things which cannot be seen, and believe the things which cannot be understood.

FAITH LIVES IN A COMMANDING POSITION

where you know God will work the miracle, if you dare to stand upon the Word.

Paul related his conversion many times over and I believe it is good to rehearse what God has done for you. I have been privileged to be dropped in every part of the world, and have seen that God has arranged a plan for me. I said to our people, "The Lord is moving me to go out through the States and Canada." When the Lord told me I said, "Lord, You have three things to do, You have to find money for home, and find money to go, and you have to give me a real change, for You know that sometimes my mind or memory is no good at all to me." Straight away money came from all over and I said, "It is true God is sending me. I have already 50 pounds." My son George said, "Father, Mother's gone to heaven, and you are leaving us; what shall we do?" A letter came and I said, "George, you open the letter." And for six weeks a cheque had been coming for 25 pounds. I went to Liverpool and a man said, "Here is 5 pounds for you." When I was on the ship a lady, poorly dressed, gave me a red sugar bag and there were 25 sovereigns. Just as I was getting on the ship a man came and gave me a book, and said, "There is a leaf for every day in the year." And the Lord said to me, "Put down everything that takes place in the month." I did so, and I had a memory like an encyclopedia. You see, I never learned geography, and God sent me all over the world to see it. The Lord has a way of making you equal to

LIVE IN A PLACE OF COMMAND

in the power of the Holy Ghost so long as you have learned the lesson needed. God will make us know how to live. I went to a Quakers' meeting, quiet and still, and there was such a silence that I was moved. You know it is of faith, and so I jumped up and I had the time of my life. All these Quakers came round me and they said, "You are the first man that we have ever seen in this place who was so quickly led by the Spirit." I said, "If the Spirit does not move me, I move the Spirit. John says it is the unction of the Holy One, and you need no man to reach you, it is the Holy Ghost who teaches. It is simplicity itself."

When the ship began to move I said to the people, "I am going to preach on this ship on Sunday, will you come and hear me preach?" They said no. Later they came around again and said, "We are going to have an entertainment, and we would like you to be in it. So I said, "Come in a quarter of an hour and I will tell you." They came round again and said, "Are you ready?" "Yes," I told them, "I have got a clear witness that I have to be in the entertainment." They said, "Well, what can you do?" I replied, "I can sing." They said, "Now we want to know what position you would like to have on the programme." I answered, "Tell me what you are going to have on the programme." They said, "Recitations, instruments, and many things." I asked, "What do you finish up with?" "A dance." "Well, put me down just before the dance."

I went to the entertainment, and when I saw the clerical gentlemen trying to please the people it turned me to prayer. When they had all done their pieces, my turn came and I went up to the piano with my "Redemption Songs," and the lady, who was rather less than half dressed, when she saw the music said, "I cannot play this kind of music." I said, "Be at peace, young lady, I have music and words inside." So I sang:

> If I could only tell Him as I know Him.
> My Redeemer Who has brightened all my way;
> If I could tell how precious in His presence,
> I am sure that you would make Him yours today.
> Could I tell it, Could I tell it,
> How the sunshine of His presence lights my way.
> I would tell it, I would tell it,
> And I'm sure that you would make Him yours today.

God took it up, and from the least to the greatest they were weeping. They never had a dance, but they had a prayer meeting, and

SIX YOUNG MEN WERE SAVED

by the power of God in my cabin.

Every day God was saving people on that ship. I never can forget a young man and woman who came to me. They were paid to look after a lady and gent in the first class. They said, "Our lady is in great distress. She is a Christian Scientist and she gets no relief. She has brought a doctor and he gives her no hope and now she is in despair and we have told her about you." They brought me to the door which they opened and

I went in and stood at the door just inside, and I looked at the lady who was in a poor state of health. I said, "I am not going to preach, I am going to stand here and pray, and I believe as I pray you will be perfectly healed." While I was praying God healed her, and she shouted. She said, "This is something new; come over, will you?" I had the opportunity of bringing that woman into the fulness of redemption. God delivered her and she said she would not rest until she had gone through all England in Christian Science and told them about the blood of Jesus.

Live in the Acts of the Apostles and you will see every day some miracle wrought by the power of the living God. It comes right to the threshold and God brings everything along to you. Do not fail to

CLAIM YOUR HOLY POSITION

so that you will overcome the power of the devil. The best time you have is when you have the most difficult position. You know sometimes it seems as though the strangest things happen for the furtherance of the Gospel. I was at Southampton station and there were four men to see me into the train. They knew everything and I knew nothing, only I soon found that I was in the wrong carriage. There was a man in the carriage, and I said to him, I have been to Bournemouth before, but I do not seem to be on the way. Where are you going? He said, "I am going to South Wales." I said, "Well, if I am wrong I am right. I have never once been wrong in my life only when I have been right." I asked, "What is the Lord Jesus Christ to you? He is my personal Friend and Saviour." He replied, "I do not thank you to speak to me about these things." The train stopped and I said to the porter, "Am I right for Bournemouth? How many stops?" He said three. I said to the man, "It has to be settled before I leave the train; you are going to hell." That man wished he had never met me. The train stopped and I had to get out. I said, "What are you going to do?" He answered, "I will make Him my own."

We are both of the incorruptible Word of God which liveth and abideth forever, which made the world and brought into existence things that were not there, and there was nothing made but what He made, and so I realize I am made twice. I was made first by the creation of God. The next time I was begotten in a moment of time, eternally begotten, and if you believe in your heart you can begin to say, and whatsoever you say will come to pass if you believe in your heart.

Ask God to give you the grace to use the faith you have. Peter had like precious faith, wonderful faith.

THE ACTIVE LIFE OF THE SPIRIT-FILLED BELIEVER

August 17, 1940

These are the last days; the days of the falling away. These are days when Satan is having a great deal of power. But we must keep in mind that Satan has no power only as he is allowed.

It is a great thing to know that God is loosing you from the world, loosing you from a thousand things. You must seek to have the mind of God on all things. If you don't, you will stop His working. I had to learn that as I was on the water en route to Australia. We stopped at a place called Aden, where they were selling all kinds of ware. Among other things were some beautiful rugs and ostrich feathers in great quantities. There was a gentleman in "first class" who wanted feathers. He bought one lot and the next lot put up was too big; he did not want so many. He said to me, "Will you join me?" I knew I did not want feathers for I had no room or use for them and wouldn't know what to do with them if I got them. However, he pleaded with me to join him. I perceived it was the Spirit as clearly as anything and I said, "Yes, I will." So the feathers were knocked down for fifteen dollars. Then I found the man had no money on him. He had plenty in his cabin. I perceived it was the Spirit again, so it fell to my lot to pay for the feathers. He said to me, "I will get the money and give it to one of the stewards." I replied: "No, that is not business. I am known all over the ship. You seek me out."

The man came and brought the money. I said, "God wants me to talk to you. Now sit down." So he sat down and in ten minutes' time the whole of his life was unhinged, unraveled, broken up, so broken that like a big baby he wept and cried for salvation. It was "feathers" that did it. But you know we shall never know the mind of God till we learn to know the voice of God. The striking thing about Moses is that it took him forty years to learn human wisdom, forty years to know his helplessness, and forty years to live in the power of God. One hundred and twenty years it took to teach that man, and sometimes it seems to me it will take many years to bring us just where we can tell the voice of God, the leadings of God, and all His will concerning us.

I see that all revelation, all illumination, everything that God had in Christ was to be brought forth into perfect light that we might be able to live the same, produce the same, and be in every activity sons of God with power. It must be so. We must not limit the Holy One. And we must clearly see that God brought us forth to make us supernatural, that we might be changed all the time on the line of the supernatural, that we may every day live so in the Spirit, that all of the revelations of God are just like a canvas thrown before our eyes, on which we see clearly step by step all the divine will of God.

Any assembly that puts its hand upon the working of the Spirit will surely dry up. The assembly must be as free in the Spirit as possible, and you must allow a certain amount of extravagance when people are getting through to God. Unless we are very wise, we can easily interfere and quench the power of God which is upon us. It is an evident fact that one man in a meeting, filled with unbelief, can make a place for the devil to have a seat. And it is very true, that if we are not careful we may quench the Spirit of some person who is innocent but incapable of helping himself. "We then that are strong ought to bear the infirmities of the weak..." (Romans 15:1). If you want an assembly full of life you must have one in which the Spirit of God is manifested. And in order to keep at the boiling pitch of that blessed incarnation of the Spirit, you must be as simple as babies; you must be as harmless as doves and as wise as serpents (Matthew 10:16).

I always ask God for a leading of grace. It takes grace to be in a meeting because it is so easy if you are not careful, to get on the natural side. The man who is a preacher, if he has lost the unction, will be well repaid if he will repent and get right with God and get the unction back. It never pays us to be less than always spiritual, and we must have a divine language and the language must be of God. Beloved, if you come into real perfect line with the grace of God, one thing will certainly take place in your life. You will change from that old position of the world's line where you were judging everybody, and where you were not trusting anyone, and come into a place where you will have a heart that will believe all things; a heart that under no circumstances reviles again when you are reviled.

I know many of you think many times before you speak once. Here is a great word: "For your obedience is come abroad unto all men. I am glad therefore on your behalf: but yet I would have you wise unto that which is good, and simple concerning evil" (Romans 16:19). Innocent. No inward corruption or defilement, that is full of distrusts, but just a holy, divine likeness of Jesus that dares believe that God Almighty will surely watch over all. Hallelujah! "There shall no evil befall thee, neither shall any plague come nigh thy dwelling. For He shall give his angels charge over thee, to keep thee in all thy ways" (Psalm 91:10,11). The child of God who is rocked in the bosom of the Father has the sweetest touch of heaven, and the honey of the Word is always in it.

If the saints only knew how precious they are in the sight of God they would scarcely be able to sleep for thinking of His watchful, loving care. Oh, He is a precious Jesus! He is a lovely Savior! He is divine in all His attitude toward us, and makes our hearts to burn. There is nothing like it. "Oh," they said on the road to Emmaus, "did not our heart burn within us, as He walked with us and talked with us?" (Luke 24:32). Oh beloved, it must be so today.

Always keep in your mind the fact that the Holy Ghost must bring manifestation. We must understand that the Holy Ghost is breath, the Holy Ghost is Person, and it is the most marvelous thing to me to know that this Holy Ghost power can be in every part of your body. You can feel it from the crown of your head to the soles of your feet. Oh, it is lovely to be burning all over with the Holy Ghost! And when that takes place there is nothing but the operation of the tongue that must give forth the glory and the praise.

You must be in the place of magnifying the Lord. The Holy Ghost is the great Magnifier of Jesus, the great Illuminator of Jesus. And so after the Holy Ghost comes in, it is impossible to keep your tongue still. Why, you would burst if you didn't give Him utterance. Talk about a dumb baptized soul? Such a person is not to be found in the Scriptures. You will find that when you speak unto God in the new tongue He gives you, you enter into a close communion with Him hitherto never experienced. Talk about preaching! I would like to know how it will be possible for all the people filled with the Holy Ghost to stop preaching. Even the sons and daughters must prophesy. After the Holy Ghost comes in, a man is in a new order in God. And you will find it so real that you will want to sing, talk, laugh, and shout. We are in a strange place when the Holy Ghost comes in.

If the incoming of the Spirit is lovely, what must be the onflow? The incoming is only to be an onflow. I am very interested in scenery. When I was in Switzerland I wouldn't be satisfied till I went to the top of the mountain, though I like the valleys also. On the summit of the mountain the sun beats on the snow and sends the water trickling down the mountains right through to the meadows. Go there and see if you can stop it. Just so in the spiritual. God begins with the divine flow of His eternal power which is the Holy Ghost, and you cannot stop it.

We must always clearly see that the baptism with the Spirit must make us ministering spirits.

Peter and John had been baptized only a short time. Did they know what they had? No, I defy you to know what you have. No one knows what he has in the baptism with the Holy Ghost. You have no conception of it. You cannot measure it by an human standards. It is greater than any man has any idea of, and consequently those two disciples had no idea what they had. For the first time after they were baptized in the Holy Ghost they came down to the Gate Beautiful. There they saw the man sitting who for forty years had been lame. What was the first thing after they saw him? Ministration. What was the second? Operation. What was the third? Manifestation, of course. It could not be otherwise. You will always find that this order in the Scripture will be carried out in everybody.

I clearly see that we ought to have spiritual giants in the earth, mighty in apprehension, amazing in activity, always having a wonderful report because of their activity in faith. I find instead that there are many people who perhaps have better discernment than you, better knowledge of the Word than you, but they have failed to put it into practice, so these gifts lie dormant. I am here to help you to begin on the sea of life with mighty acts in the power of God through the gifts of the Spirit. You will find that this which I am speaking on is out of knowledge derived from a wonderful experience in many lands. The man who is filled with the Holy Ghost is always acting. You read the first verse of the Acts of the Apostles, "Jesus began both to do and teach." He began to do first, and so must we.

OUTWARD MANIFESTATION

Beloved, we must see that the baptism with the Holy Ghost is an activity with an outward manifestation. When I was in Norway, God was mightily moving there, though I had to talk by interpretation. However, God always worked in a wonderful way. One day we met a man who stopped the three men I was with, one being the interpreter. I was walking on, but I saw he was in a dilemma, so I turned back and said to the interpreter, "What is the trouble?" "This man," he said, "is so full of neuralgia that he is almost blind and he is in a terrible state." As soon as ever they finished the conversation I said to the spirit that was afflicting him, "Come out of him in the name of Jesus." And the man said, "It is all gone! It is all gone! I am free." Ah, brothers, we have no conception of what God has for us!

I will tell you what happened in Sydney, Australia. A man with a stick passed a friend and me. He had to get down and then twist over, and the tortures on his face made a deep impression on my soul. I asked myself, "Is it right to pass this man?" So I said to my friend, "There is a man in awful distress, and I cannot go further. I must speak to him." I went over to this man and said to him, "You seem to be in great trouble." "Yes," he said, "I am no good and never will be." I said, "You see that hotel. Be in front of that door in five minutes and I will pray for you, and you shall be as straight as any man in this place." This is on the line of activity in the faith of Jesus. I came back after paying a bill, and he was there. I will never forget him wondering if he was going to be trapped, or what was up that a man should stop him in the street and tell him he should be made straight. I had said it, so it must be. If you say anything you must stand with God to make it so. Never say anything for bravado, without you have the right to say it. Always be sure of your ground, and that you are honouring God. If there is anything about it to make you anything, it will bring you sorrow. Your whole ministry will have to be on the line of grace and blessing. We helped him up the two steps, passed him through to the elevator, and took him upstairs. It seemed difficult to get him from the elevator to my bedroom, as though Satan was making the last stroke for his life, but we got him there. Then in five minutes' time this man walked out of that bedroom as straight as any man in this place. He walked perfectly and declared he hadn't a pain in his body.

Oh, brother, it is ministration, it is operation, it is manifestation! Those are three of the leading principles of the baptism with the Holy Ghost. And we must see to it that God is producing these three through us.

The Bible is the Word of God, it has the truths and whatever people may say of them they stand stationary, unmovable. Not one jot or tittle shall fail of all His good promises. His word will come forth. In heaven it is settled, on earth it must be made manifest that He is the God of everlasting power.

God wants manifestation and He wants His glory to be seen. He wants us all to be filled with that line of thought that He can look upon us and delight in us subduing the world unto Him. And so you are going to miss a great deal if you don't begin to act. But once you begin to act in the order of God, you will find that God establishes your faith and from that day starts you on the line of the promises. When will you begin?

WHAT IF WE BELIEVED?

In a place in England I was dealing on the lines of faith and what would take place if we believed God. Many things happened. But when I got away it appeared one man who worked in the colliery had heard me. He was in trouble with a stiff knee. He said to his wife, "I cannot help but think every day that that message of Wigglesworth's was to stir us to do something. I cannot get away from it. All the men in the pit know how I walk with a stiff knee, and you know how you have wrapped it around with yards of flannel. Well, I am going to act. You have to be the congregation." He got his wife in front of him. "I am going to act and do just as Wigglesworth did." He got hold of his leg unmercifully, saying, "Come out, you devils, come out! In the name of Jesus. Now, Jesus, help me. Come out, you devils, come out." Then he said, "Wife they are gone! Wife, they are gone. This is too good. I am going to act now." So he went to his place of worship and all the collier boys were there. It was a prayer meeting. As he told them this story these men became delighted. They said, "Jack, come over here and help me." And Jack went. As soon a he was through in one home he was invited to another, loosing these people of the pains they had gotten in the colliery.

Ah, brothers and sisters, we have no idea what God has for us if we will only begin! But oh, the grace we need! We may make a mishap. If you do it outside of Him, if you do it for yourself, and if you want to be some one, it will be a failiure. We shall only be able to do well as we do it in the name of Jesus. Oh, the love that God's Son can put into us if we are only humble enough, weak enough, and helpless enough to know that except He does it, it will not be done! "What things soever ye desire when ye pray, believe that ye receive and ye shall have them."

Live in the Spirit, walk in the Spirit, walk in communion with the Spirit, talk with God. All leadings of the divine order are for you. I pray that if there are any who have turned to their own way and have made God second, they will come to repentance on all lines. Separate yourself from every earthly touch, and touch ideas. And God will bring you to an end of yourself. Begin with God this moment.

Published in *The Pentecostal Evangel*

AFTER YOU HAVE RECEIVED POWER

March 1, 1941

In Acts 1:8 we read: "But ye shall receive power, after that the Holy Ghost is come upon you...."

Oh, the power of the Holy Ghost! the power that quickens, that reveals, and prevails! I love to think that Jesus wanted all His people to have power, that He wanted all men to be overcomers. Nothing but this power will do it. Power over sin, power over sickness, power over the devil, power over all the powers of the devil!

In order to understand what it means to have power there are two things necessary; one is to have ears to hear and the other is to have hearts to receive. Every born-again saint of God, filled with the Spirit has a real revelation of that truth, "...greater is he that is in you, than he that is in the world" (1 John 4:4). I say this with as much audacity as I please. I know evil spirits are in abundance and in multitudes; Jesus cast them out as legion. The believer, because of the Spirit that is in him, has the power to cast out the evil spirit. It must be so; God wants us to have this power in us; we must be able to destroy Satan's power wherever we go.

One day as I came into the house my wife said, "Which way did you come?" I answered that I had come in by the back way. "Oh," she said, "if you had come in by the front you would have seen a man there in a terrible state. There is a crowd of people around him and he is in terrible straits." Then the doorbell rang and she said, "There he is again. What shall we do?" I said, "Just be still." I rushed to the door and just as I was opening it the Spirit said, "This is what I baptized you for." I was very careful then in opening the door, and then I heard the man crying outside, "Oh, I have committed the unpardonable sin, I am lost, I am lost." I asked him to come in and when he got inside he said again in awful distress, "I am lost, I am lost." Then the Spirit came upon me and I commanded the lying spirit to come out of the man in the name of Jesus. Suddenly he lifted up his arms and said, "I never did it." The moment the lying spirit was out he was able to speak the truth. I then realized the power in the baptism of the Holy Spirit. It was the Spirit that said, "This is what I baptized you for," and I believe we ought to be in the place where we shall always be able to understand the mind of the Spirit amid all the other voices in the world.

After the Holy Ghost has come upon you, you have power. I believe a great mistake is made in these days by people tarrying and tarrying after they have received. After you have received it is, "Go ye." Not "sit still," but "go ye into all the world, and preach the Gospel." We shall make serious havoc of the whole thing if we turn back again and crawl into a corner seeking something we already have. I want you to see that God depends on us in these last days. There is no room for anyone to boast and the man who goes about saying, "Look at me for I am somebody," is of no value whatever. God is done with that man altogether. He will have a people to glorify Him. He is doing what He can with what He has, but we are so unwilling to move in the plan of God that He has to grind us many times to get us where He can use us.

Jesus was so filled with the Holy Ghost that He stood in the place where He was always ready. He was always in the attitude where He brought victory out of every opportunity. The power of the Holy Spirit is within us, but it can be manifested only as we go in obedience to the opportunity before us. I believe if you wait until you think you have power after you have received the Holy Ghost you will never know you have it. Don't you know that the child of God who has the baptism is inhabited by the Spirit? You will remember one time when they tried to throw Jesus from the brow of the hill, that He pressed through the midst of them and as soon as He got through He healed the man with the blind eyes. Pressing through the crowd which was trying to kill Him, He showed forth His power. Some people might think that Jesus should have run away altogether but He stopped to heal. This thought has comforted me over and over again.

One day as I was waiting for a car I stepped into a shoemaker's shop. I had not been there long when I saw a man with a green shade over his eyes, crying pitifully and in great agony. It was heart-rending and the shoemaker told me that the inflammation was burning out his eyes. I jumped up and went to the man and said, "You devil, come out of this man in the name of Jesus." Instantly the man said, "It is all gone, I can see now." That is the only scriptural way, to begin to work at once, and preach afterwards. You will find as the days go by that the miracles and healings will be manifested. Because the Master was touched with the feeling of the infirmities of the multitudes they instantly gathered around Him to hear what He had to say concerning the Word of God. However, I would rather see one man saved than ten thousand people healed. If you ask me why, I call to your attention the Word which says, "There was a certain rich man... and [he] fared sumptuously every day" (Luke 16:19). Now we don't hear of this man having any diseases but it says, "...in hell he lift up his eyes..." (v. 23). We also read that there was a poor man full of sores and "he lifted up his eyes in heaven," so we see that a man can die practically in good health but be lost, and a man can die in disease and be saved; so it is more important to be saved than anything else.

But Jesus was sent to bear the infirmities and the afflictions of the people and to destroy the works of the devil. He said that the thief (which is the devil) cometh to steal and to kill and to destroy, "...I am come that they might have life, and... have it more abundantly" (John 10:10). I maintain that God wishes all His people to have the life more abundant. We have the remedy for all sickness in the Word of God! Jesus paid the full price and the full redemption for every need and where sin abounds, grace can come in and much more abound, and dispel all the sickness.

When I was traveling from England to Australia, I witnessed for Jesus, and it was not long before I had plenty of room to myself. If you want a whole seat to yourself just begin to preach Jesus. However, some people listened and began to be much affected. One of the young men said to me, "I have never heard these truths before. You have so moved me that I must have a good conversation with you." The young man told me that his wife was a great believer in Christian Science but was very sick now and although she had tried everything she had been unable to get relief, so was having a doctor. But the doctor gave her no hope whatever and in her dilemma and facing the realities of death she asked that she might have an appointment with me.

When I got to her I felt it would be unwise to say anything about Christian Science so I said, "You are in bad shape." She said, "Yes, they give me no hope." I said, "I will not speak to you about anything but will just lay my hands upon you in the name of Jesus and when I do you will be healed." That woke her up and she began to think seriously. For three days she was lamenting over the things she might have to give up. "Will I have to give up the cigarettes?" "No," I said. "Will I have to give up the dance?" and again I replied, "No." "Well, we have a little drinking sometimes and then we play cards also. Will I have to give — ?" "No," I said, "you will not have to give up anything. Only let us see Jesus." And right then she got such a vision of her crucified Saviour and Jesus was made so real to her that she at once told her friends that she could not play cards anymore, could not drink or dance anymore, and she said she would have to go back to England to preach against this awful thing, Christian Science. Oh, what a revelation Jesus gave her! Now if I had refused to go when called for, saying that I first had to go to my cabin and pray about it, the Lord might have let that opportunity slip by. After you have received the Holy Ghost you have power; you don't have to wait.

The other day we were going through a very thickly populated part of San Francisco when we noticed a large crowd gathered. I saw it from the window of the car and said I had to get out, which I did. There in the midst was a boy in the agonies of death. As I threw my arms around the boy I asked what the trouble was and he answered that he had cramps. In the name of Jesus I commanded the devils to come out of him and at once he jumped up and not even taking time to thank me, ran off perfectly healed. We are God's own children, quickened by His Spirit and He has given us power over all the powers of darkness; Christ in us the open evidence of eternal glory, Christ in us the life, the truth, and the way.

We have a wonderful salvation that fits everybody. I believe that a baptized person has no conception of the power God has given him until he uses what he has. I maintain that Peter and John had no idea of the greatness of the power they had but they began to speculate. They said, "Well, as far as money goes, we have none of that, but we do have something; we don't exactly know what it is, but we shall try it on you, in the name of Jesus of Nazareth, rise up and walk," and it worked. In order to make yourself realize what you have in your possession you will have to try it, and I can assure you it will work all right.

I said one time to a man that the Acts of the Apostles would never have been written if the apostles had not acted, and the Holy Spirit is still continuing His acts through us. May God help us to have some acts.

There is nothing like Pentecost, and if you have never been baptized you are making a big mistake by waiting. Don't you know that the only purpose for which God saved you was that you might be a saviour of others? And for you to think that you have to remain stationary and just get to heaven is a great mistake. The baptism is to make you a witness for Jesus. The hardest way is the best way; you never hear anything about the person who is always having an easy time. The preachers always tell of how Moses crossed the Red Sea when he was at wit's end. I cannot find the record of anyone in the Scriptures whom God used who was not first tried. So if you never have any trials it is because you are not worth them.

God wants us to have power. When I was traveling in Sweden at a certain station early in the morning a little lady and her daughter got into the train. I saw at once that the lady was in dreadful agony and asked my interpreter to inquire as to the trouble. With tears running down her face she told how her daughter was taking her to the hospital to have her leg amputated. Everything that was possible had been done for her. I told her Jesus could heal. Just then the train stopped and a crowd of people entered until there was hardly standing room, but friends, we never get into a place that is too awkward for God, though it seemed to me that the devil had sent these people in at that time to hinder. However, when the train began to move along I got down, although it was terribly crowded, and putting my hands upon the woman's leg I prayed for her in the name of Jesus. At once she said to her daughter, "I am healed. It is all different now; I felt the power go down my leg," and she began to walk about. Then the train stopped at the next station and this woman got out and walked up and down the platform, saying, "I am healed. I am healed."

Jesus was the *firstfruits* and God has chosen us in Christ and has revealed His Son in us that we might manifest Him in power. God gives us power over the devil and when we say the devil, we mean everything that is not of God. Some people say we can afford to do without the baptism with the Spirit but I say we cannot. I believe any person who thinks there is a stop between Calvary and the glory has made a big mistake.

Published in *The Pentecostal Evangel*

THE FAITH OF GOD
(Hebrews 11:1-6)
December 1941

Y ou know, beloved, that there are many wonderful treasures in the storehouse of God that we have not yet gotten. But praise God, we have the promise in Corinthians:

> *...Eye hath not seen, nor ear heard, neither have entered into the heart of man, the things which God hath prepared for them that love him.*
>
> *1 Corinthians 2:9*

I pray God that there may be within us a deep hunger and thirst with the penetration which is centered entirely upon the axle of Him, for surely He is all and in all. I pray God that we may be able to understand the opening of this chapter.

A REAL FOUNDATION

Now, beloved, you will clearly see that God wants to bring us to a foundation. If we are ever going to make any progress in divine life we shall have to have a real foundation. And there is no foundation, only the foundation of faith for us.

All our movements, and all that ever will come to us, which is of any importance, will be because we have a *Rock*. And if you are on the Rock, no powers can move you. And the need of today is the Rock to have our faith firm upon.

On any line or principle of your faith you must have something established in you to bring that forth. And there is no establishment outside God's Word for you. Everything else is sand. Everything else shall sunder.

If you build on anything else but the Word of God — on imaginations, sentimentality, or any feelings, or any special joy, it will mean nothing without you have a foundation, and the foundation will have to be in the Word of God.

We must have something better than sand, and everything is sand except the Word. There isn't anything that will remain — we are told the heaven and earth will be melted up as a scroll as fervent heat. But we are told the Word of God shall be forever, and not one jot or tittle of the Word of God shall fail. And if there is anything that is satisfying me today more than another, it is, "Thy Word is settled in heaven."

And another word in the 138th Psalm says: "...thou hast magnified thy word above all thy name" (v. 2). The very establishment for me is the Word of God. It is not on any other line.

Let us come to the principle of it. If you turn to John's gospel you will find a wonderful word there. It is worth our notice and great consideration.

> *In the beginning was the Word, and the Word was with God, and the Word was God. The same was in the beginning with God. All things were made by him; and without him was not any thing made that was made.*
>
> *John 1:1-3*

THE WORD

There we have the foundation of all things, which is the Word. It is a substance. It is a power. It is more than relationship. It is personality. It is a divine injunction to every soul that enters into this privilege to be born of this Word. What it means to us will be very important for us. For remember, it is a substance, it is an evidence of things not seen. It bringeth about that which you cannot see. It brings forth that which is not there, and takes away that that is there, and substitutes it. God took the Word and made the world of the things which did not appear. And we live in the world which was made by the Word of God, and it is inhabited by millions of people. And you say it is a substance. Jesus, the Word of God, made it of the things which did not appear. And there is not anything made that is made that has not been made by the Word. And when we come to the truth of what that Word means, we shall be able not only to build but to know, not only to know, but to have. For if there is anything helping me today more than another, it is the fact that I am living in facts, I am moving in facts, I am in the knowledge of the principles of the Most High.

God is making manifest His power. God is a reality and proving His mightiness in the midst of us. And as we open ourselves to divine revelation and get rid of all things which are not of the Spirit, then we shall understand how mightily God can take us on in the Spirit, and move the things which are, and bring the things which are not into prominence.

Oh, the riches, the depths of the wisdom of the Most High God! May this morning enlarge us. Jabus knew that there were divine principles that we need to know, and he says, "Enlarge me."

David knew that there was a mightiness beyond and within, and he says, "Thou has dealt bountifully with me," knowing that all the springs came from God that were in Him which made His face to shine.

And God is an inward witness of a power, of a truth, of a revelation, of an inward presence, of a divine knowledge. He is! He is!

Then I must understand. I must clearly understand. I must have a basis of knowledge for everything that I say. We must, as preachers, never preach what we think. We must say what we know. Any man can think. You must be beyond the thinking. You must be in the teaching. You must have the knowledge. And God wants to make us so in fidelity with Him that He unveils Himself. He rolls the clouds away, the mists disappear at His presence. He is almighty in His movements.

God has nothing small. He is all large, immensity of wisdom, unfolding the grandeur of His design or plan for humanity, that humanity may sink into insignificance, and the mightiness of the mighty power of God may move upon us till we are the sons of God with power, in revelation, and might and strength in the knowledge of God.

THE PRINCIPLE OF GOD

I think John has a wonderful word on this which is to edification at this moment — very powerful in its revelation to me so often as I gaze into the perfect law of liberty.

Let me read from the first epistle of John:

> *That which was from the beginning, which we have heard, which we have seen with our eyes, which we have looked upon, and our hands have handled, of the Word of life; (For the life was manifested, and we have seen it, and bear witness, and show unto you that eternal life, which was with the Father, and was manifested unto us;) That which we have seen and heard declare we unto you, that ye also may have fellowship with us: and truly our fellowship is with the Father, and with his Son Jesus Christ (verses 1-3).*

Oh beloved, He is the Word! He is the principle of God. He is the revelation sent forth from God. All fulness dwelt in Him. This is a grand word, of His fulness we have all received, and grace for grace.

In weakness, strength. In poverty, wealth. Oh, brother, this Word! It is a flame of fire. It may burn in your bones. It may move in every tissue of your life. It may bring out of you so forcibly the plan and purpose and life of God, till you cease to be, for God has taken you.

It is a fact we may be taken, hallelujah! into all the knowledge of the wisdom of God. Then I want to build, if I am created anew, for it is a great creation. It took nine months to bring us forth into the world after we were conceived, but it only takes one moment to beget us as sons. The first formation was a long period of nine months. The second formation is a moment, is an act, is a faith, for "He that believeth hath." And as you receive Him, you are begotten, not made.

Oh, the fact that I am begotten again, wonderful! Begotten of the same seed that begot Him. Remember, as He was conceived in the womb by the Holy Ghost, so we were conceived the moment we believed and became in a principle of the like-mindedness of an open door to become sons of God with promise.

Sons must have power. We must have power with God, power with man. We must be above all the world. We must have power over Satan, power over the evils. I want you just for a moment to think with me because it will help you with this thought.

You can never make evil pure. Anything which is evil never becomes pure in that sense. There is no such a thing as ever creating impurity into purity. The carnal mind is never subject to the will of God, and cannot be. There is only one thing, it must be destroyed.

But I want you to go with me to when God cast out that which was not pure. I want you to think about Satan in the glory with all the chances, and nothing spoiled him but his pride. And pride is an awful thing. Pride in the heart, thinking we are something when we are nothing. Building up a human constitution out of our own.

Oh yes, it is true the devil is ever trying to make you think what you are. You never find God doing it. It is always Satan who comes on and says, "What a wonderful address you gave! How wonderful he did that, and how wonderful he prayed, and sang that song." It is all of the devil. There is not an atom of God in it, not from beginning to end.

VISION DAY BY DAY

Oh, the vision is so needy today, more needy than anything that man should have the visions of God. The people have always perished when there is no vision. God wants us to have visions and revelations and manifestations.

You cannot have the Holy Ghost without having revelations. You cannot have the Holy Ghost without being turned into another nature. It was the only credentials by which Joshua and Caleb could enter the land because they were of another spirit.

And we must live in an unction, in a power, in a transformation, and a divine attainment where we cease to be, where God becomes enthroned so richly.

"It is He! He came forth, emptied Himself of all, but love brought to us the grace and then offered up Himself to purge us that we might be entire and free from all things. That we should see Him who was invisible, and changed by the power which is divine, and be lost to everything but the immensity of the mightiness of a godlikeness, for we must be in the world sons of God with promise."

We must be — we must be! We must not say it is not for me. Oh, no; we must say, "It is for us."

And God cast Satan out. Oh, I do thank God for that. Yes, beloved, but God could not have cast him out if he had even been equal of power. I tell you, beloved, we can never bind the strong man till we are in the place of binding.

Thank God Satan had to come out. Yes, and how did he come out? By the Word of His power. And, beloved, if we get to know and understand the principles of our inheritance by faith, we shall find out Satan will always be cast out by the same power that cast him out in the beginning. He will be cast out to the end because Satan has not become more holy but more vile.

If you think about the last day upon earth, you will find out that the greatest war — not Armageddon, the war beyond that — will be betwixt the hosts of Satan and the hosts of God. And how will it take place? With swords, dynamite, or any human power? No! By the brightness of His presence, the holiness of His holiness, the purity of His purity, where darkness cannot remain, where sin cannot stand, where only holiness, purity will remain. All else will flee from the presence of God into the abyss for ever.

And God has saved us with this Word of power over the powers of sin. I know there is a teaching and a need of teaching of the personality of the presence of the fidelity of the Word of God with power. And we need to eat and drink of this Word. We need to feed upon it in our hearts. We need that holy revelation that ought always to take away the mists from our eyes and reveal Him.

Remember, beloved, don't forget that every day must be a day of advancement. If you have not made any advancement since yesterday, in a measure you are a backslider. There is only one way for you between Calvary and the glory, and it is forward. It is every day forward. It is no day back. It is advancement with God. It is cooperation with Him in the Spirit.

Beloved, we must see these things, because if we live on the same plane day after day, the vision is stale, the principles lose their earnestness. But we must be like those who are catching the vision of the Master day by day. And we must make inroads into every passion that would interfere and bring everything to the slaughter that is not holy. For God would have us in these days to know that He wishes to seat us on high. Don't forget it.

The principles remain with us (if we will only obey) to seat us on high, hallelujah! And let us still go on building because we must build this morning. We must know our foundation. We must be able to take the Word of God and so make it clear to people because we shall be confronted with evil powers.

RECONSTRUCTED

I am continually confronted with things which God must clear away. Every day something comes before me that has to be dealt with on these lines. For instance, when I was at Cazadero seven or eight years ago, amongst the first people that came to me in those meetings was a man who was stone deaf. And every time we had the meeting — suppose I was rising up to say a few words, this man would take his chair from off the ordinary row and place it right in front of me. And the devil used to say, "Now, you are done." I said, "No, I am not done. It is finished."

The man was as deaf as possible for three weeks. And then in the meetings, as we were singing about three weeks afterwards, this man became tremendously disturbed as though in a storm. He looked in every direction, and he became as one that had almost lost his mind. And then he took a leap. He started on the run and went out amongst the people, and right up one of the hills. When he got about 60 yards ago he heard singing. And the Lord said, "Thy ears are open." And he came back, and we were still singing. That stopped our singing. And then he told us that when his ears were opened he could not understand what it was. There was such a tremendous noise he could not understand it whatever. He thought something had happened to the world, and so he ran out of the whole thing. Then, when he got away, he heard singing.

Oh, the devil said for three weeks, "You cannot do it." I said, "It is done!" As though God would ever forget! As though God could ever forget! As if it were possible for God to ever ignore our prayers!

The most trying time is the most helpful time. Most preachers say something about Daniel, and about the Hebrew children, and especially about Moses when he was in a tried corner. Beloved, if you read the

Scriptures you will never find anything about the easy time. All the glories came out of hard times.

And if you are really reconstructed it will be in a hard time — it won't be in a singing meeting, but at a time when you think all things are dried up, when you think there is no hope for you, and you have passed everything, then that is the time that God makes the man, when tried by fire that God purges you, takes the dross away and brings forth the pure gold. Only melted gold is minted. Only moistened clay receives the mould. Only soft wax receives the seal. Only broken, contrite hearts receive the mark as the potter turns us on his wheel, shaped and burnt to take and keep the heavenly mould, the stamp of God's pure gold.

We must have the stamp of our blessed Lord, who was marred more than any man. And when He touched human weakness it was reconstructed. He spoke out of the depths of trial and mockery, and became the initiative of a world's redemption. Never man spoke like He spake! He was full of order and made all things move till they said, "We never saw it like this."

He is truly the Son of God with power, with blessing, with life, with maturity, and He can take the weakest and make them into strength.

Published in *Revival News*

HOW TO BECOME AN OVERCOMER

January 17, 1942

The first chapter of Mark. We read of John the Baptist who was filled with the Holy Spirit from his mother's womb. Because of this mighty infilling there was mighty message on his lips. It was foretold of John by the prophet Isaiah, that he would be the voice of one crying in the wilderness. He was to lift up his voice with strength, and cry to the cities of Judah, "Behold your God!" (Isaiah 40:9).

And so we find John as he pointed to Jesus, crying out, "Behold the Lamb of God," proclaiming Him the One of whom Abraham prophesied when he said to his son Isaac, "The Lord will provide *Himself* a Lamb" — the Lamb of God and God the Lamb.

John was so filled with the Spirit of God that the cry he raised moved all Israel. This shows that when God gets hold of a man and fills him with the Spirit, he can have a message, a proclamation of the Gospel that will move people. The man who does have the Spirit of the Lord may cry for many years and nobody take notice of him. The man who is filled with the Spirit of God needs to cry out but once and people will feel the effect of it.

This should teach us that there is a necessity for everyone of us to be filled with the Spirit of God. It is not sufficient just to have a touch or to have usually a little. There is only one thing that will meet the needs of the people today, and that is to be immersed in the life of God — God filling you with His Spirit, then you live right in God and God lives in you so whether you eat or drink or whatever you do, it shall be all for the glory of God. In that place you will find that all your strength and all your mind and all your soul are filled with zeal, not only for worship but to proclaim the Gospel message, a proclamation that is accompanied by the power of God which must defeat satanic power, discomfit the world, and redound the glory of God.

The reason the world today is not seeing this is because *Christian people are not filled with the Spirit of Christ*. They are satisfied with going to church, occasionally reading the Bible, and sometimes praying. Beloved, if God lays hold of you by the Spirit, you will find that there is an end to everything in the old life. All the old things will have passed away, and all things will have become new — all things are of God. You will see that as you are wholly yielded to God, your whole being will be transformed by the Spirit's indwelling. He will take you in hand so that you may become a vessel unto honor. Our lives are not to be for ourselves, for if we live for self, we shall die. If we seek to save our lives we shall lose them, but if we lose our lives we shall save them. If we through the Spirit mortify the deeds of the body, we shall live, live a life of freedom and joy and blessing and service, a life that will bring blessing to others. God would have us to see that we must be filled with the Spirit, every day live in the Spirit and walk in the Spirit, and be continually renewed in the Spirit.

Study the life of Jesus. It was quite a natural thing for Him after He had served the whole day among the multitude, to want to go to His Father to pray all night. Why? He wanted a renewing of divine strength and power. He wanted fellowship with His Father. His Father would speak to Him the word that He was to bring to others, and would empower Him afresh for new ministry. He would come from those hours of sweet communion and fellowship with His Father, clothed with His holy presence and Spirit, and anointed with the Holy Spirit and power He would go about doing good and healing all that were oppressed of the enemy.

When He met sickness it had to leave. He came from that holy time of communion with power to meet the needs of the people, whatever they were. It is an awful thing for me to see people who profess to be Christians lifeless and powerless. The place of holy communion is open to us all. There is a place where we can be daily refreshed and renewed and reempowered.

In the fourth chapter of Hebrews we are told, "There remaineth therefore a rest to the people of God. For he that is entered into his rest, he also hath ceased from his own works..." (vv. 9-10). Oh, what a blessed rest that is, to cease from your own works, to come to the place where God is now enthroned in your life, working in you day by day to will and to do His good pleasure, working in you an entirely new order of things.

God wants to bring you forth as a flame of fire, with a message from God, with the truth that shall defeat the powers of Satan, with an unlimited supply for every needy soul. So, just as John moved the whole of Israel with a mighty cry, you too by the power of the Holy Ghost will move the people so that they repent and cry, "What shall we do?"

This is what Jesus meant when He said to Nicodemus, "Except a man be born again, he cannot see the kingdom of God...that which is born of the flesh is flesh; and that which is born of the Spirit is spirit. Marvel not that I said unto thee, Ye must be born again." If we only knew what these words mean to us, to be born of God! An infilling of the life of God, a new life from God, a new creation, living in the world but not of the world, knowing the blessedness of that word, "Sin shall not have dominion over you." How shall we reach this place in the Spirit? By the provision of the Holy Spirit that He makes. If we live in the Spirit, we shall find all that is carnal swallowed up in life. There is an infilling of the Spirit which quickens our mortal bodies.

Give God your life, and you will see that sickness has to go when God comes in fully. Then you are to walk before God and you will find that He will perfect that which concerns you. That is the place where He wants believers to live, the place where the Spirit of the Lord comes into your whole being. That is the place of victory.

Look at the disciples. Before they received the Holy Spirit they were in bondage. When Christ said, "One of you shall betray Me," they were all doubtful of themselves and said, "Is it I?" They were conscious of their human depravity and helplessness. Peter said, "Though I should die with Thee, yet will I not deny Thee." The others declared the same; yet they all forsook Him and fled. But after the power of God fell upon them in the upper room, they were like lions to meet difficulty. They were bold. What made them so? The purity and power that is by the Spirit.

God can make you an overcomer. When the Spirit of God comes into your surrendered being He transforms you. There is a life in the Spirit that makes you free and there is an audacity about it, and there is a personality in it — it is God in you.

God is able to so transform you and change you, that all the old order has to go before God's new order. Do you think that God will make you to be a failure? God never made man to be a failure. He made man to be a son, to walk the earth in the power of the Spirit, master over the flesh and the devil, until nothing arises within him except that which will magnify and glorify the Lord.

Jesus came to set us free from sin, and free us from sickness, so that we should go forth in the power of the Spirit and minister to the needy, sick, and afflicted. Through the revelation of the Word of God, I find that divine healing is solely for the glory of God, and that salvation is walking in newness of life so that we are inhabited by Another, even God.

Published in *The Pentecostal Evangel*

he motto of a cold, indifferent, worldly church is, "Respectability and decorum," respectability inspired by one who is far from respectable — Satan.

PENTECOSTAL MANIFESTATIONS

May 27, 1944

The birth of the Church was announced by a rushing mighty wind, a tornado from heaven. Moffatt translates Acts 2:1, "During the course of Pentecost they were all together, when suddenly there came a sound from heaven like a *violent blast of wind*...." And all of the assembled company came under the power of that which was symbolized as a mighty tornado, a violent blast. Their whole beings were moved by it, so that onlookers thought they were full of new wine. The unnatural movement of their bodies was followed by a supernatural movement of their tongues, for they spoke in other tongues as the Spirit gave them utterance. Thus they received the enduement of power from on high.

The crowd saw the movements and heard the sounds. The sounds were comprehensible — some of them. The movements were incomprehensible — most of them. Some were amazed — those who could comprehend the languages — and the others were confounded. They could not understand the languages, but they thought they could understand the motions, and they interpreted them as the actions of drunken people. Some were amazed, others mocked — none understood.

A generation that prides itself upon its outer respectability and decorum despises the manifestations of the Spirit of God. Nevertheless it is written, "...the manifestation of the Spirit is given to every man to profit withal" (1 Corinthians 12:7).

David danced or leaped before the ark of the Lord, and he was considered vile by the daughter of the former king. The daughter of Saul accused the anointed of God of vileness in manifestation, want of respectability, of lack of decorum, before the ark of the Lord.

Did David stop when the wife of his bosom derided him? Did he acquiesce to the formalism she represented? He declared, "...I will yet be more vile than thus..." (2 Samuel 6:22). It was as if he had said, "If occasion requires it, I will leap higher and dance more."

There is great danger when some churches who have known the manifestation of the Spirit in days gone by desire to become so respectable and decorous that the supernatural is ruled out of their meetings. We need Peters today who can say in explanation of the Pentecostal phenomena in our midst, "...these are not drunken, as ye suppose...*this is that...*" (Acts 2:15,16). If we become so ultra-respectable and decorous that we rule out the supernatural, Peter will have nothing to apologize for. He will have to say, "This was that, but it is gone." We may as well write upon our assemblies, "Ichabod" — the glory has departed. We cease to be vile, and Michal will welcome us home.

There must be no compromise with Michals, with those who hate the supernatural, or they will draw us from the presence of the ark and cause us to cease to be joyful in the presence of the Lord. Michal would have been quite content to have the ark stay where it was.

Pentecost came with the sound of a mighty rushing wind, a violent blast from heaven! Heaven has not exhausted its blasts, but our danger is we are getting frightened of them. The apostles were not. They had a repetition. When they had been threatened to speak no more in the name of Jesus, they lifted up their voices to God in one accord, and prayed,

> *...behold their threatenings: and grant unto thy servants, that with all boldness they may speak thy word, By stretching forth thine hand to heal; and that signs and wonders may be done by the name of thy holy child Jesus.*
>
> *Acts 4:29,30*

And the place was shaken where they were assembled together, and all were filled afresh with the Holy Ghost. Pentecost repeated! Manifestation again! All filled — mouths and all! "And they spake the Word of God with" — what? hesitation, moderation, timidity? No, they were yet more vile. "They spake the Word of God with *boldness.*" And the signs and wonders increased. They never resented the first manifestations on their body on the day of Pentecost, and they prayed and received the second experience — building and all. Even the place was shaken this time.

Our God is an active God. His thunder is just as loud today as it was in the first century. His lightning is just as vivid as it was in the days of the early church. The sound of the mighty rushing wind is just the same today as it was on the day of the Pentecost. Pray for the violent blasts of wind from heaven, expect them, and you will get them. And do not be afraid of them.

Let God deal with the Michals. David did not compromise. He was willing to have yet more manifestations of the Spirit. "I will yet be more vile." We can have Pentecost plus Pentecost, if we wish. God's arm is not shortened, nor is His ear heavy. He wants to show His hand and the strength of His arm today in convincing a gainsaying world by sight, sound, and instruction. Take note of Conybeare's translation of 1 Thessalonians 5:19, *"Quench not the manifestation of the Spirit."*

Published in *The Pentecostal Evangel*

POWER FROM ON HIGH

May 27, 1944

We have a remarkable word in Matthew 3:11,

I indeed baptize you with water unto repentance: but he that cometh after me is mightier than I, whose shoes I am not worthy to bear: he shall baptize you with the Holy Ghost, and with fire.

This was the word of one who was filled with the Holy Ghost even from his mother's womb, who was so filled with the power of the Spirit of God that they came from east and west and from north and south to the banks of the Jordan to hear him.

You have seen water baptism, and you know what it means. This later baptism taught by this wilderness preacher means that we shall be so immersed, covered, and flooded with the blessed Holy Ghost, that He fills our whole body.

Now turn to John 7:37-39:

> *In the last day, that great day of the feast, Jesus stood and cried, saying, If any man thirst, let him come unto me, and drink. He that believeth on me, as the scripture hath said, out of his belly shall flow rivers of living water. (But this spake he of the Spirit,*

which they that believe on him should receive: for the Holy Ghost
was not yet given; because that Jesus was not yet glorified.)
                                                         John 7:37-39

Jesus saw that the people who had come to the feast, expecting blessing, were going back dissatisfied. He had come to help the needy, to bring satisfaction to the unsatisfied. He does not want any of us to be thirsty, famished, naked, full of discord, full of disorder, full of evil, full of carnality, full of sensuality. And so He sends out in His own blessed way the old prophetic cry: "Ho, every one that thirsteth, come ye to the waters, and he that hath no money; come ye, buy, and eat..." (Isaiah 55:1).

The Master can give you that which will satisfy. He has in Himself just what you need at this hour. He knows your greatest need. You need the blessed Holy Ghost, not merely to satisfy your thirst, but to satisfy the needs of thirsty ones everywhere; for as the blessed Holy Spirit flows through you like rivers of living water, these floods will break what needs to be broken, they will bring to death that which should be brought to death, but they will bring life and fruitage where there is none.

What do you have? A well of water? That is good as far as it goes. But Christ wants to see a plentiful supply of the river of the Holy Ghost flowing through you. Here, on this last day of the feast, we find Him preparing them for the Pentecostal fulness that was to come, the fulness that He should shed forth from the glory after His ascension.

Note the condition necessary — "He that *believeth on Me.*" This is the root of the matter. *Believe on Him.* Believing on Him will bring forth this river of blessedness. Abraham believed God, and we are all blessed through faithful Abraham. As we believe God, many will be blessed through our faith. Abraham was an extraordinary man of faith. He believed God in the face of everything. God wants to bring us to the place of believing, where, despite all contradictions around, we are strong in faith, giving God glory. As we *fully believe God*, He will be glorified, and we will prove a blessing to the whole world as was our father Abraham.

Turn to John 14. Here we see the promise that ignorant and unlearned fisherman were to be clothed with the Spirit, anointed with power from on high, and endued with the Spirit of wisdom and knowledge. As He imparts divine wisdom, you will not act foolishly. The Spirit of God will give you a sound mind, and He will impart to you the divine nature.

How could these weak and helpless fishermen, poor and needy, ignorant and unlearned, do the works of Christ and greater works than He had done? They were incapable. None of us is able. But our emptiness has to be clothed with divine fulness, and our helplessness has to be filled with the power of His helpfulness. Paul knew this when he gloried in all that brought him down in weakness, for flowing into his weakness came a mighty deluge of divine power.

Christ knew that His going away would leave His disciples like a family of orphans. But He told them it was expedient, it was best, for after His return to the Father He would send the *Comforter*, and He Himself would come to indwell them. "...ye in me, and I in you" (John 14:20).

Christ said, "And I will pray the Father, and he shall send you another Comforter, that he may abide with you for ever; even the Spirit of truth..." (John 14:16,17). What a fitting name for the One who was coming to them at the time they were bereft — Comforter. After Christ had left them there was a great need, but that need was met on the day of Pentecost when the Comforter came.

You will always find that in the moment of need the Holy Spirit is a comforter. When my dear wife was lying dead, the doctors could do nothing. They said to me, "She's gone; we cannot help you." My heart was so moved that I said, "Oh God, I cannot spare her!" I went up to her and said, "Oh, come back, come back, and speak to me! Come back, come back!" The Spirit of the Lord moved, and she came back and smiled again. But then the Holy Ghost said to me, "She's mine. Her work is done. She is mine."

Oh, that comforting word! No one else could have spoken it. The Comforter came. From that moment my dear wife passed out. And in this day the Comforter has a word for every bereaved one.

Christ further said,

> *But the Comforter, which is the Holy Ghost, whom the Father will send in my name, he shall teach you all things, and bring all things to your remembrance, whatsoever I have said unto you.*
>
> *John 14:26*

How true this is. From time to time He takes of the words of Christ and makes them life to us. And, empowered with this blessed Comforter, the words that we spake under the anointing are spirit and life.

There are some who come to our meetings who, when you ask them whether they are seekers, reply, "Oh, I am ready for anything." I tell them, "You will never get anything." It is necessary to have the purpose that the psalmist had when he said, *"One thing have I desired of the Lord, that will I seek after..."* (Psalm 27:4). When the Lord reveals to you that you must be filled with the Holy Ghost, seek that one thing until God gives you that gift.

I spoke to two young men in a meeting one day. They were preachers. They had received their degrees. I said to them, "Young men, what about it?"

"Oh," they said, "we do not believe in receiving the Holy Ghost in the same way as you people do."

I said to them, "You are dressed up like preachers, and it is a pity having to have the dress without the presence."

"Well, we do not believe it the way you do," they said.

"But look," I said, "the apostles believed it that way. Wouldn't you like to be like the apostles? You have read how they received at the beginning, haven't you?"

Always remember this, that the baptism will always be as at the beginning. It has not changed. If you want a real baptism, expect it just the same way as they had it at the beginning.

These preachers asked, "What had they at the beginning?"

I quoted from the tenth chapter of Acts where it says,

> *...on the Gentiles also was poured out the gift of the Holy Ghost. For they heard them speak with tongues, and magnify God....*
> *Acts 10:45,46*

The Jews knew that these Gentiles had the same kind of experience as they themselves had at the beginning on the day of Pentecost. The experience has not changed, it is still the same as at the beginning.

When these two young men realized that Peter and John and the rest of the disciples had received the mighty enduement at the beginning, and that it was for them, they walked up to the front where folk were tarrying. They were finely dressed, but in about half an hour they looked different. They had been prostrated. I had not caused them to do it. But they had been so lost and so controlled by the power of God, and were so filled with the glory of God, they just rolled over, and their fine clothes were soiled — but their faces were radiant. What caused the change? They had received what the hundred and twenty received at the beginning.

These young preachers had been ordained by men. Now they received an ordination that was better. The Lord had ordained them that they should go and bring forth much fruit. The person who receives this ordination goes forth with fresh feet — his feet shod with the preparation of the Gospel of peace; he goes forth with a fresh voice — it speaks as the Spirit gives utterance; he goes forth with a fresh mind — a mind illuminated by the power of God; he goes forth with a fresh vision, and sees all things new.

When I was in Switzerland, a woman came to me and said, "Now that I am healed and have been delivered from that terrible carnal oppression that bound and fettered me, I feel that I have a new mind. I should like to receive the Holy Ghost; but when I hear these people at the altar making so much noise, I feel like running away."

Shortly after this we were in another place in Switzerland where there was a great hotel joined to the building where we were ministering. At the close of one of the morning services, the power of God fell. That is the only way I can describe it — the power of God *fell*. This poor, timid creature, who could not bear to hear any noise, screamed so loud that all the waiters in this big hotel came out, with their aprons on and their trays, to see what was up. Nothing especially was "up," something had come down, and it so altered the situation that this woman could stand anything after that.

When you receive the baptism, remember the words in 1 John 2:20. "...ye have an unction from the Holy One...." God grant that we may not forget that. Many people, instead of standing on the rock of faith to believe that they have received this unction, say, "Oh, if I could only feel the unction!"

Brother, your feeling robs you of your greatest unction. Your feelings are often on the line of discouragement. You have to get away from the walk by sense, for God has said, "The just shall live by faith" (Habakkuk 2:4; Romans 1:17; Galatians 3:11; and Hebrews 10:38). Believe what God says, "Ye have an unction from the Holy One," an unction from above. All thoughts of holiness, all thoughts of purity, all thoughts of power are from above.

Frequently I see a condition of emergency. Here is a woman dying; here is a man who has lost all the powers of his faculties; here is a person apparently in death. God does not want me to be filled with anxiety. What does He want me to do? To *believe* only. After you have received, only believe. Dare to believe the One who has declared, "I will do it." Christ says,

> *...verily I say unto you, That whosoever shall say unto this mountain, Be thou removed, and be thou cast into the sea; and shall not doubt in his heart, but shall believe that those things which he saith shall come to pass; he shall have whatsoever he saith.*
>
> *Mark 11:23*

God declares, "Ye have an unction." Believe God, and you will see this happen. What you say will come to pass. Speak the Word and the bound shall be free, the sick shall be healed. "...he shall have whatsoever he saith" (Mark 11:23). "Ye have an unction." The unction has come, the unction abides, the unction is with us.

But what about it, if you have not lived in the place where the unction can be increased? What is the matter? There is something between you and the Holy One — some uncleanness, some impurity, some desire that is not of Him, something that has come in the way? The Spirit is grieved. Has the unction left? No. When He comes in, He comes to abide. Make confession of your sin, of your failure, and once more the precious blood of Jesus Christ will cleanse, and the grieved Spirit will once more manifest Himself.

John further says, "...the anointing which ye have received of him abideth in you..." (1 John 2:27). We have an anointing, the same anointing which Jesus Christ Himself received. For "God anointed Jesus of Nazareth with the Holy Ghost and with power: who went about doing good..." (Acts 10:38). The same anointing is for us.

It means much to have a continuous faith for the manifestation of the anointing. At the death of Lazarus, when it seemed that Mary and Martha and all around them had lost faith, Jesus turned to the Father and said, "Father, I thank thee that thou hast heard me. And I knew that thou hearest me always..." (John 11:41,42). Before that supreme faith that counted on God, that counted on His anointing, death had to give up Lazarus.

Through a constant fellowship with the Father, through bold faith in the Son, through a mighty unction of the blessed Holy Spirit, there will come a right of way for God to be enthroned in your hearts, purifying us so thoroughly that there is no room for anything but the divine presence within. And through the manifestation of this presence, the works of Christ and greater works shall be accomplished for the glory of our triune God.

Published in *The Pentecostal Evangel*

 e read in the Word that *by faith* Abel offered unto God a more excellent sacrifice than Cain; *by faith* Enoch was translated that he should not see death; *by faith* Noah prepared an ark to the

BY FAITH
April 21, 1945

saving of his house; *by faith* Abraham, when he was called to go out into a place which he should after receive for an inheritance, obeyed (Hebrews 11). There is only one way to all the treasures of God, and that is *the way of faith*. All things are possible, the fulfilling of all promises, *to him that believeth*. And it is all by grace.

> *...by grace are ye saved through faith; and that not of yourselves: it is the gift of God.*
>
> Ephesians 2:8

There will be failure in our lives if we do not build on the base, the Rock Christ Jesus. He is the only way. He is the truth. He is the life. And the Word He gives us is life-giving. As we receive the Word of life, it quickens, it opens, it fills us, it moves us, it changes us; and it brings us into a place where we dare to say amen to all that God has said. Beloved, there is a lot in an "Amen." You never get any place until you have the Amen inside of you. That was the difference between Zacharias and Mary. When the Word came to Zacharias he was filled with unbelief until the angel said, "thou shalt be dumb...because thou believest not my words" (Luke 1:20). Mary said, "...be it unto me according to thy Word" (Luke 1:38). And the Lord was pleased that she believed that there would be a performance. When we believe what God has said, *there shall be a performance.*

Read the twelfth chapter of Acts, and you will find that there were people waiting all night and praying that Peter might come out of prison. But there seemed to be one thing missing despite all their praying, and that was faith. Rhoda had more faith than all the rest of them. When the knock came at the door, she ran to it for she was expecting an answer to her prayers; and the moment she heard Peter's voice, she ran back and announced to them that Peter was standing at the door. And all the people said, "You are mad. It isn't so." That was not faith. When she insisted that he was there, they said, "Well, perhaps God has sent his angel." But Rhoda insisted, "It is Peter." And Peter continued knocking. And they went out and found it so. What Rhoda had believed for had become a glorious fact.

Beloved, we may do much praying and groaning, but we do not receive from God because of that; we receive because we believe. And yet sometimes it takes God a long time to bring us through the groaning and the crying before we can believe.

I know this, that no man by his praying can change God — for you cannot change Him. Finney said, "Can a man who is full of sin and all kinds of ruin in his life, change God when he starts to pray?" No, it is impossible. But when a man labors in prayer, he groans and travails because his tremendous sin is weighing him down, and he becomes broken in the presence of God; and when properly melted he comes into perfect harmony with the divine plan of God, and then God can work in that clay. He could not before. Prayer changes hearts, but it never changes God. He is the same yesterday, and today, and forever — full of love, full of compassion, full of mercy, full of grace, and ready to bestow this and communicate that to us as we come in faith to Him.

Believe that when you come into the presence of God you can have all you came for. You can take it away; and you can use it, for all the power of God is at your disposal in response to your faith. The price for all was paid by the blood of Jesus Christ at Calvary. Oh, He is the living God, the One who has power to change us! "...it is he that hath made us, and not we ourselves..." (Psalm 100:3). And He purposes to transform us so that the greatness of His power may work through us. Oh, beloved! God delight in us, and when a man's ways please the Lord, then He makes all things to move according to His own blessed purpose.

We read in Hebrews 11:5, "By faith Enoch was translated that he should not see death...before his translation he had this testimony, that he pleased God." I believe it is in the mind of God to prepare us for translation. But remember this, translation comes only on the line of holy obedience and a walk according to the good pleasure of God. We are called to walk together with God through the Spirit. It is delightful to know that we can talk with God and hold communion with Him. Through this wonderful baptism in the Spirit which the Lord gives us, He enables us to talk to Himself in a language that the Spirit has given, a language which no man understands but which He understands, a language of love. Oh, how wonderful it is to speak to Him in the Spirit, to let the Spirit lift, and lift and lift us until He takes us into the very presence of God! I pray that God by His Spirit may move all of us so that we walk with God even as Enoch walked with Him. But beloved, it is a walk by faith and not by sight, a walk of believing the Word of God.

I believe there are two kinds of faith. All people are born with a natural faith but God calls us to a supernatural faith which is a gift from Himself. In the twenty-sixth chapter of Acts Paul tells us of his call, how God spoke to him and told him to go to the Gentiles, "To open their eyes, and to turn them from darkness to light, and from the power of Satan unto God, that they may receive forgiveness of sins, and inheritance among them which are sanctified *by faith that is in me*" (Acts 26:18). The faith which was in Christ was by the Holy Spirit to be given to those who believed. Henceforth, as Paul yielded his life to God, he could say,

> *I am crucified with Christ: nevertheless I live; yet not I, but Christ liveth in me: and the life which I now live in the flesh I live by the faith of the Son of God, who loved me, and gave himself for me.*
>
> *Galatians 2:20*

The faith of the Son of God communicated by the Spirit to the one who puts his trust in God and in His Son.

I want to show you the difference between our faith and the faith of Jesus. Our faith is limited and comes to an end. Most people have experienced coming to the place where they have said, "Lord, I can go no further. I have gone so far, and I cannot go on." But God can help us and take us beyond this. I remember one night, being in the north of England and going around to see some sick people, I was taken into a house where there was a young woman lying on her bed, a very helpless case. Her reason was gone and many things were manifested that were absolutely satanic, and I knew it.

She was a beautiful young woman. Her husband was quite a young man. He came in with a baby in his arms, leaned over and kissed his wife. The moment he did so she threw herself over on the other side of the bed, just as a lunatic would do, with no consciousness of the presence of her husband. It was heartbreaking. The husband took the baby and pressed the baby's lips to the mother. Again there was a wild frenzy. I said to the sister who was attending her, "Have you anybody to help?" She answered, "We have done everything we could." I said, "Have you no spiritual help?" Her husband stormed and said, "Spiritual help? Do you think we believe in God after we have had seven weeks of no sleep and this maniac condition? If you think we believe in God, you are mistaken. You have come to the wrong house."

There was a young woman about eighteen who grinned at me as she passed out of the door, as much as to say, "You cannot do anything." But this brought me to a place of compassion for this poor young woman. And then with what faith I had I began to penetrate the heavens. I was soon out on the heights, and I tell you I never saw a man get anything from God who prayed on the earth level. If you get anything from God you will have to pray right into heaven, for all you want is there. If you are living an earthly life, all taken up with sensual things, and expect things from heaven, they will never come. God wants us to be a heavenly people, seated with Him in the heavenlies, and laying hold of all the things in heaven that are at our disposal.

I saw there, in the presence of that demented girl, limitations to my faith; but as I prayed there came another faith into my heart that could not be denied, a faith that grasped the promises, a faith that believed God's Word. I came from the presence of the glory back to earth. I was not the same man. I confronted the same conditions I had seen before, but in the name of Jesus. With a faith that could shake hell and move anything else, I cried to the demon power that was making this young woman a maniac, "Come out of her, in the name of Jesus!" She rolled over and fell asleep, and awakened in fourteen hours, perfectly sane and perfectly whole.

Enoch walked with God. During those many years of his life he was penetrating the heavens, laying hold of and believing God, living with such cooperation and such a touch of God upon him that things moved on earth and things moved in heaven. He became such a heavenly being that it was not possible for him to stay here any longer. Oh, hallelujah! I believe God wants to bring all of us into line with His will, so that we shall penetrate into the heavenlies and become so empowered that we shall see signs and wonders and divers gifts of the Holy Spirit in our midst. These are wonderful days — these days of the outpouring of the Holy Spirit. You ask me, "When would you have liked to come to earth?" My answer is, "Just now. It suits me beautifully to know that I can be filled with the Holy spirit, that I can be a temple in which He dwells, and that through this temple there shall be a manifestation of the power of God that will bring glory to His name."

Enoch conversed with God. I want to live in constant conversation with God. I am so grateful that from my youth up, God has given me a relish for the Bible. I find the Bible food for my soul. It is strength to the believer. It builds up our character in God. And as we receive with meekness the Word of God, we are being changed by the Spirit from glory to glory. And by this Book comes faith for faith cometh by hearing, and hearing by the Word of God (Romans 10:17). And we know that "...without faith it is impossible to please him... (Hebrews 11:6)."

I believe that all our failures come because of an imperfect understanding of God's Word. I see that it is impossible to please God on any other line but by faith, and everything that is not of faith is sin. You say, "How can I obtain this faith?" You see the secret in Hebrews 12:2, *"Looking unto Jesus the author and finisher of our faith...."* He is the author of faith. Oh, the might of our Christ who created the universe and upholds it all by the might of His power! God has chosen Him and ordained Him and clothed Him, and He who made this vast universe will make us a new creation. He spoke the Word and the stars came into being, can He not speak the Word that will produce a mighty faith in us? Ah, this One who is the author and finisher of our faith comes and dwells within us, quickens us by His Spirit, and molds us by His will. He comes to live His life of faith within us and to be to us all that we need. And He who has begun a good work within us will complete it and perfect it; for He not only is the author but the finisher and perfecter of our faith.

> *...the word of God is quick, and powerful, and sharper than any twoedged sword, piercing even to the dividing asunder of soul and spirit, and of the joints and marrow, and is a discerner of the thoughts and intents of the heart.*
>
> *Hebrews 4:12*

How the Word of God severs the soul and the spirit — the soul which has a lot of carnality, a lot of selfishness in it, a lot of evil in it! Thank God, the Lord can sever from us all that is earthly and sensual, and make us a spiritual people. He can bring all our selfishness to the place of death, and bring the life of Jesus into our being to take the place of that earthly and sensual thing that is destroyed by the living Word.

The living Word pierces right to the very marrow. When I was in Australia, so many people came to me with double curvature of the spine; but the Word of the Lord came right down to the very marrow of their spines, and instantly they were healed and made straight, as I laid hands on them in the name of Jesus. The divine son of God, the living Word, through His power, moved upon those curvatures of the spine and straightened them out. Oh, thank God for the mighty power of the Word!

The Word of God comes in to separate us from everything that is not of God. It destroys. It also gives life. He must bring to death all that is carnal in us. It was after the death of Christ that God raised Him up on high, and as we are dead with Him we are raised up and made to sit in heavenly places in the new life that the Spirit gives.

God has come to lead us out of ourselves into Himself, and to take us from the ordinary into the extraordinary, from the human into the divine, and make us after the image of His Son. Oh, what a Savior! What an ideal Savior! It is written,

> *...now are we the sons of God, and it doth not yet appear what we shall be: but we know that, when he shall appear, we shall be like him; for we shall see him as he is.*
>
> *1 John 3:2*

But even now, the Lord wants to transform us from glory to glory, by the Spirit of the living God. Have faith in God, have faith in the Son, have faith in the Holy spirit; and the triune God will work in you, working in you to will and to do all the good pleasure of His will.

Published in *The Pentecostal Evangel*

EXPERIENCES WROUGHT OUT BY HUMILITY

June 8, 1945

irst Peter 5 — What a privilege to care for the flock of God, to be used by God to encourage the people, to help stand against the manifold trials that affect the needy. What a holy calling! We each have our own work and we must do it, so that boldness may be ours in the day of the Master's appearing, and that no man take our crown. As the Lord is always encouraging us, we have that which can encourage others. There must be a willingness, a ready mind, a yielding to the mind of the Spirit. There is no place for the child of God in God's great plan except in humility.

JACOB AS OUR EXAMPLE

God can never do all He wants to do, all that He came to do through the Word, until He gets us to the place where He can trust us, and we are in *abiding fellowship with Him* in His great plan for the world's redemption. We have this illustrated in the life of Jacob. It took God twenty-one years to bring Jacob to the place of contrition of heart, humility, and brokenness of spirit. God even gave him power to wrestle with strength, and he said, "I think I can manage after all," until God touched his thigh, making him know that he was mortal and that he was dealing with immortality. As long as we can save ourselves, we will do it.

In Mark 5:25, we have the story of the woman who had suffered many things of many physicians and had spent all that she had, and was nothing bettered but rather grew worse. She said, "...If I may touch but his clothes, I shall be whole" (Mark 5:28). She came to know her need. Our full cupboard is often our greatest hindrance. It is when we are *empty and undone* and come to God in our nothingness and helplessness, He picks us up.

Peter says, "Humble yourselves therefore under the mighty hand of God, that he may exalt you in due time" (1 Peter 5:6). Look at the Master at Jordan, submitting Himself to the baptism of John, then again submitting Himself to the cruel cross. Truly, angels desire to look into these things, and all heaven is waiting for the man who will burn all the bridges behind him and allow God to begin a plan in righteousness, so full, so sublime, beyond all human thought, but according to the revelation of the Spirit.

"Casting all your care upon him; for he careth for you" (1 Peter 5:7). He careth! We sometimes forget this. If we descend into the natural all goes wrong, but when we trust Him and abide beneath His shadow, how blessed it is. Oh, the times I have experienced my helplessness and nothingness and casting my care upon Him have proved He careth.

Then verse eight tells us to be sober. Wheat does it mean, to be sober? It is to have a clear knowledge that you are powerless to manage, but a rest of faith, knowing God is near at hand to deliver all the time. The adversary's opportunity is when you are something and try to open your own door. Our thoughts, words, acts, and deeds must all be in the power of the Holy Ghost. Oh, yes, we have need to be sober, not only sober, but vigilant, not only to be filled with the Spirit but with a *"go forth"* in you, a knowledge that God's Holy presence is with you. Sober, vigilant, an ability to judge, dissect, and balance things that differ.

"...your adversary the devil, as a roaring lion, walketh about, seeking whom he may devour: whom resist stedfast in the faith..." (1 Peter 5:8-9). Resist in the hour when by his wiles we may be bewildered, almost swept off our feet and darkness is upon us to such a degree that it seems as if some evil thing had overtaken us. Whom resist steadfast in the faith.

He that keepeth Israel neither slumbers nor sleeps. God covers us, for no humanity can stand against the powers of hell.

TONGUES AND INTERPRETATION: "The strongholds of God are stronger than the strength of man and He never faileth to interpose on behalf of His own."

"...after that ye have suffered..." (1 Peter 5:10). Then there is some suffering? Yes! But not to be compared to the glory that is to be revealed to us. The difference is so great that it is not even worthy of mention. *Ours is an eternal glory*, from glory to glory, until we are swallowed up, until we are swallowed up in Him, the Lord of glory.

FIX YOUR HEARTS

Then in this same verse we have four other things for the heart to be fixed in God. 1. Perfect. 2. Establish. 3. Strengthen. 4. Settle.

1. *Perfect.* In Hebrews 13:21, we read, "Make you perfect in every good work to do his will, working in you that which is wellpleasing in his sight, through Jesus Christ...." Keep in mind the fact that when perfection is spoken of in the Word, it is always through a joining up with eternal things. Perfection is a working in us of the will of God. There are some of us here that would be faint-hearted if we thought we had to be perfect to get in the blessing with God. How is it going to be? We find as we follow on that the purpose of eternal life is an advancement, for we are saved by the blood. Our actions, our mind, covered by the blood of Jesus, and as we yield and yield we find ourselves in possession of another mind, even the mind of Christ, to cause us to understand the perfection of His will.

Someone says, "I can never be perfect! It is beyond my furtherest thought." Just so! It is! But as we press on, the Holy Ghost enlightens and we enter in as Paul says according to the revelation of the Spirit. I am perfected as I launch out into God by faith, His blood covering my sin, His righteousness covering my unrighteousness, His perfection covering my imperfection. *I am holy and perfect in him.*

2. *Establish.* You must be established in the fact that it is His life, not yours. Faith in His Word, faith in His life; you are supplanted by another, you are disconnected from the earth, insulated by faith.

3. *Strengthen.* Strengthened in the fact that God is doing the business, not you, you are in the plan, which God is working out.

TONGUES AND INTERPRETATION: "There is nothing in itself that can bring out that which God designs. What God intends is always a going on to perfection until we are like unto Him. It is an establishment of righteousness on His own Word."

4. *Settled.* What is it to be settled? A knowledge that I am in union with His will, that I am established in the knowledge of it, that day by day I am strengthened. It is an eternal work of righteousness, until by the Spirit you are perfected. First enduring, then an establishing, a strengthening, a settling. It is according to your faith. It is as you believe. Now a closing word.

To God be all the glory. What does it mean, for it all to be realized in my case? That I live for His glory, that there be no withdrawal, no relinquishing, no looking back, but going on, on, on, for His glory now and forever, until as Enoch, we walk with God and are not, for God has taken us.

Published in *Redemption Tidings*

HOW TO BE TRANSFORMED

July 14, 1945

Jacob was on his way to the land of his fathers, but he was very troubled at the thought of meeting his brother Esau. Years before, Jacob and his mother had formed a plan to secure the blessing that Isaac was going to give Esau. How inglorious was the fulfilling of this carnal plan! It resulted in Esau's hating Jacob and saying in his heart, "When my father is dead, then will I slay my brother Jacob" (Genesis 27:41). Our own plans lead us frequently into disaster.

Jacob had to flee from the land, but how good the Lord was to the fleeing fugitive. He gave him a vision of a ladder, and angels ascending and descending. How gracious is our God! He refused to have His plans of grace frustrated by the carnal workings of Jacob's mind, and that night He revealed Himself to Jacob saying, "...I am with thee, and will keep thee in all places whither thou goest, and will bring thee again into this land; for I will not leave thee, until I have done that which I have spoken to thee of" (Genesis 28:15). It is the goodness of the Lord that leads to repentance. I believe that Jacob really did some repenting that night as he was made conscious of his own meanness.

Many things may happen in our lives to show us how depraved we are by nature, but when the veil is lifted we see how merciful and tender God is. His tender compassion is over us all the time.

Since the time when Jacob had had the revelation of the ladder and the angels, he had had twenty-one years of testing and trial. But God had been faithful to His promise all through these years. Jacob could say to his wives, "...your father hath deceived me, and changed my wages ten times; but God suffered him not to hurt me" (Genesis 31:7). He said to his father-in-law, "Except the God of my father, the God of Abraham, and the fear of Isaac, had been with me, surely thou hadst sent me away now empty. God hath seen mine affliction and the labour of my hands..." (Genesis 31:42).

Now that Jacob was returning to the land of his birth, his heart was filled with fear. If he ever needed the Lord, it was just at this time. And he wanted to be alone with God. His wives, his children, his sheep, his kine (cattle), his camels, and his asses, gone on, "And Jacob was left alone; and there wrestled a man with him until the breaking of the day" (Genesis 32:24). The Lord saw Jacob's need, and came down to meet him. It was He who wrestled with the supplanter, breaking him, changing him, transforming him.

Jacob knew that his brother Esau had power to take away all that he had, and to execute vengeance upon him. He knew that no one could deliver him but God. And there alone, lean in soul and impoverished in spirit, he met with God. Oh, how we need to get alone with God, to be broken, to be changed, to be transformed! And when we do meet with Him, He interposes, and all care and strife are at an end. Get alone with God and receive the revelation of His infinite grace, and of His wonderful purposes and plans for your life.

This picture of Jacob left alone is so real to me, I can imagine his thoughts that night. He would think about the ladder and the angels. I somehow think that as he would begin to pray, his tongue would cleave to the roof of his mouth. He knew he had to get rid of a lot of things. In days gone by, it had all been Jacob! Jacob! When you get alone with God, what a place of revelation it is. What a revelation of self we receive. And then

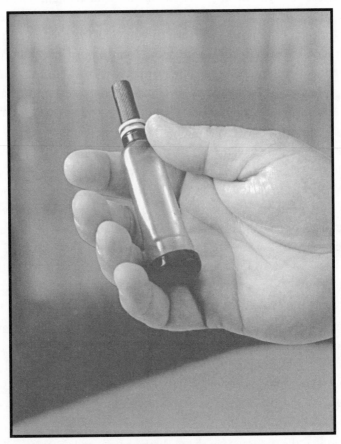

Anointing oil bottle used by Smith Wigglesworth.

"It was not that there was any virtue in me—the people's faith was exercised as it was at Jerusalem when they said Peter's shadow would heal them."

what a revelation of the provision made for us at Calvary. It is here that we get a revelation of a life crucified with Christ, buried with Him, raised with Him, transformed by Christ, and empowered by the Spirit.

Hour after hour passed. Oh, that we might spend all nights alone with God! We are occupied too much with the things of time and sense. We need to spend time alone in the presence of God. We need to give God much time in order to receive new revelations from Him. We need to get past all the thoughts of earthly matters that crowd in so rapidly. It takes God time to deal with us. If He would only deal with us as He dealt with Jacob, then we should have power with Him, and prevail.

Jacob was not dry-eyed that night. Hosea tells us, "…he wept, and made supplication…" (Hosea 12:4). He knew that he had been a disappointment to the Lord, that he had been a groveler, but in the revelation he received that night he saw the possibility of being transformed from a supplanter to a prince with God. The testing hour came when, at the break of day, the Angel, who was none other than the Lord and Master, said, "…Let me go, for the day breaketh…" (Genesis 32:26). This is where we so often fail. Jacob knew that if God went without blessing him, Esau could not be met. You cannot meet the terrible things that await you in the world unless you secure the blessing of God.

You must never let go. Whatever you are seeking — a fresh revelation, light on the path, some particular thing — never let go. Victory is yours if you are earnest enough. If you are in darkness, if you need a fresh revelation, if your mind needs relief, if there are problems you cannot solve, lay hold of God and declare, "…I will not let thee go, except thou bless me" (Genesis 32:26).

In wrestling, the strength is in the neck, the breast, and the thigh, but the greatest strength is in the thigh. The Lord touched Jacob's thigh. With his human strength gone, surely defeat was certain. What did Jacob do? He hung on. God means to have people who are broken. The divine power can only come when there is an end of our own self-sufficiency. But when we are broken, we must hold fast. If we let go then we shall fall short.

Jacob cried, "…I will not let thee go, except thou bless me…." And God blessed him, saying, "…Thy name shall be called no more Jacob, but Israel: for as a prince hast thou power with God and with men, and hast prevailed" (Genesis 32:28). Now a new order begins. The old supplanter has passed away, there is a new creation: Jacob the supplanter has been transformed into Israel the prince.

When God comes into your life, you will find Him enough. As Israel came forth, the sun rose upon him, and he had power over all the things of the world, and power over Esau. Esau met him, but there was no fight now, there was reconciliation. They kissed each other. How true it is, "When a man's ways please the Lord, he maketh even his enemies to be at peace with him" (Proverbs 16:7). Esau inquired, "What about all these cattle, Jacob? "Oh, that's a present." "Oh, I have plenty; I don't want your cattle. What a joy to see your face again!" What a wonderful change! The material things did not count for much after the night of revelation. Who wrought the change? God.

Can you hold on to God as did Jacob? You certainly can if you are sincere, if you are dependent, if you are broken, if you are weak. It is when you are weak that you are strong (2 Corinthians 12:10). But if you are self-righteous, if you are proud, if you are highminded, if you are puffed up in your own imagination, you can receive nothing from Him. If you become lukewarm instead of being at white heat, you can become a disappointment to God. And He says, "...I will spue thee out of my mouth" (Revelation 3:16).

But there is a place of holiness, a place of meekness, a place of faith, where you can call to God, "I will not let thee go, except thou bless me" (Genesis 32:26). And in response He will bless you exceeding abundantly above all you ask or think.

Sometimes we are tempted to think that He has left us. Oh, no. He has promised never to leave us, and He will not fail. Jacob held on until the blessing came. We can do the same.

If God does not help us, we are no good for this world's need; we are no longer salt, we lose our savor. But as we spend time alone with God, and cry to Him to bless us, He re-salts us, He re-empowers us; but He brings us to brokenness and moves us into the orbit of His own perfect will.

The next morning as the sun rose, Jacob "...halted upon his thigh" (Genesis 32:31). You may ask, "What is the use of a lame man?" It is those who have seen the face of God and have been broken by Him, who can meet the forces of the enemy and break down the bulwarks of Satan's kingdom. The Word declares, "...the lame take the prey" (Isaiah 33:23). On that day Jacob was brought to a place of dependence upon God.

Oh, the blessedness of being brought into a life of dependence upon the power of the Holy Spirit. Henceforth we know that we are nothing without Him; we are absolutely dependent upon Him. I am absolutely nothing without the power and unction of the Holy Ghost. Oh, for a life of absolute dependence! It is through a life of dependence there is a life of power. If you are not there, get alone with God. If need be, spend a whole night alone with God, and let Him change and transform you. Never let Him go until He blesses you, until He makes you an Israel, a prince with God.

Published in *The Pentecostal Evangel*

AFLAME FOR GOD

October 17, 1942

Christ said to His disciples just before He ascended, "...ye shall receive power, after that the Holy Ghost is come upon you: and ye shall be witnesses unto me..." (Acts 1:8). On the day of Pentecost He sent the power, and the remainder of the Acts of the Apostles tells of the witnessing of these Spirit-filled disciples, the Lord working with them, and confirming the Word with signs following.

The Lord Jesus is just the same today. The anointing is just the same. The Pentecostal experience is just the same, and we are to look for like results as set forth in Luke's record of what happened in the days of the early church.

John the Baptist said concerning Jesus, "...he shall baptize you with the Holy Ghost, and with fire" (Matthew 3:11). God's ministers are to be a flame of fire — a perpetual flame, a constant fire, a continual burning, burning and shining lights. God has nothing less for us than to be flames. We must have a living faith in God, a faith that God's great might and power may flame through us until our whole life is energized by the power of God.

I realize that when the Holy Ghost comes, He comes to enable us to show forth Jesus Christ in all His glory, to make Him known as the One who heals today as in the days of old. The baptism in the Spirit is to enable us to preach as they did at the beginning, through the power of the Holy Ghost sent down from heaven and with the manifestation of the gifts of the Spirit. Oh, if we would only let the Lord work in us, melting us until a new order arises, moved with His compassion!

I was traveling from Egypt to Italy. God was wonderfully on that ship with me, and every hour I was conscious of His blessed presence. A man on the ship suddenly collapsed and his wife was terribly alarmed, and everybody else seemed to be. Some said that he was about to expire. But I saw it was just a glorious opportunity for the power of God to be manifested. Oh, what it means to be a flame of fire, to be indwelt by the living Christ! We are a back number if we have to pray for poker when an occasion like that comes, or if we have to wait until we feel a sense of His presence. The Lord's promise was, "...ye shall receive power, after that the Holy Ghost is come upon you..." and if we will believe, the power of God will be always manifested when there is a definite need. When you exercise your faith, you will find that there is a greater power than there is in the world. Oh, to be awakened out of unbelief into a place of daring for God on the authority of His blessed Book!

So right there on board that ship, in the name of Jesus I rebuked the devil, and to the astonishment of the man's wife and the man himself, he was able to stand. He said, "What is this? It is going all over me. I have never felt anything like this before." From the top of his head to the soles of his feet the power of God shook him. God has given us authority over all the power of the devil. Oh, that we may live in the place where we realize this always!

Christ, who is the express image of God, has come to our human weaknesses, to change them and us into divine likeness, to be partakers of the divine nature, so that by the power of His might we may not only overcome, but rejoice in the fact that we are more than conquerors. God wants you to know by experience what it means to be more than a conqueror. The baptism in the Holy spirit has come for nothing less than to empower us, to give the very power that Christ Himself had, so that you, a yielded vessel, may continue the same type of ministry that He had when He walked this earth in the days of His flesh. He purposes that we should come behind in no gift. There are gifts of healing and the working of miracles, but we must apprehend these. There is the gift of faith by the same Spirit which we are to receive.

The need in the world today is that we should be burning and shining lights to reflect the glory of Christ. We cannot do it with a cold indifferent experience, and we never shall. His servants are to be flames of fire. Christ came that we might have life, and life more abundantly. And we are to give that life to others, to be ministers of the life and power and healing virtue of Jesus Christ wherever we go.

Some years ago I was in Ceylon. In one place the folk complained, "Four days is not much to give us." "No," I said, "but it is a good share." They said to me, "We are not touching the people here at all." I said, "Can you have a meeting early in the morning, at eight o"clock?" They said they would. So I said, "Tell all the mothers who want their babies to be healed to come, and all the people over seventy to come, and after that we hope to give an address to the people to make them ready for the baptism in the Spirit."

It would have done you good to see the four hundred mothers coming at eight o'clock with their babies, and then to see the hundred and fifty old people, with their white hair, coming to be healed. We need to have something more than smoke to touch the people; we need to be a burning fire for God. His ministers must be flames of fire. In those days there were thousands out to hear the Word of God. I believe there were about three thousand persons crying for mercy at once. It was a great sight.

From that first morning on the meetings grew to such an extent that I would estimate every time some 5,000 to 6,000 gathered; and I had to preach in a temperature of 110°. Then I had to pray for these people who were sick. But I can tell you, a flame of fire can do anything. Things change in the fire. This was Pentecost. But what moved me more than anything else was this: there were hundreds who tried to touch me, they were so impressed with the power of God that was present. And many testified that with the touch they were healed. It was not that there was any virtue in me — the people's faith was exercised as it was at Jerusalem when they said Peter's shadow would heal them.

You can receive something in three minutes that you can carry with you into glory. What do you want? Is anything too hard for God. God can meet you now. God sees inwardly. He knows all about you. Nothing is hidden from Him, and He can satisfy the soul and give you a spring of eternal blessing that will carry you right through.

Published in *The Pentecostal Evangel*

THE POWER OF CHRIST'S RESURRECTION

March 28, 1947

That I may know him, and the power of his resurrection, and the fellowship of his sufferings, being made conformable unto his death...I count not myself to have apprehended: but this one thing I do, forgetting those things which are behind, and reaching forth unto those things which are before, I press toward the mark for the prize of the high calling of God in Christ Jesus.

Philippians 3:10,13-14

What a wonderful Word! This surely means to press on to be filled with all the fulness of God. If we leak out here we shall surely miss God, and shall fail in fulfilling the ministry He would give us.

PRESSING ON FOR FULLER POWER

The Lord would have us preach by life, and by deed, always abounding in service; living epistles, bringing forth to men the knowledge of God. If we went all the way with God, what would happen? What should we see if we would only seek to bring honor to the name of our God? Here we see Paul pressing in for this. There is no standing still. We must move on to a fuller power of the Spirit, never satisfied that we have apprehended all, but filled with the assurance that God will take us on to the goal we desire to reach, as we press on for the prize ahead.

Abraham came out from Ur of the Chaldees. We never get into a new place until we come out from the old one. There is a place where we leave the old life behind, and where the life in Christ fills us and we are filled with His glorious personality.

On the road to Damascus, Saul of Tarsus was apprehended by Christ. From the first he sent up a cry, "Lord, what wilt thou have me to do?" He desired always to do the will of God, but here he realized a place of closer intimacy, a place of fuller power, of deeper crucifixion. He sees a prize ahead and every fiber of his being is intent on securing that prize. Jesus Christ came to be the firstfruits; the firstfruits of a great harvest of like fruit, like unto Himself. How zealous is the farmer as he watches his crops and sees the first shoots and blades. They are the earnest of the great harvest that is coming. Paul here is longing that the Father's heart shall be satisfied, for in that first resurrection the Heavenly Husbandman will see a firstfruits harvest, firstfruits like unto Christ, sons of God made conformable to the only begotten Son of God.

You say, "I am in a needy place." It is in needy places that God delights to work. For three days the people that were with Christ were without food, and He asked Philip, "From whence shall we buy bread that these may eat?" That was a hard place for Philip, but not for Jesus, for He knew perfectly what He would do. The hard place is where He delights to show forth His miraculous power. And how fully was the need provided for. Bread enough and to spare!

THE PRESENCE OF THE RISEN CHRIST

Two troubled, baffled travelers are on the road to Emmaus. As they communed together and reasoned, Jesus Himself drew near, and He opened up the Word to them in such a way that they saw light in His light. Their eyes were holden that they could not recognize who it was talking with them. But, oh how their hearts burned within as He opened up the Scripture to them. And at the breaking of bread He was made known to them. Always seek to be found in the place where He manifests His presence and power.

The resurrected Christ appeared to Peter and a few more of them early one morning on the shore of the lake. He prepared a meal for the tired, tried disciples. This is just like Him. Count on His presence.

Count on His power. Count on His provision. He is always there just where you need Him.

Have you received *Him*? Are you to be found *"in Him"*? Have you received *His righteousness*, which is by faith? Abraham got to this place, for God gave this righteousness to him because he believed, and as you believe God He puts His righteousness to your account. He will put His righteousness right within you. He will keep you in perfect peace as you stay your mind upon Him and trust in Him. He will bring you to a rest of faith, to a place of blessed assurance that all that happens is working for your eternal good.

Here is the widow's son on the road to burial. Jesus meets that unhappy procession. He has compassion on that poor woman who is taking her only son to the cemetery. His great heart had such compassion that death had no power — it could not longer hold its prey. Compassion is greater than suffering. Compassion is greater than death. O God, give us this compassion! In His infinite compassion Jesus stopped that funeral procession and cried to that widow's son, "Young man, I say unto thee, Arise." And he who was dead sat up, and Jesus delivered him to his mother.

CHANNELS FOR HIS POWER

Paul got a vision and revelation of the resurrection power of Christ, and so he was saying, "I will not stop until I have laid hold of what God has laid hold of me for." For what purpose has God laid hold of us? To be channels for His power. He wants to manifest the power of the Son of God through you and me. God helps us to manifest the faith of Christ, the compassion of Christ, the resurrection power of Christ.

One morning about eleven o'clock I saw a woman who was suffering with a tumor. She could not live through the day. A little blind girl led me to the bedside. Compassion broke me up and I wanted that woman to live for the child's sake. I said to the woman, "Do you want to live?" She could not speak. She just moved her finger. I anointed her with oil and said, "In the name of Jesus." There was a stillness of death that followed; and the pastor, looking at the woman, said to me, "She is gone."

When God pours in His compassion it has resurrection power in it. I carried that woman across the room, put her against a wardrobe, and held her there. I said, "In the name of Jesus, death, come out." And soon her body began to tremble like a leaf. "In Jesus' name, walk," I said. She did and went back to bed.

I told this story in the assembly. There was a doctor there and he said, "I'll prove that." He went to the woman and she told him it was perfectly true. She said, "I was in heaven, and I saw countless numbers all like Jesus. Then I heard a voice saying, 'Walk, in the name of Jesus.'"

There is power in the name of Jesus. Let us apprehend it, the power of His resurrection, the power of His compassion, the power of His love. Love will break the hardest thing — there is nothing it will not break.

Published in *Redemption Tidings*

 bide in the presence of power where victory is assured. If we keep in the right place with God, God can do anything with us. There is a power and majesty falling on Jesus. He is no longer the same. He has now received the mighty anointing power of God. And He realizes submission, and as He submits He is more and more covered with the power and led by the Spirit. He came out of the wilderness more full of God, more clothed with the Spirit and ready for the fight. The enduement with power had such an effect upon Him that other people saw it and flocked to hear Him, and great blessing came to the land.

ABIDING IN POWER

The Holy Ghost coming upon an individual changes him and fertilizes his spiritual life. What is possible if we reach this place and keep in it — abide in it. Only one thing is going to accomplish the purpose of God — that is, to be filled with the Spirit we must yield and submit, until our bodies are saturated with God, that at any moment God's will can be revealed. We want a great hunger and thirst for God.

Thousands must be brought to a knowledge of the truth; that will only be brought about by human instrumentality, when the instrument is at a place where he will say all the Holy Ghost directs him to; be still and know that I am God, the place of tranquility, where we know He is controlling, and moves us by the mighty power of His Spirit.

Ezekiel said, "I prophesied as I was commanded." He did what he was told to do. It takes more to live in that place than any other I know of. To live in the place where you hear God's voice. Only by the power of the Spirit can you do as you are told quickly.

We must keep at the place where we see God, always hearing His voice — where He sends us with messages bringing life and power and victory.

I desire you all to follow me in reading the first twelve verses of the eleventh chapter of Matthew's gospel:

CHRIST IN US

And it came to pass, when Jesus had made an end of commanding his twelve disciples, he departed thence to teach and to preach in their cities. Now when John had heard in the prison the works of Christ, he sent two of his disciples, And said unto him, Art thou he that should come, or do we look for another? Jesus answered and said unto them, Go and show John again those things which ye do hear and see: The blind receive their sight, and the lame walk, the lepers are cleansed, and the deaf hear, the dead are raised up, and the poor have the gospel preached to them. And blessed is he, whosoever shall not be offended in me. And as they departed, Jesus began to say unto the multitudes concerning John, What went ye out into the wilderness to see? A reed shaken with the wind? But what went ye out for to see? A man clothed in soft raiment? behold, they that wear soft clothing are in kings' houses. But what went ye out for to see? A prophet? yea, I say unto you, and more than a prophet. For this is he, of whom it is written, Behold, I send my messenger before thy face, which shall prepare thy way before thee. Verily I say unto you, Among them that are born of women there hath not risen a greater than John the Baptist: notwithstanding he that is least in the kingdom of heaven is greater than he. And from the days of John the Baptist until now the kingdom of heaven suffereth violence, and the violent take it by force.

I believe that God wants to bring to our eyes and our ears a living realization of what the Word of God is, what the Lord God means, and what we may expect if we believe it. Tonight I am certain that the Lord wishes to put before us a living fact which shall by faith, bring into action a principle which is within our own hearts, so that Christ can dethrone every power of Satan.

It is only this truth revealed to our hearts that can make us so much greater that we had ever any idea we were. I believe there are volumes of truth right in the midst of our own hearts; only there is the need of revelation and of stirring ourselves up to understand the mightiness which God has within us: we may prove what He has accomplished in us if we will only be willing to accomplish that which He has accomplished in us.

For God has not accomplished something in us that should lie dormant, but He has brought within us a power, a revelation, a life that is so great, that I believe God wants to reveal the greatness of it. The possibilities of man in the hands of God! There isn't anything you can imagine greater than what the man may accomplish.

But everything on a natural basis is very limited to what God has for us on a spiritual basis. If man can accomplish much in a short time, what may we accomplish if we will have the revealed Word tonight, and take it as truth which God has given us and that he wants to bring out in revelation and force?

JOHN THE BAPTIST

In the first place, notice the fact that John the Baptist was the forerunner of Jesus. Within his own short history, John the Baptist had the power of God revealed to him as no man in the old dispensation probably. He had a wonderful revelation, he had a mighty anointing.

I want you to see how he moved Israel. I want you to see how the power of God rested upon him. I want you to see how he had the vision of Jesus, and went forth with power and turned the hearts of Israel to Him. And yet Jesus says about John:

> *...Among them that are born of women there hath not risen a greater than John the Baptist: notwithstanding he that is least in the kingdom of heaven is greater than he.*
>
> *Matthew 11:11*

Then I want you to see how satanic power can work in the mind. I find that Satan comes to John when he is in prison. I find that Satan can come to any of us. Without we are filled, or divinely insulated with the power of God, we may go under by the power of Satan.

But I want to prove tonight that we have a greater power than Satan's, in imagination, in thought, in everything. Satan comes to John the Baptist in prison, and says to John:

"Don't you think you have made a mistake? Here you are in prison. You hear nothing about Jesus. Isn't there something wrong with the whole business? After all, you may be greatly deceived about being a forerunner of the Christ."

I find men who might be giants of faith, who might be leaders of society, who might rise to subdue kingdoms, who might be noble amongst princes, but they go down, because they allow suggestions of Satan to dethrone their better knowledge of the power of God. God, help us tonight.

See what John the Baptist did:

> *Now when John had heard in the prison the works of Christ, he sent two of his disciples, And said unto him, Art thou he that should come, or do we look for another?*
> *Matthew 11:2,3*

How could Jesus send those men back with a stimulating truth, with a personal, effective power that should stir their hearts to know that they had met Him whom all the prophets had spoken about? What would declare it? How shall they know? How can they tell it?

> *Jesus answered and said unto them, Go and show John again those things which ye do hear and see: The blind receive their sight, and the lame walk, the lepers are cleansed, and the deaf hear, the dead are raised up, and the poor have the gospel preached to them.*
> *Matthew 11:4,5*

And when they saw the miracles and wonders, and heard the gracious words He spoke as the power of God rested upon Him, they were ready.

Has that work to cease? If it hasn't to cease, then I must put before you tonight a living fact. I must have you see why it shall not cease. Instead of ceasing, it had to continue to be. It is only by the grace of God that I dare put these truths before you because of facts which will be proved.

Tonight, I have a message for the saved people, and a message for the unsaved, but I want you to hear. There are none so deaf as those who won't hear, and none so blind as those who won't see. But God has given you ears, and He wants you to hear. What shall you hear?

> *And ye shall know the truth, and the truth shall make you free.*
> *John 8:32*

Hear what Jesus said:

> *And as they departed, Jesus began to say unto the multitudes concerning John, What went ye out into the wilderness to see? A reed shaken with the wind?*
> *Matthew 11:7*

Did you ever see a man of God like a reed? If ever you did I should say he was only an imitator. Has God ever made a man to be a reed, or to be like smoking flax? No. God wants to make men as flames of fire. God wants to make men strong in the Lord, and in the power of His might.

Therefore, beloved, if you will hear the truth of the Gospel, you will see that God has made provision for you to be strong, to be on fire, to be as though you were quickened from the dead, as those who have seen the King, as those who have a resurrection touch. We know we are the sons of God with power as we believe His Word and stand in the truth of His Word.

TONGUES AND INTERPRETATION: "The Spirit of the Lord breathes upon the slain, and upon the dry bones, and upon the things which are not, and changes them in the flesh in a moment of time, and makes that which is weak, strong. And behold, He is amongst us tonight to quicken that which is dead and make the dead alive."

He is here! "The dead shall hear the voice of the Son of God: and they that hear shall live." Praise the Lord!

We pass on to another thought in the next verse which is very important:

And from the days of John the Baptist until now the kingdom
of heaven suffereth violence, and the violent take it by force.

Matthew 11:12

HID IN CHRIST

This is a message to every believer. Every believer is belonging to the kingdom of heaven. Every believer has the life of the Lord in him. And if Jesus were to come, who is our life, instantly our life would go out to meet His life because we exist and consist of the life of the Son of God. "And your life is hid with Christ, in God."

There is a wonderful word in Luke's gospel, the twenty-second chapter, which if all believers understood, there would be great joy in their hearts:

> *And he said unto them, With desire I have desired to eat this*
> *passover with you before I suffer: For I say unto you, I will not*
> *any more eat thereof, until it be fulfilled in the kingdom of God.*
>
> *Luke 22:15,16*

Everyone in Christ Jesus shall be there when He sits down the first time to break bread in the kingdom of heaven. It is not possible for any child of God to remain when Jesus comes. The Lord help us to believe it.

I know there is a great deal of speculation on the rapture, and on the coming of the Lord. But let me tell you to hope for edification and consolation, for the Scripture by the Holy Ghost won't let me speak but on edification, and consolation, and comfort of the Spirit. Why? Because we are here for the purpose of giving everybody in the meeting "consolation."

I don't mean to cover sin up. God won't let us do that. But we must unveil truth. And what is truth? The Word of God is truth. "I am the way, the truth, and the life."

> *Search the Scriptures; for in them ye think ye have eternal life:*
> *and they are they which testify of me.*
>
> *John 5:39*

What does the truth say? That when He appears, all that are Christ's at His coming, will be changed in a moment, in the twinkling of an eye.

And we will be presented the same moment along with all those that sleep in Him, and we will all go together.

> *...the Lord shall not prevent them which are asleep...and the dead in Christ shall rise first: Then we which are alive and remain shall be caught up together with them in the clouds, to meet the Lord in the air: and so shall we ever be with the Lord. Wherefore comfort one another with these words.*
>
> *1 Thessalonians 4:15-18*

> *For I say unto you, I will not drink of the fruit of the vine, until the kingdom of God shall come.*
>
> *Luke 22:18*

Two thousand years will soon be up since the Lord broke bread around the table with His disciples.

I am longing, the saints are longing, for the grand union when millions, billions, trillions will again with Him unite in that great fellowship supper. Praise the Lord! But now, the stimulation, the power that must be working every day till that day appears!

Come, this is my point. (Nay, it is not my point, it is God's revelation to us. I am going to be out of it. If ever I say, "I" or "my," you must look upon it, and forgive me. I don't want to be here tonight to speak my own words, my own thoughts. I want the Lord to be glorified in bringing every thought so that we shall all be comforted and edified tonight. But this is a strong message for us, and a very helpful one especially for the sick and needy believer.) The kingdom of heaven is within us, within every believer. The kingdom of heaven is the Christ, is the Word of God.

THE KINGDOM

The kingdom of heaven is to outstrip everything else, even your own lives. It has to be so manifested that you have to realize even the death of Christ brings forth the life of Christ.

"The kingdom of heaven suffereth violence."

How? Every suffering one, every needy one, every paralyzed condition, every weakness of the head, of the loins, or of any part of the body —

if you feel distress in any way, it means that the kingdom of heaven is suffering violence at the hand of the adversary.

Could the kingdom of heaven bring weaknesses? diseases? Could it bring imperfection on the body? Could it bring consumption? Could it bring extreme burnings, cancers, tumors?

"Behold, the kingdom of God is within you."

The kingdom of heaven is the life of Jesus, it is the power of the Highest. The kingdom of heaven is pure, it is holy. It has no disease, no imperfection. It is as holy as God is. And Satan with his evil power "cometh not, but for to steal, and to kill, and to destroy" that body.

Every ailment that any one has tonight is from satanic source. It is foolish and ridiculous to think that sickness purifies you. There is no purification in disease. Scientists and doctors of the last days have told you that they can make a child purer by putting impure matter into it on the line of vaccination. It is ridiculous and foolish for any sane person to put impure matter into a child that is pure.

I have seen blindness, and idiocy, and all kinds of evil come from that evil construction of what they call science, hideous science, foolish science. God deliver us from such foolishness.

A little girl was brought to me who was as perfect and pure a child as there ever was. From the days of its vaccination it was blind.

I have before my mind a beautiful girl of nine years. From the days of her vaccination an evil spirit possessed her so that she screamed and moaned for years and years. The neighbors said to her father, "We cannot bear to hear your child, night after night, day after day, screaming and moaning." They pleaded with him to have the child put in an asylum. The father lifted up his big hands and said, "These fingers shall work till there is no flesh on them if necessary, so that my child shall not have to go to an asylum."

One day I went by invitation to this home, taking with me a much stronger and bigger man than myself. There we saw this child crying and rolling about from place to place. I got hold of the child to comfort it, only a father or mother knows how to help the poor things.

In a moment it twisted out of my hands like a serpent. How strange! The big man that was with me said, "I'll take hold of the child." He took it, but the child, in a mysterious way, got out of his hands and went up some steps, crying bitterly, and with a moaning that went right through you.

The Spirit of the Lord came upon me; I went up the staircase, took hold of the child, looked right in its eyes, and said, "Come out, you evil spirit, in the name of Jesus!" She went to a couch close by and fell asleep, and from that day was perfect.

I know the deliverance came, but I want you to see the wiles of Satan, and the power of the devil. And I want to show you tonight, in the name of Jesus, your power of dethronement.

Oh, this blessed Lord! Oh, this lovely Jesus! Oh, this incarnation of the Lamb slain!

Beloved, I wouldn't stand on this platform without I knew that all the Bible is true. Jesus said, "The devil cometh not, but for to steal, and to kill, and to destroy: I am come that they might have life, and that they might have it more abundantly" (John 10:10).

I want us to see the difference between the life abundant of Jesus and the power of Satan. Then — by the grace of God — to help us in our position — I want to keep before you, "The kingdom of heaven suffereth."

It is only fair and reasonable that I put before you the almightiness of God, against the might of Satan. If Satan was almighty we shall all have to quake. But when we know that Satan in everything is subject to the powers of God, we can get the truth right in our hearts and go away from this meeting conquerors over the situation. I want to make every man in this meeting strong in the Lord and in the power of His might.

THE POWER IN YOU

I want to bring before you an inward knowledge of a power in you greater than any power. And I trust by the help of the Spirit that I may bring you into a place of deliverance, a place of holy sanctification where you dare stand against the wiles of the devil, and drive them back, and cast them out. The Lord help us!

If I can wake you up! You ask, "Are we not awake?" You may be sensible to what I am saying. You may be able to tell when I lift my hand and put it down. Still you may be asleep concerning the deep things of God. I want God to give you an inward awakening, a revealing of truth within you, an audacity, a flaming indignation against the powers of Satan.

Lot had a righteous indignation from day to day, but it was too late. He ought to have had it when he went into Sodom, and not when he was coming out. But I don't want any one of you to go away downcast because you haven't taken sooner a step in the right direction. Always be thankful that you are alive to hear, and to change the situation.

It would be a serious thing for us to pay so much for this place and that you should come in and sit from an hour and a half to two hours, and then go out as you came in. I couldn't stand it. It would all be the biggest foolishness possible, and we would all need to be in the asylum.

There must be something take place tonight in this meeting, of an inward knowledge of God over the power of Satan on every line. When I speak about you waking up, the thought in my heart is this: I don't doubt your sincerity about being saved, about being just. It is out of my life to question a man's sincerity on his righteousness.

And yet, as I preach to you, I feel I have a right to say that there is a deeper sincerity to reach to, there is a greater audacity of faith and fact to reach. There is something that you have to wake up to; where you will never allow disease to have you, or sin to have you, or a weak heart to have you, or a pain in the back. You will never allow anything that isn't perfect life to have anything to do with you.

I am going on now to show you the weakness of believers. Does God know all about you? Is He acquainted with you altogether? Why not trust Him who knows all about you, instead of telling somebody else who knows only what you have told them.

Again, why should you — under any circumstances — believe that you will be better by being diseased? When disease is impurity, why should you ever believe that you would be sanctified by having a great deal of sickness?

Some people talk about God being pleased to put disease on His children. "Here is a person I love," says God. "I will break his arm. In order that he should love Me more, I will break his leg. In order that he should love Me still more, I will give him a weak heart. And in order to increase that love, I will make him so that he cannot eat anything without having indigestion."

The whole thing won't stand daylight. And yet people are always talking thus, and they never think to read the Word of God, which says, "Before I was afflicted I went astray..." (Psalm 119:67). And they have never read the following words into their lives, "Fools because of their transgression, and because of their iniquities, are afflicted. Their soul abhorreth all manner of meat; and they draw near unto the gates of death. Then they cry unto the Lord in their trouble, and he saveth them out of their distresses" (Psalm 107:17-19).

Yes, we have that to praise the Lord for. Is it right now to say, "You know, my brother, I have suffered so much in this affliction that it has made me know God better"? Well, now, before you get up, ask God for a lot more affliction, so you will get to know Him better still. If you won't ask for more affliction to make you purer still, I won't believe that the first affliction made you purer; because if it had, you would have more faith in it. It appears you haven't faith in your afflictions. It is only language, but language doesn't count unless it works out a fact. But if the people can see that your language is working out a fact, then they have some grounds for believing in it.

I have looked through my Bible, and I cannot find where God brings disease and sickness. I know there is glory, and I know it is the power of God that brings the glory; but it isn't God at all, but the devil that brings sickness and disease. Why does he? I know this, that Satan is God's whip, and if you don't obey God, God stands on one side and Satan will devour you. "But so far shalt thou go, and no further. Don't touch his life."

"...let God be true, but every man a liar..." (Romans 3:4). I am going to take it on its real basis, on the truth as it is revealed unto me in the scriptures, "The kingdom of heaven suffereth violence."

Then why is Satan allowed to bring sickness? Because we know better than we do. And if all the people would do as well as they know, they would have no sickness. If we would be true to our convictions, walk according to our light, God would verify His presence in the midst of us, and we should know that sickness should not come nigh thy dwelling. "For he shall give his angels charge over thee, to keep thee in all thy ways" (Psalm 91:11). Then, again, if there are weak persons in the place tonight, and they are suffering terribly, I know they are sorry for their sickness, but if they would be as sorry for their sins as they are for their sickness, they would be out of it tonight. If ever we get desperate about having our sins destroyed, they will go. God help us!

Well, if you are whole from top to bottom and don't know you have a body, it is easy to shout, "Glory!" But if some people shouted "Glory," one side of them would ache. And so it is with these people who are not free tonight. I want to put you in a place where you will shout "Glory"!

It is true that God keeps me, as it were, without knowing I have a body. I believe that is "redemption." But I am not going to condemn people who are not there. I am here to help them. But I cannot help you out unless I give you scripture. If I can lay down a basis, I can send you home and know that you will deliver yourself.

If I could only get you to catch faith, by the grace of God, every person in the place would be delivered. But I find out this, that Satan has a tremendous power over certain functions of the body, and I want to play on that for a moment to help you.

When Satan can get to your body he will, if possible, make the pain, or the weakness, so distracting that it will affect your mind, and always bring your mind down to where the pain is. When that takes place, you haven't the same freedom in the Spirit to lift up your heart and shout, and praise the Lord, because the distraction of the pain brings the elementary power which ought to be full of praise to God, down into the body. And by that means — concerning everybody who is afflicted — "the kingdom of heaven suffereth violence."

Beloved, I mean precisely this: Anything that takes me from a position where I am in an attitude of worship, of peace, of joy, of a consciousness of the presence of God, of an inward moving of the powers of God that makes me able to lift myself up and live in the world as though I was not of it (because I am not of it); anything that dethrones me from that attitude is evil, is Satan.

Tonight, I want to prove how the kingdom of heaven suffereth violence. If it is only a finger or a tooth that aches, if it is only a corn that pinches you, or anything in the body that detracts from the highest spiritual attainment, the kingdom of heaven is dethroned in a measure, "the kingdom of heaven suffereth violence."

By the Word of God I am proving to you the kingdom of heaven is within you. "Greater is He that is in you," which is the kingdom of heaven, which is the Son of God, "than he that is in the world," the power of Satan outside you.

Disease or weakness, or any distraction in you, is a power of violence that can take it by force. The same spiritual power that shall reveal it to you, shall relieve you here in this meeting. For instance, I would like a manifestation of this distraction.

HEALED

Is there a person here who is saved by the power of God, but who is suffering in his back, in his legs, in his head, or shoulders? (A man raises his hand.)

Stand up, young man. Where are you suffering?

"In my leg."

Stand out in the aisle; this is an example for all the people.

Are you saved?

"I am."

Do you believe the kingdom of God is within you?

"I do."

I can prove the Scriptures to be true. Here the kingdom of heaven in this man is suffering violence because he has a pain in his leg which takes his mind a hundred times a day, off the highest throned position — where he is seated in heavenly places with Christ Jesus — on to his leg; and I am going to tell this young man that tonight he has to treat that as an enemy, as the power of Satan down in his legs; and in the name of Jesus he has to say that he is free. He has to say it by the power that is within him, in fact, the personality, the presence of God, the power against Satan, the name of Jesus. I want you to say, "In the name of Jesus, come out!" Shout! Put your hand upon your leg and say, "In the name of Jesus, I command you to come out!" Go right to the bottom of your leg. Amen! Praise the Lord! Now walk around. Has he come out? Are you free?

"Yes."

Praise God! On the authority of the Word of God, I maintain that "Greater is He that is in you," than any power of Satan about you. Suppose five or six were standing up tonight, and I prayed with the facts in my heart that in me — by the power of Jesus — is a greater power than the power that is binding you. I pray, I believe, and the evil power goes out while I am praying. How much more would be done if you people would inwardly claim your right and deliver yourself?

You see that Bible. I believe it from front to back. But it won't have an atom of power in you if you don't put the Bible in practice in yourself. If, by the power of God, I put in you an audacity, a determination that you won't let Satan rest there, you will be free. Praise the Lord!

Why do I take this attitude? Because every step of my life since my baptism I have had to pay the price of everything for others. God has to take me through to the place that I may be able to show the people how to do it. Some people come up to me and say, "I have been waiting for the baptism, and I am having such a struggle, I am having to fight for every inch of it." "Isn't it strange?" No, a thousand to one God is preparing you to help somebody else who is desiring to receive it.

The reason I am so rigid about the necessity of getting the baptism in the Holy Ghost, and about the significance of the Spirit making manifestation when He comes in, is this: I fought it. I pressed myself on the attention of the meeting almost like a man who was mad. I told the people where I was, "This meeting of yours is nothing. I have left better conditions at home. I am hungry and thirsty for something." "What do you want?" they asked. "I want tongues." "You want the baptism?" they asked. "Not I," I said. "I have the baptism. I want tongues." I could have had a row with anybody. The whole position was this: God was training me for something else. The power of God fell upon my body with such ecstasy of joy that I could not satisfy the joy within, with the natural tongue, then I found the Spirit speaking through me in other tongues.

What did it mean? I knew that I have had anointings of joy before this, and expressions of the blessed attitude of the Spirit of life, and joy in the Holy Spirit; I felt it all the way through my life, but when the fulness came with a high tide, with an overflowing life, I knew that was different from anything else. And I knew that was the baptism, but God had to show me.

People ask, "Do all speak with tongues?" Certainly not. But all the people may speak as the Spirit gives utterance as in the upper room, and as in the house of Cornelius, and at Ephesus when they were filled with the Holy Ghost.

There is quite a difference between having a gift, and speaking as the Spirit gives utterance. If I had had a gift when I was filled with the Holy Ghost, wherever I went, I could have spoken, because gifts and calling remain. But I couldn't speak in tongues. Why? Because I had gotten the Holy Ghost, but I hadn't gotten the gift.

But I got the Holy Ghost, who is the Giver of all gifts. And nine months afterwards, God gave me the gift of tongues, so that I could speak in tongues any time. But do I? God forbid! Why? Because no man ought to use a gift; but the Holy Ghost uses the gift.

I shall not make you to be "extraordinary" on this line that I have brought before you, without I can make you "vexed." You ask why? If I could make every person who has a bad leg, to be so vexed at the devil that they will kick that leg off with the other, then I should get something through. You say that is extravagant. Well, I only use the extravagance to wake you up.

I have a reason for talking like this. People are all the time coming up to me and saying, "I have been prayed for, and I am just the same." It is enough to make you kick them. I mean more than I say. I am the last man to kick anybody in this place. God forbid. "For the weapons of our warfare are not carnal, but mighty through God to the pulling down of strong holds" (2 Corinthians 10:4).

If I can get you enraged against the powers of darkness, and the powers of disease, if I can wake you up, you won't go to bed without you prove that there is a master in you — greater than the power that is hanging round about you.

So many times I have gone into houses and been shut up with insane people. I have gone in — determined that they should be delivered. In the middle of the night chiefly, sometimes in the middle of the day, these demon powers would come and bite me, and handle me terribly rough. But I never gave in. It would dethrone a higher principle if I had to give in.

There is a great cloud of witnesses of the satanic powers from hell. We are here on probation to slay the enemy, and destroy the kingdoms of darkness, to move amongst satanic forces and subdue them in the name of Jesus.

May the God of grace and mercy strengthen us. If the 500, or 600 in this place tonight were — in the will of God — to rise as one man to slay the enemy, the host round about would feel the power. And in the measure that we destroy these evil powers, we make it easier for weak believers; for every time Satan overcomes a saint it gives him ferocity for another attack, but when he is subdued he will come to the place where defeat is written against him.

If you know God is within you, and you are suffering in any part of your body, please stand. I would like to take another case to prove my position in order to help all the people here.

IT IS GONE!

(A sister stands.)

You know you are saved?

"Yes, sir."

Praise God! Do you know that truth in the fourth chapter of the first epistle of John, "Greater is he that is in you, than he that is in the world"?

What is the trouble with you?

"I am suffering neuralgic pains."

Then by the authority of Jesus, where the neuralgia is, you go like this: "I rebuke you in the name of Jesus! I am against you! In the name of Jesus, come out and leave me!" Now, go on.

"I rebuke you in the name of Jesus! I refuse this pain to remain in the name of Jesus."

I believe it is gone. Is it gone?

"It is gone!"

Let me read to you what I have been preaching, because I want to prove that it is the Word of God. It is in the eleventh chapter of Matthew: "And from the days of John the Baptist until now," right up to this moment, "the kingdom of heaven suffereth violence...." That is, the inward presence of God suffereth violence by the power of Satan. "...and the violent take it by force" (v. 12).

How many people in this meeting are going to try that before going to bed? Glory to God! That is faith.

> Oh, I know the Lord, I know the Lord,
>
> I know the Lord's laid His hand on me.

If anyone said to me, "Wigglesworth, I will give you ten thousand dollars," in my estimation it would be as dust compared to the rising faith

I have seen. What I have seen by your uplifted hands on the lines of faith is of more value to me than anything you could count.

In your home, with your wife and your children, you will have audacity of determination, with a righteous indignation against the power of disease to cast it out. That is worth more to you than anything you could buy on any line.

I have a clear conviction that through the preached Word there are people going to take a new step on other lines. By the grace of God, we have seen tonight that we have to keep authority over the body, making the body subject to the higher powers. What about you who are in sickness, or bound in other ways; don't you long to come into a fulness of God? Aren't you longing to know a Saviour who can preserve you in the world over the powers of the enemy? I pray tonight, in the name of Jesus, that you will yield.

Everyone who has an inward knowledge of an indwelling Christ, lift your right hand. Thank God! Put them down. No one can have a knowledge of an inward Christ without having a longing for an increase of souls saved. The very first principle is that you have a first love. And if you don't lose that love it will keep you on winning souls all the time.

Dare those who did not put up their hands, put up their hands now, and let all those 400 believers pray for them? While we all appreciate the penitent form being filled, yet I know that if you cannot be saved in your seats you cannot be saved here. You are not saved by coming out, although it is a help for you to come out, but if these 400 saved people pray for you who have no knowledge of salvation, you can be saved just where you are.

So I am going to give you a real live opportunity to get near God by standing on your feet with these 400, and sweep into the kingdom of heaven by faith. Let us rise.

> Jesus paid it all,
> All to Him I owe;
> Sin had left a crimson stain;
> He washed it white as snow.

THE DELIVERANCE OF MULTITUDES — HOW? (Matthew 8)

acts are stubborn things. We want all unbelief cut away that the mind does not interfere with God's plan. The devil has been at work. For today try to put away what God has established. God has established truth in His Word. Men have tried to bring it to nought. God has His Word in the earth, it is also settled in heaven. If you are on the Word you are eternally fixed. God has said it, it is established, the Word of God abideth forever. Men pass away, things change, but God's Word abideth forever. Examine yourselves in the faith. "If thou wilt, thou canst make me clean." Who was it? A leper. An incurable and loathsome condition, limbs rotting and dropping off. When a man had leprosy he was doomed for life, like consumption or cancer it was the devil manifest in the flesh. And the devil never lets go of the flesh until he is made to. For deliverance you must have a mightier than Satan. Here in our midst is one greater than Satan. If you believe it, it will make all the difference to you. No more trouble, no more sickness, God's plan is wonderful, if you allow God to do a deep work cutting away unbelief. His ways are perfect. He always goes to the right place. Doctors say sometimes they begin at the wrong place and when they get to the right place they cannot do it. When the patient dies they say the operation was successful, but they died after it. None die after the operation of Jesus. Rather hard on the doctors, some say. No, they need not quake, they will have plenty to do while the world is rolling on in sin. But the believer is in quite a different place to the world. Jesus said to the woman, "Can we take of the children's bread and give it to the dogs." Children of God have bread, it is the life of Jesus. Jesus has all the bread you want, for spirit, soul, and body.

I went into an hotel where there was a man whose arm had been poisoned. I looked at the arm, it was very much swollen. His arm, neck, and face were blue. He opened his eyes and said, "Can you save me, I am dying?" I took hold of the arm and turned it round twice. It was an act of faith. I said, "In the name of Jesus you are free." He swang his arm round and round and said, "Look! Jesus, that mighty wonderful name which God has said is greater than all." This same Jesus, the Deliverer of all humanity.

You often hear people say "Run and fetch my purse, I cannot do without my purse." Mother, did you ever run back for your Bible? It contains richer gold, more manifest power. If the Word of God is in your heart you will be free. God is always making you free. The Gospel is full of liberality, and no bondage. Full of liberty. How long does it take to get clean? Jesus said, "I will, be thou clean," and immediately his leprosy was cleansed.

Lots of people have a great block in their way. They say, "I wonder if it is God's will," and they hang their harp on the willow. Is it the will of God? It comes on the line of redemption. Is it the will of God to save? Some men say, "All men will be saved." That is not scriptural. Who will be saved and who will be lost? The lost are those who believe not. To all who believe, God's plan is clear. The plan is, "I will when you will." The difference between personality and reality as to faith.

There was a woman sick unto death. She went to service, I went with two mission leaders to her house. There she was, laid in the bed, dying. The Lord revealed to me that nothing could save her but His power. I bent near to her. She said, "I have faith, I have faith." She repeated this continually, "I have faith." I said, "You have no faith, you are dying and you know it. You have only words." I said, "Do you want to live?" "Yes," she said, "but I have no power." The Spirit of the Lord came upon me and I said, "In the name of Jesus." The Spirit of God raised her up.

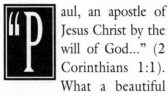

"Paul, an apostle of Jesus Christ by the will of God..." (2 Corinthians 1:1). What a beautiful thought, we are here by the will of God. By the will of God we are saved, by the will of God we are sanctified, by the will of God we are baptized in the Holy Ghost.

IN A HARD PLACE
Changing Strengths to Save Another

> *Blessed be God, even the Father of our Lord Jesus Christ, the Father of mercies, and the God of all comfort.*
>
> 2 Corinthians 1:3

Jesus could not have breathed any greater words than John 14:16:

> *...I will pray the Father, and he shall give you another Comforter, that he may abide with you for ever.*

IN ALL OUR TRIBULATION

The Father of mercies and the God of all comfort. A revelation of a greater power, an abiding presence sustaining and comforting in the hour of trial, ready at the moment, an unbreathing of God in the human life. What more do we need in these last days when perilous times are upon us than to be filled saturated. Baptized with the Holy Ghost. Baptized. Baptized into. Never to come out. How comforting! Exhilarating! Joyful! May it please the Lord to establish us in this state of grace, knowing nothing among men but Jesus and Him crucified. Clothed upon with His Spirit — nothing outside of the blessed Holy Ghost. This beloved is God's ideal for us.

> *Who comforteth us in all our tribulation, that we may be able to comfort them which are in any trouble, by the comfort wherewith we ourselves are comforted of God.*
>
> 2 Corinthians 1:4

Are we here in this experience?
Where He may lead me I will go,

> For I have learned to trust Him so,
> And I remember it was for me,
> That He was slain on Calvary.

Who comforteth us in all our tribulation! My life is that which God has chosen, to go through certain experiences to profit others. In all ages God has had His witnesses and He is teaching, chastening, correcting, moving upon me just up to the measure I am able to bear, in order to meet a needy soul that would go down without such comfort. All the chastening and the hardship is because we are able, not we, but yielding to another — even the Holy Ghost. We are strengthened unto endurance that we may comfort others by the comfort wherewith we ourselves are comforted of God.

What is the need of brokenness, of travail? The need is Psalms 119:67.

> *Before I was afflicted I went astray: but now have I kept thy word. Fools because of their transgression, and because of their iniquities, are afflicted. Their soul abhorreth all manner of meat; and they draw near unto the gates of death. Then they cry....*
> *Psalms 107:17-19*

He saves them? Fool — what is the word? One who knows better than he is doing. "The fool hath said in his heart, There is no God..." (Psalm 53:1). But He knows better. It is only the hardened heart and the stiff neck that are destroyed without remedy. "Now chastening for the present seemeth to be joyous, but grievous: nevertheless afterward it yieldeth the peaceable fruit of righteousness unto them that are exercised thereby" (Hebrews 12:11). It worketh out to provoke or to bestow upon us fruits unto holiness. It is in the hard places where we see no help, we cry out to God. He delivers us? What for? To the end that we can succor the tempted. It was said of Jesus that He was in all points tempted as we are. Where did He receive strength to comfort us? It was at the end of strong crying and tears, when the angel came and ministered just in time and saved Him from death just at the end. Is He not able? Oh, God highly exalted Him. Now He can send angels to us. When? Just when we should go right down, did He not stretch out to us a helping hand?

TONGUES AND INTERPRETATION: "It is God who seeth into the depths of the human heart. He seeth and saveth such in trouble. There is in it a plan and a purpose for others. How is it worked out? On the time of submission and yielding and a yielding to the unfolding of God's plan, then we shall be able to save others."

> *Who comforteth us in all our tribulation, that we may be able to comfort them which are in any trouble, by the comfort where-with we ourselves are comforted of God.*
>
> *2 Corinthians 1:4*

There is a sense of the power of God in humanity bringing you through necessities, never touching the mortal body, only the mind. We must have the mind of Christ.

Full of Consolation Towards the Needy

> *For as the sufferings of Christ abound in us, so our consolation also aboundeth by Christ.*
>
> *2 Corinthians 1:5*

God takes us to a place of need, and before you are hardly aware of it, you are full of consolation towards the needy. How? The sufferings of Christ abound! The ministry of the Spirit aboundeth so often. It is a great bless-ing we do not know our vocation in the Spirit. It is so much greater than our appreciation of it. Then a word in season — here and there, a min-istry, a sowing beside all waters as the Holy Spirit directeth our path.

> *And whether we be afflicted, it is for your consolation and sal-vation, which is effectual in the enduring of the same sufferings which we also suffer: or whether we be comforted, it is for your consolation and salvation.*
>
> *2 Corinthians 1:6*

Cooperated one with another. Here is the value of testing, resulting in a great flow of life one to another. John Wesley woke up to the con-sciousness of the need of one establishing another, bearing witness to the ministry of the Spirit, by this means multitudes were born again in the class meetings when they heard thus the wonderful works of God. Hearing stories pouring out consolation by the revelation of the Spirit. We are members one of another. When God's breath is upon us and we are quickened by the Holy Ghost, we can pour into each other wonderful ministries of grace and helpfulness. We need a strong ministry of consolation, not deterioration — a living below our privileges. These consolations come out of privation, endurance, affliction.

> *But we had the sentence of death in ourselves, that we should not trust in ourselves, but in God which raiseth the dead.*
>
> 2 Corinthians 1:9

Have we gone as far as Paul? Not one of us. Could you see how Paul could help and comfort and sustain because he yielded to God all the hurts (or trust) as Jesus did. Yielded to the Holy Ghost to work out the sentence of death — he could help others. I pray God, He may never find us kicking against the pricks. We may have to go through the testing. For the truths you stand for, you are tried for. Divine healing, pure heart, baptism, Holy Ghost, and fire — we are tested with it — rising up and tested on it, we could get out of it. In every meeting the glory rises. We go down also to be sustained and brought out for the glory of God. If God be for us, who can be against us?

> *For our light affliction, which is but for a moment, worketh for us a far more exceeding and eternal weight of glory.*
>
> 2 Corinthians 4:17

Oh, the joy of being worthy of suffering! How shall I stand the glory that shall be after? There are many more of God's people that are victorious in suffering — which fail or leak out in the summer day. Privation is often easier than success. We need a sound mind all the time to balance us that we trade not with our liberty all the time we get glimpses of the glory.

To Paul in the glory the presence of the Lord was so wonderful — lest I be exalted! There was given the thorn in the flesh. That was the mercy of God. He knoweth how to deliver the godly out of temptation and saveth such as be of a contrite spirit. What a revelation for the time to come. If Satan had his way, we should be devoured.

> *Who delivered us from so great a death, and doth deliver: in whom we trust that he will yet deliver us.*
>
> 2 Corinthians 1:10

Oh, God is! He will never fail us. He has been faithful with this moment and He will keep us to the end. Who delivered us from so great a death and doth deliver, in whom we trust that He will yet deliver us. Ye also helping together by prayer for us, for the gift bestowed upon us by the means of many persons. Thanks may be given by many on our behalf. Who delivered us and doth deliver, in whom we trust that He will yet deliver. Amen. Amen.

PRAISE

The new man created in Christ is God's masterpiece, His poem (Ephesians 2:10) set to music — a song. Singing and making melody in your heart unto the Lord. Praise is God's sunlight in the heart. It destroys sin germs. It ripens the fruits of the Spirit. It is the oil of gladness that lubricates life's activities. There can be no holy life without it. It keeps the heart pure and the eye clear. Praise is essential to the knowledge of God and His will. The strength of a life is the strength of its song. When the pressure is heavy that is the time to sing. Pressure is permitted to strengthen the attitude and spirit of praise. It takes a man to sing in the dark when the storm and battle are raging, and it is such singing that makes the man.

UNCONDITIONAL SURRENDER

It is Pentecost which has made me rejoice in Jesus. God has been vindicating His power by His Holy Spirit. I have a yearning intensity to see Pentecost and I am not seeing it. I may feel a little of the glow, what we need is a deeper work of the Holy Spirit, God's message to come full of life and power and keener than a two-edged sword (Hebrews 4:12). Peter stood up in the power of the Holy Spirit and 3,000 people were saved, again, and 5,000.

I am positive of the fact that we are on the wrong side of the cross. We talk about love, love, love — it ought to be repent, repent, repent. John the Baptist came and his message was repent! Jesus came — the same message — *repent!* The Holy Spirit came — the same message — repent, repent, repent, and believe. What has this to do with Pentecost? Everything! It is the secret of failure.

Daniel carried on his heart the burden of the people, he mourned for the captivity of Zion, he confessed his sin and the people's sin, he identified himself with Israel until God made him a flame of fire. The result — a remnant returned to Zion to walk in the despised way of obedience to God.

Nehemiah was brokenhearted when he learned of the desolations of Jerusalem. He pleaded months before God, his sin and the sin of his people, and God opened the way and the gates were built up, etc.

It is the spirit of deep repentance that is needed. You had an offering for foreign missionary work here yesterday. £50 was subscribed and you all seemed satisfied. The Lord bless you for your gifts. They mean something, but not Pentecost. A lack of compassion, God says, "And ye shall seek me, and find me, when ye shall search for me with all your heart" (Jeremiah 29:13), then the dry bones will move and the Spirit will be poured out upon us, not by measure (John 3:34).

The baptism of the Holy Spirit is a smashing of the whole man and a compassion for the world. "Bring ye all the tithes into the storehouse...and prove me now herewith, saith the Lord... (Malachi 3:10). Where is the fault for the state of things we see today? The lack of a deep spirit of repentance. Weeping is not repentance, sorrow is not repentance. Repentance is a turning away and doing the work of righteousness and holiness.

Much that I see in the children of God today is strange to me. The baptism of the Holy Ghost brings a deep repentance and a smashed and impoverished spirit.

What shall we do to receive it? Don't ask any more! *Repent, repent, repent.* God will hear and God will baptize. Will you? Is it possible after we have been baptized with the Holy Ghost to be satisfied with what we see? What made Jesus weep over Jerusalem? Because He had a heart of compassion — sin sick souls everywhere — we want a baptism of love which goes to the bottom of the disease. To cry unto God until He brings us up to the measure of the stature of the fulness of Christ.

There was a man who went down from Jerusalem to Jericho and fell among thieves. Who was his brother? He that relieved him. Are you awake to the great fact that God has given you eternal life? With the power God has put at your disposal, how can you rest as you look out upon your brethren? How we have sinned against God! How we lack this spirit of compassion. Do we weep as we look forth upon the unsaved? If not we are not Pentecost-full. Jesus was moved with compassion, are you?

We are not seeing the heathen yet. Since my only daughter went to Africa, I have a little less dim idea of what it meant, when I read God so loved the world that He gave Jesus. God gave Jesus. What does it mean? Compassion. After ye have received the Holy Ghost, ye shall have power (Acts 1:8). If you have no power, you have not repented. You say, "That's hard language." It is truth. Who is thy brother's keeper? Who is the son and the heir? Are you salted? Have you a pure life? Don't be fooled, don't live in a false position. The world wants to know — power is at our disposal. Will we meet the condition? God says, "If you will, I will." God will do it.

Daniel responded to God and knew his time and a nation was saved. Nehemiah met God's conditions for his time and the city was built. God has made the conditions. He will pour out His Spirit.

If we do not go on, we shall have it to face. It may depend on us to be the means. "Not by might, nor by power, but by my spirit, saith the Lord of hosts" (Zechariah 4:6). The world for Jesus, we can turn the tap on — the condition — *unconditional surrender.* Be quit with sin, holiness opens the windows of heaven. The Spirit of God shall be poured out not by measure, until the people say, "What must we do to be saved?"

e shall receive power, after that the Holy Ghost is come upon you..." (Acts 1:8). The disciples had been asking whether the Lord would at that time restore again the kingdom to Israel. Christ told them that it was not for them to know the times and seasons which the Father had put in His own power, but He promised them that when

YE SHALL RECEIVE POWER

they received the Holy Ghost they should receive power to witness for Him in all the world. To receive the Holy Ghost is to receive power with God, and power with men.

POWER FROM ON HIGH

There is a power of God and there is a power which is of Satan. When the Holy Spirit fell in the early days, a number of spiritists came to our meetings. They thought we had received something like they had and they were coming to have a good time. They filled the two front rows of our mission. When the power of God fell, these imitators began their shaking and muttering under the power of the devil. The Spirit of the Lord came mightily upon me and I cried, "Now, you devils, clear out of this!" And out they went. I followed them right out into the street and then they turned round and cursed me. There was power from below, but it was no match for the power of the Holy Ghost, and they soon had to retreat.

The Lord wants all saved people to receive power from on High — power to witness, power to act, power to live, and power to show forth the divine manifestation of God within. The power of God will take you out of your own plans and put you into the plan of God. You will be unmantled and divested of that which is purely of yourself and put into a divine order. The Lord will change you and put His mind where yours was, and thus enable you to have the mind of Christ. Instead of your laboring according to your own plan, it will be God working in you and through you to do His own good pleasure through the power of the Spirit within. Someone has said that you are no good until you have your "I" knocked out. Christ must reign within, and the life in the Holy Ghost means at all times the subjection of your own will to make way for the working out of the good and acceptable and perfect will of God within.

The Lord Jesus gave commandment that the disciples should tarry until they were endued with power from on high and in Acts 2 we read how the Spirit of God came. He comes the same way today and we don't know of the Holy Ghost coming any other way.

I was holding a meeting, once, in London, and at the close a man came to me and said, "We are not allowed to hold meetings in this hall after 11 o'clock, and we would like you to come home with us, I am so hungry for God." The wife said she, too, was hungry, and so I agreed to go with them. At about 12:30 we arrived at their house. The man began stirring up the fire and said, "Now we will have a good supper." I said to them, "I did not come here for your warm fire, your supper, or your bed. I came here because I thought you were hungry to get more of God." We got down to pray and at about 3:30 the Lord baptized the wife, and she spoke in tongues as the Spirit gave utterance. At about five o'clock I spoke to the husband and asked how he was getting on. He replied, "God has broken my iron, stubborn will." He had not received the baptism, but God had wrought a mighty work within him.

The following day, at his business, everyone could tell that a great change had come to him. Before he had been a walking terror. The men who labored for him had looked upon him as a regular devil because of the way he had acted; but coming into contact with the power of God that night completely changed him. Before this he had made a religious profession, but he had never truly entered into the experience of the new birth until that night, when the power of God surged so mightily through his home. A short while afterwards I went to this man's home, and his two sons ran to me and kissed me, saying, "We have a new father." Previous to this these boys had often said to their mother, "Mother, we cannot stand it in the home any longer. We will have to leave." But the Lord changed the whole situation that night as we prayed together. On the second visit the Lord baptized this man in the Holy Ghost. The Holy Spirit will reveal false positions, pull the mask off any refuge of lies and clean up and remove all false conditions. When the Holy Spirit came in, that man's house and business and he himself were entirely changed.

An Effective Witness

When the Holy Spirit comes He comes to empower you to be an effective witness. At one time we were holding some special meetings and I was out distributing bills. I went into a shoemaker's store and there was a man with a green shade over his eyes and also a cloth. My heart looked up to the Lord and I had the witness within that He was ready to change any condition. The man was crying, "Oh! Oh!! Oh!!!" I asked, "What's the trouble?" He told me he was suffering with great inflammation and burning. I said, "I rebuke this condition in Jesus' name." Instantly the Lord healed him. He took off the shade and cloth and said, "Look, it is all gone." I believe the Lord wants us to enter into real activity and dare to do for Him. "Ye shall receive power after that the Holy Ghost is come upon you."

At one time a lady wrote and asked if I could go and help her. She said that she was blind, having two blood clots behind her eyes. When I reached the house they brought the blind woman to me. We were together for some time and then the power of God fell. Rushing to the window she exclaimed, "I can see! Oh, I can see! The blood is gone, I can see." She then inquired about receiving the Holy Spirit and confessed that for ten years she had been fighting our position. She said, "I could not bear these tongues, but God has settled the whole thing today. I now want the baptism in the Holy Ghost." The Lord graciously baptized her in the Spirit.

The Holy Spirit will come when a man is cleansed. There must be a purging of the old life. I never saw anyone baptized who was not clean within. I never saw a man baptized who smoked. We take it for granted that anyone who is seeking the fulness of the Spirit is free from such things as these. You cannot expect the Third Person of the Trinity to come into an unclean temple. There first must be a confession of all that is wrong and a cleansing in the precious blood of Jesus Christ.

I remember being in a meeting at one time, where there was a man seeking the baptism, and he looked like he was in trouble. He was very restless, and finally he said to me, "I will have to go." I said, "What's up?" He said, "God is unveiling things to me, and I feel so unworthy." I said, "Repent of everything that is wrong." He continued to tarry and the Lord continued to search his heart. These times of waiting on God for the fulness of the Spirit are times when He searches the heart and tries the reins. Later the man said to me, "I have a hard thing to do, the hardest thing I have ever had to do." I said to him, "Tell the Lord you will do it, and never mind the consequences." He agreed, and the next morning he had to take a ride of thirty miles and go with a bag of gold to a certain party with whom he dealt. This man had a hundred head of cattle and he bought all his feed at a certain place. He always paid his accounts on a certain day, but one day he missed. He was always so punctual in paying his accounts that when later the people of his firm went over their books, they thought they must have made a mistake in not crediting the man with the money and so they sent him a receipt.

The man never intended not to pay the account, but if you defer to do a right thing the devil will see that you never do it. But when that man was seeking the Lord that night the Lord dealt with him on this point, and he had to go and straighten the thing the next morning. He paid the account and then the Lord baptized him in the Spirit. They that bear the vessels of the Lord must be clean, must be holy.

When the Holy Spirit comes He always brings a rich revelation of Christ. Christ becomes so real to you that, when, under the power of the Spirit, you begin to express your love and praise to Him, you find yourself speaking in another tongue. Oh, it is a wonderful thing! At one time I belonged to a class who believed that they had received the baptism in the Spirit without the speaking in tongues. There are many folks like that today, but if you can go with them to a prayer meeting you will find them asking the Lord again and again to baptize them in the Spirit. Why all this asking if they really have received the baptism? I have never heard anyone who has received the baptism in the Holy Ghost after the original pattern asking the Lord to give them the Holy Ghost. They know of a surety that He has come.

I was once traveling from Belgium to England. As I landed I received a request to stop at a place between Harwich and Colchester. The people were delighted that God had sent me, and told me of a special case they wanted me to pray for. They said, "We have a brother here who believes in the Lord, and he is paralyzed from his loins downward. He cannot stand on his legs and he has been twenty years in this condition." They took me to this man and as I saw him there in his chair I put the question to him, "What is the greatest desire in your heart?" He said, "Oh, if I could only receive the Holy Ghost!" I was somewhat surprised at this answer, and I laid my hands on his head and said, "Receive ye the Holy Ghost." Instantly the power of God fell upon him and he began breathing very heavily. He rolled off the chair and there he lay like a bag of potatoes, utterly helpless. I like anything that God does. I like to watch God working. There he was with his great, fat body, and his head was working just as though it was on a swivel. Then to our joy he began speaking in tongues. I had my eyes on every bit of him and as I saw the condition of his legs I said, "Those legs can never carry that body." Then I looked up and said, "Lord, tell me what to do." The Holy Ghost is the executive of Jesus Christ and the Father. If you want to know the mind of God you must have the Holy Ghost to bring God's latest thought to you and to tell you what to do. The Lord said to me, "Command him in My name to walk." But I missed it, of course. I said to the people there, "Let's see if we can lift him up." But we could not lift him, he was like a ton weight. I cried, "Oh Lord, forgive me." I repented of doing the wrong thing, and then the Lord said to me again, "Command him to walk." I said to him, "Arise in the name of Jesus." His legs were immediately strengthened. Did he walk? He ran all round. A month after this he walked ten miles and back. He has a Pentecostal work now. When the power of the Holy Ghost is present, things will happen.

There is more for us all yet, praise the Lord. This is only the beginning. So far we have only touched the fringe of things. There is so much more for us if we will but yield to God.

Do you want to receive the Spirit?

> *If ye then, being evil, know how to give good gifts unto your children: how much more shall your heavenly Father give the Holy Spirit to them that ask him?*
>
> *Luke 11:13*

I am a father and I want to give my boys the very best. We human fathers are but finite, but our heavenly Father is infinite. There is not limit to the power and blessing He has laid up for them that love Him. Be filled with the Spirit.

Alphabetical Index

Topical Index

About the Author

Roberts Liardon is President of Roberts Liardon Ministries, and Founder and Senior Pastor of Embassy Christian Center in Irvine, California. He is also Founder of Spirit Life Bible College and Life Ministerial Association in Irvine.

Roberts Liardon received his call to ministry as an eight-year-old boy. Since then, he has diligently endeavored to follow that call through preaching and teaching God's Word. He has preached in over eighty nations with extensive ministry in Europe, Asia, and Africa.

As a bestselling author, Roberts has expanded his ministry onto the printed page. His books have been translated into over twenty-seven languages and have been circulated throughout the world. Roberts' books reflect his belief that the Church can fulfill its call and bring revival to the nations by combining God's Word with the moving of His Spirit.

As a historian, Roberts possesses a wealth of knowledge regarding the great leaders of three Christian movements — Pentecostal, Divine Healing, and Charismatic. He embarked on his in-depth studies as a fourteen-year-old boy and continued those studies into adulthood. Roberts has established on-going research through the founding of the Reformers and Revivalist Historical Museum in California.

Through his compilation of *Smith Wigglesworth: The Complete Collection of His Life Teachings,* Roberts preserves the treasure of our Christian heritage.

Other Books by Roberts Liardon

God's Generals

God's Generals Workbook

How to Survive an Attack

Religious Politics

The Invading Force

The Price of Spiritual Power

Learning to Say No Without Feeling Guilty

Run to the Battle

Kathryn Kuhlman
A Spiritual Biography of Gods Miracle Working Power

Breaking Controlling Powers

Cry of the Spirit
Unpublished Sermons by Smith Wigglesworth

I Saw Heaven

A Call to Action

Spiritual Timing

The Quest for Spiritual Hunger

Forget Not His Benefits

Haunted Houses, Ghosts & Demons

Holding to the Word of the Lord

Roberts Liardon Ministries International Offices:

Roberts Liardon Ministries — Europe
P.O. Box 2043
Hove, Brighton
East Sussex, BN3 6JU England
Phone and Fax: 44 1273 562395

Roberts Liardon Ministries – South Africa
P.O. Box 3155
Kimberly 8300, South Africa
Phone and Fax: 27 531 82 1207

Roberts Liardon Ministries — USA
P.O. Box 30710
Laguna Hills, California 92654
Phone: (714) 833-3555
Fax: (714) 833-9555

Additional copies of this book and other book titles from
ALBURY PUBLISHING are available at your local bookstore.

Albury Publishing
P.O. Box 470406
Tulsa, Oklahoma 74147-0406

In Canada books are available from:
Word Alive
P.O. Box 670
Niverville, Manitoba
CANADA ROA 1EO